The baby names almanac

2013

Emily Larson

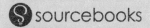

sourcebooks

Copyright © 2010, 2011, 2012 by Sourcebooks, Inc.
Cover and internal design © 2010 by Sourcebooks, Inc.
Cover design by Dawn Adams/Sourcebooks
Cover image © hannamariah/shutterstock

Sourcebooks and the colophon are registered trademarks of Sourcebooks, Inc.

This publication is designed to provide accurate and authoritative information in regard to the subject matter covered. It is sold with the understanding that the publisher is not engaged in rendering legal, accounting, or other professional service. If legal advice or other expert assistance is required, the services of a competent professional person should be sought.—*From a Declaration of Principles Jointly Adopted by a Committee of the American Bar Association and a Committee of Publishers and Associations*

Published by Sourcebooks, Inc.
P.O. Box 4410, Naperville, Illinois 60567-4410
(630) 961-3900
Fax: (630) 961-2168
www.sourcebooks.com

Library of Congress Cataloging-in-Publication Data

Larson, Emily.
  The baby names almanac, 2013 / Emily Larson.
    p. cm.
  (pbk. : alk. paper) 1. Names, Personal--Dictionaries. I. Title.
  CS2377.L384 2013
  929.4'4--dc23

                              2012037239

                   Printed and bound in Canada.
                   WC 10 9 8 7 6 5 4 3 2 1

Contents

So, you've got a baby to name.

As if preparing for the arrival of the baby isn't enough, you're dealing with all the pressure of figuring out what, exactly, to call the little bundle of joy. It can be stressful to find a name that will do justice to the hope you have for your child.

After all, names influence first impressions. They can trigger great—or unpleasant—nicknames. They can affect your child's self-esteem. They can be a tangible, lasting link to a family legacy.

But let's not forget that they can be fun. And that's what this book is all about.

Remember *The Old Farmer's Almanac*, which comes out annually as a guide to each year's trends, forecasts, and hot spots? Aimed at farmers, of course, the book provides a way to put the year into context, to navigate the shifting seasons, and to understand all the factors swirling in the atmosphere.

The 2013 Baby Names Almanac aims to be a similar lifeline for parents. With a finger on the pulse of pop culture and an ear to the ground of what's hip, new, and relevant, this book offers you an instant, idiosyncratic snapshot of how the world today is shaping what you may want to name your child tomorrow.

Jam-packed with information and ideas, plus thousands of names to browse, this book analyzes the most recent trends and fads in baby naming, offering up forecasts and predictions. You'll find our take on questions like these (and much more!):

- Which cutting-edge names are on the rise?
- Which popular names are on the decline?
- What influence do celebrities have on names?

- *Names in music:* Could you name your daughter **Blue Ivy**? Could **Carly** call your name, maybe? Will **Brantley** continue to climb?
- *Names in movies:* Will **Katniss** be the hot new girls' name of 2012? How long can **Bella** last now that the movie franchise is over?
- *Names in sports:* Watch out, **Iker**! Spanish goalkeeper Iker Casillas is inspiring a host of parents, and the 2012 Olympic Games in London may bring a new crop of babies named **Ryan**, **Michael**, or **Gabrielle**.

- How many babies get the most popular name, anyway?
- Which letter do most girls' names start with? How about boys' names?
- What are the most popular "gender-neutral" names today—and which gender uses each name more often? (If you name your daughter **Jordan**, will she find herself playing with lots of other little girls named **Jordan**—or little boys instead?)
- How can you take a trend and turn it into a name you love? (How about a little **Archer** of your own?)

We understand that sometimes this information on trends and popularity is hard to digest, so we've created some easy-to-visualize graphics. Turn to page 4, for example, to see a map of the United States showing where **Sophia** reigns and where little **Mason** is king.

And what baby name book would be complete without the names? Flip to page 69 to begin browsing through more than 20,000 names, including entries for the most popular names for girls and boys as reported by the Social Security Administration (www.ssa.gov/OACT/babynames).

A little bit of a mishmash and a screenshot of the world today, *The 2013 Baby Names Almanac* is like no other book out there. Stuffed with ideas on what's hip and hot and how you can take a trend and turn it into a name you love, this book is your all-in-one guide to baby names now.

The Top 10

Let's start with the most popular names in the country. Ranked by the Social Security Administration (SSA), these names are released around Mother's Day each year. (The top 10 names get the most attention, but you may also hear about the top 100. The total number of names widely reported is 1,000.) In 2011 the top 10 girl names were similar to—but not identical to—the top 10 for 2010. For example, for the first time ever, **Sophia** took over the top spot, booting 2010's winner **Isabella** to second. The boy's list had more changes. **Jacob** remained the most popular, but **Mason** catapulted into the number two spot (in 2010 it wasn't even in the top 10!) and **Anthony** slid out of the top 10 to number 11. Here's a quick comparison of 2010 and 2011:

2011 Girls	2010 Girls	2011 Boys	2010 Boys
1. Sophia	1. Isabella	1. Jacob	1. Jacob
2. Isabella	2. Sophia	2. Mason	2. Ethan
3. Emma	3. Emma	3. William	3. Michael
4. Olivia	4. Olivia	4. Jayden	4. Jayden
5. Ava	5. Ava	5. Noah	5. William
6. Emily	6. Emily	6. Michael	6. Alexander
7. Abigail	7. Abigail	7. Ethan	7. Noah
8. Madison	8. Madison	8. Alexander	8. Daniel
9. Mia	9. Chloe	9. Aiden	9. Aiden
10. Chloe	10. Mia	10. Daniel	10. Anthony

Just How Many Jacobs Are There, Anyway?

Sure, these names are popular, but what does that mean? Well, it seems that new parents are increasingly looking for off-the-beaten-path names for their little ones, and it shows. According to the SSA, the top 1,000 names represent 72.98 percent of all babies born and named in the United States in 2011—a significant drop from the 77.84 percent recorded in 2000.

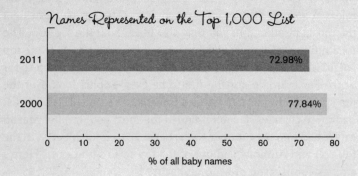

Names Represented on the Top 1,000 List

Although parents of either gender have always been looking beyond the top 1,000, parents of boys are more likely to pick a name in that mix—78.77 percent of boys' names are represented on the top 1,000 list, while only 66.90 percent of girls' names are.

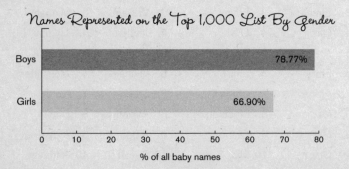

Names Represented on the Top 1,000 List By Gender

Plus, although it may seem like you know a zillion people with daughters named **Mia** or **Ava**, the most popular names are actually bestowed upon a relatively small number of babies each year. For example, in 2011 only 1.0013 percent of all male babies born in the United States (that's 20,153 little guys total) got the most popular name, **Jacob**. There are slightly more girls (21,695) with the most popular name, **Sophia**, but even that's only 1.1297 percent of all girls born. Only a fifth of the Jacob total—3,777 babies—were given the 100th most popular name, **Jaden**. The number of babies with the number one name is dropping swiftly—back in 1999, the first year Jacob hit number one, more than 35,000 boys got that name,

> ## Mary, Mary Quite Contrary
>
> **Mary** has been the most popular girl's name in the last 100 years, with 3.6 million babies given the name since 1912. For boys, **James** reigns, with 4.8 million namesakes in the last century.

which is more than 14,000 additional babies compared to 2011. And back in 1970, 4.48 percent of all male babies (a staggering 85,298 tots) were named **Michael**, the most popular name of that year. So if you've got your heart set on naming your son **Ethan** but you're worried that he'll be surrounded by Ethans wherever he goes, take heart!

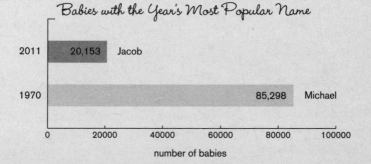

Babies with the Year's Most Popular Name

What's Popular in My State?

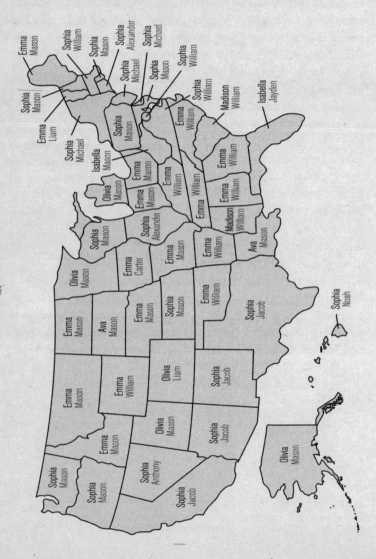

It's interesting to see how some names are more popular in certain states than in others. For example, **Carter** ranks 41st nationally for boys, but in Iowa it's the most popular name. Likewise, **Camila** ranks eleventh among California's baby girls, but only 48th in the nation.

The following chart lists the top five names for girls and boys for each of the 50 states, and it also shows the actual number of births for each of those names in each state. Check out how many girl babies got the number one name in Wyoming (**Emma**, 42) compared to the number of girl babies with the same name in California, where it was only the fifth most popular name (2,103):

Top Five Names by State

State	Girl	Births	Boy	Births
Alabama	Emma	281	William	442
	Ava	275	Mason	300
	Madison	255	James	298
	Olivia	229	Jacob	281
	Isabella	221	John	275
Alaska	Olivia	59	Mason	58
	Emma	55	James	51
	Isabella	49	William	51
	Madison	46	Liam	47
	Sophia	44	Ethan	45
Arizona	Sophia	553	Jacob	414
	Isabella	500	Anthony	393
	Emma	367	Daniel	388
	Emily	340	Michael	360
	Mia	335	Ethan	356

State	Girl	Births	Boy	Births
Arkansas	Emma	184	William	213
	Isabella	152	Jacob	184
	Addison	140	Mason	182
	Madison	137	Aiden	165
	Abigail	132	Noah	158
California	Sophia	3,538	Jacob	3,142
	Isabella	3,040	Daniel	2,880
	Emily	2,389	Jayden	2,740
	Mia	2,297	Anthony	2,680
	Emma	2,103	Matthew	2,450
Colorado	Olivia	316	Liam	288
	Sophia	298	Mason	283
	Emma	280	Noah	281
	Isabella	274	Elijah	277
	Abigail	230	William	270
Connecticut	Sophia	256	Alexander	234
	Isabella	232	Michael	230
	Olivia	225	Mason	229
	Ava	196	Ryan	224
	Emma	196	Jacob	195
Delaware	Sophia	70	Michael	64
	Olivia	60	Mason	61
	Ava	59	Ryan	60
	Emma	56	William	60
	Emily	49	Noah	56
District of Columbia	Sophia	50	William	71
	Ava	41	Alexander	63
	Elizabeth	38	Daniel	61
	Olivia	35	James	61
	Sofia	34	Christopher	60

State	Girl	Births	Boy	Births
Florida	Isabella	1,564	Jayden	1,228
	Sophia	1,406	Jacob	1,208
	Emma	981	Daniel	985
	Olivia	905	Noah	977
	Emily	830	Michael	975
Georgia	Emma	524	William	823
	Isabella	521	Christopher	595
	Madison	513	Mason	590
	Olivia	488	Joshua	580
	Ava	473	Jayden	575
Hawaii	Sophia	65	Noah	89
	Olivia	63	Mason	88
	Chloe	55	Elijah	80
	Emma	54	Aiden	71
	Isabella	54	Ethan	68
Idaho	Emma	116	Mason	118
	Sophia	108	Jacob	92
	Olivia	90	Liam	86
	Ava	78	Benjamin	84
	Emily	69	Alexander	80
Illinois	Sophia	889	Alexander	895
	Olivia	846	Michael	792
	Isabella	814	Jacob	773
	Emma	688	Noah	731
	Emily	621	Daniel	700
Indiana	Emma	450	Mason	507
	Olivia	446	Liam	390
	Ava	442	Elijah	367
	Sophia	428	Noah	361
	Isabella	376	William	361

State	Girl	Births	Boy	Births
Iowa	Emma	202	Carter	195
	Olivia	192	Mason	185
	Sophia	187	Owen	170
	Ava	174	Noah	167
	Addison	142	Jacob	160
Kansas	Sophia	218	Mason	185
	Emma	198	William	173
	Olivia	184	Jacob	166
	Isabella	163	Ethan	162
	Ava	157	Jackson	161
Kentucky	Emma	330	William	393
	Isabella	305	Mason	327
	Sophia	259	Elijah	323
	Olivia	240	Jacob	294
	Addison	236	Brayden	276
Louisiana	Ava	286	Mason	309
	Emma	256	Jayden	284
	Isabella	254	Aiden	255
	Sophia	232	William	230
	Olivia	215	Landon	225
Maine	Emma	102	Mason	94
	Sophia	88	Liam	74
	Isabella	82	Jacob	72
	Olivia	79	Benjamin	71
	Ava	71	Wyatt	68
Maryland	Sophia	364	Mason	431
	Olivia	298	Jacob	340
	Isabella	296	Michael	321
	Madison	288	Ethan	316
	Ava	283	Ryan	308

State	Girl	Births	Boy	Births
Massachusetts	Sophia	554	William	468
	Olivia	452	Benjamin	458
	Isabella	437	Jacob	449
	Emma	430	Michael	445
	Ava	401	Ryan	431
Michigan	Olivia	611	Mason	685
	Sophia	607	Jacob	591
	Emma	555	Noah	520
	Isabella	531	Logan	503
	Ava	522	Liam	470
Minnesota	Olivia	366	Mason	445
	Sophia	355	William	365
	Emma	338	Jacob	325
	Ava	337	Liam	325
	Isabella	255	Benjamin	319
Mississippi	Madison	159	William	286
	Emma	149	James	206
	Ava	124	Jayden	205
	Addison	115	John	176
	Olivia	113	Christopher	169
Missouri	Emma	415	Mason	480
	Sophia	412	William	413
	Olivia	385	Noah	348
	Ava	378	Jacob	344
	Isabella	319	Liam	344
Montana	Emma	69	Mason	74
	Madison	45	Liam	62
	Olivia	45	Wyatt	55
	Ava	42	Jacob	52
	Harper	39	Noah	46

State	Girl	Births	Boy	Births
Nebraska	Emma	141	Mason	131
	Sophia	126	Jackson	118
	Olivia	118	William	116
	Ava	116	Alexander	108
	Ella	104	Jacob	108
Nevada	Sophia	221	Anthony	192
	Isabella	201	Jacob	179
	Olivia	132	Daniel	173
	Emily	129	Mason	173
	Emma	128	Jayden	171
New Hampshire	Sophia	123	Mason	107
	Olivia	101	Logan	91
	Emma	95	Liam	84
	Ava	77	Jackson	83
	Isabella	69	Noah	76
New Jersey	Sophia	658	Michael	695
	Isabella	632	Ryan	591
	Olivia	538	Anthony	587
	Ava	481	Jayden	583
	Emily	462	Jacob	576
New Mexico	Sophia	140	Jacob	158
	Isabella	124	Elijah	127
	Mia	106	Michael	127
	Nevaeh	88	Aiden	115
	Emma	85	Noah	115
New York	Sophia	1,450	Michael	1,442
	Isabella	1,406	Jacob	1,393
	Olivia	1,168	Jayden	1,366
	Emma	1,119	Matthew	1,247
	Ava	950	Joseph	1,244

State	Girl	Births	Boy	Births
North Carolina	Emma	609	William	760
	Ava	554	Mason	725
	Olivia	522	Jacob	595
	Isabella	490	Elijah	578
	Sophia	481	Noah	570
North Dakota	Emma	64	Mason	71
	Ava	63	Carter	52
	Sophia	53	Jacob	50
	Olivia	49	Liam	49
	Harper	47	Ethan	48
Ohio	Emma	781	Mason	886
	Sophia	772	Jacob	700
	Ava	738	Noah	661
	Olivia	717	William	635
	Isabella	644	Liam	623
Oklahoma	Emma	259	William	226
	Sophia	223	Mason	225
	Isabella	198	Jacob	219
	Olivia	185	Noah	212
	Ava	173	Elijah	207
Oregon	Sophia	270	Mason	220
	Emma	220	Liam	212
	Olivia	216	Logan	187
	Ava	167	Jacob	185
	Isabella	164	Alexander	183
Pennsylvania	Sophia	872	Mason	911
	Emma	814	Michael	823
	Ava	801	Jacob	752
	Olivia	736	Logan	667
	Isabella	683	Ryan	646

State	Girl	Births	Boy	Births
Rhode Island	Sophia	95	Mason	85
	Olivia	70	Michael	71
	Isabella	69	Benjamin	66
	Emma	61	William	61
	Ava	56	Jayden	60
South Carolina	Madison	250	William	403
	Emma	242	Mason	267
	Isabella	231	Jayden	263
	Olivia	223	James	257
	Ava	192	Aiden	252
South Dakota	Ava	73	Mason	80
	Emma	60	Carter	60
	Olivia	54	William	53
	Sophia	51	Logan	51
	Brooklyn	48	Elijah	50
Tennessee	Emma	458	William	598
	Isabella	391	Mason	466
	Ava	359	Elijah	439
	Olivia	354	Jacob	416
	Madison	346	James	393
Texas	Sophia	2,180	Jacob	2,030
	Isabella	2,060	Jayden	1,876
	Emma	1,713	Daniel	1,728
	Mia	1,480	Jose	1,702
	Emily	1,439	David	1,604
Utah	Olivia	235	Mason	272
	Sophia	224	William	265
	Emma	214	James	223
	Lily	184	Jacob	212
	Abigail	173	Samuel	204

State	Girl	Births	Boy	Births
Vermont	Emma	39	Liam	41
	Olivia	38	William	38
	Sophia	36	Mason	37
	Ava	29	Carter	35
	Isabella	28	Benjamin	33
Virginia	Sophia	508	William	585
	Emma	493	Jacob	509
	Olivia	452	Mason	483
	Isabella	444	Noah	472
	Abigail	411	Ethan	435
Washington	Sophia	440	Mason	444
	Olivia	426	Liam	386
	Emma	422	Alexander	375
	Isabella	330	Jacob	354
	Emily	328	Ethan	352
West Virginia	Isabella	159	Mason	160
	Emma	135	Jacob	131
	Madison	119	Landon	128
	Sophia	109	Noah	117
	Addison	99	Aiden	115
Wisconsin	Sophia	361	Mason	512
	Emma	335	Liam	325
	Ava	326	William	310
	Olivia	301	Logan	299
	Isabella	266	Owen	298
Wyoming	Emma	42	William	32
	Olivia	29	Jacob	30
	Addison	27	Jackson	27
	Sophia	26	Parker	27
	Isabella	22	Liam	26

What Joined—and Dropped Off—the Hot 100 in 2010?

One of the easiest ways to spot name trends is to watch what joins the Hot 100 and what drops off. For the (young) ladies, several new names joined in 2011: **Harper** (a nod to the newest Beckham, we bet!), **Scarlett**, **Kennedy**, **London**, **Lydia**, **Ellie**, and **Aubree** (a 124-slot jump in popularity, from 223 in 2010 to 99 in 2011).

Another bunch dropped off the list: **Rachel** and **Jessica**, two hugely popular names from the '80s and '90s, lost their Hot 100 spots, as did **Angelina**, **Gabrielle**, **Natalia**, and **Paige**. **Mary**, the girls' name that has been number one more often than any other name in the past 100 years, continued its slide, going from 109 in 2010 to 112 in 2011. **Jennifer**, which held the number-one spot from 1970 to 1984, continued to slide, dropping from 120 in 2010 to 134 in 2011. For the boys, **Nolan**, **Grayson**, and **Bryson** joined the list, and **Eric**, **Bryan**, and **Aidan** fell off (though the variant Aiden held on to number 9 for the second year in a row).

New to the Hot 100

Aubree	Kennedy
Ellie	London
Harper	Bryson
Lydia	Grayson
Scarlett	Nolan

Off the Hot 100

Angelina	Rachel
Gabrielle	Valeria
Jessica	Aidan
Natalia	Bryan
Paige	Eric

New to the Top 1,000 This Year

These names are fresh faces in the top 1,000 list this year. Some of them have never set foot on the list before, but odds are they'll keep moving up.

Girls

Renata:	757	Kailynn:	898	Leigha:	966
Aviana:	762	Bentley:	905	Juniper:	970
Braylee:	796	Aubri:	910	Malaysia:	971
Milania:	813	Audrianna:	934	Rivka:	976
Blake:	815	Blakely:	935	Alianna:	977
Kensley:	824	Julieta:	938	Kendyl:	979
Avianna:	831	Kyndal:	940	Sariyah:	983
Saanvi:	844	Temperance:	941	Kamille:	986
Nahla:	861	Tinley:	942	Amalia:	992
Aubrianna:	867	Liv:	956	Hattie:	993
Elliot:	875	Samiya:	963	Milana:	998
Nova:	884	Abrielle:	964		
Sloan:	889	Annabell:	965		

Boys

Raylan:	701	Miller:	925	Brecken:	962
Crosby:	747	Otto:	930	Zeke:	971
Rylen:	849	Vihaan:	932	Maksim:	973
Callan:	885	Enoch:	933	Cristiano:	975
Brysen:	900	Benton:	938	Hendrix:	976
Nixon:	901	Graysen:	940	Princeton:	978
Arlo:	918	Crew:	943	Corban:	986
Braylin:	919	Flynn:	946	Cayson:	991
Arian:	922	Maxton:	949	Kohen:	995

Biggest Jumper: Briella and Brantley

The 394-slot rise for **Briella** might be due to TV star Briella Calafiore, the fashionable hairstylist on the reality shows *Jerseylicious* and *Glam Fairy*. Jumping from 891 to 497, it's not as big a rise as **Brantley**, which shot up 416 slots, from 736 to 320. Perhaps rising country music star Brantley Gilbert is propelling the jump?

How Do You Spell Aydin?

When you take into account that the male name **Jayden** has nine spelling variations in the top 1,000 (see the list that follows), that means that this one name actually shows up on the list nine different times! We broke down the top 1,000 names for boys and girls this way, counting all the different spelling variations as one name, and we got some surprising results. Looking from that perspective, there aren't 1,000 unique names at all! We counted roughly 670 unique girls' names and approximately 764 unique boys' names. The girls have fewer unique names, spelled in more ways, whereas parents of boys reach into a bigger pool of names. Let's take a look at some of the names with the most (or most interesting!) variations in the top 1,000.

Note: Some of these names could be pronounced slightly differently from one another. Also, names are listed in order of popularity.

Boys

It's no surprise that the "-ayden" names (such as **Aiden**, **Jayden**, **Brayden**, and **Kaden**) offer lots of spelling variety, but the changes in **Tristan** and **Kason** struck us as a little more unusual.

Aiden	Jayden	Cameron	Kayden
1. Aiden	1. Jayden	1. Cameron	1. Kayden
2. Ayden	2. Jaden	2. Kameron	2. Kaden
3. Aidan	3. Jaiden	3. Camryn	3. Caden
4. Aden	4. Jaydon	4. Kamryn	4. Cayden
5. Adan	5. Jadon	5. Camron	5. Kaiden
6. Aidyn	6. Jaidyn	6. Camren	6. Caiden
7. Aydin	7. Jaeden	7. Kamron	7. Kaedan
8. Aydan	8. Jaydan	8. Kamren	
9. Aaden	9. Jaydin		

Brayden
1. Brayden
2. Braden
3. Braydon
4. Braeden
5. Braiden
6. Bradyn

Devin
1. Devin
2. Devon
3. Davin
4. Deven
5. Devan
6. Davon

Kason
1. Kason
2. Kasen
3. Cason
4. Kayson
5. Casen
6. Cayson

Tristan
1. Tristan
2. Tristen
3. Triston
4. Tristian
5. Tristin
6. Trystan

Connor
1. Connor
2. Conner
3. Conor
4. Konner
5. Konnor

Jackson
1. Jackson
2. Jaxon
3. Jaxson
4. Jaxen
5. Jaxton

Top 643 Names, Not Top 1,000

Only 67 percent of the top 1,000 girls' names are unique names. Only 77 percent of the top 1,000 boys' names are unique names. The rest of the names are spelling variations of those names.

Here are the three names with the most spelling variations:

Girls
1. Kaelynn
2. Hailey, Madelyn
3. Carly, Kaitlyn, Kaylee

Boys
1. Aiden
2. Jayden
3. Cameron

Girls

Some of these seemed more obvious—**Kailynn**, for one—but others, like **Leah**, surprised us with their robust variety. And quite a few new names popped up on our radar this year: **Annabelle**, **Kendall**, **Leah**, **Maya**, **Jayden**, and **Charlee**.

Kaelyn
1. Kaelyn
2. Kailyn
3. Kaylin
4. Kaylynn
5. Kaylyn
6. Kaylen
7. Cailyn
8. Kailynn
9. Kaelynn

Hailey
1. Hailey
2. Haley
3. Haylee
4. Hayley
5. Hailee
6. Haleigh
7. Haylie
8. Hayleigh

Madelyn
1. Madelyn
2. Madeline
3. Madilyn
4. Madeleine
5. Madelynn
6. Madalyn
7. Madilynn
8. Madalynn

Carly
1. Carly
2. Karlee
3. Carlee
4. Carlie
5. Carley
6. Carleigh
7. Karly

Kaitlyn
1. Kaitlyn
2. Katelyn
3. Caitlyn
4. Katelynn
5. Caitlin
6. Kaitlynn
7. Kaitlin

Kaylee
1. Kaylee
2. Kayleigh
3. Kailey
4. Kaylie
5. Caylee
6. Kailee
7. Kaleigh

Aaliyah
1. Aaliyah
2. Aliyah
3. Aleah
4. Aliya
5. Alia
6. Aleigha

Adalyn
1. Adalyn
2. Adeline
3. Adelyn
4. Adalynn
5. Adelynn
6. Addilyn

Eliana
1. Eliana
2. Elliana
3. Aliana
4. Iliana
5. Elianna
6. Alianna

Liliana
1. Liliana
2. Lilliana
3. Lilyana
4. Lilianna
5. Lillianna
6. Lilyanna

Laila
1. Laila
2. Layla
3. Leila
4. Laylah
5. Lailah
6. Leyla

Allison
1. Allison
2. Alison
3. Allyson
4. Alyson
5. Alisson

Emily
1. Emily
2. Emely
3. Emilee
4. Emilie
5. Emmalee

Annabelle
1. Annabel
2. Annabel
3. Anabel
4. Annabell
5. Anabelle

Charlee
1. Charlee
2. Charlie
3. Charley
4. Charli
5. Charleigh

Jaelyn
1. Jaelyn
2. Jaelynn
3. Jaylynn
4. Jaylin
5. Jaylyn

Jasmine
1. Jasmine
2. Jazmine
3. Jazmin
4. Jasmin
5. Jazmyn

Jayden
1. Jayden
2. Jaiden
3. Jadyn
4. Jaidyn
5. Jaden

Kendall
1. Kendall
2. Kendal
3. Kyndall
4. Kyndal
5. Kendyl

Leah
1. Leah
2. Lia
3. Lea
4. Leia
5. Leigha

Maya
1. Maya
2. Mya
3. Myah
4. Maia
5. Miya

Makayla
1. Makayla
2. Mikayla
3. Michaela
4. Mikaela
5. Mckayla

Natalie
1. Natalie
2. Nataly
3. Nathalie
4. Natalee
5. Nathaly

What Do the Most Popular Names Start With?

You may find it surprising, but only four of the names in the top 1,000 girl baby names for 2011 start with a *W*: **Wendy**, **Whitney**, **Willa**, and **Willow**. At the same time, you probably won't find it surprising that the most popular letter that girls' names start with is *A* (167 of the top 1,000), with *M* as a close second with 97 names. Among the boys' names, 109 start with *J*, and *A* names comprise 87 of the total 1,000 names. In 2009, every single letter in the alphabet had at least one boy and girl name, as **Unique** hopped back on the chart (929) for the first time in four years. But in 2011, no *U* names made it on the girls' list (but the boys are covered, with **Uriah**, **Uriel**, and **Urijah**). And only one Q (**Quinn**) or X (**Ximena**) for girls.

Gender-Neutral Options

Lots of names are popular for both boys and girls, but they're generally more popular for one gender than the other. Here's a list of names that appeared on both the boys' top 1,000 and the girls' top 1,000, plus how they ranked in 2011 for each gender. Some interesting trends here—perhaps because of the waning popularity of NFL quarterback Peyton Manning, **Payton/Peyton** are both more popular for girls! And four names are roughly given to equal numbers of boys and girls: **Dakota**, **Jaidyn**, **Jessie**, and **Justice**. We'd suggest that 2013 will be a great year for Landen (#225 for boys in 2011) to hit the girls' list).

Spelling Matters!

If you're going to choose...

Cameron/Camryn/Kamryn: Camryn and Kamryn are the more popular choices for girls, Cameron for boys

Jayden, etc: Jayden, Jaden, and Jaiden are more popular for boys. Jadyn is more popular for girls.

Casey/Kasey: Casey is the winner for boys, Kasey for girls

Jordan/Jordyn: Jordyn is more popular for girls, Jordan for boys

---

Nearly Equal

Name	Girl Rank	Boy Rank
Dakota	297	313
Jaidyn	906	873
Jessie	690	696
Justice	512	529

More Popular for Girls

Name	Girl Rank	Boy Rank
Alexis	26	242
Ariel	220	625
Avery	18	201
Camryn	294	832
Eden	181	833
Emerson	276	387
Emery	272	708
Finley	364	511
Harley	436	647
Harper	54	607
Jamie	437	801
Jaylin	709	783
Jordyn	121	656
Kamryn	312	863
Kendall	123	606

Name	Girl Rank	Boy Rank
Leighton	526	920
London	94	561
Morgan	75	539
Payton	95	397
Peyton	53	166
Quinn	188	297
Reagan	122	892
Reese	130	543
Riley	47	111
Rylee	102	741
Sidney	678	896
Skylar	145	543
Tatum	345	726
Taylor	44	337
Teagan	213	758

More Popular for Boys

Name	Girl Rank	Boy Rank
Ali	713	369
Amari	514	307
Angel	216	52
Armani	727	500
Bentley	905	75
Blake	815	73

Name	Girl Rank	Boy Rank
Cameron	442	52
Casey	620	423
Charlie	376	236
Dylan	492	33
Elliot	875	272
Hayden	185	90

Name	Girl Rank	Boy Rank
Jaden	982	100
Jaiden	876	186
Jayden	292	4
Jordan	196	46
Kai	887	202
Kayden	531	105
Logan	524	20
Micah	912	104
Parker	366	79
Phoenix	645	388

Name	Girl Rank	Boy Rank
River	913	424
Rory	900	598
Rowan	535	309
Ryan	575	25
Rylan	702	146
Sawyer	719	172
Skyler	456	287
Zion	612	245

Which Names are Moving Up—and Falling Down—the Fastest?

The SSA compiles a list of names that have made the biggest moves when compared to their rank the previous year (assuming the name has made the top 500 at least once in the last two years). Some of these jumpers have obvious triggers, while the reasons for other jumps and declines are more open to interpretation. Take a look and see what you think.

40 Girls' Names Heating Up

Name	Number of Spots It Moved Up	Name	Number of Spots It Moved Up
Briella	394	Nylah	149
Angelique	247	Raelynn	133
Aria	196	Brynlee	130
Mila	190	Olive	127
Elsie	165	June	126

Name	Number of Spots It Moved Up	Name	Number of Spots It Moved Up
Bristol	126	Charlie	85
Aubree	124	Dylan	82
Charlee	119	Londyn	80
Adalynn	119	Eloise	80
Aubrie	108	Adelyn	80
Mckinley	105	Caylee	79
Parker	99	Lyric	74
Brynn	96	Cora	72
Gemma	93	Quinn	67
Gia	91	Brielle	66
Nyla	90	Luna	65
Kinsley	90	Kenzie	64
Aylin	90	Harper	64
Willow	87	Hanna	63
Elliana	87	Liana	62

40 Girls' Names Cooling Down

Name	Number of Spots It Moved Down	Name	Number of Spots It Moved Down
Brisa	343	Brenda	104
Dana	147	Erika	103
Desiree	121	Miley	99
Denise	114	Danna	98
Kimora	109	Janiya	91

Name	Number of Spots It Moved Down
Ciara	89
Tatiana	87
Kendra	86
Cassandra	84
Jayden	80
Johanna	79
Aniya	78
Jasmin	75
Jayda	73
Madisyn	72
Anahi	70
Katelynn	68
Nataly	65
Kiera	65
Alejandra	65

Name	Number of Spots It Moved Down
Shayla	64
Courtney	64
Sierra	63
Jamie	62
Angie	61
Madalyn	59
Lindsey	59
Madyson	58
Erica	57
Melany	55
Marissa	55
Tiana	54
Breanna	54
Jaylynn	53
Amari	52

40 Boys' Names Heating Up

Name	Number of Spots It Moved Up
Brantley	416
Iker	267
Maximiliano	173
Zaiden	131
Kamden	109

Name	Number of Spots It Moved Up
Barrett	106
Archer	101
Declan	97
Atticus	96
Nico	95

Name	Number of Spots It Moved Up	Name	Number of Spots It Moved Up
Abram	87	Axel	55
Amare	83	Braylen	54
Maverick	80	Karter	53
Jayce	75	Brooks	53
Dexter	70	Arthur	52
Jameson	67	Mateo	51
Remington	65	Emmett	51
Kieran	65	Ronan	50
Kason	64	Xander	49
Finnegan	64	Waylon	49
Adriel	64	Greyson	49
Bruce	62	Brycen	49
Milo	61	Gideon	48
Abel	56	Zayden	46
Chandler	55	Matteo	44

40 Boys' Names Cooling Down

Name	Number of Spots It Moved Down	Name	Number of Spots It Moved Down
Brett	119	Brenden	81
Jamarion	112	Davion	76
Shaun	105	Braiden	76
Jaydon	100	Salvador	75
Nickolas	86	Braeden	67

Name	Number of Spots It Moved Down	Name	Number of Spots It Moved Down
Chris	66	Frederick	46
Dane	59	Jimmy	45
Cullen	58	Darius	42
Jamari	57	Byron	42
Brayan	57	Quinton	41
Reese	56	Emiliano	41
Justice	56	Dillon	41
Ty	54	Isaias	40
Talon	53	Andy	40
Braden	52	Terry	39
Payton	51	Joe	39
Kobe	49	Devon	39
Orlando	48	Malik	38
Zackary	46	Jonas	38
Johan	46	Drew	38

What's Hot (or Not) Today (And What Will—and Won't!—Be Tomorrow)

Now that we've seen the state of baby names today, let's take a look at a snapshot of some interesting trends we've spotted, as well as some predictions as to what might play out on the playground sometime soon.

You'll notice that within some fads, certain names are on the rise and certain names are on the decline, showing how trends are morphing over time (how religious names like **Mary** and **Rachel** are on the decline, while **Trinity** and **Genesis** are climbing the ranks). We've also included some offbeat and unique ways to take each of these trends and find a name that really fits you and your family.

Trends Today

WE'RE KEEPING UP WITH THE KARDASHIANS!

There's no question that the oldest Kardashian sister, Kourtney, bears responsibility for the second most popular boys' name of 2011. Mason Dash Disick, Kourtney's son, was born December 14, 2009. Since his birth, the name **Mason** shot up from number 34 in 2009 to number 12 in 2010, all the way to number 2 in 2011! Now that Kourtney has had a daughter, **Penelope**, we can't wait to see how quickly the name flies up the charts in the coming years.

Other Kardashian names are making a splash, too. In 2006, **Khloe** barely made the list at 954. Only five years later, it's holding steady in the top 50 at number 49. **Kourtney** wasn't even in the top 1000 for 2005, 2006, or 2007. Today, it is 656.

THE RISE OF IKER

The name **Iker** first debuted on the charts—it had never even been in the top 1000!—in 2010, at number 646. In 2011, Iker had the second highest jump up the list, landing at 379. The rise in popularity of the name might be due to Spanish soccer team Real Madrid's talented (and extremely handsome!) goalkeeper, Iker Casillas, who led the Spanish national team to their first World Cup title in 2010.

THE BECKHAM EFFECT

Victoria and David Beckham added a fourth child, daughter **Harper**, to their brood in 2011, and, as usual, the name struck a chord with many new parents and made big gains in popularity. Let's look at the history of the Beckham clan: Their first child, **Brooklyn**, was born in 1999. While Brooklyn Beckham is a boy, the name has been rising steadily on the girls' name chart for the past decade, getting as high as 21 in 2011. **Romeo**, the second Beckham son, was born in 2002, and that name started climbing in 2006 after years of sitting in the 600s. **Cruz**, the name of Beckham son number three, jumped into the top 500 in 2006, just after the Beckhams used it a year earlier. And finally **Harper**, arrived in 2011. That same year, the name made its first appearance in the top 100, shooting from number 118 in 2010 all the way to 54 in 2011. Take a look at this chart, which tracks all the Beckham children names (and their last name) through the decades.

Year	2001	2002	2003	2004	2005	2006	2007	2008	2009	2010	2011
Brooklyn	172	152	118	101	78	67	57	47	37	34	21
Romeo	509	567	639	602	610	573	500	465	410	358	360
Cruz	597	641	597	561	516	496	429	367	346	321	300
Harper	–	–	–	887	745	508	439	296	172	118	54
Beckham	–	–	–	–	–	–	–	898	845	750	655

A dash means that the name did not make the list that year.

NEW SUPERSTARS INSPIRING NAMES—AND NOT

Justin Bieber is inarguably one of the world's biggest stars, but his name isn't translating into a major hit in the baby names department. Despite his fame—and Justin Timberlake's, too, of course—**Justin** has continued to slide in popularity. The name landed at 59 in 2011, down from 50 in 2010.

A superstar name that got a boost a few years ago, **Rihanna**, is on a definite downtrend. The girls' name made it all the way to 310 in 2008 but has been dropping steadily since, sliding 144 spaces to 729 in 2011.

One hot musical act of 2011 most definitely *did* have an effect on the baby girl names that year. **Adele** debuted in the top 1000 in 2010 at number 909 and skyrocketed to 627 in 2011. Now that the singer is expecting a little one herself in 2013, we'll be keeping watch to see if the name she chooses for her new addition has a similar effect.

GO WEST, YOUNG MAN

The FX cable show *Justified*, starring Timothy Olyphant, is a surprising trendsetter in 2011. The name of Olyphant's character, **Raylan**, made the top 1000 for the first time in 2011, debuting at 701. **Arlo**, another *Justified* character name, debuted in 2011 at 918. (Celebs Johnny Knoxville and Toni Collette both welcomed baby Arlos this year. Knoxville's Arlo is a girl, while Collette used it more traditionally, for a boy.) Another *Justified* character shares a name with the number 5 spot since 2008: Ava.

Justified is a show about the world of the Wild West, and other names traditionally associated with cowboys and saloons are also heating up. Even the direction itself is inspiring popular names. (**Weston** is up to number 203!) Check out these new popular names for the littlest cowboys and cowgirls:

Name	2010	2011
Raylan	–	701
Arlo	–	918
Wyatt	57	48
Zeke	–	971
Colt	331	326
Amos	–	860
Levi	70	66
Maverick	505	425
Milo	422	361
Hattie	–	993
Elsie	645	480
Raelynn	629	496
Rose	337	291
Pearl	960	814
Lillian	22	22
Josephine	184	182
Charley	830	623
Annie	396	386

Ways to Make This Trend Your Own
Options still off the radar: Boyd, Kirby, Buck, Nell, Clint, Peggy, Loretta, May

IS THERE AN FX MOVEMENT?

Not only did *Justified* introduce two big names to the top 1000, but two other shows from the cable network made a clear impact on the hot new names. **Gemma**, the matriarch character of the popular show *Sons of Anarchy*, jumped 93 slots to 356 on the girls list, while **Archer**, the title character from the animated series, rose 101 slots to 447.

COLORFUL KIDS

In early 2012, Beyonce and Jay-Z gave birth to their first child, a daughter named **Blue Ivy**. While the name Blue hasn't cracked the top 1000 (yet!), Ivy has been slowly climbing the ranks and is currently 266. And the superstar couple were clearly on trend—girl names that are also colors of the rainbow are becoming increasingly popular. Check out the chart below:

Name	2010	2011
Violet	122	101
Rose	337	291
Jade	115	113
Olive	543	416
Ruby	113	109
Hazel	263	211
Raven	610	591
Scarlet	414	370

Way To Make This Trend Your Own
Options still off the radar: Clementine, Coral, Goldie, Lavender, Silver, Azure, Cyan

REVERING A LEGEND

Many parents are looking to superstars' last names to find inspiration for their tots. For example, **Lennon** (for John) is on the rise for boys (up 175 spots to 745 in 2011!), and last year, Mariah Carey and Nick Cannon named one of their twins **Monroe**, in honor of Mariah's beloved Marilyn. **Marley** (in honor of Bob) is a popular choice for girls (258 in 2011), while **Jackson** (for Michael) is a big hit for boys (23 in 2011). And, after falling off the top 1000 completely in 2010, there has been another **Elvis** spotting in 2011—at number 904!

K NAMES ARE OK!

We already mentioned how influential the Kardashians have been—we're not only borrowing their names, but also their first letter! Celebrities love the offbeat *K* options as well; actress Allyson Hannigan named her daughter **Keeva**, while actor Kevin James named his son **Kannon**. And they're not alone—a lot of *K* names are really making the scene, including a few that don't start with a *K* but have a prominent *K* sound. For boys, the name **Kamden** has really exploded in popularity and is up 109 slots; for girls, **Kinsley** shot up 90 spots. Check out the following charts:

Boys' Names Starting with a *K*	2010 Rank	2011 Rank
Kamden	557	448
Kieran	540	475
Kason	480	416
Karter	444	391
Khalil	502	466
Knox	459	434

Boys' Names with a Prominent *K* Sound	2010 Rank	2011 Rank
Iker	646	379
Declan	274	177
Atticus	558	462
Maverick	505	425

Ways to Make This Trend Your Own
Options still off the radar: Keane, Keegan, Kal, Kel, Kenn, Kasimir, Kasim, Kione, Kincaid, Kiefer

Girls' Names Starting with a K	2010 Rank	2011 Rank
Kinsley	307	217
Kenzie	372	308
Kennedi	490	445
Kali	537	493
Kailyn	443	399
Kinley	231	194

Girls' Names with a Prominent K Sound	2010 Rank	2011 Rank
Angelique	627	380
Mckinley	556	451
Caylee	523	444

Ways to Make This Trend Your Own
Options still off the radar: Kezia, Kimball, Kearney, Kerensa, Kalinda, Karsten, Kalifa, Khalida, Kismet, Kolette, Kiele

REVENGE IS SWEET

The TV show *Revenge* was a breakout hit of the 2011 season, and the story of Emily Thorne and her vendetta against the Grayson family seems to have inspired a number of baby names. Perhaps we'll be seeing these well-dressed tots populating the Hamptons soon enough!

Name	2010	2011
Grayson	122	97
Victoria	32	23
Nolan	104	93
Charlotte	46	27
Declan	274	177

DESTINATION NAMES

Ten years ago, naming a child after a location was quite unusual. Now, **Brooklyn** is number 21 on the list for girls! Naming tots after places is a hot idea these days—it's even a big trend among celebrities. In 2012, Mike Tyson named his son **Morocco**, Jillian Michaels welcomed a son **Phoenix**, Chris Hemsworth named his daughter **India**, and Fantasia Barrino named her son **Dallas**. Here are some place names on the rise:

Girls' Names	2000 Rank	2011 Rank
Brooklyn (New York)	177	21
Charlotte (North Carolina)	37	27
Savannah (Georgia)	289	41
London (England)	828	94
Paris (France)	473	338
Adelaide (Australia)	–	407
Aspen (Colorado)	570	519

Ways to Make This Trend Your Own
Options still off the radar: Orleans (New Orleans, Louisiana), Helena (Montana), Olympia (Washington), Juneau (Alaska), Valletta (Malta), Dublin (Ireland), Pristina (Kosovo)

Boys' Names	2000 Rank	2011 Rank
Jackson (Mississippi)	72	23
Santiago (Chile)	359	131
Lincoln (Nebraska)	710	178
Israel	244	221
Kingston, Jamaica	–	226
Phoenix (Arizona)	876	388
London (England)	895	508
Boston (Massachusetts)	–	557
Memphis (Tennessee)	–	720
Milan (Italy)	–	608

Ways to Make This Trend Your Own
Options still off the radar: Richmond (Virginia), Salem (Oregon), Montgomery (Alabama), Wellington (New Zealand), Dakar (Senegal), Cairo (Egypt)

IT'S A BIRD, IT'S A PLANE, IT'S A...BABY

Superheroes are always huge hits at the box office—and now they are hitting it big in the name department, too. In 2012, *The Avengers* had the biggest opening weekend of all time, and some of our favorite superheroes are inspiring increasingly popular names. **Clark**, Superman's alter ego, rose 77 spots in 2011 to 616. **Parker**, the last name of Spider-Man's alter ego Peter, climbed to

79. And Batman did a double jump: **Bruce** shot from 532 in 2010 to 470 in 2011, while **Wayne** went from 786 to 704.

NAMES FROM THE ANCIENT GREEKS AND ROMANS

When we say these names are old, we're not kidding. They have been around for a long, long time...and while many girls' names are becoming more popular (with some traditional exceptions—**Diana** and **Helen** are on the slide), the boys' names are surprisingly less popular (and perfect for someone looking for the cutting edge).

Girls' Names	1998 Rank	2011 Rank
Chloe	87	10
Athena	550	313
Phoebe	606	310
Paris	457	338
Daphne	757	450
Diana	83	203
Helen	349	427

Ways to Make This Trend Your Own

Options still off the radar: Artemis, Antigone, Aphrodite, Ariadne, Calliope, Cassandra, Circe, Cleopatra, Echo, Electra, Eurydice, Euterpe, Gaia, Halcyone, Ione, Iris, Juno, Lavinia, Maia, Medea, Minerva, Persephone, Psyche, Rhea, Selene, Thalia, Venus

Boys' Names	1998 Rank	2011 Rank
Alexander	22	8
Cassius	–	876
Jason	40	71

Boys' Names	1998 Rank	2011 Rank
Marcus	96	145
Hector	185	247
Antony	832	957

Ways to Make This Trend Your Own
Options still off the radar: Achilles, Aeneas, Apollo, Cadmus, Dionysus, Endymion, Hercules, Hermes, Hyperion, Icarus, Janus, Mercury, Midas, Minos, Morpheus, Odysseus, Orion, Orpheus, Pegasus, Perseus, Prometheus, Ptolemy, Theseus, Vulcan, Zeus

THE PALIN FAMILY

Like the Beckhams, one family with lots of members has inspired quite a few baby names. Sarah Palin's first name might be much less popular these days than it once was, but the names of her extended family have been on the rise since she became a household name in the summer of 2008. **Track** and **Trig** haven't made the chart, and **Kyla**, the newest addition (son Track's daughter, born in 2011), was already on the rise. Check out these other Palin-inspired names:

Name	2007 Rank	2008 Rank	2009 Rank	2010 Rank	2011 Rank
Bristol (girl)	–	–	666	560	434
Piper (girl)	240	172	147	144	110
Willow (girl)	429	407	313	290	202
Tripp (boy)	–	933	672	669	670
Levi (boy)	132	116	85	70	66

TO KILL A MOCKINGBIRD

2010 was the fiftieth anniversary of the publication of *To Kill a Mockingbird*, and 2011 saw a huge rise in two names inspired by the classic novel. Fans named their sons **Atticus** (which jumped from 558 in 2010 to 462 in 2011), after the heroic father and lawyer at the center of the story. **Harper**, the first name of the book's author, continues to climb the ranks—currently at number 54. Fans of the novel should know that **Scout**, **Dill**, **Finch**, **Boo**, and **Radley** still remain off the radar.

A CORNUCOPIA OF PURITAN NAMES

Many names have remained popular for hundreds of years, such as **Emily**, **Olivia**, **Michael**, and **Matthew**. However, in recent years, names with a Puritan bent in particular have become all the rage. You probably know at least one **Ethan** or **Emma**—names that would be equally at home in 1700s Salem, Massachusetts, and on today's playgrounds. In 2011, the name **Temperance** made its first ever appearance on the top 1000, possibly helped along by the character of Temperance Brennan on *Bones*. These names are particularly hot for boys. Here's a look at trends in Puritan names.

Girls' Names	2000 Rank	2011 Rank
Abigail	14	7
Leah	96	29
Emma	17	3
Grace	19	16
Charlotte	289	27

Ways to Make This Trend Your Own

Options still off the radar: Honor, Mercy, Providence, Constance, Verity, Prudence, Providence, Damaris

Boys' Names	2000 Rank	2011 Rank
Caleb	38	32
Levi	172	66
Asher	579	113
Silas	602	183
Tobias	589	538
Asa	655	554
Elias	242	139
Eli	235	58

Ways to Make This Trend Your Own
Options still off the radar: Ebenezer, Abner, Enoch, Sylas, Cyrus, Ariel, Abel

NAMES ENDING IN –LYNN

For girls, names that end in *–lynn* or *–lyn* have been on the rise for years and had an especially notable explosion in 2011. Perhaps because the syllable gives a feminine edge to almost any name, parents are choosing both traditional variants (Evelyn) and some that are more unusual (Braelynn).

Girls' Names	2000 Rank	2011 Rank
Brooklyn	177	21
Evelyn	150	24
Adalyn	–	214
Madilyn	642	301
Kaelyn	651	385
Jaelyn	616	417
Braelyn	–	425

Girls' Names	2000 Rank	2011 Rank
Gracelyn	919	482
Raelynn	–	496
Joselyn	650	359

Ways To Make This Trend Your Own:
Options still off the radar: Lynn, Carlyn, Fallyn, Ugolyn, Newlyn

WHO'S RESPONSIBLE FOR BRANTLEY?

The biggest jumper for a boys' name in 2011 was Brantley, which first appeared in the top 1000 in 2010 at 736. In 2011, the name shot up 416 spots to 320. So what's responsible for the name's explosion? Depends who you talk to! Country music fans attribute the popular boys' name to chart-topper Brantley Gilbert, whose hit song "Country Must Be Country Wide" hit number one in 2011. Sports enthusiasts would argue the name comes from Baltimore Raven John Brantley, who was the starting quarterback for the University of Florida during the 2011 season.

HAS *TWILIGHT* SEEN ITS END?

In 2009, names inspired by the *Twilight* series saw a huge bump in popularity. **Cullen** rose a stunning 71 spots in 2010 after another meteoric rise in 2009, accelerating from 782 in 2008 to 413 in 2010. It's a no-brainer why: the ladies get all swoony from *Twilight* vampire Edward Cullen, played by Robert Pattinson in the *Twilight* film series. (Not surprisingly, the Gaelic name means "good-looking boy.") But 2012 brought the final installments of the film franchise, so we can't help wondering: has the *Twilight* trend peaked? In 2011, **Cullen** dropped a whopping 58 spots to 471; the name **Bella**, shared with *Twilight* heroine Bella Swan, dropped from 48 to 60; and **Edward** fell 12 spots to 148.

Then, of course, there's **Jacob**. The boys' name has been number one for thirteen years, starting long before the *Twilight* books. But what's more, Jacob is actually *declining*, even though it's still number one. As we mentioned earlier, more than 35,000 babies were named Jacob when it hit number one in 1999. In 2011, a mere 20,153 babies received the name.

The one *Twilight* name still climbing the ranks? **Emmett**. This dowdyish name ranked at 740 in 2000 but is now at 222, up another 51 slots from 2010.

LAST NAMES FIRST

We've already looked at gender-neutral names, and the surname-as-first name fad is a deeper twist on that. In fact, perhaps due to women naming their children with their maiden names, last names as first names is perhaps one of the biggest trends of the past ten years—especially for boys. One of the more unusual celebrity takes on this was Tony Romo and Candice Crawford's son, Hawkins. Take a look at some of the more popular last-name choices for boys and girls.

Girls' Names	2011 Rank
Avery	18
Riley	47
Mackenzie	68
Bailey	88
Paisley	195
Presley	227
Kelsey	254
Parker	366
Sawyer	719

Ways to Make This Trend Your Own
Options still off the radar: Golden, Kingsley, Sheridan, Easton, Curtis, Banfield, Robinson

Boys' Names	2011 Rank
Logan	20
Landon	34
Connor	54
Hunter	55
Chase	69
Bentley	75
Parker	79
Cooper	82
Carson	85
Bryson	98
Easton	102
Hudson	112

Ways to Make This Trend Your Own
Options still off the radar: Foster, Ford, Albee, Burroughs, Pelham, Wilder, Barnes, Hopper

DOWNTON ABBEY

The British TV series about life on the fictional estate of Downton Abbey premiered on PBS in January 2011 and was an overnight sensation. Its impact on names seems undeniable. In fact, Elsie, the first name of head housekeeper Mrs. Hughes, was the fifth highest jumper of 2011—catapulting 165 spots to 480.

Name	2010	2011
Cora	276	204
Violet	122	101
Edith	824	771
Elsie (Mrs. Hughes)	645	480
Branson	852	731

Ways to Make This Trend Your Own

Options still off the radar: Rosamund, Sybil, Lavinia, Bates

RELIGIOUS NAMES

Religious names have become quite a bit more popular in recent years, and the trend is reflected in the different kinds of religious names that are popular now versus years ago. As a prime example, **Sarah** is down ten slots from its 2010 rank, but **Nevaeh** (*heaven* backwards) is holding strong at 35. In fact, in 2009, **Muhammad** was the most popular British baby name (once all the spelling variants are taken into account). Here's a look at some religious names and how they've changed in popularity over the past fifteen years.

Girls' Names	1995 Rank	2011 Rank
Sarah	5	39
Nevaeh*	–	35
Trinity	662	77
Mary	40	112
Rebecca	28	148
Rachel	12	117
Heaven	558	317

*Heaven spelled backward

Girls' Names	1995 Rank	2011 Rank
Eve	–	546
Genesis	333	82
Eden	658	181

Ways to Make This Trend Your Own
Options still off the radar: Khadija, Dinah, Seraphina

Boys' Names	1995 Rank	2011 Rank
Noah	100	5
Daniel	9	10
Joshua	5	14
Gabriel	65	24
Benjamin	31	19
Isaac	98	35
Isaiah	109	43
Adam	38	81
Zion	–	245
Moses	598	522
Muhammad	779	480
Messiah	–	629
Jesus	76	92
Cain	–	841

Ways to Make This Trend Your Own
Options still off the radar: Aasif, Esau, Tabor

X MARKS THE SPOT
One hot trend for boys are names with the letter X. Actress
January Jones was right on trend in 2011 when she named her son

Xander. But the names don't have to start with an *X* to have that something special the *X* adds. Check these lists out:

Boys' Names	2000 Rank	2010 Rank
Xavier	103	77
Jaxon	476	86
Max	164	96
Axel	361	132
Braxton	336	153
Maddox	–	169
Xander	928	205
Maximus	850	212
Paxton	943	273
Felix	376	311
Jax	–	319
Dexter	756	384
Phoenix	876	388
Knox	–	434
Xzavier	873	552
Rex	–	617
Daxton	–	665
Xavi	–	806
Lennox	–	823
Nixon	–	901

Ways to Make This Trend Your Own

Options still off the radar: Xesus, Xanthus, Xachary

PRESIDENTIAL PEDIGREES

One of the hottest trends in names these days is presidential surnames, at least the ones that differ from already popular names (**Madison, Taylor**). Other presidential options are popping up everywhere—**Nixon** entered the top 1000 in 2011 (it debuted at number 901). Even *Twilight* actor Jackson Rathbone had a son who bears the presidential name **Monroe**.

You might also want to consider changing the spelling to create your own spin on this trend. For example, if you don't want to name your darling Reagan because your politics are more to the left, consider **Regan** (2011 rank: 930) or even **Teagan** (2011 rank: 213).

Girls' Names	2000 Rank	2011 Rank
Madison (James)	3	8
Taylor (Zachary)	10	44
Kennedy (John F.)	139	90
Reagan (Ronald)	286	122
McKinley (William)	–	451

Ways to Make This Trend Your Own
Options still off the radar: Taft (William), Carter (Jimmy)

Boys' Names	2000 Rank	2011 Rank
Jackson (Andrew)	72	25
Tyler (John)	10	38
Grant (Ulysses)	123	151
Lincoln (Honest Abe)	710	178
Harrison (Benjamin or William Henry)	184	234
Pierce (Franklin)	498	474

Boys' Names	2000 Rank	2011 Rank
Hayes (Rutherford)	–	776
Carter (Jimmy)	152	41
Truman (Harry S.)	–	994

Ways to Make This Trend Your Own

Options still off the radar: Buchanan (James), Johnson (Andrew), Garfield (James)

Crowdsourcing a Name

Kim Zolciak, star of *Don't Be Tardy for the Wedding*, took to Twitter for a baby name guessing game. She tweeted: "Big Question?!! What do u think we are naming our son due in a couple months? Starts with a K of course?! #startguessing." Kaden was the most popular guess, though Zolciak said no one guessed the name they chose, which was Kash Kade. Likewise, in fall of 2011, Lindsey and Dave Meske of Crystal Lake, Illinois, made national headlines when they took to Facebook to decide their baby's name. The couple couldn't agree on a name, so they posted a poll online. The choices were McKenna, Madelyn, Emily, and Addilynne. More than four thousand people from around the world voted, and in February 2012, the Menskes welcomed baby Madelyn (the name beat out McKenna by only 45 votes!). Maybe you could do the same—get your Facebook and Twitter pals started with a first letter and let them do all the work!

ERIN GO BRAGH!

Irish names have become quite popular for boys, but interestingly enough, traditional Irish girls' names are dropping in popularity. Poor **Colleen**, which consistently ranked in the top 200 names from 1948 to 1993, has dropped like a stone since then (from 207 in 1994 to falling off the top 1,000 list entirely in 2007). The counterpoint to this is **Malachi**, a name that first appeared on the top 1,000 in 1987 ranked at 992. Since then, it's taken off in popularity to be ranked at 164 in 2011.

Girls' Names	2000 Rank	2011 Rank
Erin	60	233
Kelly	111	336
Bridget	273	474
Kathleen	204	632
Eileen	627	748
Colleen	455	–

Ways to Make This Trend Your Own
Options still off the radar: Deirdre, Saoirse, Siobhan, Nuala

Boys' Names	2000 Rank	2011 Rank
Liam	140	15
Riley	109	47
Malachi	351	164
Declan	545	177
Finn	834	304

Ways to Make This Trend Your Own
Options still off the radar: Conan, Daire, Lorcan

ENDS WITH AN -O
Many boys' names with Spanish or Italian heritage end in an −o suffix, which can go beautifully with countless last names. Plus, they're O-so-romantic. Penelope Cruz and Javier Bardem's son's name, **Leo** (2011 rank: 167 and a steady climber since 2000), is an example of this trend.

Not many popular girls' names end in –*o*, and the ones that are fairly common might be nicknames for another name (**Coco**, **Cleo**, or **Margo**, for example). Why? Well, one contributing factor is that Spanish and Italian girls' names end with an –*a* (Maria, Ana, Isabella, Antoinetta, and so on).

Here's another tip: these –*o* names make fantastic middle names, too.

Name	2011 Rank
Diego	99
Antonio	118
Alejandro	130
Santiago	131
Leonardo	149
Leo	167
Mateo	171
Eduardo	184
Fernando	208
Francisco	211
Ricardo	214
Mario	224
Sergio	278
Marco	280
Emiliano	281
Maximiliano	289
Roberto	295
Angelo	298
Emilio	303
Pedro	306

Name	2011 Rank
Lorenzo	310
Armando	343
Gerardo	356
Pablo	357
Romeo	360
Milo	361
Julio	362
Rocco	402
Arturo	431

Ways to Make This Trend Your Own

Options still off the radar: Carmelo, Cosmo (remember Kramer from *Seinfeld?*), Dario, Stasio, Viggo

Predictions: Hot Names

Okay, so you've read about the trends. But what other names might be taking off in the near future? Here are some we think could be gaining ground.

BOYS AND GIRLS

The Hunger Games

The first film of *The Hunger Games* series hit theaters in March 2012, setting plenty of box office records and laying the foundation for what could be a slew of new names for young boys and girls. Currently, none of the character names are even in the top 1000, but we wouldn't be surprised if, in a couple of years, classrooms are filled with kids named **Katniss**, **Primrose**, **Peeta**, and **Gale**. The biggest *Hunger Games* name to watch? Our money is on **Rue**, the name of Katniss's lovable ally in the first book of the series.

Options for girls: Katniss, Kat, Primrose, Prim, Rue, Effie, Octavia
Options for boys: Gale, Peeta, Haymitch, Cato, Cinna, Finnick

GIRLS

Anastasia

We see 2013 as a big year for **Anastasia** (and its shorter variant **Ana**), thanks to the 2012 breakout book series *Fifty Shades of Grey*. The books from author E. L. James heated up plenty of bedrooms, and we expect to see the result of that in nurseries soon! Anastasia was 371 on the list in 2011, while Ana sat at 238. We think the names will be as hot as those books!

Variants: Anna, Anya, Anastase, Anastasha, Stasia, Stacey

Carly, Ellie, Perry

These musical acts—Carly Rae Jepsen, Ellie Goulding, and The Band Perry—were all the rage in 2012, and the names seem ripe for a surge in popularity. **Carly** has been slowly dropping over the last five years, but that seems likely to turn around. **Ellie** has been quietly climbing, breaking into the top 100 for the first time in 2011 (rank: 97). And **Perry** has never been on the girls' list, but we expect to see it—or its variants **Perri** or **Peri**—quite soon.

Carly variants: Carley, Carlie, Charlie, Karlie, Caroline
Ellie variants: Elle, Ellen, Eli, Elliot
Perry variants: Parry, Parrea, Peri, Perri

Ivy

Naming a child Blue might be too unusual for expectant parents, but fans of Beyonce and Jay-Z are going to be borrowing the couple's daughter's middle name plenty. **Ivy** has all the qualities of a girls' name that plenty of people love—the *-ee* ending sound, a reference to nature, and it's still just uncommon enough, at 266, to stand out.

Bryn

Bethenny Frankel's adorable daughter **Bryn** steals the screen on *Bethenny Ever After*—she's happy-go-lucky, always laughing, and hardly ever cranky, so it's no wonder her name appeared on the top 1000 this year for the first time since 2004. Coming in at 745, we see a meteoric rise in this name's future. The more common variant, Brynn, is also on an upswing, hitting 190 this year. Watch out for Brynn to hit the top 100 in 2013!

BRYNN/BRYN RISING	
Year	**Rank**
2000	615/–
2001	652/–
2002	584/–
2003	291/–
2004	358/912
2005	421/–
2006	401/–
2007	350/–
2008	323/–
2009	344/–
2010	286/–
2011	190/745

Penelope

It's been a big decade for the name **Penelope**, and we think 2013 could be the year it finally breaks into the top 100. In 2001, Penelope barely made the top 1000, landing at 946. The girls' name has been slowly climbing the ranks, reaching 169 in 2011. But with two A-list superstar endorsements—Tina Fey named her daughter **Penelope Athena** in 2011 and Kourtney Kardashian (the celebumom behind the **Mason** surge!) named her baby girl **Penelope Scotland** in 2012—we expect Penelope (and its variant Penny) to go through the roof!

POPULAR PENELOPE	
Year	**Rank**
2001	946
2002	717
2003	712
2004	647
2005	560
2006	482
2007	409
2008	359
2009	252
2010	200
2011	169

More 2013 Forecasts: Getting Hotter

Maxwell: The name hasn't yet hit the top 1000 for girls, but we expect to credit Jessica Simpson (and actress Lindsay Sloane) for adding it to the ever-growing gender-neutral name list in 2013.

Eloise: This throwback to the beloved children's book—and the name of Denise Richards's most recent addition—is growing in popularity right now. It debuted on the top 1000 in 2009 at 913 and climbed all the way to 449 over the next two years.

Winter: Autumn is in the top 100 (rank: 69), and Summer isn't far behind (rank: 173). The next seasonal name will be Winter, and it should come storming onto the list next year. It was nipping on the heels of the top 1000 in 2011, and now that Gretchen Mol named her baby girl Winter and Nicole Richie used it as a middle name for Harlow, the season will finally shine.

Stella: Names ending in *-a* are always huge for girls—just look at the top 10!—and Stella is in shouting distance of the top 10 at number 73. It's been quite a decade for the name—in 2000, it ranked at only 656!

BOYS

Nolan

It broke the top 100 for the first time this year—number 93!—and our bet is that **Nolan** will keep rising. Maybe it's superstar director Christopher Nolan, or maybe the character on *Revenge* (names from the show are collectively on the rise), or maybe it's young *Modern Family* actor Nolan Gould...but whatever is influencing the name, it's working! We see no limits for Nolan.

Variants: Nolyn, Noland, Nolen

Theodore

The name Theodore lends itself to a few different popular nicknames—Theo, Ted, Teddy—so it's almost like getting a four-for-one deal! Actress Ali Larter used the name for her son, and the 2012 box office hit *Ted* will only help catapult the name up the ranks.

Variants: Ted, Teddy, Theo

More 2013 Forecasts: Getting Hotter

Bryce: Teen phenom **Bryce** Harper graced the cover of *Sports Illustrated* when he was sixteen years old and made his major league baseball debut with the Washington Nationals in 2012, when he was only nineteen. The name Bryce has been hanging just outside the top 100 for nine years now, and we think this athletic namesake is just what **Bryce** needs to make a run for the top.

Barrett: We love this last name as a first name, and we're not alone. It's been rising by leaps and bounds over the past decade, and, at 435, **Barrett** was the fifth biggest jumper of 2011.

Miles: Naming children after musical legends is a growing trend, and we think 2013 will be the year of **Miles** Davis namesakes. The name jumped 22 spots in 2011 and is a variant of another popular jumper, Milo.

Enzo: *Jersey Shore*'s Snooki gave birth to her first child, a son, and she named him **Lorenzo**, but plans to call him **Enzo** for short. Considering Enzo is already on the rise—it has climbed from 872 in 2003 to 400 in 2011—we think Snooki's endorsement will be just the ticket to a breakout year.

Channing

If box office sales are any indication, 2012 will be a breakout year for the name **Channing**. Actor Channing Tatum starred in three hit films and won over fans, and his name is just unusual enough to woo prospective parents. The name broke into the top 1000 in 2010, after more than fifteen years off the list (2011 rank: 672), but we think it finally has a chance to break the top 500.

Anderson

The popular CNN news anchor **Anderson** Cooper got his own talk show this year, and his daytime presence might be the reason for his name's continuing surge in popularity. We see 2013 as an even bigger year for the last-name-as-first-name (and don't forget, the journalist's last name, **Cooper**, is also on the rise!).

All About Anderson	
Year	**Rank**
2000	781
2001	751
2002	664
2003	613
2004	594
2005	500
2006	399
2007	346
2008	324
2009	288
2010	312
2011	294

Hidden Climbers

These names aren't necessarily the biggest jumpers in popularity, and we've mentioned some of them already, but we wanted to bring them to your attention because they have steadily climbed the charts over the past few years. Look for them to gain even more ground in 2013.

Girls		Boys	
Alaina	Maci	Asher	Ryder
Alice	Mila	Axel	Rylan
Aliyah	Paisley	Bradley	Sawyer
Annabelle	Penelope	Braxton	Silas
Aria	Piper	Declan	Tucker
Aurora	Quinn	Easton	Vincent
Brielle	Reagan	Elias	
Clara	Reese	Ezekiel	
Delilah	Ruby	Greyson	
Eleanor	Skylar	Hudson	
Elena	Valentina	Jace	
Eliana	Violet	Jaxon	
Elise	Vivian	Kayden	
Hadley		Leo	
Josephine		Leonardo	
Kendall		Lincoln	
Kinley		Maddox	
Liliana		Micah	
Lyla		Roman	

Predictions: The Coldest Baby Names

We think these names are over with a capital *O*. In some cases, they became really hot really fast, and now they're oh-so-out-of-style. Others are surprisingly low in popularity considering their perceived "commonality." Perhaps you might want to consider some of these options if you want your baby to stand out in a crowd. See if you agree.

BOYS

Brett: The legendary football player Brett Favre officially retired in early 2011, and it seems his name retired with him. The name plummeted 119 slots in 2011, landing at 508.

Lance: Perhaps it's Lance Armstrong backlash. The name has dropped 200 spots since 2000. At 467, we think Lance will soon be out of the top 500.

Colby: Likely a *Survivor* effect, this name was hugely popular ten years ago. It has been slowing sliding since it peaked at 99 in 2001, and we don't see the downward trend turning around anytime soon.

Braiden/Braeden/Braden: All spellings of the popular name took a plunge this year—76, 67, and 52 spots respectively, to 544, 476, and 259. In fact, most of the "rhymes with Aiden" names are cooling down significantly.

GIRLS

Miley: As Miley Cyrus grows up, her name continues to fade out. The name—which burst into the top 1000 in 2007—dropped 99 slots in 2011.

Denise/Dana/Danna/Desiree: Have D names been D-listed? These four names were all in the top 10 list of girls' names that dropped the most in 2011.

Kimora: Fashion model and reality star Kimora Lee Simmons was behind the name's rise from 2005 to 2008, but Kimora dropped out of the top 500 in 2011.

Lindsay/Lindsey: As Lindsey Lohan continues to make headlines, the name continues to slide. Lindsay and Lindsey fell 56 and 59 slots respectively.

Gold Medal Names

Searching for a name that's destined for greatness? Look no further than the 2012 U.S. Olympic team. The following names have served these athletes well—and made their country proud. Most of these names are on the decline, but we think an Olympic run will be just the ticket to a major comeback. Because, like the athletes themselves, these names may be down, but they're never out! Whether you are looking to go traditional or off the beaten path, there's a name here for your future superstar.

Boys' Name	Athlete	Sport	2005 Rank	2011 Rank
Ryan	Lochte	Swimming	14	25
Terrence	Jennings	Tae Kwon Do	577	646
Tyson	Gay	Track and Field	267	251
Danell	Leyva	Gymnastics	–	–
Ashton	Eaton	Track and Field	107	109
Kevin	Durant	Basketball	33	67
Ellis	Coleman	Wrestling	788	724

Boys' Name	Athlete	Sport	2005 Rank	2011 Rank
Trey	Hardee	Track and Field	229	324
Clay	Stanley	Volleyball	653	727
Brady	Ellison	Archery	110	135

Girls' Name	Athlete	Sport	2005 Rank	2011 Rank
Gabrielle (Gabby)	Douglas	Gymnastics	55	119
Allyson	Felix	Track and Field	257	264
Hope	Solo	Soccer	184	231
Lori (Lolo)	Jones	Track and Field	–	–
Alexandra	Morgan	Soccer	37	76
"	Raisman	Gymnastics	"	"
Mariel	Zagunis	Fencing	–	–
Melissa (Missy)	Franklin	Swimming	104	184
Kimberly	Rhode	Shooting	63	67
Jordyn	Wieber	Gymnastics	188	121
Maya	Moore	Basketball	73	64

If you'd rather go more global with your name choices, check out some of these superstar athletes from around the world. The names of the world's best athletes might spark some Olympic babies whose names will hit the charts next year.

Worldly Names That Might Medal

Boys

Kenenisa (Bekele), Track and Field, Ethiopia
Usain (Bolt), Track and Field, Jamaica
Lin (Dan), Badminton, China
Dayron (Robles), Track and Field, Cuba
Rafael (Nadal), Tennis, Spain
Oscar (Pistorius), South Africa, Track and Field
Ous (Mellouli), Swimming, Tunisia

Girls

Oksana (Chusovitina), Gymnastics, Germany
Bahiya (Al-Hamad), Shooting, Qatar
Larisa (Iordache), Gymnastics, Romania
Carolina (Mendoza), Diving, Mexico
Fabiana (Murer), Track and Field, Brazil
Aliya (Mustafina), Gymnastics, Russia
Sally (Pearson), Track and Field, Australia

And what about the gold-medal names that the Olympians them-selves are choosing? Here is what some Olympic athletes named their kids:

Athlete Name / Sport	Baby Name (Boy or Girl)	Year of Birth	YOB Rank	2011 Rank
Kerri Walsh, beach volleyball	Joseph (B)	2009	15	22
	Sundance (B)	2010	–	–
Jason Lezak, swimming	Ryan (B)	2009	19	25
	Blake (B)	2011	87	73
Lebron James, basketball	Lebron Jr. (B)	2004	–	–
	Bryce (B)	2007	111	114
Candace Parker, basketball	Lailaa (G)	2009	–	–
Kristin Armstrong, cycling	Lucas (B)	2010	35	29
Christie Rampone, soccer	Rylie (G)	2005	338	358
	Reece (G)	2010	–	–

Celebrity-Inspired Names on the Rise

Dax (Shepard): Entered the list at 932 in 2007, now stands at 712.

Giuliana (Rancic): Entered the list at 902 in 2007, now stands at 323.

Carmelo (Anthony): Entered the list at 914 in 2004, now stands at 580.

Leighton (Meester): Debuted at 674 in 2009 and rose to 526 in 2011.

Kellan (Lutz): Entered the list at 883 in 2007, now stands at 363.

Evangeline (Lilly): 598 in 2006, at 286 in 2011.

(Jonathan) **Rhys** (Meyers): Entered the list at 940 in 2004, now at 486.

Liv (Tyler): Entered the list in 2011 at 956.

Recent Celebrity Babies

Here's a quick overview of what the celebustork has dropped off.

Adaline (Joclyn Towne and Simon Helberg)

Arlo (Naomi Nelson and Johnny Knoxville)

Bastian Kick (Addie Lane and Jeremy Sisto)

Beatrice Jean (Bryce Dallas Howard and Seth Gabel)

Blue Ivy (Beyonce and Jay-Z)

Boone McCoy (Katharine and Eric Church)

Brit Madison (Susan and David Chokachi)

Brooks Alan (Molly Sims and Scott Stuber)

Callen Christian (Drew and Brittany Brees)

Camden Jack (Kristin Cavallari and Jay Cutler)

Camden John (Nick Lachey and Vanessa Minnillo)

Clover Clementine (Natasha Gregson Wagner and Barry Watson)

Colt Daniel (Joan and John Rich)

Dallas Xavier (Fantasia Barrino)

Dixie Pearly (Lily Aldridge and Caleb Followill)

Dylan River (Heather and Joe Nichols)
Edward Duke (Giuliana and Bill Rancic)
Eliza (Caterina Scorsone and Rob Giles)
Elliotte Anne (Marla Sokoloff and Alec Puro)
Emet Kuli (Lisa Loeb and Roey Hershkovitz)
Etta Jones (Carson Daly and Siri Pinter)
Exton Elias (Susan and Robert Downey Jr.)
Fiona Leigh (Bridget and Danny Pudi)
Finn Davey (Tori Spelling and Dean McDermott)
James Timothy (Bridget and Danny Pudi)
Kaya Emory (Lindsay Davenport and Jonathan Leach)
Keeva Jane (Allyson Hannigan and Alexis Denisoff)
Kennedy Faye (Kate and Justin Moore)
Kez Sunday (Nia Long and Ime Udoka)
Gloria Ray (Maggie Gyllenhaal and Peter Sarsgaard)
Gray Audrey (Jenna von Oy and Brad Bratcher)
Halcyon Juna (Beth Littleford and Rob Fox)
Hattie Margaret (Tori Spelling and Dean McDermott)
Haven Garner (Jessica Alba and Cash Warren)
Hawkins Crawford (Candice Crawford and Tony Romo)
Hudson (Lindsay Price and Curtis Stone)
India Rose (Elsa Pataky and Chris Hemsworth)
Lauryn Anabelle (Diana Gonzalez-Jones and J. R. Martinez)
Leo Grey (Kaitlin Olson and Rob McElhenny)
Lillian McCormack (Mary McCormack and Michael Morris)
Lorenzo Dominic (Nicole Polizzi and Jionni LaValle)
Luca Cruz (Hilary Duff and Mike Comrie)
Lucia (Mira Sorvino and Christopher Backus)
Mabel Ray (Emma Heming-Willis and Bruce Willis)
Mapel Sylvie (Amanda Anka and Jason Bateman)
Marcelo Alejandro (Ali Landry and Alejandro Monteverde)
Maxwell Drew (Jessica Simpson and Eric Johnson)

Maxwell Lue (Lindsay Sloane and Dar Rollins)
Micah Emmanuel (Sarah Drew and Peter Lanfer)
Milo Thomas (Alyssa Milano and David Bugliari)
Monroe Jackson (Sheila Hafsadi and Jackson Rathbone)
Noah Phoenix (Allesandra Ambrosio and Jamie Mazur)
Noah Rev (Jessica and Josh Lucas)
Nolan River (Colette and Thomas Ian Nicholas)
Pearl Clementine (Lisa Stelly and Jack Osbourne)
Penelope Athena (Tina Fey and Jeffrey Richmond)
Penelope Scotland (Kourtney Kardashian and Scott Disick)
Phoenix (Jillian Michaels and Heidi Rhoades)
Poppy James (Jessica Capshaw and Christopher Gavigan)
Rafael (Ana Ortiz and Noah Lebenzon)
Rex Harrison (Niki Taylor and Burney Lamar)
Ruby Jeanne (Marley Shelton and Beau Flynn)
Russell Wallace (Mary Elizabeth Ellis and Charlie Day)
Samuel (Jennifer Garner and Ben Affleck)
Sebella Rose (Roselyn Sanchez and Eric Winter)
Sonny (Ceren and Jason Lee)
Talia Serafina (Erica Cerra and Raffaele Fiore)
Truman (Alexis Stewart)
West Yantz (Jessa Lee and Randy Houser)
Weston Lee (Jenna Fischer and Lee Kirk)
Willa Lue (Keri Russell and Shane Deary)
Xander Dane (January Jones)

Girls

* — All names with a * in the text denote Top 100 Names of 2011.
ᵀ — All names with a ᵀ in the text denote Top Twin Names of 2011.
^ — All names with a ^ in the text denote hot names rising in popularity in 2011.

A

Aadi (Hindi) Child of the beginning
Aadie, Aady, Aadey, Aadee, Aadea, Aadeah, Aadye

*Aaliyah (Arabic) An ascender, one having the highest social standing
Aaleyah, Aaliya, Aliyah, Alliyah, Alieya, Aliyiah, Alliyia, Aleeya, Alee, Aleiya, Alia, Aleah, Alea, Aliya

Aaralyn (American) Woman with song
Aaralynn, Aaralin, Aaralinn, Aaralinne, Aralyn, Aralynn

Aba (African) Born on a Thursday
Abah, Abba, Abbah

Abarrane (Hebrew) Feminine form of Abraham; mother of a multitude; mother of nations
Abarrayne, Abarraine, Abarane, Abarayne, Abaraine, Abame, Abrahana

Abena (African) Born on a Tuesday
Abenah, Abeena, Abyna, Abina, Abeenah, Abynah, Abinah

Abiela (Hebrew) My father is Lord
Abielah, Abiella, Abiellah, Abyela, Abyelah, Abyella, Abyellah

*ᵀAbigail (Hebrew) The source of a father's joy
Abagail, Abbigail, Abigael, Abigale, Abbygail, Abygail, Abygayle, Abbygayle, Abbegale, Abby, Abbagail, Abbey, Abbie, Abbi, Abigayle

Abijah (Hebrew) My father is Lord
Abija, Abisha, Abishah, Abiah, Abia, Aviah, Avia

Abila (Spanish) One who is beautiful
Abilah, Abyla, Abylah

Abilene (American / Hebrew) From a town in Texas / resembling grass
Abalene, Abalina, Abilena, Abiline, Abileene, Abileen, Abileena, Abilyn

Abir (Arabic) Having a fragrant scent
Abeer, Abyr, Abire, Abeere, Abbir, Abhir

Abira (Hebrew) A source of strength; one who is strong
Abera, Abyra, Abyrah, Abirah, Abbira, Abeerah

Abra (Hebrew / Arabic)
Feminine form of Abraham;
mother of a multitude;
mother of nations / lesson;
example
Abri, Abrah, Abree, Abria,
Abbra, Abrah, Abbrah

Abril (Spanish / Portuguese)
Form of April, meaning
opening buds of spring

Academia (Latin) From a com-
munity of higher learning
Akademia, Academiah,
Akademiah

Acantha (Greek) Thorny; in
mythology, a nymph who was
loved by Apollo
Akantha, Ackantha, Acanthah,
Akanthah, Ackanthah

Accalia (Latin) In mythology,
the foster mother of Romulus
and Remus
Accaliah, Acalia, Accalya,
Acalya, Acca, Ackaliah, Ackalia

Adah (Hebrew) Ornament;
beautiful addition to the
family
Adda, Adaya, Ada

Adanna (African) Her father's
daughter; a father's pride
Adana, Adanah, Adannah,
Adanya, Adanyah

Adanne (African) Her
mother's daughter; a
mother's pride
Adane, Adayne, Adaine,
Adayn, Adain, Adaen, Adaene

Adara (Greek / Arabic)
Beautiful girl / chaste one;
virgin
Adair, Adare, Adaire, Adayre,
Adarah, Adarra, Adaora, Adar

Addin (Hebrew) One who is
adorned; voluptuous
Addine, Addyn, Addyne

*T**Addison** (English) Daughter
of Adam
Addeson, Addyson, Adison,
Adisson, Addisyn, Adyson

Adeen (Irish) Little fire shin-
ing brightly
Adeene, Adean, Adeane, Adein,
Adeine, Adeyn, Adeyne

Adela (German) Of the nobil-
ity; serene; of good humor
Adele, Adelia, Adella, Adelle,
Adelie, Adelina, Adali

^**Adelaide** (German) Of the
nobility; serene; of good
humor
Adelaid

^**Adeline** (German) Form of
Adela, meaning of the nobility
*Adalyn, **Adalynn**, Adelyn,*
Adelynn

Adianca (Native American)
One who brings peace
Adianka, Adyanca, Adyanka

Adira (Hebrew / Arabic)
Powerful, noble woman /
having great strength
*Adirah, Adeera, Adyra,
Adeerah, Adyrah, Adeira,
Adeirah, Adiera*

Admina (Hebrew) Daughter of
the red earth
*Adminah, Admeena, Admyna,
Admeenah, Admynah,
Admeina*

Adoración (Spanish) Having
the adoration of all

Adra (Arabic) One who is
chaste; a virgin

ᵀ**Adriana** (Greek) Feminine
form of Adrian; from the
Adriatic Sea region; woman
with dark features
*Adria, Adriah, Adrea, Adreana,
Adreanna, Adrienna, Adriane,
Adriene, Adrie, Adrienne,
Adrianna, Adrianne, Adriel*

Adrina (Italian) Having great
happiness
*Adrinna, Adreena, Adrinah,
Adryna, Adreenah, Adrynah*

Aegea (Latin / Greek) From the
Aegean Sea / in mythology, a
daughter of the sun who was
known for her beauty

Aegina (Greek) In mythology,
a sea nymph
Aeginae, Aegyna, Aegynah

Aelwen (Welsh) Woman with
a fair brow
*Aelwenn, Aelwenne, Aelwin,
Aelwinn, Aelwinne, Aelwyn,
Aelwynn, Aelwynne*

Aerwyna (English) A friend of
the ocean

Afra (Hebrew / Arabic) Young
doe / white; an earth color
*Affra, Affrah, Afrah, Afrya,
Afryah, Afria, Affery, Affrie*

Afrodille (French) Daffodil;
showy and vivid
*Afrodill, Afrodil, Afrodile,
Afrodilla, Afrodila*

Afton (English) From the
Afton river

Agave (Greek) In mythology, a
queen of Thebes

Agnes (Greek) One who is
pure; chaste
*Agneis, Agnese, Agness, Agnies,
Agnus, Agna, Agne, Agnesa,
Nessa, Oona*

Agraciana (Spanish) One who
forgives
*Agracianna, Agracyanna,
Agracyana, Agraciann,
Agraciane, Agracyann,
Agracyane, Agracianne*

Agrona (Celtic) In mythology, the goddess of war and death
Agronna, Agronia, Agrone

Ahelia (Hebrew) Breath; a source of life
Ahelie, Ahelya, Aheli, Ahelee, Aheleigh, Ahelea, Aheleah, Ahely

Ahellona (Greek) Woman who has masculine qualities
Ahelona, Ahellonna, Ahelonna

Ahinoam (Hebrew) In the Bible, one of David's wives

Ahuva (Hebrew) One who is dearly loved
Ahuvah, Ahuda, Ahudah

Aida (English / French / Arabic) One who is wealthy; prosperous / one who is helpful / a returning visitor
Ayda, Aydah, Aidah, Aidee, Aidia, Aieeda, Aaida

Aidan (Gaelic) One who is fiery; little fire
Aiden, Adeen, Aden, Aideen, Adan, Aithne, Aithnea, Ajthne

Aiko (Japanese) Little one who is dearly loved

Ailbhe (Irish) Of noble character; one who is bright

Aileen (Irish / Scottish) Light bearer / from the green meadow
Ailean, Ailein, Ailene, Ailin, Aillen, Ailyn, Alean, Aleane

Ailis (Irish) One who is noble and kind
Ailish, Ailyse, Ailesh, Ailisa, Ailise

Ailna (German) One who is sweet and pleasant; of the nobility
Ailne

Ain (Irish / Arabic) In mythology, a woman who wrote laws to protect the rights of women / precious eye

Aine (Celtic) One who brings brightness and joy

Aingeal (Irish) Heaven's messenger; angel
Aingealag

Ainsley (Scottish) One's own meadow
Ainslie, Ainslee, Ainsly, Ainslei, Aynslie, Aynslee, Aynslie, Ansley

Aionia (Greek) Everlasting life
Aioniah, Aionea, Aioneah, Ayonia, Ayoniah, Ayonea, Ayoneah

Airic (Celtic) One who is pleasant and agreeable
Airick, Airik, Aeric, Aerick, Aerik

Aisha (Arabic / African) lively / womanly
Aiesha, Ayisha, Myisha

Aisling (Irish) A dream or vision; an inspiration
Aislin, Ayslin, Ayslinn, Ayslyn, Ayslynn, Aislyn, Aisylnn, Aislinn, Isleen

Aitheria (Greek) Of the wind
Aitheriah, Aitherea, Aithereah, Aytheria, Aytheriah, Aytherea, Aythereah

Ajaya (Hindi) One who is invincible; having the power of a god
Ajay

Aka (Maori / Turkish) Affectionate one / in mythology, a mother goddess
Akah, Akka, Akkah

Akili (Tanzanian) Having great wisdom
Akilea, Akilee, Akilie, Akylee, Akylie, Akyli, Akileah

Akilina (Latin) Resembling an eagle
Akilinah, Akileena, Akilyna, Akilinna, Ackilina, Acilina, Akylina, Akylyna

Akira (Scottish) One who acts as an anchor
Akera, Akerra, Akiera, Akirah, Akiria, Akyra, Akirrah, Akeri, Akeira, Akeara

Aksana (Russian) Form of Oksana, meaning "hospitality"
Aksanna, Aksanah, Aksannah

Alaia (Arabic / Basque) One who is majestic, of high worth joy
Alaya, Alayah, Alaiah

Alaina (French) Beautiful and fair woman; dear child
Alayna, Alaine, Alayne, Alainah, Alana, Alanah, Alanna, Alannah, Alanis, Alyn, Alani, Alanni, Alaney; Alanney; Alanie

Alair (French) One who has a cheerful disposition
Alaire, Allaire, Allair, Aulaire, Alayr, Alayre, Alaer

Alanza (Spanish) Feminine form of Alonzo; noble and ready for battle

Alarice (German) Feminine form of Alaric; ruler of all
Alarise, Allaryce, Alarica, Alarisa, Alaricia, Alrica

Alcina (Greek) One who is strong-willed and opinionated
Alceena, Alcyna, Alsina, Alsyna, Alzina, Alcine, Alcinia, Alcyne

Alda (German / Spanish) Long-lived, old / wise; an elder
Aldah, Aldine, Aldina, Aldinah, Aldene, Aldona

Aldis (English) From the ancient house
Aldys, Aldiss, Aldisse, Aldyss, Aldysse

Aldonsa (Spanish) One who is kind and gracious
Aldonza, Aldonsia, Aldonzia

Aleah (Arabic) Exalted
Alea, Alia, Aliah, Aliana, Aleana

Aleen (Celtic) Form of Helen, meaning "the shining light"
Aleena, Aleenia, Alene, Alyne, Alena, Alenka, Alynah, Aleine

Alegria (Spanish) One who is cheerful and brings happiness to others
Alegra, Aleggra, Allegra, Alleffra, Allecra

Alera (Latin) Resembling an eagle
Alerra, Aleria, Alerya, Alerah, Alerrah

Alethea (Greek) One who is truthful
Altheia, Lathea, Lathey, Olethea

*Alexa (Greek) Form of Alexandra, meaning "helper and defender of mankind"
Aleka, Alexia

^*Alexandra (Greek) Feminine form of Alexander; a helper and defender of mankind
*Alexandria, Alexandrea, Alixandra, **Alessandra**, **Alexis**, Alondra, Aleksandra, Alejandra, Sandra, Sandrine, Sasha*

*Alexis (Greek) Form of Alexandra, meaning "helper and defender of mankind"
Alexus, Alexys, Alexia

Ali (English) Form of Allison or Alice, meaning "woman of the nobility"
Allie, Alie, Alli, Ally

Aliana (English) Form of Eliana, meaning "the Lord answers our prayers"
Alianna

^Alice (German) Woman of the nobility; truthful; having high moral character
Ally, Allie, Alyce, Alesia, Aleece

Alicia (Spanish) Form of Alice, meaning "woman of the nobility"
Alecia, Aleecia, Aliza, Aleesha, Alesha, Alisha, Alisa

Alika (Hawaiian) One who is honest
Alicka, Alicca, Alyka, Alycka, Alycca

Alina (Arabic / Polish) One who is noble / one who is beautiful and bright
Aline, Aleena, Alena, Alyna

Alivia (Spanish) Form of Olivia, meaning of the olive tree

*****Allison** (English) Form of Alice, meaning "woman of the nobility, truthful; having high moral character"
Alisanne, Alison, Alicen, Alisen, Alisyn, Allyson, Alyson, Allisson

Alma (Latin / Italian) One who is nurturing and kind / refers to the soul
Almah

Almira (English) A princess; daughter born to royalty
Almeera, Almeira, Almiera, Almyra, Almirah, Almeerah, Almeirah

Aloma (Spanish) Form of Paloma, meaning "dove-like"
Alomah, Alomma, Alommah

Alondra (Spanish) Form of Alexandra, meaning "helper and defender of mankind"

Alpha (Greek) The firstborn child; the first letter of the Greek alphabet

Alphonsine (French) Feminine form of Alphonse; one who is ready for battle
Alphonsina, Alphonsyne, Alphonsyna, Alphonseene, Alphonseena, Alphonseane, Alphonseana, Alphonsiene

Alura (English) A divine counselor
Allura, Alurea, Alhraed

Alvera (Spanish) Feminine of Alvaro; guardian of all; speaker of the truth
Alveria, Alvara, Alverna, Alvernia, Alvira, Alvyra, Alvarita, Alverra

*****Alyssa** (German) Form of Alice, meaning "woman of the nobility, truthful; having high moral character"
Alisa, Alissya, Alyssaya, Alishya, Alisia, Alissa, Allisa, Allyssa, Alysa, Alysse, Alyssia

Amada (Spanish) One who is loved by all
Amadia, Amadea, Amadita, Amadah

Amadea (Latin) Feminine form of Amedeo; loved by God
Amadya, Amadia, Amadine, Amadina, Amadika, Amadis

Amadi (African) One who rejoices
Amadie, Amady, Amadey, Amadye, Amadee, Amadea, Amadeah

Amalia (German) One who is industrious and hardworking
Amelia, Amalya, Amalie, Amalea, Amylia, Amyleah, Amilia, Neneca

Amalthea (Greek) One who soothes; in mythology, the foster mother of Zeus
Amaltheah, Amalthia, Amalthya

Amanda (Latin) One who is much loved
Amandi, Amandah, Amandea, Amandee, Amandey, Amande, Amandie, Amandy, Mandy

Amani (African / Arabic) One who is peaceful / one with wishes and dreams
Amanie, Amany, Amaney, Amanee, Amanye, Amanea, Amaneah

Amara (Greek) One who will be forever beautiful
Amarah, Amarya, Amaira, Amaria, Amar

Amari (African) Having great strength, a builder
Amaree, Amarie

Amaya (Japanese) Of the night rain
Amayah, Amaia, Amaiah

Amber (French) Resembling the jewel; a warm honey color
Ambur, Ambar, Amberly, Amberlyn, Amberli, Amberlee, Ambyr, Ambyre

Ambrosia (Greek) Immortal; in mythology, the food of the gods
Ambrosa, Ambrosiah, Ambrosyna, Ambrosina, Ambrosyn, Ambrosine, Ambrozin, Ambrozyn, Ambrozyna, Ambrozyne, Ambrozine, Ambrose, Ambrotosa, Ambruslne, Amhrosine

*Amelia (German) Form of Amalia or (Latin) form of Emily, meaning "one who is industrious and hardworking"
Amelie, Amelita, Amylia, Amely

America (Latin) A powerful ruler
Americus, Amerika, Amerikus

Amina (Arabic) A princess, one who commands; truthful, trustworthy
Amirah, Ameera, Amyra, Ameerah, Amyrah, Ameira, Ameirah, Amiera

Amissa (Hebrew) One who is honest; a friend
Amisa, Amise, Amisia, Amiza, Amysa, Amysia, Amysya, Amyza

Amiyah (American) Form of Amy, meaning "beloved"
Amiah, Amiya, Amya

Amrita (Hindi) Having immortality; full of ambrosia
Amritah, Amritta, Amryta, Amrytta, Amrytte, Amritte, Amryte, Amreeta

Amser (Welsh) A period of time

Amy (Latin) Dearly loved
Aimee, Aimie, Aimi, Aimy, Aimya, Aimey, Amice, Amicia

Anaba (Native American) A woman returning from battle
Anabah, Annaba, Annabah

Anabal (Gaelic) One who is joyful
Anaball, Annabal, Annaball

Anahi (Latin) Immortal

Analia (Spanish) Combination of Ana and Lea or Lucia
Annalee, Annali, Annalie, Annaleigh, Annalea, Analeigh, Anali, Analie, Annalina, Anneli, Annaleah, Annaliese, Annalise, Annalisa, Analise, Analiese, Analisa

Anarosa (Spanish) A graceful rose
Annarosa, Anarose, Annarose

Anastasia (Greek) One who shall rise again
Anastase, Anastascia, Anastasha, Anastasie, Stacia, Stasia, Stacy, Stacey

Ancina (Latin) Form of Ann, meaning "a woman graced with God's favor"
Ancyna, Anncina, Anncyna, Anceina, Annceina, Anciena, Annciena, Anceena

*Andrea (Greek / Latin) Courageous and strong / feminine form of Andrew; womanly
Andria, Andrianna, Andreia, Andreina, Andreya, Andriana, Andreana, Andera

Angel (Greek) A heavenly messenger

^**Angela** (Greek) A heavenly messenger; an angel
*Angelica, **Angelina**, **Angelique**, Anjela, Anjelika, Angella, Angelita, Angeline, Angie, Angy*

Angelina (Greek) Form of Angela, meaning "a heavenly messenger, an angel"
Angeline, Angelyn, Angelene, Angelin

Ani (Hawaiian) One who is very beautiful
Aneesa, Aney, Anie, Any, Aany, Aanye, Anea, Aneah

Aniceta (French) One who is unconquerable
Anicetta, Anniceta, Annicetta

Aniya (American) Form of Anna, meaning "a woman graced with God's favor"
Aniyah, Anaya

*^**Anna** (Latin) A woman graced with God's favor
Annah, Ana, Ann, Anne, Anya, Ane, Annika, Anouche, Annchen, Ancina, Annie, Anika

^**Annabel** (Italian) Graceful and beautiful woman
***Annabelle**, Annabell, **Annabella**, Annabele, Anabel, Anabell, Anabelle, Anabella*

Annabeth (English) Graced with God's bounty
Anabeth, Annabethe, Annebeth, Anebeth, Anabethe

Annalynn (English) From the graceful lake
Analynn, Annalyn, Annaline, Annalin, Annalinn, Analyn, Analine, Analin

Annmarie (English) Filled with bitter grace
Annemarie, Annmaria, Annemaria, Annamarie, Annamaria, Anamarie, Anamaria, Anamari

Annora (Latin) Having great honor
Anora, Annorah, Anorah, Anoria, Annore, Annorya, Anorya, Annoria

Anouhea (Hawaiian) Having a soft, cool fragrance

Ansley (English) From the noble's pastureland
Ansly, Anslie, Ansli, Anslee, Ansleigh, Anslea, Ansleah, Anslye, Ainsley

Antalya (Russian) Born with the morning's first light
Antaliya, Antalyah, Antaliyah, Antalia, Antaliah

Antea (Greek) In mythology, a woman who was scorned and committed suicide
Anteia, Anteah

Antje (German) A graceful woman

Antoinette (French) Praiseworthy
Toinette

Anwen (Welsh) A famed beauty
Anwin, Anwenne, Anwinne, Anwyn, Anwynn, Anwynne, Anwenn, Anwinn

Anya (Russian) Form of Anna, meaning "a woman graced with God's favor"

Aphrah (Hebrew) From the house of dust
Aphra

Aphrodite (Greek) Love; in mythology, the goddess of love and beauty
Afrodite, Afrodita, Aphrodita, Aphrodyte, Aphhrodyta, Aphrodytah

Aponi (Native American) Resembling a butterfly
Aponni, Apponni, Apponi

Apphia (Hebrew) One who is productive
Apphiah

Apple (American) Sweet fruit; one who is cherished
Appel, Aple, Apel

April (English) Opening buds of spring, born in the month of April
Avril, Averel, Averill, Avrill, Apryl, Apryle, Aprylle, Aprel, Aprele, Aprila, Aprile, Aprili, Aprilla, Aprille, Aprielle, Aprial, Abrielle, Avrielle, Avrial, Abrienda, Avriel, Averyl, Averil, Avryl, Apryll

Aquene (Native American) One who is peaceful
Aqueena, Aqueene, Aqueen

Arabella (Latin) An answered prayer; beautiful altar
Arabela, Arabel, Arabell

Araceli (Spanish) From the altar of heaven
Aracely, Aracelie, Areli, Arely

Aranka (Hungarian) The golden child

Ararinda (German) One who is tenacious
Ararindah, Ararynda, Araryndah

Arava (Hebrew) Resembling a willow; of an arid land
Aravah, Aravva, Aravvah

Arcadia (Greek / Spanish)
Feminine form of Arkadios;
woman from Arcadia / one
who is adventurous
*Arcadiah, Arkadia, Arcadya,
Arkadya, Arckadia, Arckadya*

Ardara (Gaelic) From the
stronghold on the hill
*Ardarah, Ardarra, Ardaria,
Ardarrah, Ardariah*

Ardel (Latin) Feminine form of
Ardos; industrious and eager
*Ardelle, Ardella, Ardele,
Ardelia, Ardelis, Ardela, Ardell*

Arden (Latin / English) One
who is passionate and enthusiastic / from the valley of the
eagles
*Ardin, Ardeen, Ardena, Ardene,
Ardan, Ardean, Ardine, Ardun*

Ardra (Celtic / Hindi) One
who is noble / the goddess of
bad luck and misfortune

Argea (Greek) In mythology,
the wife of Polynices
Argeia

^**Aria** (English) A beautiful
melody
Ariah

*ᵀ**Ariana** (Welsh / Greek)
Resembling silver / one who
is holy
*Ariane, Arian, **Arianna**, Arianne,
Aerian, Aerion, Arianie,
Arieon, Aryana, Aryanna*

Ariel (Hebrew) A lionness of
God
*Arielle, Ariele, Airial, Ariela,
Ariella, Aryela, Arial, Ari,
Ariely, Arely, Arieli, Areli*

Arietta (Italian) A short but
beautiful melody
*Arieta, Ariete, Ariet, Ariett,
Aryet, Aryeta, Aryetta, Aryette*

Arin (English) Form of Erin,
meaning "woman of Ireland"
Aryn

Arisje (Danish) One who is
superior

Arissa (Greek) One who is
superior
Arisa, Aris, Aryssa, Arysa, Arys

Arizona (Native American)
From the little spring / from
the state of Arizona

Armani (Persian) One who is
desired
*Armanee, Armahni, Armaney,
Armanie, Armaney*

Arnette (English) A little eagle
*Arnett, Arnetta, Arnete, Arneta,
Arnet*

Aroha (Maori) One who loves and is loved

Arona (Maori) One who is colorful and vivacious
Aronah, Aronnah, Aronna

Arrosa (Basque) Sprinkled with dew from heaven; resembling a rose
Arrose

Artis (Irish / English / Icelandic) Lofy hill; noble / rock / follower of Thor
Artisa, Artise, Artys, Artysa, Artyse, Artiss, Arti, Artina

Arusi (African) A girl born during the time of a wedding
Arusie, Arusy, Arusey, Arusee, Arusea, Aruseah, Arusye

Arwa (Arabic) A female mountain goat

Arya (Indian) One who is noble and honored
Aryah, Aryana, Aryanna, Aryia

Ascención (Spanish) Refers to the Ascension

Ashby (English) Home of the ash tree
Ashbea, Ashbie, Ashbeah, Ashbey, Ashbi, Ashbee

Asherat (Syrian) In mythology, goddess of the sea

Ashima (Hebrew) In the Bible, a deity worshipped at Hamath
Ashimah, Ashyma, Asheema, Ashimia, Ashymah, Asheemah, Asheima, Asheimah

Ashira (Hebrew) One who is wealthy; prosperous
Ashyra, Ashyrah, Ashirah, Asheera, Asheerah, Ashiera, Ashierah, Asheira

*T**Ashley** (English) From the meadow of ash trees
Ashlie, Ashlee, Ashleigh, Ashly, Ashleye, Ashlya, Ashala, Ashleay

Ashlyn (American) Combination of Ashley and Lynn
Ashlynn, Ashlynne

Asia (Greek / English) Resurrection / the rising sun; in the Koran, the woman who raised Moses; a woman from the east
Aysia, Asya, Asyah, Azia, Asianne

Asis (African) Of the sun
Asiss, Assis, Assiss

Asli (Turkish) One who is genuine and original
Aslie, Asly, Asley, Aslee, Asleigh, Aslea, Asleah, Alsye

Asma (Arabic) One of high status

Aspen (English) From the aspen tree
Aspin, Aspine, Aspina, Aspyn, Aspyna, Aspyne

Assana (Irish) From the waterfall
Assane, Assania, Assanna, Asanna, Asana

Astra (Latin) Of the stars; as bright as a star
Astera, Astrea, Asteria, Astrey, Astara, Astraea, Astrah, Astree

Astrid (Scandinavian / German) One with divine strength
Astryd, Estrid

Asunción (Spanish) Refers to the Virgin Mary's assumption into heaven

^**Athena** (Greek) One who is wise; in mythology, the goddess of war and wisdom
Athina, Atheena, Athene

^***Aubrey** (English) One who rules with elf-wisdom
Aubree, Aubrie, Aubry, Aubri, Aubriana

***Audrey** (English) Woman with noble strength
Audree, Audry, Audra, Audrea, Adrey, Audre, Audray, Audrin, **Audrina**

Augusta (Latin) Feminine form of Augustus; venerable, majestic
Augustina, Agustina, Augustine, Agostina, Agostine, Augusteen, Augustyna, Agusta

Aulis (Greek) In mythology, a princess of Attica
Auliss, Aulisse, Aulys, Aulyss, Aulysse

Aurora (Latin) Morning's first light; in mythology, the goddess of the dawn
Aurore, Aurea, Aurorette

*T**Autumn** (English) Born in the fall
Autum

*T**Ava** (German / Iranian) A birdlike woman / from the water
Avah, Avalee, Avaleigh, Avali, Avalie, Avaley, Avelaine, Avelina

Avasa (Indian) One who is independent
Avasah, Avassa, Avasia, Avassah, Avasiah, Avasea, Avaseah

Avena (English) From the oat field
Avenah, Aviena, Avyna, Avina, Avinah, Avynah, Avienah, Aveinah

Avera (Hebrew) One who transgresses
Averah, Avyra, Avira

*ᵀAvery (English) One who is a wise ruler; of the nobility
Avrie, Averey, Averie, Averi, Averee, Averea, Avereah

Aviana (Latin) Blessed with a gracious life
Avianah, Avianna, Aviannah, Aviane, Avianne, Avyana, Avyanna, Avyane

Aviva (Hebrew) One who is innocent and joyful; resembling springtime
Avivi, Avivah, Aviv, Avivie, Avivice, Avni, Avri, Avyva

Awel (Welsh) One who is as refreshing as a breeze
Awell, Awele, Awela, Awella

Awen (Welsh) A fluid essence; a muse; a flowing spirit
Awenn, Awenne, Awin, Awinn, Awinne, Awyn, Awynn, Awynne

Axelle (German / Latin / Hebrew) Source of life; small oak / axe / peace
Axella, Axell, Axele, Axl, Axela, Axelia, Axellia

^Ayala (Hebrew) Resembling a gazelle
*Ayalah, Ayalla, Ayallah, **Aylin**, Ayleen, Ayline, Aileen*

Ayanna (Hindi / African) One who is innocent / resembling a beautiful flower
Ayana, Ayania, Ahyana, Ayna, Anyaniah, Ayannah, Aiyanna, Aiyana

Ayla (Hebrew) From the oak tree
Aylah, Aylana, Aylanna, Aylee, Aylea, Aylene, Ayleena, Aylena, Aylin, Ayleen, Ayline, Aileen

Aza (Arabic / African) One who provides comfort / powerful
Azia, Aiza, Aizia, Aizha

Azana (African) One who is superior
Azanah, Azanna, Azannah

Azar (Persian) One who is fiery; scarlet
Azara, Azaria, Azarah, Azarra, Azarrah, Azarr

Aznii (Chechen) A famed beauty
Azni, Aznie, Azny, Azney, Aznee, Aznea, Azneah

Azriel (Hebrew) God is my helper
Azrael, Azriell, Azrielle, Azriela, Azriella, Azraela

Azul (Spanish) Blue

B

Badia (Arabic) An elegant lady; one who is unique
Badiah, Badi'a, Badiya, Badea, Badya, Badeah

Bahija (Arabic) A cheerful woman
Bahijah, Bahiga, Bahigah, Bahyja, Bahyjah, Bahyga, Bahygah

Bailey (English) From the courtyard within castle walls; a public official
Bailee, Bayley, Baylee, Baylie, Baili, Bailie, Baileigh, Bayleigh

Baka (Indian) Resembling a crane
Bakah, Bakka, Backa, Bacca

Baligha (Arabic) One who is forever eloquent
Balighah, Baleegha, Balygha, Baliegha, Baleagha, Baleigha

Banba (Irish) In mythology, a patron goddess of Ireland

Bansuri (Indian) One who is musical
Bansurie, Bansari, Banseri, Bansurri, Bansury, Bansurey, Bansuree

Bara (Hebrew) One who is chosen
Barah, Barra, Barrah

Barbara (Latin) A traveler from a foreign land; a stranger
Barbra, Barbarella, Barbarita, Baibin, Babette, Bairbre, Barbary, Barb

Barika (African) A flourishing woman; one who is successful
Barikah, Baryka, Barikka, Barykka, Baricka, Barycka, Baricca, Barycca

Barr (English) A lawyer
Barre, Bar

Barras (English) From among the trees

Beatrice (Latin) One who blesses others
Beatrix, Beatriz, Beatriss, Beatrisse, Bea, Beatrize, Beatricia, Beatrisa

Becky (English) Form of Rebecca, meaning "one who is bound to God"
Beckey, Becki, Beckie, Becca, Becka, Bekka, Beckee, Beckea

Bel (Indian) From the sacred wood

Belen (Spanish) Woman from Bethlehem

Belinda (English) A beautiful and tender woman
Belindah, Belynda, Balynda, Belienda, Bleiendah, Balyndah, Belyndah

Belisama (Celtic) In mythology, a goddess of rivers and lakes
Belisamah, Belisamma, Belysama, Belisma, Belysma, Belesama

*Bella (Italian) A woman famed for her beauty
Belle, Bela, Bell, Belita, Bellissa, Belia, Bellanca, Bellany

Bena (Native American) Resembling a pheasant
Benah, Benna, Bennah

Benigna (Spanish) Feminine form of Benigno; one who is kind; friendly

Bernice (Greek) One who brings victory
Berenisa, Berenise, Berenice, Bernicia, Bernisha, Berniss, Bernyce, Bernys

Bertha (German) One who is famously bright and beautiful
Berta, Berthe, Berth, Bertina, Bertyna, Bertine, Bertyne, Birte

Bertilda (English) A luminous battle maiden
Bertilde, Bertild

Beryl (English) Resembling the pale-green precious stone
Beryll, Berylle, Beril, Berill, Berille

Bess (English) Form of Elizabeth, meaning "my God is bountiful; God's promise"
Besse, Bessi, Bessie, Bessy, Bessey, Bessee, Bessea

Beth (English) Form of Elizabeth, meaning "my God is bountiful; God's promise"
Bethe

Bethany (Hebrew) From the house of figs
Bethan, Bethani, Bethanie, Bethanee, Bethaney, Bethane, Bethann, Bethanne

Beyonce (American) One who surpasses others
Beyoncay, Beyonsay, Beyonsai, Beyonsae, Beyonci, Beyoncie, Beyoncee, Beyoncea

Bianca (Italian) A shining, fair-skinned woman
Bianka, Byanca, Byanka

Bibiana (Italian) Form of Vivian, meaning "lively woman"
Bibiane, Bibianna

Bijou (French) As precious as a jewel

Billie (English) Feminine form of William; having a desire to protect
Billi, Billy, Billey, Billee, Billeigh, Billea, Billeah

Blaine (Scottish / Irish) A saint's servant / a thin woman
Blayne, Blane, Blain, Blayn, Blaen, Blaene

Blair (Scottish) From the field of battle
Blaire, Blare, Blayre, Blaer, Blaere, Blayr

Blake (English) A dark beauty
Blayk, Blayke, Blaik, Blaike, Blaek, Blaeke

Blue (English) A color, lighter than purple-indigo but darker than green

Blythe (English) Filled with happiness
Blyth, Blithe, Blith

Bonamy (French) A very good friend
Bonamey, Bonami, Bonamie, Bonamee, Bonamei, Bonamea, Bonameah

Bonnie (English) Pretty face
Boni, Bona, Bonea, Boneah, Bonee

Brady (Irish) A large-chested woman
Bradey, Bradee, Bradi, Bradie, Bradea, Bradeah

Braelyn (American) Combination of Braden and Lynn
Braylin, Braelin, Braylyn, Braelen, Braylen

Braima (African) Mother of multitudes
Braimah, Brayma, Braema, Braymah, Braemah

Brandy (English) A woman wielding a sword; an alcoholic drink
Brandey, Brandi, Brandie, Brandee, Branda, Brande, Brandelyn, Brandilyn

Brazil (Spanish) Of the ancient tree
Brasil, Brazile, Brazille, Brasille, Bresil, Brezil, Bresille, Brezille

Brencis (Slavic) Crowned with laurel

Brenda (Irish) Feminine form of Brendan; a princess; wielding a sword
Brynda, Brinda, Breandan, Brendalynn, Brendolyn, Brend, Brienda

Brenna (Welsh) A raven-like woman
Brinna, Brenn, Bren, Brennah, Brina, Brena, Brenah

*ᵀ**Brianna** (Irish) Feminine form of Brian; from the high hill; one who ascends
Breanna, Breanne, Breana, Breann, Breeana, Breeanna, Breona, Breonna, Bryana, Bryanna, Briana

Brice (Welsh) One who is alert; ambitious
Bryce

Bridget (Irish) A strong and protective woman; in mythology, goddess of fire, wisdom, and poetry
Bridgett, Bridgette, Briget, Brigette, Bridgit, Bridgitte, Birgit, Birgitte

Brie (French) Type of cheese
Bree, Breeyah, Bria, Briya, Briah, Briyah, Brya

^**Briella** (Italian/Spanish) Form of Gabriella, meaning "heroine of God"

Brielle (French) Form of Brie, meaning "type of cheese"

Brilliant (American) A dazzling and sparkling woman

^**Brisa** (Spanish) Beloved
Brisia, Brisha, Brissa, Briza, Bryssa, Brysa

^**Bristol** (English) From the city in England
Brystol, Bristow, Brystow

Brittany (English) A woman from Great Britain
Britany, Brittanie, Brittaney, Brittani, Brittanee, Britney, Britnee, Britny

***Brook** (English) From the running stream
Brooke, Brookie

*ᵀ**Brooklyn** (American) Borough of New York City
Brooklin, Brooklynn, Brooklynne

Brylee (American) Variation of Riley
Brilee, Brylie, Briley, Bryli

^**Brynley** (English) From the burnt meadow
Brynlee, Brynly, Brinley, Brinli, Brynlie

^**Brynn** (Welsh) Hill
Brin, Brinn, Bryn, Brynlee, Brynly, Brinley, Brinli, Brynlie

Bryony (English) Of the healing place
Briony, Brionee

C

Cabrina (American) Form of Sabrina, meaning "a legendary princess"
Cabrinah, Cabrinna

Cabriole (French) An adorable girl
Cabriolle, Cabrioll, Cabriol, Cabryole, Cabryolle, Cabryoll, Cabryol, Cabriola

Cacalia (Latin) Resembling the flowering plant
Cacaliah, Cacalea, Cacaleah

Caden (English) A battle maiden
Cadan, Cadin, Cadon

Cadence (Latin) Rhythmic and melodious; a musical woman
Cadena, Cadenza, Cadian, Cadienne, Cadianne, Cadiene, Caydence, Cadencia, Kadence, Kaydence

Caia (Latin) One who rejoices
Cai, Cais

Cailyn (Gaelic) A young woman
Cailin

Cainwen (Welsh) A beautiful treasure
Cainwenn, Cainwenne, Cainwin, Cainwinn, Cainwinne, Cainwyn, Cainwynn, Cainwynne

Cairo (African) From the city in Egypt

Caitlin (English) Form of Catherine, meaning one who is pure, virginal
Caitlyn, Catlin, Catline, Catlyn, Caitlan, Caitlinn, Caitlynn

Calais (French) From the city in France

Cale (Latin) A respected woman
Cayl, Cayle, Cael, Caele, Cail, Caile

Caledonia (Latin) Woman of
Scotland
*Caledoniah, Caledoniya,
Caledona, Caledonya, Calydona*

California (Spanish) From
paradise; from the state of
California
Califia

Calise (Greek) A gorgeous
woman
Calyse, Calice, Calyce

Calista (Greek) Most beautiful; in mythology, a nymph
who changed into a bear
and then into the Great Bear
constellation
*Calissa, Calisto, Callista, Calyssa,
Calysta, Calixte, Colista, Collista*

Calla (Greek) Resembling a
lily; a beautiful woman
Callah

Callie (Greek) A beautiful girl
Cali, Callee, Kali, Kallie

Calypso (Greek) A woman
with secrets; in mythology,
a nymph who captivated
Odysseus for seven years

Camassia (American) One
who is aloof
*Camassiah, Camasia,
Camasiah, Camassea,
Camasseah, Camasea,
Camaseah*

Cambay (English) From the
town in India
Cambaye, Cambai, Cambae

Cambria (Latin) A woman of
Wales
*Cambriah, Cambrea, Cambree,
Cambre, Cambry, Cambrey,
Cambri, Cambrie, Cambreah*

Camdyn (English) Of the
enclosed valley
*Camden, Camdan, Camdon,
Camdin*

Cameron (Scottish) Having a
crooked nose
*Cameryn, Camryn, Camerin,
Camren, Camrin, Camron*

*Camila (Italian) Feminine
form of Camillus; a ceremo-
nial attendant; a noble virgin
*Camile, Camille, Camilla,
Camillia, Caimile, Camillei,
Cam, Camelai*

Campbell (Scottish) Having a
crooked mouth
Campbel, Campbelle, Campbele

Candace (Ethiopian / Greek) A
queen / one who is white and
glowing
*Candice, Candiss, Candyce,
Candance, Candys, Candyss,
Candy*

Candida (Latin) White-skinned

Candra (Latin) One who is glowing

Candy (English) A sweet girl; form of Candida, meaning "white-skinned"; form of Candace, meaning "a queen / one who is white and glowing"
Candey, Candi, Candie, Candee, Candea, Candeah

Caneadea (Native American) From the horizon
Caneadeah, Caneadia, Caneadiah

Canika (American) A woman shining with grace
Canikah, Caneeka, Canicka, Canyka, Canycka, Caneekah, Canickah, Canykah

Canisa (Greek) One who is very much loved
Canisah, Canissa, Canysa, Caneesa, Canyssa

Cannes (French) A woman from Cannes

Cantabria (Latin) From the mountains
Cantabriah, Cantebria, Cantabrea, Cantebrea

Caprina (Italian) Woman of the island Capri
Caprinah, Caprinna, Capryna, Capreena, Caprena, Capreenah, Caprynah, Capriena

Cara (Italian / Gaelic) One who is dearly loved / a good friend
Carah, Caralee, Caralie, Caralyn, Caralynn, Carrah, Carra, Chara

Carina (Latin) Little darling
Carinna, Cariana, Carine, Cariena, Caryna, Carinna, Carynna

Carissa (Greek) A woman of grace
Carisa, Carrisa, Carrissa, Carissima

Carla (Latin) Feminine form of Carl; a free woman
Carlah, Carlana, Carleen, Carlena, Carlene, Carletta

Carlessa (American) One who is restless
Carlessah, Carlesa, Carlesah

Carly (American) Form of Carla, meaning "a free woman"
Carlee, Carleigh, Carli, Carlie, Carley

Carmel (Hebrew) Of the fruitful orchid
Carmela, Carmella, Karmel

Carmen (Latin) A beautiful song
Carma, Carmelita, Carmencita, Carmia, Carmie, Carmina, Carmine, Carmita

Carna (Latin) In mythology, a goddess who ruled the heart

Carni (Latin) One who is vocal
Carnie, Carny, Carney, Carnee, Carnea, Carneah, Carnia, Carniah

Carol (English) Form of Caroline, meaning "joyous song"; feminine form of Charles; a small, strong woman
Carola, Carole, Carolle, Carolla, Caroly, Caroli, Carolie, Carolee

*Caroline (Latin) Joyous song; feminine form of Charles; a small, strong woman
Carol, Carolina, Carolyn, Carolann, Carolanne, Carolena, Carolene, Carolena, Caroliana

Carrington (English) A beautiful woman; a woman of Carrington
Carington, Carryngton, Caryngton

Carson (Scottish) Son of the marshland
Carsan, Carsen, Carsin, Carsyn

Carys (Welsh) One who loves and is loved
Caryss, Carysse, Caris, Cariss, Carisse, Cerys, Ceryss, Cerysse

Casey (Greek / Irish) A vigilant woman
Casie, Casy, Caysie, Kasey

Cason (Greek) A seer
Cayson, Caison, Caeson

Cassandra (Greek) An unheeded prophetess; in mythology, King Priam's daughter who foretold the fall of Troy
Casandra, Cassandrea, Cassaundra, Cassondra, Cass, Cassy, Cassey, Cassi, Cassie

Cassidy (Irish) Curly-haired girl
Cassady, Cassidey, Cassidi, Cassidie, Cassidee, Cassadi, Cassadie, Cassadee, Casidhe, Cassidea, Cassadea

Casta (Spanish) One who is pure; chaste
Castah, Castalina, Castaleena, Castaleina, Castaliena, Castaleana, Castalyna, Castara

Catherine (English) One who is pure; virginal
Catharine, Cathrine, Cathryn, Catherin, Catheryn, Catheryna, Cathi, Cathy, Katherine, Catalina

Catrice (Greek) A wholesome woman
Catrise, Catryce, Catryse, Catreece, Catreese, Catriece

Cayenne (French) Resembling the hot and spicy pepper

Cayla (American) Form of Kaila, meaning "crowned with laurel"
Caila, Caylah, Cailah

Caylee (American) Form of Kayla, meaning "crowned with laurel"
Caleigh, Caley, Cayley, Cailey, Caili, Cayli

Cecilia (Latin) Feminine form of Cecil; one who is blind; patron saint of music
Cecelia, Cecile, Cecilee, Cicely, Cecily, Cecille, Cecilie, Cicilia, Sheila, Silka, Sissy, Celia

Celand (Latin) One who is meant for heaven
Celanda, Celande, Celandia, Celandea

Celandine (English) Resembling a swallow
Celandyne, Celandina, Celandyna, Celandeena, Celandena, Celandia

Celeste (Latin) A heavenly daughter
Celesta, Celestia, Celisse, Celestina, Celestyna, Celestine

Celia (Latin) Form of Cecelia, meaning patron saint of music

Celina (Latin) In mythology, one of the daughters of Atlas who was turned into a star of the Pleiades constellation; of the heavens; form of Selena, meaning "of the moon"
Celena, Celinna, Celene, Celenia, Celenne, Celicia

Celosia (Greek) A fiery woman; burning; aflame
Celosiah, Celosea, Celoseah

Cera (French) A colorful woman
Cerah, Cerrah, Cerra

Cerina (Latin) Form of Serena, meaning "having a peaceful disposition"
Cerinah, Ceryna, Cerynah, Cerena, Cerenah, Ceriena

Cerise (French) Resembling the cherry
Cerisa

Chadee (French) A divine woman; a goddess
Chadea, Chadeah, Chady, Chadey, Chadi, Chadie

Chai (Hebrew) One who gives life
Chae, Chaili, Chailie, Chailee, Chaileigh, Chaily, Chailey, Chailea

Chailyn (American)
Resembling a waterfall
Chailynn, Chailynne, Chaelyn,
Chaelynn, Chaelynne, Chaylyn

Chakra (Arabic) A center of
spiritual energy

Chalette (American) Having
good taste
Chalett, Chalet, Chalete,
Chaletta, Chaleta

Chalina (Spanish) Form
of Rosalina, meaning
"resembling a gentle horse /
resembling the beautiful and
meaningful flower"
Chalinah, Chalyna, Chaleena,
Chalena, Charo, Chaliena,
Chaleina, Chaleana

Chameli (Hindi) Resembling
jasmine
Chamelie, Chamely, Chameley,
Chamelee

Chan (Sanskrit) A shining
woman

Chana (Hebrew) Form of
Hannah, meaning "having
favor and grace"
Chanah, Channa, Chaanach,
Chaanah, Chanach, Channah

Chance (American) One who
takes risks
Chanci, Chancie, Chancee,
Chancea, Chanceah, Chancy,
Chancey

Chanda (Sanskrit) An enemy
of evil
Chandy, Chaand, Chand,
Chandey, Chandee, Chandi,
Chandie, Chandea

Chandra (Hindi) Of the moon;
another name for the goddess
Devi
Chandara, Chandria,
Chaundra, Chandrea,
Chandreah

Chanel (French) From the
canal; a channel
Chanell, Chanelle, Channelle,
Chenelle, Chenel, Chenell

Channary (Cambodian) Of the
full moon
Channarie, Channari, Channarey,
Channaree, Chantrea, Chantria

Chantrice (French) A singer
Chantryce, Chantrise, Chantryse

Charisma (Greek) Blessed with
charm
Charismah, Charizma,
Charysma, Karisma

Charity (Latin) A woman of
generous love
Charitey, Chariti, Charitie,
Charitee

Charlesia (American) Feminine form of Charles; small, strong woman
Charlesiah, Charlesea, Charleseah, Charlsie, Charlsi

^**Charlie** (English) Form of Charles, meaning "one who is strong"
Charlee, Charli, Charley, Charlize, Charlene, Charlyn, Charlaine, Charlisa, Charlena

*ᵀ**Charlotte** (French) Form of Charles, meaning "a small, strong woman"
Charlize, Charlot, Charlotta

Charlshea (American) Filled with happiness
Charlsheah, Charlshia, Charlshiah

Charnee (American) Filled with joy
Charny, Charney, Charnea, Charneah, Charni, Charnie

Charnesa (American) One who gets attention
Charnessa, Charnessah

Charsetta (American) An emotional woman
Charsett, Charsette, Charset, Charsete, Charseta

Chartra (American) A classy lady
Chartrah

Charu (Hindi) One who is gorgeous
Charoo, Charou

Chasia (Hebrew) One who is protected; sheltered
Chasiah, Chasea, Chaseah, Chasya, Chasyah

Chasidah (Hebrew) A religious woman; pious
Chasida, Chasyda, Chasydah

Chavi (Egyptian) A precious daughter
Chavie, Chavy, Chavey, Chavee, Chavea, Chaveah

Chaya (Hebrew) Life
Chaia

Chedra (Hebrew) Filled with happiness
Chedrah

Cheer (American) Filled with joy
Cheere

Chekia (American) A saucy woman
Cheekie, Checki, Checkie, Checky, Checkey, Checkee, Checkea, Checkeah

Chelone (English) Resembling a flowering plant

Chelsea (English) From the landing place for chalk
Chelcie, Chelsa, Chelsee, Chelseigh, Chelsey, Chelsi, Chelsie, Chelsy

Chemarin (French) A dark beauty
Chemarine, Chemaryn, Chemareen, Chemarein, Chemarien

Chemda (Hebrew) A charismatic woman
Chemdah

Chenille (American) A soft-skinned woman
Chenill, Chenil, Chenile, Chenilla, Chenila

Cherika (French) One who is dear
Chericka, Cheryka, Cherycka, Cherieka, Cheriecka, Chereika, Chereicka, Cheryka

Cherish (English) To be held dear, valued

Cherry (English) Resembling a fruit-bearing tree
Cherrie, Cherri, Cherrey, Cherree, Cherrea, Cherreah

Chesney (English) One who promotes peace
Chesny, Chesni, Chesnie, Chesnea, Chesneah, Chesnee

Cheyenne (Native American) Unintelligible speaker
Chayanne, Cheyane, Cheyene, Shayan, Shyann

Chiante (Italian) Resembling the wine
Chianti, Chiantie, Chiantee, Chianty, Chiantey, Chiantea

Chiara (Italian) Daughter of the light
Chiarah, Chiarra, Chiarrah

Chiba (Hebrew) One who loves and is loved
Chibah, Cheeba, Cheebah, Cheiba, Cheibah, Chieba, Chiebah, Cheaba

Chidi (Spanish) One who is cheerful
Chidie, Chidy, Chidey, Chidee, Chidea, Chideah

Chidori (Japanese) Resembling a shorebird
Chidorie, Chidory, Chidorey, Chidorea, Chidoreah, Chidoree

Chikira (Spanish) A talented dancer
Chikirah, Chikiera, Chikierah, Chikeira, Chikeirah, Chikeera, Chikeerah, Chikyra

Chiku (African) A talkative girl

Chinara (African) God receives
Chinarah, Chinarra, Chinarrah

Chinue (African) God's own
blessing
Chinoo, Chynue, Chynoo

Chiriga (African) One who is
triumphant
Chyriga, Chyryga, Chiryga

Chislaine (French) A faithful
woman
*Chislain, Chislayn, Chislayne,
Chislaen, Chislaene, Chyslaine,
Chyslain, Chyslayn*

Chitsa (Native American) One
who is fair
Chitsah, Chytsa, Chytsah

Chizoba (African) One who is
well-protected
Chizobah, Chyzoba, Chyzobah

*ᵀ**Chloe** (Greek) A flourishing
woman; blooming
Clo, Cloe, Cloey, Chloë

Christina (English) Follower of
Christ
*Christinah, Cairistiona,
Christine, Christin, Christian,
Christiana, Christiane,
Christianna, Kristina, Cristine,
Christal, Crystal, Chrystal,
Cristal*

Chula (Native American)
Resembling a colorful flower
Chulah, Chulla, Chullah

Chulda (Hebrew) One who can
tell fortunes
Chuldah

Chun (Chinese) Born during
the spring

Chyou (Chinese) Born during
autumn

Ciara (Irish) A dark beauty
*Ceara, Ciaran, Ciarra, Ciera,
Cierra, Ciere, Ciar, Ciarda*

Cidrah (American) One who is
unlike others
Cidra, Cydrah, Cydra

Cinnamon (American)
Resembling the reddish-
brown spice
Cinnia, Cinnie

Ciona (American) One who is
steadfast
Cionah, Cyona, Cyonah

Claennis (Anglo-Saxon) One
who is pure
*Claenis, Claennys, Claenys,
Claynnis, Claynnys, Claynys,
Claynyss*

***Claire** (French) Form of Clara,
meaning "famously bright"
Clare, Clair

Clancey (American) A light-
hearted woman
*Clancy, Clanci, Clancie,
Clancee, Clancea, Clanceah*

*Clara (Latin) One who is famously bright
Clarie, Clarinda, Clarine, Clarita, Claritza, Clarrie, Clarry, Clarabelle, **Claire,** *Clarice*

Clarice (French) A famous woman; also a form of Clara, meaning "one who is famously bright"
Claressa, Claris, Clarisa, Clarise, Clarisse, Claryce, Clerissa, Clerisse, Clarissa

Claudia (Latin / German / Italian) One who is lame
Claudelle, Gladys

Clelia (Latin) A glorious woman
Cloelia, Cleliah, Clelea, Cleleah, Cloeliah, Cloelea, Cloeleah

Clementine (French) Feminine form of Clement; one who is merciful
Clem, Clemence, Clemency, Clementia, Clementina, Clementya, Clementyna, Clementyn

Cleodal (Latin) A glorious woman
Cleodall, Cleodale, Cleodel, Cleodell, Cleodelle

Cleopatra (Greek) A father's glory; of the royal family
Clea, Cleo, Cleona, Cleone, Cleonie, Cleora, Cleta, Cleoni

Clever (American) One who is quick-witted and smart

Cloris (Greek) A flourishing woman; in mythology, the goddess of flowers
Clores, Clorys, Cloriss, Clorisse, Cloryss, Clorysse

Cloud (American) A light-hearted woman
Cloude, Cloudy, Cloudey, Cloudee, Cloudea, Cloudeah, Cloudi, Cloudie

Clydette (American) Feminine form of Clyde, meaning "from the river"
Clydett, Clydet, Clydete, Clydetta, Clydeta

Clymene (Greek) In mythology, the mother of Atlas and Prometheus
Clymena, Clymyne, Clymyn, Clymyna, Clymeena, Clymeina, Clymiena, Clymeana

Clytie (Greek) The lovely one; in mythology, a nymph who was changed into a sunflower
Clyti, Clytee, Clyty, Clytey, Clyte, Clytea, Clyteah

Coby (Hebrew) Feminine form of Jacob; the supplanter
Cobey, Cobi, Cobie, Cobee, Cobea, Cobeah

Coffey (American) A lovely woman
Coffy, Coffe, Coffee, Coffea, Coffeah, Coffi, Coffie

Coira (Scottish) Of the churning waters
Coirah, Coyra, Coyrah

Colanda (American) Form of Yolanda, meaning "resembling the violet flower; modest"
Colande, Coland, Colana, Colain, Colaine, Colane, Colanna, Corlanda, Calanda, Calando, Calonda, Colantha, Colanthe, Culanda, Culonda, Coulanda, Colonda

Cole (English) A swarthy woman; having coal-black hair
Col, Coal, Coale, Coli, Colie, Coly, Coley, Colee

Colette (French) Victory of the people
Collette, Kolette

Coligny (French) Woman from Cologne
Coligney, Colignie, Coligni, Colignee, Colignea, Coligneah

Colisa (English) A delightful young woman
Colisah, Colissa, Colissah, Colysa, Colysah, Colyssa, Colyssah

Colola (American) A victorious woman
Colo, Cola

Comfort (English) One who strengthens or soothes others
Comforte, Comfortyne, Comfortyna, Comforteene, Comforteena, Comfortene, Comfortena, Comfortiene

Conary (Gaelic) A wise woman
Conarey, Conarie, Conari, Conaree, Conarea, Conareah

Concordia (Latin) Peace and harmony; in mythology, goddess of peace
Concordiah, Concordea, Concord, Concorde, Concordeah

Constanza (American) One who is strong-willed
Constanzia, Constanzea

Consuela (Spanish) One who provides consolation
Consuelia, Consolata, Consolacion, Chela, Conswela, Conswelia, Conswelea, Consuella

Contessa (Italian) A titled
woman; a countess
*Countess, Contesse, Countessa,
Counteaa, Contesa*

Cooper (English) One who
makes barrels
Couper

Copper (American) A redheaded woman
Coper, Coppar, Copar

^**Cora** (English) A young
maiden
Corah, Coraline, Corra

Coral (English) Resembling
the semiprecious sea growth;
from the reef
*Coralee, Coralena, Coralie,
Coraline, Corallina, Coralline,
Coraly, Coralyn*

Corazon (Spanish) Of the
heart
Corazana, Corazone, Corazona

Cordelia (Latin) A good-
hearted woman; a woman of
honesty
*Cordella, Cordelea, Cordilia,
Cordilea, Cordy, Cordie, Cordi,
Cordee*

Corey (Irish) From the hollow;
of the churning waters
*Cory, Cori, Coriann, Corianne,
Corie, Corri, Corrianna, Corrie*

Corgie (American) A humor-
ous woman
*Corgy, Corgey, Corgi, Corgee,
Corgea, Corgeah*

Coriander (Greek) A romantic
woman; resembling the spice
*Coryander, Coriender,
Coryender*

Corina (Latin) A spear-wielding
woman
*Corinne, Corine, Corinna,
Corrinne, Corryn, Corienne,
Coryn, Corynna*

Corinthia (Greek) A woman of
Corinth
*Corinthiah, Corinthe,
Corinthea, Corintheah,
Corynthia, Corynthea, Corynthe*

Cornelia (Latin) Feminine
form of Cornelius; referring
to a horn
*Cornalia, Corneelija, Cornela,
Cornelija, Cornelya, Cornella,
Cornelle, Cornie*

Cota (Spanish) A lively woman
Cotah, Cotta, Cottah

Coty (French) From the river-
bank
*Cotey, Coti, Cotie, Cotee, Cotea,
Coteah*

Courtney (English) A courteous woman; courtly
Cordney, Cordni, Cortenay, Corteney, Cortland, Cortnee, Cortneigh, Cortney, Courteney

Covin (American) An unpredictable woman
Covan, Coven, Covyn, Covon

Coy (English) From the woods, the quiet place
Coye, Coi

Cree (Native American) A tribal name
Crei, Crey, Crea, Creigh

Cressida (Greek) The golden girl; in mythology, a woman of Troy
Cressa, Criseyde, Cressyda, Crissyda

Cristos (Greek) A dedicated and faithful woman
Crystos, Christos, Chrystos

Cwen (English) A royal woman; queenly
Cwene, Cwenn, Cwenne, Cwyn, Cwynn, Cwynne, Cwin, Cwinn

Cylee (American) A darling daughter
Cyleigh, Cyli, Cylie, Cylea, Cyleah, Cyly, Cyley

Cynthia (Greek) Moon goddess
Cinda, Cindy, Cinthia, Cindia Cinthea

Cyrene (Greek) In mythology, a maiden-huntress loved by Apollo
Cyrina, Cyrena, Cyrine, Cyreane, Cyreana, Cyreene, Cyreena

Czigany (Hungarian) A gypsy girl; one who moves from place to place
Cziganey, Czigani, Cziganie, Cziganee

D

Dacey (Irish) Woman from the south
Daicey, Dacee, Dacia, Dacie, Dacy, Daicee, Daicy, Daci

Daffodil (French) Resembling the yellow flower
Daffodill, Daffodille, Dafodil, Dafodill, Dafodille, Daff, Daffodyl, Dafodyl

Dagmar (Scandinavian) Born on a glorious day
Dagmara, Dagmaria, Dagmarie, Dagomar, Dagomara, Dagomaria, Dagmarr, Dagomarr

Dahlia (Swedish) From the valley; resembling the flower
Dahlea, Dahl, Dahiana, Dayha, Daleia, Dalia

Daira (Greek) One who is well-informed
Daeira, Danira, Dayeera

Daisy (English) Of the day's eye; resembling a flower
Daisee, Daisey, Daisi, Daisie, Dasie, Daizy, Daysi, Deysi

Dakota (Native American) A friend to all
Dakotah, Dakotta, Dakoda, Dakodah

Damali (Arabic) A beautiful vision
Damalie, Damaly, Damaley, Damalee, Damaleigh, Damalea

Damani (American) Of a bright tomorrow
Damanie, Damany, Damaney, Damanee, Damanea, Damaneah

Damaris (Latin) A gentle woman
Damara, Damaress, Damariss, Damariz, Dameris, Damerys, Dameryss, Damiris

Dana (English) Woman from Denmark
Danna, Daena, Daina, Danaca, Danah, Dane, Danet, Daney, Dania

Danica (Slavic) Of the morning star
Danika

Daniela (Spanish) Form of Danielle, meaning "God is my judge"
Daniella

Danielle (Hebrew) Feminine form of Daniel; God is my judge
Daanelle, Danee, Danele, Danella, Danelle, Danelley, Danette, Daney

^**Danna** (American) Variation of Dana, meaning woman from Denmark
Dannah

Daphne (Greek) Of the laurel tree; in mythology, a virtuous woman transformed into a laurel tree to protect her from Apollo
Daphna, Daphney, Daphni, Daphnie, Daffi, Daffie, Daffy, Dafna

Darby (English) Of the deer park
Darb, Darbee, Darbey, Darbie, Darrbey, Darrbie, Darrby, Derby, Larby

Daria (Greek) Feminine form of Darius; possessing good fortune; wealthy
Dari, Darian, Dariane, Darianna, Dariele, Darielle, Darien, Darienne

Daring (American) One who takes risks; a bold woman
Daryng, Derring, Dering, Deryng

Darlene (English) Our little darling
Dareen, Darla, Darleane, Darleen, Darleena, Darlena, Darlenny, Darlina

Daryn (Greek) Feminine form of Darin; a gift of God
Darynn, Darynne, Darinne, Daren, Darenn, Darene

Dawn (English) Born at day-break; of the day's first light
Dawna, Dawne, Dawnelle, Dawnetta, Dawnette, Dawnielle, Dawnika, Dawnita

Day (American) A father's hope for tomorrow
Daye, Dai, Dae

Daya (Hebrew) Resembling a bird of prey
Dayah, Dayana, Dayaṇara, Dayania, Dayaniah, Dayanea, Dayaneah

Dayton (English) From the sunny town
Dayten, Daytan

Dea (Greek) Resembling a goddess
Deah, Diya, Diyah

Deborah (Hebrew) Resembling a bee; in the Bible, a prophetess
Debbera, Debbey, Debbi, Debbie, Debbra, Debby

Deidre (Gaelic) A broken-hearted or raging woman
Deadra, Dede, Dedra, Deedra, Deedre, Deidra, Deirdre, Deidrie

Deiondre (American) From the lush valley
Deiondra, Deiondria, Deiondrea, Deiondriya

Deja (French) One of remem-brance
Dayja, Dejah, Daejah, Daijia, Daija, Daijah, Deijah, Deija

Dekla (Latvian) In mythology, a trinity goddess
Decla, Deckla, Deklah, Decklah, Declah

Delaney (Irish / French) The dark challenger / from the elder-tree grove
Delaina, Delaine, Delainey, Delainy, Delane, Delanie, Delany, Delayna

Delaware (English) From the state of Delaware
Delawair, Delaweir, Delwayr, Delawayre, Delawaire, Delawaer, Delawaere

Delilah (Hebrew) A seductive woman
Delila, Delyla, Delylah

Delta (Greek) From the mouth of the river; the fourth letter of the Greek alphabet
Dellta, Deltah, Delltah

Delyth (Welsh) A pretty young woman
Delythe, Delith, Delithe

Demeter (Greek) In mythology, the goddess of the harvest
Demetra, Demitra, Demitras, Dimetria, Demetre, Demetria, Dimitra, Dimitre

Demi (Greek) A petite woman
Demie, Demee, Demy, Demiana, Demianne, Demianna, Demea

Denali (Indian) A superior woman
Denalie, Denaly, Denally, Denalli, Denaley, Denalee, Denallee, Denallie

Dendara (Egyptian) From the town on the river
Dendera, Dendaria, Denderia, Dendarra

Denise (French) Feminine form of Dennis; a follower of Dionysus
Denese, Denyse, Denice, Deniece, Denisa, Denissa, Denize, Denyce, Denys

Denver (English) From the green valley

Derora (Hebrew) As free as a bird
Derorah, Derorra, Derorit, Drora, Drorah, Drorit, Drorlya, Derorice

Derry (Irish) From the oak grove
Derrey, Derri, Derrie, Derree, Derrea, Derreah

Deryn (Welsh) A birdlike woman
Derran, Deren, Derhyn, Deron, Derrin, Derrine, Derron, Derrynne

Desiree (French) One who is desired
Desaree, Desirae, Desarae, Desire, Desyre, Dezirae, Deziree, Desirat

*Destiny (English) Recognizing one's certain fortune; fate
Destanee, Destinee, Destiney, Destini, Destinie, Destine, Destina, Destyni

Deva (Hindi) A divine being
Devi, Daeva

Devera (Latin) In mythology, goddess of brooms
Deverah

Devon (English) From the beautiful farmland; of the divine
Devan, Deven, Devenne, Devin, Devona, Devondra, Devonna, Devonne, Devyn

Dextra (Latin) Feminine form of Dexter; one who is skillful
Dex

Dharma (Hindi) The universal law of order
Darma

Dhisana (Hindi) In Hinduism, goddess of prosperity
Dhisanna, Disana, Disanna, Dhysana

Dhyana (Hindi) One who meditates

Diamond (French) Woman of high value
Diamanta, Diamonique, Diamante

Diana (Latin) Of the divine; in mythology, goddess of the moon and the hunt
Dianna, Dayanna, Dayana, Deanna

Diane (Latin) Form of Diana, meaning "of the divine"
Dayann, Dayanne, Deana, Deane, Deandra, Deann

Diata (African) Resembling a lioness
Diatah, Dyata, Diatta, Dyatah, Dyatta, Diattah, Dyattah

Dido (Latin) In mythology, the queen of Carthage who committed suicide
Dydo

Dielle (Latin) One who worships God
Diele, Diell, Diella, Diela, Diel

Dimity (English) Resembling a sheer cotton fabric
Dimitee, Dimitey, Dimitie, Dimitea, Dimiteah, Dimiti

Dimona (Hebrew) Woman from the south
Dimonah, Dymona, Demona, Demonah, Dymonah

Disa (English) Resembling an orchid

Discordia (Latin) In mythology, goddess of strife
Dyscordia, Diskordia, Dyskordia

Diti (Hindi) In Hinduism, an earth goddess
Dyti, Ditie, Dytie, Dity, Dyty, Ditey, Dytey, Ditee

Dixie (English) Woman from the South
Dixi, Dixy, Dixey, Dixee

Dolores (Spanish) Woman of sorrow; refers to the Virgin Mary
Dalores, Delora, Delores, Deloria, Deloris, Dolorcita, Dolorcitas, Dolorita

Domina (Latin) An elegant lady
Dominah, Domyna, Domynah

Dominique (French) Feminine form of Dominic; born on the Lord's day
Domaneke, Domanique, Domenica, Domeniga, Domenique, Dominee, Domineek, Domineke

Doreen (French / Gaelic) The golden one / a brooding woman
Dorene, Doreyn, Dorine, Dorreen, Doryne, Doreena, Dore, Doirean, Doireann, Doireanne, Doireana, Doireanna

Dorothy (Greek) A gift of God
Dasha, Dasya, Dodie, Dody, Doe, Doll, Dolley, Dolli

Dove (American) Resembling a bird of peace
Duv

Drisana (Indian) Daughter of the sun
Dhrisana, Drisanna, Drysana, Drysanna, Dhrysana, Dhrisanna, Dhrysanna

Drury (French) One who is greatly loved
Drurey, Druri, Drurie, Druree, Drurea, Drureah

Duana (Irish) Feminine form of Dwayne; little, dark one
Duane, Duayna, Duna, Dwana, Dwayna, Dubhain, Dubheasa

Duena (Spanish) One who acts as a chaperone

Dulce (Latin) A very sweet woman
Dulcina, Dulcee, Dulcie

Dumia (Hebrew) One who is silent
Dumiya, Dumiah, Dumiyah, Dumea, Dumeah

Duvessa (Irish) A dark beauty
Duvessah, Duvesa, Dubheasa, Duvesah

^**Dylan** (Welsh) Daughter of the waves
Dylana, Dylane, Dyllan, Dyllana, Dillon, Dillan, Dillen, Dillian

Dympna (Irish) Fawn; the patron saint of the insane
Dymphna, Dimpna, Dimphna

Dyre (Scandinavian) One who is dear to the heart

Dysis (Greek) Born at sunset
Dysiss, Dysisse, Dysys, Dysyss, Dysysse

E

Eadlin (Anglo-Saxon) Born into royalty
Eadlinn, Eadlinne, Eadline, Eadlyn, Eadlynn, Eadlynne, Eadlina, Eadlyna

Eadrianne (American) One who stands out
Eadrian, Eadriann, Edriane, Edriana, Edrianna

Eara (Scottish) Woman from the east
Earah, Earra, Earrah, Earia, Earea, Earie, Eari, Earee

Earla (English) A great leader
Earlah

Earna (English) Resembling an eagle
Earnah, Earnia, Earnea, Earniah, Earneah

Easter (American) Born during the religious holiday
Eastere, Eastre, Eastir, Eastar, Eastor, Eastera, Easteria, Easterea

Easton (American) A wholesome woman
Eastan, Easten, Eastun, Eastyn

Eathelin (English) Noble woman of the waterfall
Eathelyn, Eathelinn, Eathelynn, Eathelina, Eathelyna, Ethelin, Ethelyn, Eathelen

Eber (Hebrew) One who moves beyond

Ebere (African) One who shows mercy
Eberre, Ebera, Eberia, Eberea, Eberria, Eberrea, Ebiere, Ebierre

Ebony (Egyptian) A dark
beauty
*Eboni, Ebonee, Ebonie,
Ebonique, Eboney, Ebonea,
Eboneah*

Ebrill (Welsh) Born in April
*Ebrille, Ebril, Evril, Evrill,
Evrille*

Edana (Irish) Feminine form
of Aidan; a fiery woman
*Edanah, Edanna, Ena,
Eideann, Eidana*

Eden (Hebrew) Place of pleasure
Edan, Edin, Edon

Edith (English) The spoils of
war; one who is joyous; a
treasure
*Edyth, Eda, Edee, Edie, Edita,
Edelina, Edeline, Edelyne,
Edelynn, Edalyn, Edalynn,
Edita, Edyta, Eydie*

Edna (Hebrew) One who
brings pleasure; a delight
Ednah, Edena, Edenah

Edra (English) A powerful and
mighty woman
*Edrah, Edrea, Edreah, Edria,
Edriah*

Eduarda (Portugese) Feminine
form of Edward; a wealthy
protector
*Eduardia, Eduardea, Edwarda,
Edwardia, Edwardea,
Eduardina, Eduardyna,
Edwardina*

Edurne (Basque) Feminine form
of Edur; woman of the snow
*Edurna, Edurnia, Edurnea,
Edurniya*

Egan (American) A wholesome
woman
Egann, Egen, Egun, Egon

Egeria (Latin) A wise counselor; in mythology, a water
nymph
*Egeriah, Egerea, Egereah,
Egeriya, Egeriyah*

Eileen (Gaelic) Form of Evelyn,
meaning "a birdlike woman"
*Eila, Eileene, Eilena, Eilene,
Eilin, Eilleen, Eily, Eilean*

Eiluned (Welsh) An idol wor-
shipper
Luned

Eilwen (Welsh) One with a fair
brow
*Eilwenne, Eilwin, Eilwinne,
Eilwyn, Eilwynne*

Eirene (Greek) Form of Irene, meaning "a peaceful woman"
Eireen, Eireene, Eiren, Eir, Eireine, Eirein, Eirien, Eiriene

Eires (Greek) A peaceful woman
Eiress, Eiris, Eiriss, Eirys, Eiryss

Eirian (Welsh) One who is bright and beautiful
Eiriann, Eiriane, Eiriana, Eirianne, Eirianna

Ekron (Hebrew) One who is firmly rooted
Eckron, Ecron

Elaine (French) Form of Helen, meaning "the shining light"
Ellaine, Ellayne, Elaina, Elayna, Elayne, Elaene, Elaena, Ellaina

Elana (Hebrew) From the oak tree
Elanna, Elanah, Elanie, Elani, Elany, Elaney, Elanee, Elan

Elata (Latin) A high-spirited woman
Elatah, Elatta, Elattah, Elatia, Elatea, Elatiah, Elateah

Elath (Hebrew) From the grove of trees
Elathe, Elatha, Elathia, Elathea

Eldora (Greek) A gift of the sun
Eleadora, Eldorah, Eldorra, Eldoria, Eldorea

Eldoris (Greek) Woman of the sea
Eldorise, Eldoriss, Eldorisse, Eldorys, Eldoryss, Eldorysse

Eleacie (American) One who is forthright
Eleaci, Eleacy, Eleacey, Eleacee, Eleacea

Eleanor (Greek) Form of Helen, meaning "the shining light"
Eleanora, Eleni, Eleonora, Eleonore, Elinor, Elnora, Eleanore, Elinora, Nora

Elena (Spanish) Form of Helen, meaning "the shining light"
Elenah, Eleena, Eleenah, Elyna, Elynah, Elina, Elinah, Eleni, Eliana

Eliana (Hebrew) The Lord answers our prayers
Eleana, Elia, Eliane, Elianna, Elianne, Eliann, Elyana, Elyanna, Elyann, Elyan, Elyanne

Elica (German) One who is noble
Elicah, Elicka, Elika, Elyca, Elycka, Elyka, Elsha, Elsje

Elida (English) Resembling a winged creature
Elidah, Elyda, Eleeda, Eleda, Elieda, Eleida, Eleada

Elika (Hebrew) God will judge
Elikah, Elyka, Elicka, Elycka, Elica, Elyca

^**Elisa** (English) Form of Elizabeth, meaning "my God is bountiful"
Elisha, Elishia, Elissa, Elisia, Elysa, Elysha, Elysia, Elyssa

Elise (English) Form of Elizabeth, meaning "my God is bountiful"
Elle, Elice, Elisse, Elyse, Elysse, Ilyse

Elita (Latin) The chosen one
Elitah, Elyta, Elytah, Eleta, Eletah, Elitia, Elitea, Electa

*ᵀ**Elizabeth** (Hebrew) My God is bountiful; God's promise
Liz, Elisabet, Elisabeth, Elisabetta, Elissa, Eliza, Elizabel, Elizabet, Elsa, Beth, Babette, Libby, Lisa, Itzel, Ilsabeth, Ilsabet

*ᵀ**Ella** (German) From a foreign land
Elle, Ellee, Ellesse, Elli, Ellia, Ellie, Elly, Ela

Ellen (English) Form of Helen, meaning "the shining light"
Elin, Elleen, Ellena, Ellene, Ellyn, Elynn, Elen, Ellin

Ellery (English) Form of Hilary, meaning "a cheerful woman"
Ellerey, Elleri, Ellerie, Elleree, Ellerea, Ellereah

Elliana (Hebrew) The Lord answers our prayers
Eliana

*****Ellie** (English) Form of Eleanor, meaning "the shining light"
Elli, Elly, Elley, Elleigh

^**Ellyanne** (American) A shining and gracious woman
*Ellianne, Ellyanna, **Ellianna**, Ellyann, Elliann, Ellyan, Ellian*

Elma (German) Having God's protection
Elmah

^**Eloisa** (Latin) Form of Louise, meaning "a famous warrior"
***Eloise**, Eloiza, Eloisee, Eloize, Eloizee, Aloisa, Aloise*

Elrica (German) A great ruler
Elricah, Elrika, Elrikah, Elryca, Elrycah, Elryka, Elrykah, Elrick

^**Elsie** (English) Form of Elizabeth, meaning "my god is bountiful"

Elvia (Irish) A friend of the elves
Elva, Elvie, Elvina, Elvinia, Elviah, Elvea, Elveah, Elvyna

Elvira (Latin) A truthful woman; one who can be trusted
Elvera, Elvita, Elvyra

Ema (Polynesian / German) One who is greatly loved / a serious woman

Ember (English) A low-burning fire
Embar, Embir, Embyr

Emerson (German) Offspring of Emery
Emmerson, Emyrson

Emery (German) Industrious
Emeri, Emerie, Emori, Emorie, Emory

ᵀEmily** (Latin) An industrious and hardworking woman
Emilee, Emilie, Emilia, Emelia, Emileigh, Emeleigh, Emeli, Emelie, Emely, Emmalee

ᵀEmma** (German) One who is complete; a universal woman
Emmy, Emmajean, Emmalee, Emmi, Emmie, Emmaline, Emelina, Emeline

Emmylou (American) A universal ruler
Emmilou, Emmielou, Emylou, Emilou, Emielou

Ena (Irish) A fiery and passionate woman
Enah, Enat, Eny, Enya

Encarnación (Spanish) Refers to the Incarnation festival

Engracia (Spanish) A graceful woman
Engraciah, Engracea, Engraceah

Enslie (American) An emotional woman
Ensli, Ensley, Ensly, Enslee, Enslea, Ensleigh

Eranthe (Greek) As delicate as a spring flower
Erantha, Eranth, Eranthia, Eranthea

Erasta (African) A peaceful woman

Ercilia (American) One who is frank
Erciliah, Ercilea, Ercileah, Ercilya, Ercilyah, Erciliya, Erciliyah

Erendira (Spanish) Daughter born into royalty
Erendirah, Erendiria, Erendirea, Erendyra, Erendyria, Erendyrea, Erendeera, Erendiera

Erica (Scandinavian / Latin) Feminine form of Eric; ever the ruler / resembling heather
Erika, Ericka, Erikka, Eryka, Erike, Ericca, Erics, Eiric, Rica

Erimentha (Greek) A devoted protector
Erimenthe, Erimenthia, Erimenthea

Erin (Gaelic) Woman from Ireland
Erienne, Erina, Erinn, Erinna, Erinne, Eryn, Eryna, Erynn, Arin

Ernestina (German) Feminine form of Ernest; one who is determined; serious
Ernesta, Ernestine, Ernesha

Esdey (American) A warm and caring woman
Essdey, Esdee, Esdea, Esdy, Esdey, Esdi, Esdie, Esday

Eshah (African) An exuberant woman
Esha

Eshe (African) Giver of life
Eshey, Eshay, Esh, Eshae, Eshai

Esme (French) An esteemed woman
Esmai, Esmae, Esmay, Esmaye, Esmee

Esmeralda (Spanish) Resembling a prized emerald
Esmerald, Emerald, Emeralda, Emelda, Esma

Esne (English) Filled with happiness
Esnee, Esney, Esnea, Esni, Esnie, Esny

Essence (American) A perfumed woman
Essince, Esense, Esince, Essynce, Esynce

Esthelia (Spanish) A shining woman
Estheliah, Esthelea, Estheleah, Esthelya, Esthelyah, Estheliya, Estheliyah

Esther (Persian) Resembling the myrtle leaf
Ester, Eszter, Eistir, Eszti

Estrella (Spanish) Star
Estrela

Estrid (Norse) Form of Astrid, meaning "one with divine strength"
Estread, Estreed, Estrad, Estri, Estrod, Estrud, Estryd, Estrida

Etana (Hebrew) A strong and dedicated woman
Etanah, Etanna, Etannah, Etania, Etanea, Ethana, Ethanah, Ethania

Etaney (Hebrew) One who is focused
Etany, Etanie, Etani, Etanee, Etanea

Eternity (American) Lasting forever
Eternitie, Eterniti, Eternitey, Eternitee, Eternyty, Eternyti, Eternytie, Eternytee

Ethna (Irish) A graceful woman
Ethnah, Eithne, Ethne, Eithna, Eithnah

Eudlina (Slavic) A generous woman
Eudlinah, Eudleena, Eudleenah

Eudocia (Greek) One who is esteemed
Eudociah, Eudocea, Eudoceah

Eugenia (Greek) A well-born woman
Eugenie, Gina, Zenechka

Eulanda (American) A fair woman
Eulande, Euland, Eulandia, Eulandea

Eunice (Greek) One who conquers
Eunise, Eunyce, Eunis, Euniss, Eunyss, Eunysse

Eurybia (Greek) In mythology, a sea goddess and mother of Pallas, Perses, and Astraios
Eurybiah, Eurybea, Eurybeah

Eurynome (Greek) In mythology, the mother of the Graces
Eurynomie, Eurynomi

Euvenia (American) A hardworking woman

*Eva (Hebrew) Giver of life; a lively woman
Eve, Evetta, Evette, Evia, Eviana, Evie, Evita, Eeva

^Evangeline (Greek) A bringer of good news
Evangelina, Evangelyn

*ᵀEvelyn (German) A bird-like woman
Evaleen, Evalina, Evaline, Evalyn, Evelin, Evelina, Eveline, Evelyne, Eileen, Evelynn

Evline (French) One who loves nature
Evleen, Evleene, Evlean, Evleane, Evlene, Evlyn, Evlyne

F

Faillace (French) A delicate and beautiful woman
Faillase, Faillaise, Falace, Falase, Fallase, Fallace

Fairly (English) From the far meadow
Fairley, Fairlee, Fairleigh, Fairli, Fairlie, Faerly, Faerli, Faerlie

***Faith** (English) Having a belief and trust in God
Faythe, Faithe, Faithful, Fayana, Fayanna, Fayanne, Fayane, Fayth

Fakhira (Arabic) A magnificent woman
Fakhirah, Fakhyra, Fakhyrah, Fakheera, Fakira, Fakirah, Fakeera, Fakyra

Fala (Native American) Resembling a crow
Falah, Falla, Fallah

Fallon (Irish) A commanding woman
Fallyn, Faline, Falinne, Faleen, Faleene, Falynne, Falyn, Falina

Fantasia (Latin) From the fantasy land
Fantasiah, Fantasea, Fantasiya, Fantazia, Fantazea, Fantaziya

Farley (English) From the fern clearing
Farly, Farli, Farlie, Farlee, Farleigh, Farlea, Farleah

Fate (Greek) One's destiny
Fayte, Faite, Faete, Faet, Fait, Fayt

Fatima (Arabic) The perfect woman
Fatimah, Fahima, Fahimah

Fatinah (Arabic) A captivating woman
Fatina, Fateena, Fateenah, Fatyna, Fatynah, Fatin, Fatine, Faatinah, Fateana, Fateanah, Fatiena, Fatienah, Fateina, Fateinah

Favor (English) One who grants her approval
Faver, Favar, Favorre

Fay (English) From the fairy kingdom; a fairy or an elf
Faye, Fai, Faie, Fae, Fayette, Faylinn, Faylyn, Faylynn

Fayina (Russian) An independent woman
Fayinah, Fayena, Fayeena, Fayeana, Fayiena, Fayeina

February (American) Born in the month of February
Februari, Februarie, Februarey, Februaree, Februarea

Feechi (African) A woman who worships God
Feechie, Feechy, Feechey, Feechee, Fychi, Fychie, Fychey, Fychy

Felicity (Latin) Form of Felicia, meaning "happy"
Felicy, Felicie, Felisa

Femi (African) God loves me
Femmi, Femie, Femy, Femey, Femee, Femea, Femeah

Fenia (Scandinavian) A gold worker
Feniah, Fenea, Feneah, Feniya, Feniyah, Fenya, Fenyah, Fenja

Fernanda (Spanish) Feminine form of Fernando; an adventurous woman

Fernilia (American) A successful woman
Ferniliah, Fernilea, Fernileah, Fernilya, Fernilyah

Fia (Portuguese / Italian / Scottish) A weaver / from the flickering fire / arising from the dark of peace
Fiah, Fea, Feah, Fya, Fiya, Fyah, Fiyah

Fianna (Irish) A warrior huntress
Fiannah, Fiana, Fianne, Fiane, Fiann, Fian

Fielda (English) From the field
Fieldah, Felda, Feldah

Fife (American) Having dancing eyes
Fyfe, Fifer, Fify, Fifey, Fifee, Fifea, Fifi, Fifie

Fifia (African) Born on a Friday
Fifiah, Fifea, Fifeah, Fifeea, Fifeeah

Filipa (Spanish) Feminine form of Phillip; a friend of horses
Filipah, Filipina, Filipeena, Filipyna, Filippa, Fillipa, Fillippa

Fina (English) Feminine form of Joseph; God will add
Finah, Feena, Fyna, Fifine, Fifna, Fifne, Fini, Feana

^Finley (Gaelic) A fair-haired hero
Finlay, Finly, Finlee, Finli, Finlie, Finnley, Finnlee, Finnli, Finn, Fin

Finnea (Gaelic) From the stream of the wood
Finneah, Finnia, Fynnea, Finniah, Fynnia

Fiona (Gaelic) One who is fair; a white-shouldered woman
Fionna, Fione, Fionn, Finna, Fionavar, Fionnghuala, Fionnuala, Fynballa

Firdaus (Arabic) From the garden in paradise

Flair (English) An elegant woman of natural talent
Flaire, Flare, Flayr, Flayre, Flaer, Flaere

Flame (American) A passionate and fiery woman
Flaym, Flayme, Flaime, Flaim, Flaem, Flaeme

Flannery (Gaelic) From the flatlands
Flanery, Flanneri, Flannerie, Flannerey, Flannaree, Flannerea

Fleming (English) Woman from Belgium
Flemyng, Flemming, Flemmyng

Fleta (English) One who is swift
Fletah, Flete, Fleda, Flita, Flyta

Florence (Latin) A flourishing woman; a blooming flower
Florencia, Florentina, Florenza, Florentine, Florentyna, Florenteena, Florenteene, Florentyne

Florizel (English) A young woman in bloom
Florizell, Florizelle, Florizele, Florizel, Florizella, Florizela, Florazel, Florazell

Fola (African) Woman of honor
Folah, Folla, Follah

Fontenot (French) One who is special

Forest (English) A woodland dweller
Forrest

Forever (American) Everlasting

Francesca (Italian) Form of Frances, meaning "one who is free"
Francia, Francina, Francisca, Franchesca, Francie, Frances

Frederica (German) Peaceful ruler
Freda, Freida, Freddie, Rica

Freira (Spanish) A sister
Freirah, Freyira, Freyirah

Freya (Norse) A lady
Freyah, Freyja, Freja

Freydis (Norse) Woman born into the nobility
Freydiss, Freydisse, Freydys, Fredyss, Fraidis, Fradis, Fraydis, Fraedis

Frida (German) Peaceful
Frieda, Fryda

Fuchsia (Latin) Resembling the flower
Fusha, Fushia, Fushea, Fewsha, Fewshia, Fewshea

Fury (Greek) An enraged woman; in mythology, a winged goddess who punished wrongdoers
Furey, Furi, Furie, Furee

G

*ᵀGabriella (Italian / Spanish) Feminine form of Gabriel; heroine of God
Gabriela, Gabriellia, Gabrila, Gabryela, Gabryella

Gabrielle (Hebrew) Feminine form of Gabriel; heroine of God
Gabriel, Gabriela, Gabriele, Gabriell, Gabriellen, Gabriellia, Gabrila

Galena (Greek) Feminine form of Galen; one who is calm and peaceful
Galene, Galenah, Galenia, Galenea

Galiana (Arabic) The name of a Moorish princess
Galianah, Galianna, Galianne, Galiane, Galian, Galyana, Galyanna, Galyann

Galila (Hebrew) From the rolling hills
Galilah, Gelila, Gelilah, Gelilia, Gelilya, Glila, Glilah, Galyla

Galilee (Hebrew) From the sacred sea
Galileigh, Galilea, Galiley, Galily, Galili, Galilie

Galina (Russian) Form of Helen, meaning "the shining light"
Galinah, Galyna, Galynah, Galeena, Galeenah, Galine, Galyne, Galeene

Garbi (Basque) One who is pure; clean
Garbie, Garby, Garbey, Garbee, Garbea, Garbeah

Gardenia (English) Resembling the sweet-smelling flower
Gardeniah, Gardenea, Gardyna

Garima (Indian) A woman of importance
Garimah, Garyma, Gareema

Garnet (English) Resembling the dark-red gem
Garnette, Granata, Grenata, Grenatta

Gasha (Russian) One who is well-behaved
Gashah, Gashia, Gashea, Gashiah, Gasheah

Gavina (Latin) Feminine form of Gavin; resembling the white falcon; woman from Gabio

Gaza (Hebrew) Having great strength
Gazah, Gazza, Gazzah

Geila (Hebrew) One who brings joy to others
Geela, Geelah, Geelan, Geilah, Geiliya, Geiliyah, Gelisa, Gellah

^**Gemma** (Latin) As precious as a jewel
Gemmalyn, Gemmalynn, Gem, Gema, Gemmaline, Jemma

***Genesis** (Hebrew) Of the beginning; the first book of the Bible
Genesies, Genesiss, Genessa, Genisis

Genevieve (French) White wave; fair-skinned
Genavieve, Geneve, Genevie, Genivee, Genivieve, Genoveva, Gennie, Genny

Georgia (Greek) Feminine form of George; one who works the earth; a farmer; from the state of Georgia
Georgeann, Georgeanne, Georgina, Georgena, Georgene, Georgetta, Georgette, Georgiana, Jeorjia

Gerardine (English) Feminine form of Gerard; one who is mighty with a spear
Gerarda, Gerardina, Gerardyne, Gererdina, Gerardyna, Gerrardene, Gerhardina, Gerhardine

Gertrude (German) Adored warrior
Geertruide, Geltruda, Geltrudis, Gert, Gerta, Gerte, Gertie, Gertina, Trudy

^**Gia** (Italian) Form of Gianna, meaning "God is Gracious"
Giah

Giada (Italian) Jade
Giadda

***Gianna** (Italian) Feminine form of John, meaning "God is gracious"
Gia, Giana, Giovana

Gillian (Latin) One who is
youthful
*Gilian, Giliana, Gillianne,
Ghilian*

Gina (Japanese / English)
A silvery woman / form of
Eugenia, meaning "a well-
born woman"; form of Jean,
meaning "God is gracious"
*Geana, Geanndra, Geena,
Geina, Gena, Genalyn,
Geneene, Genelle*

Ginger (English) A lively
woman; resembling the spice
*Gingee, Gingie, Ginjer, Gingea,
Gingy, Gingey, Gingi*

Ginny (English) Form of
Virginia, meaning "one who
is chaste; virginal"
*Ginnee, Ginnelle, Ginnette,
Ginnie, Ginnilee, Ginna,
Ginney, Ginni*

Giona (Italian) Resembling the
bird of peace
*Gionah, Gionna, Gyona,
Gyonna, Gionnah, Gyonah,
Gyonnah*

Giovanna (Italian) Feminine
form of Giovanni; God is gra-
cious
*Geovana, Geovanna,
Giavanna, Giovana, Giovani,
Giovanni, Giovanie, Giovanee*

Giselle (French) One who
offers her pledge
Gisel, Gisela, Gisella, Jiselle

Gita (Hindi / Hebrew) A beau-
tiful song / a good woman
*Gitah, Geeta, Geetah, Gitika,
Gatha, Gayatri, Gitel, Gittel*

Gitana (Spanish) A gypsy
woman
*Gitanah, Gitanna, Gitannah,
Gitane*

Githa (Anglo-Saxon) A gift
from God
Githah, Gytha

^**Giulia** (Italian) Form of Julia,
meaning "one who is youth-
ful, daughter of the sky"
*Giuliana, Giulie, Giulietta,
Giuliette*

Gladys (Welsh) Form of
Claudia, meaning "one who
is lame"
*Gladdis, Gladdys, Gladi,
Gladis, Gladyss, Gwladys,
Gwyladyss, Gleda*

Glenna (Gaelic) From the val-
ley between the hills
*Gleana, Gleneen, Glenene,
Glenine, Glen, Glenn, Glenne,
Glennene*

Glenys (Welsh) A holy woman
*Glenice, Glenis, Glennice,
Glennis, Glennys, Glynis*

Gloria (Latin) A renowned and
highly praised woman
*Gloriana, Glorianna, Glorya,
Glorie, Gloree, Gloriane*

Golda (English) Resembling
the precious metal
*Goldarina, Goldarine, Goldee,
Goldi, Goldie, Goldina, Goldy,
Goldia*

Gordana (Serbian / Scottish)
A proud woman / one who is
heroic
*Gordanah, Gordanna,
Gordania, Gordaniya,
Gordanea, Gordannah,
Gordaniah, Gordaniyah*

ᵀ*Grace** (Latin) Having God's
favor; in mythology, the Graces
were the personification of
beauty, charm, and grace
*Gracee, Gracella, Gracelynn,
Gracelynne, Gracey, Gracia,
Graciana, Gracie, Gracelyn*

Gracie (Latin) Form of Grace,
meaning "having God's favor"
Gracee, Gracey, Graci

Granada (Spanish) From the
Moorish kingdom
Granadda, Grenada, Grenadda

Greer (Scottish) Feminine
form of Gregory; one who is
alert and watchful
Grear, Grier, Gryer

Gregoria (Latin) Feminine
form of Gregory; one who is
alert and watchful
*Gregoriana, Gregorijana,
Gregorina, Gregorine, Gregorya,
Gregoryna, Gregorea, Gregoriya*

Greta (German) Resembling
a pearl
*Greeta, Gretal, Grete, Gretel,
Gretha, Grethe, Grethel,
Gretna, Gretchen*

Guadalupe (Spanish) From
the valley of wolves
Guadelupe, Lupe, Lupita

Gudny (Swedish) One who is
unspoiled
*Gudney, Gudni, Gudnie,
Gudne, Gudnee, Gudnea,
Gudneah*

Guinevere (Welsh) One who
is fair; of the white wave; in
mythology, King Arthur's
queen
*Guenever, Guenevere, Gueniver,
Guenna, Guennola, Guinever,
Guinna, Gwen*

Guiseppina (Italian) Feminine form of Guiseppe; the Lord will add
Giuseppyna, Giuseppa, Giuseppia, Giuseppea, Guiseppie, Guiseppia, Guiseppa, Giuseppina

Gulielma (German) Feminine form of Wilhelm; determined protector
Guglielma, Guillelmina, Guillielma, Gulielmina, Guillermina

Gulinar (Arabic) Resembling the pomegranate
Gulinare, Gulinear, Gulineir, Gulinara, Gulinaria, Gulinarea

Gwendolyn (Welsh) One who is fair; of the white ring
Guendolen, Guendolin, Guendolinn, Guendolynn, Guenna, Gwen, Gwenda, Gwendaline, Wendy

Gwyneth (Welsh) One who is blessed with happiness
Gweneth, Gwenith, Gwenyth, Gwineth, Gwinneth, Gwinyth, Gwynith, Gwynna

Gytha (English) One who is treasured
Gythah

Habbai (Arabic) One who is much loved
Habbae, Habbay, Habbaye

Habiba (Arabic) Feminine form of Habib; one who is dearly loved; sweetheart
Habibah, Habeeba, Habyba

Hachi (Native American / Japanese) From the river / having good fortune
Hachie, Hachee, Hachiko, Hachiyo, Hachy, Hachey, Hachikka

Hadara (Hebrew) A spectacular ornament; adorned with beauty
Hadarah, Hadarit, Haduraq, Hadarra, Hadarrah

Hadassah (Hebrew) From the myrtle tree
Hadassa, Hadasah, Hadasa

Hadiya (Arabic) A gift from God; a righteous woman
Hadiyah, Hadiyyah, Haadiyah, Haadiya, Hadeeya, Hadeeyah, Hadieya, Hadieyah

Hadlai (Hebrew) In a resting state; one who hinders
Hadlae, Hadlay, Hadlaye

^**Hadley** (English) From the field of heather
Hadlea, Hadleigh, Hadly, Hedlea, Hedleigh, Hedley, Hedlie, Hadlee

Hadria (Latin) From the town in northern Italy
Hadrea, Hadriana, Hadriane, Hadrianna, Hadrien, Hadrienne, Hadriah, Hadreah

Hafthah (Arabic) One who is protected by God
Haftha

Hagab (Hebrew) Resembling a grasshopper
Hagabah, Hagaba, Hagabe

Hagai (Hebrew) One who has been abandoned
Hagae, Hagay, Hagaye, Haggai, Haggae, Hagie, Haggie, Hagi

Hagen (Irish) A youthful woman
Hagan, Haggen, Haggan

Haggith (Hebrew) One who rejoices; the dancer
Haggithe, Haggyth, Haggythe, Hagith, Hagithe, Hagyth, Hagythe

Haidee (Greek) A modest woman; one who is well-behaved
Hadee, Haydee, Haydy, Haidi, Haidie, Haydi, Haydie, Haidy

*ᵀ**Hailey** (English) from the field of hay
*Haley, Hayle, Hailee, **Haylee**, Haylie, Haleigh, Hayley, Haeleigh*

Haimati (Indian) A queen of the snow-covered mountains
Haimatie, Haimaty, Haimatey, Haimatee, Haymati, Haymatie, Haymatee, Haimatea

Haimi (Hawaiian) One who searches for the truth
Haimie, Haimy, Haimey, Haimee, Haymi, Haymie, Haymee, Haimea

Hakana (Turkish) Feminine form of Hakan; ruler of the people; an empress
Hakanah, Hakanna, Hakane, Hakann, Hakanne

Hakkoz (Hebrew) One who has the qualities of a thorn
Hakoz, Hakkoze, Hakoze, Hakkoza, Hakoza

Halak (Hebrew) One who is bald; smooth

Haleigha (Hawaiian) Born with the rising sun
Haleea, Haleya, Halya

Hall (American) One who is distinguished
Haul

Hallie (Scandinavian / Greek / English) From the hall / woman of the sea / from the field of hay
Halley, Hallie, Halle, Hallee, Hally, Halleigh, Hallea, Halleah

Halo (Latin) Having a blessed aura
Haylo, Haelo, Hailo

Halsey (American) A playful woman
Halsy, Halsee, Halsea, Halsi, Halsie, Halcie, Halcy, Halcey

Halyn (American) A unique young woman
Halynn, Halynne, Halin, Halinn, Halinne

Hammon (Hebrew) Of the warm springs

Hamula (Hebrew) Feminine form of Hamul; spared by God
Hamulah, Hamulla, Hamullah

Hana (Japanese / Arabic) Resembling a flower blossom / a blissful woman
Hanah, Hanako

Hanan (Arabic) One who shows mercy and compassion

Hang (Vietnamese) Of the moon

Hanika (Hebrew) A graceful woman
Hanikah, Haneeka, Haneekah, Hanyka, Hanykah, Haneika, Haneikah, Hanieka

Hanita (Indian) Favored with divine grace
Hanitah, Hanyta, Haneeta, Hanytah, Haneetah, Haneita, Haneitah, Hanieta

Haniyah (Arabic) One who is pleased; happy
Haniya, Haniyyah, Haniyya, Hani, Hanie, Hanee, Hany, Haney

*ᵀHannah (Hebrew) Having favor and grace; in the Bible, mother of Samuel
Hanalee, Hanalise, Hanna, Hanne, Hannele, Hannelore, Hannie, Hanny, Chana

Hanya (Aboriginal) As solid as a stone

Happy (American) A joyful woman
Happey, Happi, Happie, Happee, Happea

Hara (Hebrew) From the mountainous land
Harah, Harra, Harrah

Haradah (Hebrew) One who is filled with fear
Harada

Harika (Turkish) A superior woman
Harikah, Haryka, Hareeka, Harykah, Hareekah, Hareaka, Hareakah

Hariti (Indian) In mythology, the goddess for the protection of children
Haritie, Haryti, Harytie, Haritee, Harytee, Haritea, Harytea

Harley (English) From the meadow of the hares
Harlea, Harlee, Harleen, Harleigh, Harlene, Harlie, Harli, Harly

Harlow (American) An impetuous woman

Harmony (English / Latin) Unity / musically in tune
Harmonie, Harmoni, Harmonee

*Harper (English) One who plays or makes harps

Harriet (German) Feminine form of Henry; ruler of the house
Harriett, Hanriette, Hanrietta, Harriette, Harrietta, Harrette

Harva (English) A warrior of the army

Hasibah (Arabic) Feminine form of Hasib; one who is noble and respected
Hasiba, Hasyba, Hasybah, Haseeba, Haseebah

Hasina (African) One who is good and beautiful
Hasinah, Hasyna, Hasynah

Haurana (Hebrew) Feminine form of Hauran; woman from the caves
Hauranna, Hauranah, Haurann, Hauranne

Haven (English) One who provides a safe haven
Hayven, Havan, Hayvan, Havon, Hayvon, Havin, Hayvin, Havyn, Hayvyn, Haeven, Haevin, Haevan

Havva (Turkish) A giver of the breath of life
Havvah, Havvia, Havviah

Hayden (English) From the hedged valley
Haden, Haydan, Haydn, Haydon, Haeden, Haedyn, Hadyn

Hayud (Arabic) From the mountain
Hayuda, Hayudah, Hayood, Hayooda

Hazel (English) From the hazel tree
Hazell, Hazelle, Haesel, Hazle, Hazal, Hayzel, Haezel, Haizel

Heartha (Teutonic) A gift from Mother Earth

Heather (English) Resembling the evergreen flowering plant
Hether, Heatha, Heath, Heathe

ᵀHeaven (American) From paradise; from the sky
Heavely, Heavenly, Hevean, Hevan, Heavynne, Heavenli, Heavenlie, Heavenleigh, Heavenlee, Heavenley, Heavenlea, Heavyn

Hecate (Greek) In mythology, a goddess of fertility and witchcraft
Hekate

Heidi (German) Of the nobility, serene
Heidy, Heide, Hydie

Heirnine (Greek) Form of Helen, meaning "the shining light"
Heirnyne, Heirneine, Heirniene, Heirneene, Heirneane

Helen (Greek) The shining light; in mythology, Helen was the most beautiful woman in the world
Helene, Halina, Helaine, Helana, Heleena, Helena, Helenna, Hellen, Aleen, Elaine, Eleanor, Elena, Ellen, Galina, Heirnine, Helice, Leanna, Yalena

Helia (Greek) Daughter of the sun
Heliah, Helea, Heleah, Heliya, Heliyah, Heller, Hellar

Helice (Greek) Form of Helen, meaning "the shining light"
Helyce, Heleece, Heliece, Heleace

Helike (Greek) In mythology, a willow nymph who nurtured Zeus
Helica, Helyke, Helika, Helyka, Helyca

Helle (Greek) In mythology, the daughter of Athamas who escaped sacrifice on the back of a golden ram

Helma (German) Form of Wilhelmina, meaning "determined protector"
Helmah, Helmia, Helmea, Helmina, Helmyna, Helmeena, Helmine, Helmyne

Heloise (French) One who is famous in battle
Helois, Heloisa, Helewidis

Hen (English) Resembling the mothering bird

Henrietta (German) Feminine form of Henry; ruler of the house
Henretta, Henrieta, Henriette, Henrika, Henryetta, Hetta, Hette, Hettie

Hephzibah (Hebrew) She is my delight
Hepsiba, Hepzibeth, Hepsey

Herdis (Scandinavian) A battle maiden
Herdiss, Herdisse, Herdys

Hermelinda (Spanish) Bearing a powerful shield
Hermelynda, Hermalinda, Hermalynda, Hermelenda

Hermia (Greek) Feminine form of Hermes; a messenger of the gods
Hermiah, Hermea, Hermila

Hermona (Hebrew) From the mountain peak
Hermonah, Hermonna

Hernanda (Spanish) One who is daring
Hernandia, Hernandea, Hernandiya

Herra (Greek) Daughter of the earth
Herrah

Hersala (Spanish) A lovely woman
Hersalah, Hersalla, Hersallah, Hersalia, Hersaliah, Hersalea, Hersaleah

Hesiena (African) The first-born of twins
Hesienna, Hesienah, Heseina

Hesione (Greek) In mythology, a Trojan princess saved by Hercules from a sea monster

Hester (Greek) A starlike woman
Hestere, Hesther, Hesta, Hestar

Heven (American) A pretty young woman
Hevin, Hevon, Hevun, Hevven, Hevvin, Hevvon, Hevvun

Hezer (Hebrew) A woman of great strength
Hezir, Hezyr, Hezire, Hezyre, Hezere

Hiah (Korean) A bright woman
Heija, Heijah, Hia

Hibiscus (Latin) Resembling the showy flower
Hibiskus, Hibyscus, Hibyskus, Hybiscus, Hybiskus, Hybyscus, Hybyskus

Hikmah (Arabic) Having great wisdom
Hikmat, Hikma

Hilan (Greek) Filled with happines
Hylan, Hilane, Hilann, Hilanne, Hylane, Hylann, Hylanne

Hilary (Latin) A cheerful woman
Hillary, Hillery, Ellery

Hina (Polynesian) In mythology, a dual goddess symbolizing day and night
Hinna, Henna, Hinaa, Hinah, Heena, Hena

Hind (Arabic) Owning a group of camels; a wife of Muhammed
Hynd, Hinde, Hynde

Hinda (Hebrew) Resembling a doe
Hindah, Hindy, Hindey, Hindee, Hindi, Hindie, Hynda, Hyndy

Hiriwa (Polynesian) A silvery woman

Hitomi (Japanese) One who has beautiful eyes
Hitomie, Hitomee, Hitomea, Hitomy, Hitomey

Holda (German) A secretive woman; one who is hidden
Holde

Hollander (Dutch) A woman from Holland
Hollynder, Hollender, Holander, Holynder, Holender, Hollande, Hollanda

Holly (English) Of the holly tree
Holli, Hollie, Hollee, Holley, Hollye, Hollyanne, Holle, Hollea

Holton (American) One who is whimsical
Holten, Holtan, Holtin, Holtyn, Holtun

Holy (American) One who is pious or sacred
Holey, Holee, Holeigh, Holi, Holie, Holye, Holea, Holeah

ᵀ**Hope** (English) One who has high expectations through faith

Hortensia (Latin) Woman of the garden
Hartencia, Hartinsia, Hortencia, Hortense, Hortenspa, Hortenxia, Hortinzia, Hortendana

Hova (African) Born into the middle class

Hoyden (American) A spirited woman
Hoiden, Hoydan, Hoidan, Hoydyn, Hoidyn, Hoydin, Hoidin

Hudson (English) One who is adventurous; an explorer
Hudsen, Hudsan, Hudsun, Hudsyn, Hudsin

Hueline (German) An intelligent woman
Huelene, Huelyne, Hueleine, Hueliene, Hueleene, Huleane

Huhana (Maori) Form of Susannah, meaning "white lily"
Huhanah, Huhanna, Huhanne, Huhann, Huhane

Humita (Native American) One who shells corn
Humitah, Humyta, Humeeta, Humieta, Humeita, Humeata, Humytah, Humeetah

Hutena (Hurrian) In mythology, the goddess of fate
Hutenah, Hutenna, Hutyna, Hutina

Huwaidah (Arabic) One who is gentle
Huwaydah, Huwaida

Huyen (Vietnamese) A woman with jet-black hair

Hypatia (Greek) An intellectually superior woman
Hypasia, Hypacia, Hypate

Hypermnestra (Greek) In mythology, the mother of Amphiareos

I

Ianthe (Greek) Resembling the violet flower; in mythology, a sea nymph, a daughter of Oceanus
Iantha, Ianthia, Ianthina

Ibtesam (Arabic) One who smiles often
Ibtisam, Ibtysam

Ibtihaj (Arabic) A delight; bringer of joy
Ibtehaj, Ibtyhaj

Ida (Greek) One who is diligent; hardworking; in mythology, the nymph who cared for Zeus on Mount Ida
Idania, Idaea, Idalee, Idaia, Idania, Idalia, Idalie, Idana

Idil (Latin) A pleasant woman
Idyl, Idill, Idyll

Idoia (Spanish) Refers to the Virgin Mary
Idoea, Idurre, Iratze, Izazkun

Idona (Scandinavian) A fresh-faced woman
Idonah, Idonna, Idonnah

Ife (African) One who loves and is loved
Ifeh, Iffe

Ignatia (Latin) A fiery woman; burning brightly
Igantiah, Ignacia, Ignazia

Iheoma (Hawaiian) Lifted up by God

Ikeida (American) A spontaneous woman
Ikeidah, Ikeyda, Ikeydah

Ilamay (French) From the island
Ilamaye, Ilamai, Ilamae

Ilandere (American) Moon woman
Ilander, Ilanderre, Ilandera, Ilanderra

Ilia (Greek) From the ancient city
Iliah, Ilea, Ileah, Iliya, Iliyah, Ilya, Ilyah

Iliana (English) Form of Aileen, meaning, "the light-bearer"
Ilianna, Ilyana, Ilyanna, Ilene, Iline, Ilyne

Ilithyia (Greek) In mythology, goddess of childbirth
Ilithya, Ilithiya, Ilithyiah

Ilma (German) Form of Wilhelmina, meaning "determined protector"
Ilmah, Illma, Illmah

Ilori (African) A special child; one who is treasured
Illori, Ilorie, Illorie, Ilory, Illory, Ilorey, Illorey, Iloree

Ilta (Finnish) Born at night
Iltah, Illta

Ilyse (German / Greek) Born into the nobility / form of Elyse, meaning "blissful"
Ilysea, Ilysia, Ilysse, Ilysea

Imala (Native American) One who disciplines others
Imalah, Imalla, Imallah, Immala, Immalla

Iman (Arabic) Having great faith
Imani, Imanie, Imania, Imaan, Imany, Imaney, Imanee, Imanea, Imain, Imaine, Imayn

Imanuela (Spanish) A faithful woman
Imanuella, Imanuel, Imanuele, Imanuell

Imari (Japanese) Daughter of today
Imarie, Imaree, Imarea, Imary, Imarey

Imelda (Italian) Warrior in the universal battle
Imeldah, Imalda, Imaldah

Imperia (Latin) A majestic woman
Imperiah, Imperea, Impereah, Imperial, Imperiel, Imperielle, Imperialle

Ina (Polynesian) In mythology, a moon goddess
Inah, Inna, Innah

Inaki (Asian) Having a generous nature
Inakie, Inaky, Inakey, Inakea, Inakee

Inanna (Sumerian) A lady of the sky; in mythology, goddess of love, fertility, war, and the earth
Inannah, Inana, Inanah, Inann, Inanne, Inane

Inara (Arabic) A heaven-sent daughter; one who shines with light
Inarah, Innara, Inarra, Innarra

Inari (Finnish / Japanese) Woman from the lake / one who is successful
Inarie, Inaree, Inary, Inarey, Inarea, Inareah

Inaya (Arabic) One who cares for the well-being of others
Inayah, Inayat

Inca (Indian) An adventurer
Incah, Inka, Inkah, Incka, Inckah

India (English) From the river; woman from India
Indea, Indiah, Indeah, Indya, Indiya, Indee, Inda, Indy

Indiana (English) From the land of the Indians; from the state of Indiana
Indianna, Indyana, Indyanna

Indiece (American) A capable woman
Indeice, Indeace, Indeece, Indiese, Indeise, Indeese, Indease

Indigo (English) Resembling the plant; a purplish-blue dye
Indygo, Indeego

Ineesha (American) A sparkling woman
Ineeshah, Ineisha, Ineishah, Iniesha, Inieshah, Ineasha, Ineashah, Ineysha

Ingalls (American) A peaceful woman

Ingelise (Danish) Having the grace of the god Ing
Ingelisse, Ingeliss, Ingelyse, Ingelisa, Ingelissa, Ingelysa, Ingelyssa

Inghean (Scottish) Her father's daughter
Ingheane, Inghinn, Ingheene, Ingheen, Inghynn

Ingrid (Scandinavian) Having the beauty of the God Ing
Ingred, Ingrad, Inga, Inge, Inger, Ingmar, Ingrida, Ingria, Ingrit, Inkeri

Inis (Irish) Woman from Ennis
Iniss, Inisse, Innis, Inys, Innys, Inyss, Inysse

Intisar (Arabic) One who is victorious; triumphant
Intisara, Intisarah, Intizar, Intizara, Intizarah, Intisarr, Intysarr, Intysar

Iolanthe (Greek) Resembling a violet flower
Iolanda, Iolanta, Iolantha, Iolante, Iolande, Iolanthia, Iolanthea

Iona (Greek) Woman from the island
Ionna, Ioane, Ioann, Ioanne

Ionanna (Hebrew) Filled with grace
Ionannah, Ionana, Ionann, Ionane, Ionanne

Ionia (Greek) Of the sea and islands
Ionya, Ionija, Ioniah, Ionea, Ionessa, Ioneah, Ioniya

Iosepine (Hawaiian) Form of Josephine, meaning "God will add"
Iosephine, Iosefa, Iosefena, Iosefene, Iosefina, Iosefine, Iosepha, Iosephe

Iowa (Native American) Of the Iowa tribe; from the state of Iowa

Iphedeiah (Hebrew) One who is saved by the Lord

Iphigenia (Greek) One who is born strong; in mythology, daughter of Agamemnon
Iphigeneia, Iphigenie

Ipsa (Indian) One who is desired
Ipsita, Ipsyta, Ipseeta, Ipseata, Ipsah

Iratze (Basque) Refers to the Virgin Mary
Iratza, Iratzia, Iratzea, Iratzi, Iratzie, Iratzy, Iratzey, Iratzee

Ireland (Celtic) The country of
the Irish
Irelan, Irelann

Irem (Turkish) From the heavenly gardens
Irema, Ireme, Iremia, Iremea

Irene (Greek) A peaceful
woman; in mythology, the
goddess of peace
*Ira, Irayna, Ireen, Iren, Irena,
Irenea, Irenee, Irenka, Eirene*

Ireta (Greek) One who is
serene
*Iretah, Iretta, Irettah, Irete,
Iret, Irett, Ireta*

Iris (Greek) Of the rainbow; a
flower; a messenger goddess
*Irida, Iridiana, Iridianny,
Irisa, Irisha, Irita, Iria, Irea,
Iridian, Iriss, Irys, Iryss*

Irma (German) A universal
woman

Irta (Greek) Resembling a
pearl
Irtah

Irune (Basque) Refers to the
Holy Trinity
Iroon, Iroone, Iroun, Iroune

*T**Isabel** (Spanish) Form of
Elizabeth, meaning "my God
is bountiful; God's promise"
*Isabeau, Isabela, Isabele,
Isabelita, Isabell, Isabelle,
Ishbel, Ysabel*

*T**Isabella** (Italian / Spanish)
Form of Isabel, meaning consecrated to God
*Isabela, Isabelita, Isobella,
Izabella, Isibella, Isibela*

Isadore (Greek) A gift from
the goddess Isis
*Isadora, Isador, Isadoria,
Isidor, Isidoro, Isidorus, Isidro,
Isidora*

Isana (German) A strong-willed woman
Isanah, Isanna, Isane, Isann

Isela (American) A giving
woman
Iselah, Isella, Isellah

Isis (Egyptian) In mythology,
the most powerful of all goddesses

Isla (Gaelic) From the island
Islae, Islai, Isleta

Isleen (Gaelic) Form of
Aisling, meaning "a dream or
vision; an inspiration"
*Isleene, Islyne, Islyn, Isline,
Isleine, Isliene, Islene, Isleyne*

Isolde (Celtic) A woman known for her beauty; in mythology, the lover of Tristan
Iseult, Iseut, Isold, Isolda, Isolt, Isolte, Isota, Isotta

Isra (Arabic) One who travels in the evening
Israh, Isria, Isrea, Israt

Itiah (Hebrew) One who is comforted by God
Itia, Iteah, Itea, Itiyah, Itiya, Ityah, Itya

Itidal (Arabic) One who is cautious
Itidalle, Itidall, Itidale

Itsaso (Basque) Woman of the ocean
Itasasso, Itassaso, Itassasso

Iudita (Hawaiian) An affectionate woman
Iuditah, Iudyta, Iudytah, Iudeta, Iudetah

Iuginia (Hawaiian) A high-born woman
Iuginiah, Iuginea, Iugineah, Iugynia

Ivana (Slavic) Feminine form of Ivan; God is gracious
Iva, Ivah, Ivania, Ivanka, Ivanna, Ivanya, Ivanea, Ivane, Ivanne

Ivory (English) Having a creamy-white complexion; as precious as elephant tusks
Ivorie, Ivorine, Ivoreen, Ivorey, Ivoree, Ivori, Ivoryne, Ivorea

Ivy (English) Resembling the evergreen vining plant
Ivie, Ivi, Ivea

Iwilla (American) She shall rise
Iwillah, Iwilah, Iwila, Iwylla, Iwyllah, Iwyla, Iwylah

Ixchel (Mayan) The rainbow lady; in mythology, the goddess of the earth, moon, and healing
Ixchell, Ixchelle, Ixchela, Ixchella, Ixchal, Ixchall, Ixchalle, Ixchala

Iyabo (African) The mother is home

Izanne (American) One who calms others
Izann, Izane, Izana, Izan, Izanna

Izolde (Greek) One who is philosophical
Izold, Izolda

J

Jacey (American) Form of Jacinda, meaning "resembling the hyacinth"
Jacee, Jacelyn, Jaci, Jacine, Jacy, Jaicee, Jaycee, Jacie

Jacinda (Spanish) Resembling the hyacinth
Jacenda, Jacenia, Jacenta, Jacindia, Jacinna, Jacinta, Jacinth, Jacintha, Jacinthe, Jacinthia, Jacynth, Jacyntha, Jacynthe, Jacynthia, Jakinda, Jakinta, Jaikinda, Jaekinda

Jacqueline (French) Feminine form of Jacques; the supplanter
Jackie, Xaquelina, Jacalin, Jacalyn, Jacalynn, Jackalin, Jackalinne, Jackelyn, Jacquelyn

Jade (Spanish) Resembling the green gemstone
Jadeana, Jadee, Jadine, Jadira, Jadrian, Jadrienne, Jady

Jaden (Hebrew / English) One who is thankful to God / form of Jade, meaning "resembling the green gemstone"
Jadine, Jadyn, Jadon, Jayden, Jadyne, Jaydyn, Jaydon, Jaidyn

Jadzia (Polish) A princess; born into royalty
Jadziah, Jadzea, Jadzeah

Jae (English) Feminine form of Jay; resembling a jaybird
Jai, Jaelana, Jaeleah, Jaelyn, Jaenelle, Jaya

Jael (Hebrew) Resembling a mountain goat
Jaella, Jaelle, Jayel, Jaele, Jayil

Jaen (Hebrew) Resembling an ostrich
Jaena, Jaenia, Jaenea, Jaenne

Jaffa (Hebrew) A beautiful woman
Jaffah, Jafit, Jafita

Jalila (Arabic) An important woman; one who is exalted
Jalilah, Jalyla, Jalylah, Jaleela

Jamaica (American) From the island of springs
Jamaeca, Jamaika, Jemaica, Jamika, Jamieka

Jamie (Hebrew) Feminine form of James; she who supplants
Jaima, Jaime, Jaimee, Jaimelynn, Jaimey, Jaimi, Jaimie, Jaimy

Janan (Arabic) Of the heart and soul

Jane (Hebrew) Feminine form of John; God is gracious
Jaina, Jaine, Jainee, Janey, Jana, Janae, Janaye, Jandy, Sine, Janel, Janelle

Janet (Scottish) Feminine form of John, meaning "God is gracious"
Janetta, Jenetta, Janeta, Janette, Janit

Janis (English) Feminine form of John; God is gracious
Janice, Janeece, Janess, Janessa, Janesse, Janessia, Janicia, Janiece

Janiyah (American) Form of Jana, meaning gracious, merciful
Janiya, Janiah

Jarah (Hebrew) A sweet and kind woman

Jasher (Hebrew) One who is righteous; upright
Jashiere, Jasheria, Jasherea

Jaslene (American) Form of Jocelyn, meaning joy
Jaslin, Jaslyn, Jazlyn, Jazlynn

*__Jasmine__ (Persian) Resembling the climbing plant with fragrant flowers
Jaslyn, Jaslynn, Jasmin, Jasmyn, Jazmin, Jazmine, Jazmyn

Javiera (Spanish) Feminine form of Xavier; one who is bright; the owner of a new home
Javierah, Javyera, Javyerah, Javeira, Javeirah

ᵀ**Jayda** (English) Resembling the green gemstone
__Jada__, Jaydah, Jaida, Jaidah

^ᵀ**Jayla** (Arabic) One who is charitable
Jaela, Jaila, Jaylah, Jaylee, Jaylen, Jaylene, __Jayleen__, Jaylin, Jaylyn, Jaylynn

Jean (Hebrew) Feminine form of John; God is gracious
Jeanae, Jeanay, Jeane, Jeanee, Jeanelle, Jeanetta, Jeanette, Jeanice, Gina

Jemima (Hebrew) Our little dove; in the Bible, the eldest of Job's daughters
Jemimah, Jamina, Jeminah, Jemmimah, Jemmie, Jemmy, Jem, Jemmi, Jemmey, Jemmee, Jemmea

Jemma (English) Form of Gemma, meaning "as precious as a jewel"
Jemmah, Jema, Jemah, Jemmalyn, Jemalyn

Jena (Arabic) Our little bird
Jenna, Jenah

Jendayi (Egyptian) One who is thankful
Jendayie, Jendayey, Jendayee

Jennifer (Welsh) One who is fair; a beautiful girl
*Jenefer, Jeni, Jenifer, Jeniffer, Jenn, Jennee, Jenni, Jen, **Jenna**, Jenny*

Jeorjia (American) Form of Georgia, meaning "one who works the earth; a farmer"
Jeorgia, Jeorja, Jorja, Jorjette, Jorgette, Jorjeta, Jorjetta, Jorgete

Jereni (Slavic) One who is peaceful
Jerenie, Jereny, Jereney, Jerenee

Jermaine (French) Woman from Germany
Jermainaa, Jermane, Jermayne, Jermina, Jermana, Jermayna

Jessica (Hebrew) The Lord sees all
Jess, Jessa, Jessaca, Jessaka, Jessalin, Jessalyn, Jesse, Jesseca, Yessica, Jessie

Jetta (Danish) Resembling the jet-black lustrous gemstone
Jette, Jett, Jeta, Jete, Jettie, Jetty, Jetti, Jettey

Jewel (French) One who is playful; resembling a precious gem
Jewell, Jewelle, Jewelyn, Jewelene, Jewelisa, Jule, Jewella, Juelline

Jezebel (Hebrew) One who is not exalted; in the Bible, the queen of Israel punished by God
Jessabell, Jetzabel, Jezabel, Jezabella, Jezebelle, Jezibel, Jezibelle, Jezybell

Jie (Chinese) One who is pure; chaste

Jiera (Lithuanian) A lively woman
Jierah, Jyera, Jyerah, Jierra, Jyerra

Jillian (English) Form of Gillian, meaning "one who is youthful"
Jilian, Jiliana, Jillaine, Jillan, Jillana, Jillane, Jillanne, Jillayne, Jillene, Jillesa, Jilliana, Jilliane, Jilliann, Jillianna, Jill

Jimena (Spanish) One who is heard

Jinelle (Welsh) Form of Genevieve, meaning "white wave; fair-skinned"
Jinell, Jinele, Jinel, Jynelle, Jynell, Jynele, Jynel

Jiselle (American) Form of Giselle, meaning "one who offers her pledge"
Jisell, Jisele, Jisela, Jizelle, Joselle, Jisella, Jizella, Jozelle

Jo (English) Feminine form of Joseph; God will add
Jobelle, Jobeth, Jodean, Jodelle, Joetta, Joette, Jolinda, Jolisa

Joanna (French) Feminine form of John, meaning "God is Gracious"
Joana

*Jocelyn (German / Latin) From the tribe of Gauts / one who is cheerful, happy
Jocelin, Jocelina, Jocelinda, Joceline, Jocelyne, Jocelynn, Jocelynne, Josalind, Joslyn, Joslynn, Joselyn

Joda (Hebrew) An ancestor of Christ

Jolan (Greek) Resembling a violet flower
Jola, Jolaine, Jolande, Jolanne, Jolanta, Jolantha, Jolandi, Jolanka

Jolene (English) Feminine form of Joseph; God will add
Joeline, Joeleen, Joeline, Jolaine, Jolean, Joleen, Jolena, Jolina

Jolie (French) A pretty young woman
Joly, Joely, Jolee, Joleigh, Joley, Joli

Jonina (Israeli) Resembling a little dove
Joninah, Jonyna, Jonynah, Joneena, Joneenah, Jonine, Jonyne, Joneene

Jorah (Hebrew) Resembling an autumn rose
Jora

Jord (Norse) In mythology, goddess of the earth
Jorde

Jordan (Hebrew) Of the down-flowing river; in the Bible, the river where Jesus was baptized
Jardena, Johrdan, Jordain, Jordaine, Jordana, Jordane, Jordanka, Jordyn, Jordin

Josephine (French) Feminine form of Joseph; God will add
Josefina, Josephene, Jo, Josie, Iosepine

Journey (American) One who likes to travel
Journy, Journi, Journie, Journee

Jovana (Spanish) Feminine form of Jovian; daughter of the sky
Jeovana, Jeovanna, Jovanna, Jovena, Jovianne, Jovina, Jovita, Joviana

Joy (Latin) A delight; one who brings pleasure to others
Jioia, Jioya, Joi, Joia, Joie, Joya, Joyann, Joyanna

Joyce (English) One who brings joy to others
Joice, Joyceanne, Joycelyn, Joycelynn, Joyse, Joyceta

Judith (Hebrew) Woman from Judea
Judithe, Juditha, Judeena, Judeana, Judyth, Judit, Judytha, Judita, Hudes

*★**Julia** (Latin) One who is youthful; daughter of the sky
Jiulia, Joleta, Joletta, Jolette, Julaine, Julayna, Julee, Juleen, Julie, Julianne

Juliana (Spanish) Form of Julia, meaning "one who is youthful"
Julianna

Juliet (French) Form of Julia, meaning one who is youthful
Juliette, Julitta, Julissa

July (Latin) Form of Julia, meaning "one who is youthful; daughter of the sky"; born during the month of July
Julye

^**June** (Latin) One who is youthful; born during the month of June
Junae, Junel, Junelle, Junette, Junita, Junia

Justice (English) One who upholds moral rightness and fairness
Justyce, Justiss, Justyss, Justis, Justus, Justise

K

Kachina (Native American) A spiritual dancer
Kachine, Kachinah, Kachineh, Kachyna, Kacheena, Kachynah, Kacheenah, Kacheana

Kadin (Arabic) A beloved companion
Kadyn, Kadan, Kaden, Kadon, Kadun, Kaedin, Kaeden, Kaydin

Kaelyn (English) A beautiful girl from the meadow
Kaelynn, Kaelynne, Kaelin, Kailyn, Kaylyn, Kaelinn, Kaelinne

Kagami (Japanese) Displaying one's true image
Kagamie, Kagamy, Kagamey, Kagamee, Kagamea

Kailasa (Indian) From the silver mountain
Kailasah, Kailassa, Kaylasa, Kaelasa, Kailas, Kailase

*Kaitlyn (Greek) Form of Katherine, meaning "one who is pure, virginal"
*Kaitlin, Kaitlan, Kaitleen, Kaitlynn, Katalin, Katalina, Katalyn, Katelin, Kateline, Katelinn, **Katelyn**, Katelynn, Katilyn, Katlin*

Kakra (Egyptian) The younger of twins
Kakrah

Kala (Arabic / Hawaiian) A moment in time / form of Sarah, meaning "a princess; lady"
Kalah, Kalla, Kallah

Kalifa (Somali) A chaste and holy woman
Kalifah, Kalyfa, Kalyfah, Kaleefa, Kaleefah, Kalipha, Kalypha, Kaleepha, Kaleafa, Kaleafah, Kaleapha

Kalinda (Indian) Of the sun
Kalindah, Kalynda, Kalinde, Kalindeh, Kalindi, Kalindie, Kalyndi, Kalyndie

Kallie (English) Form of Callie, meaning "a beautiful girl"
Kalli, Kallita, Kally, Kalley, Kallee, Kalleigh, Kallea, Kalleah

Kalma (Finnish) In mythology, goddess of the dead

Kalyan (Indian) A beautiful and auspicious woman
Kalyane, Kalyanne, Kalyann, Kaylana, Kaylanna, Kalliyan, Kaliyan, Kaliyane

Kama (Indian) One who loves and is loved
Kamah, Kamma, Kammah

Kamala (Arabic) A woman of perfection
Kamalah, Kammala, Kamalla

Kamaria (African) Of the moon
Kamariah, Kamarea, Kamareah, Kamariya, Kamariyah

Kambiri (African) Newest addition to the family
Kambirie, Kambiry, Kambyry

Kamea (Hawaiian) The one and only; precious one
Kameo

^**Kamila** (Spanish) Form of Camilla, meaning ceremonial attendant
Kamilah

Kamyra (American) Surrounded by light
Kamira, Kamera, Kamiera, Kameira, Kameera, Kameara

Kanda (Native American) A magical woman
Kandah

Kanika (African) A dark, beautiful woman
Kanikah, Kanyka, Kanicka

Kantha (Indian) A delicate woman
Kanthah, Kanthe, Kantheh

Kanya (Thai) A young girl; a virgin

Kaoru (Japanese) A fragrant girl
Kaori

Kara (Greek / Italian / Gaelic) One who is pure / dearly loved / a good friend
Karah, Karalee, Karalie, Karalyn, Karalynn, Karrah, Karra, Khara

Karcsi (French) A joyful singer
Karcsie, Karcsy, Karcsey, Karcsee, Karcsea

Karen (Greek) Form of Katherine, meaning "one who is pure; virginal"
Karan, Karena, Kariana, Kariann, Karianna, Karianne, Karin, Karina

Karina (Scandinavian / Russian) One who is dear and pure
Karinah, Kareena, Karyna

Karisma (English) Form of Charisma, meaning "blessed with charm"
Kharisma, Karizma, Kharizma

Karissa (Greek) Filled with grace and kindness; very dear
Karisa, Karyssa, Karysa, Karessa, Karesa, Karis, Karise

Karla (German) Feminine form of Karl; a small strong, woman
Karly, Karli, Karlie, Karleigh, Karlee, Karley, Karlin, Karlyn, Karlina, Karleen

Karmel (Latin) Form of Carmel, meaning "of the fruitful orchard"
Karmelle, Karmell, Karmele, Karmela, Karmella

Karoline (English) A small and strong woman
Karolina, Karolinah, Karolyne, Karrie, Karie, Karri, Kari, Karry

Karsen (American) Variation of the Scottish Carson, meaning "from the swamp"
Karsyn, Karsin

Karsten (Greek) The anointed one
Karstin, Karstine, Karstyn, Karston, Karstan, Kiersten, Keirsten

Kasey (Irish) Form of Casey, meaning "a vigilant woman"
Kacie, Kaci, Kacy, KC, Kacee, Kacey, Kasie, Kasi

Kasi (Indian) From the holy city; shining

Kasmira (Slavic) A peacemaker
Kasmirah, Kasmeera

Kate (English) Form of Katherine, meaning "one who is pure, virginal"
Katie, Katey, Kati

*ᵀKatherine (Greek) Form of Catherine, meaning "one who is pure; virginal"
Katharine, Katharyn, Kathy, Kathleen, Katheryn, Kathie, Kathrine, Kathryn, Karen, Kay

Katniss (American) From the young adult novel series *The Hunger Games*

Katriel (Hebrew) Crowned by God
Katriele, Katrielle, Katriell

Kaveri (Indian) From the sacred river
Kaverie, Kauveri, Kauverie, Kavery, Kaverey, Kaveree, Kaverea, Kauvery

Kay (English / Greek) The keeper of the keys / form of Katherine, meaning "one who is pure; virginal"
Kaye, Kae, Kai, Kaie, Kaya, Kayana, Kayane, Kayanna

Kayden (American) Form of Kaden, meaning "a beloved companion"

*ᵀKayla (Arabic / Hebrew) Crowned with laurel
Kaylah, Kalan, Kalen, Kalin, Kalyn, Kalynn, Kaylan, Kaylana, Kaylin, Kaylen, Kaylynn, Kaylyn, Kayle

*ᵀKaylee (American) Form of Kayla, meaning "crowned with laurel"
Kaleigh, Kaley, Kaelee, Kaeley, Kaeli, Kailee, Kailey, Kalee, Kayleigh, Kayley, Kayli, Kaylie

Kearney (Irish) The winner
Kearny, Kearni, Kearnie, Kearnee, Kearnea

Keaton (English) From a shed
town
Keatan, Keatyn, Keatin, Keatun

Keavy (Irish) A lovely and
graceful girl
*Keavey, Keavi, Keavie, Keavee,
Keavea*

Keeya (African) Resembling a
flower
Keeyah, Kieya, Keiya, Keyya

Kefira (Hebrew) Resembling a
young lioness
Kefirah, Kefiera, Kefeira

Keira (Irish) Form of Kiera,
meaning "little dark-haired
one"
*Kierra, Kyera, Kyerra,
Keiranne, Kyra, Kyrie, Kira,
Kiran*

Keisha (American) The favorite child; form of Kezia,
meaning "of the spice tree"
*Keishla, Keishah, Kecia, Kesha,
Keysha, Keesha, Kiesha, Keshia*

Kelly (Irish) A lively and
bright-headed woman
*Kelley, Kelli, Kellie, Kellee,
Kelliegh, Kellye, Keely, Keelie,
Keeley, Keelyn*

Kelsey (English) From the
island of ships
*Kelsie, Kelcey, Kelcie, Kelcy,
Kellsie, Kelsa, Kelsea, Kelsee,
Kelsi, Kelsy, Kellsey*

Kendall (Welsh) From the
royal valley
*Kendal, Kendyl, Kendahl,
Kindall, Kyndal, Kenley*

Kendra (English) Feminine
form of Kendrick; having
royal power; from the high
hill
*Kendrah, Kendria, Kendrea,
Kindra, Kindria*

^**Kenley** (American) Variation
of Kinley and McKinley

*****Kennedy** (Gaelic) A helmeted
chief
*Kennedi, Kennedie, Kennedey,
Kennedee, Kenadia, Kenadie,
Kenadi, Kenady, Kenadey*

Kensington (English) A brash
lady
*Kensyngton, Kensingtyn,
Kinsington, Kinsyngton,
Kinsingtyn*

^**Kenzie** (American)
Diminutive of McKenzie

Kerensa (Cornish) One who
loves and is loved
*Kerinsa, Keransa, Kerensia,
Kerensea, Kerensya, Kerenz,
Kerenza, Keranz*

Kerr (Scottish) From the marshland

Keshon (American) Filled with happiness
Keyshon, Keshawn, Keyshawn, Kesean, Keysean, Keshaun, Keyshaun, Keshonna

Kevina (Gaelic) Feminine form of Kevin; a beautiful and beloved child
Kevinah, Keva, Kevia, Kevinne, Kevyn, Kevynn

Keyla (English) A wise daughter

Kezia (Hebrew) Of the spice tree
Keziah, Kesia, Kesiah, Kesi, Kessie, Ketzia, Keisha

Khai (American) Unlike the others; unusual
Khae, Khay, Khaye

Khalida (Arabic) Feminine form of Khalid; an immortal woman
Khalidah, Khaleeda, Khalyda

Khaliqa (Arabic) Feminine form of Khaliq; a creator; one who is well-behaved
Khaliqah, Khalyqa, Khaleeqa

Khayriyyah (Arabic) A charitable woman
Khayriyah, Khariyyah, Khariya, Khareeya

Khepri (Egyptian) Born of the morning sun
Kheprie, Kepri, Keprie, Khepry, Kepry, Khepree, Kepree, Kheprea

Khiana (American) One who is different
Khianna, Khiane, Khianne, Khian, Khyana, Khyanna, Kheana, Kheanna

*Khloe (Greek) Form of Chloe, meaning "a flourishing woman, blooming"

Kiara (American) Form of Chiara, meaning "daughter of the light"

Kichi (Japanese) The fortunate one

Kidre (American) A loyal woman
Kidrea, Kidreah, Kidria, Kidriah, Kidri, Kidrie, Kidry, Kidrey

Kiele (Hawaiian) Resembling the gardenia
Kielle, Kiel, Kiell, Kiela, Kiella

Kikka (German) The mistress of all
Kika, Kykka, Kyka

ᵀKiley (American) Form of Kylie, meaning "a boomerang"
Kylie

Kimana (American) Girl from the meadow
Kimanah, Kimanna

Kimball (English) Chief of the warriors; possessing royal boldness
Kimbal, Kimbell, Kimbel, Kymball, Kymbal

***Kimberly** (English) Of the royal fortress
Kimberley, Kimberli, Kimberlee, Kimberleigh, Kimberlin, Kimberlyn, Kymberlie, Kymberly

Kimeo (American) Filled with happiness
Kimeyo

Kimetha (American) Filled with joy
Kimethah, Kymetha

Kimiko (Japanese) A noble child; without equal

Kimora (American) Form of Kimberly, meaning "royal"

Kina (Hawaiian) Woman of China

Kinley (American) Variation of McKinley, Scottish, meaning offspring of the fair hero

Kinsey (English) The king's victory
Kinnsee, Kinnsey, Kinnsie, Kinsee, Kinsie, Kinzee, Kinzie, Kinzey

^**Kinsley** (English) From the king's meadow
Kinsly, Kinslee, Kinsleigh, Kinsli, Kinslie, Kingsley, Kingslee, Kingslie

Kioko (Japanese) A daughter born with happiness

Kirima (Eskimo) From the hill
Kirimah, Kiryma, Kirymah, Kirema, Kiremah, Kireema, Kireemah, Kireama

Kismet (English) One's destiny; fate

Kiss (American) A caring and compassionate woman
Kyss, Kissi, Kyssi, Kissie, Kyssie, Kissy, Kyssy, Kissey

Kobi (American) Woman from California
Kobie, Koby, Kobee, Kobey, Kobea

Kolette (English) Form of Colette, meaning "victory of the people"
Kolete, Kolett, Koleta, Koletta, Kolet

Komala (Indian) A delicate and tender woman
Komalah, Komalla, Komal, Komali, Komalie, Komalee

Kona (Hawaiian) A girly
woman
*Konah, Konia, Koniah, Konea,
Koneah, Koni, Konie, Koney*

Konane (Hawaiian) Daughter
of the moonlight

Kreeli (American) A charming
and kind girl
*Kreelie, Krieli, Krielie, Kryli,
Krylie, Kreely, Kriely, Kryly*

Krenie (American) A capable
woman
Kreni, Kreny, Kreney, Krenee

Kristina (English) Form of
Christina, meaning "follower
of Christ"
*Kristena, Kristine, Kristyne,
Kristyna, Krystina, Krystine*

Kumi (Japanese) An everlasting beauty
Kumie, Kumy, Kumey, Kumee

Kyla (English) Feminine form
of Kyle; from the narrow
channel
Kylah, Kylar, Kyle

*Kylie (Australian) A boomer-
ang
*Kylee, Kyleigh, Kyley, Kyli,
Kyleen, Kyleen, Kyler,
Kily,Kileigh, Kilee, Kilie, Kili,
Kilea, Kylea*

Kyra (Greek) Form of Cyrus,
meaning "noble"
*Kyrah, Kyria, Kyriah, Kyrra,
Kyrrah*

Lacey (French) Woman from
Normandy; as delicate as lace
*Lace, Lacee, Lacene, Laci,
Laciann, Lacie, Lacina, Lacy*

Lael (Hebrew) One who
belongs to God
Laele, Laelle

*Laila (Arabic) A beauty of the
night, born at nightfall
Layla, Laylah

Lainil (American) A soft-hearted
woman
*Lainill, Lainyl, Lainyll, Laenil,
Laenill, Laenyl, Laenyll, Laynil*

Lais (Greek) A legendary cour-
tesan
*Laise, Lays, Layse, Laisa, Laes,
Laese*

Lajita (Indian) A truthful
woman
Lajyta, Lajeeta, Lajeata

Lake (American) From the still waters
Laken, Laiken, Layken, Layk, Layke, Laik, Laike, Laeken

Lala (Slavic) Resembling a tulip
Lalah, Lalla, Lallah, Laleh

Lalaine (American) A hard-working woman
Lalain, Lalaina, Lalayn, Lalayne, Lalayna, Lalaen, Lalaene, Lalaena

Lalia (Greek) One who is well-spoken
Lali, Lallia, Lalya, Lalea, Lalie, Lalee, Laly, Laley

Lalita (Indian) A playful and charming woman
Lalitah, Laleeta, Laleetah, Lalyta, Lalytah, Laleita, Laleitah, Lalieta

Lamia (Greek) In mythology, a female vampire
Lamiah, Lamiya, Lamiyah, Lamea, Lameah

Lamya (Arabic) Having lovely dark lips
Lamyah, Lamyia, Lama

Lanassa (Russian) A light-hearted woman; cheerful
Lanasa, Lanassia, Lanasia, Lanassiya, Lanasiya

Landon (English) From the long hill
Landyn, Landen

Lang (Scandinavian) Woman of great height

Lani (Hawaiian) From the sky; one who is heavenly
Lanikai

Lanza (Italian) One who is noble and willing
Lanzah, Lanzia, Lanziah, Lanzea, Lanzeah

Lapis (Egyptian) Resembling the dark-blue gemstone
Lapiss, Lapisse, Lapys, Lapyss, Lapysse

Laquinta (American) The fifth-born child

Laramie (French) Shedding tears of love
Larami, Laramy, Laramey, Laramee, Laramea

Larby (American) Form of Darby, meaning "of the deer park"
Larbey, Larbi, Larbie, Larbee, Larbea

Larch (American) One who is full of life
Larche

Lark (English) Resembling the songbird
Larke

Larue (American) Form of Rue, meaning "a medicinal herb"
LaRue, Laroo, Larou

Lashawna (American) Filled with happiness
Lashauna, Laseana, Lashona, Lashawn, Lasean, Lashone, Lashaun

Lata (Indian) Of the lovely vine
Latah

Latanya (American) Daughter of the fairy queen
Latanyah, Latonya, Latania, Latanja, Latonia, Latanea

LaTeasa (Spanish) A flirtatious woman
Lateasa, Lateaza

Latona (Latin) In mythology, the Roman equivalent of Leto, the mother of Artemis and Apollo
Latonah, Latonia, Latonea, Lantoniah, Latoneah

Latrelle (American) One who laughs a lot
Latrell, Latrel, Latrele, Latrella, Latrela

Laudonia (Italian) Praises the house
Laudonea, Laudoniya, Laudomia, Laudomea, Laudomiya

Laura (Latin) Crowned with laurel; from the laurel tree
Lauraine, Lauralee, Laralyn, Laranca, Larea, Lari, Lauralee, Lauren, Loretta

*Lauren (French) Form of Laura, meaning "crowned with laurel; from the laurel tree"
Laren, Larentia, Larentina, Larenzina, Larren, Laryn, Larryn, Larrynn

*Leah (Hebrew) One who is weary; in the Bible, Jacob's first wife
Leia, Leigha, Lia, Liah, Leeya

Leanna (Gaelic) Form of Helen, meaning "the shining light"
Leana, Leann, Leanne, Lee-Ann, Leeann, Leeanne, Leianne, Leyanne

Lecia (English) Form of Alice, meaning "woman of the nobility; truthful; having high moral character"
Licia, Lecea, Licea, Lisha, Lysha, Lesha

Ledell (Greek) One who is queenly
Ledelle, Ledele, Ledella, Ledela, Ledel

Legend (American) One who is memorable
Legende, Legund, Legunde

Legia (Spanish) A bright woman
Legiah, Legea, Legeah, Legiya, Legiyah, Legya, Legyah

Leila (Persian) Night, dark beauty
Leela, Lela

Lenis (Latin) One who has soft and silky skin
Lene, Leneta, Lenice, Lenita, Lennice, Lenos, Lenys, Lenisse

Leona (Latin) Feminine form of Leon; having the strength of a lion
Leeona, Leeowna, Leoine, Leola, Leone, Leonelle, Leonia, Leonie

Lequoia (Native American) Form of Sequoia, meaning "of the giant redwood tree"
Lequoya, Lequoiya, Lekoya

Lerola (Latin) Resembling a blackbird
Lerolla, Lerolah, Lerolia, Lerolea

Leslie (Gaelic) From the holly garden; of the gray fortress
Leslea, Leslee, Lesleigh, Lesley, Lesli, Lesly, Lezlee, Lezley

Leucippe (Greek) In mythology, a nymph
Lucippe, Leucipe, Lucipe

Leucothea (Greek) In mythology, a sea nymph
Leucothia, Leucothiah, Leucotheah

Levora (American) A homebody
Levorah, Levorra, Levorrah, Levoria, Levoriah, Levorea, Levoreah, Levorya

Lewa (African) A very beautiful woman
Lewah

Lewana (Hebrew) Of the white moon
Lewanah, Lewanna, Lewannah

Lia (Italian) Form of Leah, meaning "one who is weary"

Libby (English) Form of Elizabeth, meaning "my God is bountiful; God's promise"
Libba, Libbee, Libbey, Libbie, Libet, Liby, Lilibet, Lilibeth

Liberty (English) An independent woman; having freedom
Libertey, Libertee, Libertea, Liberti, Libertie, Libertas, Libera, Liber

Libra (Latin) One who is balanced; the seventh sign of the zodiac
Leebra, Leibra, Liebra, Leabra, Leighbra, Lybra

Librada (Spanish) One who is free
Libradah, Lybrada, Lybradah

Lieu (Vietnamese) Of the willow tree

Ligia (Greek) One who is musically talented
Ligiah, Ligya, Ligiya, Lygia, Ligea, Lygea, Lygya, Lygiya

^Lila (Arabic / Greek) Born at night / resembling a lily
Lilah, Lyla, Lylah

Lilac (Latin) Resembling the bluish-purple flower
Lilack, Lilak, Lylac, Lylack, Lylak, Lilach

Lilette (Latin) Resembling a budding lily
Lilett, Lilete, Lilet, Lileta, Liletta, Lylette, Lylett, Lylete

Liliana (Italian, Spanish) Form of Lillian, meaning "resembling the lily"
Lilliana, Lillianna, Liliannia, Lilyana, Lilia

Lilith (Babylonian) Woman of the night
Lilyth, Lillith, Lillyth, Lylith, Lyllith, Lylyth, Lyllyth, Lilithe

*Lillian (Latin) Resembling the lily
Lilian, Liliane, Lilianne, Lilias, Lilas, Lillas, Lillias

Lilo (Hawaiian) One who is generous
Lylo, Leelo, Lealo, Leylo, Lielo, Leilo

*Lily (English) Resembling the flower; one who is innocent and beautiful
Leelee, Lil, Lili, Lilie, Lilla, Lilley, Lilli, Lillie, Lilly

Limor (Hebrew) Refers to myrrh
Limora, Limoria, Limorea, Leemor, Leemora, Leemoria, Leemorea

Lin (Chinese) Resembling jade; from the woodland

Linda (Spanish) One who is soft and beautiful
Lindalee, Lindee, Lindey, Lindi, Lindie, Lindira, Lindka, Lindy, Lynn

Linden (English) From the hill of lime trees
Lindenn, Lindon, Lindynn, Lynden, Lyndon, Lyndyn, Lyndin, Lindin

Lindley (English) From the pastureland
Lindly, Lindlee, Lindleigh, Lindli, Lindlie, Leland, Lindlea

Lindsay (English) From the island of linden trees; from Lincoln's wetland
Lind, Lindsea, Lindsee, Lindseigh, Lindsey, Lindsy, Linsay, Linsey

Lisa (English) Form of Elizabeth, meaning "my God is bountiful; God's promise"
Leesa, Liesa, Lisebet, Lise, Liseta, Lisette, Liszka, Lisebeth

Lishan (African) One who is awarded a medal
Lishana, Lishanna, Lyshan, Lyshana, Lyshanna

Lissie (American) Resembling a flower
Lissi, Lissy, Lissey, Lissee, Lissea

Liv (Scandinavian / Latin) One who protects others / from the olive tree
Livia, Livea, Liviya, Livija, Livvy, Livy, Livya, Lyvia

Liya (Hebrew) The Lord's daughter
Liyah, Leeya, Leeyah, Leaya, Leayah

Lo (American) A fiesty woman
Loe, Low, Lowe

Loicy (American) A delightful woman
Loicey, Loicee, Loicea, Loici, Loicie, Loyce, Loice, Loyci

Lokelani (Hawaiian) Resembling a small red rose
Lokelanie, Lokelany, Lokelaney, Lokelanee, Lokelanea

Loki (Norse) In mythology, a trickster god
Lokie, Lokee, Lokey, Loky, Lokea, Lokeah, Lokia, Lokiah

Lola (Spanish) Form of Dolores, meaning "woman of sorrow"
Lolah, Loe, Lolo

^*T**London** (English) From the capital of England
Londyn

Lorelei (German) From the rocky cliff; in mythology, a siren who lured sailors to their deaths
Laurelei, Laurelie, Loralee, Loralei, Loralie, Loralyn

Loretta (Italian) Form of Laura, meaning "crowned with laurel; from the laurel tree"
Laretta, Larretta, Lauretta, Laurette, Leretta, Loreta, Lorette, Lorretta

Lorraine (French) From the kingdom of Lothair
Laraine, Larayne, Laurraine, Leraine, Lerayne, Lorain, Loraina, Loraine

Love (English) One who is full of affection
Lovey, Loveday, Lovette, Lovi, Lovie, Lov, Luv, Luvey

Lovely (American) An attractive and pleasant woman
Loveli, Loveley, Lovelie, Lovelee, Loveleigh, Lovelea

Luana (Hawaiian) One who is content and enjoys life
Lewanna, Lou-Ann, Louann, Louanna, Louanne, Luanda, Luane, Luann

Lucretia (Latin) A bringer of light; a successful woman; in mythology, a maiden who was raped by the prince of Rome
Lacretia, Loucrecia, Loucrezia, Loucresha, Loucretia, Lucrece, Lucrecia, Lucreecia

^*Lucy** (Latin) Feminine form of Lucius; one who is illuminated
*Luce, Lucetta, Lucette, Luci, Lucia, Luciana, Lucianna, Lucida, **Lucille***

Lucylynn (American) A lighthearted woman
Lucylyn, Lucylynne, Lucilynn, Lucilyn, Lucilynne

^**Luna** (Latin) Of the moon
Lunah

Lunet (English) Of the crescent moon
Lunett, Lunette, Luneta, Lunete, Lunetta

Lupita (Spanish) Form of Guadalupe, meaning "from the valley of wolves"
Lupe, Lupyta, Lupelina, Lupeeta, Lupieta, Lupeita, Lupeata

Lurissa (American) A beguiling woman
Lurisa, Luryssa, Lurysa, Luressa, Luresa

Luyu (Native American) Resembling the dove

*****Lydia** (Greek) A beautiful woman from Lydia
Lidia, Lidie, Lidija, Lyda, Lydie, Lydea, Liddy, Lidiy

Lyla (Arabic) Form of Lila, meaning "born at night, resembling a lily"
Lylah

Lynn (English) Woman of the lake; form of Linda, meaning "one who is soft and beautiful"
Linell, Linnell, Lyn, Lynae, Lyndel, Lyndell, Lynell, Lynelle

^**Lyric** (French) Of the lyre; the words of a song
Lyrica, Lyricia, Lyrik, Lyrick, Lyrika, Lyricka

Lytanisha (American) A scintillating woman
Lytanesha, Lytaniesha, Lytaneisha, Lytanysha, Lytaneesha, Lytaneasha

M

Macanta (Gaelic) A kind and gentle woman
Macan, Macantia, Macantea, Macantah

Machi (Taiwanese) A good friend
Machie, Machy, Machey, Machee, Machea

Mackenna (Gaelic) Daughter of the handsome man
Mackendra, Mackennah, McKenna, McKendra, Makenna, Makennah

*^**Mackenzie** (Gaelic) Daughter of a wise leader; a fiery woman; one who is fair
*Mckenzie, Mackenzey, Makensie, **Makenzie**, M'Kenzie, **McKenzie**, Meckenzie, Mackenzee, Mackenzy*

^**McKinley** (English) Offspring of the fair hero

^**Macy** (French) One who wields a weapon
*Macee, Macey, **Maci**, Macie, Maicey, Maicy, Macea, Maicea*

Madana (Ethiopian) One who heals others
Madayna, Madaina, Madania, Madaynia, Madainia

Maddox (English) Born into wealth and prosperity
Madox, Madoxx, Maddoxx

*****Madeline** (Hebrew) Woman from Magdala
*Mada, Madalaina, Madaleine, Madalena, Madalene, **Madelyn**, Madalyn, Madelynn, Madilyn*

Madhavi (Indian) Feminine form of Madhav; born in the springtime
Madhavie, Madhavee, Madhavey, Madhavy, Madhavea

Madini (Swahili) As precious as a gemstone
Madinie, Madiny, Madiney, Madinee, Madyny, Madyni, Madinea, Madynie

*ᵀMadison (English) Daughter of a mighty warrior
Maddison, Madisen, Madisson, Madisyn, Madyson

Madonna (Italian) My lady; refers to the Virgin Mary
Madonnah, Madona, Madonah

Maeve (Irish) An intoxicating woman
Mave, Meave, Medb, Meabh

Maggie (English) Form of Margaret, meaning "resembling a pearl"
Maggi

Magnolia (French) Resembling the flower
Magnoliya, Magnoliah, Magnolea, Magnoleah, Magnoliyah, Magnolya, Magnolyah

Mahal (Native American) A tender and loving woman
Mahall, Mahale, Mahalle

Mahari (African) One who offers forgiveness
Maharie, Mahary, Maharey

Mahesa (Indian) A powerful and great lady
Maheshvari

Mahira (Arabic) A clever and adroit woman
Mahirah, Mahir, Mahire

Maia (Latin / Maori) The great one; in mythology, the goddess of spring / a brave warrior
Maiah, Mya, Maja

Maida (English) A maiden; a virgin
Maidel, Maidie, Mayda, Maydena, Maydey, Mady, Maegth, Magd

Maiki (Japanese) Resembling the dancing flower
Maikie, Maikei, Maikki, Maikee

Maimun (Arabic) One who is lucky; fortunate
Maimoon, Maimoun

Maine (French) From the mainland; from the state of Maine

Maiolaine (French) As delicate as a flower
Maiolainie, Maiolani

Maisha (African) Giver of life
Maysha, Maishah, Mayshah, Maesha, Maeshah

Maisie (Scottish) Form of Margaret, meaning "resembling a pearl"
Maisee, Maisey, Maisy, Maizie, Mazey, Mazie, Maisi, Maizi

Majaya (Indian) A victorious woman
Majayah

Makala (Hawaiian) Resembling myrtle
Makalah, Makalla, Makallah

*T**Makayla** (Celtic / Hebrew / English) Form of Michaela, meaning "who is like God?"
Macaela, MacKayla, Mak, Mechaela, Meeskaela, Mekea, Mekelle

Makani (Hawaiian) Of the wind
Makanie, Makaney, Makany, Makanee

Makareta (Maori) Form of Margaret, meaning "resembling a pearl / the child of light"
Makaretah, Makarita

Makea (Finnish) One who is sweet
Makeah, Makia, Makiah

Makelina (Hawaiian) Form of Madeline, meaning "woman from Magdala"
Makelinah, Makeleena, Makelyna, Makeleana

Makena (African) One who is filled with happiness
Makenah, Makeena, Makeenah, Makeana, Makeanah, Makyna, Makynah, Mackena

Makenna (Irish) Form of McKenna, meaning "of the Irish one"
Makennah

Malak (Arabic) A heavenly messenger; an angel
Malaka, Malaika, Malayka, Malaeka, Malake, Malayk, Malaek, Malakia

Malati (Indian) Resembling a fragrant flower
Malatie, Malaty, Malatey, Malatee, Malatea

Mali (Thai / Welsh) Resembling a flower / form of Molly, meaning "star of the sea / from the sea of bitterness"
Malie, Malee, Maleigh, Maly, Maley

Malia (Hawaiian) Form of Mary, meaning "star of the sea / from the sea of bitterness"
Maliah, Maliyah, Maleah

Malika (Arabic) Destined to be queen
Malikah, Malyka, Maleeka, Maleika, Malieka, Maliika, Maleaka

Malina (Hawaiian) A peaceful woman
Malinah, Maleena, Maleenah, Malyna, Malynah, Maleina, Maliena, Maleana

Malinka (Russian) As sweet as a little berry
Malinkah, Malynka, Maleenka, Malienka, Maleinka, Maleanka

Mana (Polynesian) A charismatic and prestigious woman
Manah

Manal (Arabic) An accomplished woman
Manala, Manall, Manalle, Manalla, Manali

Mandoline (English) One who is accomplished with the stringed instrument
Mandalin, Mandalyn, Mandalynn, Mandelin, Mandellin, Mandellyn, Mandolin, Mandolyn

Mangena (Hebrew) As sweet as a melody
Mangenah, Mangenna, Mangennah

Manyara (African) A humble woman
Manyarah

Maola (Irish) A handmaiden
Maoli, Maole, Maolie, Maolia, Maoly, Maoley, Maolee, Maolea

Mapenzi (African) One who is dearly loved
Mpenzi, Mapenzie, Mapenze, Mapenzy, Mapenzee, Mapenzea

Maram (Arabic) One who is wished for
Marame, Marama, Marami, Maramie, Maramee, Maramy, Maramey, Maramea

Marcella (Latin) Dedicated to Mars, the God of war
Marcela, Marsela, Marsella, Maricela, Maricel

Marcia (Latin) Feminine form of Marcus; dedicated to Mars, the god of war
Marcena, Marcene, Marchita, Marciana, Marciane, Marcianne, Marcilyn, Marcilynn

Marely (American) form of Marley, "meaning of the marshy meadow"

Margaret (Greek / Persian) Resembling a pearl / the child of light
Maighread, Mairead, Mag, Maggi, Maggie, Maggy, Maiga, Malgorzata, Megan, Marwarid, Marjorie, Marged, Makareta

Marged (Welsh) Form of Margaret, meaning "resembling a pearl / the child of light"
Margred, Margeda, Margreda

*Maria (Spanish) Form of Mary, meaning "star of the sea / from the sea of bitterness"
Mariah, Marialena, Marialinda, Marialisa, Maaria, Mayria, Maeria, Mariabella

*Mariah (Latin) Form of Mary, meaning "star of the sea"

Mariana (Spanish / Italian) Form of Mary, meaning "star of the sea"
Marianna

Mariane (French) Blend of Mary, meaning "star of the sea / from the sea of bitterness," and Ann, meaning "a woman graced with God's favor"
Mariam, Mariana, Marian, Marion, Maryann, Maryanne, Maryanna, Maryane

Marietta (French) Form of Mary, meaning "star of the sea / from the sea of bitterness"
Mariette, Maretta, Mariet, Maryetta, Maryette, Marieta

Marika (Danish) Form of Mary, meaning "star of the sea / from the sea of bitterness"

Mariko (Japanese) Daughter of Mari; a ball or sphere
Maryko, Mareeko, Marieko, Mareiko

Marilyn (English) Form of Mary, meaning "star of the sea / from the sea of bitterness"
Maralin, Maralyn, Maralynn, Marelyn, Marilee, Marilin

Marissa (Latin) Woman of the sea
Maressa, Maricia, Marisabel, Marisha, Marisse, Maritza, Mariza, Marrissa

Marjam (Slavic) One who is merry
Marjama, Marjamah, Marjami, Marjamie, Marjamy, Marjamey, Marjamee, Marjamea

Marjani (African) Of the coral reef
Marjanie, Marjany, Marjaney, Marjanee, Marjean, Marjeani, Marjeanie, Marijani

Marjorie (English) Form of Margaret, meaning "resembling a pearl / the child of light"
Marcharie, Marge, Margeree, Margerie, Margery, Margey, Margi

Marlene (German) Blend of Mary, meaning "star of the sea / from the sea of bitterness," and Magdalene, meaning "woman from Magdala"
Marlaina, Marlana, Marlane, Marlayna

Marley (English) Of the marshy meadow
Marlee, Marleigh, Marli, Marlie, Marly

Marlis (German) Form of Mary, meaning "star of the sea / from the sea of bitterness"
Marlisa, Marliss, Marlise, Marlisse, Marlissa, Marlys, Marlyss, Marlysa

Marlo (English) One who resembles driftwood
Marloe, Marlow, Marlowe, Marlon

Marsala (Italian) From the place of sweet wine
Marsalah, Marsalla, Marsallah

Martha (Aramaic) Mistress of the house; in the Bible, the sister of Lazarus and Mary
Maarva, Marfa, Marhta, Mariet, Marit, Mart, Marta, Marte

Mary (Latin / Hebrew) Star of the sea / from the sea of bitterness
Mair, Mal, Mallie, Manette, Manon, Manya, Mare, Maren, Maria, Marietta, Marika, Marilyn, Marlis, Maureen, May, Mindel, Miriam, Molly, Mia

Masami (African / Japanese) A commanding woman / one who is truthful
Masamie, Masamee, Masamy, Masamey, Masamea

Mashaka (African) A troublemaker; a mischievous woman
Mashakah, Mashakia

Massachusetts (Native American) From the big hill; from the state of Massachusetts
Massachusets, Massachusette, Massachusetta, Massa, Massachute, Massachusta

Matana (Hebrew) A gift from God
Matanah, Matanna, Matannah, Matai

Matangi (Hindi) In Hinduism, the patron of inner thought
Matangy, Matangie, Matangee, Matangey, Matangea

Matsuko (Japanese) Child of the pine tree

Maureen (Irish) Form of Mary, meaning "star of the sea / from the sea of bitterness"
Maura, Maurene, Maurianne, Maurine, Maurya, Mavra, Maure, Mo

Mauve (French) Of the mallow plant
Mawve

Maven (English) Having great knowledge
Mavin, Mavyn

Maverick (American) One who is wild and free
Maverik, Maveryck, Maveryk, Mavarick, Mavarik

Mavis (French) Resembling a songbird
Mavise, Maviss, Mavisse, Mavys, Mavyss, Mavysse

May (Latin) Born during the month of May; form of Mary, meaning "star of the sea / from the sea of bitterness"
Mae, Mai, Maelynn, Maelee, Maj, Mala, Mayana, Maye

*Maya (Indian / Hebrew) An illusion, a dream / woman of the water
Mya

Mayumi (Japanese) One who embodies truth, wisdom, and beauty

Mazarine (French) Having deep-blue eyes
Mazareen, Mazareene, Mazaryn, Mazaryne, Mazine, Mazyne, Mazeene

Mazhira (Hebrew) A shining woman
Mazhirah, Mazheera

McKayla (Gaelic) A fiery woman
McKale, McKaylee, McKaleigh, McKay, McKaye, McKaela

Meara (Gaelic) One who is filled with happiness
Mearah

Medea (Greek) A cunning ruler; in mythology, a sorceress
Madora, Medeia, Media, Medeah, Mediah, Mediya, Mediyah

Medini (Indian) Daughter of the earth
Medinie, Mediny, Mediney, Medinee, Medinea

Meditrina (Latin) The healer; in mythology, goddess of health and wine
Meditreena, Meditryna, Meditriena

Medora (Greek) A wise ruler
Medoria, Medorah, Medorra, Medorea

Medusa (Greek) In mythology, a Gorgon with snakes for hair
Medoosa, Medusah, Medoosah, Medousa, Medousah

Meenakshi (Indian) Having beautiful eyes

Megan (Welsh) Form of Margaret, meaning "resembling a pearl / the child of light"
Maegan, Meg, Magan, Magen, Megin, Maygan, Meagan, Meaghan, Meghan

Mehalia (Hebrew) An affectionate woman
Mehaliah, Mehalea, Mehaleah, Mehaliya, Mehaliyah

Melangell (Welsh) A sweet messenger from heaven
Melangelle, Melangela, Melangella, Melangele, Melangel

*Melanie (Greek) A dark-skinned beauty
Malaney, Malanie, Mel, Mela, Melaina, Melaine, Melainey, Melany

Meli (Native American) One who is bitter
Melie, Melee, Melea, Meleigh, Mely, Meley

Melia (Hawaiian / Greek) Resembling the plumeria / of the ash tree; in mythology, a nymph
Melidice, Melitine, Meliah, Meelia, Melya

Melika (Turkish) A great beauty
Melikah, Melicka, Melicca, Melyka, Melycka, Meleeka, Meleaka

Melinda (Latin) One who is sweet and gentle
Melynda, Malinda, Malinde, Mallie, Mally, Malynda, Melinde, Mellinda, Mindy

Melisande (French) Having the strength of an animal
Malisande, Malissande, Malyssandre, Melesande, Melisandra, Melisandre

Melissa (Greek) Resembling a honeybee; in mythology, a nymph
Malissa, Mallissa, Mel, Melesa, Melessa, Melisa, Melise, Melisse

Melita (Greek) As sweet as
honey
Malita, Malitta, Melida,
Melitta, Melyta, Malyta,
Meleeta, Meleata

Melody (Greek) A beautiful
song
Melodee, Melodey, Melodi,
Melodia, Melodie, Melodea

Merana (American) Woman of
the waters
Meranah, Meranna, Merannah

Mercer (English) A prosperous
merchant

Meredith (Welsh) A great
ruler; protector of the sea
Maredud, Meridel, Meredithe,
Meredyth, Meridith, Merridie,
Meradith, Meredydd

Meribah (Hebrew) A quarrel-
some woman
Meriba

Meroz (Hebrew) From the
cursed plains
Meroza, Merozia, Meroze

Merry (English) One who is
lighthearted and joyful
Merree, Merri, Merrie,
Merrielle, Merrile, Merrilee,
Merrili, Merrily

Mertice (English) A well-
known lady

Merton (English) From the village near the pond
Mertan, Mertin, Mertun

Metea (Greek) A gentle
woman
Meteah, Metia, Metiah

Metin (Greek) A wise counselor
Metine, Metyn, Metyne

Metis (Greek) One who is
industrious
Metiss, Metisse, Metys, Metyss,
Metysse

Mettalise (Danish) As graceful
as a pearl
Metalise, Mettalisse, Mettalisa,
Mettalissa

*⋆ᵀ**Mia** (Israeli / Latin) Who
is like God? / form of Mary,
meaning "star of the sea /
from the sea of bitterness"
Miah, Mea, Meah, Meya

^**Michaela** (Celtic, Gaelic,
Hebrew, English, Irish)
Feminine form of Michael;
who is like God?
Macaela, MacKayla, Mak,
Mechaela, Meeskaela, Mekea,
Micaela, **Mikaela**

ᵀ**Michelle** (French) Feminine form of Michael; who is like God?
Machelle, Mashelle, M'chelle, Mechelle, Meechelle, Me'Shell, Meshella, Mischa

Michewa (Tibetan) Sent from heaven
Michewah

Mide (Irish) One who is thirsty
Meeda, Mida

Midori (Japanese) Having green eyes
Midorie, Midory, Midorey, Midoree, Midorea

Mignon (French) One who is cute and petite

Mikayla (English) Feminine form of Michael, meaning "who is like God?"

^**Mila** (Slavic) One who is industrious and hardworking
Milaia, Milaka, Milla, Milia

Milan (Latin) From the city in Italy; one who is gracious
Milaana

Milena (Slavic) The favored one
Mileena, Milana, Miladena, Milanka, Mlada, Mladena

Miley (American) Form of Mili, meaning "a virtuous woman"
Milee, Mylee, Mareli

Miliana (Latin) Feminine of Emeliano; one who is eager and willing
Milianah, Milianna, Miliane, Miliann, Milianne

Milima (Swahili) Woman from the mountains
Milimah, Mileema, Milyma

Millo (Hebrew) Defender of the sacred city
Milloh, Millowe, Milloe

Mima (Hebrew) Form of Jemima, meaning "our little dove"
Mimah, Mymah, Myma

Minda (Native American / Hindi) Having great knowledge
Mindah, Mynda, Myndah, Menda, Mendah

Mindel (Hebrew) Form of Mary, meaning "star of the sea / from the sea of bitterness"
Mindell, Mindelle, Mindele, Mindela, Mindella

Mindy (English) Form of Melinda, meaning "one who is sweet and gentle"
Minda, Mindee, Mindi, Mindie, Mindey, Mindea

Ming Yue (Chinese) Born beneath the bright moon

Minka (Teutonic) One who is resolute; having great strength
Minkah, Mynka, Mynkah, Minna, Minne

Minowa (Native American) One who has a moving voice
Minowah, Mynowa, Mynowah

Minuit (French) Born at midnight
Minueet

Miracle (American) An act of God's hand
Mirakle, Mirakel, Myracle, Myrakle

Mirai (Basque / Japanese) A miracle child / future
Miraya, Mirari, Mirarie, Miraree, Mirae

Miranda (Latin) Worthy of admiration
Maranda, Myranda, Randi

Miremba (Ugandan) A promoter of peace
Mirembe, Mirem, Mirembah, Mirembeh, Mirema

Miriam (Hebrew) Form of Mary, meaning "star of the sea / from the sea of bitterness"
Mariam, Maryam, Meriam, Meryam, Mirham, Mirjam, Mirjana, Mirriam

Mirinesse (English) Filled with joy
Miriness, Mirinese, Mirines, Mirinessa, Mirinesa

Mirit (Hebrew) One who is strong-willed

Mischa (Russian) Form of Michelle, meaning "who is like God?"
Misha

Mistico (Italian) A mystical woman
Mistica, Mystico, Mystica, Mistiko, Mystiko

Mitali (Indian) A friendly and sweet woman
Mitalie, Mitalee, Mitaleigh, Mitaly, Mitaley, Meeta, Mitalea

Miya (Japanese) From the sacred temple
Miyah

Miyo (Japanese) A beautiful daughter
Miyoko

Mizar (Hebrew) A little woman; petite
Mizarr, Mizarre, Mizare, Mizara, Mizaria, Mizarra

Mliss (Cambodian) Resembling a flower
Mlissa, Mlisse, Mlyss, Mlysse, Mlyssa

Mocha (Arabic) As sweet as chocolate
Mochah

Modesty (Latin) One who is without conceit
Modesti, Modestie, Modestee, Modestus, Modestey, Modesta, Modestia, Modestina

Moesha (American) Drawn from the water
Moisha, Moysha, Moeesha, Moeasha, Moeysha

Mohini (Indian) The most beautiful
Mohinie, Mohinee, Mohiny

Moladah (Hebrew) A giver of life
Molada

*Molly (Irish) Form of Mary, meaning "star of the sea / from the sea of bitterness"
Moll, Mollee, Molley, Molli, Mollie, Molle, Mollea, Mali

Mona (Gaelic) One who is born into the nobility
Moina, Monah, Monalisa, Monalissa, Monna, Moyna, Monalysa, Monalyssa

Moncha (Irish) A solitary woman
Monchah

Monica (Greek / Latin) A solitary woman / one who advises others
Monnica, Monca, Monicka, Monika, Monike

Monique (French) One who provides wise counsel
Moniqua, Moneeque, Moneequa, Moneeke, Moeneek, Moneaque, Moneaqua, Moneake

Monisha (Hindi) Having great intelligence
Monishah, Monesha, Moneisha, Moniesha, Moneysha, Moneasha

Monroe (Gaelic) Woman from the river
Monrow, Monrowe, Monro

Monserrat (Latin) From the jagged mountain
Montserrat

Montana (Latin) Woman of the mountains; from the state of Montana
Montanna, Montina, Monteene, Montese

Morcan (Welsh) Of the bright sea
Morcane, Morcana, Morcania, Morcanea

Moreh (Hebrew) A great archer; a teacher

*[★T]Morgan** (Welsh) Circling the bright sea; a sea dweller
Morgaine, Morgana, Morgance, Morgane, Morganica, Morgann, Morganne, Morgayne

Morguase (English) In Arthurian legend, the mother of Gawain
Marguase, Margawse, Morgawse, Morgause, Margause

Morina (Japanese) From the woodland town
Morinah, Moreena, Moryna, Moriena, Moreina, Moreana

Mubarika (Arabic) One who is blessed
Mubaarika, Mubaricka, Mubaryka, Mubaricca, Mubarycca

Mubina (Arabic) One who displays her true image
Mubeena, Mubinah, Mubyna, Mubeana, Mubiena

Mudan (Mandarin) Daughter of a harmonious family
Mudane, Mudana, Mudann, Mudaen, Mudaena

Mufidah (Arabic) One who is helpful to others
Mufeeda, Mufeyda, Mufyda, Mufeida, Mufieda, Mufeada

Mugain (Irish) In mythology, the wife of the king of Ulster
Mugayne, Mugaine, Mugane

Muirne (Irish) One who is dearly loved
Muirna

Munay (African) One who loves and is loved
Manay, Munaye, Munae, Munai

Munazza (Arabic) An independent woman; one who is free
Munazzah, Munaza, Munazah

Muriel (Irish) Of the shining sea
Merial, Meriel, Merrill

Murphy (Celtic) Daughter of a great sea warrior
Murphi, Murphie, Murphey

Musoke (African) Having the beauty of a rainbow

ᵀ**Mya** (American) Form of Maya, meaning "an illusion, woman of the water"
Myah

Myisha (Arabic) Form of Aisha, meaning "lively; womanly"
Myesha, Myeisha, Myeshia, Myiesha, Myeasha

Myka (Hebrew) Feminine of Micah, meaning "who is like God?"
Micah, Mika

Myrina (Latin) In mythology, an Amazon
Myrinah, Myreena, Myreina, Myriena, Myreana

Myrrh (Egyptian) Resembling the fragrant oil

N

Naama (Hebrew) Feminine form of Noam; an attractive woman; good-looking
Naamah

Naava (Hebrew) A lovely and pleasant woman
Naavah, Nava, Navah, Navit

Nabila (Arabic) Daughter born into nobility; a highborn daughter
Nabilah, Nabeela, Nabyla, Nabeelah, Nabylah, Nabeala, Nabealah

Nadda (Arabic) A very generous woman
Naddah, Nada, Nadah

Nadia (Slavic) One who is full of hope
Nadja, Nadya, Naadiya, Nadine, Nadie, Nadiyah, Nadea, Nadija

Nadirah (Arabic) One who is precious; rare
Nadira, Nadyra, Nadyrah, Nadeera, Nadeerah, Nadra

Naeva (French) Born in the evening
Naevah, Naevia, Naevea, Nayva, Nayvah

Nagge (Hebrew) A radiant woman

Nailah (Arabic) Feminine form of Nail; a successful woman; the acquirer
Na'ila, Na'ilah, Naa'ilah, Naila, Nayla, Naylah, Naela, Naelah

Najia (Arabic) An independent woman; one who is free
Naajia

Najja (African) The second-born child
Najjah

Namid (Native American) A star dancer
Namide, Namyd, Namyde

Namita (Papuan) In mythology, a mother goddess
Namitah, Nameeta, Namyta

Nana (Hawaiian / English) Born during the spring; a star / a grandmother or one who watches over children

Nancy (English) Form of Anna, meaning "a woman graced with God's favor"
Nainsey, Nainsi, Nance, Nancee, Nancey, Nanci, Nancie, Nancsi

Nandalia (Australian) A fiery woman
Nandaliah, Nandalea, Nandaleah, Nandali, Nandalie, Nandalei, Nandalee, Nandaleigh

Nandita (Indian) A delightful daughter
Nanditah, Nanditia, Nanditea

*Naomi (Hebrew / Japanese) One who is pleasant / a beauty above all others
Namoie, Nayomi, Naomee

Narella (Greek) A bright woman; intelligent
Narellah, Narela, Narelah, Narelle, Narell, Narele

Nascio (Latin) In mythology, goddess of childbirth

Natalia (Spanish / Latin) form of Natalie; born on Christmas day
Natalya, Natalja

*ᵀNatalie (Latin) Refers to Christ's birthday; born on Christmas Day
Natala, Natalee, Nathalie, Nataline, Nataly, Natasha

Natane (Native American) Her father's daughter
Natanne

Natasha (Russian) Form of Natalie, meaning "born on Christmas Day"
Nastaliya, Nastalya, Natacha, Natascha, Natashenka, Natashia, Natasia, Natosha

Navida (Iranian) Feminine form of Navid; bringer of good news
Navyda, Navidah, Navyda, Naveeda, Naveedah, Naveada, Naveadah

Navya (Indian) One who is youthful
Navyah, Naviya, Naviyah

Nawal (Arabic) A gift of God
Nawall, Nawalle, Nawala, Nawalla

Nawar (Arabic) Resembling a flower
Nawaar

Nazahah (Arabic) One who is pure and honest
Nazaha, Nazihah, Naziha

Nechama (Hebrew) One who provides comfort
Nehama, Nehamah, Nachmanit, Nachuma, Nechamah, Nechamit

Neda (Slavic) Born on a Sunday
Nedda, Nedah, Nedi, Nedie, Neddi, Neddie, Nedaa

Neena (Hindi) A woman who has beautiful eyes
Neenah, Neanah, Neana, Neyna, Neynah

Nefertiti (Egyptian) A queenly woman
Nefertari, Nefertyty, Nefertity, Nefertitie, Nefertitee, Nefertytie, Nefertitea

Neith (Egyptian) In mythology, goddess of war and hunting
Neitha, Neytha, Neyth, Neit, Neita, Neitia, Neitea, Neithe, Neythe

Nekana (Spanish) Woman of sorrow
Nekane, Nekania, Nekanea

Neo (African) A gift from God

Nerissa (Italian / Greek) A black-haired beauty / sea nymph
Narissa, Naryssa, Nericcia, Neryssa, Narice, Nerice, Neris

Nessa (Hebrew / Greek) A miracle child / form of Agnes, meaning "one who is pure; chaste"
Nesha, Nessah, Nessia, Nessya, Nesta, Neta, Netia, Nessie

Netis (Native American) One who is trustworthy
Netiss, Netisse, Netys, Netyss, Netysse

*ᵀNevaeh (American) Child from heaven

Nevina (Scottish) Feminine form of Nevin; daughter of a saint
Nevinah, Neveena, Nevyna, Nevinne, Nevynne, Neveene, Neveana, Neveane

Newlyn (Gaelic) Born during the spring
Newlynn, Newlynne, Newlin, Newlinn, Newlinne, Newlen, Newlenn, Newlenne

Neziah (Hebrew) One who is pure; a victorious woman
Nezia, Nezea, Nezeah, Neza, Nezah, Neziya, Neziyah

Niabi (Native American) Resembling a fawn
Niabie, Niabee, Niabey, Niaby

Niagara (English) From the famous waterfall
Niagarah, Niagarra, Niagarrah, Nyagara, Nyagarra

ᵀ**Nicole** (Greek) Feminine form of Nicholas; of the victorious people
Necole, Niccole, Nichol, Nichole, Nicholle, Nickol, Nickole, Nicol

Nicosia (English) Woman from the capital of Cyprus
Nicosiah, Nicosea, Nicoseah, Nicotia, Nicotea

Nidia (Spanish) One who is gracious
Nydia, Nidiah, Nydiah, Nidea, Nideah, Nibia, Nibiah, Nibea

Nike (Greek) One who brings victory; in mythology, goddess of victory
Nikee, Nikey, Nykee, Nyke

Nilam (Arabic) Resembling a precious blue stone
Neelam, Nylam, Nilima, Nilyma, Nylyma, Nylima, Nealam, Nealama

Nilsine (Scandinavian) Feminine form of Neil; a champion

Nimeesha (African) A princess; daughter born to royalty
Nimeeshah, Nimiesha

Nini (African) As solid as a stone
Ninie, Niny, Niney, Ninee, Ninea

Nishan (African) One who wins awards
Nishann, Nishanne, Nishana, Nishanna, Nyshan, Nyshana

Nitya (Indian) An eternal beauty
Nithya, Nithyah, Nityah

Nixie (German) A beautiful water sprite
Nixi, Nixy, Nixey, Nixee, Nixea

Noelle (French) Born at Christmastime
Noel, Noela, Noele, Noe

Nolcha (Native American) Of the sun
Nolchia, Nolchea

Nomusa (African) One who is merciful
Nomusah, Nomusha, Nomusia, Nomusea, Nomushia, Nomushea

Nora (English) Form of Eleanor, meaning "the shining light"
Norah, Noora, Norella, Norelle, Norissa, Norri, Norrie, Norry

Nordica (German) Woman from the north
Nordika, Nordicka, Nordyca, Nordyka, Nordycka, Norda, Norell, Norelle

Nosiwe (African) Mother of the homeland

Noura (Arabic) Having an inner light
Nureh, Nourah, Nure

Nyala (African) Resembling an antelope
Nyalah, Nyalla, Nyallah

^Nylah (Gaelic) Cloud or champion

Nyneve (English) In Arthurian legend, another name for the lady of the lake
Nineve, Niniane, Ninyane, Nyniane, Ninieve, Niniveve

O

Oaisara (Arabic) A great ruler; an empress
Oaisarah, Oaisarra, Oaisarrah

Oamra (Arabic) Daughter of the moon
Oamrah, Oamira, Oamyra, Oameera

Oba (African) In mythology, the goddess of rivers
Obah, Obba, Obbah

Octavia (Latin) Feminine form of Octavius; the eighth-born child
Octaviana, Octavianne, Octavie, Octiana, Octoviana, Ottavia, Octavi, Octavy

Ode (Egyptian / Greek) Traveler of the road / a lyric poem
Odea

Odessa (Greek) Feminine form of Odysseus; one who wanders; an angry woman
Odissa, Odyssa, Odessia, Odissia, Odyssia, Odysseia

Odina (Latin / Scandinavian) From the mountain / feminine form of Odin, the highest of the gods
Odinah, Odeena, Odeene, Odeen, Odyna, Odyne, Odynn, Odeana

Ogin (Native American) Resembling the wild rose

Oheo (Native American) A beautiful woman

Oira (Latin) One who prays to God
Oyra, Oirah, Oyrah

Okalani (Hawaiian) Form of Kalani, meaning "from the heavens"
Okalanie, Okalany, Okalaney, Okalanee, Okaloni, Okalonie, Okalonee, Okalony, Okaloney, Okeilana, Okelani, Okelani, Okelanie, Okelany, Okelaney, Okelanee, Okalanea, Okalonea, Okelanea

Okei (Japanese) Woman of the ocean

Oksana (Russian) Hospitality
Oksanah, Oksie, Aksana

Ola (Nigerian / Hawaiian / Norse) One who is precious / giver of life; well-being / a relic of one's ancestors
Olah, Olla, Ollah

Olaide (American) A thoughtful woman
Olaid, Olaida, Olayd, Olayde, Olayda, Olaed, Olaede, Olaeda

Olathe (Native American) A lovely young woman

Olayinka (Yoruban) Surrounded by wealth and honor
Olayenka, Olayanka

Oleda (English) Resembling a winged creature
Oldedah, Oleta, Olita, Olida, Oletah, Olitah, Olidah

Olethea (Latin) Form of Alethea, meaning "one who is truthful"
Oletheia, Olethia, Oletha, Oletea, Olthaia, Olithea, Olathea, Oletia

Olina (Hawaiian) One who is joyous
Oline, Oleen, Oleene, Olyne, Oleena, Olyna, Olin

^*ᵀ**Olivia** (Latin) Feminine form of Oliver; of the olive tree; one who is peaceful
*Oliviah, Oliva, **Olive**, Oliveea, Olivet, Olivetta, Olivette, Olivija*

Olwen (Welsh) One who leaves a white footprint
Olwynn, Olvyen, Olvyin

Olympia (Greek) From Mount Olympus; a goddess
Olympiah, Olimpe, Olimpia, Olimpiada, Olimpiana, Olypme, Olympie, Olympi

Omri (Arabic) A red-haired woman
Omrie, Omree, Omrea, Omry, Omrey

Ona (Hebrew) Filled with grace
Onit, Onat, Onah

Ondrea (Slavic) Form of Andrea, meaning "courageous and strong / womanly"
Ondria, Ondrianna, Ondreia, Ondreina, Ondreya, Ondriana, Ondreana, Ondera

Oneida (Native American) Our long-awaited daughter
Onieda, Oneyda, Onida, Onyda

Onida (Native American) The one who has been expected
Onidah, Onyda, Onydah

Ontina (American) An open-minded woman
Ontinah, Onteena, Onteenah, Onteana, Onteanah, Ontiena, Ontienah, Onteina

Oona (Gaelic) Form of Agnes, meaning "one who is pure; chaste"

Opal (Sanskrit) A treasured jewel; resembling the iridescent gemstone
Opall, Opalle, Opale, Opalla, Opala, Opalina, Opaline, Opaleena

Ophelia (Greek) One who offers help to others
Ofelia, Ofilia, OphElie, Ophelya, Ophilia, Ovalia, Ovelia, Opheliah

Ophrah (Hebrew) Resembling a fawn; from the place of dust
Ofra, Ofrit, Ophra, Oprah, Orpa, Orpah, Ofrat, Ofrah

Orange (Latin) Resembling the sweet fruit
Orangetta, Orangia, Orangina, Orangea

Orbelina (American) One who brings excitement
Orbelinah, Orbeleena

Orea (Greek) From the mountains
Oreah

Orenda (Iroquois) A woman with magical powers

Oriana (Latin) Born at sunrise
Oreana, Orianna, Oriane, Oriann, Orianne

Oribel (Latin) A beautiful golden child
Orabel, Orabelle, Orabell, Orabela, Orabella, Oribell, Oribelle, Oribele

Orin (Irish) A dark-haired beauty
Orine, Orina, Oryna, Oryn, Oryne

Orinthia (Hebrew / Gaelic) Of the pine tree / a fair lady
Orrinthia, Orenthia, Orna, Ornina, Orinthea, Orenthea, Orynthia, Orynthea

Oriole (Latin) Resembling the gold-speckled bird
Oreolle, Oriolle, Oreole, Oriola, Oriolla, Oriol, Oreola, Oreolla

Orion (Greek) The huntress; a constellation

Orithna (Greek) One who is natural
Orithne, Orythna, Orythne, Orithnia, Orythnia, Orithnea, Orythnea

Orla (Gaelic) The golden queen
Orlah, Orrla, Orrlah, Orlagh, Orlaith, Orlaithe, Orghlaith, Orghlaithe

Orna (Irish / Hebrew) One who is pale-skinned / of the cedar tree
Ornah, Ornette, Ornetta, Ornete, Orneta, Obharnait, Ornat

Ornella (Italian) Of the flowering ash tree

Ornice (Irish) A pale-skinned woman
Ornyce, Ornise, Orynse, Orneice, Orneise, Orniece, Orniese, Orneece

Orva (Anglo-Saxon / French) A courageous friend / as precious as gold

Orynko (Ukrainian) A peaceful woman
Orinko, Orynka, Orinka

Osaka (Japanese) From the city of industry
Osaki, Osakie, Osakee, Osaky, Osakey, Osakea

Osma (English) Feminine form of Osmond; protected by God
Osmah, Ozma, Ozmah

Otina (American) A fortunate woman
Otinah, Otyna, Otynah, Oteena, Oteenah, Oteana, Oteanah, Otiena

Overton (English) From the upper side of town
Overtown

Owena (Welsh) A high-born woman
Owenah, Owenna, Owennah, Owenia, Owenea

Ozora (Hebrew) One who is wealthy
Ozorah, Ozorra, Ozorrah

P

Pace (American) A charismatic young woman
Paice, Payce, Paece, Pase, Paise, Payse, Paese

Pacifica (Spanish) A peaceful woman
Pacifika, Pacyfyca, Pacyfyka, Pacifyca, Pacifyka, Pacyfica, Pacyfika

Pageant (American) A dramatic woman
Pagent, Padgeant, Padgent

Paige (English) A young assistant
Page, Payge, Paege

Paisley (English) Woman of the church

Paki (African) A witness of God
Pakki, Packi, Pacci, Pakie, Pakkie, Paky, Pakky, Pakey

Palba (Spanish) A fair-haired woman

Palemon (Spanish) A kind-hearted woman
Palemond, Palemona, Palemonda

Palesa (African) Resembling a flower
Palessa, Palesah, Palysa, Palisa, Paleesa

Paloma (Spanish) Dove-like
Palloma, Palomita, Palometa, Peloma, Aloma

Pamela (English) A woman who is as sweet as honey
Pamelah, Pamella, Pammeli, Pammelie, Pameli, Pamelie, Pamelia, Pamelea

Panagiota (Greek) Feminine form of Panagiotis; a holy woman

Panchali (Indian) A princess; a high-born woman
Panchalie, Panchaly, Panchalli

Panda (English) Resembling the bamboo-eating animal
Pandah

Pandara (Indian) A good wife
Pandarah, Pandarra, Pandaria, Pandarea

Pandora (Greek) A gifted, talented woman; in mythology, the first mortal woman, who unleashed evil upon the world
Pandorah, Pandorra, Pandoria, Pandorea, Pandoriya

Pantxike (Latin) A woman who is free
Pantxikey, Pantxikye, Pantxeke, Pantxyke

Paras (Indian) A woman against whom others are measured

^T**Paris** (English) Woman of the city in France
Pariss, Parisse, Parys, Paryss, Parysse

^**Parker** (English) The keeper of the park
Parkyr

Parry (Welsh) Daughter of Harry
Parri, Parrie, Parrey, Parree, Parrea

Parvani (Indian) Born during a full moon
Parvanie, Parvany, Parvaney, Parvanee, Parvanea

Parvati (Hindi) Daughter of the mountain; in Hinduism, a name for the wife of Shiva
Parvatie, Parvaty, Parvatey, Parvatee, Pauravi, Parvatea, Pauravie, Pauravy

Paterekia (Hawaiian) An upper-class woman
Paterekea, Pakelekia, Pakelekea

Patience (English) One who is patient; an enduring woman
Patiencia, Paciencia, Pacencia, Pacyncia, Pacincia, Pacienca

Patricia (English) Feminine form of Patrick; of noble descent
Patrisha, Patrycia, Patrisia, Patsy, Patti, Patty, Patrizia, Pattie, Trisha

Patrina (American) Born into the nobility
Patreena, Patriena, Patreina, Patryna, Patreana

Paula (English) Feminine form of Paul; a petite woman
Paulina, Pauline, Paulette, Paola, Pauleta, Pauletta, Pauli, Paulete

Pausha (Hindi) Resembling the moon
Paushah

Pax (Latin) One who is peaceful; in mythology, the goddess of peace
Paxi, Paxie, Paxton, Paxten, Paxtan, Paxy, Paxey, Paxee

^***Payton** (English) From the warrior's village
Paton, Paeton, Paiton, Payten, Paiten

Pearl (Latin) A precious gem of the sea
Pearla, Pearle, Pearlie, Pearly, Pearline, Pearlina, Pearli, Pearley

Pelopia (Greek) In mythology, the wife of Thyestes and mother of Aegisthus
Pelopiah, Pelopea, Pelopeah, Pelopiya

Pembroke (English) From the broken hill
Pembrook, Pembrok, Pembrooke

Pendant (French) A decorated woman
Pendent, Pendante, Pendente

Penelope (Greek) Resembling a duck; in mythology, the faithful wife of Odysseus
Peneloppe, Penelopy, Penelopey, Penelopi, Penelopie, Penelopee, Penella, Penelia

Penia (Greek) In mythology, the personification of poverty
Peniah, Penea, Peniya, Peneah, Peniyah

Penthesilea (Greek) In mythology, a queen of the Amazons

Peony (Greek) Resembling the flower
Peoney, Peoni, Peonie, Peonee, Peonea

Pepin (French) An awe-inspiring woman
Peppin, Pepine, Peppine, Pipin, Pippin, Pepen, Pepan, Peppen

Pepita (Spanish) Feminine form of Joseph; God will add
Pepitah, Pepitta, Pepitia, Pepitina

Perdita (Latin) A lost woman
Perditah, Perditta, Perdy, Perdie, Perdi, Perdee, Perdea, Perdeeta

Perdix (Latin) Resembling a partridge
Perdixx, Perdyx, Perdyxx

Peri (Persian / English) In mythology, a fairy / from the pear tree
Perry, Perri, Perie, Perrie, Pery, Perrey, Perey, Peree

Perpetua (Latin) One who is constant; steadfast

Persephone (Greek) In mythology, the daughter of Demeter and Zeus who was abducted to the underworld
Persephoni, Persephonie, Persephony, Persephoney, Persephonee, Persefone, Persefoni, Persefonie

Persis (Greek) Woman of Persia
Persiss, Persisse, Persys, Persyss, Persysse

Pesha (Hebrew) A flourishing woman
Peshah, Peshia, Peshiah, Peshea, Pesheah, Peshe

Petronela (Latin) Feminine form of Peter, as solid and strong as a rock
Petronella, Petronelle, Petronia, Petronilla, Petronille, Petrona, Petronia, Petronel

Petunia (English) Resembling the flower
Petuniah, Petuniya, Petunea, Petoonia, Petounia

*****Peyton** (English) From the warrior's village
Peyten

Phaedra (Greek) A bright woman; in mythology, the wife of Theseus
Phadra, Phaidra, Phedra, Phaydra, Phedre, Phaedre

Phailin (Thai) Resembling a sapphire
Phaylin, Phaelin, Phalin

Phashestha (American) One who is decorated
Phashesthea, Phashesthia, Phashesthiya

Pheakkley (Vietnamese) A faithful woman
Pheakkly, Pheakkli, Pheakklie, Pheakklee, Pheakkleigh, Pheakklea

Pheodora (Greek) A supreme gift
Pheodorah, Phedora, Phedorah

Phernita (American) A well-spoken woman
Pherneeta, Phernyta, Phernieta, Pherneita, Pherneata

Phia (Italian) A saintly woman
Phiah, Phea, Pheah

Philippa (English) Feminine form of Phillip; a friend of horses
Phillippa, Philipa, Phillipa, Philipinna, Philippine, Phillipina, Phillipine, Pilis

Philomena (Greek) A friend of strength
Filomena, Philomina, Mena

Phoebe (Greek) A bright, shining woman; in mythology, another name for the goddess of the moon
Phebe, Phoebi, Phebi, Phoebie, Phebie, Pheobe, Phoebee, Phoebea

Phoena (Greek) Resembling a mystical bird
Phoenah, Phoenna, Phena, Phenna

Phoenix (Greek) A dark-red color; in mythology, an immortal bird
Phuong, Phoenyx

Phyllis (Greek) Of the foliage; in mythology, a girl who was turned into an almond tree
Phylis, Phillis, Philis, Phylys, Phyllida, Phylida, Phillida, Philida

Pili (Egyptian) The second-born child
Pilie, Pily, Piley, Pilee, Pilea, Pileigh

Pililani (Hawaiian) Having great strength
Pililanie, Pililany, Pililaney, Pililanee, Pililanea

Piluki (Hawaiian) Resembling a small leaf
Pilukie, Piluky, Pilukey, Pilukee, Pilukea

Pineki (Hawaiian) Resembling a peanut
Pinekie, Pineky, Pinekey, Pinekee, Pinekea

Ping (Chinese) One who is peaceful
Pyng

Pinga (Inuit) In mythology, goddess of the hunt, fertility, and healing
Pingah, Pyngah, Pyngah

Pinquana (Native American) Having a pleasant fragrance
Pinquan, Pinquann, Pinquanne, Pinquanna, Pinquane

Piper (English) One who plays the flute
Pipere, Piperel, Piperell, Piperele, Piperelle, Piperela, Piperella, Pyper

Pippi (French / English) A friend of horses / a blushing young woman
Pippie, Pippy, Pippey, Pippee, Pippea

Pirouette (French) A ballet dancer
Piroette, Pirouett, Piroett, Piroueta, Piroeta, Pirouetta, Piroetta, Pirouet

Pisces (Latin) The twelfth sign of the zodiac; the fishes
Pysces, Piscees, Pyscees, Piscez, Pisceez

Pithasthana (Hindi) In Hinduism, a name for the wife of Shiva

Platinum (English) As precious as the metal
Platynum, Platnum, Platie, Plati, Platee, Platy, Platey, Platea

Platt (French) From the plains
Platte

Pleshette (American) An extravagent woman
Pleshett, Pleshet, Pleshete, Plesheta, Pleshetta

Pleun (American) One who is good with words
Pleune

Po (Italian) A lively woman

Podarge (Greek) In mythology, one of the Harpies

Poetry (American) A romantic woman
Poetrey, Poetri, Poetrie, Poetree, Poetrea

Polete (Hawaiian) A kind young woman
Polet, Polett, Polette, Poleta, Poletta

Polina (Russian) A small woman
Polinah, Poleena, Poleenah, Poleana, Poleanah, Poliena, Polienah, Poleina

Polyxena (Greek) In mythology, a daughter of Priam and loved by Achilles
Polyxenah, Polyxenia, Polyxenna, Polyxene, Polyxenea

Pomona (Latin) In mythology, goddess of fruit trees
Pomonah, Pomonia, Pomonea, Pamona, Pamonia, Pamonea

Poni (African) The second-born daughter
Ponni, Ponie, Ponnie, Pony, Ponny, Poney, Ponney, Ponee

Poodle (American) Resembling the dog; one with curly hair
Poudle, Poodel, Poudel

Poonam (Hindi) A kind and caring woman
Pounam

Porter (Latin) The doorkeeper

Posala (Native American) Born at the end of spring
Posalah, Posalla, Posallah

Posh (American) A fancy young woman
Poshe, Posha

Potina (Latin) In mythology, goddess of children's food and drink
Potinah, Potyna, Potena, Poteena, Potiena, Poteina, Poteana

Powder (American) A light-hearted woman
Powdar, Powdir, Powdur, Powdor, Powdi, Powdie, Powdy, Powdey

Praise (Latin) One who expresses admiration
Prayse, Praize, Prayze, Praze, Praese, Praeze

Pramada (Indian) One who is indifferent

Pramlocha (Hindi) In Hinduism, a celestial nymph

Precious (American) One who is treasured
Preshis, Preshys

Presley (English) Of the priest's town
Presly, Preslie, Presli, Preslee

Primola (Latin) Resembling a primrose
Primolah, Primolia, Primoliah, Primolea, Primoleah

Princess (English) A high-born daughter; born to royalty
Princessa, Princesa, Princie, Princi, Princy, Princee, Princey, Princea

Prisca (Latin) From an ancient family
Priscilla, Priscella, Precilla, Presilla, Prescilla, Prisilla, Prisella, Prissy, Prissi

Promise (American) A faithful woman
Promice, Promyse, Promyce, Promis, Promiss, Promys, Promyss

Prudence (English) One who is cautious and exercises good judgment
Prudencia, Prudensa, Prudensia, Prudentia, Predencia, Predentia, Prue, Pru

Pryce (American / Welsh) One who is very dear / an enthusiastic child
Price, Prise, Pryse

Pulcheria (Italian) A chubby
baby
*Pulcheriah, Pulcherea,
Pulchereah, Pulcherya,
Pulcheryah, Pulcheriya*

Pulika (African) An obedient
and well-behaved girl
*Pulikah, Pulicca, Pulicka,
Pulyka, Puleeka, Puleaka*

Pyrena (Greek) A fiery woman
*Pyrenah, Pyrina, Pyrinah,
Pyryna, Pyrynah, Pyreena,
Pyreenah, Pyriena*

Pyria (American) One who is
cherished
*Pyriah, Pyrea, Pyreah, Pyriya,
Pyriyah, Pyra*

Qadesh (Syrian) In mythology,
goddess of love and sensuality
*Quedesh, Qadesha, Quedesha,
Qadeshia, Quedeshia,
Quedeshiya*

Qamra (Arabic) Of the moon
*Qamrah, Qamar, Qamara,
Qamrra, Qamaria, Qamrea,
Qamria*

Qimat (Indian) A valuable
woman
*Qimate, Qimatte, Qimata,
Qimatta*

Qitarah (Arabic) Having a nice
fragrance
*Qitara, Qytarah, Qytara,
Qitaria, Qitarra, Qitarria,
Qytarra, Qytarria*

Qoqa (Chechen) Resembling
a dove

Quana (Native American)
One who is aromatic; sweet-
smelling
*Quanah, Quanna, Quannah,
Quania, Quaniya, Quanniya,
Quannia, Quanea*

Querida (Spanish) One who is
dearly loved; beloved
*Queridah, Queryda, Querydah,
Querrida, Queridda,
Querridda, Quereeda,
Quereada*

Queta (Spanish) Head of the
household
Quetah, Quetta, Quettah

Quiana (American) Living
with grace; heavenly
*Quianah, Quianna, Quiane,
Quian, Quianne, Quianda,
Quiani, Quianita*

Quincy (English) The fifth-born child
Quincey, Quinci, Quincie, Quincee, Quincia, Quinncy, Quinnci, Quyncy

^**Quinn** (English / Irish) Woman who is queenly
Quin, Quinne

Quintana (Latin / English) The fifth girl / queen's lawn
Quintanah, Quinella, Quinta, Quintina, Quintanna, Quintann, Quintara, Quintona

Quintessa (Latin) Of the essence
Quintessah, Quintesa, Quintesha, Quintisha, Quintessia, Quyntessa, Quintosha, Quinticia

Quinyette (American) The fifth-born child
Quinyett, Quinyet, Quinyeta, Quinyette, Quinyete

Quirina (Latin) One who is contentious
Quirinah, Quiryna, Quirynah, Quireena, Quireenah, Quireina, Quireinah, Quiriena

Quiritis (Latin) In mythology, goddess of motherhood
Quiritiss, Quiritisse, Quirytis, Quirytys, Quiritys, Quirityss

R

Rabiah (Egyptian / Arabic) Born in the springtime / of the gentle wind
Rabia, Raabia, Rabi'ah, Rabi

Rachana (Hindi) Born of the creation
Rachanna, Rashana, Rashanda, Rachna

Rachel (Hebrew) The innocent lamb; in the Bible, Jacob's wife
Rachael, Racheal, Rachelanne, Rachelce, Rachele, Racheli, Rachell, Rachelle, Raquel

Radcliffe (English) Of the red cliffs
Radcleff, Radclef, Radclif, Radclife, Radclyffe, Radclyf, Radcliphe, Radclyphe

Radella (English) An elfin counselor
Radell, Radel, Radele, Radela, Raedself, Radself, Raidself

Radmilla (Slavic) Hard-working for the people
Radilla, Radinka, Radmila, Redmilla, Radilu

Rafi'a (Arabic) An exalted
woman
*Rafia, Rafi'ah, Rafee'a, Rafeea,
Rafeeah, Rafiya, Rafiyah*

Ragnara (Swedish) Feminine
form of Ragnar; one who pro-
vides counsel to the army
*Ragnarah, Ragnarra,
Ragnaria, Ragnarea, Ragnari,
Ragnarie, Ragnary, Ragnarey*

Rahi (Arabic) Born during the
springtime
*Rahii, Rahy, Rahey, Rahee,
Rahea, Rahie*

Rahimah (Arabic) A compas-
sionate woman; one who is
merciful
*Rahima, Raheema, Raheemah,
Raheima, Rahiema, Rahyma,
Rahymah, Raheama*

Raina (Polish) Form of Regina,
meaning "a queenly woman"
*Raenah, Raene, Rainah, Raine,
Rainee, Rainey, Rainelle, Rainy*

Raja (Arabic) One who is filled
with hope
Rajah

Raleigh (English) From the
clearing of roe deer
*Raileigh, Railey, Raley, Rawleigh,
Rawley, Raly, Rali, Ralie*

Ramona (Spanish) Feminine
form of Ramon; a wise pro-
tector
*Ramee, Ramie, Ramoena,
Ramohna, Ramonda,
Ramonde, Ramonita,
Ramonna*

Randi (English) Feminine
form of Randall; shielded
by wolves; form of Miranda,
meaning "worthy of admiration"
*Randa, Randee, Randelle,
Randene, Randie, Randy,
Randey, Randilyn*

Raquel (Spanish) Form of
Rachel, meaning "the inno-
cent lamb"
*Racquel, Racquell, Raquela,
Raquelle, Roquel, Roquela,
Rakel, Rakell*

Rasha (Arabic) Resembling a
young gazelle
*Rashah, Raisha, Raysha,
Rashia, Raesha*

Ratana (Thai) Resembling a
crystal
*Ratanah, Ratanna, Ratannah,
Rathana, Rathanna*

Rati (Hindi) In Hinduism,
goddess of passion and lust
*Ratie, Ratea, Ratee, Raty,
Ratey*

Ratri (Indian) Born in the evening
Ratrie, Ratry, Ratrey, Ratree, Ratrea

Rawiyah (Arabic) One who recites ancient poetry
Rawiya, Rawiyya, Rawiyyah

Rawnie (English) An elegant lady
Rawni, Rawny, Rawney, Rawnee, Rawnea

Raya (Israeli) A beloved friend
Rayah

Raymonde (German) Feminine form of Raymond; one who offers wise protection
Raymondi, Raymondie, Raymondee, Raymondea, Raymonda, Raymunde, Raymunda

Rayna (Hebrew / Scandinavian) One who is pure / one who provides wise counsel
Raynah, Raynee, Rayni, Rayne, Raynea, Raynie

Reba (Hebrew) Form of Rebecca, meaning "one who is bound to God"
Rebah, Reeba, Rheba, Rebba, Ree, Reyba, Reaba

Rebecca (Hebrew) One who is bound to God; in the Bible, the wife of Isaac
Rebakah, Rebbeca, Rebbecca, Rebbecka, Rebeca, Rebeccah, Rebeccea, Becky, Reba

Reese (American) Form of Rhys, meaning "having great enthusiasm for life"
Rhyss, Rhysse, Reece, Reice, Reise, Reace, Rease, Riece

ᵀ**Reagan** (Gaelic) Born into royalty; the little ruler
Raegan, Ragan, Raygan, Reganne, Regann, Regane, Reghan, Regan

Regina (Latin) A queenly woman
Regeena, Regena, Reggi, Reggie, Régine, Regine, Reginette, Reginia, Raina

Rehan (Armenian) Resembling a flower
Rehane, Rehann, Rehanne, Rehana, Rehanna, Rehanan, Rehannan, Rehania

Rehoboth (Hebrew) From the city by the river
Rehobothe, Rehobotha, Rehobothia

Rekha (Indian) One who walks a straight line
Rekhah, Reka, Rekah

Remy (French) Woman from the town of Rheims
Remi, Remie, Remmy, Remmi, Remmie, Remmey, Remey

Ren (Japanese) Resembling a water lily

Renée (French) One who has been reborn
Ranae, Ranay, Ranée, Renae, Renata, Renay, Renaye, René

Reseda (Latin) Resembling the mignonette flower
Resedah, Reselda, Resedia, Reseldia

Resen (Hebrew) From the head of the stream; refers to a bridle

Reshma (Arabic) Having silky skin
Reshmah, Reshman, Reshmane, Reshmann, Reshmanne, Reshmana, Reshmanna, Reshmaan

Reya (Spanish) A queenly woman
Reyah, Reyeh, Reye, Reyia, Reyiah, Reyea, Reyeah

Reza (Hungarian) Form of Theresa, meaning "a harvester"
Rezah, Rezia, Reziah, Rezi, Rezie, Rezy, Rezee, Resi

Rezeph (Hebrew) As solid as a stone
Rezepha, Rezephe, Rezephia, Rezephah, Rezephiah

Rhea (Greek) Of the flowing stream; in mythology, the wife of Cronus and mother of gods and goddesses
Rea, Rhae, Rhaya, Rhia, Rhiah, Rhiya, Rheya

Rheda (Anglo-Saxon) A divine woman; a goddess
Rhedah

Rhiannon (Welsh) The great and sacred queen
Rheanna, Rheanne, Rhiana, Rhiann, Rhianna, Rhiannan, Rhianon, Rhyan

Rhonda (Welsh) Wielding a good spear
Rhondelle, Rhondene, Rhondiesha, Rhonette, Rhonnda, Ronda, Rondel, Rondelle

Rhys (Welsh) Having great enthusiasm for life
Rhyss, Rhysse, Reece, Reese, Reice, Reise, Reace, Rease

Ria (Spanish) From the river's mouth
Riah

Riane (Gaelic) Feminine form
of Ryan; little ruler
*Riana, Rianna, Rianne,
Ryann, Ryanne, Ryana,
Ryanna, Riann*

Rica (English) Form of
Frederica, meaning "peaceful
ruler"; form of Erica, meaning "ever the ruler / resembling heather"
*Rhica, Ricca, Ricah, Rieca,
Riecka, Rieka, Riqua, Ryca*

Riddhi (Indian) A prosperous
woman
*Riddhie, Riddhy, Riddhey,
Riddhee, Riddhea*

Rihanna (Arabic) Resembling
sweet basil
Rihana

*ᵀRiley (Gaelic) From the
rye clearing; a courageous
woman
*Reilley, Reilly, Rilee, Rileigh,
Ryley, Rylee, Ryleigh, Rylie*

Rini (Japanese) Resembling a
young rabbit
*Rinie, Rinee, Rinea, Riny,
Riney*

Rio (Spanish) Woman of the
river
Rhio

Risa (Latin) One who laughs
often
*Risah, Reesa, Riesa, Rise, Rysa,
Rysah, Riseh, Risako*

Rita (Greek) Precious pearl
*Ritta, Reeta, Reita, Rheeta,
Riet, Rieta, Ritah, Reta*

Roberta (English) Feminine
form of Robert; one who is
bright with fame
Robertah, Robbie, Robin

Rochelle (French) From the
little rock
*Rochel, Rochele, Rochell,
Rochella, Rochette, Roschella,
Roschelle, Roshelle*

Roja (Spanish) A red-haired
lady
Rojah

Rolanda (German) Feminine
form of Roland; well-known
throughout the land
*Rolandah, Rolandia,
Roldandea, Rolande, Rolando,
Rollanda, Rollande*

Romhilda (German) A glorious
battle maiden
*Romhilde, Romhild, Romeld,
Romelde, Romelda, Romilda,
Romild, Romilde*

Ronli (Hebrew) My joy is the Lord
Ronlie, Ronlee, Ronleigh, Ronly, Ronley, Ronlea, Ronia, Roniya

Ronni (English) Form of Veronica, meaning "displaying her true image"
Ronnie, Ronae, Ronay, Ronee, Ronelle, Ronette, Roni, Ronica, Ronika

Rosalind (German / English) Resembling a gentle horse / form of Rose, meaning "resembling the beautiful and meaningful flower"
Ros, Rosaleen, Rosalen, Rosalin, Rosalina, Rosalinda, Rosalinde, Rosaline, Chalina

Rose (Latin) Resembling the beautiful and meaningful flower
Rosa, Rosie, Rosalind

Roseanne (English) Resembling the graceful rose
Ranna, Rosana, Rosanagh, Rosanna, Rosannah, Rosanne, Roseann, Roseanna

Rosemary (Latin / English) The dew of the sea / resembling a bitter rose
Rosemaree, Rosemarey, Rosemaria, Rosemarie, Rosmarie, Rozmary, Rosamaria, Rosamarie

Rowan (Gaelic) Of the red-berry tree
Rowann, Rowane, Rowanne, Rowana, Rowanna

Rowena (Welsh / German) One who is fair and slender / having much fame and happiness
Rhowena, Roweena, Roweina, Rowenna, Rowina, Rowinna, Rhonwen, Rhonwyn

Ruana (Indian) One who is musically inclined
Ruanah, Ruanna, Ruannah, Ruane, Ruann, Ruanne

Ruby (English) As precious as the red gemstone
Rubee, Rubi, Rubie, Rubyna, Rubea

Rudella (German) A well-known woman
Rudela, Rudelah, Rudell, Rudelle, Rudel, Rudele, Rudy, Rudie

Rue (English, German) A medicinal herb
Ru, Larue

Rufina (Latin) A red-haired woman
Rufeena, Rufeine, Ruffina, Rufine, Ruffine, Rufyna, Ruffyna, Rufyne

Ruhi (Arabic) A spiritual woman
Roohee, Ruhee, Ruhie, Ruhy, Ruhey, Roohi, Roohie, Ruhea

Rukmini (Hindi) Adorned with gold; in Hinduism, the first wife of Krishna
Rukminie, Rukminy, Rukminey, Rukminee, Rukminea, Rukminni, Rukminii

Rumah (Hebrew) One who has been exalted
Ruma, Rumia, Rumea, Rumiah, Rumeah, Rumma, Rummah

Rumina (Latin) In mythology, a protector goddess of mothers and babies
Ruminah, Rumeena, Rumeenah, Rumeina, Rumiena, Rumyna, Rumeinah, Rumienah

Rupali (Indian) A beautiful woman
Rupalli, Rupalie, Rupalee, Rupallee, Rupal, Rupa, Rupaly, Rupaley

Ruqayyah (Arabic) A gentle woman; a daughter of Muhammad
Ruqayya, Ruqayah, Ruqaya

Ruth (Hebrew) A beloved companion
Ruthe, Ruthelle, Ruthellen, Ruthetta, Ruthi, Ruthie, Ruthina, Ruthine

Ryba (Slavic) Resembling a fish
Rybah, Rybba, Rybbah

Ryder (American) An accomplished horsewoman
Rider

Rylee (American) Form of Riley, meaning "from the rye clearing / a courageous woman"

Saba (Greek / Arabic) Woman from Sheba / born in the morning
Sabah, Sabaa, Sabba, Sabbah, Sabaah

Sabana (Spanish) From the open plain
Sabanah, Sabanna, Sabann, Sabanne, Sabane, Saban

Sabi (Arabic) A lovely young lady
Sabie, Saby, Sabey, Sabee, Sabbi, Sabbee, Sabea

Sabirah (Arabic) Having great patience
Sabira, Saabira, Sabeera, Sabiera, Sabeira, Sabyra, Sabirra, Sabyrra

Sabra (Hebrew) Resembling the cactus fruit; to rest
Sabrah, Sebra, Sebrah, Sabrette, Sabbra, Sabraa, Sabarah, Sabarra

Sabrina (English) A legendary princess
Sabrinah, Sabrinna, Sabreena, Sabriena, Sabreina, Sabryna, Sabrine, Sabryne, Cabrina, Zabrina

Sachet (Hindi) Having consciousness
Sachett, Sachette

Sada (Japanese) The pure one
Sadda, Sadaa, Sadako, Saddaa

Sadella (American) A beautiful fairylike princess
Sadel, Sadela, Sadelah, Sadele, Sadell, Sadellah, Sadelle, Sydel

Sadhana (Hindi) A devoted woman
Sadhanah, Sadhanna, Sadhannah, Sadhane, Sadhanne, Sadhann, Sadhan

Sadhbba (Irish) A wise woman
Sadhbh, Sadhba

Sadie (English) Form of Sarah, meaning "a princess; lady"
Sadi, Sady, Sadey, Sadee, Saddi, Saddee, Sadiey, Sadye

Sadiya (Arabic) One who is fortunate; lucky
Sadiyah, Sadiyyah, Sadya, Sadyah

Sadzi (American) Having a sunny disposition
Sadzee, Sadzey, Sadzia, Sadziah, Sadzie, Sadzya, Sadzyah, Sadzy

Safa (Arabic) One who is innocent and pure
Safah, Saffa, Sapha, Saffah, Saphah

Saffron (English) Resembling the yellow flower
Saffrone, Saffronn, Saffronne, Safron, Safronn, Safronne, Saffronah, Safrona

Saheli (Indian) A beloved
friend
*Sahelie, Sahely, Saheley,
Sahelee, Saheleigh, Sahyli,
Sahelea*

Sahila (Indian) One who pro-
vides guidance
*Sahilah, Saheela, Sahyla,
Sahiela, Saheila, Sahela,
Sahilla, Sahylla*

Sahkyo (Native American)
Resembling the mink
Sakyo

Saida (Arabic) Fortunate one;
one who is happy
*Saidah, Sa'ida, Sayida, Saeida,
Saedah, Said, Sayide, Sayidea*

Saihah (Arabic) One who is
useful; good
Saiha, Sayiha

Sailor (American) One who
sails the seas
*Sailer, Sailar, Saylor, Sayler,
Saylar, Saelor, Saeler, Saelar*

Saima (Arabic) A fasting
woman
Saimah, Saimma, Sayima

Sajni (Indian) One who is
dearly loved
*Sajnie, Sajny, Sajney, Sajnee,
Sajnea*

Sakae (Japanese) One who is
prosperous
Sakai, Sakaie, Sakay, Sakaye

Sakari (Native American) A
sweet girl
*Sakarie, Sakary, Sakarri,
Sakarey, Sakaree, Sakarree,
Sakarah, Sakarrie*

Sakina (Indian / Arabic) A
beloved friend / having God-
inspired peace of mind
*Sakinah, Sakeena, Sakiena,
Sakeina, Sakyna, Sakeyna,
Sakinna, Sakeana*

Sakti (Hindi) In Hinduism,
the divine energy
*Saktie, Sakty, Sakkti, Sackti,
Saktee, Saktey, Saktia, Saktiah*

Saku (Japanese) Remembrance
of the Lord
Sakuko

Sakura (Japanese) Resembling
a cherry blossom
Sakurah, Sakurako, Sakurra

Sala (Hindi) From the sacred
sala tree
Salah, Salla, Sallah

Salal (English) An evergreen
shrub with flowers and ber-
ries
*Sallal, Salall, Sallall, Salalle,
Salale, Sallale*

Salamasina (Samoan) A princess; born to royalty
Salamaseena, Salamasyna, Salamaseana, Salamaseina, Salamasiena

Salina (French) One of a solemn, dignified character
Salin, Salinah, Salinda, Salinee, Sallin, Sallina, Sallinah, Salline

Saloma (Hebrew) One who offers peace and tranquility
Salomah, Salome, Salomia, Salomiah, Schlomit, Shulamit, Salomeaexl, Salomma

Salus (Latin) In mythology, goddess of health and prosperity; salvation
Saluus, Salusse, Saluss

Salwa (Arabic) One who provides comfort; solace
Salwah

Samah (Arabic) A generous, forgiving woman
Sama, Samma, Sammah

*Samantha (Aramaic) One who listens well
Samanthah, Samanthia, Samanthea, Samantheya, Samanath, Samanatha, Samana, Samanitha

Sameh (Arabic) One who forgives
Sammeh, Samaya, Samaiya

Samina (Arabic) A healthy woman
Saminah, Samine, Sameena, Samyna, Sameana, Sameina, Samynah

Samone (Hebrew) Form of Simone, meaning "one who listens well"
Samoan, Samoane, Samon, Samona, Samonia

Samuela (Hebrew) Feminine form of Samuel; asked of God
Samuelah, Samuella, Samuell, Samuelle, Sammila, Sammile, Samella, Samielle

Sana (Persian / Arabic) One who emanates light / brilliance; splendor
Sanah, Sanna, Sanako, Sanaah, Sane, Saneh

Sanaa (Swahili) Beautiful work of art
Sanae, Sannaa

Sandeep (Punjabi) One who is enlightened
Sandeepe, Sandip, Sandipp, Sandippe, Sandeyp, Sandeype

Sandhya (Hindi) Born at twilight; name of the daughter of the god Brahma
Sandhiya, Sandhyah, Sandya, Sandyah

Sandra (Greek) Form of Alexandra, meaning "a helper and defender of mankind"
Sandrah, Sandrine, Sandy, Sandi, Sandie, Sandey, Sandee, Sanda, Sandrica

Sandrica (Greek) Form of Alexandra, meaning "a helper and defender of mankind"
Sandricca, Sandricah, Sandricka, Sandrickah, Sandrika, Sandrikah, Sandryca, Sandrycah

Sandrine (Greek) Form of Alexandra, meaning "a helper and defender of mankind"
Sandrin, Sandreana, Sandreanah, Sandreane, Sandreen, Sandreena, Sandreenah, Sandreene

Sangita (Indian) One who is musical
Sangitah, Sangeeta, Sangeita, Sangyta, Sangieta, Sangeata

Saniya (Indian) A moment in time preserved
Saniyah, Sanya, Sanea, Sania

Sanjna (Indian) A conscientious woman

Santana (Spanish) A saintly woman
Santa, Santah, Santania, Santaniah, Santaniata, Santena, Santenah, Santenna

Saoirse (Gaelic) An independent woman; having freedom
Saoyrse

Sapna (Hindi) A dream come true
Sapnah, Sapnia, Sapniah, Sapnea, Sapneah, Sapniya, Sapniyah

*ᵀSarah (Hebrew) A princess; lady; in the Bible, wife of Abraham
Sara, Sari, Sariah, Sarika, Saaraa, Sarita, Sarina, Sarra, Kala, Sadie

Saraid (Irish) One who is excellent; superior
Saraide, Saraed, Saraede, Sarayd, Sarayde

Sarama (African / Hindi) A kind woman / in Hinduism, Indra's dog
Saramah, Saramma, Sarrama, Sarramma

Saran (African) One who brings joy to others
Sarane, Sarran, Saranne, Saranna, Sarana, Sarann

Sarasvati (Hindi) In Hinduism, goddess of learning and the arts
Sarasvatti, Sarasvatie, Sarasvaty, Sarasvatey, Sarasvatee, Sarasvatea

Saraswati (Hindi) Owning water; in Hinduism, a river goddess
Saraswatti, Saraswatie, Saraswaty, Saraswatey, Saraswatee, Saraswatea

Sardinia (Italian) Woman from a mountainous island
Sardiniah, Sardinea, Sardineah, Sardynia, Sardyniah, Sardynea, Sardyneah

Sasa (Japanese) One who is helpful; gives aid
Sasah

Sasha (Russian) Form of Alexandra, meaning "a helper and defender of mankind"
Sascha, Sashenka, Saskia

Sauda (Swahili) A dark beauty
Saudaa, Sawda, Saudda

*Savannah (English) From the open grassy plain
Savanna, Savana, Savanne, Savann, Savane, Savanneh

Savarna (Hindi) Daughter of the ocean
Savarnia, Savarnea, Savarniya, Savarneia

Savitri (Hindi) In Hinduism, the daughter of the god of the sun
Savitari, Savitrie, Savitry, Savitarri, Savitarie, Savitree, Savitrea, Savitrey

Savvy (American) Smart and perceptive woman
Savy, Savvi, Savvie, Savvey, Savee, Savvee, Savvea, Savea

Sayyida (Arabic) A mistress
Sayyidah, Sayida, Sayyda, Seyyada, Seyyida, Seyada, Seyida

^*Scarlett (English) Vibrant red color; a vivacious woman
Scarlet, Scarlette, Skarlet

Scota (Irish) Woman of Scotland
Scotta, Scotah, Skota, Skotta, Skotah

Sea'iqa (Arabic) Thunder and lightning
Seaqa, Seaqua

Season (Latin) A fertile woman; one who embraces change
Seazon, Seeson, Seezon, Seizon, Seasen, Seasan, Seizen, Seizan

Sebille (English) In Arthurian legend, a fairy
Sebylle, Sebill, Sebile, Sebyle, Sebyl

Secunda (Latin) The second-born child
Secundah, Secuba, Secundus, Segunda, Sekunda

Seda (Armenian) Voices of the forest
Sedda, Sedah, Seddah

Sedona (American) Woman from a city in Arizona
Sedonah, Sedonna, Sedonnah, Sedonia, Sedonea

Seema (Greek) A symbol; a sign
Seyma, Syma, Seama, Seima, Siema

Sefarina (Greek) Of a gentle wind
Sefarinah, Sefareena, Sefareenah, Sefaryna, Sefarynah, Sefareana, Sefareanah

Seiko (Japanese) The force of truth

Selene (Greek) Of the moon
Sela, Selena, Selina, Celina, Zalina

Sema (Arabic) A divine omen; a known symbol
Semah

Senalda (Spanish) A sign; a symbol
Senaldah, Senaldia, Senaldiya, Senaldea, Senaldya

September (American) Born in the month of September
Septimber, Septymber, Septemberia, Septemberea

Sequoia (Native American) Of the giant redwood tree
Sekwoya, Lequoia

Serafina (Latin) A seraph; a heavenly winged angel
Serafinah, Serafine, Seraphina, Serefina, Seraphine, Sera

Serena (Latin) Having a peaceful disposition
Serenah, Serene, Sereena, Seryna, Serenity, Serenitie, Serenitee, Serepta, Cerina, Xerena

Serendipity (American) A fateful meeting; having good fortune
Serendipitey, Serendipitee, Serendipiti, Serendipitie, Serendypyty

*ᵀ**Serenity** (Latin) Peaceful

Sevati (Indian) Resembling
the white rose
*Sevatie, Sevatti, Sevate, Sevatee,
Sevatea, Sevaty, Sevatey, Sevti*

Shabana (Arabic) A maiden
belonging to the night
*Shabanah, Shabanna,
Shabaana, Shabanne, Shabane*

Shabnan (Persian) A falling
raindrop
*Shabnane, Shabnann,
Shabnanne*

Shadha (Arabic) An aromatic
fragrance
Shadhah

Shafiqa (Arabic) A compas-
sionate woman
*Shafiqah, Shafiqua, Shafeeqa,
Shafeequa*

Shai (Gaelic) A gift of God
*Shay, Shae, Shayla, Shea,
Shaye*

Sha'ista (Arabic) One who is
polite and well-behaved
*Shaistah, Shaista, Shaa'ista,
Shayista, Shaysta*

Shakila (Arabic) Feminine
form of Shakil; beautiful one
*Shakilah, Shakela, Shakeela,
Shakeyla, Shakyla, Shakeila,
Shakiela, Shakina*

Shakira (Arabic) Feminine
form of Shakir; grateful;
thankful
*Shakirah, Shakiera, Shaakira,
Shakeira, Shakyra, Shakeyra,
Shakura, Shakirra*

Shakti (Indian) A divine
woman; having power
*Shaktie, Shakty, Shaktey,
Shaktee, Shaktye, Shaktea*

Shaliqa (Arabic) One who is
sisterly
*Shaliqah, Shaliqua, Shaleeqa,
Shaleequa, Shalyqa, Shalyqua*

Shamima (Arabic) A woman
full of flavor
*Shamimah, Shameema,
Shamiema, Shameima,
Shamyma, Shameama*

Shandy (English) One who is
rambunctious; boisterous
*Shandey, Shandee, Shandi,
Shandie, Shandye, Shandea*

Shani (African) A marvelous
woman
*Shanie, Shany, Shaney,
Shanee, Shanni, Shanea,
Shannie, Shanny*

Shanley (Gaelic) Small and
ancient woman
*Shanleigh, Shanlee, Shanly,
Shanli, Shanlie, Shanlea*

Shannon (Gaelic) Having ancient wisdom; river name
Shanon, Shannen, Shannan, Shannin, Shanna, Shannae, Shannun, Shannyn

Shaquana (American) Truth in life
Shaqana, Shaquanah, Shaquanna, Shaqanna, Shaqania

Sharifah (Arabic) Feminine form of Sharif; noble; respected; virtuous
Sharifa, Shareefa, Sharufa, Sharufah, Sharyfa, Sharefa, Shareafa, Shariefa

Sharik (African) One who is a child of God
Shareek, Shareake, Sharicke, Sharick, Sharike, Shareak, Sharique, Sharyk

Sharikah (Arabic) One who is a good companion
Sharika, Shareeka, Sharyka, Shareka, Shariqua, Shareaka

Sharlene (French) Feminine form of Charles; petite and womanly
Sharleene, Sharleen, Sharla, Sharlyne, Sharline, Sharlyn, Sharlean, Sharleane

Sharon (Hebrew) From the plains; a flowering shrub
Sharron, Sharone, Sharona, Shari, Sharis, Sharne, Sherine, Sharun

Shasta (Native American) From the triple-peaked mountain
Shastah, Shastia, Shastiya, Shastea, Shasteya

Shawnee (Native American) A tribal name
Shawni, Shawnie, Shawnea, Shawny, Shawney, Shawnea

Shayla (Irish) Of the fairy palace; form of Shai, meaning "a gift of God"
Shaylah, Shaylagh, Shaylain, Shaylan, Shaylea, Shayleah, Shaylla, Sheyla

Shaylee (Gaelic) From the fairy palace; a fairy princess
Shalee, Shayleigh, Shailee, Shaileigh, Shaelee, Shaeleigh, Shayli, Shaylie

Sheehan (Celtic) Little peaceful one; peacemaker
Shehan, Sheyhan, Shihan, Shiehan, Shyhan, Sheahan

Sheela (Indian) One of cool conduct and character
Sheelah, Sheetal

Sheena (Gaelic) God's gracious gift
Sheenah, Shena, Shiena, Sheyna, Shyna, Sheana, Sheina

Sheherezade (Arabic) One who is a city dweller

Sheila (Irish) Form of Cecilia, meaning "one who is blind"
Sheilah, Sheelagh, Shelagh, Shiela, Shyla, Selia, Sighle, Sheiletta

Shelby (English) From the willow farm
Shelbi, Shelbey, Shelbie, Shelbee, Shelbye, Shelbea

Sheridan (Gaelic) One who is wild and untamed; a searcher
Sheridann, Sheridanne, Sherydan, Sherridan, Sheriden, Sheridon, Sherrerd, Sherida

Sheshebens (Native American) Resembling a small duck

Shifra (Hebrew) A beautiful midwife
Shifrah, Shiphrah, Shiphra, Shifria, Shifriya, Shifrea

Shikha (Indian) Flame burning brightly
Shikhah, Shikkha, Shekha, Shykha

Shima (Native American) Little mother
Shimah, Shimma, Shyma, Shymah

Shina (Japanese) A virtuous woman; having goodness
Shinah, Shinna, Shyna, Shynna

Shobha (Indian) An attractive woman
Shobhah, Shobbha, Shoba, Shobhan, Shobhane

Shoshana (Arabic) Form of Susannah, meaning "white lily"
Shosha, Shoshan, Shoshanah, Shoshane, Shoshanha, Shoshann, Shoshanna, Shoshannah

Shradhdha (Indian) One who is faithful; trusting
Shraddha, Shradha, Shradhan, Shradhane

Shruti (Indian) Having good hearing
Shrutie, Shruty, Shrutey, Shrutee, Shrutye, Shrutea

Shunnareh (Arabic) Pleasing in manner and behavior
Shunnaraya, Shunareh, Shunarreh

Shyann (English) Form of Cheyenne, meaning "unintelligible speaker"
Shyanne, Shyane, Sheyann, Sheyanne, Sheyenne, Sheyene

Shysie (Native American) A quiet child
Shysi, Shysy, Shysey, Shysee, Shycie, Shyci, Shysea, Shycy

Sibyl (English) A prophetess; a seer
Sybil, Sibyla, Sybella, Sibil, Sibella, Sibilla, Sibley, Sibylla

Siddhi (Hindi) Having spiritual power
Sidhi, Syddhi, Sydhi

Sidero (Greek) In mythology, stepmother of Pelias and Neleus
Siderro, Sydero, Sideriyo

Sieglinde (German) Winning a gentle victory

Sienna (Italian) Woman with reddish-brown hair
Siena, Siennya, Sienya, Syenna, Syinna

Sierra (Spanish) From the jagged mountain range
Siera, Syerra, Syera, Seyera, Seeara

Sigfreda (German) A woman who is victorious
Sigfreeda, Sigfrida, Sigfryda, Sigfreyda, Sigfrieda, Sigfriede, Sigfrede

Sigismonda (Teutonic) A victorious defender
Sigismunda

Signia (Latin) A distinguishing sign
Signiya, Signea, Signeia, Signeya, Signa

Sigyn (Norse) In mythology, the wife of Loki

Sihu (Native American) As delicate as a flower

Silka (Latin) Form of Cecelia, meaning "one who is blind"
Silke, Silkia, Silkea, Silkie, Silky, Silkee, Sylka, Sylke

Sima (Arabic) One who is treasured; a prize
Simma, Syma, Simah, Simia, Simiya

Simone (French) One who listens well
Sim, Simonie, Symone, Samone

Sine (Scottish) Form of Jane, meaning "God is gracious"
Sinead, Sineidin, Sioned, Sionet, Sion, Siubhan, Siwan, Sineh

Sinobia (Greek) Form of
Zenobia, meaning "child of
Zeus"
*Sinobiah, Sinobya, Sinobe,
Sinobie, Sinovia, Senobia,
Senobya, Senobe*

Sinopa (Native American)
Resembling a fox

Sinope (Greek) In mythology, one of the daughters of
Asopus

Siran (Armenian) An alluring
and lovely woman

Siren (Greek) In mythology, a
sea nymph whose beautiful
singing lured sailors to their
deaths; refers to a seductive
and beautiful woman
*Sirene, Sirena, Siryne, Siryn,
Syren, Syrena, Sirine, Sirina*

Siria (Spanish / Persian)
Bright like the sun / a
glowing woman
*Siriah, Sirea, Sireah, Siriya,
Siriyah, Sirya, Siryah*

Siroun (Armenian) A lovely
woman
Sirune

Sirpuhi (Armenian) One who
is holy; pious
*Sirpuhie, Sirpuhy, Sirpuhey,
Sirpuhea, Sirpuhee*

Sissy (English) Form of
Cecilia, meaning "one who is
blind"
*Sissey, Sissie, Sisley, Sisli,
Sislee, Sissel, Sissle, Syssy*

Sita (Hindi) In Hinduism,
goddess of the harvest and
wife of Rama

Sive (Irish) A good and sweet
girl
*Sivney, Sivny, Sivni, Sivnie,
Sivnee, Sivnea*

Skylar (English) One who is
learned, a scholar
*Skylare, Skylarr, Skyler, Skylor,
Skylir*

Sloane (Irish) A strong
protector; a woman warrior
Sloan, Slone

Smita (Indian) One who
smiles a lot

Snow (American) Frozen rain
*Snowy, Snowie, Snowi, Snowey,
Snowee, Snowea, Sno*

Snowdrop (English)
Resembling a small white
flower

Solana (Latin / Spanish) Wind
from the east / of the sunshine
*Solanah, Solanna, Solann,
Solanne*

Solange (French) One who is religious and dignified

Solaris (Greek) Of the sun
Solarise, Solariss, Solarisse, Solarys, Solaryss, Solarysse, Sol, Soleil

Solita (Latin) One who is solitary
Solitah, Solida, Soledad, Soledada, Soledade

Somatra (Indian) Of the excellent moon

Sona (Arabic) The golden one
Sonika, Sonna

Sonora (Spanish) A pleasant-sounding woman
Sonorah, Sonoria, Sonorya, Sonoriya

Soo (Korean) Having an excellent long life

*⋆ᵀ**Sophia** (Greek) Form of Sophie, meaning great wisdom and foresight
Sofia, Sofiya

*⋆ᵀ**Sophie** (Greek) Wisdom
Sophia, Sofiya, Sofie, Sofia, Sofi, Sofiyko, Sofronia, Sophronia, Zofia

Sorina (Romanian) Feminine form of Sorin; of the sun
Sorinah, Sorinna, Sorinia, Soriniya, Sorinya, Soryna, Sorynia, Sorine

Sorrel (French) From the surele plant
Sorrell, Sorrelle, Sorrele, Sorrela, Sorrella

Sparrow (English) Resembling a small songbird
Sparro, Sparroe, Sparo, Sparow, Sparowe, Sparoe

Sslama (Egyptian) One who is peaceful

Stacey (English) Form of Anastasia, meaning "one who shall rise again"
Stacy, Staci, Stacie, Stacee, Stacia, Stasia, Stasy, Stasey

*⋆**Stella** (English) Star of the sea
Stela, Stelle, Stele, Stellah, Stelah

Stephanie (Greek) Feminine form of Stephen; crowned in victory
Stephani, Stephany, Stephaney, Stephanee, Stephene, Stephana, Stefanie, Stefani

Stevonna (Greek) A crowned lady
Stevonnah, Stevona, Stevonah, Stevonia, Stevonea, Stevoniya

Styx (Greek) In mythology, the river of the underworld
Stixx, Styxx, Stix

Suave (American) A smooth and courteous woman
Swave

Subhadra (Hindi) In Hinduism, the sister of Krishna

Subhaga (Indian) A fortunate person

Subhuja (Hindi) An auspicious celestial damsel

Subira (African) One who is patient
Subirah, Subirra, Subyra, Subyrra, Subeera, Subeara, Subeira, Subiera

Suhaila (Arabic) Feminine form of Suhail; the second brightest star
Suhayla, Suhaela, Suhala, Suhailah, Suhaylah, Suhaelah, Suhalah

Sulwyn (Welsh) One who shines as bright as the sun
Sulwynne, Sulwynn, Sulwinne, Sulwin, Sulwen, Sulwenn, Sulwenne

Sumana (Indian) A good-natured woman
Sumanah, Sumanna, Sumane, Sumanne, Sumann

Sumi (Japanese) One who is elegant and refined
Sumie

Sumitra (Indian) A beloved friend
Sumitrah, Sumita, Sumytra, Sumyta, Sumeetra, Sumeitra, Sumietra, Sumeatra

ᵀ**Summer** (American) Refers to the season; born in summer
Sommer, Sumer, Somer, Somers

Suna (Turkish) A swan-like woman

Sunanda (Indian) Having a sweet character
Sunandah, Sunandia, Sunandiya, Sunandea, Sunandya

Sunila (Indian) Feminine form of Sunil; very blue
Sunilah, Sunilla, Sunilya, Suniliya

Sunniva (English) Gift of the sun
Synnove, Synne, Synnove, Sunn

Surabhi (Indian) Having a lovely fragrance
Surbhii, Surabhie, Surabhy, Surabhey, Surabhee, Surabhea

Susannah (Hebrew) White lily
Susanna, Susanne, Susana,
Susane, Susan, Suzanna,
Suzannah, Suzanne,
Shoshana, Huhana

Sushanti (Indian) A peaceful
woman; tranquil
Sushantie, Sushanty,
Sushantey, Sushantee,
Sushantea

Suzu (Japanese) One who is
long-lived
Suzue, Suzuko

Swanhilda (Norse) A woman
warrior; in mythology, the
daughter of Sigurd
Swanhild, Swanhilde,
Svanhilde, Svanhild, Svenhilde,
Svenhilda

Swarupa (Indian) One who is
devoted to the truth

*Sydney (English) Of the wide
meadow
Sydny, Sydni, Sydnie, Sydnea,
Sydnee, Sidney, Sidne, Sidnee

T

Taariq (Swahili) Resembling
the morning star
Tariq, Taarique, Tarique

Tabia (African / Egyptian) One
who makes incantations / a
talented woman
Tabiah, Tabya, Tabea, Tabeah,
Tabiya

Tabita (African) A graceful
woman
Tabitah, Tabyta, Tabytah,
Tabeeta, Tabeata, Tabieta,
Tabeita

Tabitha (Greek) Resembling a
gazelle; known for beauty and
grace
Tabithah, Tabbitha, Tabetha,
Tabbetha, Tabatha, Tabbatha,
Tabotha, Tabbotha

Tabora (Spanish) One who
plays a small drum
Taborah, Taborra, Taboria,
Taborya

Tacincala (Native American)
Resembling a deer
Tacincalah, Tacyncala,
Tacyncalah, Tacincalla,
Tacyncalla

Tahsin (Arabic) Beautification; one who is praised
Tahseen, Tahsene, Tahsyne, Tasine, Tahseene, Tahsean, Tahseane

Tahzib (Arabic) One who is educated and cultured
Tahzeeb, Tahzebe, Tahzybe, Tazib, Tazyb, Tazeeb, Tahzeab, Tazeab

Taithleach (Gaelic) A quiet and calm young lady

Takako (Japanese) A lofty child

Takoda (Native American) Friend to everyone
Takodah, Takodia, Takodya, Takota

Tala (Native American) A stalking wolf
Talah, Talla

Talia (Hebrew / Greek) Morning dew from heaven / blooming
Taliah, Talea, Taleah, Taleya, Tallia, Talieya, Taleea, Taleia

Talihah (Arabic) One who seeks knowledge
Taliha, Talibah, Taliba, Talyha, Taleehah, Taleahah

Taline (Armenian) Of the monestary
Talene, Taleen, Taleene, Talyne, Talinia, Talinya, Taliniya

Talisa (American) Consecrated to God
Talisah, Talysa, Taleesa, Talissa, Talise, Taleese, Talisia, Talisya

Talisha (American) A damsel; an innocent
Talesha, Taleisha, Talysha, Taleesha, Tylesha, Taleysha, Taleshia, Talishia

Talitha (Arabic) A maiden; young girl
Talithah, Taletha, Taleetha, Talytha, Talithia, Talethia, Tiletha, Talith

Tamanna (Indian) One who is desired
Tamannah, Tamana, Tamanah, Tammana, Tammanna

Tamasha (African) Pageant winner
Tamasha, Tomosha, Tomasha, Tamashia, Tamashya

Tamesis (Celtic) In mythology, the goddess of water; source of the name for the river Thames
Tamesiss, Tamesys, Tamesyss

Tangia (American) The angel
Tangiah, Tangya, Tangiya, Tangeah

Tani (Japanese / Melanesian / Tonkinese) From the valley / a sweetheart / a young woman
Tanie, Tany, Taney, Tanee, Tanni, Tanye, Tannie, Tanny

Tania (Russian) Queen of the fairies
Tanya, Tannie, Tanny, Tanika

Tanner (English) One who tans hides
Taner, Tannar, Tannor, Tannis

Tansy (English / Greek) An aromatic yellow flower / having immortality
Tansey, Tansi, Tansie, Tansee, Tansye, Tansea, Tancy, Tanzy

Tanushri (Indian) One who is beautiful; attractive
Tanushrie, Tanushry, Tanushrey, Tanushree, Tanushrea

Tanvi (Indian) Slender and beautiful woman
Tanvie, Tanvy, Tanvey, Tanvee, Tanvye, Tannvi, Tanvea

Tapati (Indian) In mythology, the daughter of the sun god
Tapatie, Tapaty, Tapatey, Tapatee, Tapatye, Tapatea

Taphath (Hebrew) In the Bible, Solomon's daughter
Tafath, Taphathe, Tafathe

Tara (Gaelic / Indian) Of the tower; rocky hill / star; in mythology, an astral goddess
Tarah, Tarra, Tayra, Taraea, Tarai, Taralee, Tarali, Taraya

Tarachand (Indian) Silver star
Tarachande, Tarachanda, Tarachandia, Tarachandea, Tarachandiya, Tarachandya

Taree (Japanese) A bending branch
Tarea, Tareya

Taregan (Native American) Resembling a crane
Tareganne, Taregann

Tareva-chine(shanay) (Native American) One with beautiful eyes

Tariana (American) From the holy hillside
Tarianna, Taryana, Taryanna

Tarika (Indian) A starlet
Tarikah, Taryka, Tarykah, Taricka, Tarickah

Tarisai (African) One to behold; to look at
Tarysai

Tasanee (Thai) A beautiful view
Tasane, Tasani, Tasanie, Tasany, Tasaney, Tasanye, Tasanea

Taskin (Arabic) One who provides peace; satisfaction
Taskine, Taskeen, Taskeene, Taskyne, Takseen, Taksin, Taksyn

Tasnim (Arabic) From the fountain of paradise
Tasnime, Tasneem, Tasneeme, Tasnyme, Tasnym, Tasneam, Tasneame

Tatum (English) Bringer of joy; spirited
Tatom, Tatim, Tatem, Tatam, Tatym

Tavi (Aramaic) One who is well-behaved
Tavie, Tavee, Tavy, Tavey, Tavea

*ᵀTaylor (English) Cutter of cloth; one who alters garments
Tailor, Taylore, Taylar, Tayler, Talour, Taylre, Tailore, Tailar

Teagan (Gaelic) One who is attractive
Teegan

Tehya (Native American) One who is precious
Tehyah, Tehiya, Tehiyah

Teigra (Greek) Resembling a tiger
Teigre

Telephassa (Latin) In mythology, the queen of Tyre
Telephasa, Telefassa, Telefasa

Temperance (English) Having self-restraint
Temperence, Temperince, Temperancia, Temperanse, Temperense, Temperinse

Tendai (African) Thankful to God
Tenday, Tendae, Tendaa, Tendaye

Tender (American) One who is sensitive; young and vulnerable
Tendere, Tendera, Tenderia, Tenderre, Tenderiya

Teranika (Gaelic) Victory of the earth
Teranikah, Teranieka, Teraneika, Teraneeka, Teranica, Teranicka, Teranicca, Teraneaka

Teresa (Greek) A harvester
Theresa, Theresah, Theresia, Therese, Thera, Tresa, Tressa, Tressam, Reese, Reza

Terpsichore (Greek) In mythology, the muse of dancing and singing
Terpsichora, Terpsichoria, Terpsichoriya

Terra (Latin) From the earth; in mythology, an earth goddess
Terrah, Terah, Teralyn, Terran, Terena, Terenah, Terenna, Terrena

Terrian (Greek) One who is innocent
Terriane, Terrianne, Terriana, Terianna, Terian, Terianne

Tessa (Greek) Form of Teresa, meaning "a harvester"

Tetsu (Japanese) A strong woman
Tetsue

Tetty (English) Form of Elizabeth, meaning "my God is bountiful; God's promise"
Tettey, Tetti, Tettie, Tettee, Tettea

Tevy (Cambodian) An angel
Tevey, Tevi, Tevie, Tevee, Tevea

Thandiwe (African) The loving one
Thandywe, Thandiewe, Thandeewe, Thandie, Thandi, Thandee, Thandy, Thandey

Thara (Arabic) One who is wealthy; prosperous
Tharah, Tharra, Tharrah, Tharwat

Thelma (Greek) One who is ambitious and willful
Thelmah, Telma, Thelmai, Thelmia, Thelmalina

Thelred (English) One who is well-advised
Thelrede, Thelread, Thelredia, Thelredina, Thelreid, Thelreed, Thelryd

Thema (African) A queen
Themah, Theema, Thyma, Theyma, Theama

Theora (Greek) A watcher
Theorra, Theoria, Theoriya, Theorya

Theta (Greek) Eighth letter of the Greek alphabet
Thetta

Thistle (English) Resembling the prickly, flowered plant
Thistel, Thissle, Thissel

Thomasina (Hebrew) Feminine form of Thomas; a twin
Thomasine, Thomsina, Thomasin, Tomasina, Tomasine, Thomasa, Thomaseena, Thomaseana

Thoosa (Greek) In mythology, a sea nymph
Thoosah, Thoosia, Thoosiah, Thusa, Thusah, Thusia, Thusiah, Thousa

Thorberta (Norse) Brilliance
of Thor
Thorbiartr, Thorbertha

Thordia (Norse) Spirit of Thor
Thordiah, Thordis, Tordis,
Thordissa, Tordissa, Thoridyss

Thuy (Vietnamese) One who is
gentle and pure
Thuye, Thuyy, Thuyye

Thy (Vietnamese / Greek) A
poet / one who is untamed
Thye

^**Tia** (Spanish / Greek) An aunt /
daughter born to royalty
*Tiah, Tea, Teah, **Tiana**, Teea,*
Tya, Teeya, Tiia

Tiberia (Italian) Of the Tiber
river
Tiberiah, Tiberiya, Tiberya,
Tibeeria, Tibearia, Tibieria,
Tibeiria

Tiegan (Aztec) A little princess
in a big valley
Tiegann, Tieganne

Tierney (Gaelic) One who is
regal; lordly
Tiernie, Tierni, Tiernee, Tierny,
Tiernea

Tiffany (Greek) Lasting love
Tiffaney, Tiffani, Tiffanie,
Tiffanee, Tifany, Tifaney,
Tifanee, Tifani

Timothea (English) Feminine
form of Timothy; honoring
God
Timotheah, Timothia,
Timothya, Timothiya

Tina (English) From the river;
also shortened form of names
ending in -tina
Tinah, Teena, Tena, Teyna,
Tyna, Tinna, Teana

Ting (Chinese) Graceful and
slim woman

Tirza (Hebrew) One who is
pleasant; a delight
Tirzah

Tisa (African) The ninth-born
child
Tisah, Tiza

Tita (Latin) Holding a title of
honor
Titah, Teeta, Tyta, Teata

Tivona (Hebrew) Lover of
nature
Tivonna, Tivone, Tivonia,
Tivoniya

Toan (Vietnamese) Form of
An-toan, meaning "safe and
secure"
Toane, Toanne

Toinette (French) Form of Antoinette, meaning "praiseworthy"
Toinett, Toinete, Toinet, Toineta, Toinetta, Tola

Toki (Japanese / Korean) One who grasps opportunity; hopeful / resembling a rabbit
Tokie, Toky, Tokey, Tokye, Tokiko, Tokee, Tokea

Tola (Polish / Cambodian) Form of Toinette, meaning "praiseworthy" / born during October
Tolah, Tolla, Tollah

Topanga (Native American) From above or a high place
Topangah

Topaz (Latin) Resembling a yellow gemstone
Topazz, Topaza, Topazia, Topaziya, Topazya, Topazea

Tordis (Norse) A goddess
Tordiss, Tordisse, Tordys, Tordyss, Tordysse

Torny (Norse) New; just discovered
Torney, Tornie, Torni, Torne, Torn, Tornee, Tornea

Torunn (Norse) Thor's love
Torun, Torrun, Torrunn

Tory (American) Form of Victoria, meaning "victorious woman; winner; conqueror"
Torry, Torey, Tori, Torie, Torree, Tauri, Torye, Toya

Tosca (Latin) From the Tuscany region
Toscah, Toscka, Toska, Tosckah, Toskah

Tosha (English) Form of Natasha, meaning "born on Christmas"
Toshah, Toshiana, Tasha, Tashia, Tashi, Tassa

Tourmaline (Singhalese) A stone of mixed colors
Tourmalyne, Tourmalina, Tourmalinia

Tova (Hebrew) One who is well-behaved
Tovah, Tove, Tovi, Toba, Toibe, Tovva

Treasa (Irish) Having great strength
Treasah, Treesa, Treisa, Triesa, Treise, Treese, Toirease

**Trinity (Latin) The holy three
Trinitey, Triniti, Trinitie, Trinitee, Trynity, Trynitey, Tryniti, Trynitie

Trisha (Latin) Form of Patricia, meaning "of noble descent"
Trishah, Trishia, Tricia, Trish, Trissa, Trisa

Trishna (Polish) In mythology, the goddess of the deceased, protector of graves
Trishnah, Trishnia, Trishniah, Trishnea, Trishneah, Trishniya, Trishniyah, Trishnya

Trisna (Indian) The one desired
Trisnah, Trisnia, Trisniah, Trisnea, Trisneah, Trisniya, Trisniyah, Trisnya

Trudy (German) Form of Gertrude, meaning "adored warrior"
Trudey, Trudi, Trudie, Trude, Trudye, Trudee, Truda, Trudia

Trupti (Indian) State of being satisfied
Truptie, Trupty, Truptey, Truptee, Trupte, Truptea

Tryamon (English) In Arthurian legend, a fairy princess
Tryamonn, Tryamonne, Tryamona, Tryamonna

Tryna (Greek) The third-born child
Trynah

Tsifira (Hebrew) One who is crowned
Tsifirah, Tsifyra, Tsiphyra, Tsiphira, Tsipheera, Tsifeera

Tuccia (Latin) A vestal virgin

Tula (Hindi) Balance; a sign of the zodiac
Tulah, Tulla, Tullah

Tullia (Irish) One who is peaceful
Tulliah, Tullea, Tulleah, Tullya, Tulia, Tulea, Tuleah, Tulya

Tusti (Hindi) One who brings happiness and peace
Tustie, Tusty, Tustey, Tustee, Tuste, Tustea

Tutilina (Latin) In mythology, the protector goddess of stored grain
Tutilinah, Tutileena, Tutileana, Tutilyna, Tutileina, Tutiliena, Tutilena, Tutylina

Tuuli (Finnish) Of the wind
Tuulie, Tuulee, Tuula, Tuuly, Tuuley, Tuulea

Tuyet (Vietnamese) Snow white woman
Tuyett, Tuyete, Tuyette, Tuyeta, Tuyetta

Tyler (English) Tiler of roofs

Tyme (English) The aromatic herb thyme
Time, Thyme, Thime

Tyne (English) Of the river
Tyna

Tyro (Greek) In mythology, a woman who bore twin sons to Poseidon

Tzidkiya (Hebrew) Righteousness of the Lord
Tzidkiyah, Tzidkiyahu

Tzigane (Hungarian) A gypsy
Tzigan, Tzigain, Tzigaine, Tzigayne

U

Uadjit (Egyptian) In mythology, a snake goddess
Ujadet, Uajit, Udjit, Ujadit

Ualani (Hawaiian) Of the heavenly rain
Ualanie, Ualany, Ualaney, Ualanee, Ualanea, Ualania, Ualana

Udavine (American) A thriving woman
Udavyne, Udavina, Udavyna, Udevine, Udevyne, Udevina, Udevyna

Udele (English) One who is wealthy; prosperous
Udelle, Udela, Udella, Udelah, Udellah, Uda, Udah

Uela (American) One who is devoted to God
Uelah, Uella, Uellah

Uganda (African) From the country in Africa
Ugandah, Ugaunda, Ugaundah, Ugawnda, Ugawndah, Ugonda, Ugondah

Ugolina (German) Having a bright spirit; bright mind
Ugolinah, Ugoleena, Ugoliana, Ugolyna, Ugoline, Ugolyn, Ugolyne

Ulalia (Greek) Form of Eulalia, meaning "well-spoken"
Ulaliah, Ulalya, Ulalyah

Ulan (African) Firstborn of twins
Ulann, Ulanne

Ulima (Arabic) One who is wise and astute
Ulimah, Ullima, Ulimma, Uleema, Uleama, Ulyma, Uleima, Uliema

Ulla (German) A willful woman
Ullah, Ullaa, Ullai, Ullae

Uma (Hindi) Mother; in mythology, the goddess of beauty and sunlight
Umah, Umma

Umberla (French) Feminine form of Umber; providing shade; of an earth color
Umberlah, Umberly, Umberley, Umberlee, Umberleigh, Umberli, Umberlea, Umberlie

Ummi (African) Born of my mother
Ummie, Ummy, Ummey, Ummee, Umi

Unity (American) Woman who upholds oneness; togetherness
Unitey, Unitie, Uniti, Unitee, Unitea, Unyty, Unytey, Unytie

Ura (Indian) Loved from the heart
Urah, Urra

Ural (Slavic) From the mountains
Urall, Urale, Uralle

Urbai (American) One who is gentle
Urbae, Urbay, Urbaye

Urbana (Latin) From the city; city dweller
Urbanah, Urbanna, Urbane, Urbania, Urbanya, Urbanne

Uriela (Hebrew) The angel of light
Uriella, Urielle, Uriel, Uriele, Uriell

Urta (Latin) Resembling the spiny plant
Urtah

Utah (Native American) People of the mountains; from the state of Utah

Uzoma (African) One who takes the right path
Uzomah, Uzomma, Uzommah

Uzzi (Hebrew / Arabic) God is my strength / a strong woman
Uzzie, Uzzy, Uzzey, Uzzee, Uzi, Uzie, Uzy, Uzey

V

Vala (German) The chosen one; singled out
Valah, Valla

Valda (Teutonic / German) Spirited in battle / famous ruler
Valdah, Valida, Velda, Vada, Vaida, Vayda, Vaeda

Valdis (Norse) In mythology, the goddess of the dead
Valdiss, Valdys, Valdyss

Valencia (Spanish) One who is powerful; strong; from the city of Valencia
Valenciah, Valyncia, Valencya, Valenzia, Valancia, Valenica, Valanca, Valecia

ᵀ**Valentina** (Latin) One who is vigorous and healthy
Valentinah, Valentine, Valenteena, Valenteana, Valentena, Valentyna, Valantina, Valentyne

ᵀ**Valeria** (Latin) Form of Valerie, meaning "strong and valiant"
Valara, Valera, Valaria, Valeriana, Veleria, Valora

Valerie (Latin) Feminine form of Valerius; strong and valiant
Valeri, Valeree, Valerey, Valery, Valarie, Valari, Vallery

Vandani (Hindi) One who is honorable and worthy
Vandany, Vandaney, Vandanie, Vandanee, Vandania, Vandanya

ᵀ**Vanessa** (Greek) Resembling a butterfly
Vanessah, Vanesa, Vannesa, Vannessa, Vanassa, Vanasa, Vanessia, Vanysa, Yanessa

Vanity (English) Having excessive pride
Vanitey, Vanitee, Vaniti, Vanitie, Vanitty, Vanyti, Vanyty, Vanytie

Vanmra (Russian) A stranger; from a foreign place
Vanmrah

Varda (Hebrew) Resembling a rose
Vardah, Vardia, Vardina, Vardissa, Vardita, Vardysa, Vardyta, Vardit

Varuna (Hindi) Wife of the sea
Varunah, Varuna, Varun, Varunani, Varuni

Vashti (Persian) A lovely woman
Vashtie, Vashty, Vashtey, Vashtee

Vasta (Persian) One who is pretty
Vastah

Vasteen (American) A capable woman
Vasteene, Vastiene, Vastien, Vastein, Vasteine, Vastean, Vasteane

Vasuda (Hindi) Of the earth
*Vasudah, Vasudhara,
Vasundhara, Vasudhra,
Vasundhra*

Vayu (Hindi) A vital life force;
the air
Vayyu

Vedette (French) From the
guard tower
*Vedete, Vedett, Vedet, Vedetta,
Vedeta*

Vedi (Sanskrit) Filled with
wisdom
*Vedie, Vedy, Vedey, Vedee,
Vedea, Vedeah*

Vega (Latin) A falling star
Vegah

Vellamo (Finnish) In mythology, the goddess of the sea
Velamo, Vellammo

Ventana (Spanish) As trans-
parent as a window
*Ventanah, Ventanna, Ventane,
Ventanne*

Venus (Greek) In mythology, the goddess of love and
beauty
*Venis, Venys, Vynys, Venusa,
Venusina, Venusia*

Veradis (Latin) One who is
genuine; truthful
*Veradise, Veradys, Veradisa,
Verdissa, Veradysa, Veradyssa,
Veradisia, Veraditia*

Verda (Latin) Springlike; one
who is young and fresh
*Verdah, Verdea, Virida, Verdy,
Verdey, Verde, Verdi, Verdie*

Verenase (Swedish) One who
is flourishing
*Verenese, Verennase, Vyrenase,
Vyrennase, Vyrenese, Verenace,
Vyrenace*

Veronica (Latin) Displaying
her true image
*Veronicah, Veronic, Veronicca,
Veronicka, Veronika,
Veronicha, Veronique,
Veranique, Ronni*

Vesna (Slavic) Messenger; in
mythology, the goddess of
spring
Vesnah, Vezna, Vesnia, Vesnaa

Vespera (Latin) Evening star;
born in the evening
*Vesperah, Vespira, Vespeera,
Vesperia, Vesper*

Vevila (Gaelic) Woman with a
melodious voice
*Vevilah, Veveela, Vevyla,
Vevilla, Vevylla, Vevylle, Vevyle,
Vevillia*

Vibeke (Danish) A small
woman
*Vibekeh, Vibeek, Vibeeke,
Vybeke, Viheke*

Vibhuti (Hindi) Of the sacred
ash; a symbol
Vibuti, Vibhutie, Vibhutee

*Victoria (Latin) Victorious
woman; winner; conqueror
*Victoriah, Victorea, Victoreah,
Victorya, Victorria, Victoriya,
Vyctoria, Victorine, Tory*

Vidya (Indian) Having great
wisdom
Vidyah

Viet (Vietnamese) A woman
from Vietnam
Vyet, Viett, Vyett, Viette, Vyette

Vigilia (Latin) Wakefulness;
watchfulness
*Vigiliah, Vygilia, Vygylia,
Vijilia, Vyjilia*

Vignette (French) From the
little vine
*Vignete, Vignet, Vignetta,
Vignett, Vigneta, Vygnette,
Vygnete, Vygnet*

Vilina (Hindi) One who is
dedicated
*Vilinah, Vileena, Vileana,
Vylina, Vyleena, Vyleana,
Vylyna, Vilinia*

Villette (French) From the
small village
*Vilette, Villete, Vilete, Vilet,
Vilett, Villet, Villett, Vylet*

Vimala (Indian) Feminine
form of Vamal; clean and
pure
Vimalah, Vimalia, Vimalla

Vincentia (Latin) Feminine
form of Vincent; conquerer;
triumphant
*Vincentiah, Vincenta,
Vincensia, Vincenzia,
Vyncentia, Vyncyntia,
Vyncenzia, Vycenzya*

Violet (French) Resembling
the purplish-blue flower
*Violett, Violette, Violete, Vyolet,
Vyolett, Vyolette, Vyolete,
Violeta*

Virginia (Latin) One who is
chaste; virginal; from the state
of Virginia
*Virginiah, Virginnia, Virgenya,
Virgenia, Virgeenia, Virgeena,
Virgena, Ginny*

Virtue (Latin) Having moral
excellence, chastity, and
goodness
*Virtu, Vyrtue, Vyrtu, Vertue,
Vertu*

Viveka (German) Little woman of the strong fortress
Vivekah, Vivecka, Vyveka, Viveca, Vyveca, Vivecca, Vivika, Vivieka

^**Vivian** (Latin) Lively woman
*Viv, Vivi, **Vivienne**, Bibiana*

Vixen (American) A flirtatious woman
Vixin, Vixi, Vixie, Vixee, Vixea, Vixeah, Vixy, Vixey

Vlasta (Slavic) A friendly and likeable woman
Vlastah, Vlastia, Vlastea, Vlastiah, Vlasteah

Voleta (Greek) The veiled one
Voletah, Voletta, Volita, Volitta, Volyta, Volytta, Volet, Volett

Volva (Scandinavian) In mythology, a female shaman
Volvah, Volvya, Volvaa, Volvae, Volvai, Volvay, Volvia

Vondila (African) Woman who lost a child
Vondilah, Vondilla, Vondilya, Vondilia, Vondyla, Vondylya

Vonna (French) Form of Yvonne, meaning "young archer"
Vonnah, Vona, Vonah, Vonnia, Vonnya, Vonia, Vonya, Vonny

Vonshae (American) One who is confident
Vonshay, Vonshaye, Vonshai

Vor (Norse) In mythology, an omniscient goddess
Vore, Vorr, Vorre

Vulpine (English) A cunning woman; like a fox
Vulpyne, Vulpina, Vulpyna

Vyomini (Indian) A gift of the divine
Vyominie, Vyominy, Vyominey, Vyominee, Vyomyni, Vyomyny, Viomini, Viomyni

W

Wafa (Arabic) One who is faithful; devoted
Wafah, Wafaa, Waffa, Wapha, Waffah, Waphah

Wagaye (African) My sense of value; my price
Wagay, Wagai, Wagae

Wainani (Hawaiian) Of the beautiful waters
Wainanie, Wainany, Wainaney, Wainanee, Wainanea, Wainaneah

Wajihah (Arabic) One who is
distinguished; eminent
*Wajiha, Wajeeha, Wajyha,
Wajeehah, Wajyhah, Wajieha,
Wajiehah, Wajeiha*

Wakanda (Native American)
One who possesses magical
powers
*Wakandah, Wakenda,
Wakinda, Wakynda*

Wakeishah (American) Filled
with happiness
*Wakeisha, Wakieshah,
Wakiesha, Wakesha*

Walda (German) One who has
fame and power
*Waldah, Wallda, Walida,
Waldine, Waldina, Waldyne,
Waldyna, Welda*

Walker (English) Walker of the
forests
Wallker, Walkher

Walta (African) One who acts
as a shield
Waltah

Wanetta (English) A pale-
skinned woman
*Wanettah, Wanette, Wannette,
Wannetta, Wonetta, Wonette,
Wonitta, Wonitte*

Wangari (African) Resembling
the leopard
*Wangarie, Wangarri, Wangary,
Wangarey, Wangaria,
Wangaree*

Wanyika (African) Of the bush
*Wanyikka, Wanyicka,
Wanyicca, Wanyica*

Waqi (Arabic) Falling;
swooping
Waqqi

Warma (American) A caring
woman
*Warm, Warme, Warmia,
Warmiah, Warmea, Warmeah*

Warna (German) One who
defends her loved ones
Warnah

Washi (Japanese) Resembling
an eagle
*Washie, Washy, Washey,
Washee, Washea, Washeah*

Waynette (English) One who
makes wagons
*Waynett, Waynet, Waynete,
Wayneta, Waynetta*

Wednesday (American) Born
on a Wednesday
*Wensday, Winsday,
Windnesday, Wednesdae,
Wensdae, Winsdae,
Windnesdae, Wednesdai*

Welcome (English) A welcome guest
Welcom, Welcomme

Wendy (Welsh) Form of Gwendolyn, meaning "one who is fair; of the white ring"
Wendi, Wendie, Wendee, Wendey, Wenda, Wendia, Wendea, Wendya

Wesley (English) From the western meadow
Wesly, Weslie, Wesli, Weslee, Weslia, Wesleigh, Weslea, Weslei

Whisper (English) One who is soft-spoken
Whysper, Wisper, Wysper

Whitley (English) From the white meadow
Whitly, Whitlie, Whitli, Whitlee, Whitleigh, Whitlea, Whitlia, Whitlya

Whitney (English) From the white island
Whitny, Whitnie, Whitni, Whitnee, Whittney, Whitneigh, Whytny, Whytney

Wicapi (Native American) A holy star

Wijida (Arabic) An excited seeker
Wijidah, Weejida, Weejidah, Wijeeda, Wijeedah, Wijyda, Wijydah, Wijieda

Wileen (Teutonic) A firm defender
Wiline, Wilean, Wileane, Wilyn, Wileene, Wilene, Wyleen, Wyline

Wilhelmina (German) Feminine form of Wilhelm; determined protector
Wilhelminah, Wylhelmina, Wylhelmyna, Willemina, Wilhelmine, Wilhemina, Wilhemine, Helma, Ilma

Willa (English) Feminine version of William, meaning "protector"
Willah, Wylla

Willow (English) One who is hoped for; desired
Willo, Willough

Winetta (American) One who is peaceful
Wineta, Wynetta, Wyneta, Winet, Winett, Winette, Wynet, Wynett

Winnielle (African) A victorious woman
Winniell, Winniele, Winniel, Winniella

Winola (German) Gracious and charming friend
Winolah, Wynola, Winolla, Wynolla, Wynolah, Winollah, Wynollah

Winta (African) One who is desired
Wintah, Whinta, Wynta, Whynta, Whintah, Wyntah, Whyntah

Wisconsin (French) Gathering of waters; from the state of Wisconsin
Wisconsyn, Wisconsen

Woody (American) A woman of the forest
Woodey, Woodi, Woodie, Woodee, Woodea, Woodeah, Woods

Wren (English) Resembling a small songbird
Wrenn, Wrene, Wrena, Wrenie, Wrenee, Wreney, Wrenny, Wrenna

Wynda (Scottish) From the narrow passage
Wyndah, Winda, Windah

Xalvadora (Spanish) A savior
Xalvadorah, Xalbadora, Xalbadorah, Xalvadoria, Xalbadoria

Xanadu (African) From the exotic paradise

Xantara (American) Protector of the Earth
Xantarah, Xanterra, Xantera, Xantarra, Xantarrah, Xanterah, Xanterrah

Xaquelina (Galician) Form of Jacqueline, meaning "the supplanter"
Xaqueline, Xaqueleena, Xaquelyna, Xaquelayna, Xaqueleana

Xerena (Latin) Form of Serena, meaning "having a peaceful disposition"
Xerenah, Xerene, Xeren, Xereena, Xeryna, Xereene, Xerenna

Xhosa (African) Leader of a nation
Xosa, Xhose, Xhosia, Xhosah, Xosah

Xiang (Chinese) Having a nice fragrance
Xyang, Xeang, Xhiang, Xhyang, Xheang

Xiao Hong (Chinese) Of the morning rainbow

Xin Qian (Chinese) Happy and beautiful woman

Xinavane (African) A mother;
to propagate
*Xinavana, Xinavania,
Xinavain, Xinavaine,
Xinavaen, Xinavaene*

Xirena (Greek) Form of Sirena,
meaning "enchantress"
*Xirenah, Xireena, Xirina,
Xirene, Xyrena, Xyreena,
Xyrina, Xyryna*

Xi-Wang (Chinese) One with
hope

Xochiquetzal (Aztec)
Resembling a flowery feather;
in mythology, the goddess of
love, flowers, and the earth

Xola (African) Stay in peace
Xolah, Xolia, Xolla, Xollah

Xue (Chinese) Woman of
snow

Y

Yachne (Hebrew) One who is
gracious and hospitable
*Yachnee, Yachney, Yachnie,
Yachni, Yachnea, Yachneah*

Yadra (Spanish) Form of
Madre, meaning "mother"
Yadre, Yadrah

Yaffa (Hebrew) A beautiful
woman
Yaffah, Yaffit, Yafit, Yafeal

Yakini (African) An honest
woman
*Yakinie, Yakiney, Yakiny,
Yackini, Yackinie, Yackiney,
Yackiny, Yakinee*

Yalena (Greek) Form of Helen,
meaning "the shining light"
*Yalenah, Yalina, Yaleena,
Yalyna, Yalana, Yaleana,
Yalane, Yaleene*

Yama (Japanese) From the
mountain
Yamma, Yamah, Yammah

Yamin (Hebrew) Right hand
*Yamine, Yamyn, Yamyne,
Yameen, Yameene, Yamein,
Yameine, Yamien*

Yana (Hebrew) He answers
Yanna, Yaan, Yanah, Yannah

Yanessa (American) Form of
Vanessa, meaning "resem-
bling a butterfly"
*Yanessah, Yanesa, Yannesa,
Yannessa, Yanassa, Yanasa,
Yanessia, Yanysa*

Yanka (Slavic) God is good
Yancka, Yancca, Yankka

Yara (Brazilian) In mythology, the goddess of the river; a mermaid
Yarah, Yarrah, Yarra

Yareli (American) The Lord is my light
Yarelie, Yareley, Yarelee, Yarely, Yaresly, Yarelea, Yareleah

Yaretzi (Spanish) Always beloved
Yaretzie, Yaretza, Yarezita

Yashira (Japanese) Blessed with God's grace
Yashirah, Yasheera, Yashyra, Yashara, Yashiera, Yashierah, Yasheira, Yasheirah

Yashona (Hindi) A wealthy woman
Yashonah, Yashawna, Yashauna, Yaseana, Yashawnah, Yashaunah, Yaseanah

Yasmine (Persian) Resembling the jasmine flower
Yasmin, Yasmene, Yasmeen, Yasmeene, Yasmen, Yasemin, Yasemeen, Yasmyn

Yatima (African) An orphan
Yatimah, Yateema, Yatyma, Yateemah, Yatymah, Yatiema, Yatiemah, Yateima

Yedidah (Hebrew) A beloved friend
Yedida, Yedyda, Yedydah, Yedeeda, Yedeedah

Yeira (Hebrew) One who is illuminated
Yeirah, Yaira, Yeyra, Yairah, Yeyrah

Yenge (African) A hardworking woman
Yenga, Yengeh, Yengah

Yeshi (African) For a thousand
Yeshie, Yeshey, Yeshy, Yeshee, Yeshea, Yesheah

Yessica (Hebrew) Form of Jessica, meaning "the Lord sees all"
Yesica, Yessika, Yesika, Yesicka, Yessicka, Yesyka, Yesiko

Yetta (English) Form of Henrietta, meaning "ruler of the house"
Yettah, Yeta, Yette, Yitta, Yettie, Yetty

Yi Min (Chinese) An intelligent woman

Yi Ze (Chinese) Happy and shiny as a pearl

Yihana (African) One deserving congratulations
Yihanah, Yhana, Yihanna, Yihannah, Yhanah, Yhanna, Yhannah

Yinah (Spanish) A victorious
woman
Yina, Yinna, Yinnah

Yitta (Hebrew) One who
emanates light
Yittah, Yita, Yitah

Ynes (French) Form of Agnes,
meaning "pure; chaste"
Ynez, Ynesita

Yogi (Hindi) One who
practices yoga
*Yogini, Yoginie, Yogie, Yogy,
Yogey, Yogee, Yogea, Yogeah*

Yohance (African) A gift from
God
Yohanse

Yoki (Native American) Of the
rain
*Yokie, Yokee, Yoky, Yokey,
Yokea, Yokeah*

Yolanda (Greek) Resembling
the violet flower
*Yola, Yolana, Yolandah,
Colanda*

Yomaris (Spanish) I am the
sun
Yomariss, Yomarise, Yomarris

Yon (Korean) Resembling a
lotus blossom

Yoruba (African) Woman from
Nigeria
Yorubah, Yorubba, Yorubbah

Yoshi (Japanese) One who is
respectful and good
*Yoshie, Yoshy, Yoshey, Yoshee,
Yoshiyo, Yoshiko, Yoshino,
Yoshea*

Ysabel (Spanish) Form of
Isabel, meaning "my God is
bountiful; God's promise"
*Ysabelle, Ysabela, Ysabele,
Ysabell, Ysabella, Ysbel, Ysibel,
Ysibela*

Ysbail (Welsh) A spoiled girl
*Ysbale, Ysbayle, Ysbaile, Ysbayl,
Ysbael, Ysbaele*

Yue (Chinese) Of the
moonlight

Yuette (American) A capable
woman
*Yuett, Yuete, Yuet, Yueta,
Yuetta*

Yulan (Spanish) A splendid
woman
Yulann

Yuna (African) A gorgeous
woman
Yunah, Yunna, Yunnah

Yuta (Hebrew / Japanese) One
who is awarded praise / one
who is superior
Yutah, Yoota, Yootah

Yvonne (French) Young archer
Yvone, Vonne, Vonna

Zabrina (American) Form of Sabrina, meaning "a legendary princess"
Zabreena, Zabrinah, Zabrinna, Zabryna, Zabryne, Zabrynya, Zabreana, Zabreane

Zachah (Hebrew) Feminine form of Zachary; God is remembered
Zacha, Zachie, Zachi, Zachee, Zachea, Zacheah

Zafara (Hebrew) One who sings
Zaphara, Zafarra, Zapharra, Zafarah, Zafarrah, Zapharah, Zapharrah

Zagir (Armenian) Resembling a flower
Zagiri, Zagirie, Zagiree, Zagirea, Zagireah, Zagiry, Zagirey, Zagira

Zahiya (Arabic) A brilliant woman; radiant
Zahiyah, Zehiya, Zehiyah, Zeheeya, Zaheeya, Zeheeyah, Zaheeyah, Zaheiya

Zahra (Arabic / Swahili) White-skinned / flowerlike
Zahrah, Zahraa, Zahre, Zahreh, Zahara, Zaharra, Zahera, Zahira

Zainab (Arabic) A fragrant flowering plant
Zaynab, Zaenab

Zainabu (Swahili) One who is known for her beauty
Zaynabu, Zaenabu

Zalina (French) Form of Selene, meaning "of the moon"; in mythology Selene was the Greek goddess of the moon
Zalinah, Zaleana, Zaleena, Zalena, Zalyna, Zaleen, Zaleene, Zalene

Zama (Latin) One from the town of Zama
Zamah, Zamma, Zammah

Zambda (Hebrew) One who meditates
Zambdah

Zamella (Zulu) One who strives to succeed
Zamellah, Zamy, Zamie, Zami, Zamey, Zamee, Zamea, Zameah

Zamilla (Greek) Having the strength of the sea
Zamillah, Zamila, Zamilah, Zamylla, Zamyllah, Zamyla, Zamylah

Zamora (Spanish) From the city of Zamora
Zamorah, Zamorrah, Zamorra

Zana (Romanian / Hebrew) In mythology, the three graces / shortened form of Susanna, meaning "lily"
Zanna, Zanah, Zannah

Zane (Scandinavian) One who is bold
Zain, Zaine, Zayn, Zayne, Zaen, Zaene

Zanta (Swahili) A beautiful young woman
Zantah

Zarahlinda (Hebrew) Of the beautiful dawn
Zaralinda, Zaralynda, Zarahlindah, Zaralyndah, Zarahlynda, Zarahlyndah, Zaralenda, Zarahlenda

Zariah (Russian / Slavic) Born at sunrise
Zarya, Zariah, Zaryah

Zarifa (Arabic) One who is successful; moves with grace
Zarifah, Zaryfa, Zaryfah, Zareefa, Zareefah, Zariefa, Zariefah, Zareifa

Zarna (Hindi) Resembling a spring of water
Zarnah, Zarnia, Zarniah

Zarqa (Arabic) Having bluish-green eyes; from the city of Zarqa
Zarqaa

Zaylee (English) A heavenly woman
Zayleigh, Zayli, Zaylie, Zaylea, Zayleah, Zayley, Zayly, Zalee

Zaypana (Tibetan) A beautiful woman
Zaypanah, Zaypo, Zaypanna, Zaypannah

Zaza (Hebrew / Arabic) Belonging to all / one who is flowery
Zazah, Zazu, Zazza, Zazzah, Zazzu

Zdenka (Slovene) Feminine form of Zdenek, meaning "from Sidon"
Zdena, Zdenuska, Zdenicka, Zdenika, Zdenyka, Zdeninka, Zdenynka

Zebba (Persian) A known
beauty
*Zebbah, Zebara, Zebarah,
Zebarra, Zebarrah*

Zelia (Greek / Spanish)
Having great zeal / of the
sunshine
*Zeliah, Zelya, Zelie, Zele,
Zelina, Zelinia*

Zenaida (Greek) White-winged
dove; in mythology, a daugh-
ter of Zeus
*Zenaidah, Zenayda, Zenaide,
Zenayde, Zinaida, Zenina,
Zenna, Zenaydah*

Zenechka (Russian) Form
of Eugenia, meaning "a
well-born woman"

Zenobia (Greek) Child of Zeus
Sinobia

Zephyr (Greek) Of the west
wind
*Zephyra, Zephira, Zephria,
Zephra, Zephyer, Zefiryn,
Zefiryna, Zefyrin*

Zera (Hebrew) A sower of
seeds
*Zerah, Zeria, Zeriah, Zera'im,
Zerra, Zerrah*

Zeraldina (Polish) One who
rules with the spear
*Zeraldinah, Zeraldeena,
Zeraldeenah, Zeraldiena,
Zeraldienah, Zeraldeina,
Zeraldeinah, Zeraldyna*

Zerdali (Turkish) Resembling
the wild apricot
*Zerdalie, Zerdaly, Zerdaley,
Zerdalya, Zerdalia, Zerdalee,
Zerdalea*

Zesta (American) One with
energy and gusto
*Zestah, Zestie, Zestee, Zesti,
Zesty, Zestey, Zestea, Zesteah*

Zetta (Portuguese) Resembling
the rose
Zettah

Zhen (Chinese) One who is
precious and chaste
Zen, Zhena, Zenn, Zhenni

Zhi (Chinese) A woman of
high moral character

Zhong (Chinese) An honorable
woman

Zi (Chinese) A flourishing
young woman

Zia (Arabic) One who
emanates light; splendor
Ziah, Zea, Zeah, Zya, Zyah

Zilias (Hebrew) A shady
woman; a shadow
Zilyas, Zylias, Zylyas

Zillah (Hebrew) The shadowed
one
*Zilla, Zila, Zyla, Zylla, Zilah,
Zylah, Zyllah*

Zilpah (Hebrew) One who
is frail but dignified; in the
Bible, a concubine of Jacob
*Zilpa, Zylpa, Zilpha, Zylpha,
Zylpah, Zilphah, Zylphah*

Zimbab (African) Woman
from Zimbabwe
Zymbab, Zimbob, Zymbob

Zinat (Arabic) A decoration;
graceful beauty
*Zeenat, Zynat, Zienat, Zeinat,
Zeanat*

Zinchita (Incan) One who is
dearly loved
*Zinchitah, Zinchyta,
Zinchytah, Zincheeta,
Zincheetah, Zinchieta,
Zinchietah, Zincheita*

Zintkala Kinyan (Native
American) Resembling a
flying bird
Zintkalah Kinyan

Ziona (Hebrew) One who
symbolizes goodness
Zionah, Zyona, Zyonah

Zipporah (Hebrew) A beauty;
little bird; in the Bible, the
wife of Moses
*Zippora, Ziporah, Zipora,
Zypora, Zyppora, Ziproh,
Zipporia*

Zira (African) The pathway
*Zirah, Zirra, Zirrah, Zyra,
Zyrah, Zyrra, Zyrrah*

Zisel (Hebrew) One who is
sweet
*Zissel, Zisal, Zysel, Zysal,
Zyssel, Zissal, Zyssal*

Zita (Latin / Spanish) Patron
of housewives and servants /
little rose
Zitah, Zeeta, Zyta, Zeetah

Ziwa (Swahili) Woman of the
lake
Ziwah, Zywa, Zywah

Zizi (Hungarian) Dedicated to
God
*Zeezee, Zyzy, Ziezie, Zeazea,
Zeyzey*

Zoa (Greek) One who is full of
life; vibrant

*★ᵀ***Zoe** (Greek) A life-giving
woman; alive
*Zoee, Zowey, Zowie, Zowe,
Zoelie, Zoeline, Zoelle,* **Zoey**

Zofia (Slavic) Form of Sophia, meaning "wisdom"
Zofiah, Zophia, Zophiah, Zophya, Zofie, Zofee, Zofey

Zora (Slavic) Born at dawn; aurora
Zorah, Zorna, Zorra, Zorya, Zorane, Zory, Zorrah, Zorey

Zoria (Basque) One who is lucky
Zoriah

Zoriona (Basque) One who is happy

Zubeda (Swahili) The best one
Zubedah

Zudora (Arabic) A laborer; hardworking woman
Zudorah, Zudorra

Zula (African) One who is brilliant; from the town of Zula
Zul, Zulay, Zulae, Zulai, Zulah, Zulla, Zullah

Zuni (Native American) One who is creative
Zunie, Zuny, Zuney, Zunee, Zunea, Zuneah

Zurafa (Arabic) A lovely woman
Zurafah, Zirafa, Zirafah, Ziraf, Zurufa, Zurufah

Zuri (Swahili / French) A beauty / lovely and white
Zurie, Zurey, Zuria, Zuriaa, Zury, Zuree, Zurya, Zurisha

Zuwena (African) One who is pleasant and good
Zuwenah, Zwena, Zwenah, Zuwenna, Zuwennah, Zuwyna, Zuwynah

Zuyana (Sioux) One who has a brave heart
Zuyanah, Zuyanna

Zuzena (Basque) One who is correct
Zuzenah, Zuzenna

Zwi (Scandinavian) Resembling a gazelle
Zui, Zwie, Zwee, Zwey

Boys

A

Aabha (Indian) One who shines
Abha, Abbha

Aabharan (Hindu) One who is treasured; jewel
Abharan, Abharen, Aabharen, Aabharon

Aaden (Irish) Form of Aidan, meaning "a fiery young man"
Adan, Aden

Aage (Norse) Representative of ancestors
Age, Ake, Aake

Aarif (Arabic) A learned man
Arif, Aareef, Areef, Aareaf, Areaf, Aareif, Areif, Aarief

*Aaron (Hebrew) One who is exalted; from the mountain of strength
Aaran, Aaren, Aarin, Aaro, Aaronas, Aaronn, Aarron, Aaryn, Eron, Aron, Eran

Abdi (Hebrew) My servant
Abdie, Abdy, Abdey, Abdee

Abdul (Arabic) A servant of God
Abdal, Abdall, Abdalla, Abdallah, Abdel, Abdell, Abdella, Abdellah

Abedi (African) One who worships God
Abedie, Abedy, Abedey, Abedee, Abedea

Abednago (Aramaic) Servant of the god of wisdom, Nabu
Abednego

Abejundio (Spanish) Resembling a bee
Abejundo, Abejundeo, Abedjundiyo, Abedjundeyo

^Abel (Hebrew) The life force, breath
Abele, Abell, Abelson, Able, Avel, Avele

Abraham (Hebrew) Father of a multitude; father of nations
Abarran, Avraham, Aberham, Abrahamo, Abrahan, Abrahim, Abram, Abrami, Ibrahim

Abram (Hebrew) Form of Abraham, meaning "father of nations"

Absalom (Hebrew) The father of peace
Absalon, Abshalom, Absolem, Absolom, Absolon, Avshalom, Avsholom

Abu (African) A father
Abue, Aboo, Abou

Abundio (Spanish) A man of
plenty
*Abbondio, Abondio, Aboundio,
Abundo, Abundeo, Aboundeo*

Adael (Hebrew) God witnesses
Adaele, Adayel, Adayele

*Adam (Hebrew) Of the earth
*Ad, Adamo, Adams, Adan,
Adao, Addam, Addams, Addem*

Adamson (English) The son of
Adam
*Adamsson, Addamson,
Adamsun, Adamssun*

Addy (Teutonic) One who is
awe-inspiring
*Addey, Addi, Addie, Addee,
Addea, Adi, Ady, Adie*

Adelpho (Greek) A brotherly
man
*Aldelfo, Adelfus, Adelfio,
Adelphe*

Adil (Arabic) A righteous man;
one who is fair and just
*Adyl, Adiel, Adeil, Adeel, Adeal,
Adyeel*

Aditya (Hindi) Of the sun
*Adithya, Adithyan, Adityah,
Aditeya, Aditeyah*

Adonis (Greek) In mythology,
a handsome young man loved
by Aphrodite
Addonia, Adohnes, Adonys

*Adrian (Latin) A man from
Hadria
*Adrien, Adrain, Adrean,
Adreean, Adreyan, Adreeyan,
Adriaan*

^Adriel (Hebrew) From God's
flock
*Adriell, Adriele, Adryel, Adryell,
Adryele*

Afif (Arabic) One who is
chaste; pure
*Afeef, Afief, Afeif, Affeef, Affif,
Afyf, Afeaf*

Agamemnon (Greek) One who
works slowly; in mythology,
the leader of the Greeks at
Troy
Agamemno, Agamenon

^Ahmad (Arabic) One who
always thanks God; a name of
Muhammed
Ahmed

*ᵀAidan (Irish) A fiery young
man
*Aiden, Aedan, Aeden, Aidano,
Aidyn, **Ayden**, Aydin, Aydan*

Aiken (English) Constructed of oak; sturdy
Aikin, Aicken, Aickin, Ayken, Aykin, Aycken, Ayckin

Ainsworth (English) From Ann's estate
Answorth, Annsworth, Ainsworthe, Answorthe, Annsworthe

Ajax (Greek) In mythology, a hero of the Trojan war
Aias, Aiastes, Ajaxx, Ajaxe

Ajit (Indian) One who is invincible
Ajeet, Ajeat, Ajeit, Ajiet, Ajyt

Akiko (Japanese) Surrounded by bright light
Akyko

Akin (African) A brave man; a hero
Akeen, Akean, Akein, Akien, Akyn

Akiva (Hebrew) One who protects or provides shelter
Akyva, Akeeva, Akeava, Akieva, Akeiva, Akeyva

Akmal (Arabic) A perfect man
Aqmal, Akmall, Aqmall, Acmal, Acmall, Ackmal, Ackmall

Alaire (French) Filled with joy
Alair, Alaer, Alaere, Alare, Alayr, Alayre

Alamar (Arabic) Covered with gold
Alamarr, Alemar, Alemarr, Alomar, Alomarr

Alan (German / Gaelic) One who is precious / resembling a little rock
Alain, Alann, Allan, Alson, Allin, Allen, Allyn

Alard (German) Of noble strength
Aliard, Allard, Alliard

Albert (German) One who is noble and bright
Alberto, Albertus, Alburt, Albirt, Aubert, Albyrt, Albertos, Albertino

Alden (English) An old friend
Aldan, Aldin, Aldyn, Aldon, Aldun

Aldo (German) Old or wise one; elder
Aldous, Aldis, Aldus, Alldo, Aldys

Aldred (English) An old advisor
Alldred, Aldraed, Alldraed, Aldread, Alldread

Alejandro (Spanish) Form of
Alexander, meaning "a helper
and defender of mankind"
Alejandrino, Alejo

TAlex** (English) Form of
Alexander, meaning "a helper
and defender of mankind"
*Aleks, Alecks, Alecs, Allex,
Alleks, Allecks, **Alexis***

TAlexander** (Greek) A helper
and defender of mankind
*Alex, Alec, Alejandro,
Alaxander, Aleksandar,
Aleksander, Aleksandr,
Alessandro, Alexzander, Zander*

Alfonso (Italian) Prepared for
battle; eager and ready
*Alphonso, Alphonse, Affonso,
Alfons, Alfonse, Alfonsin,
Alfonsino, Alfonz, Alfonzo*

Ali (Arabic) The great one; one
who is exalted
Alie, Aly, Aley, Alee

Alijah (American) Form of
Elijah, meaning "Jehovah is
my god"

Alon (Hebrew) Of the oak tree
Allona, Allon, Alonn

Alonzo (Spanish) Form of
Alfonso, meaning "prepared
for battle; eager and ready"
*Alonso, Alanso, Alanzo,
Allonso, Allonzo, Allohnso,
Allohnzo, Alohnso*

Aloysius (German) A famous
warrior
*Ahlois, Aloess, Alois, Aloisio,
Aloisius, Aloisio, Aloj, Alojzy*

Alpha (Greek) The first-born
child; the first letter of the
Greek alphabet
Alphah, Alfa, Alfah

Alter (Hebrew) One who is old
Allter, Altar, Alltar

Alton (English) From the old
town
*Aldon, Aldun, Altun, Alten,
Allton, Alltun, Allten*

Alvin (English) Friend of the
elves
Alven, Alvan, Alvyn

Amani (African / Arabic) One
who is peaceful / one with
wishes and dreams
*Amanie, Amany, Amaney,
Amanee, Amanye, Amanea,
Amaneah*

^**Amari** (African) Having great
strength; a builder
*Amare, Amarie, Amaree,
Amarea, Amary, Amarey*

Amil (Hindi) One who is
invaluable
*Ameel, Ameal, Ameil, Amiel,
Amyl*

Amit (Hindi) Without limit;
endless
*Ameet, Ameat, Ameit, Amiet,
Amyt*

Amory (German) Ruler and
lover of one's home
*Aimory, Amery, Amorey,
Amry, Amori, Amorie, Amoree,
Amorea*

Amos (Hebrew) To carry;
hardworking
Amoss, Aymoss, Aymos

Andino (Italian) Form of
Andrew, meaning "one who
is manly; a warrior"
*Andyno, Andeeno, Andeano,
Andieno, Andeino*

Andre (French) Form of
Andrew, meaning "manly,
a warrior"
*Andreas, Andrei, Andrej,
Andres, Andrey*

*****Andrew** (Greek) One who is
manly; a warrior
*Andy, Aindrea, Andreas, Andie,
Andonia, Andor, Andresj,
Anderson*

Andrik (Slavic) Form of
Andrew, meaning "one who
is manly; a warrior"
*Andric, Andrick, Andryk,
Andryck, Andryc*

*****Angel** (Greek) A messenger
of God
*Andjelko, Ange, Angelino,
Angell, Angelmo, Angelo, Angie,
Angy*

Angus (Scottish) One force;
one strength; one choice
Aengus, Anngus, Aonghus

Anicho (German) An ancestor
*Anico, Anecho, Aneco, Anycho,
Anyco*

Ankur (Indian) One who is
blossoming; a sapling

Annan (Celtic) From the brook
Anan

Ansley (English) From the
noble's pastureland
*Ansly, Anslie, Ansli, Anslee,
Ansleigh, Anslea, Ansleah,
Anslye*

Antenor (Spanish) One who
antagonizes
*Antener, Antenar, Antenir,
Antenyr, Antenur*

*****Anthony** (Latin) A flourishing
man; of an ancient Roman
family
*Antal, Antony, Anthoney,
Anntoin, Antin, Anton, Antone,
Antonello, **Antonio***

Antoine (French) Form of Anthony, meaning "a flourishing man; of an ancient Roman family"
Antione, Antjuan, Antuan, Antuwain, Antuwaine, Antuwayne, Antuwon, Antwahn

Antonio (Italian) Form of Anthony, meaning "a flourishing man, from an ancient Roman family"
Antonin, Antonino, Antonius, Antonyo

Ara (Armenian / Latin) A legendary king / of the altar; the name of a constellation
Araa, Aira, Arah, Arae, Ahraya

Aram (Assyrian) One who is exalted
Arram

Arcadio (Greek) From an ideal country paradise
Alcadio, Alcado, Alcedio, Arcadios, Arcadius, Arkadi, Arkadios, Arkadius

Arcelio (Spanish) From the altar of heaven
Arcelios, Arcelius, Aricelio, Aricelios, Aricelius

Archard (German) A powerful holy man
Archerd, Archird, Archyrd

Archelaus (Greek) The ruler of the people
Archelaios, Arkelaos, Arkelaus, Arkelaios, Archelaos

^Archer (Latin) A skilled bowman

Ardell (Latin) One who is eager
Ardel, Ardelle, Ardele

Arden (Latin / English) One who is passionate and enthusiastic / from the valley of the eagles
Ardan, Arrden, Arrdan, Ardin, Arrdin, Ard, Ardyn, Arrdyn

Arduino (German) A valued friend
Ardwino, Arrduino, Ardueno

Ari (Hebrew) Resembling a lion or an eagle
Aree, Arie, Aristide, Aristides, Arri, Ary, Arye, Arrie

Ariel (Hebrew) A lion of God
Arielle, Ariele, Ariell, Arriel, Ahriel, Airial, Arieal, Arial

Aries (Latin) Resembling a ram; the first sign of the zodiac; a constellation
Arese, Ariese

Arion (Greek) A poet or musician
Arian, Arien, Aryon

Aristotle (Greek) Of high quality
Aristotelis, Aristotellis

Arius (Greek) Enduring life; everlasting; immortal
Areos, Areus, Arios

Arley (English) From the hare's meadow
Arlea, Arleigh, Arlie, Arly, Arleah, Arli, Arlee

^**Armani** (Persian) One who is desired

Arnold (German) The eagle ruler
Arnaldo, Arnaud, Arnauld, Arnault, Arnd, Arndt, Arnel, Arnell

^**Arthur** (Celtic) As strong as a bear; a hero
Aart, Arrt, Art, Artair, Arte, Arther, Arthor, Arthuro

Arvad (Hebrew) A wanderer; voyager
Arpad

Arvin (English) A friend to everyone
Arvinn, Arvinne, Arven, Arvenn, Arvenne, Arvyn, Arvynn, Arvynne

Asa (Hebrew) One who heals others
Asah

Asaph (Hebrew) One who gathers or collects
Asaf, Asaphe, Asafe, Asiph, Asiphe, Asif, Asife

Ash (English) From the ash tree
Ashe

Asher (Hebrew) Filled with happiness
Ashar, Ashor, Ashir, Ashyr, Ashur

Ashley (English) From the meadow of ash trees
Ashely, Asheley, Ashelie, Ashlan, Ashleigh, Ashlen, Ashli, Ashlie

Ashton (English) From the ash-tree town
Asheton, Ashtun, Ashetun, Ashtin, Ashetin, Ashtyn, Ashetyn, Aston

Aslan (Turkish) Resembling a lion
Aslen, Azlan, Azlen

Athens (Greek) From the capital of Greece
Athenios, Athenius, Atheneos, Atheneus

^**Atticus** (Latin) A man from Athens
Attikus, Attickus, Aticus, Atickus, Atikus

Atwell (English) One who lives at the spring
Attwell, Atwel, Attwel

Aubrey (English) One who rules with elf-wisdom
Aubary, Aube, Aubery, Aubry, Aubury, Aubrian, Aubrien, Aubrion

Auburn (Latin) Having a reddish-brown color
Aubirn, Auburne, Aubyrn, Abern, Abirn, Aburn, Abyrn, Aubern

Audley (English) From the old meadow
Audly, Audleigh, Audlee, Audlea, Audleah, Audli, Audlie

August (Irish) One who is venerable; majestic
Austin, Augustine, Agoston, Aguistin, Agustin, Augustin, Augustyn, Avgustin, Augusteen, Agosteen

*ᵀAustin (English) Form of August, meaning "one who is venerable; majestic"
Austen, Austyn, Austan, Auston, Austun

Avery (English) One who is a wise ruler; of the nobility
Avrie, Averey, Averie, Averi, Averee

Aviram (Hebrew) My Father is mighty
Avyram, Avirem, Avyrem

^Axel (German / Latin / Hebrew) Source of life; small oak / axe / peace
Aksel, Ax, Axe, Axell, Axil, Axill, Axl

Aya (Hebrew) Resembling a bird
Ayah

*Ayden (Irish) Form of Aiden, meaning "a fiery young man"

Ayo (African) Filled with happiness
Ayoe, Ayow, Ayowe

Azamat (Arabic) A proud man; one who is majestic

Azi (African) One who is youthful
Azie, Azy, Azey, Azee, Azea

Azmer (Islamic) Resembling a lion
Azmar, Azmir, Azmyr, Azmor, Azmur

B

Baakir (African) The eldest child
Baakeer, Baakyr, Baakear, Baakier, Baakeir

Bachir (Hebrew) The oldest son
Bacheer, Bachear, Bachier, Bacheir, Bachyr

Baha (Arabic) A glorious and splendid man
Bahah

Bailintin (Irish) A valiant man
Bailinten, Bailentin, Bailenten, Bailintyn, Bailentyn

Bain (Irish) A fair-haired man
Baine, Bayn, Bayne, Baen, Baene, Bane, Baines, Baynes

Bajnok (Hungarian) A victorious man
Bajnock, Bajnoc

Bakari (Swahili) One who is promised
Bakarie, Bakary, Bakarey, Bakaree, Bakarea

Bakhit (Arabic) A lucky man
Bakheet, Bakheat, Bakheit, Bakhiet, Bakhyt, Bakht

Bala (Hindi) One who is youthful
Balu, Balue, Balou

Balark (Hindi) Born with the rising sun

Balasi (Basque) One who is flat-footed
Balasie, Balasy, Balasey, Balasee, Balasea

Balbo (Latin) One who mutters
Balboe, Balbow, Balbowe, Ballbo, Balbino, Balbi, Balbie, Balby

Baldwin (German) A brave friend
Baldwine, Baldwinn, Baldwinne, Baldwen, Baldwenn, Baldwenne, Baldwyn, Baldwynn

Balint (Latin) A healthy and strong man
Balent, Balin, Balen, Balynt, Balyn

Balloch (Scottish) From the grazing land

Bancroft (English) From the bean field
Bancrofte, Banfield, Banfeld, Bankroft, Bankrofte

Bandana (Spanish) A brightly colored headwrap
Bandanah, Bandanna, Bandannah

Bandy (American) A fiesty man
Bandey, Bandi, Bandie, Bandee, Bandea

Bansi (Indian) One who plays the flute
Bansie, Bansy, Bansey, Bansee, Bansea

Bao (Vietnamese / Chinese) To order / one who is prized

Baqir (Arabic) A learned man
Baqeer, Baqear, Baqier, Baqeir, Baqyr, Baqer

Barak (Hebrew) Of the lightning flash
Barrak, Barac, Barrac, Barack, Barrack

Baram (Hebrew) The son of the nation
Barem, Barum, Barom, Barim, Barym

Bard (English) A minstrel; a poet
Barde, Bardo

Barden (English) From the barley valley; from the boar's valley
Bardon, Bardun, Bardin, Bardyn, Bardan, Bardene

Bardol (Basque) A farmer
Bardo, Bartol

Bardrick (Teutonic) An axe ruler
Bardric, Bardrik, Bardryck, Bardryk, Bardryc, Bardarick, Bardaric, Bardarik

Barek (Arabic) One who is noble
Barec, Bareck

Barend (German) The hard bear
Barende, Barind, Barinde, Barynd, Barynde

Barnett (English) Of honorable birth
Barnet, Baronet, Baronett

Baron (English) A title of nobility
Barron

Barr (English) A lawyer
Barre, Bar

Barra (Gaelic) A fair-haired man

^**Barrett** (German / English) Having the strength of a bear / one who argues
Baret, Barrat, Barratt, Barret, Barrette

Barry (Gaelic) A fair-haired man
Barrey, Barri, Barrie, Barree, Barrea, Barrington, Barryngton, Barringtun

Bartholomew (Aramaic) The son of the farmer
Bart, Bartel, Barth, Barthelemy, Bartho, Barthold, Bartholoma, Bartholomaus, Bartlett, Bartol

Bartlett (French) Form of Bartholomew, meaning "the son of the farmer"
Bartlet, Bartlitt, Bartlit, Bartlytt, Bartlyt

Bartley (English) From the meadow of birch trees
Bartly, Bartli, Bartlie, Bartlee, Bartlea, Bartleah, Bartleigh

Bartoli (Spanish) Form of Bartholomew, meaning "the son of the farmer"
Bartolie, Bartoly, Bartoley, Bartolee, Bartoleigh, Bartolea, Bartolo, Bartolio

Barton (English) From the barley town
Bartun, Barten, Bartan, Bartin, Bartyn

Barwolf (English) The ax-wolf
Barrwolf, Barwulf, Barrwulf

Basant (Arabic) One who smiles often
Basante

Bassett (English) A little person
Baset, Basset, Basett

Basy (American) A homebody
Basey, Basi, Basie, Basee, Basea, Basye

Baurice (American) Form of Maurice, meaning "a dark-skinned man; Moorish"
Baurell, Baureo, Bauricio, Baurids, Baurie, Baurin

Bay (Vietnamese / English) The seventh-born child; born during the month of July / from the bay
Baye, Bae, Bai

Beal (French) A handsome man
Beals, Beale, Beall, Bealle

Beamer (English) One who plays the trumpet
Beamor, Beamir, Beamyr, Beamur, Beamar, Beemer, Beemar, Beemir

Beau (French) A handsome man, an admirer
Bo

Becher (Hebrew) The firstborn son

Beckett (English) From the small stream; from the brook
Becket

Bedar (Arabic) One who is attentive
Beder, Bedor, Bedur, Bedyr, Bedir

Beircheart (Anglo-Saxon) Of the intelligent army

Bela (Slavic) A white-skinned man
Belah, Bella, Bellah

Belden (English) From the beautiful valley
Beldan, Beldon, Beldun, Beldin, Beldyn, Bellden, Belldan, Belldon, Belldun, Belldin, Belldyn

Belen (Greek) Of an arrow
Belin, Belyn, Belan, Belon, Belun

Belindo (English) A handsome and tender man
Belyndo, Belindio, Belyndio, Belindeo, Belyndeo, Belindiyo, Belyndiyo, Belindeyo

Bellarmine (Italian) One who is handsomely armed
Bellarmin, Bellarmeen, Bellarmeene, Bellarmean, Bellarmeane, Bellarmyn, Bellarmyne

Belton (English) From the beautiful town
Bellton, Beltun, Belltun, Belten, Bellten

Belvin (American) Form of Melvin, meaning "a friend who offers counsel"
Belven, Belvyn, Belvon, Belvun, Belvan

Bem (African) A peaceful man

Ben (English) Form of Benjamin, meaning "son of the south; son of the right hand"
Benn, Benni, Bennie, Bennee, Benney, Benny, Bennea, Benno

*ᵀBenjamin (Hebrew) Son of the south; son of the right hand
Ben, Benejamen, Beniamino, Benjaman, Benjamen, Benjamino, Benjamon, Benjiman, Benjimen

Bennett (English) Form of Benedict, meaning "one who is blessed"
Benett, Bennet, Benet

^*Bentley (English) From the meadow of bent grass
Bently, Bentleigh, Bentlee, Bentlie

Berdy (German) Having a brilliant mind
Berdey, Berdee, Berdea, Berdi, Berdie

Beresford (English) From the barley ford
Beresforde, Beresfurd, Beresfurde, Beresferd, Beresferde, Berford, Berforde, Berfurd

Berkeley (English) From the meadow of birch trees
Berkely, Berkeli, Berkelie, Berkelea, Berkeleah, Berkelee, Berkeleigh, Berkley

Bernard (German) As strong and brave as a bear
Barnard, Barnardo, Barnhard, Barnhardo, Bearnard, Bernardo, Bernarr, Bernd

Berry (English) Resembling a berry fruit
Berrey, Berri, Berrie, Berree, Berrea

Bert (English) One who is illustrious
Berte, Berti, Bertie, Bertee, Bertea, Berty, Bertey

Bethel (Hebrew) The house of God
Bethell, Bethele, Bethelle, Betuel, Betuell, Betuele, Betuelle

Bevis (Teutonic) An archer
Beviss, Bevys, Bevyss, Beavis, Beaviss, Beavys, Beavyss

Biagio (Italian) One who has a stutter
Biaggio

Birney (English) From the island with the brook
Birny, Birnee, Birnea, Birni, Birnie

Black (English) A dark-skinned man
Blak, Blac, Blacke

Blackwell (English) From the dark spring
Blackwel, Blackwelle, Blackwele

Blade (English) One who wields a sword or knife
Blayd, Blayde, Blaid, Blaide, Blaed, Blaede

Blagden (English) From the dark valley
Blagdon, Blagdan, Blagdun, Blagdin, Blagdyn

Blaine (Scottish / Irish) A saint's servant / a thin man
Blayne, Blane, Blain, Blayn, Blaen, Blaene, Blainy, Blainey

Blaise (Latin / American) One with a lisp or a stutter / a fiery man
Blaze, Blaize, Blaiz, Blayze, Blayz, Blaez, Blaeze

*ᵀBlake (English) A dark, handsome man
Blayk, Blayke, Blaik, Blaike, Blaek, Blaeke

Bliss (English) Filled with happiness
Blis, Blyss, Blys

Blondell (English) A fair-haired boy
Blondel, Blondele, Blondelle

Boaz (Hebrew) One who is swift
Boaze, Boas, Boase

Bob (English) Form of Robert, meaning "one who is bright with fame"
Bobbi, Bobbie, Bobby, Bobbey, Bobbee, Bobbea

Bogart (French) One who is strong with the bow
Bogaard, Bogaart, Bogaerd, Bogey, Bogie, Bogi, Bogy, Bogee

Bolivar (Spanish) A mighty warrior
Bolevar, Bolivarr, Bolevarr, Bollivar, Bollivarr, Bollevar, Bollevarr

Bonaventure (Latin) One who undertakes a blessed venture
Bonaventura, Buenaventure, Buenaventura, Bueaventure, Bueaventura

Booker (English) One who binds books; a scribe
Bookar, Bookir, Bookyr, Bookur, Bookor

Bosley (English) From the meadow near the forest
Bosly, Boslee, Boslea, Bosleah, Bosleigh, Bosli, Boslie, Bozley

Boston (English) From the town near the forest; from the city of Boston
Bostun, Bostin, Bostyn, Bosten, Bostan

Boyce (French) One who lives near the forest
Boice, Boyse, Boise

Boyd (Celtic) A blond-haired man
Boyde, Boid, Boide, Boyden, Boydan, Boydin, Boydyn, Boydon

Boynton (Irish) From the town near the river Boyne
Boyntun, Boynten, Boyntin, Boyntan, Boyntyn

Bracken (English) Resembling the large fern
Braken, Brackan, Brakan, Brackin, Brakin, Brackyn

Braddock (English) From the broadly spread oak
Bradock, Braddoc, Bradoc, Braddok, Bradok

Braden (Gaelic / English) Resembling salmon / from the wide valley
Bradan, Bradon, Bradin, Bradyn, Braeden, Brayden

Bradford (English) From the wide ford
Bradforde, Bradferd, Bradferde

Bradley (English) From the wide meadow
Bradly, Bradlea, Bradleah, Bradlee, Bradleigh, Bradli

Brady (Irish) The son of a large-chested man
Bradey, Bradee, Bradea, Bradi, Bradie, Braidy, Braidey, Braidee

Bramley (English) From the wild gorse meadow; from the raven's meadow
Bramly, Bramlee, Bramlea

*ᵀ**Brandon** (English) From the broom or gorse hill
Brandun, Brandin, Brandyn, Brandan, Branden, Brannon, Brannun, Brannen

Branson (English) The son of Brand or Brandon
Bransun, Bransen, Bransan, Bransin, Bransyn

Brant (English) Steep, tall

^**Brantley** (English) Form of Brant, meaning "steep, tall"
Brantly

Braxton (English) From Brock's town
Braxtun, Braxten, Braxtan, Braxtyn

*****Brayden** (Gaelic / English) Form of Braden, meaning "resembling salmon / from the wide valley"
Braydon, Braydan, Braydin, Braydyn

^**Braylen** (American) Combination of Brayden and Lynn
Braylon

Brendan (Irish) Born to royalty; a prince
Brendano, Brenden, Brendin, Brendon, Brendyn, Brendun

Brennan (Gaelic) A sorrowful man; a teardrop
Brenan, Brenn, Brennen, Brennin, Brennon, Brenin, Brennun, Brennyn

Brent (English) From the hill
Brendt, Brennt, Brentan, Brenten, Brentin, Brenton, Brentun, Brentyn

Brett (Latin) A man from Britain or Brittany
Bret, Breton, Brette, Bretton, Brit, Briton, Britt, Brittain

Brewster (English) One who brews
Brewer, Brewstere

ᵀ**Brian** (Gaelic / Celtic) Of noble birth / having great strength
Briano, Briant, Brien, Brion, Bryan, Bryant, Bryen, Bryent

Briar (English) Resembling a thorny plant
Brier, Bryar, Bryer

Brock (English) Resembling a badger
Broc

Broderick (English) From the wide ridge
Broderik, Broderic, Brodrick, Brodryk, Brodyrc, Brodrik, Broderyc, Brodrig

***Brody** (Gaelic / Irish) From the ditch
Brodie, Brodey, Brodi, Brodee

Brogan (Gaelic) One who is sturdy
Broggan, Brogen, Broggen, Brogon, Broggon, Brogun, Broggun, Brogin, Broggin, Brogyn

^**Brooks** (English) From the running stream
Brookes

^**Bruce** (Scottish) A man from Brieuse; one who is well-born; from an influential family
Brouce, Brooce, Bruci, Brucie, Brucey, Brucy

Bruno (German) A brown-haired man
Brunoh, Brunoe, Brunow, Brunowe, Bruin, Bruine, Brunon, Brunun

Bryce (Scottish / Anglo-Saxon) One who is speckled / the son of a nobleman
Brice, Bricio, Brizio, Brycio

^***Bryson** (Welsh) The son of Brice
Brisen, Brysin, Brysun, Brysyn, Brycen

Bud (English) One who is brotherly
Budd, Buddi, Buddie, Buddee, Buddey, Buddy

Budha (Hindi) Another name for the planet Mercury
Budhan, Budhwar

Bulat (Russian) Having great strength
Bulatt

Burbank (English) From the riverbank of burrs
Burrbank, Burhbank

Burgess (German) A free citizen of the town
Burges, Burgiss, Burgis, Burgyss, Burgys, Burgeis

Burne (English) Resembling a bear; from the brook; the brown-haired one
Burn, Beirne, Burnis, Byrn, Byrne, Burns, Byrnes

Burnet (French) Having brown hair
Burnett, Burnete, Burnette, Bernet, Bernett, Bernete, Bernette

Burton (English) From the fortified town
Burtun, Burten, Burtin, Burtyn, Burtan

Butler (English) The keeper of the bottles (wine, liquor)
Buttler, Butlar, Butlor, Butlir, Buttlir, Butlyr

Byron (English) One who lives near the cow sheds
Byrom, Beyren, Beyron, Biren, Biron, Buiron, Byram, Byran

C

Cable (French) One who makes rope
Cabel, Caibel, Caible, Caybel, Cayble, Caebel, Caeble, Cabe

Caddis (English) Resembling a worsted fabric
Caddys, Caddiss, Caddice

Cade (English / French) One who is round / of the cask
Caid, Caide, Cayd, Cayde, Caed, Caede

Cadell (Welsh) Having the spirit of battle
Cadel, Caddell, Caddel

Caden (Welsh) Spirit of Battle
Caiden, Cayden

Cadmus (Greek) A man from the east; in mythology, the man who founded Thebes
Cadmar, Cadmo, Cadmos, Cadmuss

Cadogan (Welsh) Having glory and honor during battle
Cadogawn, Cadwgan, Cadwgawn, Cadogaun

Caesar (Latin) An emperor
Caezar, Casar, Cezar, Chezare, Caesarius, Ceasar, Ceazer

Cain (Hebrew) One who wields a spear; something acquired; in the Bible, Adam and Eve's first son who killed his brother Abel
Cayn, Caen, Cane, Caine, Cayne, Caene

Caird (Scottish) A traveling metal worker
Cairde, Cayrd, Cayrde, Caerd, Caerde

Cairn (Gaelic) From the mound of rocks
Cairne, Cairns, Caern, Caerne, Caernes

Caith (Irish) Of the battlefield
Caithe, Cayth, Caythe, Cathe, Caeth, Caethe

Calbert (English) A cowboy
Calberte, Calburt, Calburte, Calbirt, Calbirte, Calbyrt, Calbyrte

Cale (English) Form of Charles, meaning "one who is manly and strong / a free man"
Cail, Caile, Cayl, Cayle, Cael, Caele

*^T**Caleb** (Hebrew) Resembling a dog
Cayleb, Caileb, Caeleb, Calob, Cailob, Caylob, Caelob, Kaleb

Calian (Native American) A warrior of life
Calien, Calyan, Calyen

Callum (Gaelic) Resembling a dove
Calum

Calvin (French) The little bald one
Cal, Calvyn, Calvon, Calven, Calvan, Calvun, Calvino

Camara (African) One who teaches others

Camden (Gaelic) From the winding valley
Camdene, Camdin, Camdyn, Camdan, Camdon, Camdun

Cameo (English) A small, perfect child
Cammeo

***Cameron** (Scottish) Having a crooked nose
Cameren, Cameran, Camerin, Cameryn, Camerun, Camron, Camren, Camran, Tameron

Campbell (Scottish) Having a crooked mouth
Campbel, Cambell, Cambel, Camp, Campe, Cambeul, Cambeull, Campbeul

Candan (Turkish) A sincere
man
*Canden, Candin, Candyn,
Candon, Candun*

Cannon (French) An official of
the church
*Canon, Cannun, Canun,
Cannin, Canin*

Canyon (Spanish / English)
From the footpath / from the
deep ravine
Caniyon, Canyun, Caniyun

Capricorn (Latin) The tenth
sign of the zodiac; the goat

Cargan (Gaelic) From the
small rock
*Cargen, Cargon, Cargun,
Cargin, Cargyn*

Carl (German) Form of Karl,
meaning "a free man"
*Carel, Carlan, Carle, Carlens,
Carlitis, Carlin, Carlo, **Carlos***

*Carlos (Spanish) Form of
Karl, meaning "a free man"
Carolos, Carolo, Carlito

Carlsen (Scandinavian) The
son of Carl
*Carlssen, Carlson, Carlsson,
Carlsun, Carllsun, Carlsin,
Carllsin, Carlsyn*

Carlton (English) From the
free man's town
*Carltun, Carltown, Carston,
Carstun, Carstown, Carleton,
Carletun, Carlten*

Carmichael (Scottish) A
follower of Michael

Carmine (Latin / Aramaic)
A beautiful song / the color
crimson
*Carman, Carmen, Carmin,
Carmino, Carmyne, Carmon,
Carmun, Carmyn*

*Carson (Scottish) The son of
a marsh dweller
*Carsen, Carsun, Carsan,
Carsin, Carsyn*

*Carter (English) One who
transports goods; one who
drives a cart
*Cartar, Cartir, Cartyr, Cartor,
Cartur, Cartere, Cartier,
Cartrell*

Cartland (English) From
Carter's land
*Carteland, Cartlan, Cartlend,
Cartelend, Cartlen*

Cary (Celtic / Welsh / Gaelic)
From the river / from the
fort on the hill / having dark
features
*Carey, Cari, Carie, Caree,
Carea, Carry, Carrey, Carri*

Case (French) Refers to a chest or box
Cace

Cash (Latin) money

^**Cason** (Greek) A seer
Casen

Cassander (Spanish) A brother of heroes
Casander, Casandro, Cassandro, Casandero

Cassius (Latin) One who is empty; hollow; vain
Cassios, Cassio, Cach, Cache, Cashus, Cashos, Cassian, Cassien

Castel (Spanish) From the castle
Castell, Castal, Castall, Castol, Castoll, Castul, Castull, Castil

Castor (Greek) Resembling a beaver; in mythology, one of the Dioscuri
Castur, Caster, Castar, Castir, Castyr, Castorio, Castoreo, Castoro

Cat (American) Resembling the animal
Catt, Chait, Chaite

Cathmore (Irish) A renowned fighter
Cathmor, Cathemore

Cato (Latin) One who is all-knowing
Cayto, Caito, Caeto

Caton (Spanish) One who is knowledgable
Caten, Catun, Catan, Catin, Catyn

Cavell (Teutonic) One who is bold
Cavel, Cavele, Cavelle

Caxton (English) From the lump settlement
Caxtun, Caxten

Celesto (Latin) From heaven
Célestine, Celestino, Celindo, Celestyne, Celestyno

Cephas (Hebrew) As solid as a rock

Cesar (Spanish) Form of Caesar, meaning "emperor"
Cesare, Cesaro, Cesario

Chad (English) One who is warlike
Chaddie, Chadd, Chadric, Chadrick, Chadrik, Chadryck, Chadryc, Chadryk

Chadwick (English) From Chad's dairy farm
Chadwik, Chadwic, Chadwyck, Chadwyk, Chadwyc

Chai (Hebrew) A giver of life
Chaika, Chaim, Cahyim, Cahyyam

Chalkley (English) From the chalk meadow
Chalkly, Chalkleigh, Chalklee, Chalkleah, Chalkli, Chalklie, Chalklea

Champion (English) A warrior; the victor
Champeon, Champiun, Champeun, Champ

Chan (Spanish / Sanskrit) Form of John, meaning "God is gracious" / a shining man
Chayo, Chano, Chawn, Chaun

Chanan (Hebrew) God is compassionate
Chanen, Chanin, Chanyn, Chanun, Chanon

ᵀ**Chance** (English) Having good fortune

^**Chandler** (English) One who makes candles
Chandlar, Chandlor

Chaniel (Hebrew) The grace of God
Chanyel, Chaniell, Chanyell

Channing (French / English) An official of the church / resembling a young wolf
Channyng, Canning, Cannyng

Chao (Chinese) The great one

Chappel (English) One who works in the chapel
Capel, Capell, Capello, Cappel, Chappell

*****Charles** (English / German) One who is manly and strong / a free man
Charls, Chas, Charli, Charlie, Charley, Charly, Charlee, Charleigh, Cale, Chuck, Chick

Charleson (English) The son of Charles
Charlesen, Charlesin, Charlesyn, Charlesan, Charlesun

Charlton (English) From the free man's town
Charleton, Charltun, Charletun, Charleston, Charlestun

Charro (Spanish) A cowboy
Charo

*ᵀ**Chase** (English) A huntsman
Chace, Chasen, Chayce, Chayse, Chaise, Chaice, Chaece, Chaese

Chatwin (English) A warring friend
Chatwine, Chatwinn, Chatwinne, Chatwen, Chatwenn, Chatwenne, Chatwyn, Chatwynn

Chaviv (Hebrew) One who is dearly loved
Chaveev, Chaveav, Chaviev, Chaveiv, Chavyv, Chavivi, Chavivie, Chavivy

Chay (Gaelic) From the fairy place
Chaye, Chae

Chelsey (English) From the landing place for chalk
Chelsee, Chelseigh, Chelsea, Chelsi, Chelsie, Chelsy, Chelcey, Chelcy

Cheslav (Russian) From the fortified camp
Cheslaw

Chester (Latin) From the camp of the soldiers
Chet, Chess, Cheston, Chestar, Chestor, Chestur, Chestir, Chestyr

Chico (Spanish) A boy; a lad

Chien (Vietnamese) A combative man

Chiron (Greek) A wise tutor
Chyron, Chirun, Chyrun

Chogan (Native American) Resembling a blackbird
Chogen, Chogon, Chogun, Chogin, Chogyn

Choni (Hebrew) A gracious man
Chonie, Chony, Choney, Chonee, Chonea

*ᵀ**Christian** (Greek) A follower of Christ
Chrestien, Chretien, Chris, Christan, Christer, Christiano, Cristian

*ᵀ**Christopher** (Greek) One who bears Christ inside
Chris, Kit, Christof, Christofer, Christoffer, Christoforo, Christoforus, Christoph, Christophe, Cristopher, Cristofer

Chuchip (Native American) A deer spirit

Chuck (English) Form of Charles, meaning "one who is manly and strong / a free man"
Chucke, Chucki, Chuckie, Chucky, Chuckey, Chuckee, Chuckea

Chul (Korean) One who stands firm

Chun (Chinese) Born during the spring

Cid (Spanish) A lord
Cyd

Cillian (Gaelic) One who suffers strife

Ciqala (Native American) The little one

Cirrus (Latin) A lock of hair; resembling the cloud
Cyrrus

Clair (Latin) One who is bright
Clare, Clayr, Claer, Clairo, Claro, Claero

Clancy (Celtic) Son of the red-haired warrior
Clancey, Clanci, Clancie, Clancee, Clancea, Clansey, Clansy, Clansi

Clark (English) A cleric; a clerk
Clarke, Clerk, Clerke, Clerc

Claude (English) One who is lame
Claud, Claudan, Claudell, Claidianus, Claudicio, Claudien, Claudino, Claudio

Clay (English) Of the earth's clay

Clayton (English) From the town settled on clay
Claytun, Clayten, Claytin, Claytyn, Claytan, Cleyton, Cleytun, Cleytan

Cleon (Greek) A well-known man
Cleone, Clion, Clione, Clyon, Clyone

Clifford (English) From the ford near the cliff
Cliff, Clyfford, Cliford, Clyford

Cliffton (English) From the town near the cliff
Cliff, Cliffe, Clyff, Clyffe, Clifft, Clift, Clyfft, Clyft

Clinton (English) From the town on the hill
Clynton, Clintun, Clyntun, Clint, Clynt, Clinte, Clynte

Clive (English) One who lives near the cliff
Clyve, Cleve

Cluny (Irish) From the meadow
Cluney, Cluni, Clunie, Clunee, Clunea, Cluneah

Cobden (English) From the cottage in the valley
Cobdenn, Cobdale, Cobdail, Cobdaile, Cobdell, Cobdel, Cobdayl, Cobdayle

Coby (English) Form of Jacob, meaning "he who supplants"
Cobey

Cody (Irish / English) One who is helpful; a wealthy man / acting as a cushion
Codi, Codie, Codey, Codee, Codeah, Codea, Codier, Codyr

Colbert (French) A famous
and bright man
*Colvert, Culbert, Colburt,
Colbirt, Colbyrt, Colbart,
Culburt, Culbirt*

Colby (English) From the coal
town
*Colbey, Colbi, Colbie, Colbee,
Collby, Coalby, Colbea, Colbeah*

*****Cole** (English) Having dark
features; having coal-black
hair
*Coley, Coli, Coly, Colie, Colee,
Coleigh, Colea, Colson*

Coleridge (English) From the
dark ridge
Colerige, Colridge, Colrige

Colgate (English) From the
dark gate
*Colegate, Colgait, Colegait,
Colgayt, Colegayt, Colgaet*

Colin (Scottish) A young man;
a form of Nicholas, meaning
"of the victorious people"
*Cailean, Colan, Colyn, Colon,
Colen, Collin, Collan*

Colt (English) A young horse;
from the coal town
Colte

Colter (English) A horse
herdsman
*Coltere, Coltar, Coltor, Coltir,
Coltyr, Coulter, Coultar, Coultir*

*****ᵀColton** (English) From the
coal town
*Colten, Coltun, Coltan, Coltin,
Coltyn, Coltrain*

Comanche (Native American)
A tribal name
*Comanchi, Comanchie,
Comanchee, Comanchea,
Comanchy, Comanchey*

Comus (Latin) In mythology,
the god of mirth and revelry
Comas, Comis, Comys

Conan (English / Gaelic)
Resembling a wolf / one who
is high and mighty
Conant

Condon (Celtic) A dark,
wise man
*Condun, Condan, Conden,
Condin, Condyn*

Cong (Chinese) A clever man

Conn (Irish) The chief
Con

Connecticut (Native American)
From the place beside the
long river / from the state of
Connecticut

Connery (Scottish) A daring
man
*Connary, Connerie, Conneri,
Connerey, Connarie, Connari,
Connarey, Conary*

*ᵀ**Connor** (Gaelic) A wolf lover
Conor, Conner, Coner, Connar, Conar, Connur, Conur, Connir, Conir

Conroy (Irish) A wise adviser
Conroye, Conroi

Constantine (Latin) One who is steadfast; firm
Dinos

Consuelo (Spanish) One who offers consolation
Consuel, Consuelio, Consueleo, Consueliyo, Consueleyo

Conway (Gaelic) The hound of the plain; from the sacred river
Conwaye, Conwai, Conwae, Conwy

Cook (English) One who prepares meals for others
Cooke

Cooney (Irish) A handsome man
Coony, Cooni, Coonie, Coonee, Coonea

*****Cooper** (English) One who makes barrels
Coop, Coopar, Coopir, Coopyr, Coopor, Coopur, Coopersmith, Cupere

Corbett (French) Resembling a young raven
Corbet, Corbete, Corbette, Corbit, Corbitt, Corbite, Corbitte

Corcoran (Gaelic) Having a ruddy complexion
Cochran

Cordero (Spanish) Resembling a lamb
Corderio, Corderiyo, Cordereo, Cordereyo

Corey (Irish) From the hollow; of the churning waters
Cory, Cori, Corie, Coree, Corea, Correy, Corry, Corri

Coriander (Greek) A romantic man; resembling the spice
Coryander, Coriender, Coryender

Corlan (Irish) One who wields a spear
Corlen, Corlin, Corlyn, Corlon, Corlun

Corrado (German) A bold counselor
Corrade, Corradeo, Corradio

Corridon (Irish) One who wields a spear
Corridan, Corridun, Corriden, Corridin, Corridyn

Cortez (Spanish) A courteous man
Cortes

Cosmo (Greek) The order of the universe
Cosimo, Cosmé, Cosmos, Cosmas, Cozmo, Cozmos, Cozmas

Cotton (American) Resembling or farmer of the plant
Cottin, Cotten, Cottyn, Cottun, Cottan

Courtney (English) A courteous man; courtly
Cordney, Cordni, Cortenay, Corteney, Cortni, Cortnee, Cortneigh, Cortney

Covert (English) One who provides shelter
Couvert

Covey (English) A brood of birds
Covy, Covi, Covie, Covee, Covea, Covvey, Covvy, Covvi

Covington (English) From the town near the cave
Covyngton, Covingtun, Covyngtun

Cox (English) A coxswain
Coxe, Coxi, Coxie, Coxey, Coxy, Coxee, Coxea

Coyle (Irish) A leader during battle
Coyl, Coil, Coile

Craig (Gaelic) From the rocks; from the crag
Crayg, Craeg, Craige, Crayge, Craege, Crage, Crag

Crandell (English) From the valley of cranes
Crandel, Crandale, Crandail, Crandaile, Crandayl, Crandayle, Crandael, Crandaele

Crawford (English) From the crow's ford
Crawforde, Crawferd, Crawferde, Crawfurd, Crawfurde

Creed (Latin) A guiding principle; a belief
Creede, Cread, Creade, Creedon, Creadon, Creedun, Creadun, Creedin

Creek (English) From the small stream
Creeke, Creak, Creake, Creik, Creike

Creighton (Scottish) From the border town
Creightun, Crayton, Craytun, Craiton, Craitun, Craeton, Craetun, Crichton

Crescent (French) One who creates; increasing; growing
Creissant, Crescence, Cressant, Cressent, Crescant

Cruz (Spanish) Of the cross

Cuarto (Spanish) The fourth-born child
Cuartio, Cuartiyo, Cuarteo

Cullen (Gaelic) A good-looking young man
Cullin, Cullyn, Cullan, Cullon, Cullun

Cunningham (Gaelic) Descendant of the chief
Conyngham, Cuningham, Cunnyngham, Cunyngham

Curcio (French) One who is courteous
Curceo

Cuthbert (English) One who is bright and famous
Cuthbeorht, Cuthburt, Cuthbirt, Cuthbyrt

Cyneley (English) From the royal meadow
Cynely, Cyneli, Cynelie, Cynelee, Cynelea, Cyneleah, Cyneleigh

Czar (Russian) An emperor

D

Dacey (Gaelic / Latin) A man from the south / a man from Dacia
Dacy, Dacee, Dacea, Daci, Dacie, Daicey, Daicy

Dack (English) From the French town of Dax
Dacks, Dax

Daedalus (Greek) A craftsman
Daldalos, Dedalus

Dag (Scandinavian) Born during the daylight
Dagney, Dagny, Dagnee, Dagnea, Dagni, Dagnie, Daeg, Dagget

Daijon (American) A gift of hope
Dayjon, Daejon, Dajon

Dainan (Australian) A kind-hearted man
Dainen, Dainon, Dainun, Dainyn, Dainin, Daynan, Daynen, Daynon

Daire (Irish) A wealthy man
Dair, Daere, Daer, Dayr, Dayre, Dare, Dari, Darie

Daivat (Hindi) A powerful man

Dakarai (African) Filled with happiness

Dakota (Native American) A friend to all
Daccota, Dakoda, Dakodah, Dakotah, Dakoeta, Dekota, Dekohta, Dekowta

Dallan (Irish) One who is blind
Dalan, Dallen, Dalen, Dalin, Dallin, Dallyn, Dalyn, Dallon, Dalon, Dallun, Dalun

Dallas (Scottish) From the dales
Dalles, Dallis, Dallys, Dallos

Dalton (English) from the town in the valley
Daltun, Dalten, Daltan, Daltin, Daltyn, Daleten, Dalte, Daulten

Damario (Greek / Spanish) Resembling a calf / one who is gentle
Damarios, Damarius, Damaro, Damero, Damerio, Damereo, Damareo, Damerios

^Damian (Greek) One who tames or subdues others
*Daemon, Daimen, Daimon, Daman, Damen, Dameon, Damiano, Damianos, **Damon***

Dane (English) A man from Denmark
Dain, Daine, Dayn, Dayne

Danely (Scandinavian) A man from Denmark
Daneley, Daneli, Danelie, Danelee, Daneleigh, Danelea, Daineley, Dainely

Daniachew (African) A mediator

*ᵀDaniel (Hebrew) God is my judge
Dan, Danal, Daneal, Danek, Danell, Danial, Daniele, Danil, Danilo

Danso (African) A reliable man
Dansoe, Dansow, Dansowe

Dante (Latin) An enduring man; everlasting
Dantae, Dantay, Dantel, Daunte, Dontae, Dontay, Donte, Dontae

Daoud (Arabian) Form of David, meaning "the beloved one"
Daoude, Dawud, Doud, Daud, Da'ud

Daphnis (Greek) In mythology, the son of Hermes
Daphnys

Dar (Hebrew) Resembling a pearl
Darr

Darcel (French) Having dark features
Darcell, Darcele, Darcelle, Darcio, Darceo

Dardanus (Greek) In mythology, the founder of Troy
Dardanio, Dardanios, Dardanos, Dard, Darde

Darek (English) Form of Derek, meaning "the ruler of the tribe"
Darrek, Darec, Darrec, Darreck, Dareck

Darion (Greek) A gift
Darian, Darien, Dariun, Darrion, Darrian, Darrien, Daryon, Daryan

Darius (Greek) A kingly man; one who is wealthy
Darias, Dariess, Dario, Darious, Darrius, Derrius, Derrious, Derrias

Darlen (American) A sweet man; a darling
Darlon, Darlun, Darlan, Darlin, Darlyn

Darnell (English) From the hidden place
Darnall, Darneil, Darnel, Darnele, Darnelle

Darold (English) Form of Harold, meaning "the ruler of an army"
Darrold, Derald, Derrald, Derold, Derrold

Darren (Gaelic / English) A great man / a gift from God
Darran, Darrin, Darryn, Darron, Darrun, Daren, Darin, Daran

Dart (English / American) From the river / one who is fast
Darte, Darrt, Darrte, Darti, Dartie, Dartee, Dartea, Darty

Darvell (French) From the eagle town
Darvel, Darvele, Darvelle

Dasras (Indian) A handsome man

Dasya (Indian) A servant

***David** (Hebrew) The beloved one
Dave, Davey, Davi, Davidde, Davide, Davie, Daviel, Davin, Daoud

Davis (English) The son of David
Davies, Daviss, Davys, Davyss

Davu (African) Of the beginning
Davue, Davoo, Davou, Davugh

Dawson (English) The son of David
Dawsan, Dawsen, Dawsin, Dawsun

Dax (French) From the French town Dax
Daxton

Dayton (English) From the sunny town

Deacon (Greek) The dusty one; a servant
Deecon, Deakon, Deekon, Deacun, Deecun, Deakun, Deekun, Deacan

Dean (English) From the valley; a church official
Deane, Deen, Deene, Dene, Deans, Deens, Deani, Deanie

DeAndre (American) A manly man
D'André, DeAndrae, DeAndray, Diandray, Diondrae, Diondray

Dearon (American) One who is much loved
Dearan, Dearen, Dearin, Dearyn, Dearun

Decker (German / Hebrew) One who prays / a piercing man
Deker, Decer, Dekker, Deccer, Deck, Decke

^Declan (Irish) The name of a saint

Dedrick (English) Form of Dietrich, meaning "the ruler of the tribe"
Dedryck, Dedrik, Dedryk, Dedric, Dedryc

Deegan (Irish) A black-haired man
Deagan, Degan, Deegen, Deagen, Degen, Deegon, Deagon, Degon

Deinorus (American) A lively man
Denorius, Denorus, Denorios, Deinorius, Deinorios

Dejuan (American) A talkative man
Dejuane, Dewon, Dewonn, Dewan, Dewann, Dwon, Dwonn, Dajuan

Delaney (Irish / French) The dark challenger / from the elder-tree grove
Delany, Delanee, Delanea, Delani, Delanie, Delainey, Delainy, Delaini

Delaware (English) From the state of Delaware
Delawair, Delaweir, Delwayr, Delawayre, Delawaire, Delawaer, Delawaere

Delius (Greek) A man from Delos
Delios, Delos, Delus, Delo

Dell (English) From the small valley
Delle, Del

Delmon (English) A man of the mountain
Delmun, Delmen, Delmin, Delmyn, Delmont, Delmonte, Delmond, Delmonde

Delsi (American) An easygoing guy
Delsie, Delsy, Delsey, Delsee, Delsea, Delci, Delcie, Delcee

Delvin (English) A godly friend
Delvinn, Delvinne, Delvyn, Delvynn, Delvynne, Delven, Delvenn, Delvenne

Demarcus (American) The son of Marcus
DeMarcus, DaMarkiss, DeMarco, Demarkess, DeMarko, Demarkus, DeMarques, DeMarquez

Dembe (African) A peaceful man
Dembi, Dembie, Dembee, Dembea, Dembey, Demby

Denali (American) From the national park
Denalie, Denaly, Denaley, Denalee, Denalea, Denaleigh

Denley (English) From the meadow near the valley
Denly, Denlea, Denleah, Denlee, Denleigh, Denli, Denlie

Denman (English) One who lives in the valley
Denmann, Denmin, Denmyn, Denmen, Denmon, Denmun

Dennis (French) A follower of Dionysus
Den, Denies, Denis, Dennes, Dennet, Denney, Dennie, Denys, Dennys

Dennison (English) The son of Dennis
Denison, Dennisun, Denisun, Dennisen, Denisen, Dennisan, Denisan

Deo (Greek) A godly man

Deonte (French) An outgoing man
Deontay, Deontaye, Deontae, Dionte, Diontay, Diontaye, Diontae

Deotis (American) A learned man; a scholar
Deotiss, Deotys, Deotyss, Deotus, Deotuss

Derek (English) The ruler of the tribe
Dereck, Deric, Derick, Derik, Deriq, Derk, Derreck, Derrek, Derrick

Dervin (English) A gifted friend
Dervinn, Dervinne, Dervyn, Dervynn, Dervynne, Dervon, Dervan, Dervun

Deshan (Hindi) Of the nation
Deshal, Deshad

Desiderio (Latin) One who is desired; hoped for
Derito, Desi, Desideratus, Desiderios, Desiderius, Desiderus, Dezi, Diderot

Desmond (Gaelic) A man from South Munster
Desmonde, Desmund, Desmunde, Dezmond, Dezmonde, Dezmund, Dezmunde, Desmee

Desperado (Spanish) A renegade

Destin (French) Recognizing one's certain fortune; fate
Destyn, Deston, Destun, Desten, Destan

Destrey (American) A cowboy
Destry, Destree, Destrea, Destri, Destrie

Deutsch (German) A German

Devanshi (Hindi) A divine messenger
Devanshie, Devanshy, Devanshey, Devanshee

Devante (Spanish) One who fights wrongdoing

Deverell (French) From the riverbank
Deverel, Deveral, Deverall, Devereau, Devereaux, Devere, Deverill, Deveril

Devlin (Gaelic) Having fierce bravery; a misfortunate man
Devlyn, Devlon, Devlen, Devlan, Devlun

Devon (English) From the beautiful farmland; of the divine
Devan, Deven, Devenn, Devin, Devonn, Devone, Deveon, Devonne

Dewitt (Flemish) A blond-haired man
DeWitt, Dewytt, DeWytt, Dewit, DeWit, Dewyt, DeWyt

^**Dexter** (Latin) A right-handed man; one who is skillful
Dextor, Dextar, Dextur, Dextir, Dextyr, Dexton, Dextun, Dexten

Dhyanesh (Indian) One who meditates
Dhianesh, Dhyaneshe, Dhianeshe

Dice (American) A gambling man
Dyce

Dichali (Native American) One who talks a lot
Dichalie, Dichaly, Dichaley, Dichalee, Dichalea, Dichaleigh

*Diego (Spanish) Form of James, meaning "he who supplants"
Dyego, Dago

Diesel (American) Having great strength
Deisel, Diezel, Deizel, Dezsel

Dietrich (German) The ruler of the tribe
Dedrick

Digby (Norse) From the town near the ditch
Digbey, Digbee, Digbea, Digbi, Digbie

Diji (African) A farmer
Dijie, Dijee, Dijea, Dijy, Dijey

Dillon (Gaelic) Resembling a lion; a faithful man
Dillun, Dillen, Dillan, Dillin, Dillyn, Dilon, Dilan, Dilin

Dino (Italian) One who wields a little sword
Dyno, Dinoh, Dynoh, Deano, Deanoh, Deeno, Deenoh, Deino

Dinos (Greek) Form of Constantine, meaning "one who is steadfast; firm"
Dynos, Deanos, Deenos, Deinos, Dinose, Dinoz

Dins (American) One who climbs to the top
Dinz, Dyns, Dynz

Dionysus (Greek) The god of wine and revelry
Dion, Deion, Deon, Deonn, Deonys, Deyon, Diandre

Dior (French) The golden one
D'Or, Diorr, Diorre, Dyor, Deor, Dyorre, Deorre

Diron (American) Form of Darren, meaning "a great man / a gift from God"
Dirun, Diren, Diran, Dirin, Diryn, Dyron, Dyren

Dixon (English) The son of Dick
Dixen, Dixin, Dixyn, Dixan, Dixun

Doane (English) From the rolling hills
Doan

Dobber (American) An independent man
Dobbar, Dobbor, Dobbur, Dobbir, Dobbyr

Dobbs (English) A fiery man
Dobbes, Dobes, Dobs

Domevlo (African) One who doesn't judge others
Domivlo, Domyvlo

Domingo (Spanish) Born on a Sunday
Domyngo, Demingo, Demyngo

*Dominic (Latin) A lord
Demenico, Dom, Domenic, Domenico, Domenique, Domini, Dominick, Dominico

Domnall (Gaelic) A world ruler
Domhnall, Domnull, Domhnull

Don (Scottish) Form of Donald, meaning "ruler of the world"
Donn, Donny, Donney, Donnie, Donni, Donnee, Donnea, Donne

Donald (Scottish) Ruler of the world
Don, Donold, Donuld, Doneld, Donild, Donyld

Donato (Italian) A gift from God

Donovan (Irish) A brown-haired chief
Donavan, Donavon, Donevon, Donovyn

Dor (Hebrew) Of this generation
Doram, Doriel, Dorli, Dorlie, Dorlee, Dorlea, Dorleigh, Dorly

Doran (Irish) A stranger; one who has been exiled
Doren, Dorin, Doryn

Dorsey (Gaelic) From the fortress near the sea
Dorsy, Dorsee, Dorsea, Dorsi, Dorsie

Dost (Arabic) A beloved friend
Doste, Daust, Dauste, Dawst, Dawste

Dotson (English) The son of Dot
Dotsen, Dotsan, Dotsin, Dotsyn, Dotsun, Dottson, Dottsun, Dottsin

Dove (American) A peaceful man
Dovi, Dovie, Dovy, Dovey, Dovee, Dovea

Drade (American) A serious-minded man
Draid, Draide, Drayd, Drayde, Draed, Draede, Dradell, Dradel

Drake (English) Resembling a dragon
Drayce, Drago, Drakie

Drew (Welsh) One who is wise
Drue, Dru

Driscoll (Celtic) A mediator; one who is sorrowful; a messenger
Dryscoll, Driscol, Dryscol, Driskoll, Dryskoll, Driskol, Dryskol, Driskell

Druce (Gaelic / English) A wise man; a druid / the son of Drew
Drews, Drewce, Druece, Druse, Druson, Drusen

Drummond (Scottish) One who lives on the ridge
Drummon, Drumond, Drumon, Drummund, Drumund, Drummun

Duane (Gaelic) A dark or swarthy man
Dewain, Dewayne, Duante, Duayne, Duwain, Duwaine, Duwayne, Dwain

Dublin (Irish) From the capital of Ireland
Dublyn, Dublen, Dublan, Dublon, Dublun

Duc (Vietnamese) One who has upstanding morals

Due (Vietnamese) A virtuous man

Duke (English) A title of nobility; a leader
Dooke, Dook, Duki, Dukie, Dukey, Duky, Dukee, Dukea

Dumi (African) One who inspires others
Dumie, Dumy, Dumey, Dumee, Dumea

Dumont (French) Man of the mountain
Dumonte, Dumount, Dumounte

Duncan (Scottish) A dark warrior
Dunkan, Dunckan, Dunc, Dunk, Dunck

Dundee (Scottish) From the town on the Firth of Tay
Dundea, Dundi, Dundie, Dundy, Dundey

Dung (Vietnamese) A brave man; a heroic man

Dunton (English) From the town on the hill
Duntun, Dunten, Duntan, Duntin, Duntyn

Durin (Norse) In mythology, one of the fathers of the dwarves
Duryn, Duren, Duran, Duron, Durun

Durjaya (Hindi) One who is difficult to defeat

Durrell (English) One who is strong and protective
Durrel, Durell, Durel

Dustin (English / German) From the dusty area / a courageous warrior
Dustyn, Dusten, Dustan, Duston, Dustun, Dusty, Dustey, Dusti

Duvall (French) From the valley
Duval, Duvale

Dwade (English) A dark traveler
Dwaid, Dwaide, Dwayd, Dwayde, Dwaed, Dwaede

Dwight (Flemish) A white- or blond-haired man
Dwite, Dwhite, Dwyght, Dwighte

Dyami (Native American) Resembling an eagle
Dyamie, Dyamy, Dyamey, Dyamee, Dyamea, Dyame

Dyer (English) A creative man
Dier, Dyar, Diar, Dy, Dye, Di, Die

*Dylan (Welsh) Son of the sea
Dyllan, Dylon, Dyllon, Dylen, Dyllen, Dylun, Dyllun, Dylin

Dzigbode (African) One who is patient

E

Eagan (Irish) A fiery man
Eegan, Eagen, Eegen, Eagon, Eegon, Eagun, Eegun

Eagle (Native American) Resembling the bird
Eegle, Eagel, Eegel

Eamon (Irish) Form of Edmund, meaning "a wealthy protector"
Eaman, Eamen, Eamin, Eamyn, Eamun, Eamonn, Eames, Eemon

Ean (Gaelic) Form of John, meaning "God is gracious"
Eion, Eyan, Eyon, Eian

Earl (English) A nobleman
Earle, Erle, Erl, Eorl

Easey (American) An easy-going man
Easy, Easi, Easie, Easee, Easea, Eazey, Eazy, Eazi

Eastman (English) A man from the east
East, Easte, Eeste

^Easton (English) Eastern place
Eastan, Easten, Eastyn

Eckhard (German) Of the brave sword point
Eckard, Eckardt, Eckhardt, Ekkehard, Ekkehardt, Ekhard, Ekhardt

Ed (English) Form of Edward, meaning "a wealthy protector"
Edd, Eddi, Eddie, Eddy, Eddey, Eddee, Eddea, Edi

Edan (Celtic) One who is full of fire
Edon, Edun

Edbert (English) One who is prosperous and bright
Edberte, Edburt, Edburte, Edbirt, Edbirte, Edbyrt, Edbyrte

Edenson (English) Son of Eden
Eadenson, Edensun, Eadensun, Edinson

Edgar (English) A powerful and wealthy spearman
Eadger, Edgardo, Edghur, Edger

Edison (English) Son of Edward
Eddison, Edisun, Eddisun, Edisen, Eddisen, Edisyn, Eddisyn, Edyson

Edlin (Anglo-Saxon) A wealthy friend
Edlinn, Edlinne, Edlyn, Edlynn, Edlynne, Eadlyn, Eadlin, Edlen

Edmund (English) A wealthy protector
Ed, Eddie, Edmond, Eamon

Edom (Hebrew) A red-haired man
Edum, Edam, Edem, Edim, Edym

Edred (Anglo-Saxon) A king
Edread, Edrid, Edryd

Edward (English) A wealthy protector
Ed, Eadward, Edik, Edouard, Eduard, Eduardo, Edvard, Edvardas, Edwardo

Edwardson (English) The son of Edward
Edwardsun, Eadwardsone, Eadwardsun

Edwin (English) A wealthy friend
Edwinn, Edwinne, Edwine, Edwyn, Edwynn, Edwynne, Edwen, Edwenn

Effiom (African) Resembling a crocodile
Efiom, Effyom, Efyom, Effeom, Efeom

Efigenio (Greek) Form of Eugene, meaning "a well-born man"
Ephigenio, Ephigenios, Ephigenius, Efigenios

Efrain (Spanish) Form of Ephraim, meaning "one who is fertile; productive"
Efraine, Efrayn, Efrayne, Efraen, Efraene, Efrane

Efrat (Hebrew) One who is honored
Efratt, Ephrat, Ephratt

Egesa (Anglo-Saxon) One who creates terror
Egessa, Egeslic, Egeslick, Egeslik

Eghert (German) An intelligent man
Egherte, Eghurt, Eghurte, Eghirt, Eghirte, Eghyrt

Egidio (Italian) Resembling a young goat
Egydio, Egideo, Egydeo, Egidiyo, Egydiyo, Egidius

Eilert (Scandinavian) Of the hard point
Elert, Eilart, Elart, Eilort, Elort, Eilurt, Elurt, Eilirt

Eilon (Hebrew) From the oak tree
Eilan, Eilin, Eilyn, Eilen, Eilun

Einar (Scandinavian) A leading warrior
Einer, Ejnar, Einir, Einyr, Einor, Einur, Ejnir, Ejnyr

Einri (Teutonic) An intelligent man
Einrie, Einry, Einrey, Einree, Einrea

Eisig (Hebrew) One who laughs often
Eisyg

Eladio (Spanish) A man from Greece
Eladeo, Eladiyo, Eladeyo

Elbert (English / German) A well-born man / a bright man
Elberte, Elburt, Elburte, Elbirt, Elbirte, Ethelbert, Ethelburt, Ethelbirt

Eldan (English) From the valley of the elves

Eldon (English) From the sacred hill
Eldun

Eldorado (Spanish) The golden man

Eldred (English) An old, wise advisor
Eldrid, Eldryd, Eldrad, Eldrod, Edlrud, Ethelred

Eldrick (English) An old, wise ruler
Eldrik, Eldric, Eldryck, Eldryk, Eldryc, Eldrich

Eleazar (Hebrew) God will help
Elazar, Eleasar, Eliezer, Elazaro, Eleazaro, Elazer

*Eli (Hebrew) One who has ascended; my God on High
Ely

Eliachim (Hebrew) God will establish
Eliakim, Elyachim, Elyakim, Eliakym

Elian (Spanish) A spirited man
Elyan, Elien, Elyen, Elion, Elyon, Eliun, Elyun

Elias (Hebrew) Form of Elijah, meaning "Jehovah is my god"
Eliyas

Elihu (Hebrew) My God is He
Elyhu, Elihue, Elyhue

*TElijah (Hebrew) Jehovah is my God
Elija, Eliyahu, Eljah, Elja, Elyjah, Elyja, Elijuah, Elyjuah

Elimu (African) Having knowledge of science
Elymu, Elimue, Elymue, Elimoo, Elymoo

Elisha (Hebrew) God is my salvation
Elisee, Eliseo, Elisher, Eliso, Elisio, Elysha, Elysee, Elyseo

Elliott (English) Form of Elijah, meaning "Jehovah is my God"
Eliot, Eliott, Elliot, Elyot

Ellory (Cornish) Resembling a swan
Ellorey, Elloree, Ellorea, Ellori, Ellorie, Elory, Elorey

Ellsworth (English) From the nobleman's estate
Elsworth, Ellswerth, Elswerth, Ellswirth, Elswirth, Elzie

Elman (English) A nobleman
Elmann, Ellman, Ellmann

Elmo (English / Latin) A protector / an amiable man
Elmoe, Elmow, Elmowe

Elmot (American) A lovable man
Elmott, Ellmot, Ellmott

Elof (Swedish) The only heir
Eluf, Eloff, Eluff, Elov, Ellov, Eluv, Elluv

Elois (German) A famous warrior
Eloys, Eloyis, Elouis

Elpidio (Spanish) A fearless man; having heart
Elpydio, Elpideo, Elpydeo, Elpidios, Elpydios, Elpidius

Elroy (Irish / English) A red-haired young man / a king
Elroi, Elroye, Elric, Elryc, Elrik, Elryk, Elrick, Elryck

Elston (English) From the nobleman's town
Ellston, Elstun, Ellstun, Elson, Ellson, Elsun, Ellsun

Elton (English) From the old town
Ellton, Eltun, Elltun, Elten, Ellten, Eltin, Elltin, Eltyn

Eluwilussit (Native American) A holy man

Elvey (English) An elf warrior
Elvy, Elvee, Elvea, Elvi, Elvie

Elvis (Scandinavian) One who is wise
Elviss, Elvys, Elvyss

Elzie (English) Form of Ellsworth, meaning "from the nobleman's estate"
Elzi, Elzy, Elzey, Elzee, Elzea, Ellzi, Ellzie, Ellzee

Emest (German) One who is serious
Emeste, Emesto, Emestio, Emestiyo, Emesteo, Emesteyo, Emo, Emst

Emil (Latin) One who is eager; an industrious man
Emelen, Emelio, Emile, Emilian, Emiliano, Emilianus, Emilio, Emilion

Emiliano (Spanish) Form of Emil, meaning "one who is eager"

Emmanuel (Hebrew) God is with us
Manuel, Manny, Em, Eman, Emmannuel

^Emmett (German) A universal man
Emmet, Emmit, Emmitt, Emmot

Emrys (Welsh) An immortal man

Enapay (Native American) A brave man
Enapaye, Enapai, Enapae

Enar (Swedish) A great warrior
Ener, Enir, Enyr, Enor, Enur

Engelbert (German) As bright as an angel
Englebert, Englbert, Engelburt, Engleburt, Englburt, Englebirt, Engelbirt, Englbirt

Enoch (Hebrew) One who is dedicated to God
Enoc, Enok, Enock

Enrique (Spanish) The ruler of
the estate
*Enrico, Enriko, Enricko,
Enriquez, Enrikay, Enreekay,
Enrik, Enric*

Enyeto (Native American) One
who walks like a bear

^**Enzo** (Italian) The ruler of the
estate
Enzio, Enzeo, Enziyo, Enzeyo

Eoin Baiste (Irish) Refers to
John the Baptist

Ephraim (Hebrew) One who is
fertile; productive
*Eff, Efraim, Efram, Efrem,
Efrain*

Eric (Scandinavian) Ever the
ruler
*Erek, Erich, Erick, Erik, Eriq,
Erix, Errick, Eryk*

Ernest (English) One who
is sincere and determined;
serious
*Earnest, Ernesto, Ernestus,
Ernst, Erno, Ernie, Erni, Erney*

Eron (Spanish) Form of Aaron,
meaning "one who is exalted"
Erun, Erin, Eran, Eren, Eryn

Errigal (Gaelic) From the small
church
*Errigel, Errigol, Errigul, Errigil,
Errigyl, Erigal, Erigel, Erigol*

Erskine (Gaelic) From the high
cliff
*Erskin, Erskyne, Erskyn,
Erskein, Erskeine, Erskien,
Erskiene*

Esam (Arabic) A safeguard
Essam

Esben (Scandinavian) Of God
*Esbin, Esbyn, Esban, Esbon,
Esbun*

Esmé (French) One who is
esteemed
*Esmay, Esmaye, Esmai, Esmae,
Esmeling, Esmelyng*

Esmun (American) A kind
man
*Esmon, Esman, Esmen, Esmin,
Esmyn*

Esperanze (Spanish) Filled
with hope
*Esperance, Esperence,
Esperenze, Esperanzo,
Esperenzo*

Estcott (English) From the
eastern cottage
Estcot

Esteban (Spanish) One who is
crowned in victory
*Estebon, Estevan, Estevon,
Estefan, Estefon, Estebe,
Estyban, Estyvan*

*T**Ethan** (Hebrew) One who is
firm and steadfast
*Ethen, Ethin, Ethyn, Ethon,
Ethun, Eitan, Etan, Eithan*

Ethanael (American) God has
given me strength
*Ethaniel, Ethaneal, Ethanail,
Ethanale*

Ethel (Hebrew) One who is
noble
Ethal, Etheal

Etlelooaat (Native American)
One who shouts

Eudocio (Greek) One who is
respected
*Eudoceo, Eudociyo, Eudoceyo,
Eudoco*

***Eugene** (Greek) A well-born
man
*Eugean, Eugenie, Ugene,
Efigenio, Gene, **Owen***

Eulogio (Greek) A reasonable
man
*Eulogiyo, Eulogo, Eulogeo,
Eulogeyo*

Euodias (Greek) Having good
fortune
Euodeas, Euodyas

Euphemios (Greek) One who
is well-spoken
*Eufemio, Eufemius, Euphemio,
Eufemios, Euphemius,
Eufemius*

Euphrates (Turkish) From the
great river
*Eufrates, Euphraites, Eufraites,
Euphraytes, Eufraytes*

Eusebius (Greek) One who is
devout
*Esabio, Esavio, Esavius, Esebio,
Eusabio, Eusaio, Eusebio,
Eusebios*

Eustace (Greek) Having an
abundance of grapes
*Eustache, Eustachios,
Eustachius, Eustachy,
Eustaquio, Eustashe, Eustasius,
Eustatius*

***Evan** (Welsh) Form of John,
meaning "God is gracious"
*Evann, Evans, Even, Evin,
Evon, Evyn, Evian, Evien*

Evander (Greek) A benevolent
man
*Evandor, Evandar, Evandir,
Evandur, Evandyr*

Everett (English) Form of
Everhard, meaning "as strong
as a bear"

Evett (American) A bright man
*Evet, Evatt, Evat, Evitt, Evit,
Evytt, Evyt*

Eyal (Hebrew) Having great
strength

Eze (African) A king

Ezeji (African) The king of yams
Ezejie, Ezejy, Ezejey, Ezejee, Ezejea

Ezekiel (Hebrew) Strengthened by God
Esequiel, Ezechiel, Eziechiele, Eziequel, Ezequiel, Ezekial, Ezekyel, Esquevelle, Zeke

F

Factor (English) A business-man
Facter, Factur, Factir, Factyr, Factar

Fairbairn (Scottish) A fair-haired boy
Fayrbairn, Faerbairn, Fairbaern, Fayrbaern, Faerbaern, Fairbayrn, Fayrbayrn, Faerbayrn

Fairbanks (English) From the bank along the path
Fayrbanks, Faerbanks, Farebanks

Faisal (Arabic) One who is decisive; resolute
Faysal, Faesal, Fasal, Feisal, Faizal, Fasel, Fayzal, Faezal

Fakhir (Arabic) A proud man
Fakheer, Fakhear, Fakheir, Fakhier, Fakhyr, Faakhir, Faakhyr, Fakhr

Fakih (Arabic) A legal expert
Fakeeh, Fakeah, Fakieh, Fakeih, Fakyh

Falco (Latin) Resembling a falcon; one who works with falcons
Falcon, Falconer, Falconner, Falk, Falke, Falken, Falkner, Faulconer

Fam (American) A family-oriented man

Fang (Scottish) From the sheep pen
Faing, Fayng, Faeng

Faraji (African) One who provides consolation
Farajie, Farajy, Farajey, Farajee, Farajea

Fardoragh (Irish) Having dark features

Fargo (American) One who is jaunty
Fargoh, Fargoe, Fargouh

Farha (Arabic) Filled with happiness
Farhah, Farhad, Farhan, Farhat, Farhani, Farhanie, Farhany, Farhaney

Fariq (Arabic) One who holds rank as lieutenant general
Fareeq, Fareaq, Fareiq, Farieq, Faryq, Farik, Fareek, Fareak

Farnell (English) From the fern hill
Farnel, Farnall, Farnal, Fernauld, Farnauld, Fernald, Farnald

Farold (English) A mighty traveler
Farould, Farald, Farauld, Fareld

Farran (Irish / Arabic / English) Of the land / a baker / one who is adventurous
Fairran, Fayrran, Faerran, Farren, Farrin, Farron, Ferrin, Ferron

Farrar (English) A blacksmith
Farar, Farrer, Farrier, Ferrar, Ferrars, Ferrer, Ferrier, Farer

Farro (Italian) Of the grain
Farroe, Faro, Faroe, Farrow, Farow

Fatik (Indian) Resembling a crystal
Fateek, Fateak, Fatyk, Fatiek, Fateik

Faust (Latin) Having good luck
Fauste, Faustino, Fausto, Faustos, Faustus, Fauston, Faustin, Fausten

Fawcett (American) An audacious man
Fawcet, Fawcette, Fawcete, Fawce, Fawci, Fawcie, Fawcy, Fawcey

Fawwaz (Arabic) A successful man
Fawaz, Fawwad, Fawad

Fay (Irish) Resembling a raven
Faye, Fai, Fae, Feich

Februus (Latin) A pagan god

Fedor (Russian) A gift from God
Faydor, Feodor, Fyodor, Fedyenka, Fyodr, Fydor, Fjodor

Feechi (African) One who worships God
Feechie, Feechy, Feechey, Feechee, Feachi, Feachie

Feivel (Hebrew) The brilliant one
Feival, Feivol, Feivil, Feivyl, Feivul, Feiwel, Feiwal, Feiwol

Felim (Gaelic) One who is always good
Felym, Feidhlim, Felimy, Felimey, Felimee, Felimea, Felimi, Felimie

Felipe (Spanish) Form of Phillip, meaning "one who loves horses"
Felippe, Filip, Filippo, Fillip, Flip, Fulop, Fullop, Fulip

Frederick (German) A peaceful ruler
Fred, Fredrick, Federico, Federigo, Fredek, Frederic, Frederich, Frederico, Frederik, Fredric

Freeborn (English) One who was born a free man
Freeborne, Freebourn, Freebourne, Freeburn, Freeburne, Free

Fremont (French) The protector of freedom
Freemont, Fremonte

Frigyes (Hungarian) A mighty and peaceful ruler

Frode (Norse) A wise man
Froad, Froade

Froyim (Hebrew) A kind man
Froiim

Fructuoso (Spanish) One who is fruitful
Fructo, Fructoso, Fructuso

Fu (Chinese) A wealthy man

Fudail (Arabic) Of high moral character
Fudaile, Fudayl, Fudayle, Fudale, Fudael, Fudaele

Fulbright (English) A brilliant man
Fullbright, Fulbrite, Fullbrite, Fulbryte, Fullbryte, Fulbert, Fullbert

Fulki (Indian) A spark
Fulkie, Fulkey, Fulky, Fulkee, Fulkea

Fullerton (English) From Fuller's town
Fullertun, Fullertin, Fullertyn, Fullertan, Fullerten

Fursey (Gaelic) The name of a missionary saint
Fursy, Fursi, Fursie, Fursee, Fursea

Fyfe (Scottish) A man from Fifeshire
Fife, Fyffe, Fiffe, Fibh

Fyren (Anglo-Saxon) A wicked man
Fyrin, Fyryn, Fyran, Fyron, Fyrun

G

Gabai (Hebrew) A delightful man

Gabbana (Italian) A creative man
Gabbanah, Gabana, Gabanah, Gabbanna, Gabanna

Gabbo (English) To joke or scoff
Gabboe, Gabbow, Gabbowe

Gabor (Hebrew) God is my strength
Gabur, Gabar, Gaber, Gabir, Gabyr

Gabra (African) An offering
Gabre

*ᵀ**Gabriel** (Hebrew) A hero of God
Gabrian, Gabriele, Gabrielli, Gabriello, Gaby, Gab, Gabbi, Gabbie

Gad (Hebrew / Native American) Having good fortune / from the juniper tree
Gadi, Gadie, Gady, Gadey, Gadee, Gadea

Gadiel (Arabic) God is my fortune
Gadiell, Gadiele, Gadielle, Gaddiel, Gaddiell, Gadil, Gadeel, Gadeal

Gaffney (Irish) Resembling a calf
Gaffny, Gaffni, Gaffnie, Gaffnee, Gaffnea

Gage (French) Of the pledge
Gaige, Gaege, Gauge

Gahuj (African) A hunter

Gair (Gaelic) A man of short stature
Gayr, Gaer, Gaire, Gayre, Gaere, Gare

Gaius (Latin) One who rejoices
Gaeus

Galal (Arabic) A majestic man
Galall, Gallal, Gallall

Galbraith (Irish) A foreigner; a Scot
Galbrait, Galbreath, Gallbraith, Gallbreath, Galbraithe, Gallbraithe, Galbreathe, Gallbreathe

Gale (Irish / English) A foreigner / one who is cheerful
Gail, Gaill, Gaille, Gaile, Gayl, Gayle, Gaylle, Gayll

Galen (Greek) A healer; one who is calm
Gaelan, Gaillen, Galan, Galin, Galyn, Gaylen, Gaylin, Gaylinn

Gali (Hebrew) From the fountain
Galie, Galy, Galey, Galee, Galea, Galeigh

Galip (Turkish) A victorious man
Galyp, Galup, Galep, Galap, Galop

Gallagher (Gaelic) An eager helper
Gallaghor, Gallaghar, Gallaghur, Gallaghir, Gallaghyr, Gallager, Gallagar, Gallagor

Galt (English) From the high, wooded land
Galte, Gallt, Gallte

Galtero (Spanish) Form of Walter, meaning "the commander of the army"
Galterio, Galteriyo, Galtereo, Galtereyo, Galter, Galteros, Galterus, Gualterio

Gamaliel (Hebrew) God's reward
Gamliel, Gamalyel, Gamlyel, Gamli, Gamlie, Gamly, Gamley, Gamlee

Gameel (Arabic) A handsome man
Gameal, Gamil, Gamiel, Gameil, Gamyl

Gamon (American) One who enjoys playing games
Gamun, Gamen, Gaman, Gamin, Gamyn, Gammon, Gammun, Gamman

Gan (Chinese) A wanderer

Gandy (American) An adventurer
Gandey, Gandi, Gandie, Gandee, Gandea

Gann (English) One who defends with a spear
Gan

Gannon (Gaelic) A fair-skinned man
Gannun, Gannen, Gannan, Gannin, Gannyn, Ganon, Ganun, Ganin

Garcia (Spanish) One who is brave in battle
Garce, Garcy, Garcey, Garci, Garcie, Garcee, Garcea

Gared (English) Form of Gerard, meaning "one who is mighty with a spear"
Garad, Garid, Garyd, Garod, Garud

Garman (English) A spearman
Garmann, Garmen, Garmin, Garmon, Garmun, Garmyn, Gar, Garr

Garrett (English) Form of Gerard, meaning "one who is mighty with a spear"
Garett, Garret, Garretson, Garritt, Garrot, Garrott, Gerrit, Gerritt

Garrison (French) Prepared
Garris, Garrish, Garry, Gary

Garson (English) The son of Gar (Garrett, Garrison, etc.)
Garrson, Garsen, Garrsen, Garsun, Garrsun, Garsone, Garrsone

Garth (Scandinavian) The keeper of the garden
Garthe, Gart, Garte

Garvey (Gaelic) A rough but peaceful man
Garvy, Garvee, Garvea, Garvi, Garvie, Garrvey, Garrvy, Garrvee

Garvin (English) A friend with a spear
Garvyn, Garven, Garvan, Garvon, Garvun

Gary (English) One who wields a spear
Garey, Gari, Garie, Garea, Garee, Garry, Garrey, Garree

Gassur (Arabic) A courageous man
Gassor, Gassir, Gassyr, Gassar, Gasser

Gaston (French) A man from Gascony
Gastun, Gastan, Gasten, Gascon, Gascone, Gasconey, Gasconi, Gasconie

Gate (American) One who is close-minded
Gates, Gait, Gaite, Gaits

*ᵀGavin (Welsh) A little white falcon
Gavan, Gaven, Gavino, Gavyn, Gavynn, Gavon, Gavun, Gavyno

Gazali (African) A mystic
Gazalie, Gazaly, Gazaley, Gazalee, Gazalea, Gazaleigh

Geirleif (Norse) A descendant of the spear
Geirleaf, Geerleif, Geerleaf

Geirstein (Norse) One who wields a rock-hard spear
Geerstein, Gerstein

Gellert (Hungarian) A mighty soldier
Gellart, Gellirt, Gellyrt, Gellort, Gellurt

Genaro (Latin) A dedicated man
Genaroh, Genaroe, Genarow, Genarowe

Gene (English) Form of Eugene, meaning "a well-born man"
Genio, Geno, Geneo, Gino, Ginio, Gineo

Genet (African) From Eden
Genat, Genit, Genyt, Genot, Genut

Genoah (Italian) From the city of Genoa
Genoa, Genovise, Genovize

Geoffrey (English) Form of Jeffrey, meaning "a man of peace"
Geffrey, Geoff, Geoffery, Geoffroy, Geoffry, Geofrey, Geofferi, Geofferie

George (Greek) One who works the earth; a farmer
Georas, Geordi, Geordie, Georg, Georges, Georgi, Georgie, Georgio, Yegor, Jurgen, Joren

Gerald (German) One who rules with the spear
Jerald, Garald, Garold, Gearalt, Geralde, Geraldo, Geraud, Gere, Gerek

Gerard (French) One who is mighty with a spear
Gerord, Gerrard, Gared, Garrett

Geremia (Italian) Form of Jeremiah, meaning "one who is exalted by the Lord"
Geremiah, Geremias, Geremija, Geremiya, Geremyah, Geramiah, Geramia

Germain (French / Latin) A man from Germany / one who is brotherly
Germaine, German, Germane, Germanicus, Germano, Germanus, Germayn, Germayne

Gerry (German) Short form of names beginning with Ger-, such as Gerald or Gerard
Gerrey, Gerri, Gerrie, Gerrea, Gerree

Gershom (Hebrew) One who has been exiled
Gersham, Gershon, Gershoom, Gershem, Gershim, Gershym, Gershum, Gersh

Getachew (African) Their master

Ghazi (Arabic) An invader; a conqueror
Ghazie, Ghazy, Ghazey, Ghazee, Ghazea

Ghoukas (Armenian) Form of Lucas, meaning "a man from Lucania"
Ghukas

Giancarlo (Italian) One who is gracious and mighty
Gyancarlo

^**Gideon** (Hebrew) A mighty warrior; one who fells trees
Gideone, Gidi, Gidon, Gidion, Gid, Gidie, Gidy, Gidey

Gilam (Hebrew) The joy of the people
Gylam, Gilem, Gylem, Gilim, Gylim, Gilym, Gylym, Gilom

Gilbert (French / English) Of the bright promise / one who is trustworthy
Gib, Gibb, Gil, Gilberto, Gilburt, Giselbert, Giselberto, Giselbertus

Gildas (Irish / English) One who serves God / the golden one
Gyldas, Gilda, Gylda, Gilde, Gylde, Gildea, Gyldea, Gildes

Giles (Greek) Resembling a young goat
Gyles, Gile, Gil, Gilles, Gillis, Gilliss, Gyle, Gyl

Gill (Gaelic) A servant
Gyll, Gilly, Gilley, Gillee, Gillea, Gilli, Gillie, Ghill

Gillivray (Scottish) A servant of God
Gillivraye, Gillivrae, Gillivrai

Gilmat (Scottish) One who wields a sword
Gylmat, Gilmet, Gylmet

Gilmer (English) A famous hostage
Gilmar, Gilmor, Gilmur, Gilmir, Gilmyr, Gillmer, Gillmar, Gillmor

Gilon (Hebrew) Filled with joy
Gilun, Gilen, Gilan, Gilin, Gilyn, Gilo

Ginton (Arabic) From the garden
Gintun, Gintan, Ginten, Gintin, Gintyn

Giovanni (Italian) Form of John, meaning "God is gracious"
Geovani, Geovanney, Geovanni, Geovanny, Geovany, Giannino, Giovan, Giovani, Yovanny

Giri (Indian) From the mountain
Girie, Giry, Girey, Giree, Girea

Girvan (Gaelic) The small rough one
Gyrvan, Girven, Gyrven, Girvin, Gyrvin, Girvyn, Gyrvyn, Girvon

Giulio (Italian) One who is youthful
Giuliano, Giuleo

Giuseppe (Italian) Form of Joseph, meaning "God will add"
Giuseppi, Giuseppie, Giuseppy, Giuseppee, Giuseppea, Giuseppey, Guiseppe, Guiseppi

Gizmo (American) One who is playful
Gismo, Gyzmo, Gysmo, Gizmoe, Gismoe, Gyzmoe, Gysmoe

Glade (English) From the
clearing in the woods
*Glayd, Glayde, Glaid, Glaide,
Glaed, Glaede*

Glaisne (Irish) One who is
calm; serene
*Glaisny, Glaisney, Glaisni,
Glaisnie, Glaisnee, Glasny,
Glasney, Glasni*

Glasgow (Scottish) From the
city in Scotland
Glasgo

Glen (Gaelic) From the secluded
narrow valley
*Glenn, Glennard, Glennie,
Glennon, Glenny, Glin, Glinn,
Glyn*

Glover (English) One who
makes gloves
*Glovar, Glovir, Glovyr, Glovur,
Glovor*

Gobind (Sanskrit) The cow
finder
*Gobinde, Gobinda, Govind,
Govinda, Govinde*

Goby (American) An
audacious man
*Gobi, Gobie, Gobey, Gobee,
Gobea*

Godfrey (German) God is
peace
*Giotto, Godefroi, Godfry,
Godofredo, Goffredo, Gottfrid,
Gottfried, Godfried*

Godfried (German) God is
peace
Godfreed, Gjord

Gogo (African) A grandfa-
therly man

Goldwin (English) A golden
friend
*Goldwine, Goldwinn,
Goldwinne, Goldwen,
Goldwenn, Goldwenne,
Goldwyn, Goldwynn*

Goode (English) An upstand-
ing man
*Good, Goodi, Goodie, Goody,
Goodey, Goodee, Goodea*

Gordon (Gaelic) From the
great hill; a hero
*Gorden, Gordin, Gordyn,
Gordun, Gordun, Gordi,
Gordie, Gordee*

Gormley (Irish) The blue
spearman
*Gormly, Gormlee, Gormlea,
Gormleah, Gormleigh, Gormli,
Gormlie, Gormaly*

Goro (Japanese) The fifth-born child

Gotzon (Basque) A heavenly messenger; an angel

Gower (Welsh) One who is pure; chaste
Gwyr, Gowyr, Gowir, Gowar, Gowor, Gowur

Gozal (Hebrew) Resembling a baby bird
Gozall, Gozel, Gozell, Gozale, Gozele

Grady (Gaelic) One who is famous; noble
Gradey, Gradee, Gradea, Gradi, Gradie, Graidy, Graidey, Graidee

Graham (English) From the gravelled area; from the gray home
Graem

Grand (English) A superior man
Grande, Grandy, Grandey, Grandi, Grandie, Grandee, Grandea, Grander

Granger (English) A farmer
Grainger, Graynger, Graenger, Grange, Graynge, Graenge, Grainge, Grangere

Grant (English) A tall man; a great man
Grante, Graent

Granville (French) From the large village
Granvylle, Granvil, Granvyl, Granvill, Granvyll, Granvile, Granvyle, Grenvill

Gray (English) A gray-haired man
Graye, Grai, Grae, Greye, Grey, Graylon, Graylen, Graylin

^*Grayson (English) The son of a gray-haired man
*Graysen, Graysun, Graysin, **Greyson**, Graysan, Graison, Graisun, Graisen*

Greenwood (English) From the green forest
Greenwode

Gregory (Greek) One who is vigilant; watchful
Greg, Greggory, Greggy, Gregori, Gregorie, Gregry, Grigori

Gremian (Anglo-Saxon) One who enrages others
Gremien, Gremean, Gremyan

Gridley (English) From the flat meadow
Gridly, Gridlee, Gridlea, Gridleah, Gridleigh, Gridli, Gridlie

Griffin (Latin) Having a
hooked nose
*Griff, Griffen, Griffon, Gryffen,
Gryffin, Gryphen*

Griffith (Welsh) A mighty chief
Griffyth, Gryffith, Gryffyth

Grimsley (English) From the
dark meadow
*Grimsly, Grimslee, Grimslea,
Grimsleah, Grimsleigh,
Grimsli, Grimslie*

Griswold (German) From the
gray forest
*Griswald, Gryswold, Gryswald,
Greswold, Greswald*

Guban (African) One who has
been burnt
*Guben, Gubin, Gubyn, Gubon,
Gubun*

Guedado (African) One who is
unwanted

Guerdon (English) A warring
man
*Guerdun, Guerdan, Guerden,
Guerdin, Guerdyn*

Guido (Italian) One who acts
as a guide
*Guidoh, Gwedo, Gwido,
Gwydo, Gweedo*

Guillaume (French) Form of
William, meaning "the deter-
mined protector"
*Gillermo, Guglielmo,
Guilherme, Guillermo, Gwillyn,
Gwilym, Guglilmo*

Gulshan (Hindi) From the
gardens

Gunner (Scandinavian) A bold
warrior
*Gunnar, Gunnor, Gunnur,
Gunnir, Gunnyr*

Gunnolf (Norse) A warrior
wolf
Gunolf, Gunnulf, Gunulf

Gur (Hebrew) Resembling a
lion cub
*Guryon, Gurion, Guriel,
Guriell, Guryel, Guryell, Guri,
Gurie*

Gurpreet (Indian) A devoted
follower
*Gurpreat, Gurpriet, Gurpreit,
Gurprit, Gurpryt*

Guru (Indian) A teacher; a religious head

Gurutz (Basque) Of the holy
cross
Guruts

Gus (German) A respected
man; one who is exalted
Guss

Gustav (Scandinavian) Of the staff of the gods
Gus, Gustave, Gussie, Gustaf, Gustof, Tavin

Gusty (American) Of the wind; a revered man
Gustey, Gustee, Gustea, Gusti, Gustie, Gusto

Guwayne (American) Form of Wayne, meaning "one who builds wagons"
Guwayn, Guwain, Guwaine, Guwaen, Guwaene, Guwane

Gwalchmai (Welsh) A battle hawk

Gwandoya (African) Suffering a miserable fate

Gwydion (Welsh) In mythology, a magician
Gwydeon, Gwydionne, Gwydeonne

Gylfi (Scandinavian) A king
Gylfie, Gylfee, Gylfea, Gylfi, Gylfie, Gylphi, Gylphie, Gylphey

Gypsy (English) A wanderer; a nomad
Gipsee, Gipsey, Gipsy, Gypsi, Gypsie, Gypsey, Gypsee, Gipsi

H

Habimama (African) One who believes in God
Habymama

Hadden (English) From the heather-covered hill
Haddan, Haddon, Haddin, Haddyn, Haddun

Hadriel (Hebrew) The splendor of God
Hadryel, Hadriell, Hadryell

Hadwin (English) A friend in war
Hadwinn, Hadwinne, Hadwen, Hadwenn, Hadwenne, Hadwyn, Hadwynn, Hadwynne

Hafiz (Arabic) A protector
Haafiz, Hafeez, Hafeaz, Hafiez, Hafeiz, Hafyz, Haphiz, Haaphiz

Hagar (Hebrew) A wanderer

Hagen (Gaelic) One who is youthful
Haggen, Hagan, Haggan, Hagin, Haggin, Hagyn, Haggyn, Hagon

Hagop (Armenian) Form of James, meaning "he who supplants"
Hagup, Hagap, Hagep, Hagip, Hagyp

Hagos (African) Filled with happiness

Hahnee (Native American) A beggar
Hahnea, Hahni, Hahnie, Hahny, Hahney

Haim (Hebrew) A giver of life
Hayim, Hayyim

Haines (English) From the vined cottage; from the hedged enclosure
Haynes, Haenes, Hanes, Haine, Hayne, Haene, Hane

Hajari (African) One who takes flight
Hajarie, Hajary, Hajarey, Hajaree, Hajarea

Haji (African) Born during the hajj
Hajie, Hajy, Hajey, Hajee, Hajea

Hakan (Norse / Native American) One who is noble / a fiery man

Hakim (Arabic) One who is wise; intelligent
Hakeem, Hakeam, Hakeim, Hakiem, Hakym

Hal (English) A form of Henry, meaning "the ruler of the house"; a form of Harold, meaning "the ruler of an army"

Halford (English) From the hall by the ford
Hallford, Halfurd, Hallfurd, Halferd, Hallferd

Halil (Turkish) A beloved friend
Haleel, Haleal, Haleil, Haliel, Halyl

Halla (African) An unexpected gift
Hallah, Hala, Halah

Hallberg (Norse) From the rocky mountain
Halberg, Hallburg, Halburg

Halle (Norse) As solid as a rock

Halley (English) From the hall near the meadow
Hally, Halli, Hallie, Halleigh, Hallee, Halleah, Hallea

Halliwell (English) From the holy spring
Haligwell

Hallward (English) The guardian of the hall
Halward, Hallwerd, Halwerd, Hallwarden, Halwarden, Hawarden, Haward, Hawerd

Hamid (Arabic / Indian) A praiseworthy man / a beloved friend
Hameed, Hamead, Hameid, Hamied, Hamyd, Haamid

Hamidi (Swahili) One who is commendable
Hamidie, Hamidy, Hamidey, Hamidee, Hamidea, Hamydi, Hamydie, Hamydee

Hamilton (English) From the flat-topped hill
Hamylton, Hamiltun, Hamyltun, Hamilten, Hamylten, Hamelton, Hameltun, Hamelten

Hamlet (German) From the little home
Hamlett, Hammet, Hammett, Hamnet, Hamnett, Hamlit, Hamlitt, Hamoelet

Hammer (German) One who makes hammers; a carpenter
Hammar, Hammor, Hammur, Hammir, Hammyr

Hampden (English) From the home in the valley
Hampdon, Hampdan, Hampdun, Hampdyn, Hampdin

Hancock (English) One who owns a farm
Hancok, Hancoc

Hanford (English) From the high ford
Hanferd, Hanfurd, Hanforde, Hanferde, Hanfurde

Hanisi (Swahili) Born on a Thursday
Hanisie, Hanisy, Hanisey, Hanisee, Hanisea, Hanysi, Hanysie, Hanysy

Hank (English) Form of Henry, meaning "the ruler of the house"
Hanke, Hanks, Hanki, Hankie, Hankee, Hankea, Hanky, Hankey

Hanley (English) From the high meadow
Hanly, Hanleigh, Hanleah, Hanlea, Hanlie, Hanli

Hanoch (Hebrew) One who is dedicated
Hanock, Hanok, Hanoc

Hanraoi (Irish) Form of Henry, meaning "the ruler of the house"

Hansraj (Hindi) The swan king

Hardik (Indian) One who has heart
Hardyk, Hardick, Hardyck, Hardic, Hardyc

Hare (English) Resembling a rabbit

Harence (English) One who is swift
Harince, Harense, Harinse

Hari (Indian) Resembling a lion
Harie, Hary, Harey, Haree, Harea

Harim (Arabic) A superior man
Hareem, Haream, Hariem, Hareim, Harym

Harkin (Irish) Having dark red hair
Harkyn, Harken, Harkan, Harkon, Harkun

Harlemm (American) A soulful man
Harlam, Harlom, Harlim, Harlym, Harlem

Harlow (English) From the army on the hill
Harlowe, Harlo, Harloe

Harold (Scandinavian) The ruler of an army
Hal, Harald, Hareld, Harry, Darold

Harper (English) One who plays or makes harps
Harpur, Harpar, Harpir, Harpyr, Harpor, Hearpere

Harrington (English) From Harry's town; from the herring town
Harringtun, Harryngton, Harryngtun, Harington, Haringtun, Haryngton, Haryntun

Harrison (English) The son of Harry
Harrisson, Harris, Harriss, Harryson

Harshad (Indian) A bringer of joy
Harsh, Harshe, Harsho, Harshil, Harshyl, Harshit, Harshyt

Hartford (English) From the stag's ford
Harteford, Hartferd, Harteferd, Hartfurd, Hartefurd, Hartforde, Harteforde, Hartferde

Haru (Japanese) Born during the spring

Harvey (English / French) One who is ready for battle / a strong man
Harvy, Harvi, Harvie, Harvee, Harvea, Harv, Harve, Hervey

Hasim (Arabic) One who is decisive
Haseem, Haseam, Hasiem, Haseim, Hasym

Haskel (Hebrew) An intelligent man
Haskle, Haskell, Haskil, Haskill, Haske, Hask

Hasso (German) Of the sun
Hassoe, Hassow, Hassowe

Hassun (Native American) As solid as a stone

Hastiin (Native American) A man

Hastin (Hindi) Resembling an elephant
Hasteen, Hastean, Hastien, Hastein, Hastyn

Hawes (English) From the hedged place
Haws, Hayes, Hays, Hazin, Hazen, Hazyn, Hazon, Hazan

Hawiovi (Native American) One who descends on a ladder
Hawiovie, Hawiovy, Hawiovey, Hawiovee, Hawiovea

Hawkins (English) Resembling a small hawk
Haukins, Hawkyns, Haukyn

Hawthorne (English) From the hawthorn tree
Hawthorn

*ᵀHayden (English) From the hedged valley
Haydan, Haydon, Haydun, Haydin, Haydyn, Haden, Hadan, Hadon

Haye (Scottish) From the stockade
Hay, Hae, Hai

Hazaiah (Hebrew) God will decide
Hazaia, Haziah, Hazia

Hazleton (English) From the hazel-tree town
Hazelton, Hazletun, Hazelton, Hazleten, Hazelten

Heath (English) From the untended land of flowering shrubs
Heathe, Heeth, Heethe

Heaton (English) From the town on high ground
Heatun, Heeton, Heetun, Heaten, Heeten

Heber (Hebrew) A partner or companion
Heeber, Hebar, Heebar, Hebor, Heebor, Hebur, Heebur, Hebir

Hector (Greek) One who is steadfast; in mythology, the prince of Troy
Hecter, Hekter, Heckter

Helio (Greek) Son of the sun
Heleo, Helios, Heleos

Hem (Indian) The golden son

Hemendu (Indian) Born
beneath the golden moon
Hemendue, Hemendoo

Hemi (Maori) Form of James,
meaning "he who supplants"
*Hemie, Hemy, Hemee, Hemea,
Hemey*

Henderson (Scottish) The son
of Henry
*Hendrie, Hendries, Hendron,
Hendri, Hendry, Hendrey,
Hendree, Hendrea*

Hendrick (English) Form of
Henry, meaning "the ruler of
the house"
*Hendryck, Hendrik, Hendryk,
Hendric, Hendryc*

Henley (English) From the
high meadow
*Henly, Henleigh, Henlea,
Henleah, Henlee, Henli, Henlie*

*ᵀHenry (German) The ruler of
the house
*Hal, Hank, Harry, Henny,
Henree, Henri, Hanraoi,
Hendrick*

Heraldo (Spanish) Of the
divine

Hercules (Greek) In mythol-
ogy, a son of Zeus who pos-
sessed superhuman strength
*Herakles, Hercule, Herculi,
Herculie, Herculy, Herculey,
Herculee*

Herman (German) A soldier
*Hermon, Hermen, Hermun,
Hermin, Hermyn, Hermann,
Hermie*

Herne (English) Resembling
a heron
Hern, Hearn, Hearne

Hero (Greek) The brave
defender
Heroe, Herow, Herowe

Hershel (Hebrew) Resembling
a deer
*Hersch, Herschel, Herschell,
Hersh, Hertzel, Herzel, Herzl,
Heschel*

Herwin (Teutonic) A friend of
war
*Herwinn, Herwinne, Herwen,
Herwenn, Herwenne, Herwyn,
Herwynn, Herwynne*

Hesed (Hebrew) A kind man

Hesutu (Native American) A
rising yellow-jacket nest
Hesutou, Hesoutou

Hewson (English) The son of
Hugh
Hewsun

Hiawatha (Native American) He who makes rivers
Hiawathah, Hyawatha, Hiwatha, Hywatha

Hickok (American) A famous frontier marshal
Hickock, Hickoc, Hikock, Hikoc, Hikok, Hyckok, Hyckock, Hyckoc

Hidalgo (Spanish) The noble one
Hydalgo

Hideaki (Japanese) A clever man; having wisdom
Hideakie, Hideaky, Hideakey, Hideakee, Hideakea

Hieronim (Polish) Form of Jerome, meaning "of the sacred name"
Hieronym, Hieronymos, Hieronimos, Heronim, Heronym, Heronymos, Heronimos

Hietamaki (Finnish) From the sand hill
Hietamakie, Hietamaky, Hietamakey, Hietamakee, Hietamakea

Hieu (Vietnamese) A pious man

Hikmat (Islamic) Filled with wisdom
Hykmat

Hildefuns (German) One who is ready for battle
Hildfuns, Hyldefuns, Hyldfuns

Hillel (Hebrew) One who is praised
Hyllel, Hillell, Hyllell, Hilel, Hylel, Hilell, Hylell

Hiranmay (Indian) The golden one
Hiranmaye, Hiranmai, Hiranmae, Hyranmay, Hyranmaye, Hyranmai, Hyranmae

Hiroshi (Japanese) A generous man
Hiroshie, Hiroshy, Hiroshey, Hiroshee, Hiroshea, Hyroshi, Hyroshie, Hyroshey

Hirsi (African) An amulet
Hirsie, Hirsy, Hirsey, Hirsee, Hirsea

Hisoka (Japanese) One who is secretive
Hysoka, Hisokie, Hysokie, Hisoki, Hysoki, Hisokey, Hysokey, Hisoky

Hitakar (Indian) One who wishes others well
Hitakarin, Hitakrit

Hobart (American) Form of
Hubert, meaning "having a
shining intellect"
*Hobarte, Hoebart, Hoebarte,
Hobert, Hoberte, Hoburt,
Hoburte, Hobirt*

Hohberht (German) One who
is high and bright
*Hohbert, Hohburt, Hohbirt,
Hohbyrt, Hoh*

Holcomb (English) From the
deep valley
Holcom, Holcombe

Holden (English) From a
hollow in the valley
Holdan, Holdyn, Holdon

Holland (American) From the
Netherlands
*Hollend, Hollind, Hollynd,
Hollande, Hollende, Hollinde,
Hollynde*

Hollis (English) From the
holly tree
*Hollys, Holliss, Hollyss,
Hollace, Hollice, Holli, Hollie,
Holly*

Holman (English) A man from
the valley
*Holmann, Holmen, Holmin,
Holmyn, Holmon, Holmun*

Holt (English) From the forest
*Holte, Holyt, Holyte, Holter,
Holtar, Holtor, Holtur, Holtir*

Honaw (Native American)
Resembling a bear
Honawe, Honau

Hondo (African) A warring
man
Hondoh, Honda, Hondah

Honesto (Spanish) One who is
honest
*Honestio, Honestiyo, Honesteo,
Honesteyo, Honestoh*

Honon (Native American)
Resembling a bear
*Honun, Honen, Honan,
Honin, Honyn*

Honovi (Native American)
Having great strength
*Honovie, Honovy, Honovey,
Honovee, Honovea*

Honza (Czech) A gift from
God

Horsley (English) From the
horse meadow
*Horsly, Horslea, Horsleah,
Horslee, Horsleigh, Horsli,
Horslie*

Horst (German) From the
thicket
*Horste, Horsten, Horstan,
Horstin, Horstyn, Horston,
Horstun, Horstman*

Hoshi (Japanese) Resembling a star
Hoshiko, Hoshyko, Hoshie, Hoshee, Hoshea, Hoshy, Hoshey

Hototo (Native American) One who whistles; a warrior spirit that sings

Houston (Gaelic / English) From Hugh's town / from the town on the hill
Huston, Houstyn, Hustin, Husten, Hustin, Houstun

Howard (English) The guardian of the home
Howerd, Howord, Howurd, Howird, Howyrd, Howi, Howie, Howy

Howi (Native American) Resembling a turtle dove

Hrothgar (Anglo-Saxon) A king
Hrothgarr, Hrothegar, Hrothegarr, Hrothgare, Hrothegare

Hubert (German) Having a shining intellect
Hobart, Huberte, Huburt, Huburte, Hubirt, Hubirte, Hubyrt, Hubyrte, Hubie, Uberto

Hudson (English) The son of Hugh; from the river
Hudsun, Hudsen, Hudsan, Hudsin, Hudsyn

Hugin (Norse) A thoughtful man
Hugyn, Hugen, Hugan, Hugon, Hugun

Humam (Arabic) A generous and brave man

Hungan (Haitian) A spirit master or priest
Hungen, Hungon, Hungun, Hungin, Hungyn

Hungas (Irish) A vigorous man

THunter** (English) A great huntsman and provider
Huntar, Huntor, Huntur, Huntir, Huntyr, Hunte, Hunt, Hunting

Husky (American) A big man; a manly man
Huski, Huskie, Huskey, Huskee, Huskea, Husk, Huske

Huslu (Native American) Resembling a hairy bear
Huslue, Huslou

Husto (Spanish) A righteous man
Hustio, Husteo, Hustiyo, Husteyo

Huynh (Vietnamese) An older brother

Iakovos (Hebrew) Form of Jacob, meaning "he who supplants"
Iakovus, Iakoves, Iakovas, Iakovis, Iakovys

*Ian (Gaelic) Form of John, meaning "God is gracious"
Iain, Iaine, Iayn, Iayne, Iaen, Iaene, Iahn

Iavor (Bulgarian) From the sycamore tree
Iaver, Iavur, Iavar, Iavir, Iavyr

^Ibrahim (Arabic) Form of Abraham, meaning "father of a multitude; father of nations"
Ibraheem, Ibraheim, Ibrahiem, Ibraheam, Ibrahym

Ichabod (Hebrew) The glory has gone
Ikabod, Ickabod, Icabod, Ichavod, Ikavod, Icavod, Ickavod, Icha

Ichtaca (Nahuatl) A secretive man
Ichtaka, Ichtacka

Ida (Anglo-Saxon) A king
Idah

Idi (African) Born during the holiday of Idd
Idie, Idy, Idey, Idee, Idea

Ido (Arabic / Hebrew) A mighty man / to evaporate
Iddo, Idoh, Iddoh

Idris (Welsh) An eager lord
Idrys, Idriss, Idrisse, Idryss, Idrysse

Iefan (Welsh) Form of John, meaning "God is gracious"
Iefon, Iefen, Iefin, Iefyn, Iefun, Ifan, Ifon, Ifen

Ifor (Welsh) An archer
Ifore, Ifour, Ifoure

Igasho (Native American) A wanderer
Igashoe, Igashow, Igashowe

Ignatius (Latin) A fiery man; one who is ardent
Ignac, Ignace, Ignacio, Ignacius, Ignatious, Ignatz, Ignaz, Ignazio

Igor (Scandinavian / Russian) A hero / Ing's soldier
Igoryok

Ihit (Indian) One who is honored
Ihyt, Ihitt, Ihytt

Ihsan (Arabic) A charitable man
Ihsann, Ihsen, Ihsin, Ihsyn, Ihson, Ihsun

Ike (Hebrew) Form of Isaac, meaning "full of laughter"
Iki, Ikie, Iky, Ikey, Ikee, Ikea

^Iker (Basque) A visitor
Ikar, Ikir, Ikyr, Ikor, Ikur

Ilario (Italian) A cheerful man
Ilareo, Ilariyo, Ilareyo, Ilar, Ilarr, Ilari, Ilarie, Ilary

Ilhuitl (Nahuatl) Born during the daytime

Illanipi (Native American) An amazing man
Illanipie, Illanipy, Illanipey, Illanipee, Illanipea

Iluminado (Spanish) One who shines brightly
Illuminado, Iluminato, Illuminato, Iluminados, Iluminatos, Illuminados, Illuminatos

Imaran (Indian) Having great strength
Imaren, Imaron, Imarun, Imarin, Imaryn

Inaki (Basque) An ardent man
Inakie, Inaky, Inakey, Inakee, Inakea, Inacki, Inackie, Inackee

Ince (Hungarian) One who is innocent
Inse

Indiana (English) From the land of the Indians; from the state of Indiana
Indianna, Indyana, Indyanna

Ingemar (Scandinavian) The son of Ing
Ingamar, Ingemur, Ingmar, Ingmur, Ingar, Ingemer, Ingmer

Inger (Scandinavian) One who is fertile
Inghar, Ingher

Ingo (Scandinavian / Danish) A lord / from the meadow
Ingoe, Ingow, Ingowe

Ingram (Scandinavian) A raven of peace
Ingra, Ingrem, Ingrim, Ingrym, Ingrum, Ingrom, Ingraham, Ingrahame, Ingrams

Iniko (African) Born during troubled times
Inicko, Inico, Inyko, Inycko, Inyco

Iranga (Sri Lankan) One who is special

Irenbend (Anglo-Saxon) From the iron bend
Ironbend

Irwin (English) A friend of the wild boar
Irwinn, Irwinne, Irwyn, Irwynne, Irwine, Irwen, Irwenn, Irwenne

*ᵀIsaac (Hebrew) Full of laughter
Ike, Isaack, Isaak, Isac, Isacco, Isak, Issac, Itzak

*ᵀIsaiah (Hebrew) God is my salvation
Isa, Isaia, Isais, Isia, Isiah, Issiah, Izaiah, Iziah

Iseabail (Hebrew) One who is devoted to God
Iseabaile, Iseabayl, Iseabyle, Iseabael, Iseabaele

Isham (English) From the iron one's estate
Ishem, Ishom, Ishum, Ishim, Ishym, Isenham

Isidore (Greek) A gift of Isis
Isador, Isadore, Isidor, Isidoro, Isidorus, Isidro

Iskander (Arabic) Form of Alexander, meaning "a helper and defender of mankind"
Iskinder, Iskandar, Iskindar, Iskynder, Iskyndar, Iskender, Iskendar

Israel (Hebrew) God perseveres
Israeli, Israelie, Isreal, Izrael

Istvan (Hungarian) One who is crowned
Istven, Istvin, Istvyn, Istvon, Istvun

Iulian (Romanian) A youthful man
Iulien, Iulio, Iuleo

Ivan (Slavic) Form of John, meaning "God is gracious"
Ivann, Ivanhoe, Ivano, Iwan, Iban, Ibano, Ivanti, Ivantie

Ives (Scandinavian) The archer's bow; of the yew wood
Ivair, Ivar, Iven, Iver, Ivo, Ivon, Ivor, Ivaire

Ivy (English) Resembling the evergreen vining plant
Ivee, Ivey, Ivie, Ivi, Ivea

Iyar (Hebrew) Surrounded by light
Iyyar, Iyer, Iyyer

J

Ja (Korean / African) A handsome man / one who is magnetic

Jabari (African) A valiant man
Jabarie, Jabary, Jabarey, Jabaree, Jabarea

Jabbar (Indian) One who consoles others
Jabar

Jabin (Hebrew) God has built; one who is perceptive

Jabon (American) A fiesty man
Jabun, Jabin, Jabyn, Jaben, Jaban

^**Jace** (Hebrew) God is my salvation
Jacen, Jacey, Jacian, Jacy, Jaice, Jayce, Jaece, Jase

Jacinto (Spanish) Resembling a hyacinth
Jacynto, Jacindo, Jacyndo, Jacento, Jacendo, Jacenty, Jacentey, Jacentee

*T**Jack** (English) Form of John, meaning "God is gracious"
Jackie, Jackman, Jacko, Jacky, Jacq, Jacqin, Jak, Jaq

*T**Jackson** (English) The son of Jack or John
Jacksen, Jacksun, Jacson, Jakson, Jaxen, Jaxon, Jaxun, Jaxson

*T**Jacob** (Hebrew) He who supplants
Jake, James, Kuba, Iakovos, Yakiv, Yankel, Yaqub, Jaco, Jacobo, Jacobi, Jacoby, Jacobie, Jacobey, Jacobo

Jacoby (Hebrew) Form of Jacob, meaning "he who supplants"

Jadal (American) One who is punctual
Jadall, Jadel, Jadell

Jade (Spanish) Resembling the green gemstone
Jadee, Jadie, Jayde, Jaden

^*T**Jaden** (Hebrew / English) One who is thankful to God; God has heard / form of Jade, meaning "resembling the green gemstone"
*Jaiden, Jadyn, Jaeden, Jaidyn, **Jayden**, Jaydon*

Jagan (English) One who is self-confident
Jagen, Jagin, Jagyn, Jagon, Jagun, Jago

Jahan (Indian) Man of the world
Jehan, Jihan, Jag, Jagat, Jagath

Jaidayal (Indian) The victory of kindness
Jadayal, Jaydayal, Jaedayal

Jaime (Spanish) Form of James, meaning "he who supplants"
Jamie, Jaimee, Jaimey, Jaimi, Jaimie, Jaimy, Jamee

Jaimin (French) One who is loved
Jaimyn, Jamin, Jamyn, Jaymin, Jaymyn, Jaemin, Jaemyn

Jairdan (American) One who
enlightens others
*Jardan, Jayrdan, Jaerdan,
Jairden, Jarden, Jayrden,
Jaerden*

Jaja (African) A gift from God

Jajuan (American) One who
loves God

Jake (English) Form of Jacob,
meaning "he who supplants"
*Jaik, Jaike, Jayk, Jayke, Jakey,
Jaky*

Jakome (Basque) Form of
James, meaning "he who
supplants"
*Jackome, Jakom, Jackom,
Jacome*

^T**Jalen** (American) One who
heals others; one who is
tranquil
*Jaylon, Jaelan, Jalon, Jaylan,
Jaylen, Jalan, Jaylin*

Jamal (Arabic) A handsome
man
*Jamail, Jahmil, Jam, Jamaal,
Jamy, Jamar*

Jamar (American) Form of
Jamal, meaning "a handsome
man"
*Jamarr, Jemar, Jemarr, Jimar,
Jimarr, Jamaar, Jamari,
Jamarie*

*T**James** (Hebrew) Form of
Jacob, meaning "he who
supplants"
*Jaimes, Jaymes, Jame, Jaym,
Jaim, Jaem, Jaemes, Jamese,
Jim, Jaime, Diego, Hagop,
Hemi, Jakome*

^**Jameson** (English) The son of
James
*Jaimison, Jamieson, Jaymeson,
Jamison, Jaimeson, Jaymison,
Jaemeson, Jaemison*

Jamin (Hebrew) The right
hand of favor
*Jamian, Jamiel, Jamon,
Jaymin, Jaemin, Jaymon*

Janesh (Hindi) A leader of the
people
Janeshe

Japa (Indian) One who chants
Japeth, Japesh, Japendra

Japheth (Hebrew) May he
expand; in the Bible, one of
Noah's sons
*Jaypheth, Jaepheth, Jaipheth,
Jafeth, Jayfeth*

Jarah (Hebrew) One who is as
sweet as honey
Jarrah, Jara, Jarra

Jared (Hebrew) Of the descent; descending
Jarad, Jarod, Jarrad, Jarryd, Jarred, Jarrod, Jaryd, Jerod, Jerrad, Jered

Jarman (German) A man from Germany
Jarmann, Jerman, Jermann

Jaron (Israeli) A song of rejoicing
Jaran, Jaren, Jarin, Jarran, Jarren, Jarrin, Jarron, Jaryn

Jaroslav (Slavic) Born with the beauty of spring
Jaroslaw

Jarrett (English) One who is strong with the spear
Jaret, Jarret, Jarrott, Jerett, Jarritt, Jaret

*┬Jason (Hebrew / Greek) God is my salvation / a healer; in mythology, the leader of the Argonauts
Jacen, Jaisen, Jaison, Jasen, Jasin, Jasun, Jayson, Jaysen

Jaspar (Persian) One who holds the treasure
Jasper, Jaspir, Jaspyr, Jesper, Jespar, Jespir, Jespyr

Jatan (Indian) One who is nurturing

Javan (Hebrew) Man from Greece; in the Bible, Noah's grandson
Jayvan, Jayven, Jayvon, Javon, Javern, Javen

Javier (Spanish) The owner of a new house
Javiero

Jax (American) Form of Jackson, meaning "son of Jack or John"

Jay (Latin / Sanskrit) Resembling a jaybird / one who is victorious
Jae, Jai, Jaye, Jayron, Jayronn, Jey

^Jayce (American) Form of Jason, meaning "God is my salvation"
Jayse, Jace, Jase

Jean (French) Form of John, meaning "God is gracious"
Jeanne, Jeane, Jene, Jeannot, Jeanot

Jedidiah (Hebrew) One who is loved by God
Jedadiah, Jedediah, Jed, Jedd, Jedidiya, Jedidiyah, Jedadia, Jedadiya

Jeffrey (English) A man of peace
Jeff, Geoffrey, Jeffery, Jeffree

Jelani (African) One who is mighty; strong
Jelanie, Jelany, Jelaney, Jelanee, Jelanea

Jennett (Hindi) One who is heaven-sent
Jenett, Jennet, Jenet, Jennitt, Jenitt, Jennit, Jenit

Jerald (English) Form of Gerald, meaning "one who rules with the spear"
Jeraldo, Jerold, Jerrald, Jerrold

*Jeremiah (Hebrew) One who is exalted by the Lord
Jeremia, Jeremias, Jeremija, Jeremiya, Jeremyah, Jeramiah, Jeramia, Jerram, Geremia

ᵀJeremy (Hebrew) Form of Jeremiah, meaning "one who is exalted by the Lord"
Jeramey, Jeramie, Jeramy, Jerami, Jereme, Jeromy

Jermaine (French / Latin) A man from Germany / one who is brotherly
Jermain, Jermane, Jermayne, Jermin, Jermyn, Jermayn, Jermaen, Jermaene

Jerome (Greek) Of the sacred name
Jairome, Jeroen, Jeromo, Jeronimo, Jerrome, Jerom, Jerolyn, Jerolin, Hieronim

Jerram (Hebrew) Form of Jeremiah, meaning "one who is exalted by the Lord"
Jeram, Jerrem, Jerem, Jerrym, Jerym

Jesimiel (Hebrew) The Lord establishes
Jessimiel

Jesse (Hebrew) God exists; a gift from God; God sees all
Jess, Jessey, Jesiah, Jessie, Jessy, Jese, Jessi, Jessee

*Jesus (Hebrew) God is my salvation
*Jesous, Jesues, **Jesús**, Xesus*

Jett (English) Resembling the jet-black lustrous gemstone
Jet, Jette

Jibril (Arabic) Refers to the archangel Gabriel
Jibryl, Jibri, Jibrie, Jibry, Jibrey, Jibree

Jim (English) Form of James, meaning "he who supplants"
Jimi, Jimmee, Jimmey, Jimmie, Jimmy, Jimmi, Jimbo

Jimoh (African) Born on a Friday
Jymoh, Jimo, Jymo

Jivan (Hindi) A giver of life
Jivin, Jiven, Jivyn, Jivon

Joab (Hebrew) The Lord is my father
Joabb, Yoav

Joachim (Hebrew) One who is established by God; God will judge
Jachim, Jakim, Joacheim, Joaquim, Joaquin, Josquin, Joakim, Joakeen

Joe (English) Form of Joseph, meaning "God will add"
Jo, Joemar, Jomar, Joey, Joie, Joee, Joeye

Joel (Hebrew) Jehovah is God; God is willing

Johan (German) Form of John, meaning "God is gracious"

*ᵀJohn (Hebrew) God is gracious; in the Bible, one of the Apostles
Sean, Jack, Juan, Ian, Ean, Evan, Giovanni, Hanna, Hovannes, Iefan, Ivan, Jean, Xoan, Yochanan, Yohan, Johnn, Johnny, Jhonny

ᵀJonah (Hebrew) Resembling a dove; in the Bible, the man swallowed by a whale

Jonas (Greek) Form of Jonah, meaning "resembling a dove"

*Jonathan (Hebrew) A gift of God
Johnathan, Johnathon, Jonathon, Jonatan, Jonaton, Jonathen, Johnathen, Jonaten, Yonatan

*ᵀJordan (Hebrew) Of the down-flowing river; in the Bible, the river where Jesus was baptized
Johrdan, Jordain, Jordaine, Jordane, Jordanke, Jordann, Jorden, Jordaen

Jorge (Spanish) Form of George, meaning "one who works the earth; a farmer"

*Jose (Spanish) Form of Joseph, meaning "God will add"
José, Joseito, Joselito

*ᵀJoseph (Hebrew) God will add
Joe, Guiseppe, Yosyp, Jessop, Jessup, Joop, Joos, José, Jose, Josef, Joseito

*ᵀJoshua (Hebrew) God is salvation
Josh, Joshuah, Josua, Josue, Joushua, Jozua, Joshwa, Joshuwa

*ᵀJosiah (Hebrew) God will help
Josia, Josias, Joziah, Jozia, Jozias

Journey (American) One who
likes to travel
*Journy, Journi, Journie,
Journee, Journye, Journea*

*Juan (Spanish) Form of John,
meaning "God is gracious"
Juanito, Juwan, Jwan

Judah (Hebrew) One who
praises God
*Juda, Jude, Judas, Judsen,
Judson, Judd, Jud*

Jude (Latin) Form of Judah,
meaning "one who praises
God"

*Julian (Greek) The child of
Jove; one who is youthful
*Juliano, Julianus, Julien,
Julyan, Julio, Jolyon, Jullien,
Julen*

Julius (Greek) One who is
youthful
Juleus, Yuliy

Juma (African) Born on a
Friday
Jumah

Jumbe (African) Having great
strength
*Jumbi, Jumbie, Jumby, Jumbey,
Jumbee*

Jumoke (African) One who is
dearly loved
Jumok, Jumoak

Jun (Japanese) One who is
obedient

Junaid (Arabic) A warrior
Junaide, Junayd, Junayde

Jung (Korean) A righteous man

Jurgen (German) Form of
George, meaning "one who
works the earth; a farmer"
Jorgen, Jurgin, Jorgin

Justice (English) One who
upholds moral rightness and
fairness
*Justyce, Justiss, Justyss, Justis,
Justus, Justise*

*ᵀJustin (Latin) One who is just
and upright
*Joost, Justain, Justan, Just,
Juste, Justen, Justino, Justo*

Justinian (Latin) An upright
ruler
*Justinien, Justinious, Justinius,
Justinios, Justinas, Justinus*

K

Kabir (Indian) A spiritual
leader
*Kabeer, Kabear, Kabier, Kabeir,
Kabyr, Kabar*

Kabonesa (African) One who is born during difficult times

Kacancu (African) The first-born child
Kacancue, Kakancu, Kakancue, Kacanku, Kacankue

Kacey (Irish) A vigilant man; one who is alert
Kacy, Kacee, Kacea, Kaci, Kacie, Kasey, Kasy, Kasi

Kachada (Native American) A white-skinned man

ᵀ**Kaden** (Arabic) A beloved companion
Kadan, Kadin, Kadon, Kaidan, Kaiden, Kaidon, Kaydan, Kayden

Kadmiel (Hebrew) One who stands before God
Kamiell

Kaemon (Japanese) Full of joy; one who is right-handed
Kamon, Kaymon, Kaimon

Kagen (Irish) A fiery man; a thinker
Kaigen, Kagan, Kaigan, Kaygen, Kaygan, Kaegen, Kaegan

Kahoku (Hawaiian) Resembling a star
Kahokue, Kahokoo, Kahokou

Kai (Hawaiian / Welsh / Greek) Of the sea / the keeper of the keys / of the earth
Kye

Kaimi (Hawaiian) The seeker
Kaimie, Kaimy, Kaimey, Kaimee, Kaimea

Kalama (Hawaiian) A source of light
Kalam, Kalame

Kale (English) Form of Charles, meaning "one who is manly and strong / a free man"

Kaleb (Hebrew) Resembling an aggressive dog
Kaileb, Kaeleb, Kayleb, Kalob, Kailob, Kaelob

Kalidas (Hindi) A poet or musician; a servant of Kali
Kalydas

Kalki (Indian) Resembling a white horse
Kalkie, Kalky, Kalkey, Kalkee, Kalkea

Kalkin (Hindi) The tenth-born child
Kalkyn, Kalken, Kalkan, Kalkon, Kalkun

^**Kamden** (English) From the winding valley
Kamdun, Kamdon, Kamdan, Kamdin, Kamdyn

Kane (Gaelic) The little warrior
Kayn, Kayne, Kaen, Kaene, Kahan, Kahane

Kang (Korean) A healthy man

Kano (Japanese) A powerful man
Kanoe, Kanoh

Kantrava (Indian) Resembling a roaring animal

Kaper (American) One who is capricious
Kahper, Kapar, Kahpar

Kapono (Hawaiian) A righteous man

Karcsi (French) A strong, manly man
Karcsie, Karcsy, Karcsey, Karcsee, Karcsea

Karl (German) A free man
Carl, Karel, Karlan, Karle, Karlens, Karli, Karlin, Karlo, Karlos

Karman (Gaelic) The lord of the manor
Karmen, Karmin, Karmyn, Karmon, Karmun

^**Karson** (Scottish) Form of Carson, meaning son of a marsh dweller
Karsen

^**Karter** (English) Form of Carter, meaning one who drives a cart

Kashvi (Indian) A shining man
Kashvie, Kashvy, Kashvey, Kashvee, Kashvea

Kasib (Arabic) One who is fertile
Kaseeb, Kaseab, Kasieb, Kaseib, Kasyb

Kasim (Arabic) One who is divided
Kassim, Kaseem, Kasseem, Kaseam, Kasseam, Kasym, Kassym

Kasimir (Slavic) One who demands peace
Kasimeer, Kasimear, Kasimier, Kasimeir, Kasimyr, Kaz, Kazimierz

Kason (Basque) Protected by a helmet
Kasin, Kasyn, Kasen, Kasun, Kasan

Katzir (Hebrew) The harvester
Katzyr, Katzeer, Katzear, Katzier, Katzeir

Kaushal (Indian) One who is skilled
Kaushall, Koshal, Koshall

Kazim (Arabic) An even-tempered man
Kazeem, Kazeam, Kaziem, Kazeim, Kazym

Keahi (Hawaiian) Of the flames
Keahie, Keahy, Keahey, Keahee, Keahea

Kealoha (Hawaiian) From the bright path
Keeloha, Kieloha

Kean (Gaelic / English) A warrior / one who is sharp
Keane, Keen, Keene, Kein, Keine, Keyn, Keyne, Kien

Keandre (American) One who is thankful
Kiandre, Keandray, Kiandray, Keandrae, Kiandrae, Keandrai, Kiandrai

Keanu (Hawaiian) Of the mountain breeze
Keanue, Kianu, Kianue, Keanoo, Kianoo, Keanou

Keaton (English) From the town of hawks
Keatun, Keeton, Keetun, Keyton, Keytun

Kedar (Arabic) A powerful man
Keder, Kedir, Kedyr, Kadar, Kader, Kadir, Kadyr

Kefir (Hebrew) Resembling a young lion
Kefyr, Kefeer, Kefear, Kefier, Kefeir

Keegan (Gaelic) A small and fiery man
Kegan, Keigan, Keagan, Keagen, Keegen

Keith (Scottish) Man from the forest
Keithe, Keath, Keathe, Kieth, Kiethe, Keyth, Keythe, Keithen

Kellach (Irish) One who suffers strife during battle
Kelach, Kellagh, Kelagh, Keallach

^Kellen (Gaelic / German) One who is slender / from the swamp
Kellan, Kellon, Kellun, Kellin

Kelley (Celtic / Gaelic) A warrior / one who defends
Kelly, Kelleigh, Kellee, Kellea, Kelleah, Kelli, Kellie

Kendi (African) One who is much loved
Kendie, Kendy, Kendey, Kendee, Kendea

Kendrick (English / Gaelic) A royal ruler / the champion
Kendric, Kendricks, Kendrik, Kendrix, Kendryck, Kenrick, Kenrik, Kenricks

Kenley (English) From the king's meadow
Kenly, Kenlee, Kenleigh, Kenlea, Kenleah, Kenli, Kenlie

Kenn (Welsh) Of the bright waters

Kennedy (Gaelic) A helmeted chief
Kennedi, Kennedie, Kennedey, Kennedee, Kennedea, Kenadie, Kenadi, Kenady

Kenneth (Irish) Born of the fire; an attractive man
Kennet, Kennett, Kennith, Kennit, Kennitt

Kent (English) From the edge or border
Kentt, Kennt, Kentrell

Kenton (English) From the king's town
Kentun, Kentan, Kentin, Kenten, Kentyn

Kenyon (Gaelic) A blond-haired man
Kenyun, Kenyan, Kenyen, Kenyin

Kepler (German) One who makes hats
Keppler, Kappler, Keppel, Keppeler

Kerbasi (Basque) A warrior
Kerbasie, Kerbasee, Kerbasea, Kerbasy, Kerbasey

Kershet (Hebrew) Of the rainbow

Kesler (American) An energetic man; one who is independent
Keslar, Keslir, Keslyr, Keslor, Keslur

Keung (Chinese) A universal spirit

***Kevin** (Gaelic) A beloved and handsome man
Kevyn, Kevan, Keven, Keveon, Kevinn, Kevion, Kevis, Kevon

Khairi (Swahili) A kingly man
Khairie, Khairy, Khairey, Khairee, Khairea

Khalon (American) A strong warrior
Khalun, Khalen, Khalan, Khalin, Khalyn

Khayri (Arabic) One who is charitable
Khayrie, Khayry, Khayrey, Khayree, Khayrea

Khouri (Arabic) A spiritual man; a priest
Khourie, Khoury, Khourey, Khouree, Kouri, Kourie, Koury, Kourey

Khushi (Indian) Filled with happiness
Khushie, Khushey, Khushy, Khushee

Kibbe (Native American) A nocturnal bird
Kybbe

Kibo (African) From the highest mountain peak
Keybo, Keebo, Keabo, Keibo, Kiebo

Kidd (English) Resembling a young goat
Kid, Kydd, Kyd

Kiefer (German) One who makes barrels
Keefer, Keifer, Kieffer, Kiefner, Kieffner, Kiefert, Kuefer, Kueffner

^**Kieran** (Gaelic) Having dark features; the little dark one
Keiran, Keiron, Kernan, Kieren, Kiernan, Kieron, Kierren, Kierrien, Kierron, Keeran, Keeron, Keernan, Keeren, Kearan, Kearen, Kearon, Kearnan

Kim (Vietnamese) As precious as gold
Kym

Kimoni (African) A great man
Kimonie, Kimony, Kimoney, Kimonee, Kymoni, Kymonie, Kymony, Kymoney

Kincaid (Celtic) The leader during battle
Kincade, Kincayd, Kincayde, Kincaide, Kincaed, Kincaede, Kinkaid, Kinkaide

Kindin (Basque) The fifth-born child
Kinden, Kindan, Kindyn, Kindon, Kindun

Kindle (American) To set aflame
Kindel, Kyndle, Kyndel

King (English) The royal ruler
Kyng

Kingston (English) From the king's town
Kingstun, Kinston, Kindon

Kinnard (Irish) From the tall hill
Kinard, Kinnaird, Kinaird, Kynnard, Kynard, Kynnaird, Kynaird

Kinsey (English) The victorious prince
Kynsey, Kinsi, Kynsi, Kinsie, Kynsie, Kinsee, Kynsee, Kinsea

Kione (African) One who has come from nowhere

Kioshi (Japanese) One who is quiet
Kioshe, Kioshie, Kioshy, Kioshey, Kioshee, Kyoshi, Kyoshe, Kyoshie

Kipp (English) From the small pointed hill
Kip, Kipling, Kippling, Kypp, Kyp, Kiplyng, Kipplyng, Kippi

Kiri (Vietnamese) Resembling the mountains
Kirie, Kiry, Kirey, Kiree, Kirea

Kirk (Norse) A man of the church
Kyrk, Kerk, Kirklin, Kirklyn

Kirkland (English) From the church's land
Kirklan, Kirklande, Kyrkland, Kyrklan, Kyrklande

Kirkley (English) From the church's meadow
Kirkly, Kirkleigh, Kirklea, Kirkleah, Kirklee, Kirkli, Kirklie

Kit (English) Form of Christopher, meaning "one who bears Christ inside"
Kitt, Kyt, Kytt

Kitchi (Native American) A brave young man
Kitchie, Kitchy, Kitchey, Kitchee, Kitchea

Kitoko (African) A handsome man
Kytoko

Kivi (Finnish) As solid as stone
Kivie, Kivy, Kivey, Kivee, Kivea

Knight (English) A noble solidier
Knights

^**Knox** (English) From the rounded hill

Knud (Danish) A kind man
Knude

Kobe (African / Hungarian) Tortoise / Form of Jacob, meaning "he who supplants"
Kobi, Koby

Kody (English) One who is helpful
Kodey, Kodee, Kodea, Kodi, Kodie

Koen (German) An honest advisor
Koenz, Kunz, Kuno

Kohana (Native American / Hawaiian) One who is swift / the best

Kohler (German) One who mines coal
Koler

Kojo (African) Born on a Monday
Kojoe, Koejo, Koejoe

Koka (Hawaiian) A man from Scotland

^**Kolton** (American) Form of Colton, meaning from the coal town
Kolten, Koltan

Konane (Hawaiian) Born beneath the bright moon
Konain, Konaine, Konayn, Konayne, Konaen, Konaene

Konnor (English) A wolf lover; one who is strong-willed
Konnur, Konner, Konnar, Konnir, Konnyr

Koofrey (African) Remember me
Koofry, Koofri, Koofrie, Koofree

Kordell (English) One who makes cord
Kordel, Kord, Kordale

Koresh (Hebrew) One who digs in the earth; a farmer
Koreshe

Kory (Irish) From the hollow; of the churning waters
Korey, Kori, Korie, Koree, Korea, Korry, Korrey, Korree

Kozma (Greek) One who is decorated
Kozmah

Kozue (Japanese) Of the tree branches
Kozu, Kozoo, Kozou

Kraig (Gaelic) From the rocky place; as solid as a rock
Kraige, Krayg, Krayge, Kraeg, Kraege, Krage

Kramer (German) A shop-keeper
Kramar, Kramor, Kramir, Kramur, Kramyr, Kraymer, Kraimer, Kraemer

Krany (Czech) A man of short stature
Kraney, Kranee, Kranea, Krani, Kranie

Krikor (Armenian) A vigilant watchman
Krykor, Krikur, Krykur

Kristian (Scandinavian) An annointed Christian
Kristan, Kristien, Krist, Kriste, Krister, Kristar, Khristian, Khrist

Kristopher (Scandinavian) A follower of Christ
Khristopher, Kristof, Kristofer, Kristoff, Kristoffer, Kristofor, Kristophor, Krystof

Kuba (Polish) Form of Jacob, meaning "he who supplants"
Kubas

Kuckunniwi (Native American) Resembling a little wolf
Kukuniwi

Kuleen (Indian) A high-born man
Kulin, Kulein, Kulien, Kulean, Kulyn

Kumar (Indian) A prince;
a male child

Kuri (Japanese) Resembling
a chestnut
*Kurie, Kury, Kurey, Kuree,
Kurea*

Kuron (African) One who gives
thanks
*Kurun, Kuren, Kuran, Kurin,
Kuryn*

Kurt (German) A brave
counselor
Kurte

Kushal (Indian) A talented
man; adroit
Kushall

Kwaku (African) Born on a
Wednesday
*Kwakue, Kwakou, Kwako,
Kwakoe*

Kwan (Korean) Of a bold
character
Kwon

Kwintyn (Polish) The fifth-
born child
*Kwentyn, Kwinton, Kwenton,
Kwintun, Kwentun, Kwintan,
Kwentan, Kwinten*

Kyle (Gaelic) From the narrow
channel
*Kile, Kiley, Kye, Kylan, Kyrell,
Kylen, Kily, Kili*

Kylemore (Gaelic) From the
great wood
Kylmore, Kylemor, Kylmor

Kyrone (English) Form of
Tyrone, meaning "from
Owen's land"
*Kyron, Keirohn, Keiron,
Keirone, Keirown, Kirone*

L

Lacey (French) Man from
Normandy; as delicate as lace
Lacy, Laci, Lacie, Lacee, Lacea

Lachlan (Gaelic) From the land
of lakes
*Lachlen, Lachlin, Lachlyn,
Locklan, Locklen, Locklin,
Locklyn, Loklan*

Lachman (Gaelic) A man from
the lake
*Lachmann, Lockman,
Lockmann, Lokman, Lokmann,
Lakman, Lakmann*

Ladan (Hebrew) One who is
alert and aware
*Laden, Ladin, Ladyn, Ladon,
Ladun*

Ladd (English) A servant;
a young man
*Lad, Laddey, Laddie, Laddy,
Laddi, Laddee, Laddea, Ladde*

Ladislas (Slavic) A glorious
ruler
*Lacko, Ladislaus, Laslo, Laszlo,
Lazlo, Ladislav, Ladislauv,
Ladislao*

Lagrand (American) A
majestic man
Lagrande

Laibrook (English) One who
lives on the road near the
brook
*Laebrook, Laybrook, Laibroc,
Laebroc, Laybroc, Laibrok,
Laebrok, Laybrok*

Laird (Scottish) The lord of the
manor
*Layrd, Laerd, Lairde, Layrde,
Laerde*

Laken (American) Man from
the lake
*Laike, Laiken, Laikin, Lakin,
Lakyn, Lakan, Laikyn, Laeken*

Lalam (Indian) The best
Lallam, Lalaam, Lallaam

Lam (Vietnamese) Having a
full understanding

Laman (Arabic) A bright and
happy man
Lamaan, Lamann, Lamaann

Lamar (German / French)
From the renowned land / of
the sea
*Lamarr, Lamarre, Lemar,
Lemarr*

Lambert (Scandinavian) The
light of the land
*Lambart, Lamberto, Lambirt,
Landbert, Lambirto, Lambrecht,
Lambret, Lambrett*

Lambi (Norse) In mythology,
the son of Thorbjorn
*Lambie, Lamby, Lambey,
Lambe, Lambee*

Lameh (Arabic) A shining man

Lamorak (English) In
Arthurian legend, the brother
of Percival
*Lamerak, Lamurak, Lamorac,
Lamerac, Lamurac, Lamorack,
Lamerack, Lamurack*

Lance (English) Form of
Lancelot, meaning an
attendant, a knight of the
Round Table

Lander (English) One who
owns land
*Land, Landers, Landis, Landiss,
Landor, Lande, Landry, Landri*

*ᵀLandon (English) From the
long hill
*Landyn, Landan, Landen,
Landin, Lando, Langdon,
Langden, Langdan*

Lane (English) One who takes the narrow path
Laine, Lain, Laen, Laene, Layne, Layn

Langhorn (English) Of the long horn
Langhorne, Lanhorn, Lanhorne

Langilea (Polynesian) Having a booming voice, like thunder
Langileah, Langilia, Langiliah

Langston (English) From the tall man's town
Langsten, Langstun, Langstown, Langstin, Langstyn, Langstan, Langton, Langtun

Langundo (Native American / Polynesian) A peaceful man / one who is graceful

Langworth (English) One who lives near the long paddock
Langworthe, Lanworth, Lanworthe

Lanier (French) One who works with wool

Lantos (Hungarian) One who plays the lute
Lantus

Lapidos (Hebrew) One who carries a torch
Lapydos, Lapidot, Lapydot, Lapidoth, Lapydoth, Lapidus, Lapydus

Laquinton (American) Form of Quinton, meaning "from the queen's town or settlement"
Laquinntan, Laquinnten, Laquinntin, Laquinnton, Laquintain, Laquintan, Laquintyn, Laquintynn

Lar (Anglo-Saxon) One who teaches others

Larson (Scandinavian) The son of Lawrence
Larsan, Larsen, Larsun, Larsin, Larsyn

Lasalle (French) From the hall
Lasall, Lasal, Lasale

Lashaun (American) An enthusiastic man
Lashawn, Lasean, Lashon, Lashond

Lassit (American) One who is open-minded
Lassyt, Lasset

Lathan (American) Form of Nathan, meaning "a gift from God"
Lathen, Lathun, Lathon, Lathin, Lathyn, Latan, Laten, Latun

Latimer (English) One who serves as an interpreter
Latymer, Latimor, Latymor, Latimore, Latymore, Lattemore, Lattimore

Latty (English) A generous man
Lattey, Latti, Lattie, Lattee, Lattea

Laurian (English) One who lives near the laurel trees
Laurien, Lauriano, Laurieno, Lawrian, Lawrien, Lawriano, Lawrieno

Lave (Italian) Of the burning rock
Lava

Lawford (English) From the ford near the hill
Lawforde, Lawferd, Lawferde, Lawfurd, Lawfurde

Lawler (Gaelic) A soft-spoken man; one who mutters
Lauler, Lawlor, Loller, Lawlar, Lollar, Loller, Laular, Laulor

Lawley (English) From the meadow near the hill
Lawly, Lawli, Lawlie, Lawleigh, Lawlee, Lawlea, Lawleah

Lawrence (Latin) Man from Laurentum; crowned with laurel
Larance, Laranz, Larenz, Larrance, Larrence, Larrens, Larrey, Larry

Laziz (Arabic) One who is pleasant
Lazeez, Lazeaz, Laziez, Lazeiz, Lazyz

Leaman (American) A powerful man
Leeman, Leamon, Leemon, Leamond, Leamand

Lear (Greek) Of the royalty
Leare, Leer, Leere

Leather (American) As tough as hide
Lether

Leavitt (English) A baker
Leavit, Leavytt, Leavyt, Leavett, Leavet

Leben (English) Filled with hope

Lech (Slavic) In mythology, the founder of the Polish people
Leche

Ledyard (Teutonic) The protector of the nation
Ledyarde, Ledyerd, Ledyerde

Lee (English) From the meadow
Leigh, Lea, Leah, Ley

Leeto (African) One who embarks on a journey
Leato, Leito, Lieto

Legend (American) One who is memorable
Legende, Legund, Legunde

Leighton (English) From the town near the meadow
Leightun, Layton, Laytun, Leyton, Leytun

Lekhak (Hindi) An author
Lekhan

Leland (English) From the meadow land

Lema (African) One who is cultivated
Lemah, Lemma, Lemmah

Lemon (American) Resembling the fruit
Lemun, Lemin, Lemyn, Limon, Limun, Limin, Limyn, Limen

Len (Native American) One who plays the flute

Lencho (African) Resembling a lion
Lenchos, Lenchio, Lenchiyo, Lencheo, Lencheyo

Lennon (English) Son of love
Lennan

Lennor (English) A courageous man

Lennox (Scottish) One who owns many elm trees
Lenox, Lenoxe, Lennix, Lenix, Lenixe

Lensar (English) One who stays with his parents
Lenser, Lensor, Lensur

Lenton (American) A pious man
Lentin, Lentyn, Lentun, Lentan, Lenten, Lent, Lente

Leo (Latin) Having the strength of a lion
Lio, Lyo, Leon

Leon (Greek) Form of Leo, meaning "resembling a lion"

Leonard (German) Having the strength of a lion
Len, Lenard, Lenn, Lennard, Lennart, Lennerd, Leonardo

Leor (Latin) One who listens well
Leore

Lerato (Latin) The song of my soul
Leratio, Lerateo

Leron (French / Arabic) The circle / my song
Lerun, Leran, Leren, Lerin, Leryn

Leroy (French) The king
*Leroi, Leeroy, Leeroi, Learoy,
Learoi*

*****Levi** (Hebrew) We are united
as one; in the Bible, one of
Jacob's sons
*Levie, Levin, Levyn, Levy, Levey,
Levee*

Li (Chinese) Having great
strength

*****T**Liam** (Gaelic) Form of
William, meaning "the determined protector"

Lian (Chinese) Of the willow

Liang (Chinese) A good man
Lyang

Lidmann (Anglo-Saxon) A man
of the sea; a sailor
Lidman, Lydmann, Lydman

Lif (Scandinavian) An energetic man; lively

Lihau (Hawaiian) A spirited
man

Like (Asian) A soft-spoken
man
Lyke

Lilo (Hawaiian) One who is
generous
*Lylo, Leelo, Lealo, Leylo, Lielo,
Leilo*

Lincoln (English) From the vil-
lage near the lake
*Lincon, Lyncon, Linc, Lynk,
Lync*

Lindford (English) From the
linden-tree ford
*Linford, Lindforde, Linforde,
Lyndford, Lynford, Lyndforde,
Lynforde*

Lindhurst (English) From the
village by the linden trees
*Lyndhurst, Lindenhurst,
Lyndenhurst, Lindhirst,
Lindherst, Lyndhirst, Lyndherst,
Lindenhirst*

Lindley (English) From the
meadow of linden trees
*Lindly, Lindleigh, Lindlea,
Lindleah, Lindlee, Lindli*

Lindman (English) One who
lives near the linden trees
Lindmann, Lindmon

Line (English) From the bank

Lipût (Hungarian) A brave
young man

Lisimba (African) One who
has been attacked by a lion
Lisymba, Lysimba, Lysymba

Liu (Asian) One who is quiet;
peaceful

Llewellyn (Welsh) Resembling a lion
Lewellen, Lewellyn, Llewellen, Llewelyn, Llwewellin, Llew, Llewe, Llyweilun

Lochan (Hindi / Irish) The eyes / one who is lively

*★T***Logan** (Gaelic) From the little hollow
Logann, Logen, Login, Logyn, Logenn, Loginn, Logynn

Lolonyo (African) The beauty of love
Lolonyio, Lolonyeo, Lolonio, Lolonea

Loman (Gaelic) One who is small and bare
Lomann, Loeman, Loemann

Lombard (Latin) One who has a long beard
Lombardi, Lombardo, Lombardie, Lombardy, Lombardey, Lombardee

London (English) From the capital of England
Lundon, Londen, Lunden

Lonzo (Spanish) One who is ready for battle
Lonzio, Lonzeo

Lootah (Native American) Refers to the color red
Loota, Loutah, Louta, Lutah, Luta

Lorcan (Irish) The small fierce one
Lorcen, Lorcin, Lorcyn, Lorcon, Lorcun, Lorkan, Lorken, Lorkin

Lord (English) One who has authority and power
Lorde, Lordly, Lordley, Lordlee, Lordlea, Lordleigh, Lordli, Lordlie

Lore (Basque / English) Resembling a flower / form of Lawrence, meaning "man from Laurentum; crowned with laurel"
Lorea

Lorimer (Latin) One who makes harnesses
Lorrimer, Lorimar, Lorrimar, Lorymar, Lorrymar, Lorymer, Lorrymer

Louis (German) A famous warrior
Lew, Lewes, Lewis, Lodewick, Lodovico, Lou, Louie, Lucho, Luis

Luba (Yugoslavian) One who loves and is loved
Lubah

*★T***Lucas** (English) A man from Lucania
Lukas, Loucas, Loukas, Luckas, Louckas, Lucus, Lukus, Ghoukas

Lucian (Latin) Surrounded by light
Luciano, Lucianus, Lucien, Lucio, Lucjan, Lukianos, Lukyan, Luce

Lucky (English) A fortunate man
Luckey, Luckee, Luckea, Lucki, Luckie

Ludlow (English) The ruler of the hill
Ludlowe

*Luis (Spanish) Form of Louis, meaning "a famous warrior"
Luiz

*ᵀLuke (Greek) A man from Lucania
Luc, Luken

Lunt (Scandinavian) From the grove
Lunte

Luthando (Latin) One who is dearly loved

Luther (German) A soldier of the people
Louther, Luter, Luthero, Lutero, Louthero, Luthus, Luthas, Luthos

Lux (Latin) A man of the light
Luxe, Luxi, Luxie, Luxee, Luxea, Luxy, Luxey

Ly (Vietnamese) A reasonable man

Lynn (English) A man of the lake
Linn, Lyn, Lynne, Linne

M

Maahes (Egyptian) Resembling a lion

Mac (Gaelic) The son of Mac (Macarthur, Mackinley, etc.)
Mack, Mak, Macky, Macki, Mackie, Mackee, Mackea

Macadam (Gaelic) The son of Adam
Macadhamh, MacAdam, McAdam, MacAdhamh

Macallister (Gaelic) The son of Alistair
MacAlister, McAlister, McAllister, Macalister

Macardle (Gaelic) The son of great courage
MacArdle, McCardle, Macardell, MacArdell, McCardell

Macartan (Gaelic) The son of
Artan
*MacArtan, McArtan,
Macarten, MacArten, McArten*

Macarthur (Gaelic) The son of
Arthur
*MacArthur, McArthur,
Macarther, MacArther,
McArther*

Macauslan (Gaelic) The son of
Absalon
*MacAuslan, McAuslan,
Macauslen, MacAuslen,
McAuslen*

Maccoll (Gaelic) The son of
Coll
McColl, Maccoll, MacColl

Maccrea (Gaelic) The son of
grace
*McCrea, Macrae, MacCrae,
MacCray, MacCrea*

Macedonio (Greek) A man
from Macedonia
*Macedoneo, Macedoniyo,
Macedoneyo*

Macgowan (Gaelic) The son of
a blacksmith
*MacGowan, Magowan,
McGowan, McGowen,
McGown, MacCowan,
MacCowen*

Machau (Hebrew) A gift from
God

Machenry (Gaelic) The son of
Henry
MacHenry, McHenry

Machk (Native American)
Resembling a bear

Macintosh (Gaelic) The son of
the thane
*MacIntosh, McIntosh,
Macintoshe, MacIntoshe,
McIntoshe, Mackintosh,
MacKintosh*

Mackay (Gaelic) The son of
fire
*MacKay, McKay, Mackaye,
MacKaye, McKaye*

Mackinley (Gaelic) The son of
the white warrior
*MacKinley, McKinley,
MacKinlay, McKinlay,
Mackinlay, Mackinlie,
MacKinlie*

Macklin (Gaelic) The son of
Flann
*Macklinn, Macklyn, Macklynn,
Macklen, Macklenn*

Maclaine (Gaelic) The son of
John's servant
*MacLaine, Maclain, MacLain,
Maclayn, McLaine, McLain,
Maclane, MacLane*

Macleod (Gaelic) The son of the ugly one
MacLeod, McLeod, McCloud, MacCloud

Macmurray (Gaelic) The son of Murray
MacMurray, McMurray, Macmurra, MacMurra

Macnab (Gaelic) The son of the abbot
MacNab, McNab

Macon (English / French) To make / from the city in France
Macun, Makon, Makun, Maken, Mackon, Mackun

Macqueen (Gaelic) The son of the good man
MacQueen, McQueen

Macrae (Gaelic) The son of Ray
MacRae, McRae, Macray, MacRay, McRay, Macraye, MacRaye, McRaye

Madden (Pakistani) One who is organized; a planner
Maddon, Maddan, Maddin, Maddyn, Maddun, Maden, Madon, Madun

ᵀ**Maddox** (Welsh) The son of the benefactor
Madox, Madocks, Maddocks

Madhur (Indian) A sweet man

Magee (Gaelic) The son of Hugh
MacGee, McGee, MacGhee, Maghee

Maguire (Gaelic) The son of the beige one
Magwire, MacGuire, McGuire, MacGwire, McGwire

Magus (Latin) A sorcerer
Magis, Magys, Magos, Magas, Mages

Mahan (American) A cowboy
Mahahn, Mahen, Mayhan, Maihan, Maehan, Mayhen, Maihen, Maehen

Mahant (Indian) Having a great soul
Mahante

Mahatma (Hindi) Of great spiritual development

Mahfouz (Arabic) One who is protected
Mafouz, Mahfooz, Mafooz, Mahfuz, Mafuz

Mahkah (Native American) Of the earth
Mahka, Makah, Maka

Mahmud (Arabic) One who is praiseworthy
Mahmood, Mahmoud, Mehmood, Mehmud, Mehmoud

Mailhairer (French) An
ill-fated man

Maimon (Arabic) One who
is dependable; having good
fortune
*Maymon, Maemon, Maimun,
Maymun, Maemun, Mamon,
Mamun*

Maitland (English) From the
meadow land
*Maytland, Maetland,
Maitlande, Maytlande,
Maetlande*

Majdy (Arabic) A glorious man
*Majdey, Majdi, Majdie,
Majdee, Majdea*

Makaio (Hawaiian) A gift from
God

Makena (Hawaiian) Man of
abundance
Makenah

Makin (Arabic) Having great
strength
*Makeen, Makean, Makein,
Makien, Makyn*

Makis (Hebrew) A gift from
God
*Madys, Makiss, Makyss,
Makisse, Madysse*

Malachi (Hebrew) A messen-
ger of God
*Malachie, Malachy, Malaki,
Malakia, Malakie, Malaquias,
Malechy, Maleki*

Malawa (African) A flourishing man

Malcolm (Gaelic) Follower of
St. Columbus
*Malcom, Malcolum, Malkolm,
Malkom, Malkolum*

Mali (Indian) A ruler; the
firstborn son
*Malie, Maly, Maley, Malee,
Malea*

Mamoru (Japanese) Of the
earth
*Mamorou, Mamorue,
Mamorew, Mamoroo*

Manchester (English) From
the city in England
*Manchestar, Manchestor,
Manchestir, Manchestyr,
Manchestur*

Mandan (Native American) A
tribal name
*Manden, Mandon, Mandun,
Mandin, Mandyn*

Mandhatri (Indian) A prince;
born to royalty
*Mandhatrie, Mandhatry,
Mandhatrey, Mandhatree,
Mandhatrea*

Mani (African) From the mountain
Manie, Many, Maney, Manee, Manea

Manjit (Indian) A conqueror of the mind; having great knowledge
Manjeet, Manjeat, Manjeit, Manjiet, Manjyt

Manley (English) From the man's meadow; from the hero's meadow
Manly, Manli, Manlie, Manlea, Manleah, Manlee, Manleigh

Manmohan (Indian) A handsome and pleasing man
Manmohen, Manmohin, Manmohyn

Mannheim (German) From the hamlet in the swamp
Manheim

Mano (Hawaiian) Resembling a shark
Manoe, Manow, Manowe

Manohar (Indian) A delightful and captivating man
Manoharr, Manohare

Mansel (English) From the clergyman's house
Mansle, Mansell, Mansele, Manselle, Manshel, Manshele, Manshell, Manshelle

Mansfield (English) From the field near the small river
Mansfeld, Maunfield, Maunfeld

Manton (English) From the man's town; from the hero's town
Mantun, Manten, Mannton, Manntun, Mannten

Manu (African) The second-born child
Manue, Manou, Manoo

Manuel (Spanish) Form of Emmanuel, meaning "God is with us"
Manuelo, Manuello, Manolito, Manolo, Manollo, Manny, Manni

Manya (Indian) A respected man
Manyah

Manzo (Japanese) The third son with ten-thousand-fold strength

Mar (Spanish) Of the sea
Marr, Mare, Marre

Marcel (French) The little warrior
Marceau, Marcelin, Marcellin, Marcellino, Marcell, Marcello, Marcellus, Marcelo

Marcus (Latin) Form of Mark, meaning "dedicated to Mars, the god of war"
Markus, Marcas, Marco, Markos

Mariatu (African) One who is pure; chaste
Mariatue, Mariatou, Mariatoo

Marid (Arabic) A rebellious man
Maryd

Mario (Latin) A manly man
Marius, Marios, Mariano, Marion, Mariun, Mareon

Mark (Latin) Dedicated to Mars, the god of war
Marc, Markey, Marky, Marki, Markie, Markee, Markea, Markov

Marmion (French) Our little one
Marmyon, Marmeon

Marsh (English) From the marshland
Marshe

Marshall (French / English) A caretaker of horses / a steward
Marchall, Marischal, Marischall, Marschal, Marshal, Marshell, Marshel, Marschall

Marston (English) From the town near the marsh
Marstun, Marsten, Marstin, Marstyn, Marstan

Martin (Latin) Dedicated to Mars, the god of war
Martyn, Mart, Martel, Martell, Marten, Martenn, Marti, Martie

Marvin (Welsh) A friend of the sea
Marvinn, Marvinne, Marven, Marvenn, Marvenne, Marvyn, Marvynn, Marvynne, Mervin

Maryland (English) Honoring Queen Mary; from the state of Maryland
Mariland, Maralynd, Marylind, Marilind

Masanao (Japanese) A good man

Masao (Japanese) A righteous man

*⁺Mason** (English) One who works with stone
Masun, Masen, Masan, Masin, Masyn, Masson, Massun, Massen

Masselin (French) A young Thomas
Masselyn, Masselen, Masselan, Masselon, Masselun, Maselin, Maselyn, Maselon

Masura (Japanese) A good
destiny
Masoura

Mataniah (Hebrew) A gift
from God
*Matania, Matanya,
Matanyahu, Mattania,
Mattaniah, Matanyah*

Matata (African) One who
causes trouble

Matin (Arabic) Having great
strength
*Maten, Matan, Matyn, Maton,
Matun*

Matisse (French) One who is
gifted
*Matiss, Matysse, Matyss,
Matise, Matyse*

Matlock (American) A rancher
Matlok, Matloc

^**Matteo** (Italian) Form of
Matthew, meaning "a gift
from God"
Mateo

*ᵀ**Matthew** (Hebrew) A gift
from God
*Matt, Mathew, Matvey,
Mateas, Mattix, Madteos,
Matthias, Mat, Mateo, Matteo,
Mateus*

Matunde (African) One who is
fruitful
Matundi, Matundie

Matvey (Russian) Form of
Matthew, meaning "a gift
from God"
*Matvy, Matvee, Matvea, Matvi,
Matvie, Motka, Matviyko*

Matwau (Native American)
The enemy

Maurice (Latin) A dark-
skinned man; Moorish
*Maurell, Maureo, Mauricio,
Maurids, Maurie, Maurin,
Maurio, Maurise, Baurice*

^**Maverick** (English) An
independent man; a non-
conformist
*Maveric, Maverik, Mavrick,
Mavric, Mavrik*

*****Max** (English) Form of
Maxwell, meaning from
Mack's spring

^**Maximilian** (Latin) The
greatest
*Max, Macks, Maxi, Maxie,
Maxy, Maxey, Maxee, Maxea,
Maximiliano*

Maxfield (English) From
Mack's field
Mackfield, Maxfeld, Macksfeld

ᵀ**Maxwell** (English) From
Mack's spring
*Maxwelle, Mackswell, Maxwel,
Mackswel, Mackwelle, Maxwill,
Maxwille, Mackswill*

Mayer (Latin / German / Hebrew) A large man / a farmer / one who is shining bright
Maier, Mayar, Mayor, Mayir, Mayur, Meyer, Meir, Myer

Mayfield (English) From the strong one's field
Mayfeld, Maifield, Maifeld, Maefield, Maefeld

Mayo (Gaelic) From the yew tree plain
Mayoe, Maiyo, Maeyo, Maiyoe, Maeyoe, Mayoh, Maioh

Mccoy (Gaelic) The son of Coy
McCoy

McKenna (Gaelic) The son of Kenna; to ascend
McKennon, McKennun, McKennen, McKennan

Mckile (Gaelic) The son of Kyle
McKile, Mckyle, McKyle, Mackile, Mackyle, MacKile, MacKyle

Medad (Hebrew) A beloved friend
Meydad

Medgar (German) Having great strength
Medgarr, Medgare, Medgard, Medárd

Medwin (German) A strong friend
Medwine, Medwinn, Medwinne, Medwen, Medwenn, Medwenne, Medwyn, Medwynn

Meged (Hebrew) One who has been blessed with goodness

Mehdi (Arabian) One who is guided
Mehdie, Mehdy, Mehdey, Mehdee, Mehdea

Mehetabel (Hebrew) One who is favored by God
Mehetabell, Mehitabel, Mehitabell, Mehytabel, Mehytabell

Meilyr (Welsh) A regal ruler

Meinrad (German) A strong counselor
Meinred, Meinrod, Meinrud, Meinrid, Meinryd

Meka (Hawaiian) Of the eyes
Mekah

Melancton (Greek) Resembling a black flower
Melankton, Melanctun, Melanktun, Melancten, Melankten, Melanchton, Melanchten, Melanchthon

Mele (Hawaiian) One who is happy

Melesio (Spanish) An attentive man; one who is careful
Melacio, Melasio, Melecio, Melicio, Meliseo, Milesio

Meletius (Greek) A cautious man
Meletios, Meletious, Meletus, Meletos

Meli (Native American) One who is bitter
Melie, Mely, Meley, Melee, Melea, Meleigh

Melker (Swedish) A king
Melkar, Melkor, Melkur, Melkir, Melkyr

Melton (English) From the mill town
Meltun, Meltin, Meltyn, Melten, Meltan

Melville (English) From the mill town
Melvill, Melvil, Melvile, Melvylle, Melvyll, Melvyl, Melvyle

Melvin (English) A friend who offers counsel
Melvinn, Melvinne, Melven, Melvenn, Melvenne, Melvyn, Melvynn, Melvynne, Belvin

Memphis (American) From the city in Tennessee
Memfis, Memphys, Memfys, Memphus, Memfus

Menachem (Hebrew) One who provides comfort
Menaheim, Menahem, Menachim, Menachym, Menahim, Menahym, Machum, Machem

Menassah (Hebrew) A forgetful man
Menassa, Menass, Menas, Menasse, Menasseh

Menefer (Egyptian) Of the beautiful city
Menefar, Menefir, Menefyr, Menefor, Menefur

Menelik (African) The son of a wise man
Menelick, Menelic, Menelyk, Menelyck, Menelyc

Merewood (English) From the forest with the lake
Merwood, Merewode, Merwode

Merlin (Welsh) Of the sea fortress; in Arthurian legend, the wizard and mentor of King Arthur
Merlyn, Merlan, Merlon, Merlun, Merlen, Merlinn, Merlynn, Merlonn

Merrill (English) Of the shining sea
Meril, Merill, Merrel, Merrell, Merril, Meryl, Merryll, Meryll

Merton (English) From the town near the lake
Mertun, Mertan, Merten, Mertin, Mertyn, Murton, Murtun, Murten

Mervin (Welsh) Form of Marvin, meaning "a friend of the sea"
Mervinn, Mervinne, Mervyn, Mervynn, Mervynne, Merven, Mervenn, Mervenne

Meshach (Hebrew) An enduring man
Meshack, Meshac, Meshak, Meeshach, Meeshack, Meeshak, Meeshac

Mhina (African) One who is delightful
Mhinah, Mheena, Mheenah, Mheina, Mheinah, Mhienah, Mhienah, Mhyna

Micah (Hebrew) Form of Michael, meaning "who is like God?"
Mica, Mycah

*ᵀ**Michael** (Hebrew) Who is like God?
Makai, Micael, Mical, Micha, Michaelangelo, Michail, Michal, Micheal, **Miguel**, *Mick*

Mick (English) Form of Michael, meaning "who is like God?"
Micke, Mickey, Micky, Micki, Mickie, Mickee, Mickea, Mickel

Mieko (Japanese) A bright man

Miguel (Portuguese / Spanish) Form of Michael, meaning "who is like God?"
Migel, Myguel

Milan (Latin) An eager and hardworking man
Mylan

Miles (German / Latin) One who is merciful / a soldier
Myles, Miley, Mily, Mili, Milie, Milee

Milford (English) From the mill's ford
Millford, Milfurd, Millfurd, Milferd, Millferd, Milforde, Millforde, Milfurde

Miller (English) One who works at the mill
Millar, Millor, Millur, Millir, Millyr, Myller, Millen, Millan

^**Milo** (German) Form of Miles, meaning "one who is merciful"
Mylo

Milson (English) The son of Miles
Milsun, Milsen, Milsin, Milsyn, Milsan

Mimir (Norse) In mythology, a giant who guarded the well of wisdom
Mymir, Mimeer, Mimyr, Mymeer, Mymyr, Meemir, Meemeer, Meemyr

Miner (Latin / English) One who works in the mines / a youth
Minor, Minar, Minur, Minir, Minyr

Mingan (Native American) Resembling a gray wolf
Mingen, Mingin, Mingon, Mingun, Mingyn

Minh (Vietnamese) A clever man

Minster (English) Of the church
Mynster, Minstar, Mynstar, Minstor, Mynstor, Minstur, Mynstur, Minstir

Miracle (American) An act of God's hand
Mirakle, Mirakel, Myracle, Myrakle

Mirage (French) An illusion
Myrage

Mirumbi (African) Born during a period of rain
Mirumbie, Mirumby, Mirumbey, Mirumbee, Mirumbea

Missouri (Native American) From the town of large canoes; from the state of Missouri
Missourie, Mizouri, Mizourie, Missoury, Mizoury, Missuri, Mizuri, Mizury

Mitchell (English) Form of Michael, meaning "who is like God?"
Mitch, Mitchel, Mytch, Mitchum, Mytchill, Mitcham

Mitsu (Japanese) Of the light
Mytsu, Mitsue, Mytsue

Mochni (Native American) Resembling a talking bird
Mochnie, Mochny, Mochney, Mochnee, Mochnea

Modesty (Latin) One who is without conceit
Modesti, Modestie, Modestee, Modestus, Modestey, Modesto, Modestio, Modestine

Mogens (Dutch) A powerful man
Mogen, Mogins, Mogin, Mogyns, Mogyn, Mogan, Mogans

Mohajit (Indian) A charming
man
*Mohajeet, Mohajeat, Mohajeit,
Mohajiet, Mohajyt*

Mohammed (Arabic) One who
is greatly praised; the name
of the prophet and founder of
Islam
*Mahomet, Mohamad,
Mohamed, Mohamet,
Mohammad, Muhammad,
Muhammed, Mehmet*

Mohave (Native American) A
tribal name
Mohav, Mojave

Mojag (Native American) One
who is never quiet

Molan (Irish) The servant of
the storm
Molen

Momo (American) A warring
man

Mona (African) A jealous man
Monah

Mongo (African) A well-known
man
Mongoe, Mongow, Mongowe

Mongwau (Native American)
Resembling an owl

Monroe (Gaelic) From the
mouth of the river Roe
*Monro, Monrow, Monrowe,
Munro, Munroe, Munrow,
Munrowe*

Montenegro (Spanish) From
the black mountain

Montgomery (French) From
Gomeric's mountain
*Monty, Montgomerey,
Montgomeri, Montgomerie,
Montgomeree, Montgomerea*

Monty (English) Form of
Montgomery, meaning "from
Gomeric's mountain"
*Montey, Monti, Montie,
Montee, Montea, Montes,
Montez*

Moon (American) Born
beneath the moon; a dreamer

Mooney (Irish) A wealthy man
*Moony, Mooni, Moonie,
Maonaigh, Moonee, Moonea,
Moone*

Moose (American)
Resembling the animal; a big,
strong man
Moos, Mooze, Mooz

Moran (Irish) A great man
*Morane, Morain, Moraine,
Morayn, Morayne, Moraen,
Moraene*

Morathi (African) A wise man
Morathie, Morathy, Morathey, Morathee, Morathea

Moreland (English) From the moors
Moorland, Morland

Morley (English) From the meadow on the moor
Morly, Morleigh, Morlee, Morlea, Morleah, Morli, Morlie, Moorley

Morpheus (Greek) In mythology, the god of dreams
Morfeus, Morphius, Mofius

Mortimer (French) Of the still water; of the dead sea
Mortymer, Morty, Mortey, Morti, Mortie, Mortee, Mortea, Mort, Morte

Moses (Hebrew) A savior; in the Bible, the leader of the Israelites; drawn from the water
Mioshe, Mioshye, Mohsen, Moke, Moise, Moises, Mose, Moshe

Mostyn (Welsh) From the mossy settlement
Mostin, Mosten, Moston, Mostun, Mostan

Moswen (African) A light-skinned man
Moswenn, Moswenne, Moswin, Moswinn, Moswinne, Moswyn, Moswynn, Moswynne

Moubarak (Arabian) One who is blessed
Mubarak, Moobarak

Mounafes (Arabic) A rival

Muhannad (Arabic) One who wields a sword
Muhanned, Muhanad, Muhaned, Muhunnad, Muhunad, Muhanned, Muhaned

Mukhtar (Arabic) The chosen one
Muktar

Mukisa (Ugandan) Having good fortune
Mukysa

Mulcahy (Irish) A war chief
Mulcahey, Mulcahi, Mulcahie, Mulcahee, Mulcahea

Mundhir (Arabic) One who cautions others
Mundheer, Mundhear, Mundheir, Mundhier, Mundhyr

Murdock (Scottish) From the sea
Murdok, Murdoc, Murdo, Murdoch, Murtagh, Murtaugh, Murtogh, Murtough

Murfain (American) Having a warrior spirit
Murfaine, Murfayn, Murfayne, Murfaen, Murfaene, Murfane

Muriel (Gaelic) Of the shining sea
Muryel, Muriell, Muryell, Murial, Muriall, Muryal, Muryall, Murell

Murphy (Gaelic) A warrior of the sea
Murphey, Murphee, Murphea, Murphi, Murphie, Murfey, Murfy, Murfee

Murray (Gaelic) The lord of the sea
Murrey, Murry, Murri, Murrie, Murree, Murrea, Murry

Murron (Celtic) A bitter man
Murrun, Murren, Murran, Murrin, Murryn

Murtadi (Arabic) One who is content
Murtadie, Murtady, Murtadey, Murtadee, Murtadea

Musad (Arabic) One who is lucky
Musaad, Mus'ad

Mushin (Arabic) A charitable man
Musheen, Mushean, Mushein, Mushien, Mushyn

Muskan (Arabic) One who smiles often
Musken, Muskon, Muskun, Muskin, Muskyn

Muslim (Arabic) An adherent of Islam
Muslym, Muslem, Moslem, Moslim, Moslym

Mustapha (Arabic) The chosen one
Mustafa, Mostapha, Mostafa, Moustapha, Moustafa

Muti (Arabic) One who is obedient
Mutie, Muty, Mutey, Mutee, Mutea, Muta

Myron (Greek) Refers to myrrh, a fragrant oil
Myrun, Myran, Myren, Myrin, Myryn, Miron, Mirun, Miran

Mystique (French) A man with an air of mystery
Mystic, Mistique, Mysteek, Misteek, Mystiek, Mistiek, Mysteeque, Misteeque

N

Nabendu (Indian) Born beneath the new moon
Nabendue, Nabendoo, Nabendou

Nabhi (Indian) The best
Nabhie, Nabhy, Nabhey, Nabhee, Nabhea

Nabhomani (Indian) Of the sun
Nabhomanie, Nabhomany, Nabhomaney, Nabhomanee, Nabhomanea

Nabil (Arabic) A highborn man
Nabeel, Nabeal, Nabeil, Nabiel, Nabyl

Nabu (Babylonian) In mythology, the god of writing and wisdom
Nabue, Naboo, Nabo, Nebo, Nebu, Nebue, Neboo

Nachshon (Hebrew) An adventurous man; one who is daring
Nachson

Nadav (Hebrew) A generous man
Nadaav

Nadif (African) One who is born between seasons
Nadeef, Nadief, Nadeif, Nadyf, Nadeaf

Nadim (Arabic) A beloved friend
Nadeem, Nadeam, Nadiem, Nadeim, Nadym

Naftali (Hebrew) A struggling man; in the Bible, one of Jacob's sons
Naphtali, Naphthali, Neftali, Nefthali, Nephtali, Nephthali, Naftalie, Naphtalie

Nagel (German) One who makes nails
Nagle, Nagler, Naegel, Nageler, Nagelle, Nagele, Nagell

Nahir (Hebrew) A clear-headed and bright man
Naheer, Nahear, Naheir, Nahier, Nahyr, Naher

Nahum (Hebrew) A compassionate man
Nahom, Nahoum, Nahoom, Nahuem

Naji (Arabic) One who is safe
Najea, Naje, Najee, Najie, Najy, Najey, Nanji, Nanjie

Najib (Arabic) Of noble descent; a highborn man
Najeeb, Najeab, Najeib, Najieb, Najyb, Nageeb, Nageab, Nagyb

Nally (Irish) A poor man
*Nalley, Nalli, Nallie, Nallee,
Nallea, Nalleigh*

Namir (Israeli) Resembling a
leopard
*Nameer, Namear, Namier,
Nameir, Namyr*

Nandan (Indian) One who is
pleasing
*Nanden, Nandin, Nandyn,
Nandon, Nandun*

Naotau (Indian) Our new son
Naotou

Napier (French / English) A
mover / one who takes care of
the royal linens
Neper

Napoleon (Italian / German)
A man from Naples / son of
the mists
*Napolean, Napolion,
Napoleone, Napoleane,
Napolione*

Narcissus (Greek) Resembling
a daffodil; self-love; in mythology, a youth who fell in love
with his reflection
*Narciso, Narcisse, Narkissos,
Narses, Narcisus, Narcis,
Narciss*

Naresh (Indian) A king
Nareshe, Natesh, Nateshe

Nasih (Arabic) One who
advises others
Nasyh

Natal (Spanish) Born at
Christmastime
*Natale, Natalino, Natalio,
Natall, Natalle, Nataleo, Natica*

*ᵀNathan (Hebrew) Form of
Nathaniel, meaning "a gift
from God"
*Nat, Natan, Nate, Nathen,
Nathon, Nathin, Nathyn,
Nathun, Lathan*

*Nathaniel (Hebrew) A gift
from God
*Nathan, Natanael, Nataniel,
Nathanael, Nathaneal,
Nathanial, Nathanyal,
Nathanyel, Nethanel*

Nature (American) An
outdoorsy man
Natural

Navarro (Spanish) From the
plains
*Navaro, Navarrio, Navario,
Navarre, Navare, Nabaro,
Nabarro*

Naveed (Persian) Our best
wishes
*Navead, Navid, Navied,
Naveid, Navyd*

Nazim (Arabian) Of a soft breeze
Nazeem, Nazeam, Naziem, Nazeim, Nazym

Nebraska (Native American) From the flat water land; from the state of Nebraska

Neckarios (Greek) Of the nectar; one who is immortal
Nectaire, Nectarios, Nectarius, Nektario, Nektarius, Nektarios, Nektaire

Neelotpal (Indian) Resembling the blue lotus
Nealotpal, Nielotpal, Neilotpal, Nilothpal, Neelothpal

Negm (Arabian) Resembling a star

Nehal (Indian) Born during a period of rain
Nehall, Nehale, Nehalle

Nehemiah (Hebrew) God provides comfort
Nehemia, Nechemia, Nechemiah, Nehemya, Nehemyah, Nechemya, Nechemyah

Neil (Gaelic) The champion
Neal, Neale, Neall, Nealle, Nealon, Neel, Neilan, Neile

Neirin (Irish) Surrounded by light
Neiryn, Neiren, Neerin, Neeryn, Neeren

Nelek (Polish) Resembling a horn
Nelec, Neleck

Nelson (English) The son of Neil; the son of a champion
Nealson, Neilson, Neillson, Nelsen, Nilson, Nilsson, Nelli, Nellie

Neptune (Latin) In mythology, god of the sea
Neptun, Neptoon, Neptoone, Neptoun, Neptoune

Neroli (Italian) Resembling an orange blossom
Nerolie, Neroly, Neroley, Neroleigh, Nerolea, Nerolee

Nevan (Irish) The little saint
Naomhan

Neville (French) From the new village
Nev, Nevil, Nevile, Nevill, Nevylle, Nevyl, Nevyle, Nevyll

Newcomb (English) From the new valley
Newcom, Newcome, Newcombe, Neucomb, Neucombe, Neucom, Neucome

Newlin (Welsh) From the new pond
Newlinn, Newlyn, Newlynn, Neulin, Neulinn, Neulyn, Neulynn

Newman (English) A newcomer
Newmann, Neuman, Neumann

Nhat (Vietnamese) Having a long life
Nhatt, Nhate, Nhatte

Niaz (Persian) A gift
Nyaz

Nibaw (Native American) One who stands tall
Nybaw, Nibau, Nybau

^*ᵀ**Nicholas** (Greek) Of the victorious people
Nick, Nicanor, Niccolo, Nichol, Nicholai, Nicholaus, Nikolai, Nicholl, Nichols, Colin, Nicolas, Nico

Nick (English) Form of Nicholas, meaning "of the victorious people"
Nik, Nicki, Nickie, Nickey, Nicky, Nickee, Nickea, Niki

Nickler (American) One who is swift
Nikler, Nicler, Nyckler, Nykler, Nycler

Nicomedes (Greek) One who thinks of victory
Nikomedes, Nicomedo, Nikomedo

Nihal (Indian) One who is content
Neehal, Neihal, Niehal, Neahal, Neyhal, Nyhal

Nihar (Indian) Covered with the morning's dew
Neehar, Niehar, Neihar, Neahar, Nyhar

Nikan (Persian) One who brings good things
Niken, Nikin, Nikyn, Nikon, Nikun

Nikshep (Indian) One who is treasured
Nykshep

Nikunja (Indian) From the grove of trees

Nino (Italian / Spanish) God is gracious / a young boy
Ninoshka

Nirad (Indian) Of the clouds
Nyrad

Niran (Thai) The eternal one
Nyran, Niren, Nirin, Niryn, Niron, Nirun, Nyren, Nyrin

Nirav (Indian) One who is quiet
Nyrav

Nirbheet (Indian) A fearless man
Nirbhit, Nirbhyt, Nirbhay, Nirbhaye, Nirbhai, Nirbhae

Niremaan (Arabic) One who shines as brightly as fire
Nyremaan, Nireman, Nyreman

Nishan (Armenian) A sign or symbol

Nishok (Indian) Filled with happiness
Nyshok, Nishock, Nyshock

Nissan (Hebrew) A miracle child
Nisan

Niyol (Native American) Of the wind

Njord (Scandinavian) A man from the north
Njorde, Njorth, Njorthe

*ᵀNoah (Hebrew) A peaceful wanderer
Noa

Nodin (Native American) Of the wind
Nodyn, Noden, Nodan, Nodon, Nodun

*Nolan (Gaelic) A famous and noble man; a champion of the people
Nolen, Nolin, Nolon, Nolun, Nolyn, Noland, Nolande

North (English) A man from the north
Northe

Northcliff (English) From the northern cliff
Northcliffe, Northclyf, Northclyff, Northclyffe

Norval (Scottish) From the northern valley
Norvall, Norvale, Norvail, Norvaile, Norvayl, Norvayle, Norvael, Norvaele

Norward (English) A guardian of the north
Norwarde, Norwerd, Norwerde, Norwurd, Norwurde

Noshi (Native American) A fatherly man
Noshie, Noshy, Noshey, Noshee, Noshea, Nosh, Noshe

Notaku (Native American) Resembling a growling bear
Notakou, Notakue, Notakoo

Nuhad (Arabic) A brave young man
Nuehad, Nouhad, Neuhad

Nukpana (Native American) An evil man
Nukpanah, Nukpanna, Nukpannah, Nuckpana, Nucpana

Nulte (Irish) A man from Ulster
Nulti, Nultie, Nulty, Nultey, Nultee, Nultea

Nuncio (Spanish) A messenger
Nunzio

Nuriel (Hebrew) God's light
Nuriell, Nuriele, Nurielle, Nuryel, Nuryell, Nuryele, Nuryelle, Nooriel

Nuru (African) My light
Nurue, Nuroo, Nurou, Nourou, Nooroo

Nyack (African) One who is persistent
Niack, Nyak, Niak, Nyac, Niac

Nye (English) One who lives on the island
Nyle, Nie, Nile

O

Obedience (American) A well-behaved man
Obediance, Obedyence, Obedeynce

Oberon (German) A royal bear; having the heart of a bear
Oberron

Obert (German) A wealthy and bright man
Oberte, Oberth, Oberthe, Odbart, Odbarte, Odbarth, Odbarthe, Odhert

Ochi (African) Filled with laughter
Ochie, Ochee, Ochea, Ochy, Ochey

Odam (English) A son-in-law
Odom, Odem, Odum

Ode (Egyptian / Greek) Traveler of the road / a lyric poem

Oded (Hebrew) One who is supportive and encouraging

Oder (English) From the river
Odar, Odir, Odyr, Odur

Odin (Norse) In mythology, the supreme deity
Odyn, Odon, Oden, Odun

Odinan (Hungarian) One who is wealthy and powerful
Odynan, Odinann, Odynann

Odion (African) The first-born of twins
Odiyon, Odiun, Odiyun

Odissan (African) A wanderer; traveler
Odyssan, Odisan, Odysan, Odissann, Odyssann, Odisann, Odysann

Ofir (Hebrew) The golden son
Ofeer, Ofear, Ofyr, Ofier, Ofeir, Ofer

Ogaleesha (Native American) A man wearing a red shirt
Ogaleasha, Ogaleisha, Ogaleysha, Ogalesha, Ogaliesha, Ogalisha

Oghe (Irish) One who rides horses
Oghi, Oghie, Oghee, Oghea, Oghy, Oghey

Oguz (Hungarian) An arrow
Oguze, Oguzz, Oguzze

Ohanko (Native American) A reckless man
Ohankio, Ohankiyo

Ojaswit (Indian) A powerful and radiant man
Ojaswyt, Ojaswin, Ojaswen, Ojaswyn, Ojas

Okal (African) To cross
Okall

Okan (Turkish) Resembling a horse
Oken, Okin, Okyn

Okapi (African) Resembling an animal with a long neck
Okapie, Okapy, Okapey, Okapee, Okapea, Okape

Okechuku (African) Blessed by God

Oki (Japanese) From the center of the ocean
Okie, Oky, Okey, Okee, Okea

Oklahoma (Native American) Of the red people; from the state of Oklahoma

Oktawian (African) The eighth-born child
Oktawyan, Oktawean, Octawian, Octawyan, Octawean

Olaf (Scandinavian) The remaining of the ancestors
Olay, Ole, Olef, Olev, Oluf, Uolevi

Olafemi (African) A lucky young man
Olafemie, Olafemy, Olafemey, Olafemee, Olafemea

Oleg (Russian) One who is holy
Olezka

*Oliver (Latin) From the olive tree
Oliviero, Olivero, Olivier, Oliviero, Olivio, Ollie

Olney (English) From the loner's field
Olny, Olnee, Olnea, Olni, Olnie, Ollaneg, Olaneg

Olujimi (African) One who is close to God
Olujimie, Olujimy, Olujimey, Olujimee, Olujimea

Olumide (African) God has arrived
Olumidi, Olumidie, Olumidy, Olumidey, Olumidee, Olumidea, Olumyde, Olumydi

Omar (Arabic) A flourishing man; one who is well-spoken
Omarr, Omer

Omeet (Hebrew) My light
Omeete, Omeit, Omeite, Omeyt, Omeyte, Omit, Omeat, Omeate

Omega (Greek) The last great one; the last letter of the Greek alphabet
Omegah

Onaona (Hawaiian) Having a pleasant scent

Ond (Hungarian) The tenth-born child
Onde

Ondrej (Czech) A manly man
Ondrejek, Ondrejec, Ondrousek, Ondravsek

Onkar (Indian) The purest one
Onckar, Oncar, Onkarr, Onckarr, Oncarr

Onofrio (Italian) A defender of peace
Onofre, Onofrius, Onophrio, Onophre, Onfrio, Onfroi

Onslow (Arabic) From the hill of the enthusiast
Onslowe, Ounslow, Ounslowe

Onyebuchi (African) God is in everything
Onyebuchie, Onyebuchy, Onyebuchey, Onyebuchee, Onyebuchea

Oqwapi (Native American) Resembling a red cloud
Oqwapie, Oqwapy, Oqwapey, Oqwapee, Oqwapea

Oram (English) From the enclosure near the riverbank
Oramm, Oraham, Orahamm, Orham, Orhamm

Ordell (Latin) Of the beginning
Ordel, Ordele, Ordelle, Orde

Ordway (Anglo-Saxon) A fighter armed with a spear
Ordwaye, Ordwai, Ordwae

Oren (Hebrew / Gaelic) From the pine tree / a pale-skinned man
Orenthiel, Orenthiell, Orenthiele, Orenthielle, Orenthiem, Orenthium, Orin

Orion (Greek) A great hunter

Orleans (Latin) The golden child
Orlean, Orleane, Orleens, Orleen, Orleene, Orlins, Olryns, Orlin

Orly (Hebrew) Surrounded by light
Orley, Orli, Orlie, Orlee, Orleigh, Orlea

Ormod (Anglo-Saxon) A sorrowful man

Ormond (English) One who defends with a spear / from the mountain of bears
Ormonde, Ormund, Ormunde, Ormemund, Ormemond, Ordmund, Ordmunde, Ordmond

Ornice (Irish / Hebrew) A pale-skinned man / from the cedar tree
Ornyce, Ornise, Orynse, Orneice, Orneise, Orniece, Orniese, Orneece

Orris (Latin) One who is inventive
Orriss, Orrisse, Orrys, Orryss, Orrysse

Orson (Latin) Resembling a bear; raised by a bear
Orsen, Orsin, Orsini, Orsino, Orsis, Orsonio, Orsinie, Orsiny

Orth (English) An honest man
Orthe

Orton (English) From the settlement by the shore
Ortun, Oraton, Oratun

Orville (French) From the gold town
Orvell, Orvelle, Orvil, Orvill, Orvele, Orvyll, Orvylle, Orvyl

Orwel (Welsh) Of the horizon
Orwell, Orwele, Orwelle

Os (English) The divine

Osborn (Norse) A bear of God
Osborne, Osbourn, Osbourne, Osburn, Osburne

Oscar (English / Gaelic) A spear of the gods / a friend of deer
Oskar, Osker, Oscer, Osckar, Oscker, Oszkar, Oszcar

Osher (Hebrew) A man of good fortune

Osias (Greek) Salvation
Osyas

Osileani (Polynesian) One who talks a lot
Osileanie, Osileany, Osileaney, Osileanee, Osileanea

Oswald (English) The power of God
Oswalde, Osvald, Osvaldo, Oswaldo, Oswell, Osvalde, Oswallt, Osweald

Oswin (English) A friend of God
Oswinn, Oswinne, Oswen, Oswenn, Oswenne, Oswyn, Oswynn, Oswynne

Othniel (Hebrew) God's lion
Othniell, Othnielle, Othniele, Othnyel, Othnyell, Othnyele, Othnyelle

Otmar (Teutonic) A famous warrior
Otmarr, Othmar, Othmarr, Otomar, Ottomar

Otoahhastis (Native American) Resembling a tall bull

Ottokar (German) A spirited warrior
Otokar, Otokarr, Ottokarr, Ottokars, Otokars, Ottocar, Otocar, Ottocars

Ouray (Native American) The arrow
Ouraye, Ourae, Ourai

Ourson (French) Resembling a little bear
Oursun, Oursoun, Oursen, Oursan, Oursin, Oursyn

Ovid (Latin) A shepherd; an egg
Ovyd, Ovidio, Ovido, Ovydio, Ovydo, Ovidiu, Ovydiu, Ofydd

*ᵀOwen (Welsh / Gaelic) Form of Eugene, meaning "a well-born man" / a youthful man
Owenn, Owenne, Owin, Owinn, Owinne, Owyn, Owynn, Owynne

Oxton (English) From the oxen town
Oxtun, Oxtown, Oxnaton, Oxnatun, Oxnatown

Oz (Hebrew) Having great strength
Ozz, Ozzi, Ozzie, Ozzy, Ozzey, Ozzee, Ozzea, Ozi

Ozni (Hebrew) One who knows God
Oznie, Ozny, Ozney, Oznee, Oznea

Ozuru (Japanese) Resembling a stork
Ozurou, Ozourou, Ozuroo, Ozooroo

P

Paavo (Finnish) Form of Paul, meaning "a small or humble man"
Paaveli

Pace (Hebrew / English) Refers to Passover / a peaceful man
Paice, Payce, Paece, Pacey, Pacy, Pacee, Paci, Pacie

Pacho (Spanish) An independent man; one who is free

Pachu'a (Native American) Resembling a water snake

Paco (Spanish) A man from France
Pacorro, Pacoro, Paquito

Padgett (French) One who strives to better himself
Padget, Padgette, Padgete, Padgeta, Padgetta, Padge, Paget, Pagett

Padman (Indian) Resembling the lotus
Padmann

Padruig (Scottish) Of the royal family

Paine (Latin) Man from the country; a peasant
Pain, Payn, Payne, Paen, Paene, Pane, Paien

Palamedes (English) In Arthurian legend, a knight
Palomydes, Palomedes, Palamydes, Palsmedes, Palsmydes, Pslomydes

Palban (Spanish) A blond-haired man
Palben, Palbin, Palbyn, Palbon, Palbun

Paley (English) Form of Paul, meaning "a small or humble man"
Paly, Pali, Palie, Palee, Palea

Palladin (Greek) Filled with wisdom
Palladyn, Palladen, Palladan, Paladin, Paladyn, Paladen, Paladan

Palmer (English) A pilgrim bearing a palm branch
Pallmer, Palmar, Pallmar, Palmerston, Palmiro, Palmeero, Palmeer, Palmire

Pan (Greek) In mythology, god of the shepherds
Pann

Panama (Spanish) From the canal

Pancho (Spanish) A man from France

Pankaj (Indian) Resembling the lotus flower

Panya (African) Resembling a mouse
Panyah

Panyin (African) The first-born of twins
Panyen

Paras (Hindi) A touchstone
Parasmani, Parasmanie, Parasmany, Parasmaney, Parasmanee

*Parker (English) The keeper of the park
Parkar, Parkes, Parkman, Park

Parley (Scottish) A reluctant man
Parly, Parli, Parlie, Parlee, Parlea, Parle

Parmenio (Spanish) A studious man; one who is intelligent
Parmenios, Parmenius

Parounag (Armenian) One who is thankful

Parrish (Latin) Man of the church
Parish, Parrishe, Parishe, Parrysh, Parysh, Paryshe, Parryshe, Parisch

Parry (Welsh) The son of Harry
Parrey, Parri, Parrie, Parree, Parrea

Parthenios (Greek) One who is pure; chaste
Parthenius

Parthik (Greek) One who is pure; chaste
Parthyk, Parthick, Parthyck, Parthic, Parthyc

Pascal (Latin) Born during Easter
Pascale, Pascalle, Paschal, Paschalis, Pascoe, Pascual, Pascuale, Pasqual

Patamon (Native American) Resembling a tempest
Patamun, Patamen, Pataman, Patamyn, Patamin

Patch (American) Form of Peter, meaning "as solid and strong as a rock"
Pach, Patche, Patchi, Patchie, Patchy, Patchey, Patchee

Patrick (Latin) A nobleman; patrician
Packey, Padric, Pat, Patrece, Patric, Patrice, Patreece, Patricio

Patton (English) From the town of warriors
Paten, Patin, Paton, Patten, Pattin, Paddon, Padden, Paddin

Patwin (Native American) A manly man
Patwinn, Patwinne, Patwyn, Patwynne, Patwynn, Patwen, Patwenn, Patwenne

Paul (Latin) A small or humble man
Pauley, Paulie, Pauly, Paley, Paavo

Paurush (Indian) A courageous man
Paurushe, Paurushi, Paurushie, Paurushy, Paurushey, Paurushee

Pavanjit (Indian) Resembling the wind
Pavanjyt, Pavanjeet, Pavanjeat, Pavanjete

Paxton (English) From the peaceful town
Packston, Paxon, Paxten, Paxtun, Packstun, Packsten

Pazel (Hebrew) God's gold; treasured by God
Pazell, Pazele, Pazelle

Pearroc (English) Man of the forest
Pearoc, Pearrok, Pearok, Pearrock, Pearock

Pecos (American) From the river; a cowboy
Pekos, Peckos

Pedro (Spanish) Form of Peter, meaning "as solid and strong as a rock"
Pedrio, Pepe, Petrolino, Piero, Pietro

Pelham (English) From the house of furs; from Peola's home
Pellham, Pelam, Pellam

Pell (English) A clerk or one who works with skins
Pelle, Pall, Palle

Pelon (Spanish) Filled with joy
Pellon

Pelton (English) From the town by the lake
Pellton, Peltun, Pelltun, Peltan, Pelltan, Pelten, Pellten, Peltin

Penda (African) One who is dearly loved
Pendah, Penha, Penhah

Penley (English) From the enclosed meadow
Penly, Penleigh, Penli, Penlie, Penlee, Penlea, Penleah, Pennley

Penrod (German) A respected commander

Pentele (Hungarian) A merciful man
Pentelle, Pentel, Pentell

Penuel (Hebrew) The face of God
Penuell, Penuele, Penuelle

Percival (French) One who can pierce the vale"
Purcival, Percy, Percey, Perci, Percie, Percee, Percea, Persy, Persey, Persi

Peregrine (Latin) One who travels; a wanderer
Perry, Perree, Perrea, Perri, Perrie, Perregrino

Perez (Hebrew) To break through
Peretz

Pericles (Greek) One who is in excess of glory
Perricles, Perycles, Perrycles, Periclees, Perriclees, Peryclees, Perryclees, Periclez

Perk (American) One who is cheerful and jaunty
Perke, Perky, Perkey, Perki, Perkie, Perkee, Perkea

Perkinson (English) The son of Perkin; the son of Peter
Perkynson

Perseus (Greek) In mythology, son of Zeus who slew Medusa
Persius, Persyus, Persies, Persyes

Perth (Celtic) From the thorny thicket
Perthe, Pert, Perte

Perye (English) From the pear tree

Peter (Greek) As solid and strong as a rock
Peder, Pekka, Per, Petar, Pete, Peterson, Petr, Petre, Pierce, Patch, Pedro

Petuel (Hindi) The Lord's vision
Petuell, Petuele, Petuelle

Peyton (English) From the village of warriors
Payton, Peytun, Paytun, Peyten, Payten, Paiton, Paitun, Paiten

Pharis (Irish) A heroic man
Pharys, Pharris, Pharrys

Phex (American) A kind man
Phexx

Philemon (Hebrew) A loving man
Phylemon, Philimon, Phylimon, Philomon, Phylomon, Philamon, Phylamon

Philetus (Greek) A collector
Phyletus, Philetos, Phyletos

Phillip (Greek) One who loves horses
Phil, Philip, Felipe, Filipp, Phillie, Philly

Philo (Greek) One who loves and is loved

Phoebus (Greek) A radiant man
Phoibos

Phomello (African) A successful man
Phomelo

Phong (Vietnamese) Of the wind

Phuc (Vietnamese) One who is blessed
Phuoc

Picardus (Hispanic) An adventurous man
Pycardus, Picardos, Pycardos, Picardas, Pycardas, Picardis, Pycardis, Picardys

Pickworth (English) From the woodcutter's estate
Pikworth, Picworth, Pickworthe, Pikworthe, Picworthe

Pierce (English) Form of Peter, meaning "as solid and strong as a rock"
Pearce, Pears, Pearson, Pearsson, Peerce, Peirce, Pierson, Piersson

Pin (Vietnamese) Filled with joy
Pyn

Pio (Latin) A pious man
Pyo, Pios, Pius, Pyos, Pyus

Pirro (Greek) A red-haired man
Pyrro

Pitney (English) From the island of the stubborn man
Pitny, Pitni, Pitnie, Pitnee, Pitnea, Pytney, Pytny, Pytni

Pittman (English) A laborer
Pyttman, Pitman, Pytman

Plantagenet (French) Resembling the broom flower

Poetry (American) A romantic man
Poetrey, Poetri, Poetrie, Poetree, Poetrea, Poet, Poete

Pollux (Greek) One who is crowned
Pollock, Pollok, Polloc, Pollack, Polloch

Polo (African) Resembling an alligator
Poloe, Poloh

Ponce (Spanish) The fifth-born child
Ponse

Pongor (Hungarian) A mighty man
Pongorr, Pongoro, Pongorro

Poni (African) The second-born son
Ponni, Ponie, Ponnie, Pony, Ponny, Poney, Ponney, Ponee

Pons (Latin) From the bridge
Pontius, Ponthos, Ponthus

Poornamruth (Indian) Full of sweetness
Pournamruth

Poornayu (Indian) Full of life; blessed with a full life
Pournayu, Poornayou, Pournayou, Poornayue, Pournayue

Porat (Hebrew) A productive man

Porfirio (Greek) Refers to a purple coloring
Porphirios, Prophyrios, Porfiro, Porphyrios

Powhatan (Native American) From the chief's hill

Prabhakar (Hindu) Of the sun

Prabhat (Indian) Born during the morning

Pragun (Indian) One who is straightforward; honest

Pramod (Indian) A delightful young man

Pranit (Indian) One who is humble; modest
Pranyt, Praneet, Praneat

Prasad (Indian) A gift from God

Prashant (Indian) One who is peaceful; calm
Prashante, Prashanth, Prashanthe

Pratap (Hindi) A majestic man

Pravat (Thai) History

Prem (Indian) An affectionate man

Prentice (English) A student; an apprentice
Prentyce, Prentise, Prentyse, Prentiss, Prentis

Prescott (English) From the priest's cottage
Prescot, Prestcot, Prestcott, Preostcot

Preston (English) From the priest's town
Prestin, Prestyn, Prestan, Prestun, Presten, Pfeostun

Prewitt (French) A brave young one
Prewet, Prewett, Prewit, Pruitt, Pruit, Pruet, Pruett

Prine (English) One who surpasses others
Pryne

Prometheus (Greek) In mythology, he stole fire from the heavens and gave it to man
Promitheus, Promethius, Promithius

Prop (American) A fun-loving man
Propp, Proppe

Prosper (Latin) A fortunate man
Prospero, Prosperus

Pryderi (Celtic) Son of the sea
Pryderie, Prydery, Pryderey, Pryderee, Pryderea

Prydwen (Welsh) A handsome man
Prydwenn, Prydwenne, Prydwin, Prydwinne, Prydwinn, Prydwyn, Prydwynn, Prydwynne

Pullman (English) One who works on a train
Pulman, Pullmann, Pulmann

Pyralis (Greek) Born of fire
Pyraliss, Pyralisse, Pyralys, Pyralyss, Pyralysse, Pyre

Qabil (Arabic) An able-bodied man
Qabyl, Qabeel, Qabeal, Qabeil, Qabiel

Qadim (Arabic) From an ancient family
Qadeem, Qadiem, Qadeim, Qadym, Qadeam

Qaiser (Arabic) A king; a ruler
Qeyser

Qamar (Arabic) Born beneath the moon
Qamarr, Quamar, Quamarr

Qimat (Hindi) A highly valued man
Qymat

Qing (Chinese) Of the deep water
Qyng

Quaashie (American) An ambitious man
Quashie, Quashi, Quashy, Quashey, Quashee, Quashea, Quaashi, Quaashy

Quaddus (American) A bright man
Quadus, Quaddos, Quados

Quade (Latin) The fourth-born child
Quadrees, Quadres, Quadrys, Quadries, Quadreis, Quadreys, Quadreas, Quadrhys

Quaid (Irish) Form of Walter, meaning "the commander of the army"
Quaide, Quayd, Quayde, Quaed, Quaede

Quashawn (American) A tenacious man
Quashaun, Quasean, Quashon, Quashi, Quashie, Quashee, Quashea, Quashy

Qued (Native American) Wearing a decorated robe

Quentin (Latin) The fifth-born child
Quent, Quenten, Quenton, Quentun, Quentan, Quentyn, Quente, Qwentin

Quick (American) One who is fast; a witty man
Quik, Quicke, Quic

Quillan (Gaelic) Resembling a cub
Quilan, Quillen, Quilen, Quillon, Quilon

Quilliam (Gaelic) Form of William, meaning "the determined protector"
Quilhelm, Quilhelmus, Quilliams, Quilliamson

Quimby (Norse) From the woman's estate
Quimbey, Quimbee, Quimbea, Quimbi, Quimbie

Quincy (English) The fifth-born child; from the fifth son's estate
Quincey, Quinci, Quincie, Quincee, Quinncy, Quinnci, Quyncy, Quyncey

Quinlan (Gaelic) A strong and healthy man
Quindlan, Quinlen, Quindlen, Quinian, Quinlin, Quindlin, Quinlyn, Quindlyn

Quinn (Gaelic) One who provides counsel; an intelligent man
Quin, Quinne, Qwinn, Quynn, Qwin, Quiyn, Quyn, Qwinne

Quintavius (American) The fifth-born child
Quintavios, Quintavus, Quintavies

Quinto (Spanish) The fifth-born child
Quynto, Quintus, Quintos, Quinty, Quinti, Quintie

Quinton (Latin) From the queen's town or settlement
Laquinton

Quintrell (English) An elegant and dashing man
Quintrel, Quintrelle, Quyntrell, Quyntrelle, Quyntrel, Quyntrele, Quintrele

Quirinus (Latin) One who wields a spear
Quirinos, Quirynus, Quirynos, Quirinius, Quirynius

Quito (Spanish) A lively man
Quyto, Quitos, Quytos

Quoc (Vietnamese) A patriot
Quok, Quock

Qutub (Indian) One who is tall

R

Rabbaanee (African) An easy-going man

Rabbi (Hebrew) The master

Rach (African) Resembling a frog

Radames (Egyptian) A hero
Radamays, Radamayes, Radamais, Radamaise

Radford (English) From the red ford
Radforde, Radferd, Radfurd, Radferde, Radfurde

Rafael (Spanish) Form of Raphael, meaning "one who is healed by God"
Raphael, Raphaello, Rafaello

Rafe (Irish) A tough man
Raffe, Raff, Raf, Raif, Rayfe, Raife, Raef, Raefe

Rafi (Arabic) One who is exalted
Rafie, Rafy, Rafey, Rafea, Rafee, Raffi, Raffie, Raffy

Rafiki (African) A gentle friend
Rafikie, Rafikea, Rafikee, Rafiky, Rafikey

Rafiya (African) A dignified man
Rafeeya, Rafeaya, Rafeiya, Rafieya

Raghib (Arabic) One who is desired
Ragheb, Ragheeb, Ragheab, Raghyb, Ragheib, Raghieb

Ragnar (Norse) A warrior who places judgment
Ragnor, Ragner, Ragnir, Ragnyr, Ragnur, Regnar

Rahim (Arabic) A compassionate man
Rahym, Raheim, Rahiem, Raheem, Raheam

Raiden (Japanese) In mythology, the god of thunder and lightning
Raidon, Rayden, Raydon, Raeden, Raedon, Raden

Raimi (African) A compassionate man
Raimie, Raimy, Raimey, Raimee, Raimea

Rajab (African) A glorified man

Rajan (Indian) A king
Raj, Raja, Rajah

Rajarshi (Indian) The king's sage
Rajarshie, Rajarshy, Rajarshey, Rajarshee, Rajarshea

Rajesh (Hindi) The king's rule

Rajit (Indian) One who is decorated
Rajeet, Rajeit, Rajiet, Rajyt, Rajeat

Rajiv (Hindi) To be striped
Rajyv, Rajeev, Rajeav

Ralph (English) Wolf counsel
Ralf, Ralphe, Ralfe, Ralphi, Ralphie, Ralphee, Ralphea, Ralphy, Raoul

Ram (Hebrew / Sanskrit) A superior man / one who is pleasing
Rahm, Rama, Rahma, Ramos, Rahmos, Ramm

Rambert (German) Having great strength; an intelligent man
Ramberte, Ramberth, Ramberthe, Ramburt

Rami (Arabic) A loving man
Ramee, Ramea, Ramie, Ramy, Ramey

Ramiro (Portuguese) A famous counselor; a great judge
Ramyro, Rameero, Rameyro, Ramirez, Ramyrez, Rameerez

Ramsey (English) From the raven island; from the island of wild garlic
Ramsay, Ramsie, Ramsi, Ramsee, Ramsy, Ramsea, Ramzy, Ramzey

Rand (German) One who shields others
Rande

Randall (German) The wolf shield
Randy, Randal, Randale, Randel, Randell, Randl, Randle, Randon, Rendall

Randolph (German) The wolf shield
Randy, Randolf, Ranolf, Ranolph, Ranulfo, Randulfo, Randwulf, Ranwulf, Randwolf

Randy (English) Form of Randall or Randolph, meaning "the wolf shield"
Randey, Randi, Randie, Randee, Randea

Rang (English) Resembling a raven
Range

Rangey (English) From raven's island
Rangy, Rangi, Rangie, Rangee, Rangea

Rangle (American) A cowboy
Rangel

Ranjan (Indian) A delightful boy

Raoul (French) Form of Ralph, meaning "wolf counsel"
Raoule, Raul, Roul, Rowl, Raule, Roule, Rowle

Raqib (Arabic) A glorified man
Raqyb, Raqeeb, Raqeab, Rakib, Rakeeb, Rakeab, Rakyb

Rashard (American) A good-hearted man
Rasherd, Rashird, Rashurd, Rashyrd

Rashaun (American) Form of Roshan, meaning "born during the daylight"
Rashae, Rashane, Rashawn, Rayshaun, Rayshawn, Raishaun, Raishawn, Raeshaun

Ratul (Indian) A sweet man
Ratule, Ratoul, Ratoule, Ratool, Ratoole

Raulo (Spanish) One who is wise
Rawlo

Ravi (Hindi) From the sun
Ravie, Ravy, Ravey, Ravee, Ravea

Ravid (Hebrew) A wanderer; one who searches
Ravyd, Raveed, Ravead, Raviyd, Ravied, Raveid

Ravindra (Indian) The strength of the sun
Ravyndra

Ravinger (English) One who lives near the ravine
Ravynger

Rawlins (French) From the renowned land
Rawlin, Rawson, Rawlinson, Rawlings, Rawling, Rawls, Rawl, Rawle

Ray (English) Form of Raymond, meaning "a wise protector"
Rae, Rai, Rayce, Rayder, Rayse, Raye, Rayford, Raylen

Rayfield (English) From the field of roe deer
Rayfeld

Rayhurn (English) From the roe deer's stream
Rayhurne, Rayhorn, Rayhorne, Rayhourn, Rayhourne

Raymond (German) A wise protector
Ray, Raemond, Raemondo, Raimond, Raimondo, Raimund, Raimundo, Rajmund, Ramon

Rebel (American) An outlaw
Rebell, Rebele, Rebelle, Rebe, Rebbe, Rebbi, Rebbie, Rebbea

Redwald (English) Strong counsel
Redwalde, Raedwalde, Raedwald

Reeve (English) A bailiff
Reve, Reave, Reeford, Reeves, Reaves, Reves, Reaford

Regal (American) Born into royalty
Regall

Regan (Gaelic) Born into royalty; the little ruler
Raegan, Ragan, Raygan, Reganne, Regann, Regane, Reghan, Reagan

Regenfrithu (English) A peaceful raven

Reggie (Latin) Form of Reginald, meaning "the king's advisor"
Reggi, Reggy, Reggey, Reggea, Reggee, Reg

Reginald (Latin) The king's advisor
Reggie, Reynold, Raghnall, Rainault, Rainhold, Raonull, Raynald, Rayniero, Regin, Reginaldo

Regine (French) One who is artistic
Regeen, Regeene, Regean, Regeane, Regein, Regeine, Regien, Regiene

^**Reid** (English) A red-haired man; one who lives near the reeds
Read, Reade, Reed, Reede, Reide, Raed

Reilly (Gaelic) An outgoing man
Reilley, Reilli, Reillie, Reillee, Reilleigh, Reillea

^**Remington** (English) From
the town of the raven's family
*Remyngton, Remingtun,
Remyngtun*

Renweard (Anglo-Saxon) The
guardian of the house
Renward, Renwarden, Renwerd

Renzo (Japanese) The third-
born son

Reuben (Hebrew) Behold, a
son!
*Reuban, Reubin, Reuven,
Rouvin, Rube, Ruben, Rubin,
Rubino*

Rev (American) One who is
distinct
*Revv, Revin, Reven, Revan,
Revyn, Revon, Revun*

Rex (Latin) A king
Reks, Recks, Rexs

Rexford (English) From the
king's ford
*Rexforde, Rexferd, Rexferde,
Rexfurd, Rexfurde*

Reynold (English) Form of
Reginald, meaning "the
king's advisor"
*Reynald, Reynaldo, Reynolds,
Reynalde, Reynolde*

Rhett (Latin) A well-spoken
man
Rett, Rhet

^**Rhys** (Welsh) Having great
enthusiasm for life

Richard (English) A powerful
ruler
*Rick, Rich, Ricard, Ricardo,
Riccardo, Richardo, Richart,
Richerd, Rickard, Rickert*

Richmond (French / German)
From the wealthy hill / a
powerful protector
*Richmonde, Richmund,
Richmunde*

Rick (English) Form of
Richard, meaning "a powerful
ruler"
*Ric, Ricci, Ricco, Rickie, Ricki,
Ricky, Rico, Rik*

Rickward (English) A strong
protector
*Rickwerd, Rickwood, Rikward,
Ricward, Rickweard, Rikweard,
Ricweard*

Riddock (Irish) From the
smooth field
*Ridock, Riddoc, Ridoc,
Ryddock, Rydock, Ryddoc,
Rydoc, Ryddok*

Ridgeway (English) One who
lives on the road near the
ridge
Rydgeway, Rigeway, Rygeway

Rigg (English) One who lives near the ridge
Rig, Ridge, Rygg, Ryg, Rydge, Rige, Ryge, Riggs

Riley (English) From the rye clearing
Ryly, Ryli, Rylie, Rylee, Ryleigh, Rylea, Ryleah

Riordain (Irish) A bright man
Riordane, Riordayn, Riordaen, Reardain, Reardane, Reardayn, Reardaen

Riordan (Gaelic) A royal poet; a bard or minstrel
Riorden, Rearden, Reardan, Riordon, Reardon

Ripley (English) From the noisy meadow
Riply, Ripleigh, Ripli, Riplie, Riplea, Ripleah, Riplee, Rip

Rishley (English) From the untamed meadow
Rishly, Rishli, Rishlie, Rishlee, Rishlea, Rishleah, Rishleigh

Rishon (Hebrew) The first-born son
Ryshon, Rishi, Rishie, Rishea, Rishee, Rishy, Rishey

Risley (English) From the brushwood meadow
Risly, Risli, Rislie, Risleigh, Rislea, Risleah, Rislee

Riston (English) From the brushwood settlement
Ryston, Ristun, Rystun

Ritter (German) A knight
Rytter, Ritt, Rytt

River (American) From the river
Ryver, Rivers, Ryvers

Roald (Norse) A famous ruler
Roal

Roam (American) One who wanders, searches
Roami, Roamie, Roamy, Roamey, Roamea, Roamee

Roark (Gaelic) A champion
Roarke, Rorke, Rourke, Rork, Rourk, Ruark, Ruarke

ᵀ*Robert** (German) One who is bright with fame
Bob, Rupert, Riobard, Roban, Robers, Roberto, Robertson, Robartach

Rochester (English) From the stone fortress

Rockford (English) From the rocky ford
Rockforde, Rokford, Rokforde, Rockferd, Rokferd, Rockfurd, Rokfurd

Roderick (German) A famous ruler
Rod, Rodd, Roddi, Roddie, Roddy, Roddee, Roddea

Rodney (German / English) From the famous one's island / from the island's clearing
Rodny, Rodni, Rodnie

Rogelio (Spanish) A famous soldier
Rogelo, Rogeliyo, Rogeleo, Rogeleyo, Rojelio, Rojeleo

Roland (German) From the renowned land
Roeland, Rolando, Roldan, Roley, Rollan, Rolland, Rollie, Rollin

Roman (Latin) A citizen of Rome
Romain, Romaine, Romeo

Romeo (Italian) Traveler to Rome

Ronald (Norse) The king's advisor
Ranald, Renaldo, Ronal, Ronaldo, Rondale, Roneld, Ronell, Ronello

^Ronan (Gaelic) Resembling a little seal

Rong (Chinese) Having glory

Rook (English) Resembling a raven
Rooke, Rouk, Rouke, Ruck, Ruk

Rooney (Gaelic) A red-haired man
Roony, Rooni, Roonie, Roonea, Roonee, Roon, Roone

Roosevelt (Danish) From the field of roses
Rosevelt

Roper (English) One who makes rope
Rapere

Rory (Gaelic) A red-haired man
Rori, Rorey, Rorie, Rorea, Roree, Rorry, Rorrey, Rorri

Roshan (Hindi) Born during the daylight
Rashaun

Roslin (Gaelic) A little red-haired boy
Roslyn, Rosselin, Rosslyn, Rozlin, Rozlyn, Rosling, Rozling

Roswald (German) Of the mighty horses
Rosswald, Roswalt, Rosswalt

Roswell (English) A fascinating man
Rosswell, Rozwell, Roswel, Rozwel

Roth (German) A red-haired
man
Rothe

Rousseau (French) A little red-
haired boy
*Roussell, Russo, Rousse,
Roussel, Rousset, Rousskin*

Rowdy (English) A boisterous
man
*Rowdey, Rowdi, Rowdie,
Rowdee, Rowdea*

Roy (Gaelic / French) A red-
haired man / a king
Roye, Roi, Royer, Ruy

Royce (German / French) A
famous man / son of the king
Roice, Royse, Roise

Ruadhan (Irish) A red-haired
man; the name of a saint
*Ruadan, Ruadhagan,
Ruadagan*

Ruarc (Irish) A famous ruler
*Ruarck, Ruarcc, Ruark,
Ruarkk, Ruaidhri, Ruaidri*

Rubio (Spanish) Resembling
a ruby

Rudeger (German) A friendly
man
*Rudegar, Rudger, Rudgar,
Rudiger, Rudigar*

Rudolph (German) A famous
wolf
*Rodolfo, Rodolph, Rodolphe,
Rodolpho, Rudy, Rudey, Rudi,
Rudie*

Rudyard (English) From the
red paddock

Rufus (Latin) A red-haired
man
Ruffus, Rufous, Rufino

Ruiz (Spanish) A good friend

Rujul (Indian) An honest man
*Rujool, Rujoole, Rujule, Rujoul,
Rujoule*

Rumford (English) From the
broad ford
*Rumforde, Rumferd, Rumferde,
Rumfurd*

Rupert (English) Form of
Robert, meaning "one who is
bright with fame"
Ruprecht

Rushford (English) From the
ford with rushes
*Rusheford, Rushforde,
Rusheforde, Ryscford*

Russell (French) A little red-
haired boy
*Russel, Roussell, Russ, Rusel,
Rusell*

Russom (African) The chief;
the boss
Rusom, Russome, Rusome

Rusty (English) One who
has red hair or a ruddy
complexion
*Rustey, Rusti, Rustie, Rustee,
Rustea, Rust, Ruste, Rustice*

Rutherford (English) From the
cattle's ford
*Rutherfurd, Rutherferd,
Rutherforde, Rutherfurde*

*Ryan (Gaelic) The little ruler;
little king
*Rian, Rien, Rion, Ryen, Ryon,
Ryun, Rhyan, Rhyen*

Ryder (English) An accom-
plished horseman
*Rider, Ridder, Ryden, Rydell,
Rydder*

Ryker (Danish) Form of
Richard, meaning "a powerful
ruler"
Riker

Rylan (English) Form of
Ryland, meaning "from the
place where rye is grown"
Ryelan, Ryle

^Ryland (English) From the
place where Rye is grown

S

Saarik (Hindi) Resembling a
small songbird
*Saarick, Saaric, Sarik, Sarick,
Saric, Saariq, Sareek, Sareeq*

Saber (French) Man of the
sword
Sabere, Sabr, Sabre

Sabir (Arabic) One who is
patient
*Sabyr, Sabeer, Sabear, Sabeir,
Sabier, Sabri, Sabrie, Sabree*

Saddam (Arabic) A powerful
ruler; the crusher
Saddum, Saddim, Saddym

Sadiq (Arabic) A beloved
friend
*Sadeeq, Sadyq, Sadeaq, Sadeek,
Sadeak, Sadyk, Sadik*

Saga (American) A storyteller
Sago

Sagar (Indian / English) A
king / one who is wise
Saagar, Sagarr, Saagarr

Sagaz (Spanish) One who is
clever
Sagazz

Sagiv (Hebrew) Having great strength
Sagev, Segiv, Segev

Sahaj (Indian) One who is natural

Saieshwar (Hindi) A well-known saint
Saishwar

Sailor (American) Man who sails the seas
Sailer, Sailar, Saylor, Sayler, Saylar, Saelor

Saith (English) One who is well-spoken
Saithe, Sayth, Saythe, Saeth, Saethe, Sath, Sathe

Sajal (Indian) Resembling a cloud
Sajall, Sajjal, Sajjall

Sajan (Indian) One who is dearly loved
Sajann, Sajjan, Sajjann

Saki (Japanese) One who is cloaked
Sakie, Saky, Sakey, Sakee, Sakea

Salaam (African) Resembling a peach

Salehe (African) A good man
Saleh, Salih

Salim (Arabic) One who is peaceful
Saleem, Salem, Selim

Salute (American) A patriotic man
Saloot, Saloote, Salout

Salvador (Spanish) A savior
Sal, Sally, Salvadore, Xalvador

Samanjas (Indian) One who is proper

Samarth (Indian) A powerful man; one who is efficient
Samarthe

Sameen (Indian) One who is treasured
Samine, Sameene, Samean, Sameane, Samyn, Samyne

Sami (Arabic) One who has been exalted
Samie, Samy, Samey, Samee, Samea

Sammohan (Indian) An attractive man

Sampath (Indian) A wealthy man
Sampathe, Sampat

Samson (Hebrew) As bright as the sun; in the Bible, a man with extraordinary strength
Sampson, Sansom, Sanson, Sansone

*ᵀSamuel (Hebrew) God has
heard
*Sam, Sammie, Sammy,
Samuele, Samuello, Samwell,
Samuelo, Sammey*

Samuru (Japanese) The name
of God

Sandburg (English) From the
sandy village
*Sandbergh, Sandberg,
Sandburgh*

Sandon (English) From the
sandy hill
*Sanden, Sandan, Sandun,
Sandyn, Sandin*

Sanford (English) From the
sandy crossing
*Sandford, Sanforde, Sandforde,
Sanfurd, Sanfurde, Sandfurd,
Sandfurde*

Sang (Vietnamese) A bright
man
Sange

Sanjiro (Japanese) An admirable man
Sanjyro

Sanjiv (Indian) One who lives
a long life
*Sanjeev, Sanjyv, Sanjeiv,
Sanjiev, Sanjeav, Sanjivan*

Sanorelle (American) An
honest man
Sanorell, Sanorel, Sanorele

Santana (Spanish) A saintly
man
*Santanna, Santanah,
Santannah, Santa*

Santiago (Spanish) Refers to
St. James

Santo (Italian) A holy man
*Sante, Santino, Santos, Santee,
Santi, Santie, Santea, Santy*

Sapan (Indian) A dream or
vision
Sapann

Sar (Anglo-Saxon) One who
inflicts pain
Sarlic, Sarlik

Sarbajit (Indian) The
conqueror
*Sarbajeet, Sarbajyt, Sarbajeat,
Sarbajet, Sarvajit, Sarvajeet,
Sarvajyt, Sarvajeat*

Sarojin (Hindu) Resembling
a lotus
Saroj

Sarosh (Persian) One who
prays
Saroshe

Satayu (Hindi) In Hinduism,
the brother of Amavasu and
Vivasu
Satayoo, Satayou, Satayue

Satoshi (Japanese) Born from the ashes
Satoshie, Satoshy, Satoshey, Satoshee, Satoshea

Satparayan (Indian) A good-natured man

Saturn (Latin) In mythology, the god of agriculture
Saturnin, Saturno, Saturnino

Satyankar (Indian) One who speaks the truth
Satyancar, Satyancker

Saville (French) From the willow town
Savil, Savile, Savill, Savyile, Savylle, Savyle, Sauville, Sauvile

Savir (Indian) A great leader
Savire, Saveer, Saveere, Savear, Saveare, Savyr, Savyre

Sawyer (English) One who works with wood
Sayer, Saer

Saxon (English) A swordsman
Saxen, Saxan, Saxton, Saxten, Saxtan

Sayad (Arabic) An accomplished hunter

Scadwielle (English) From the shed near the spring
Scadwyelle, Scadwiell, Scadwyell, Scadwiel, Scadwyel, Scadwiele, Scadwyele

Scand (Anglo-Saxon) One who is disgraced
Scande, Scandi, Scandie, Scandee, Scandea

Sceotend (Anglo-Saxon) An archer

Schaeffer (German) A steward
Schaffer, Shaeffer, Shaffer, Schaeffur, Schaffur, Shaeffur, Shaffur

Schelde (English) From the river
Shelde

Schneider (German) A tailor
Shneider, Sneider, Snider, Snyder

Schubert (German) One who makes shoes
Shubert, Schuberte, Shuberte, Schubirt, Shubirt, Schuburt, Shuburt

Scirocco (Italian) Of the warm wind
Sirocco, Scyrocco, Syrocco

Scott (English) A man from Scotland
Scot, Scottie, Scotto, Scotty, Scotti, Scottey, Scottee, Scottea

Scowyrhta (Anglo-Saxon) One who makes shoes

Seabury (English) From the village by the sea
Seaburry, Sebury, Seburry, Seaberry, Seabery, Seberry

Seaman (English) A mariner

Sean (Irish) Form of John, meaning "God is gracious"
Shaughn, Shawn, Shaun, Shon, Shohn, Shonn, Shaundre, Shawnel

Seanachan (Irish) One who is wise

Seanan (Hebrew / Irish) A gift from God / an old, wise man
Sinon, Senen, Siobhan

*Sebastian (Greek) The revered one
Sabastian, Seb, Sebastiano, Sebastien, Sebestyen, Sebo, Sebastyn, Sebestyen

Sedgwick (English) From the place of sword grass
Sedgewick, Sedgewyck, Sedgwyck, Sedgewic, Sedgewik, Sedgwic, Sedgwik, Sedgewyc

Seerath (Indian) A great man
Seerathe, Searath, Searathe

Sef (Egyptian) Son of yesterday
Sefe

Seferino (Greek) Of the west wind
Seferio, Sepherino, Sepherio, Seferyno, Sepheryno

Seignour (French) Lord of the house

Selas (African) Refers to the Trinity
Selassi, Selassie, Selassy, Selassey, Selassee, Selassea

Selestino (Spanish) One who is heaven-sent
Selestyno, Selesteeno, Selesteano

Sellers (English) One who dwells in the marshland
Sellars, Sellurs, Sellirs, Sellyrs

Seminole (Native American) A tribal name
Semynole

Seppanen (Finnish) A blacksmith
Sepanen, Seppenen, Sepenen, Seppanan, Sepanan

September (American) Born in the month of September
Septimber, Septymber, Septemberia, Septemberea

Septimus (Latin) The seventh-born child
Septymus

Seraphim (Hebrew) The burning ones; heavenly winged angels
Sarafino, Saraph, Serafin, Serafino, Seraph, Seraphimus, Serafim

Sereno (Latin) One who is calm; tranquil

Serfati (Hebrew) A man from France
Sarfati, Serfatie, Sarfatie, Serfaty, Sarfaty, Serfatey, Sarfatey, Serfatee

Sergio (Latin) An attendant; a servant
Seargeoh, Serge, Sergei, Sergeo, Sergey, Sergi, Sergios, Sergiu

Seth (Hebrew) One who has been appointed
Sethe, Seath, Seathe, Zeth

Seung (Korean) A victorious successor

Seven (American) Refers to the number; the seventh-born child
Sevin, Sevyn

Sewati (Native American) Resembling a bear claw
Sewatie, Sewaty, Sewatey, Sewatee, Sewatea

Sexton (English) The church's custodian
Sextun, Sextan, Sextin, Sextyn

Seymour (French) From the French town of Saint Maur
Seamore, Seamor, Seamour, Seymore

Shaan (Hebrew) A peaceful man

Shade (English) A secretive man
Shaid, Shaide, Shayd, Shayde, Shaed, Shaede

Shadi (Persian / Arabic) One who brings happiness and joy / a singer
Shadie, Shady, Shadey

Shadrach (Hebrew) Under the command of the moon god Aku
Shadrack, Shadrick, Shad

Shah (Persian) The king

Shai (Hebrew) A gift from God

Shail (Indian) A mountain rock
Shaile, Shayl, Shayle, Shael, Shaele, Shale

Shaka (African) A tribal leader
Shakah

Shakir (Arabic) One who is grateful
Shakeer, Shaqueer, Shakier, Shakeir, Shakear, Shakar, Shaker, Shakyr

Shane (English) Form of John, meaning "God is gracious"
Shayn, Shayne, Shaine, Shain

Shannon (Gaelic) Having ancient wisdom
Shanan, Shanen, Shannan, Shannen, Shanon

Shardul (Indian) Resembling a tiger
Shardule, Shardull, Shardulle

Shashi (Indian) Of the moonbeam
Shashie, Shashy, Shashey, Shashee, Shashea, Shashhi

Shavon (American) One who is open-minded
Shavaughn, Shavonne, Shavaun, Shovon, Shovonne, Shovaun

Shaw (English) From the woodland
Shawe

Shaykeen (American) A successful man
Shaykean, Shaykein, Shakeyn, Shakine

Shea (Gaelic) An admirable man / from the fairy fortress
Shae, Shai, Shay, Shaye, Shaylon, Shays

Sheen (English) A shining man
Sheene, Shean, Sheane

Sheffield (English) From the crooked field
Sheffeld

Sheldon (English) From the steep valley
Shelden, Sheldan, Sheldun, Sheldin, Sheldyn, Shel

Shelley (English) From the meadow's ledge
Shelly, Shelli, Shellie, Shellee, Shellea, Shelleigh, Shelleah

Shelton (English) From the farm on the ledge
Shellton, Sheltown, Sheltun, Shelten, Shelny, Shelney, Shelni, Shelnie

Shem (Hebrew) Having a well-known name

Shepherd (English) One who herds sheep
Shepperd, Shep, Shepard, Shephard, Shepp, Sheppard

Sheridan (Gaelic) A seeker
Sheredan, Sheridon, Sherridan, Seireadan, Sheriden, Sheridun, Sherard, Sherrard

Sherlock (English) A fairhaired man
Sherlocke, Shurlock, Shurlocke

Sherman (English) One who cuts wool cloth
Shermon, Scherman, Schermann, Shearman, Shermann, Sherm, Sherme

Sherrerd (English) From the open field
Shererd, Sherrard, Sherard

Shields (Gaelic) A faithful protector
Sheelds, Shealds

Shikha (Indian) A fiery man
Shykha

Shiloh (Hebrew) He who was sent
Shilo, Shyloh, Shylo

Shing (Chinese) A victorious man
Shyng

Shino (Japanese) A bamboo stem
Shyno

Shipton (English) From the ship town; from the sheep town

Shiro (Japanese) The fourth-born son
Shyro

Shorty (American) A man who is small in stature
Shortey, Shorti, Shortie, Shortee, Shortea

Shreshta (Indian) The best; one who is superior

Shubhang (Indian) A handsome man

Shuraqui (Arabic) A man from the east

Siamak (Persian) A bringer of joy
Syamak, Siamack, Syamack, Siamac, Syamac

Sidor (Russian) One who is talented
Sydor

Sierra (Spanish) From the jagged mountain range
Siera, Syerra, Syera, Seyera, Seeara

Sigehere (English) One who is victorious
Sygehere, Sigihere, Sygihere

Sigenert (Anglo-Saxon) A king
Sygenert, Siginert, Syginert

Sigmund (German) The victorious protector
Siegmund, Sigmond, Zsigmond, Zygmunt

Sihtric (Anglo-Saxon) A king
Sihtrik, Sihtrick, Syhtric, Syhtrik, Syhtrick, Sihtryc, Sihtryk, Sihtryck

Sik'is (Native American) A friendly man

Silas (Latin) Form of Silvanus, meaning "a woodland dweller"

Silny (Czech) Having great strength
Silney, Silni, Silnie, Silnee, Silnea

Simbarashe (African) The power of God
Simbarashi, Simbarashie, Simbarashy, Simbarashey, Simbarashee

Simcha (Hebrew) Filled with joy
Symcha, Simha, Symha

Simmons (Hebrew) The son of Simon
Semmes, Simms, Syms, Simmonds, Symonds, Simpson, Symms, Simson

Simon (Hebrew) God has heard
Shimon, Si, Sim, Samien, Semyon, Simen, Simeon, Simone

Sinai (Hebrew) From the clay desert

Sinclair (English) Man from Saint Clair
Sinclaire, Sinclare, Synclair, Synclaire, Synclare

Singer (American) A vocalist
Synger

Sion (Armenian) From the fortified hill
Sionne, Syon, Syonne

Sirius (Greek) Resembling the brightest star
Syrius

Siyavash (Persian) One who owns black horses
Siyavashe

Skerry (Norse) From the rocky island
Skereye, Skerrey, Skerri, Skerrie, Skerree, Skerrea

Slade (English) Son of the valley
Slaid, Slaide, Slaed, Slaede, Slayd, Slayde

Sladkey (Slavic) A glorious man
Sladky, Sladki, Sladkie, Sladkee, Sladkea

Smith (English) A blacksmith
Smyth, Smithe, Smythe, Smedt, Smid, Smitty, Smittee, Smittea

Snell (Anglo-Saxon) One who is bold
Snel, Snelle, Snele

Solange (French) An angel of the sun

Solaris (Greek) Of the sun
*Solarise, Solariss, Solarisse,
Solarys, Solaryss, Solarysse,
Solstice, Soleil*

Somer (French) Born during
the summer
*Somers, Sommer, Sommers,
Sommar, Somar*

Somerset (English) From the
summer settlement
*Sommerset, Sumerset,
Summerset*

Songaa (Native American)
Having great strength
Songan

Sophocles (Greek) An ancient
playwright
Sofocles

Sorley (Irish) Of the summer
vikings
*Sorly, Sorlee, Sorlea, Sorli,
Sorlie*

Soumil (Indian) A beloved
friend
*Soumyl, Soumille, Soumylle,
Soumill, Soumyll*

Southern (English) Man from
the south
Sothern, Suthern

Sovann (Cambodian) The
golden son
Sovan, Sovane

Spark (English / Latin) A
gallant man / to scatter
*Sparke, Sparki, Sparkie,
Sparky, Sparkey, Sparkee,
Sparkea*

Spencer (English) One who
dispenses provisions
Spenser

Squire (English) A knight's
companion; the shield-bearer
*Squier, Squiers, Squires,
Squyre, Squyres*

Stanford (English) From the
stony ford
*Standford, Standforde,
Standforde, Stamford*

Stanhope (English) From the
stony hollow
Stanhop

Stanton (English) From the
stone town
*Stantown, Stanten, Staunton,
Stantan, Stantun*

Stark (German) Having great
strength
Starke, Starck, Starcke

Stavros (Greek) One who is
crowned

Steadman (English) One who
lives at the farm
*Stedman, Steadmann,
Stedmann, Stedeman*

Steed (English) Resembling a stallion
Steede, Stead, Steade

Stephen (Greek) Crowned with garland
Staffan, Steba, Steben, Stefan, Stefano, Steffan, Steffen, Steffon, Steven, Steve

Sterling (English) One who is highly valued
Sterlyng, Stirling, Sterlyn

Stian (Norse) A voyager; one who is swift
Stig, Styg, Stygge, Stieran, Steeran, Steeren, Steeryn, Stieren

Stilwell (Anglo-Saxon) From the quiet spring
Stillwell, Stilwel, Stylwell, Styllwell, Stylwel, Stillwel

Stobart (German) A harsh man
Stobarte, Stobarth, Stobarthe

Stockley (English) From the meadow of tree stumps
Stockly, Stockli, Stocklie, Stocklee, Stockleigh

Storm (American) Of the tempest; stormy weather; having an impetuous nature
Storme, Stormy, Stormi, Stormie, Stormey, Stormee, Stormea

Stowe (English) A secretive man
Stow, Stowey, Stowy, Stowee, Stowea, Stowi, Stowie

Stratford (English) From the street near the river ford
Strafford, Stratforde, Straford, Strafforde, Straforde

Stratton (Scottish) A homebody
Straton, Stratten, Straten, Strattan, Stratan, Strattun, Stratun

Strider (English) A great warrior
Stryder

Striker (American) An aggressive man
Strike, Stryker, Stryke

Struthers (Irish) One who lives near the brook
Struther, Sruthair, Strother, Strothers

Stuart (English) A steward; the keeper of the estate
Steward, Stewart, Stewert, Stuert, Stu, Stew

Suave (American) A smooth and sophisticated man
Swave

Subhi (Arabic) Born during
the early morning hours
*Subhie, Subhy, Subhey,
Subhee, Subhea*

Suffield (English) From the
southern field
Suffeld, Suthfeld, Suthfield

Sullivan (Gaelic) Having dark
eyes
Sullavan, Sullevan, Sullyvan

Sully (English) From the
southern meadow
*Sulley, Sulli, Sullie, Sulleigh,
Sullee, Sullea, Sulleah, Suthley*

Sultan (African / American) A
ruler / one who is bold
*Sultane, Sulten, Sultun, Sulton,
Sultin, Sultyn*

Suman (Hindi) A wise man

Sundiata (African) Resembling
a hungry lion
*Sundyata, Soundiata,
Soundyata, Sunjata*

Sundown (American) Born at
dusk
Sundowne

Su'ud (Arabic) One who has
good luck
Suoud

Swahili (Arabic) Of the coastal
people
*Swahily, Swahiley, Swahilee,
Swahiley, Swaheeli, Swaheelie,
Swaheely, Swaheeley*

Sylvester (Latin) Man from the
forest
*Silvester, Silvestre, Silvestro,
Sylvestre, Sylvestro, Sly,
Sevester, Seveste*

Syon (Indian) One who is
followed by good fortune

Szemere (Hungarian) A man
of small stature
*Szemir, Szemeer, Szemear,
Szemyr*

T

Tabari (Arabic) A famous his-
torian
*Tabarie, Tabary, Tabarey,
Tabaree, Tabarea*

Tabbai (Hebrew) A well-
behaved boy
Tabbae, Tabbay, Tabbaye

Tabbart (German) A brilliant
man
*Tabbert, Tabart, Tabert,
Tahbert, Tahberte*

Tacari (African) As strong as a
warrior
*Tacarie, Tacary, Tacarey,
Tacaree, Tacarea*

Tadao (Japanese) One who is
satisfied

Tadeusuz (Polish) One who is
worthy of praise
Tadesuz

Tadi (Native American) Of the
wind
*Tadie, Tady, Tadey, Tadee,
Tadea*

Tadzi (American / Polish)
Resembling the loon / one
who is praised
*Tadzie, Tadzy, Tadzey, Tadzee,
Tadzea*

Taft (French / English) From
the homestead / from the
marshes
Tafte

Taggart (Gaelic) Son of a
priest
*Taggert, Taggort, Taggirt,
Taggyrt*

Taghee (Native American) A
chief
*Taghea, Taghy, Taghey, Taghi,
Taghie*

Taheton (Native American)
Resembling a hawk

Tahoe (Native American)
From the big water
Taho

Tahoma (Native American)
From the snowy mountain peak
*Tehoma, Tacoma, Takoma,
Tohoma, Tocoma, Tokoma,
Tekoma, Tecoma*

Taishi (Japanese) An ambi-
tious man
*Taishie, Taishy, Taishey,
Taishee, Taishea*

Taj (Indian) One who is
crowned
Tahj, Tajdar

Tajo (Spanish) Born during
the daytime

Taksony (Hungarian) One
who is content; well-fed
*Taksoney, Taksoni, Taksonie,
Taksonee, Taksonea, Tas*

Talasi (Native American)
Resembling a cornflower
*Talasie, Talasy, Talasey,
Talasee, Talasea*

Talford (English) From the
high ford
Talforde, Tallford, Tallforde

Talfryn (Welsh) From the high
hill
*Talfrynn, Talfrin, Talfrinn,
Talfren, Talfrenn, Tallfryn,
Tallfrin, Tallfren*

Talmai (Hebrew) From the furrows
Talmae, Talmay, Talmaye

Talmon (Hebrew) One who is oppressed
Talman, Talmin, Talmyn, Talmen

Talo (Finnish) From the homestead

Tam (Vietnamese / Hebrew) Having heart / one who is truthful

Taman (Hindi) One who is needed

Tamarius (American) A stubborn man
Tamarias, Tamarios, Tamerius, Tamerias, Tamerios

Tameron (American) Form of Cameron, meaning "having a crooked nose"
Tameren, Tameryn, Tamryn, Tamerin, Tamren, Tamrin, Bamron

Tammany (Native American) A friendly chief
Tammani, Tammanie, Tammaney, Tammanee, Tammanea

Tanafa (Polynesian) A drumbeat

Taneli (Hebrew) He will be judged by God
Tanelie, Tanely, Taneley, Tanelee, Tanelea

Tanish (Indian) An ambitious man
Tanishe, Taneesh, Taneeshe, Taneash, Taneashe, Tanysh, Tanyshe

Tanjiro (Japanese) The prized second-born son
Tanjyro

Tank (American) A man who is big and strong
Tankie, Tanki, Tanky, Tankey, Tankee, Tankea

Tanner (English) One who makes leather
Tannere, Tannor, Tannar, Tannir, Tannyr, Tannur, Tannis

Tannon (German) From the fir tree
Tannan, Tannen, Tannin, Tansen, Tanson, Tannun, Tannyn

Tano (Ghanese) From the river
Tanu

Tao (Chinese) One who will have a long life

Taos (Spanish) From the city in New Mexico

Tapani (Hebrew) A victorious man
Tapanie, Tapany, Tapaney, Tapanee, Tapanea

Tapko (American) Resembling an antelope

Tappen (Welsh) From the top of the cliff
Tappan, Tappon, Tappin, Tappyn, Tappun

Taran (Gaelic) Of the thunder
Taren, Taron, Tarin, Taryn, Tarun

Taranga (Indian) Of the waves

Taregan (Native American) Resembling a crane
Taregen, Taregon, Taregin, Taregyn

Tarit (Indian) Resembling lightning
Tarite, Tareet, Tareete, Tareat, Tareate, Taryt, Taryte

Tarn (Norse) From the mountain pool

Tarquin (Latin) One who is impulsive
Tarquinn, Tarquinne, Tarquen, Tarquenn, Tarquenne, Tarquyn, Tarquynn, Tarquynne

Tarrant (American) One who upholds the law
Tarrent, Tarrint, Tarrynt, Tarront, Tarrunt

Tarun (Indian) A youthful man
Taroun, Taroon, Tarune, Taroune, Taroone

Tashi (Tibetan) One who is prosperous
Tashie, Tashy, Tashey, Tashee, Tashea

^Tate (English) A cheerful man; one who brings happiness to others
Tayt, Tayte, Tait, Taite, Taet, Taete

Tausiq (Indian) One who provides strong backing
Tauseeq, Tauseaq, Tausik, Tauseek, Tauseak

Tavaris (American) Of misfortune; a hermit
Tavarius, Tavaress, Tavarious, Tavariss, Tavarous, Tevarus, Tavorian, Tavarian

Tavas (Hebrew) Resembling a peacock

Tavi (Aramaic) A good man
Tavie, Tavy, Tavey, Tavee, Tavea

Tavin (German) Form of Gustav, meaning "of the staff of the gods"
Tavyn, Taven, Tavan, Tavon, Tavun, Tava, Tave

Tawa (Native American) Born beneath the sun
Tawah

Tay (Scottish) From the river
Taye, Tae, Tai

Taylor (English) Cutter of cloth, one who alters garments

Teagan (Gaelic) A handsome man
Teegan, Teygan, Tegan, Teigan

Ted (English) Form of Theodore, meaning "a gift from God"
Tedd, Teddy, Teddi, Teddie, Teddee, Teddea, Teddey, Tedric

Tedmund (English) A protector of the land
Tedmunde, Tedmond, Tedmonde, Tedman, Theomund, Theomond, Theomunde, Theomonde

Teetonka (Native American) One who talks too much
Teitonka, Tietonka, Teatonka, Teytonka

Tegene (African) My protector
Tegeen, Tegeene, Tegean, Tegeane

Teiji (Japanese) One who is righteous
Teijo

Teilo (Welsh) A saintly man

Teka (African) He has replaced

Tekeshi (Japanese) A formidable and brave man
Tekeshie, Tekeshy, Tekeshey, Tekeshee, Tekeshea

Telly (Greek) The wisest man
Telley, Tellee, Tellea, Telli, Tellie

Temman (Anglo-Saxon) One who has been tamed

Temple (Latin) From the sacred place
Tempel, Templar, Templer, Templo

Teneangopte (Native American) Resembling a high-flying bird

Tennant (English) One who rents
Tennent, Tenant, Tenent

Tennessee (Native American) From the state of Tennessee
Tenese, Tenesee, Tenessee, Tennese, Tennesee, Tennesse

Teon (Anglo-Saxon) One who harms others

Teris (Irish) The son of Terence
Terys, Teriss, Teryss, Terris, Terrys, Terriss, Terryss

^**Terrance** (Latin) From an ancient Roman clan
Tarrants, Tarrance, Tarrence, Tarrenz, Terencio, Terance, Terrence, Terrey, Terry

Terrian (American) One who is strong and ambitious
Terrien, Terriun, Terriyn

Terron (English) Form of Terence, meaning "from an ancient Roman clan"
Tarran, Tarren, Tarrin

Teshi (African) One who is full of laughter
Teshie, Teshy, Teshey, Teshee, Teshea

Tessema (African) One to whom people listen

Tet (Vietnamese) Born on New Year's

Teteny (Hungarian) A chieftain

Teva (Hebrew) A natural man
Tevah

Texas (Native American) One of many friends; from the state of Texas
Texus, Texis, Texes, Texos, Texys

Teyrnon (Celtic) A regal man
Teirnon, Tayrnon, Tairnon, Taernon, Tiarchnach, Tiarnach

Thabo (African) Filled with happiness

Thackary (English) Form of Zachary, meaning "the Lord remembers"
Thackery, Thakary, Thakery, Thackari, Thackarie, Thackarey, Thackaree, Thackarea

Thaddeus (Aramaic) Having heart
Tad, Tadd, Taddeo, Taddeusz, Thad, Thadd, Thaddaios, Thaddaos

Thandiwe (African) One who is dearly loved
Thandie, Thandi, Thandy, Thandey, Thandee, Thandea

Thang (Vietnamese) One who is victorious

Thanus (American) One who owns land

Thao (Vietnamese) One who is courteous

Thatcher (English) One who fixes roofs
Thacher, Thatch, Thatche, Thaxter, Thacker, Thaker, Thackere, Thakere

Thayer (Teutonic) Of the nation's army

Theodore (Greek) A gift from God
Ted, Teddy, Teddie, Theo, Theodor

Theron (Greek) A great hunter
Therron, Tharon, Theon, Tharron

Theseus (Greek) In mythology, hero who slew the Minotaur
Thesius, Thesyus

Thinh (Vietnamese) A prosperous man

*★T**Thomas** (Aramaic) One of twins
Tam, Tamas, Tamhas, Thom, Thomason, Thomson, Thompson, Tomas

Thor (Norse) In mythology, god of thunder
Thorian, Thorin, Thorsson, Thorvald, Tor, Tore, Turo, Thorrin

Thorburn (Norse) Thor's bear
Thorburne, Thorbern, Thorberne, Thorbjorn, Thorbjorne, Torbjorn, Torborg, Torben

Thormond (Norse) Protected by Thor
Thormonde, Thormund, Thormunde, Thurmond, Thurmonde, Thurmund, Thurmunde, Thormun

Thorne (English) From the thorn bush
Thorn

Thornycroft (English) From the field of thorn bushes
Thornicroft, Thorneycroft, Thorniecroft, Thorneecroft, Thorneacroft

Thuong (Vietnamese) One who loves tenderly

Thurston (English) From Thor's town; Thor's stone
Thorston, Thorstan, Thorstein, Thorsten, Thurstain, Thurstan, Thursten, Torsten

Thuy (Vietnamese) One who is kind

Tiassale (African) It has been forgotten

Tiberio (Italian) From the Tiber river
Tibero, Tyberio, Tybero, Tiberius, Tiberios, Tyberius, Tyberios

Tibor (Slavic) From the sacred place

Tiburon (Spanish) Resembling a shark

Tiernan (Gaelic) Lord of the manor
Tiarnan, Tiarney, Tierney, Tierny, Tiernee, Tiernea, Tierni, Tiernie

Tilian (Anglo-Saxon) One who strives to better himself
Tilien, Tiliun, Tilion

Tilon (Hebrew) A generous man
Tilen, Tilan, Tilun, Tilin, Tilyn

Tilton (English) From the fertile estate
Tillton, Tilten, Tillten, Tiltan, Tilltan, Tiltin, Tilltin, Tiltun

Timir (Indian) Born in the darkness
Timirbaran

Timothy (Greek) One who honors God
Tim, Timmo, Timmothy, Timmy, Timo, Timofei, Timofeo

Tin (Vietnamese) A great thinker

Tino (Italian) A man of small stature
Teeno, Tieno, Teino, Teano, Tyno

Tip (American) A form of Thomas, meaning "one of twins"
Tipp, Tipper, Tippy, Tippee, Tippea, Tippey, Tippi, Tippie

Tisa (African) The ninth-born child
Tisah, Tysa, Tysah

^**Titus** (Greek / Latin) Of the giants / a great defender
Tito, Titos, Tytus, Tytos, Titan, Tytan, Tyto

Toa (Polynesian) A brave-hearted woman

Toan (Vietnamese) One who is safe
Toane

Tobias (Hebrew) The Lord is good
Toby

Todd (English) Resembling a fox
Tod

Todor (Bulgarian) A gift from God
Todos, Todros

Tohon (Native American) One who loves the water

Tokala (Native American) Resembling a fox
Tokalo

Tomer (Hebrew) A man of tall stature
Tomar, Tomur, Tomir, Tomor, Tomyr

Tomi (Japanese / African) A wealthy man / of the people
Tomie, Tomee, Tomea, Tomy, Tomey

Tonauac (Aztec) One who possesses the light

Torger (Norse) The power of Thor's spear
Thorger, Torgar, Thorgar, Terje, Therje

Torht (Anglo-Saxon) A bright man
Torhte

Torin (Celtic) One who acts as chief
Toran, Torean, Toren, Torion, Torran, Torrian, Toryn

Tormaigh (Irish) Having the spirit of Thor
Tormey, Tormay, Tormaye, Tormai, Tormae

Torr (English) From the tower
Torre

Torrence (Gaelic) From the little hills
Torence, Torrance, Torrens, Torrans, Toran, Torran, Torrin, Torn, Torry

Torry (Norse / Gaelic) Refers to Thor / form of Torrence, meaning "from the little hills"
Torrey, Torree, Torrea, Torri, Torrie, Tory, Torey, Tori

Toshiro (Japanese) One who is talented and intelligent
Toshihiro

Tostig (English) A well-known earl
Tostyg

Toviel (Hebrew) The Lord is good
Toviell, Toviele, Tovielle, Tovi, Tovie, Tovee, Tovea, Tovy

Toyo (Japanese) A man of plenty

Tracy (Gaelic) One who is warlike
Tracey, Traci, Tracie, Tracee, Tracea, Treacy, Trace, Tracen

Travis (French) To cross over
Travys, Traver, Travers, Traviss, Trevis, Trevys, Travus, Traves

Treffen (German) One who socializes
Treffan, Treffin, Treffon, Treffyn, Treffun

Tremain (Celtic) From the town built of stone
Tramain, Tramaine, Tramayne, Tremaine, Tremayne, Tremaen, Tremaene, Tramaen

Tremont (French) From the three mountains
Tremonte, Tremount, Tremounte

Trenton (English) From the town near the rushing rapids
Trent, Trynt, Trenten, Trentyn

Trevin (English) From the fair town
Trevan, Treven, Trevian, Trevion, Trevon, Trevyn, Trevonn

Trevor (Welsh) From the large village
Trefor, Trevar, Trever, Treabhar, Treveur, Trevir, Trevur

Trey (English) The third-born child
Tre, Trai, Trae, Tray, Traye, Trayton, Treyton, Trayson

Trigg (Norse) One who is truthful
Trygg

Tripp (English) A traveler
Trip, Trypp, Tryp, Tripper, Trypper

Tripsy (American) One who enjoys dancing
Tripsey, Tripsee, Tripsea, Tripsi, Tripsie

*ᵀTristan (Celtic) A sorrowful man; in Arthurian legend, a knight of the Round Table
Trystan, Tris, Tristam, Tristen, Tristian, Tristin, Triston, Tristram

Trocky (American) A manly man
Trockey, Trocki, Trockie, Trockee, Trockea

Trong (Vietnamese) One who is respected

Troy (Gaelic) Son of a foot-soldier
Troye, Troi

Trumbald (English) A bold man
Trumbold, Trumbalde, Trumbolde

Trygve (Norse) One who wins with bravery

Tse (Native American) As solid as a rock

Tsidhqiyah (Hebrew) The Lord is just
Tsidqiyah, Tsidhqiya, Tsdqiya

Tsubasa (Japanese) A winged being
Tsubasah, Tsubase, Tsubaseh

Tucker (English) One who makes garments
Tuker, Tuckerman, Tukerman, Tuck, Tuckman, Tukman, Tuckere, Toukere

Tuketu (Native American) Resembling a running bear
Tuketue, Tuketoo, Tuketou, Telutci, Telutcie, Telutcy, Telutcey, Telutcee

Tulsi (Indian) A holy man
Tulsie, Tulsy, Tulsey, Tulsee, Tulsea

Tumaini (African) An optimist
Tumainie, Tumainee, Tumainy, Tumainey, Tumayni, Tumaynie, Tumaynee, Tumayney

Tunde (African) One who returns
Tundi, Tundie, Tundee, Tundea, Tundy, Tundey

Tunleah (English) From the town near the meadow
Tunlea, Tunleigh, Tunly, Tunley, Tunlee, Tunli, Tunlie

Tupac (African) A messenger warrior
Tupack, Tupoc, Tupock

Turfeinar (Norse) In mythology, the son of Rognvald
Turfaynar, Turfaenar, Turfanar, Turfenar, Turfainar

Tushar (Indian) Of the snow
Tusharr, Tushare

Tusita (Chinese) One who is heaven-sent

Twrgadarn (Welsh) From the strong tower

Txanton (Basque) Form of Anthony, meaning "a flourishing man; of an ancient Roman family"
Txantony, Txantoney, Txantonee, Txantoni, Txantonie, Txantonea

Tybalt (Latin) He who sees the truth
Tybault, Tybalte, Tybaulte

Tye (English) From the fenced-in pasture
Tyg, Tyge, Tie, Tigh, Teyen

Tyfiell (English) Follower of the god Tyr
Tyfiel, Tyfielle, Tyfiele

Tyler (English) A tiler of roofs
Tilar, Tylar, Tylor, Tiler, Tilor, Ty, Tye, Tylere

Typhoon (Chinese) Of the great wind
Tiphoon, Tyfoon, Tifoon, Typhoun, Tiphoun, Tyfoun, Tifoun

Tyrone (French) From Owen's land
Terone, Tiron, Tirone, Tyron, Ty, Kyrone

Tyson (French) One who is high-spirited; fiery
Thyssen, Tiesen, Tyce, Tycen, Tyeson, Tyssen, Tysen, Tysan

U

U (Korean) A kind and gentle man

Uaithne (Gaelic) One who is innocent; green
Uaithn, Uaythne, Uaythn, Uathne, Uathn, Uaethne, Uaethn

Ualan (Scottish) Form of Valentine, meaning "one who is strong and healthy"
Ualane, Ualayn, Ualayne, Ualen, Ualon

Uba (African) One who is wealthy; lord of the house
Ubah, Ubba, Ubbah

Uberto (Italian) Form of Hubert, meaning "having a shining intellect"
Ulberto, Umberto

Udath (Indian) One who is noble
Udathe

Uddam (Indian) An exceptional man

Uddhar (Indian) One who is free; an independent man
Uddharr, Udhar, Udharr

Udell (English) From the valley of yew trees
Udale, Udel, Udall, Udayle, Udayl, Udail, Udaile, Udele

Udi (Hebrew) One who carries a torch
Udie, Udy, Udey, Udee, Udea

Udup (Indian) Born beneath the moon's light
Udupp, Uddup, Uddupp

Udyan (Indian) Of the garden
Uddyan, Udyann, Uddyann

Ugo (Italian) A great thinker

Uland (English) From the noble country
Ulande, Ulland, Ullande, Ulandus, Ullandus

Ulhas (Indian) Filled with happiness
Ulhass, Ullhas, Ullhass

Ull (Norse) Having glory; in mythology, god of justice and patron of agriculture
Ulle, Ul, Ule

Ulmer (German) Having the fame of the wolf
Ullmer, Ullmar, Ulmarr, Ullmarr, Ulfmer, Ulfmar, Ulfmaer

Ultman (Indian) A godly man
Ultmann, Ultmane

Umrao (Indian) One who is noble

Unai (Basque) A shepherd
Unay, Unaye, Unae

Unathi (African) God is with us
Unathie, Unathy, Unathey, Unathee, Unathea

Uncas (Native American) Resembling a fox
Unkas, Unckas

Ungus (Irish) A vigorous man
Unguss

Unique (American) Unlike others; the only one
Unikue, Unik, Uniqui, Uniqi, Uniqe, Unikque, Unike, Unicke

Uolevi (Finnish) Form of Olaf, meaning "the remaining of the ancestors"
Uolevie, Uolevee, Uolevy, Uolevey, Uolevea

Upchurch (English) From the upper church
Upchurche

Uranus (Greek) In mythology, the father of the Titans
Urainus, Uraynus, Uranas, Uraynas, Urainas, Uranos, Uraynos, Urainos

Uri (Hebrew) Form of Uriah, meaning "the Lord is my light"
Urie, Ury, Urey, Uree, Urea

Uriah (Hebrew) The Lord is my light
Uri, Uria, Urias, Urija, Urijah, Uriyah, Urjasz, Uriya

Urjavaha (Hindu) Of the Nimi dynasty

Urtzi (Basque) From the sky
Urtzie, Urtzy, Urtzey, Urtzee, Urtzea

Usher (Latin) From the mouth of the river
Ushar, Ushir, Ussher, Usshar, Usshir

Ushi (Chinese) As strong as an ox
Ushie, Ushy, Ushey, Ushee, Ushea

Utah (Native American) People of the mountains; from the state of Utah

Utsav (Indian) Born during a celebration
Utsavi, Utsave, Utsava, Utsavie, Utsavy, Utsavey, Utsavee, Utsavea

Utt (Arabic) One who is kind and wise
Utte

Uzi (Hebrew) Having great power
Uzie, Uzy, Uzey, Uzee, Uzea, Uzzi, Uzzie, Uzzy

Uzima (African) One who is full of life
Uzimah, Uzimma, Uzimmah, Uzyma

Uzziah (Hebrew) The Lord is my strength
Uzzia, Uziah, Uzia, Uzzya, Uzzyah, Uzyah, Uzya, Uzziel

Vachel (French) Resembling a small cow
Vachele, Vachell

Vachlan (English) One who lives near water

Vadar (Dutch) A fatherly man
Vader, Vadyr

Vadhir (Spanish) Resembling a rose
Vadhyr, Vadheer

Vadim (Russian) A good-looking man
Vadime, Vadym, Vadyme, Vadeem, Vadeeme

Vaijnath (Hindi) Refers to Lord Shiva
Vaejnath, Vaijnathe, Vaejnathe

Valdemar (German) A well-known ruler
Valdemarr, Valdemare, Valto, Valdmar, Valdmarr, Valdimar, Valdimarr

Valentine (Latin) One who is strong and healthy
Val, Valentin, Valentino, Valentyne, Ualan

Valerian (Latin) One who is strong and healthy
Valerien, Valerio, Valerius, Valery, Valeryan, Valere, Valeri, Valerii

Valin (Hindi) The monkey king

Valle (French) From the glen
Vallejo

Valri (French) One who is strong
Valrie, Valry, Valrey, Valree

Vance (English) From the marshland
Vanse

Vanderveer (Dutch) From the ferry
Vandervere, Vandervir, Vandervire, Vandervyr, Vandervyre

Vandy (Dutch) One who travels; a wanderer
Vandey, Vandi, Vandie, Vandee

Vandyke (Danish) From the dike
Vandike

Vanir (Norse) Of the ancient gods

Varante (Arabic) From the river

Vardon (French) From the green hill
Varden, Verdon, Verdun, Verden, Vardun, Vardan, Verddun, Varddun

Varg (Norse) Resembling a wolf

Varick (German) A protective ruler
Varrick, Warick, Warrick

Varius (Latin) A versatile man
Varian, Varinius

Variya (Hindi) The excellent one

Vasava (Hindi) Refers to Indra

Vashon (American) The Lord is gracious
Vashan, Vashawn, Vashaun, Vashone, Vashane, Vashayn, Vashayne

Vasin (Indian) A great ruler
Vasine, Vaseen, Vaseene, Vasyn, Vasyne

Vasuki (Hindi) In Hinduism, a serpent king
Vasukie, Vasuky, Vasukey, Vasukee, Vasukea

Vasuman (Indian) Son born of fire

Vasyl (Slavic) A king
Vasil, Vassil, Wasyl

Vatsa (Indian) Our beloved son
Vathsa

Vatsal (Indian) One who is
affectionate

Velimir (Croatian) One who
wishes for great peace
*Velimeer, Velimyr, Velimire,
Velimeere, Velimyre*

Velyo (Bulgarian) A great man
Velcho, Veliko, Velin, Velko

Vere (French) From the alder
tree

Verge (Anglo-Saxon) One who
owns four acres

Vernon (French) From the
alder-tree grove
*Vern, Vernal, Vernard, Verne,
Vernee, Vernen, Verney, Vernin*

Verrill (French) One who is
faithful
*Verill, Verrall, Verrell, Verroll,
Veryl, Veryll, Verol, Verall*

Vibol (Cambodian) A man of
plenty
*Viboll, Vibole, Vybol, Vyboll,
Vybole*

Victor (Latin) One who is
victorious; the champion
Vic, Vick, Victoriano

Vidal (Spanish) A giver of life
*Videl, Videlio, Videlo, Vidalo,
Vidalio, Vidas*

Vidar (Norse) Warrior of the
forest; in mythology, a son of
Odin
Vidarr

Vien (Vietnamese) One who is
complete; satisfied

Vincent (Latin) One who
prevails; the conqueror
*Vicente, Vicenzio, Vicenzo,
Vin, Vince, Vincens, Vincente,
Vincentius*

Viorel (Romanian) Resembling
the bluebell
Viorell, Vyorel, Vyorell

Vipin (Indian) From the forest
*Vippin, Vypin, Vypyn, Vyppin,
Vyppyn, Vipyn, Vippyn*

Vipul (Indian) A man of plenty
*Vypul, Vipull, Vypull, Vipool,
Vypool*

Virag (Hungarian) Resembling
a flower

Virgil (Latin) The staff-bearer
*Verge, Vergil, Vergilio, Virgilio,
Vergilo, Virgilo, Virgilijus*

Virginius (Latin) One who is
pure; chaste
Virginio, Virgino

Vitéz (Hungarian) A courageous warrior

Vito (Latin) One who gives life
Vital, Vitale, Vitalis, Vitaly,
Vitas, Vitus, Vitali, Vitaliy, Vid

Vitus (Latin) Giver of life
Wit

Vladimir (Slavic) A famous
prince
Vladamir, Vladimeer,
Vladimyr, Vladimyre,
Vladamyr, Vladamyre,
Vladameer, Vladimer

Vladislav (Slavic) One who
rules with glory

Volodymyr (Slavic) To rule
with peace
Wolodymyr

Vulcan (Latin) In mythology,
the god of fire
Vulkan, Vulckan

Vyacheslav (Russian) Form
of Wenceslas, meaning "one
who receives more glory"

W

Wade (English) To cross the
river ford
Wayde, Waid, Waide, Waddell,
Wadell, Waydell, Waidell, Waed

Wadley (English) From the
meadow near the ford
Wadly, Wadlee, Wadli, Wadlie,
Wadleigh

Wadsworth (English) From the
estate near the ford
Waddsworth, Wadsworthe,
Waddsworthe

Wafi (Arabic) One who is
trustworthy
Wafie, Wafy, Wafey, Wafee,
Wafiy, Wafiyy

Wahab (Indian) A big-hearted
man

Wainwright (English) One who
builds wagons
Wainright, Wainewright,
Wayneright, Waynewright,
Waynwright

Wakil (Arabic) A lawyer; a
trustee
Wakill, Wakyl, Wakyle,
Wakeel, Wakeele

Wakiza (Native American) A
desperate fighter
Wakyza, Wakeza, Wakieza,
Wakeiza

Walbridge (English) From the
Welshman's bridge
Wallbridge, Walbrydge,
Wallbrydge

Waljan (Welsh) The chosen one
Walljan, Waljen, Walljen, Waljon, Walljon

Walker (English) One who trods the cloth
Walkar, Walkir, Walkor

Wallace (Scottish) A Welshman, a man from the South
Wallach, Wallas, Wallie, Wallis, Wally, Wlash, Welch

Walter (German) The commander of the army
Walther, Walt, Walte, Walder, Wat, Wouter, Wolter, Woulter, Galtero, Quaid

Wamblee (Native American) Resembling an eagle
Wambli, Wamblie, Wambly, Wambley, Wambleigh, Wamblea

Wanikiy (Native American) A savior
Wanikiya, Wanikie, Wanikey, Waniki, Wanikee

Wanjala (African) Born during a famine
Wanjalla, Wanjal, Wanjall

Warford (English) From the ford near the weir
Warforde, Weirford, Weirforde, Weiford, Weiforde

Warley (English) From the meadow near the weir
Warly, Warleigh, Warlee, Warlea, Warleah, Warli, Warlie, Weirley

Warner (German) Of the defending army
Werner, Wernher, Warnher, Worner, Wornher

Warra (Aboriginal) Man of the water
Warrah, Wara, Warah

Warren (English / German) From the fortress

Warrick (English) Form of Varick, meaning "a protective ruler"
Warrik, Warric, Warick, Warik, Waric, Warryck, Warryk, Warryc

Warrigal (Aboriginal) One who is wild
Warrigall, Warigall, Warigal, Warygal, Warygall

Warwick (English) From the farm near the weir
Warwik, Warwyck, Warwyk

Wasswa (African) The first-born of twins
Waswa, Wasswah, Waswah

Wasyl (Ukrainian) Form of Vasyl, meaning "a king"
Wasyle, Wasil, Wasile

Watson (English) The son of Walter
Watsin, Watsen, Watsan, Watkins, Watckins, Watkin, Watckin, Wattekinson

Waylon (English) From the roadside land

Wayne (English) One who builds wagons
Wain, Wanye, Wayn, Waynell, Waynne, Guwayne

Webster (English) A weaver
Weeb, Web, Webb, Webber, Weber, Webbestre, Webestre, Webbe

Wei (Chinese) A brilliant man; having great strength

Wenceslas (Polish) One who receives more glory
Wenceslaus, Wenzel, Vyacheslav

Wendell (German) One who travels; a wanderer
Wendel, Wendale, Wendall, Wendele, Wendal, Windell, Windel, Windal

Wesley (English) From the western meadow
Wes, Wesly, Wessley, Westleigh, Westley, Wesli, Weslie, Wesleigh

Westby (English) From the western farm
Westbey, Wesby, Wesbey, Westbi, Wesbi, Westbie, Wesbie, Westbee

Weston (English) From the western town

Whit (English) A white-skinned man
White, Whitey, Whitt, Whitte, Whyt, Whytt, Whytte, Whytey

Whitby (English) From the white farm
Whitbey, Whitbi, Whitbie, Whitbee, Whytbey, Whytby, Whytbi, Whytbie

Whitfield (English) From the white field
Whitfeld, Whytfield, Whytfeld, Witfield, Witfeld, Wytfield, Wytfeld

Whitley (English) From the white meadow
Whitly, Whitli, Whitlie, Whitlee, Whitleigh, Whytley, Whytly, Whytli

Whitman (English) A white-haired man
Whitmann, Witman, Witmann, Whitmane, Witmane, Whytman, Whytmane, Wytman

Wildon (English) From the wooded hill
Willdon, Wilden, Willden

Wiley (English) One who is crafty; from the meadow by the water
Wily, Wileigh, Wili, Wilie, Wilee, Wylie, Wyly, Wyley

Wilford (English) From the willow ford
Willford, Wilferd, Willferd, Wilf, Wielford, Weilford, Wilingford, Wylingford

*ᵀWilliam (German) The determined protector
Wilek, Wileck, Wilhelm, Wilhelmus, Wilkes, Wilkie, Wilkinson, Will, Guillaume, Quilliam

Willow (English) Of the willow tree
Willowe, Willo, Willoe

Wilmer (German) A strong-willed and well-known man
Wilmar, Wilmore, Willmar, Willmer, Wylmer, Wylmar, Wyllmer, Wyllmar

Winston (English) Of the joy stone; from the friendly town
Win, Winn, Winsten, Winstonn, Wynstan, Wynsten, Wynston, Winstan

Winthrop (English) From the friendly village
Winthrope, Wynthrop, Wynthrope, Winthorp, Wynthorp

Winton (English) From the enclosed pastureland
Wintan, Wintin, Winten, Wynton, Wyntan, Wyntin, Wynten

Wirt (Anglo-Saxon) One who is worthy
Wirte, Wyrt, Wyrte, Wurt, Wurte

Wit (Polish) Form of Vitus, meaning "giver of life"
Witt

Wlodzimierz (Polish) To rule with peace
Wlodzimir, Wlodzimerz

Wolfric (German) A wolf ruler
Wolfrick, Wolfrik, Wulfric, Wulfrick, Wulfrik, Wolfryk, Wolfryck, Wolfryc

Wolodymyr (Ukrainian) Form of Volodymyr, meaning "to rule with peace"
Wolodimyr, Wolodimir, Wolodymeer, Wolodimeer

Woorak (Aboriginal) From the plains
Woorack, Woorac

*Wyatt (English) Having the strength of a warrior
Wyat, Wyatte, Wyate, Wiatt, Wiatte, Wiat, Wiate, Wyeth

Wyndham (English) From the windy village
Windham

Xakery (American) Form of Zachery, meaning "the Lord remembers"
Xaccary, Xaccery, Xach, Xacharie, Xachery, Xack, Xackarey, Xackary

Xalvador (Spanish) Form of Salvador, meaning "a savior"
Xalvadore, Xalvadoro, Xalvadorio, Xalbador, Xalbadore, Xalbadorio, Xalbadoro, Xabat

Xannon (American) From an ancient family
Xanon, Xannen, Xanen, Xannun, Xanun

Xanthus (Greek) A blond-haired man
Xanthos, Xanthe, Xanth

*Xavier (Basque / Arabic) Owner of a new house / one who is bright
Xaver, Xever, Xabier, Xaviere, Xabiere, Xaviar, Xaviare, Xavior

Xenocrates (Greek) A foreign ruler

Xesus (Galician) Form of Jesus, meaning "God is my salvation"

Xoan (Galician) Form of John, meaning "God is gracious"
Xoane, Xohn, Xon

Xue (Chinese) A studious young man

Yael (Israeli) Strength of God
Yaele

Yagil (Hebrew) One who rejoices, celebrates
Yagill, Yagyl, Yagylle

Yahto (Native American) Having blue eyes; refers to the color blue
Yahtoe, Yahtow, Yahtowe

Yahweh (Hebrew) Refers to God
Yahveh, Yaweh, Yaveh, Yehowah, Yehweh, Yehoveh

Yakiv (Ukrainian) Form of Jacob, meaning "he who supplants"
Yakive, Yakeev, Yakeeve, Yackiv, Yackeev, Yakieve, Yakiev, Yakeive

Yakout (Arabian) As precious as a ruby

Yale (Welsh) From the fertile upland
Yayle, Yayl, Yail, Yaile

Yanai (Aramaic) God will answer
Yanae, Yana, Yani

Yankel (Hebrew) Form of Jacob, meaning "he who supplants"
Yankell, Yanckel, Yanckell, Yankle, Yanckle

Yaotl (Aztec) A great warrior
Yaotyl, Yaotle, Yaotel, Yaotyle

Yaphet (Hebrew) A handsome man
Yaphett, Yapheth, Yaphethe

Yaqub (Arabic) Form of Jacob, meaning "he who supplants"
Ya'qub, Yaqob, Yaqoub

Yardley (English) From the fenced-in meadow
Yardly, Yardleigh, Yardli, Yardlie, Yardlee, Yardlea, Yarley, Yarly

Yaromir (Russian) Form of Jaromir, meaning "from the famous spring"
Yaromire, Yaromeer, Yaromeere, Yaromyr, Yaromyre

Yas (Native American) Child of the snow

Yasahiro (Japanese) One who is peaceful and calm

Yasin (Arabic) A wealthy man
Yasine, Yaseen, Yaseene, Yasyn, Yasyne, Yasien, Yasiene, Yasein

Yasir (Arabic) One who is well-off financially
Yassir, Yasser, Yaseer, Yasr, Yasyr, Yassyr, Yasar, Yassar

Yegor (Russian) Form of George, meaning "one who works the earth; a farmer"
Yegore, Yegorr, Yegeor, Yeorges, Yeorge, Yeorgis

Yehonadov (Hebrew) A gift from God
Yehonadav, Yehonedov, Yehonedav, Yehoash, Yehoashe, Yeeshai, Yeeshae, Yishai

Yenge (African) A hard-working man
Yengi, Yengie, Yengy, Yengey, Yengee

Yeoman (English) A man-servant
Youman, Yoman

Yestin (Welsh) One who is just and fair
Yestine, Yestyn, Yestyne

Yigil (Hebrew) He shall be redeemed
Yigile, Yigyl, Yigyle, Yigol, Yigole, Yigit, Yigat

Yishachar (Hebrew) He will be rewarded
Yishacharr, Yishachare, Yissachar, Yissachare, Yisachar, Yisachare

Yiska (Native American) The night has gone

Yngve (Scandinavian) Refers to the god Ing

Yo (Cambodian) One who is honest

Yoav (Hebrew) Form of Joab, meaning "the Lord is my father"
Yoave, Yoavo, Yoavio

Yochanan (Hebrew) Form of John, meaning "God is gracious"
Yochan, Yohannan, Yohanan, Yochannan

Yohan (German) Form of John, meaning "God is gracious"
Yohanan, Yohann, Yohannes, Yohon, Yohonn, Yohonan

Yonatan (Hebrew) Form of Jonathan, meaning "a gift of God"
Yonaton, Yohnatan, Yohnaton, Yonathan, Yonathon, Yoni, Yonie, Yony

Yong (Korean) One who is courageous

York (English) From the yew settlement
Yorck, Yorc, Yorke

Yosyp (Ukrainian) Form of Joseph, meaning "God will add"
Yosip, Yosype, Yosipe

Yovanny (English) Form of Giovanni, meaning "God is gracious"
Yovanni, Yovannie, Yovannee, Yovany, Yovani, Yovanie, Yovanee

Yukon (English) From the settlement of gold
Youkon, Yucon, Youcon, Yuckon, Youckon

Yuliy (Russian) Form of Julius, meaning "one who is youthful"
Yuli, Yulie, Yulee, Yuleigh, Yuly, Yuley, Yulika, Yulian

Yuudai (Japanese) A great hero
Yudai, Yuudae, Yudae, Yuuday, Yuday

Yves (French) A young archer
Yve, Yvo, Yvon, Yvan, Yvet, Yvete

Z

Zabian (Arabic) One who worships celestial bodies
Zabion, Zabien, Zaabian

Zabulon (Hebrew) One who is exalted
Zabulun, Zabulen

Zacchaeus (Hebrew) Form of Zachariah, meaning "The Lord remembers"
Zachaeus, Zachaios, Zaccheus, Zackaeus, Zacheus, Zackaios, Zaccheo

Zachariah (Hebrew) The Lord remembers
Zacaria, Zacarias, Zaccaria, Zaccariah, Zachaios, Zacharia, Zacharias, Zacherish

*ᵀZachary (Hebrew) Form of Zachariah, meaning "the Lord remembers"
Zaccary, Zaccery, Zach, Zacharie, Zachery, Zack, Zackarey, Zackary, Thackary, Xakery

Zaci (African) In mythology, the god of fatherhood

Zaden (Dutch) A sower of seeds
Zadin, Zadan, Zadon, Zadun, Zede, Zeden, Zedan

Zadok (Hebrew) One who is righteous; just
Zadoc, Zaydok, Zadock, Zaydock, Zaydoc, Zaidok, Zaidock, Zaidoc

Zador (Hungarian) An ill-tempered man
Zador, Zadoro, Zadorio

Zafar (Arabic) The conquerer; a victorious man
Zafarr, Zaffar, Zhafar, Zhaffar, Zafer, Zaffer

Zahid (Arabic) A pious man
*Zahide, Zahyd, Zahyde,
Zaheed, Zaheede, Zaheide,
Zahiede, Zaheid*

Zahir (Arabic) A radiant and
flourishing man
*Zahire, Zahireh, Zahyr,
Zahyre, Zaheer, Zaheere,
Zaheir, Zahier*

Zahur (Arabic) Resembling a
flower
*Zahure, Zahureh, Zhahur,
Zaahur*

Zale (Greek) Having the
strength of the sea
*Zail, Zaile, Zayl, Zayle, Zael,
Zaele*

Zamir (Hebrew) Resembling a
songbird
*Zamire, Zameer, Zameere,
Zamyr, Zamyre, Zameir,
Zameire, Zamier*

Zander (Slavic) Form of
Alexander, meaning "a helper
and defender of mankind"
*Zandros, Zandro, Zandar,
Zandur, Zandre*

ᵀ**Zane** (English) form of John,
meaning "God is gracious"
Zayne, Zayn, Zain, Zaine

Zareb (African) The protector;
guardian
*Zarebb, Zaareb, Zarebe,
Zarreb, Zareh, Zaareh*

Zared (Hebrew) One who has
been trapped
*Zarede, Zarad, Zarade,
Zaared, Zaarad*

Zasha (Russian) A defender of
the people
*Zashah, Zosha, Zoshah,
Zashiya, Zoshiya*

^**Zayden** (Arabic) Form of
Zayd, meaning "To become
greater, to grow"
Zaiden

Zeke (English) Form of
Ezekiel, meaning "strength-
ened by God"
Zekiel, Zeek, Zeeke, Zeeq

Zene (African) A handsome
man
Zeene, Zeen, Zein, Zeine

Zereen (Arabic) The golden
one
*Zereene, Zeryn, Zeryne, Zerein,
Zereine, Zerrin, Zerren, Zerran*

Zeroun (Armenian) One who
is respected for his wisdom
Zeroune, Zeroon, Zeroone

Zeth (English) Form of Seth, meaning "one who has been appointed"
Zethe

Zion (Hebrew) From the citadel
Zionn, Zione, Zionne

Ziv (Hebrew) A radiant man
Zive, Ziiv, Zivi, Zivie, Zivee, Zivy, Zivey

Ziyad (Arabic) One who betters himself; growth
Ziad

Zlatan (Croatian) The golden son
Zlattan, Zlatane, Zlatann, Zlatain, Zlatayn, Zlaten, Zlaton, Zlatin

Zoltan (Hungarian) A kingly man; a sultan
Zoltann, Zoltane, Zoltanne, Zsolt, Zsoltan

Zorion (Basque) Filled with happiness
Zorian, Zorien

Zoticus (Greek) Full of life
Zoticos, Zoticas

Zsigmond (Hungarian) Form of Sigmund, meaning "the victorious protector"
Zsigmund, Zsigmonde, Zsigmunde, Zsig, Zsiga

Zubair (Arabic) One who is pure
Zubaire, Zubayr, Zubayre, Zubar, Zubarr, Zubare, Zubaer

Zuberi (African) Having great strength
Zuberie, Zubery, Zuberey, Zuberee, Zubari, Zubarie, Zubary, Zubarey

Zubin (English) One with a toothy grin
Zubine, Zuben, Zuban, Zubun, Zubbin

Zuzen (Basque) One who is just and fair
Zuzenn, Zuzan, Zuzin

Zvonimir (Croatian) The sound of peace
Zvonimirr, Zvonimeer

My Favorite Names

My Favorite Names

My Favorite Names

My Favorite Names

A VALENTINE KISS

"Why are you staring at me like that?" She raised her eyes and glanced at him from behind her long lashes. She grinned, and two dimples beamed back at him.

"I can't get over your dimples. Where have you been hiding them? You look quite delectable when you smile."

"You have drunk too much wine." She reached over for the empty plate to put it into the basket.

Fitz captured her hand. "The only thing I'm drunk on is you. You are so lovely . . ." He ran the back of his hand along her soft, curved cheek.

"But I'm not. You are only being kind."

"No, just very honest." He tangled his hands in the back of her hair, pulled her face toward his and kissed her. . . .

—from "Cupid's Arrow" by Constance Hall

BOOK YOUR PLACE ON OUR WEBSITE AND MAKE THE READING CONNECTION!

We've created a customized website just for our very special readers, where you can get the inside scoop on everything that's going on with Zebra, Pinnacle and Kensington books.

When you come online, you'll have the exciting opportunity to:

- View covers of upcoming books
- Read sample chapters
- Learn about our future publishing schedule (listed by publication month *and author*)
- Find out when your favorite authors will be visiting a city near you
- Search for and order backlist books from our online catalog
- Check out author bios and background information
- Send e-mail to your favorite authors
- Meet the Kensington staff online
- Join us in weekly chats with authors, readers and other guests
- Get writing guidelines
- AND MUCH MORE!

Visit our website at
http://www.zebrabooks.com

BE MY VALENTINE

CONSTANCE HALL

CHERYL HOLT

JACKIE STEPHENS

Zebra Books
Kensington Publishing Corp.

http://www.zebrabooks.com

CONTENTS

CUPID'S ARROW

BY

CONSTANCE HALL

Though Cupid might contrive to say
This message in a better way
Twould be no truer than this line
Just: "Love me and the world is mine."

—a verse from a Victorian greeting card

CHAPTER ONE

Cornwall, England
1802

The February air bit at Brooke Lackland's face. The brim of her bonnet gave way to the force of the wind, and it whipped back against the sides of her head. One of the ribbon ties beneath her chin tore. She plopped her hand on top of her head, fighting to keep the hat from blowing away completely. Strands of raven black hair escaped the bun at her nape and lashed against her face and eyes. She shoved them back and glanced below her at the sea, turbulent in the remnants of a nor'easter. Waves pounded the craggy cliff. White foam spewed high into the air, rolled back into a sea of frothy green, and met yet another long line of breakers.

Off on the horizon, one herring boat braved Looe Bay, its topside barely visible against the backdrop of swirling gray clouds. A curlew struggled in the wind, gave up, and made an ungraceful dive onto the beach.

Brooke reached the brow of a hill and spotted the hollow of Looe below her. The village's outcropping of buildings almost seemed bent against the fierceness of the gale. She headed down the path that snaked toward the village.

With the wind at her back, she reached Looe in no time. A few fishermen fought the vigorous breeze and checked their lines, their boats banging against the bumpers along the pier. She waved to several of the sailors she knew and headed for the butcher's shop. If Mr. Sanborn didn't give her more credit, there would be no meat on the table yet again. This wind had lasted for days, making it impossible for her to go out on her skiff to fish.

The sound of pounding feet and men yelling made her glance behind her. Halfway down the block, a young boy darted out from around the side of the alehouse, skirted a parked carriage, and ran down the main street of the village.

Twelve yelling sailors scrambled after him.

"Stop the cheater!" one in the back yelled.

Afraid the men would kill the child, Brooke hiked up the hem of her dress and followed them. The sound of approaching hooves made Brooke glance behind her.

A huge bay galloped past her. She caught a fleeting blur of the rider's greatcoat whipping out behind him over the horse's back and a shiny, knee-length black boot.

Brooke watched the gentleman ride beyond the angry men, then slow as he neared the boy.

The boy glanced over his shoulder, saw the gentleman coming straight at him, and changed directions, skirting the angry crowd of men.

The rider pulled on the reins. The huge bay pawed the air in a demivolt and came down front legs stomping. One jerk on the reins from the gentleman and the bay changed directions. Then the horse ate up the distance to the boy, but not fast enough.

Captain Ball, a flat-faced, squat, sea captain speared past the other men. He raised a club and swung at the boy. Brooke sucked in her breath, sure the boy would be killed.

Inches before the child's head met the club, the gentleman rode up beside the boy and snatched the urchin off the ground by the scruff of his neck. With the child seated in front of him, the gentleman pulled back on the reins. Twelve hundred pounds of horse reared, scattering the men near its hooves. The bay pawed to a stop, flinging clods of dirt high into the air.

The boy realized his boon and didn't fight his savior, but sat heaving and acquiescent on the horse. He smiled smugly down at the men for a blink, until he turned and looked into the harsh face and fierce, frigid gray eyes of the gentleman behind him. The smile quickly faded.

Brooke couldn't let out the breath she had been holding, for she had glimpsed the gentleman's severe, chiseled features, the sandy blond hair lashed about his collar by the wind, the squared jaw coated heavily with afternoon stubble, much darker than his hair, and the corded muscles stretching against a pair of tight, doeskin riding breeches. Every raw masculine feature of the gentleman was engraved in her mind. From her first adolescent longing, Fitz Stanhope, the Marquess of Ridgefield, had been the object of her dreams. Unfortunately, he didn't know she was alive.

"What is the meaning of this?" Lord Ridgefield's ruthless gaze swept the men.

Captain Ball growled, "The thieving little bastard stole our money."

"Aye, he did," another man chimed in. "We want his hide, that's what."

" 'Tisn't right. He should be beaten wi'in an inch of his life, the little nubbin cheat," someone else called out.

A roar of hostility and curses came at the boy from the sailors, including murmurs of frustration that his lordship would stick his nose into the matter.

"If there is punishment to be given, I shall give it," Lord Ridgefield's deep voice roared above the wind.

"Ye've no right or authority here," Captain Ball said, shaking the club at the gentleman.

Lord Ridgefield drew himself up, his wide shoulders swelling beneath the eight capes of his greatcoat. "I'm afraid I do. I'm the new magistrate here in Looe. This gives me every right to"—he eyed the men who had spoken—"stick my nose in this."

Lord Ridgefield could not have elicited a more shocked response. They stared blankly and open-mouthed at him, all except the captain; he was too furious to be awed.

"We didn't know they'd replaced Northdale so soon," a bald sailor with an earring said.

"I recently took over my late uncle's duties." Frigid gray eyes turned on the man who had spoken.

The sailor stepped back from Lord Ridgefield. "That's mighty fine for the village, governor. Mighty fine."

The urchin didn't think so. His face fell at the news. His eyes darted between the new magistrate and the sailors, as if weighing the lesser of two evils.

Up until this moment, Brooke's gaze had been riveted to Lord Ridgefield, but now she eyed the boy. His short, dull, soot-caked hair straggled around a dirty oval face. A pert nose and tight-lipped rosebud mouth filled the rest of his features. For an instant, almond-shaped, impish green eyes met Brooke's. The disguise could have fooled just about anyone, save Brooke. She knew those precocious green eyes anywhere. Brooke narrowed her brows at Julia, her sister.

Julia's gaze met Brooke's and held. There was pleading in the green eyes that reached out to Brooke. For all of ten years, Brooke had not been immune to those eyes, and Julia knew it. Brooke shoved her way past several men. "My lord, I beg you to let the boy go."

Lord Ridgefield didn't bother to look at Brooke. He jerked

Julia's face around until her gaze peered into his smoldering eyes. "Are you a thief?"

Julia gulped hard. Her mischievous green eyes darted between the sailors and Lord Ridgefield, and she looked unable to speak.

"Well?" Lord Ridgefield grabbed Julia by her arms.

"He did and used these . . ." Captain Ball threw a pair of dice at Lord Ridgefield.

With a whiplike motion, Lord Ridgefield's hand lashed out and snagged the dice; then he frowned down at them.

One of the sailors said, "Go ahead, see fer yerself. They be cheaters' dispatchers, or me mother was me father. Always gets eight wit 'em. He was tryin' to take us all in hazard."

Lord Ridgefield threw the dice down on the ground. The ivories gleamed a pair of fours. His brows met over his deepset eyes as he glanced toward Julia for an answer.

"I-I didn't mean no 'arm, me lord. Just a friendly game."

"Little cheat!" Captain Ball shook his fist at Julia, which started another round of curses and gibes.

Brooke shoved the captain out of her way, the strong odor of ale and perspiration on him almost making her ill. She tried again. "Please, my lord, let me have the boy."

Lord Ridgefield turned his hard gaze on her, not an ounce of mercy in the unyielding expression. He stared at her a long moment. Recognition dawned in his eyes as if he remembered her, yet he said, "Who are you?"

"I'm Miss Lackland; my father used to be the vicar here." Brooke contained her surprise that he recognized her. Though she had been introduced to him once and had seen him on occasion when he had visited his late uncle, Lord Northdale, she had never spoken more than three words to him. Self-conscious at having his full attention, she dropped her gaze to the folds of his cravat.

"I see. Vicar McCutcheon now serves the parish, I believe?"

"Yes. My father's been dead a year now, my lord," Brooke

said, hearing the familiar catch in her voice whenever she spoke of her father's death.

This news didn't seem to rouse one bit of sympathy in Lord Ridgefield's steely gray eyes. "Do you know this urchin?"

"I do. I know his family. They winter on the moors." Brooke glanced toward heaven and hoped her father forgave her for the lie. "And I promise you, he'll be punished when I speak to his parents." She eyed Julia, who now stared at the horse's twitching ears, adroitly avoiding Brooke's gaze.

"I've never seen the brat hereabouts." Captain Ball glared at Julia as if she were a pesky garden snake.

"His family are a shy group. Rarely do they come into Looe. I let them sleep in our barn when it gets too bitter. I assure you, I know them and can vouch that this boy will be taken in hand. They may be destitute, but they still have morals."

Lord Ridgefield studied the bloodthirsty look in the captain's eyes and said, "I shall go with you to see the parents."

Brooke could not argue with him, not with Captain Ball and his men looking ready to roast her little sister over a flame, so she nodded and shared an apprehensive glance with Julia.

Brooke felt Lord Ridgefield's gaze on her, and she glanced at him. By the frown on his face, he had obviously caught her silent exchange with Julia.

"You men go about your business." Lord Ridgefield's command dispersed the group, and they started back toward the pub, grumbling under their breath.

Captain Ball shot Julia an I'll-get-you-later look, then followed the crowd. A shiver went down Brooke's spine. She knew the captain would not give up on seeking his revenge.

"Lead the way, Miss Lackland," Lord Ridgefield drawled, looking impatient.

Brooke's shiver of fear for her sister was quickly replaced by another kind of apprehension, one not so easily defined.

* * *

Fifteen minutes later, when they were well away from the village, Lord Ridgefield reined in. He dismounted and left Julia sitting in the saddle. He held the reins and waited for Brooke to come abreast of him, tapping his riding crop against the side of his boot.

"Thank you for what you did back there," Brooke spoke first, her fingers digging into the sides of her cape as she fought the wind. But the wind had nothing to do with the slight tremor in her hands.

"I did nothing." The hardness in his eyes didn't melt.

"Oh, but you did. It would have been horrible if Captain Ball and his crew knew Julia's identity."

Julia spoke from her spot on the saddle, her local brogue gone. "I'm not scared of Captain Ball."

"Well, you should be!" Brooke snapped back, giving Julia the brunt of her ire. "Did you stop one moment to think of your own safety, or what word of this would do to Mama?"

Before Julia could speak, Lord Ridgefield asked, "Who is this Captain Ball?" He stopped hitting his boot and waited for Brooke's reply.

"He took up residence here in Looe almost a month ago. He's not well liked."

Julia piped up. "Tell him the truth, Brooke, everyone believes he's in free trade."

"I see." He turned his full attention on Julia. "Captain Ball's disreputable character does not excuse your behavior, you little precocious baggage. What the devil possessed you to tempt danger and cheat cutthroat sailors out of their money?"

Julia didn't flinch under the onslaught of those piercing gray eyes. "Captain Ball and his crew are a maggoty lot. I saw no harm in fleecing them." She sounded proud of herself as she hopped down from the horse and eyed Lord Ridgefield with an admirable amount of gumption.

Awe and disbelief flashed in his eyes. "The harm is you could have been killed," he said, his voice strained as he held back his temper.

"But I wasn't."

Brooke had to admire Lord Ridgefield's restraint in the face of Julia's insolence. By the way he was slapping his boot with the riding crop and the white-knuckled grasp he had on the bay's reins, it wouldn't be long before his self-control slipped.

"I will see she is punished, my lord," she blurted, then turned to Julia. "Not another word out of you, do you hear? I'm sorely ashamed of you, speaking to Lord Ridgefield in such an impudent manner after he saved your life. How could you?"

"Go ahead, scold me. That's all you ever do. Well, I don't care. I don't!" Julia turned and stomped off.

The two adults followed Julia, the only sound between them the howl of the wind. Brooke grew aware of his arm almost touching hers, of the thud of his boots, of the sheer size of him towering next to her. She had forgotten how tall he was; her head barely reached his chest. And he looked older than his two-and-thirty years. Frown lines edged the corners of his eyes and his mouth. Still, it did nothing to mar his handsome features or the raw masculine power of his presence. His presence enveloped her like a weight, pressing against her chest, making her heart pound.

When she could stand the tension no longer, she said, "Please forgive Julia, my lord." Brooke's brows furrowed with worry as she stared after her sister. "She sometimes gets this way. I'm afraid she hasn't taken our father's death well. You really needn't see us home; 'tis but a quarter of a mile. And if you spoke to my mother, it would only upset her. Please say you will leave Julia to me."

"Very well, but I can see you're going to have your hands full."

"I can manage."

He didn't make a move to leave right away and looked over at her as if really noticing her for the first time. Brooke felt self-conscious under his scrutiny. Blood rushed to her cheeks. She couldn't help but suffer the thought he might be aware of her mismatched eyes, one green, the other light blue, both too large for her small face.

He didn't seem to notice, and the frosty glaze in his eyes melted slightly. "How long has it been since I've seen you last, Miss Lackland?"

"At least four years." Brooke raised her voice to speak to him over the wind, recalling the last time she had seen him. She had been only fourteen at the time, yet the night was as vivid in her mind as if it were yesterday. She would rue it as long as she lived.

Julia had been broodingly silent up until this point, but she proved she had been listening as she called over her shoulder, "It has been three years and eleven months to be exact—at Lord Northdale's Valentine's Ball. Brooke, I would have thought you would remember it to the hour since you've been in love with Lord Ridgefield forever."

Brooke stumbled and felt the blood drain from her face. Lord Ridgefield caught her arm before she fell. Dying a thousand deaths, she avoided his gaze and stared at Julia, who continued to walk in front of her, never missing a step. She didn't know which she wanted to do first, strangle Julia or dry up into a speck of dust and let the wind carry her away.

"Are you all right?" he asked, ignoring Julia's outburst.

Brooke hoped he hadn't heard Julia and found enough nerve to look at him. All her hopes were dashed in an instant. He wore a lopsided grin on his lips, which softened the steely gray in his eyes. She blushed down to her navel. If only she could die.

She pulled her arm back from his grasp. In a calm voice that surprised her, she said, "I'm so grateful to you for saving Julia. If you'll excuse us, I'd like to speak to my sister alone."

"Very well."

Brooke cringed at the amusement in his deep drawl. Her mortification returned a thousandfold. She covered the three yards separating her from Julia in two angry strides.

She felt Lord Ridgefield's penetrating gaze on her back. Brooke glanced over her shoulder and watched him mount his horse. As if he sensed her gaze on him, he turned and looked at her. Their gazes locked. A ghost of a smile tempered his severe chiseled features; then he turned and rode away. Now that Brooke was sure of privacy, she leaped in front of Julia and blocked her way.

Julia tried to step around her.

Brooke grabbed her by the arm. "How could you embarrass me like that?"

"I was just being honest."

"You just can't go blurting out every single thought in your head." Brooke paused and frowned at Julia. "How did you know I had a crush on him anyway?"

"I saw the way you were looking at him all cow-eyed." Julia opened her eyes wide and fluttered them.

Brooke stomped her foot in exasperation. "Sometimes I don't know what gets into you."

"I don't need a lecture from you."

"Do you not? Not only have you made it impossible for me to ever look Lord Ridgefield in the face again, but the mischief you pulled in the village is beyond anything. Where did you get the dice and these dirty clothes?"

"Billy Swenson."

"I told you to stay away from him."

"He's my friend." Julia thrust out her jaw.

"But look at you—at your hair." Brooke ruffled Julia's short locks, the wind whipping it against her hands. She felt something gritty on her skin and looked at her soot-covered palms and fingertips. "How do you think Mama will feel when she sees you've cut off your hair?"

"I could not go down there as myself."

"What possessed you to go near the alehouse or even think of playing hazards? Have you forgotten everything Papa taught us?"

Her words finally struck a nerve behind those precocious green eyes. Tears glistened, and Julia dropped her head. Hardly audible above the wind, she said, "I only did it because we needed money."

Confronted with such stark truth, Brooke wrapped her arms around her sister and hugged her. "I know," was all she could manage to say.

After a sniffle, Julia drew back and looked up at her older sister, tears streaking through the soot on her face. She wiped her nose on her sleeve and smeared the blacking on her eyebrows. After a sigh, she asked, "What were you doing in the village?"

"I was going to see if Mr. Sanborn would give us more credit."

Julia eyed Brooke's empty hands. "I see you didn't get it."

"No, thanks to your shenanigans. We'll have to eat beans again," Brooke said, trying to sound cheerful.

Julia made a face. "If I eat one more bean, I'll gag—I swear it."

"I know." Brooke's shoulders slumped in a defeated gesture, and she grimaced. "If I could only find a job."

A lengthy silence stood between them, the only sound the wind whipping the edges of Brooke's cape and dress.

"Was there no word in the post about the governess position with the Sheltons?"

"Not yet." It was all Brooke could do to keep her face straight, for there was no position. No Sheltons. Only a lie to help brighten the spirits of Julia and her mother. Times were hard, governess positions extremely rare, and then, most people required previous experience, as with all the other positions for which she had applied. To get past the awkward moment, she said, "I'm sure one will come soon."

"I hope so."

Brooke looked down into her sister's hopeful eyes, at the hunger and loss and a melancholy that she herself felt. She remembered promising her father on his death bed that she would look after Julia and her mother.

A vain promise. She had given it little thought at the time, for they had lived at the rectory and there was plenty of money to sustain them. That had all changed with the death of her father. She would never forget the apathetic, cold expression of the solicitor as he informed her that her mother's dowry had been exhausted and there was little left from her father's fortune to provide for his family. Now that little bit was gone. Unable to quell the slight bitterness she felt, she glanced toward heaven. Her father had to have known what sort of burden he had thrust upon her when he asked her to care for her sister and mother. He had to have known.

Hand in hand, Julia and Brooke trudged another quarter mile in solemn silence, the sound of their footsteps swept away in the wind. They traversed the small scrap of bottom land on the edge of Breakland Farm while leaves swirled past them. Through the row of wild nut trees and hawthorns thrashing before her, Brooke caught flashes of the faded stucco cottage they called home.

As they neared the yard, Julia said, "Look, there's Emily, and she's crying."

Brooke glanced at their longtime housekeeper. She had stayed on after the vicar's death, even though Brooke couldn't afford to pay her. Her dress whipped around her short, round frame, showing a faded, tattered petticoat and old work boots. Her round face was buried in her hands, and her shoulders shook from her sobs. A paper flapped from one of her hands.

Brooke ran toward her, a sick feeling of foreboding rising up in her. After this morning, what else could go wrong?

CHAPTER TWO

"What is the matter?" Brooke gasped out between pants. She touched the elderly servant's shoulder.

"Oh, 'tis this." Emily stopped sobbing long enough to thrust the paper at Brooke. "He didn't have the courage to come tell us himself. He sent one of his help over with it. The old liar. I'd like to give him the pointy end of me boot."

Brooke read the paper and felt the blood drain from her face. "Why would he go back on his word?"

"Greed it be, plain and simple." Emily mopped at her eyes.

"What is it?" Julia said, growing impatient.

"Mr. Breakland says we must pay rent or move." Brooke frowned down at the paper in her hand.

"But we fixed up this cottage. It's our home." Tears gleamed in Julia's eyes.

"Looks like he wants to be rid of us." Emily jammed her hands on her wide hips. "And he promising yer mother ye could stay here rent-free after we was thrown out of the rectory. Said it right there in church after yer pa's funeral—big as you please. We all heard him, but Breakland always was one for impressing others. We all know what sort he be now.'' Emily harrumphed under her breath. ''Rot him! 'Tisn't right, charging rent.''

''He has every right to charge rent for this cottage.'' Brooke lifted the notice in her hand.

Julia stomped her foot. ''He doesn't. He's nothing but a liar!''

Emily gazed at Julia, as if seeing her for the first time. She took in the blackened face and hair, the dirty, moleskin breeches with holes in the knees, the oversized boy's dingy blue shirt, and the short, woolen, moth-eaten coat. She grabbed her chest. Her eyes disappeared in her moon-shaped face as she squeezed them together. ''Curse me! What's the mite done now to herself?''

''Nothing,'' Julia said. ''I just tried to make some money, but that doesn't matter now. We'll be living in the workhouse . . .'' Julia ran into the cottage.

''What d'we do now, Miss Brooke?'' Emily's brows furrowed. ''We don't have the money to pay rent.''

''I know not, but we must keep this from Mama. This will upset her.''

As if summoned by the name, a bell tinkled above stairs.

''Rot it!'' Emily exclaimed. ''She heard the commotion.''

''I'll go to her.''

''I'll go after the mite. It'll take four baths to get that mess out of her hair.'' Emily hiked up her dress and hurried into the house.

Brooke followed, but at a slower pace, as each step brought a sinking feeling, pulling her farther and farther down.

She climbed the stairs, opened the door, and stepped into her mother's room, a small, drafty chamber with a smoking chimney. Mrs. Lackland glanced up from her bed and looked at Brooke.

Everything about Enid Lackland looked impotent and ethereal. Her hair was a lackluster blond mixed with gray, her skin sallow, her diminutive face lacked zest, and her eyes had lost the brightness and spirit that had been there prior to her husband's death. She was fingering a bolt of pink silk in her hands.

"My dear, what has happened? I heard Julia race by and slam the door. She would not come to me when I called her. Please tell me she is not in one of those belligerent moods again."

"She's just been out." Brooke stared at the new bolt of cloth. "Did Aunt Josephine send us that?"

"No, my dear," her mother explained. "A peddler came by and I bought it."

"You what?" Brooke blurted before she could stop herself.

Enid sighed airily. "I saw it and thought it would be nice to buy something new for once."

"But where did you get the money for it?"

"I had a little put away."

"Do you have any more?"

"No, I spent it all."

Brooke wanted to rail at her mother, to tell her she had had to scrimp and barter and sometimes go hungry just to feed everyone. And her mother had spent their last coin on cloth— of all things. The doctor had said to keep all harmful news at bay or her mother's fits of melancholy might worsen, so as Brooke had done for the past year, she managed to smile and said, "It's lovely."

Enid ran her hand over the silk. "I got a very good price on it. There's enough here to make all of us new dresses to wear to Lord Northdale's Valentine's Ball."

"Have you forgotten he died four months ago?"

"I didn't mean the elder, but the new Earl of Northdale, his nephew, Lord Ridgefield."

Brooke tensed at the name and half listened to her mother.

"Your Aunt Josephine intimated he has decided to settle here in Cornwall and take over Lord Northdale's position as magistrate. I always thought he was a very approachable and gallant young man the few times I met him. And we already know he's very wealthy after inheriting the title and lands from his uncle. Are we not lucky to have someone so eligible and well connected in the neighborhood?''

"I'm sure he would not like to be bothered with a ball."

Lost in her own little world, Enid did not hear her daughter, but leaned back in her bed and smiled weakly up at the ceiling. "Would it not be wonderful just for one night to forget our cares and go out in Society? I'm so looking forward to this Valentine's Ball. And of course you could find a wealthy bachelor to marry." A faint spark glistened in Enid's eyes.

Brooke didn't have the heart to tell her mother no gentleman would want a penniless vicar's daughter—an imperfect one at that with her odd-colored eyes. Enid would naturally believe her daughter flawless, no matter the evidence staring her in the face.

"Are you sure he's agreed to this Valentine's Ball?" Brooke asked, sounding incredulous.

"Oh, yes. Lady Josephine approached him on it, and he agreed. I am quite sure, knowing your aunt, she's probably already dreaming up wedding plans for Lord Ridgefield and Caroline. You know how she's been trying to marry Caroline off since her come out."

"I'm sure they'll suit. Caroline is so very pretty." Brooke managed to keep her voice toneless, though every time she thought of her perfectly beautiful cousin, she couldn't help but feel a tinge of envy. Lord Ridgefield would certainly never give her a second glance with Caroline near him. One flutter of Caroline's lashes above perfect blue eyes would have him begging at her heels like a puppy. For her own sake, Brooke knew she should forget this foolish infatuation. It would only lead to heartache, and she had had enough of that in her life. Her mother's voice broke into her thoughts.

"Yes, to be sure Caroline is lovely. And I am certain Lady

Josephine will look on Lord Ridgefield as a prospective beau
for her, even if there is a scandal attached to his lordship's
name—''

"Scandal?" Brooke perked up.

Her mother's cheeks pinked, as if she realized she had said
more than she wanted to. She cleared her throat. "Yes, one
hears naughty things.''

"What kinds of things?"

Enid eyed Brooke, weighing whether she was old enough to
hear such gossip. After a long moment, she said, "One
shouldn't repeat things, my dear. Suffice it to say, the first wife
was not a pillar of virtue. Now, will you help me cut out the
patterns for our dresses?"

Brooke nodded, the scandal the least of her worries. Aware
she still held the rent notice, she crumpled it up in her hand.

She couldn't upset her mother by informing her they might
be living out on the moors by Valentine's Day. Brooke would
have to find a way to get money, and quickly. She had to.

One week later, Brooke crept through the bracken, then
slithered down in a ditch beside the road. Her breathing came
in great shallow gasps. The frigid dampness of the night air
hung thick in her lungs and smothered her face. She tried to
still the pounding of her heart, but couldn't.

Remnants of a quarter moon curved against the backdrop of
twinkling stars. Near her ear a cricket sawed in the gorse. The
screech of a nighthawk went through her like needles. Her
fingers tightened around the hilt of the pistol in her hand, while
yet another sound pricked her heightened senses.

She stretched her neck and peered down the road. Two lan-
terns hovered in the night, their yellowish orbs swaying against
the black lacquered sides of a carriage. Squinting, she could
just make out the dark forms of a driver and a postilion. Two
of them. Brooke felt her pulse throb in her ears. She could do

this. Stiff with resolve, she pulled a dark mask over her face, gripped the pistol and edged closer to the top of the ditch.

Footsteps sounded behind Brooke; then Julia plopped down beside her.

Brooke jumped and almost squeezed the trigger of the pistol. "You scared the life out of me." Brooke glared at Julia. "You shouldn't be here. Go back home."

"I wondered what you were up to when you took Papa's pistol from his trunk and snuck out of the house. Turning highwaylady now, are you? But I thought you would know better, Brooke. Did you forget everything Papa taught us?" Julia threw Brooke's words back at her, with a flavoring of smugness added.

"Desperate people do desperate things. You can harass me later. Right now, I have to rob a carriage. Go home!"

"No, I want to help."

"What if you get caught? We both could hang. Go home!" Brooke noticed the carriage was almost upon them. A few more seconds and she would miss her chance and probably never gain enough nerve to do this again. Julia wasn't moving. The carriage was getting closer . . . closer.

She pointed at Julia. "Stay put."

Marshaling her courage, she leaped up from the ditch and raised the pistol at the postilion. "Halt or die." Her voice cracked, sounding hardly more than a squeak.

She cleared her throat, took a deep breath, and yelled, "Halt or die!"

The postilion grabbed the reins. The lead horses pawed to a halt inches from the tip of her pistol.

"Down with you! Hurry! You, too." Brooke waved the gun at the driver, who sat scowling at her. He was a burly, balding man with a flat face. He bent to reach beneath the seat. "Move one more inch to retrieve a weapon, and you'll never move again." Brooke eyed him and tried to look fierce. She saw the man's eyes dart to the seat again and blurted, "Please keep in mind my gun is already aimed at your skull, sir."

He froze, then gingerly straightened.

"Good. Now, please get down from there."

"You'll hang for this," the driver grumbled, crawling down off the box. The postilion, a young man with curly red hair, looked overcome by fear. He dismounted, his whole body trembling.

"That remains to be seen. All right, gentlemen. Drop to the road and put your hands behind your backs." They shot her an incredulous look and didn't move. "It's either lie down or be shot." Brooke aimed the gun at them. Her hand shook so hard that she was forced to grip the pistol with both hands.

As the men went down on their knees, the carriage door swung open. Brooke hadn't given a thought to who might be riding in the carriage. As she stared in fascinated dread at a pair of long black boots emerging, she could have kicked herself for not having been more cautious.

The Marquess of Ridgefield stepped out of the carriage, looking large and ominous and irritated. Crystal gray eyes gleamed out at her from the shadows of his face like shards of ice. Her dread turned to panic.

Fitz stared at the highwayman. The thief stood just inside the circular ray of light from the carriage lantern. It illuminated the robber's black baggy breeches and bulky, old dark blue coat that drooped over a thin frame, no more than five feet tall. A black hood covered a small face.

The thief looked directly at Fitz. One bright green and one bright blue eye stared out from behind the slits in the hood. His eyes widened just a little; then a cynical grin twisted up one side of his lip.

The point of the thief's gun moved between the kneeling

men and Fitz. "Kindly take off your hat, sir, and please fill it with any valuables you might have."

"A thief with manners," Fitz taunted. "That may have some sway over the hangman, but I doubt it will sway the judge."

"I do not intend to face the judge or a hangman. Now do as I say."

Entertained by her feisty audacity, Fitz found himself stifling a grin. It had been some time since he had met with such spunk from a young lady. He had to admire her courage and couldn't imagine what had driven her to such desperation. When he had first met Miss Brooke Lackland at his uncle's home, he thought her a vapid, shy, pampered vicar's daughter. But she had been just a child then. She was very much a woman now—a very fascinating one with more pluck than most men. His eyes moved over the curves he knew were hidden by the bulky coat as he said, "And what if I do not—"

At that moment, Lady Caroline hung her pretty head out the carriage window, blond curls bobbing near her perfect heart-shaped face. Her gaze snapped over to Brooke holding the gun. She screamed and jerked her head back inside the carriage. Distracted, Brooke's gaze shifted from him to the carriage.

Fitz lunged at her and knocked the gun from her hand, then reached for her.

She leaped back. With surprising reflexes for a woman, Brooke snatched a knife from her pocket and brandished it at his chest. "Stay away."

"You know I can't do that."

Fitz's driver took a step toward Brooke.

"Stay out of this; it's my fight." One look from Fitz and Rollins's expression fell.

"Aye, me lord." Rollins backed off.

The postilion, Morton, cringed against the horses, looking afraid of his own shadow. Fitz shot him a disapproving glance, then turned his gaze back on the reckless chit trying to rob him.

"I mean it. I'll cut you if you come any closer." She took a step back toward the ditch. "Just let me be on my way."

"As magistrate of this parish, I'm afraid I can't oblige you, no matter how polite you are." He lunged.

They hit the ground. He landed on top of her, knocking the knife from her hand.

She fought him with both fists, but he easily captured her wrists and snatched off the hood covering her face. She froze. The false sense of bravado the mask had provided dissolved. Heat seeped into her cheeks, down her neck. Her dark hair escaped the bun at the back of her nape, and wisps of black curls spiraled along both sides of her oval face. Long, dark, sooty lashes hooded her eyes, full of fright and hostility and humiliation, all directed at him.

"Ah, Miss Lackland, and I thought the night was going to be dull."

Fitz grew aware of her ragged breaths brushing against his lips, face, the sensitive area near his ear, of the proud, mounded softness of her breasts pressing intimately against his chest, the way her hips fitted against his own. The clean scent of a woman wafted beneath his nose. It had been over two months since he had sated his body with a woman. Too bloody long. He felt the ache in his loins down to his toes.

"Please let me go," she said, her voice shaky.

Fitz rubbed his thumb across her silken wrists, feeling the thin film of perspiration slick against his fingertip. "It's a little too late for mercy." He stared down at her lips, such a perfect rosebud shape, and so very red. "What a fool I was to let you have the care of your sister. Did you teach her everything she knows?"

"I didn't. I've never done this before. You have to believe me—"

"Leave my sister alone!" Julia charged out of the ditch, brandishing a thick stick, a martyred look in her eye.

"No, Julia!" Brooke yelled.

Fitz couldn't turn fast enough.

Crack. He felt a sharp pain in his shoulder. The stick crumbled in Julia's hand. This did not deter the little termagant. She leaped. Kicked. Bit.

Fitz was forced to turn the older sister's wrists loose to grab the younger one's arms. Brooke shoved him, rolled out from under him, and jumped to her feet. Fitz pinned Julia's hands with one hand and grabbed the seat of her sister's pants with the other.

Brooke wheeled around and struck out at his hand. Her aim was off; she hit his eye.

"Hell and damnation!" He had had all the scratching, hitting, and biting he could take. He rolled to his feet, snatched Julia up and threw her, kicking and screaming, over his shoulder.

"Run, Brooke!" Julia yelled, hitting his back.

"No. Leave her alone!" Brooke dove at Fitz.

It was just what he wanted. One quick jerk, and he pinned her against his chest, squeezing her arms down at her sides. She tried to wriggle free, but he tightened his grip on her.

"Enough!" Fitz barely whispered the command, but it cut through the air like the bark of a general.

Julia froze.

Miss Lackland stopped trying to free her arms.

Caroline stepped down from the carriage, her mother, Lady Josephine, right behind her. Caroline's gaze landed on Brooke. Her astonishment quickly gave way to a malicious look of pleasure.

"My Lawd!" Lady Josephine gasped. Her eyes grew wide in her face, and she raised her quizzing glass at Brooke, then at Julia. "You tried to rob this carriage and brought along your little sister to help?"

Caroline's blond curls shook near her ears as she said, "Shame on you, Cousin!"

Fitz dropped Julia on the ground and released Brooke, sure now the contempt on Lady Josephine's face would keep them from running. He noticed the blood drain from Miss Lackland's face as she met the abrasive censure in her aunt's eyes.

"She didn't bring me; I wanted to help her." Julia crossed her arms over her chest and thrust out her chin.

"Shut up, child. I spoke to your sister." Lady Josephine stomped her foot on the ground and puffed out her large breasts, almost popping the seams of her tight-fitting cloak. She sucked in her breath, the whalebone stays of her corset creaking, and said, "Well, Brooke, do not stand there like a dolt. Have you nothing to say, you impudent girl?"

Brooke stared down at her feet, looking pale, completely chastised, and speechless.

"I'm sure she must have a good reason," Fitz said. He watched Brooke glance up at him, an appreciative look in her eyes. Something in the forlorn, guileless way she looked at him touched a strange need in him to protect her. Perhaps knowing she had a crush on him brought about this feeling. Since her sister had blurted it out a week ago, the notion had never left his mind.

"Reason for such actions! There could be no reason!" Lady Josephine exclaimed. "I hope word of this does not get out, my lord. We just cannot have such a scandal attached to our family, especially with Caroline out."

"I can safely assure you, madam, I have no intention of relaying this to anyone." He hadn't taken his eyes off Brooke, and he saw the relief in her face.

"And a good thing, too. We are indebted to you." Lady Josephine continued her interrogation, lifting her quizzing glass and pointing it at Brooke. "Something must have driven you to such desperation. I would expect this from Julia, but not you. If my dear brother knew of this, he would turn over in his grave."

"Must we speak of this now?" Brooke cut her gaze at Fitz, then back at her aunt.

"Of course we must speak of it now. I believe Lord Ridgefield has every right to an explanation. Why did you do it, Brooke?'' Lady Josephine's small, hawklike, black eyes darted to her niece.

''Tell her, Brooke,'' Julia blurted. ''Tell her that all Papa's money is gone, you can't find a job, and now we must pay rent.''

''If you needed money, you could have come to me,'' Lady Josephine said in a patronizing tone.

''I did. Remember?'' Brooke squared her shoulders, taking on the look of a cornered soldier. ''You would not even give us a place to live on your own estate when Papa died. We had to look to Papa's parishioners to find lodgings. Farmer Breakland has decided we can no longer be a charitable concern. He's charging us more rent than we can possibly pay.''

Lady Josephine pursed her lips, looking speechless and guilty for a moment.

''You needn't worry about that now,'' Fitz drawled.

''Why?'' Brooke looked at him, her dark, finely arched brows meeting over her nose.

''As punishment, you and your sister will work for me.''

''Work for you?'' Brooke shot him a suspicious glance.

''We won't work unless you pay us.'' Julia turned and glowered at Fitz.

''We'll have to,'' Brooke muttered, looking at Julia.

''You'll earn a wage,'' Fitz added. ''Enough so you can pay your rent.'' He looked at the one stray black curl stuck to the side of Brooke's lip. He wanted very much to reach out and brush it back, and to run his thumb over her lips and feel if they were as soft as they looked.

''Oh, no, my lord,'' Lady Josephine perked up. ''If you would entrust Brooke and Julia to me, I'd see they venture into no more trouble. Brooke and her family could come to our house to live. I'll see she and Julia stay out of trouble. We need laundry maids.''

"Since she tried to rob me, Lady Josephine, I feel it my duty to keep an eye on her."

"What position am I to fill, my lord?" Brooke asked.

"We'll find one," Fitz said, unable to take his eyes off her lips.

CHAPTER THREE

An hour later, Fitz stepped into the foyer of Glen Carion. He frowned at the dark wainscoting that seemed to be everywhere in the dreary mansion he had inherited from his uncle.

"A good evening, my lord." Helms, his butler, strode toward him. He was a solidly built man, tall, with sturdy, square facial features and faded green eyes the color of an unripe lime.

"Yes, a surprisingly good evening."

Helms surveyed Fitz's black eye and raised a brow at the slight grin on his master's face. "I suppose at the card party you found the local society somewhat savage?" Helms spoke with an ease born of forty years serving Fitz and his father before him.

"Not in the least. It was an evening I shall not soon forget." Fitz touched his eye. The grin still on his face, he handed Helms his cape, cane, and hat. "And there was one individual I find very hard to get out of my mind."

"I suppose by an 'individual' you mean Lady Caroline—a

very pretty young lady." A satisfied male grin spread across Helms's lips. "I imagine men find her unforgettable."

Fitz thought of Lady Caroline's blond curls, blue flashing eyes, perfect, heart-shaped face, and pouting red lips. "I grant you, she is pretty," he said. "But I was speaking of another."

"Who?"

"Another young lady." Fitz strode down the hall, knowing Helms would be on his heels.

Helms hurried behind him. "Young, my lord?"

"Very."

This brought a smile into Helms's voice. "I suppose she was a friend of Lady Caroline and her mother?"

"Cousin, actually." Fitz thought of Brooke's tedious relatives and was glad she wasn't anything like them.

"And you met her at the card party?"

"It was a party of sorts."

"Of sorts, my lord?"

"Yes, a robbery."

"This lady robbed you?" Helms sounded as excited as an ancient dowager by the news.

"She tried."

"I suppose you arrested her."

"No, I gave her and her sister a position here at Glen Carion." Helms's footsteps paused behind Fitz, who turned and looked at the pale, gaping Helms. "No need to worry, we'll make sure they don't walk off with the silver."

"Your benevolence knows no bounds, my lord, but I suppose you have considered that it is not a wise thing to have a thief in the house, much less two of them. I think it folly to invite trouble, especially after the gossip in town about the scandal. Hiring these two young creatures will no doubt cause more trouble."

"You worry like a mother hen, Helms. I'm acquainted with the young ladies. Their father, the late vicar, was a particular friend of my uncle's. I'm sure they would not have turned to highway robbery if they were not in dire straights. That should ease your mind.''

"Not in the least, my lord. I suppose you've never heard that every time the seed of a clergyman is planted, the devil celebrates, for he uses them to anger God by tempting them into mischief. Some of the most unscrupulous people I've ever known were clergy gents.''

"I'm sure you'll keep a diligent eye on them.''

"Speaking of eyes, my lord, would you like a piece of steak for yours.''

"A little late for it, Helms. See that the carriage picks up the Miss Lacklands exactly at eight o'clock in the morning.''

"Yes, my lord.'' Helms's thick gray brows wrinkled in worry.

"Has it been quiet here?''

"Other than a few smoking chimneys, quiet is all we have here, my lord.'' Helms's dislike of Glen Carion and country life laced his voice. He set Fitz's cane in a large urn by the door, his silver hair gleaming in the candlelight from the wall sconce burning overhead.

"What of my son?'' At the thought of his son, Fitz felt tension lines pulling at his forehead.

"Last time I checked, he was in his room—moping, my lord.''

"I had so hoped moving here would lift his spirits. It has been over a year since his mother's death.''

"It will take more time.''

"I wonder if all the time in the world will help him,'' Fitz said, his despair coming through in his voice.

"At least he's away from France now and the memories of Lady Victoria . . .'' Helms grew silent and stared down at his hands.

A grandfather clock struck nine and echoed in the silence. Helms raised his head. The hopeless look on his master's face made him add, "I wouldn't worry. Master Lawford will come around. You made the right decision in bringing him here. He'll be away from the gossip that resurfaced after Lady Victoria's death. That in itself will be a benefit to him.''

"Yes, there is that advantage.''

"And this Valentine's Ball might lift his spirits.''

"Are we ready for the infernal thing?'' Fitz frowned, he had hoped to leave all routs and parties back in France, but Lady Caroline and her meddling mother had pleaded with him to keep up this absurd tradition his uncle had started. It was the highlight of the year for the local gentry. Being new to the neighborhood, Fitz felt compelled to give the ball.

"Lord Northdale stored most of his decorations in the attic, my lord. I'll go up there tomorrow and see what can be salvaged.''

"Very good. I'm going up to see Lawford.''

"Yes, my lord.'' Helms strode down the hall, Fitz's cape hanging over his arm.

As Fitz walked toward the stairs, the sound of crying made him pause. He moved toward the doorway of what used to be his uncle's study. The whimpering continued. Helms had left the candles burning in the room's sconces. Light flickered along the sofa near one wall, across the huge mahogany desk and empty leather chair.

He stepped farther into the room and frowned at the smell of cheap cigars that still permeated the air. Breedon Northdale had been a miser when it came to creature comforts, though he had spent enough money entertaining. Fitz had had to pay a five-thousand-pound lien on Glen Carion after he had inherited it and the title.

As Fitz drew near the desk, the crying grew louder. He pulled out the chair and bent down to peer at his ten-year-old son. He was curled beneath the desk, his forehead resting on his knees. Tears streamed down the sides of his pale face.

"Why are you under there?'' Fitz kept his voice even so as not to unnerve his son.

"I like it here."

"Come out and we'll talk about what is bothering you."

"No! No! No! I don't want to talk about it. I want to go back to France."

"We live here now."

"But I hate it here."

"Why?"

"I just do."

Fitz reached down to touch his son's shoulder, but Lawford shook it off. "You know we agreed to make a go of it here."

"I never agreed. You never asked me if I wanted to come here. Everything is strange here. I hate it."

"You must give it a chance."

"I won't be happy here."

Lawford bolted out from beneath the desk and tried to run past his father. Fitz snagged his son's arm and wheeled the boy around to face him. A smaller image of himself stared back at Fitz: the square jaw, the blond hair, the gray eyes. Tears glazed them, emphasizing their despair.

Fitz gripped his son's arms tighter and said, "We have to stay here. It's our home now."

"I *won't*. I hate it." Lawford knocked his hands away and stumbled out of the room, his sobs echoing down the hallway.

Fitz started to go after him, but paused. Lawford needed a chance to calm down. He stepped over to the dry bar, poured three fingers of brandy in a glass, and downed it in one gulp. For as long as Fitz could remember, Lawford had been a fearful child.

Victoria had made the situation worse, by pampering and spoiling the boy, giving in to his every wish. As he grew older, Lawford's petulance and fears worsened.

After Victoria died from consumption, Fitz had lost the ability to communicate with his son. Time and again, he had found Lawford in a corner of Victoria's bedroom, crying. In spite of Fitz's attempts to console him, Lawford closed himself off and would have nothing to do with Fitz, as if he blamed Fitz for his mother's death.

He walked over and poured himself another full glass of brandy, and thought of Victoria. She had given him unfathomable happiness and unadulterated hell, in equal measure. He had thought he would never allow himself to have feelings for another woman—until tonight.

A memory flashed of one green eye and one blue, set in an oval face, shiny raven curls, a pair of very kissable lips. He remembered the way Brooke had felt in his arms, the enticing scent of woman, the perfect curve of her lips, the way her eyes burned when she was provoked. Nor could he forget the vulnerability in those eyes that caused such protective feelings in him. Brooke had actually awakened a dormant part of him he had thought dead and buried. Fitz knew it wouldn't easily be put to rest again.

The next morning, Brooke felt the gentle sway of the carriage and watched Julia fidget on the seat.

"Please sit still." Brooke grabbed Julia's hand, which was thumping on the seat.

"I can't." Julia brushed off Brooke's hold, lifted the leather blind over the window, and poked her head out. Her short, golden curls whipped against her face. The cold air chafed her cheeks, the redness accentuating the freckles on her nose.

Julia stared up at the morning sky. "Aren't you excited? How can you sit there so calmly? He sent the carriage for us, and you tried to rob him last night. Did you ever dream he would do that?"

"He probably did it to keep an eye on us and see that we didn't rob another carriage on our way to Glen Carion."

Julia pulled her head back in and carelessly pushed a blond curl out of her eyes. "Know what I think?"

"No, and I don't want to know."

"I'm going to tell you anyway. I think he likes you and didn't want you to have to walk the two miles here."

"That is the most imbecilic thing I've ever heard come out of your mouth."

"I saw the way he knocked you on the ground and stayed on top of you. He looked *pretty* content to me."

Brooke raised a brow at her sister, feeling a blush gorging her cheeks. By now she should be used to Julia's bluntness, but this time it caught her off guard. Brooke had tried her best to forget that part of last night, but she couldn't. She had even dreamed he had stayed on top of her and kissed her until she was breathless.

"And he couldn't take his eyes off you, even when dear sweet *Caroline* was in the carriage last night. Did you see how provoked she was, stiffening her spine and poking out her lip?" Julia imitated the gesture.

"I saw no such thing."

"That's because you didn't look. And how could you with Aunt Josephine berating you all the way home. What a witchy woman, just like her daughter."

"Julia!" Brooke had said her name with reproach in it, but she was holding back a grin.

"It's true." Julia looked down her nose at Brooke and took on a very superior, proper accent, giving her voice a nasal twang. "She's a tight-fisted old prune that enjoys condescending long enough to tell others how to run their lives."

"You are cheeky and wretched." Brooke couldn't hold back the grin any longer.

Julia smiled, looking proud of herself. " 'Tis true. Did you hear her last night? Saying how she would help us." Julia rolled her eyes. "I was so proud of you when you called her on not letting us stay with her. She had no arch remarks for that."

"She didn't tell Mama what happened—you have to admit she was extremely understanding about that."

"She has her own motives; you can bank on it."

Brooke looked at her little sister. For being only ten years old, her understanding of the seedier side of human nature was uncanny. Brooke had no doubt Aunt Josephine did nothing that couldn't benefit her own situation in life.

"And I hate it when she comes to visit Mama," Julia continued. "All she does is disparage everything Mama says as if she were a rockhead. And Caroline, such a smug weed she is. Did you see her batting her eyes at Lord Ridgefield? She thinks she's so pretty." Julia laughed. "He didn't give her a second glance with you around."

"I'm sure you're wrong."

"I'm not."

"Of course you are." Brooke smiled ruefully at Julia. "Naturally Caroline would have his attentions. He must care for her if he escorted her to a card party."

"More than likely Aunt Josephine badgered him until he agreed."

They turned into the drive of Glen Carion, and the sound of a woman's laughter split the air. Julia hung her head out the window again.

"Julia, you are too far out. Get in here."

"You should see this!"

"What is it?" Brooke craned her neck, trying to peer past Julia, her curiosity overriding any sense of decorum she wished to instill in her sister. She could see only Julia's behind.

"You'll see in a moment."

The carriage rocked to a halt.

Julia wasn't expecting the sudden stop. She lost her balance. Brooke grabbed at the back of Julia's dress, and the black muslin slipped through her fingers.

Brooke screamed as Julia tumbled out the window.

CHAPTER FOUR

Brooke stood so quickly she bumped her head on top of the carriage. The fear that Julia had broken her neck dulled any sensation of pain Brooke may have felt.

"Oh, God, Julia!" she murmured and grabbed for the door. It opened as she reached for the latch.

Brooke tumbled through the opening. Strong hands grabbed her, and she was swept up into Lord Ridgefield's arms. "Julia, where is she?" Brooke turned toward the carriage and saw her sister, grinning as the driver held her. The tension in Brooke's chest eased.

Julia shrugged and tried to look coy. She patted Rollins's shoulder, and his grizzled face creased with a grin. "Rollins here happened to be coming around to open the door. What luck, hey? And you, Brooke. I thought you would certainly take a tumble on your head. If not for Lord Ridgefield's quick arms, you'd probably be raising dust. A spectacular save, my lord." She saluted him.

"Thank you." Lord Ridgefield grinned at her, then glanced down at Brooke.

With the excitement over, Brooke grew aware of the unsettling position in which she found herself. Color seeped into her cheeks. She was about to ask Lord Ridgefield to set her down, but his face was inches from hers, his hot breath brushing her neck. The words wouldn't form on her lips.

Instead she stared at the fading purple bruise beneath his right eye, evidence of her infamous robbery attempt gone awry. She grew keenly aware of each one of his breaths, the way his chest moved against her arm and side. The scent of musk from his morning shave encompassed her senses, mingling with the odors of starch, leather, horse, and his own masculine scent. She felt her hip pressing against his rock-solid abdomen, his strong arms beneath her back and knees.

And those searing gray eyes, with their strange glint, hadn't left her. They fascinated, pulled, devoured, and caused a heat to glow deep within her. A fine sheen of sweat broke out all over her. Then his gaze moved. To her neck. To her breasts. Slowly combing her body beneath her cape. She felt an urge to touch his square jaw, to run her hands through his thick blond hair, to wrap her arms around his neck and kiss him. . . .

"Rollins here couldn't have done better." Julia's voice broke into Brooke's thoughts. "Just think, Brooke, if you'd been fat or a little taller"—Julia grinned and turned a vicious look on someone behind Lord Ridgefield—"you both might have fallen. As it is, it looks as if you are the perfect size and weight for Lord Ridgefield. Wouldn't you say so, Caroline?"

Brooke wanted to strangle Julia as she glanced over Lord Ridgefield's shoulder. Caroline sat on her mare, gripping her riding crop in a white-knuckled grasp, her crystal blue eyes cutting into Brooke.

"I should say that if Lord Ridgefield wasn't so accommodating and you'd had to walk to work, none of this would ever have happened.'' Caroline shook her head haughtily, making the long curls on either side of her head bounce.

Brooke stared at Caroline in her pink riding habit that hugged her curves, at the flawless pale face, tainted only by a flush of red on the cheeks. She sat on the horse with an air of beauty and grace, perfection personified.

Brooke abruptly felt like a dowdy fool with her short, thin body and plain black dress. Lord Ridgefield had no interest in her. He had obviously been out on a morning rendezvous with Caroline.

''If you don't mind, you can put me down now,'' Brooke said, trying to keep a miffed tone from her voice.

He didn't appear at all happy about setting her down, but he did.

Brooke turned to Rollins, who was just plopping Julia on her feet. ''Thank you for delivering my sister from harm, sir.''

'' 'Twas nothing, miss.''

''And thank you for saving me.'' Brooke gave Lord Ridgefield a stiff curtsey. ''Now, we should hurry to the house. We have work to do.'' Brooke grabbed Julia's hand and pulled her up the steep curving drive. Off in the distance, the sun just peeked over the top of Glen Carion's long mansard roof, the bricks of its Georgian exterior glistening gray in the thick salty air. Behind it, the sea pounded rocky cliffs. Swallows flew and dipped near the chimneys.

''Why are we walking?'' Julia asked.

''It isn't far up the drive, and we don't want to be beholden to Lord Ridgefield in any way.'' Brooke glanced at the gentleman as he mounted his horse.

Their gazes locked for a moment.

He frowned.

She frowned.

Then he turned and spoke to Caroline.

''I care not if I'm beholden to him,'' Julia said, her tone sulky.

"You wouldn't."

"You're running away, aren't you? You're jealous."

"I'm not."

"Go ahead and keep thinking that." Julia smiled a devious smile and her eyes gleamed as she watched Brooke's shadow moving along the gravel drive.

That afternoon, Brooke strode past the dining room with a feather duster in her hand. She paused to peek inside. French brocade wallpaper covered the walls in bright blue. Sunlight streamed across the marble mantel and over a corner of a long mahogany table, large enough to seat thirty comfortably.

Brooke watched the dust motes dancing in the sunlight and heard sounds from her past echo in her mind: The clink of fine china and crystal. The sumptuous aroma of rich food. Her father's voice and that of Lord Northdale, deep in a heated discussion over politics. The good earl, a boisterous Tory, loved a good argument with her father, a staunch Whig supporter. Her family had spent many a Sunday afternoon in this room. The memory made her grin, until she remembered that particular pleasure was lost to her forever.

Brooke gulped deep in her throat. "Never look back," her father would always say. That bit of wisdom had brought her through most trials in her life—especially his death. If he had been standing here with her, he would have said in his optimistic voice, "Look at it this way, my dear, at least you have a job now."

So why didn't she feel happier? Julia might have been right this morn. Brooke had been jealous when she had seen Lord Ridgefield with Caroline. Her reaction made no sense. She had no claim on him, other than adoring him from the moment she had laid eyes on him. With Caroline around to tempt him, he probably didn't know Brooke existed. She would get over this attraction to him, for it could only end in heartbreak.

With her resolve firmly in place, she headed for the study, rubbing her fingers over the end of the feather duster. Loud, muffled voices rumbled behind the study door; then it flew open and banged against the wall.

Lord Ridgefield's son ran past her, crying, "I won't go riding! I won't! Just leave me alone!"

She watched him run down the hallway and up the staircase, his blond curls bouncing near his ears. When she glanced back into the study, she met the gaze of Lord Ridgefield. He stood near his desk, a dark frown etched into his face, his gray eyes clouded with worry.

Her face colored at having witnessed the argument. "Excuse me." She turned to leave.

"Wait! You needn't be embarrassed, Brooke," he drawled, his voice softening. "Close the door and come in."

At the familiar use of her name, she glanced up at him and stepped inside the office. "I'm sorry about your son."

"No need to be." He leaned back against the large mahogany desk and folded his hands over his chest. "You would have found out sooner or later that Lawford cannot stand me."

"Surely not."

"I'm afraid so. He blames me for his mother's death."

Brooke heard the frustration and anguish in his voice and said, "I'm sorry. Sometimes it takes time to get over death. I know Julia still hasn't come to terms with our father's passing."

"Yes, well, I don't know if Lawford can forgive me. You see, I'm sure the boy could sense the tension between his mother and me."

She sensed the loneliness and bitterness in him and his need to unburden his pain, so she asked, "You did not have a happy marriage?"

"Far from it. May I confide in you?"

"Of course." Her heart leaped that he felt comfortable enough to speak to her in such an intimate way. When she recalled he knew she was a thief and could be assured of her loyalty, her joy quickly diminished.

"I was on my grand tour and only one-and-twenty when I met Victoria. When I glimpsed her on stage, I fell madly in love with her." His eyes glistened with the bittersweet memory. "I begged her to marry me, and she agreed to be my wife. For a while we shared happiness. She was a font of liveliness and gaiety. But that was before I knew her true character. Before . . ."

He paused, his expression darkened with a scowl. For a moment he didn't speak; then he said, "I found her in a compromising position with another man. My life had suddenly turned from buoyant happiness to unadulterated hell. I wanted to walk out then, but she told me she was with child—my child."

"I'm sure you did the honorable thing and stayed with her," Brooke murmured, trying to hide her shock at his confession.

He smiled ruefully. "Yes. I couldn't sever the relationship, especially after I saw the boy, and his resemblance to me. So I stayed and helped raise him, but I never went near her again. She sought out the attentions of her numerous lovers."

"I'm so sorry, Lord Ridgefield." Brooke gripped the duster in her hand.

"I've just poured out my troubles to you; the least you could do is call me Fitz."

Brooke felt her insides melting as his gray eyes bored into her with a strange intensity. His rough fingertips touched her cheeks, then glided across her smooth skin, shooting tingles down her neck.

Brooke trembled all over as she watched him bend toward her. Would he kiss her? He was so close she could smell the clean scent of his musk cologne. . . .

A knock on the door made him draw back.

"Come," he said impatiently.

Helms opened the door and cleared his throat. He took in the blush on Brooke's cheeks and shot her a disgusted look. "Miss Lackland, there you are. I need help in the ballroom."

"But the dusting?"

"That can wait. Please come with me."

After a reluctant glance at Fitz, she followed Helms. Out of the corner of her eye she saw a lopsided grin on Fitz's face. She wondered if he was just toying with her affections because he knew she had a fancy for him, or if he truly cared for her. She smiled inwardly and hoped with all her heart the latter was true.

Above stairs, Julia was supposed to be heading up to the attic and helping Helms carry down valentine decorations for the ball. But this working business was not as much fun as she had thought it would be—especially when Helms looked at her as though she were a dirty little mouse he had caught in a flower tin. So she had slipped into one of the chambers and flopped down on the bed. With her head pillowed on her arms, she snuggled deeper into the feather mattress, wiggled her toes, and grinned up at the ceiling.

A sound drifted down the hallway.

Her head perked up. The high-pitched whimper was soft, barely audible. Either someone was crying, or a cat was having its tail pulled. Ready to do battle for the cat, she rolled off the bed, smoothed the coverlet, and left the room. She followed the mewl to a chamber two doors down.

She put her ear to the door. Knocked.

No answer. The whimpering stopped.

Julia didn't bother knocking again, but opened the door. The chamber was done all in shades of yellow. It looked like one large buttercup, with a fourposter mahogany bed in the center. A boy, appearing to be her same age, sat on a chaise longue by the window. His hands covered his face, a small ship in a bottle on his lap. Not a cat to be seen anywhere.

"Go away," the boy said, his voice muffled behind his hands.

"What are you crying about?"

"None of your business." The boy looked up at her. He was Lord Ridgefield's son all right, the same sandy-colored hair, same proud jaw, same gray eyes—well, maybe not the same. The boy's eyes looked afraid of anything and everything. He wiped a tear from his face and looked embarrassed at being caught crying.

"If you're trying to get someone's notice, you're going about it all wrong." Julia closed the door. "You have to do it like this." She put her hands over her face and let out this loud wail. Several of them. Then she dropped to the floor on her knees and rocked back and forth, bawling loudly.

Hearing him chuckle, she dropped her hands and grinned at him. "That's how you do it. None of this dibble-dabble stuff." Julia got to her feet and walked over to him. Holding out her hand, she said, "My name's Julia. What's yours?"

"Lawford."

"Lawford? What a wretched name—I suppose your father thought of it." Lawford looked lost, and Julia continued. "I'm going to call you Lawf."

"That sounds like a dog's name."

"Arf! Arf!" Julia stuck out her tongue and panted like a dog.

The boy smiled. "You're addled."

"Thank you for the compliment." Julia sat beside him and snatched up the bottle in his lap. She frowned at the ship inside. "So, why are you bawling?"

"I guess it's all right to tell you."

"I'll cut my heart out before I'd tell anyone." Julia held an imaginary knife and stabbed at the spot near her heart. "You can ask Billy Swenson how well I keep secrets—that's my best friend."

The boy looked partially convinced of her worthiness. His voice turned woeful as he said, "My father is a bully. He won't leave me alone. He hates me."

"Are you quite sure?" Julia frowned and felt his sadness.

"Yes, he's always forcing me to do things I don't want to do. It's been worse since my mother died."

"That may not be hate. He may be trying to help you."

Lawford cocked his head, confused.

Julia was so used to speaking to Brooke and elderly people that she had forgotten he was just a boy—not a very quick one at that. At least, Billy Swenson knew what she meant half the time. In a patronizing tone, Julia said, "What I mean is, he might be trying to help you forget your grief." Her tone grew softer. "I remember when my father died, I couldn't go into his office. It smelled of him, you see. I could somehow feel his presence in there, and my mother sensed that. She used to send me in his office for things she had forgotten, but I knew she was trying to get me to go in there. I was glad when we moved from the vicarage. And my mother kept all his clothes and belongings packed away in a trunk. I still can't look inside that trunk . . ." Julia's words trailed off.

A long, pensive silence stretched between them.

"I wanted to stay in France so I could go into my mother's room. I liked being in there; it made me feel like she was with me. I didn't want to ever leave it, but my father took me away. I hate him for it," Lawford said, breaking the quiet.

"You shouldn't. He only did what he thought was best for you. When the pain is less, you'll see he was right and forgive him. Just like someday I'll look in that trunk." Julia didn't like to dwell on painful things, so she forced away the gloom and teased the boy with a strained smile. "But you'll never get over your doldrums if you keep whimpering all the time and hiding in your room. Look at me, you don't see me blubbering all the time."

He stared down at his hands. His lips thinned as tears gathered in his eyes again.

"I'm sorry," Julia said, elbowing him.

"I can't help it. Since my mother died, I'm afraid of things."

"Exactly what are you afraid of?"

"This place. I hate the country—especially here. There are bees and hornets and animals. And what if the sea rises up and swallows us?"

"It hasn't swallowed me, and I've lived here for ten years."

"But it could happen. I want to go back to France, but Father says we must stay. There are ghosts here," Lawford added as he glanced around his chamber, his eyes wide with fright.

"My friend Billy's seen ghosts. He says if you aren't afraid of them, they'll go away."

"These don't."

"Well, then I'll sneak out tonight and stay here with you. We'll get those ghosts to leave. Just let one of them come around while I'm here." Julia narrowed her eyes and swept the room with a challenging look.

Lawford studied this intrepid intruder into his life as if he were positive she could drive away the fiercest of ghosts. Sounding almost afraid of her, he asked, "You would do that for me?"

"Don't think I'll do it for nothing. You have to help me."

"Do what?"

"You'll see. And it will benefit both of us."

Julia grabbed his hand and dragged him out of the room. Lawford frowned, helpless to stop her.

CHAPTER FIVE

Several days later, Brooke carried a box of valentine decorations into the ballroom and set it on a table. Morning sun streamed in through the huge windows and threw shadows over the Italian marble floor tiles, the gleam making Brooke blink. Lord Northdale never called it the ballroom, only "Cupid's Chamber." Hearts, roses, and small carvings of Venus and Cupid made up the gilded ceiling. Along one wall, a musicians' gallery hovered overhead. Above it, a sparkling crystal chandelier twinkled and winked.

She heard giggling in the hall. Master Lawford and Julia ran past the opening. She held his shoe in her hand, and he limped behind her, chasing her.

"Give me my shoe!"

"Come and get it!"

Their voices melted away. Brooke smiled, aware the friendship he had formed with Julia was the best thing for him. He seemed more affable and not so irascible. He could even carry on a conversation with his father now, though Lawford still refused all of Fitz's attempts to spend time with him. Brooke could feel the strain between them.

She frowned and thought of Fitz. Since he had confided in her a few days ago, he had spoken to her only in passing. Yet every now and then when she was in a room cleaning, she would catch him watching her intently. She truly didn't know what he was thinking.

Brooke bent down and pulled a gilded plaster cast of Cupid out of the box. She smiled at it, laid it down on the table, and searched for more of Lord Northdale's treasures. Fourteen frames formed an orderly line in the bottom. Brooke reached down and slid one out of rank. A handsome man and comely lady stared back at her, their eyes glistening with love, one of Squire Northdale's successes at playing matchmaker. She smiled, remembering how he proudly displayed the pictures on the tables at the last Valentine's Ball. Her smile turned to a frown as the painful memories of the last Valentine's Ball she had attended four years ago flooded back to her. . . .

From her usual spot—the corner—Brooke listened to the music and laughter filling Glen Carion's ballroom. Candlelight beamed off the crystal teardrops suspended from the chandelier, casting thousands of dancing lights around the large room. Perched on the musicians' gallery overhead, the orchestra performed the chords of a Scotch reel. Couples twirled past hearts and statues of Cupid that decorated the walls and tables.

She noticed Lord Ridgefield and his wife standing near the punch table. They made a striking couple, he with his blond wavy hair and handsome face, and she with her pitch black curls, flashing green eyes, and full red lips.

Brooke had to still the beating of her heart, for every time she looked at Lord Ridgefield she could not help the rush of emotion she felt. She should have gotten over this girlish infatuation, especially since he had a wife, but she couldn't.

And they didn't look at all happy. They hadn't once smiled at each other. There seemed to be an invisible barrier of tension between them. The dark scowl hadn't left Lord Ridgefield's brow since he had entered the ballroom with his wife.

Brooke noticed Julia pouring punch into the base of a palm that was very close to Lord and Lady Ridgefield. Mortified by her sister's mischief, she looked for her parents to see if they would reprimand Julia, but they were dancing. Why did Lord Northdale insist young children come to his ball? Six-year-olds—especially ones as capricious and unruly as Julia—should not be let out to terrorize Society. Frowning, she quickly made her way over to her wayward sister.

When she neared the palm, she was about to grab Julia's hand and heard Lady Ridgefield's husky voice:

"You have to agree, Fitz, Lady Caroline will make a fine match. Just look at her. She has the eye of every young swain here."

Brooke's gaze shifted across the room to her cousin. Caroline looked over the top of her fan at several young gentlemen who stood next to her. Her eyes batted at them like the perfect coquette; then her gaze darted over to Lord Ridgefield. Brooke knew Caroline, too, had a crush on Lord Ridgefield.

Julia had heard Lady Ridgefield's comment and glanced over her shoulder at Caroline also.

"I suppose she is pretty," Lord Ridgefield drawled in a bored tone.

"Much, much prettier than her cousin. Did you see the mismatched color of her eyes? No gentleman in his right mind would marry the chit. Can you imagine what her offspring would look like? No man would want a house full of children running about with different-colored eyes." Lady Ridgefield laughed in a soft, snide way.

The sound pounded Brooke like stone. The air pressed in on her as a sinking feeling twisted inside her.

"Brooke," Julia whispered and reached out to touch her sister's hand.

Brooke wheeled around and hurried out of the ballroom, tears streaming down her face. . . .

Voices echoed in the hallway now. The resonance amplified by the ballroom's vastness brought Brooke back to the present. She recognized Caroline's voice and Fitz's. Grimacing, she picked up a frame out of the box and set it on the table, trying to appear preoccupied with her work. At the sound of footsteps, she glanced up and saw Caroline and Fitz step through the doorway.

Caroline's pink silk riding habit complemented Lord Ridgefield's black breeches and coat. In spite of not wanting to admit it, she knew they made a handsome couple with their shimmering blond hair and fine Adonis and Aphrodite good looks. Brooke straightened, her fingers tightening in the sides of her black dress and maid's apron.

Caroline had a smithy's grip on Lord Ridgefield's arm as he escorted her into the room. The moment her gaze landed on Brooke, her coquette's smile melted, and a look of charming petulance fixed her expression. "Well, Cousin, how are you getting on as maid here?"

"Very well, thank you." Brooke clutched a frame to her bosom.

"Lord Ridgefield and I have been riding along the beach, what an invigorating experience."

"I hope you enjoyed your ride." Brooke addressed Fitz, who was tapping his riding crop impatiently against his boot, belying the enigmatic expression on his face.

His hair was windblown, the darker roots stark against the sun-bleached top. It waved back from his face in handsome disarray, save for one curl over his brow that arched rakishly on his forehead. Dark stubble covered his chin and added to his devastating good looks.

He opened his mouth to speak, but Caroline spoke for him.

"We did have a jolly time. I showed him some of the caves where the customs men have found smuggled goods in the past."

"How intriguing it must have been." Brooke felt Lord Ridgefield's gray eyes on her and glanced at him.

Thunk. Thunk. Thunk. His riding crop hit his boot in a rhythmic pattern, his handsome face giving away nothing. But his eyes held an impatient glint.

"I actually tripped in one of the caves, and Lord Ridgefield had to grab me."

"How fortunate." Brooke glowered at Fitz.

"I see you are starting to decorate for the Valentine's Ball. What fun it must be for you—oh, but perhaps . . ." Caroline paused and put her gloved hand over her mouth, not fooling anyone with her feigned embarrassment.

Lord Ridgefield eyed Brooke for an answer, but addressed Caroline. "Why would Miss Lackland not enjoy decorating for a ball? I thought all young ladies enjoyed such things."

Unable to stand the brunt of his scrutiny, Brooke frowned down at the floor, her cheeks coloring. Her eyes traced the dark gray marble patterns at her feet as she said, "I know not what my cousin means by it. Of course I enjoy decorating for the ball."

"Oh, I'm sure Brooke is right." Caroline brushed the subject away with a breezy swish of her hand, all the while casting an eager glance in Lord Ridgefield's direction.

"No, Lady Caroline, you never speak unless 'tis to make a point." He cut his gaze toward Caroline. "I insist you tell me why Miss Lackland would not like balls."

"Shall I tell him, Brooke?" Caroline's sweet voice held a touch of ice.

"Tell it, if you must." Brooke frowned at her cousin.

"Well, four years ago, Brooke ran out of Lord Northdale's Valentine's Ball and never frequented another."

"Is that so? Why?" His gray eyes shifted to Brooke as he waited for an answer.

Brooke said nothing, gulping past the growing lump in her throat.

Caroline continued for her. "Poor Brooke, I think she only danced with her father that night. She is so shy, so much the wallflower. Finally, near the end of the evening, she just ran out of the ballroom in tears." Caroline grinned her feline grin. "Did not you tell me someone had commented on your odd-colored eyes and offended you? Was that right, Brooke?"

Caroline's face blurred behind Brooke's tears. Up until this moment, she hadn't realized how vindictive and cruel Caroline could be. In the past Brooke had tried to overlook her cousin's flaws, for she was pretty and all pretty girls had a right to their vanity and contempt. But this was something Brooke couldn't overlook or forgive.

"I believe Helms needs my help in the attic," Brooke said, her voice trembling. Then she ran from the room.

"Brooke!" Caroline called at her back, with not much emotion. "Silly girl, she's always like this."

"Is she?" Fitz narrowed his eyes at Caroline.

"Yes."

"And do you always speak to her as you just did?"

"I was just telling you the story. I thought it might amuse you."

"Oh, I'm very amused." Fitz banged his riding crop against his boot.

"I thought you would be." Caroline smiled nervously.

"Yes, I'm amused someone could be so cruel and think it would entertain me. Now, if you don't mind, I've had all the amusement I can stomach for one day. You may leave now."

"But are we not going to ride again tomorrow?"

"It appears not. And you needn't try to accidentally come upon me as you did this morning."

"It *was* an accident. I had no idea I would run into you. And you seemed to enjoy my company; you continued to ride with me."

"An error of courteousness that I'll not soon repeat. Now you may finish your ride." Fitz jammed his riding crop toward the door.

"Well, I never." Lady Caroline thrust up her chin and flounced from the room.

Fitz ran after Brooke.

Up on the musicians' balcony, Julia and Lawford were peeking over the railing. Julia grabbed his hand and whispered, "Come on, we have to follow them."

"Why?"

"Because, I have to see how things are progressing."

Lawford shook his head in confusion. Julia rolled her eyes, then shot him a worldly-wise look. "You'll see soon enough."

Fitz spotted Brooke running along a path that snaked down the rocky cliffs of Glen Carion to the beach. Her bun had come loose, and long black hair tumbled down her back, the curly waves blowing around her arms in the wind. Her shoulders shook with each sob. Several times she tripped and stumbled.

Fitz took off after her, his boots slipping along the steep gravel on the path. She reached the beach before him and bolted. For such a short woman, she had a surprisingly long stride. Already she was ten yards ahead of him.

"Brooke, wait!"

"Go away!" she cried.

"I want to talk to you." Fitz caught her and pulled her into his arms.

She struggled.

He wouldn't let go.

After a moment, her spirit broke. Her shoulders slumped; then her head fell against his chest. He felt her body shuddering against him as sobs overtook her.

His fingers tangled in the softness of her curls. He stroked the back of her head and whispered encouragements to her. Possessive emotions rushed him, quickened him, filling every empty, bitter place Victoria had left inside him.

He clung to Brooke until her sobs turned to hiccups. Then he pulled out the handkerchief from his pocket and lifted her face to wipe the tears from her eyes. His hand paused as he looked into her face. Wind blew strands of long, raven curls across her tear-stained cheeks. She stared up at him from behind spiked black lashes, her eyes direct portals to the pain still brewing within her, to her vulnerability. Her lips glistened from the tears streaming over them.

"You are so beautiful," he whispered. Then he did what he had longed to do since that night she had tried to rob him; he bent and took possession of her mouth.

He felt her trembling all over. His arms tightened around her waist, and she was forced to lean against his body. Her lips were drawn and tight. He could tell this was her first kiss. This forced him to go slow, teasing her lips with his own. His tongue slid across her bottom lip. The saltiness of her tears lingered in his mouth.

Her lips softened and grew pliant. She wrapped her arms around his neck, and her fingers tangled in his hair. Fitz slid his tongue past her lips and ran it along the ridges of her teeth. She opened for him, and he tasted the depths of her mouth. So sweet. He groaned deep in his throat. His hand dropped to her bottom, and he pressed her tighter against his erection. His other hand cupped her breast—

She pulled back from him, looking incredulous, as if she couldn't believe what he had just done. Waves crashed against the beach, the roar like an invisible barrier between them.

"What is the matter?" Fitz reached for her again.

She jumped back. "I won't be a substitute for Caroline. And I won't be your whore." She marched past him.

"That was not my intention when I kissed you."

"And I suppose it wasn't your intention to touch my breast." She threw up her hands. "Just go back to Caroline and leave me alone." She stiffened her spine and marched past him.

He grabbed her arm and pulled her back around. "You can't possibly think I want her?"

"Of course you do. She's beautiful, flawless, and arrogant." Brooke eyed him up and down as if she felt the same way about him, and added, "Just the type of woman who would suit you."

"Thank you for clarifying what sort of woman is perfect for me, but I'd much rather do my own choosing." She was scowling at him, and her lips were drawn tight. A strand of hair blew across her mouth. He reached out to brush it back.

"Don't touch me." She jerked back from him and shoved the curl behind her ear.

"Listen to me." He grabbed her hand. She tried to pull back, but he tightened his grip. "You're every bit as attractive to me as she is. More so—"

"Don't patronize me. I don't need it from you or anyone. Leave me alone. I just want to go home! Turn my arm loose . . ." She continued to pull away.

"You can't go home yet; you have not worked out the day."

"You don't seriously believe I'll continue to work for you." Her eyes blazed with determination.

"You either work for me, my sweet, or be arrested for robbing a carriage."

"You can't do that."

"Watch me." He gazed hard at her, harder than he meant to. "You will go back up to the house now, madam."

"If I do go back, I won't have you touching me again." She eyed him warily.

"Very well. We shall forget this ever happened."

Up above on the cliff, Julia and Lawford's cherubic faces looked down on the scene from behind a thick stand of gorse. Julia watched the wind whipping Brooke's dress around her legs, and the way Lord Ridgefield's eyes were fixed on her sister's bottom. She frowned at the unyielding look on Brooke's face.

Julia pulled Lawford back so he wouldn't be seen. "See what I mean? I have to do something fast."

"Why?" Lawford looked confused.

"Really, you are very obtuse sometimes, Lawf." Julia rolled her eyes and continued in a voice she felt a simpleton could understand. "Those two. They kissed. Your father likes my sister, but she lacks confidence when it comes to men. We have to find a way to give it to her and get them together."

"I don't know if I want your sister for a mother," Lawford said, sticking out his lips in a pout, fear brewing behind his eyes. Then he glanced down at the gorse as though afraid something might leap out from behind it and scare him.

"She's very nice. You needn't be afraid of her. She would probably let you eat cookies in bed and not make you take a bath every week. And I could sleep in your room every night and keep away the ghosts. Now, don't you want me as your sister? We could all be a big happy family together."

Lawford blinked at her, sizing her up. One evil versus another. Finally, he said, "I guess it could be worse."

"That's right. Your father could have married Caroline. She's a witch. You heard what she said to Brooke."

"We shouldn't have been listening in the gallery."

"We had every right. At least we found out what your father thinks of Caroline." Julia whistled. "Be glad he doesn't like her. Believe me, you don't want her for a mother, or my Aunt Josephine for a stepgrandmama. Your life would be one ugly whirl of misery. My Aunt Josephine could nag the fleas off a dog. The first thing she would do is convince your father to send you away to school. She tried that on my mother—luckily we are too poor to send me. Come on, I hear Brooke coming. This calls for drastic measures. I'm afraid I'm going to have to use Brooke's fear against her.'' Julia strode purposely toward the house.

"What fear?" He looked lost and said, "I don't think—"

"That's right. Leave the thinking to me." Julia shook her head at him, grabbed his hand, then ran, dragging Lawford down the cobblestone path that led to Glen Carion.

Thick, gray clouds covered the sun. A foggy mist had moved up the cliffs, and the sides of Glen Carion had rounded and grayed, the long porch in the back barely visible. The moist scent of a storm lingered in the air.

Fitz strode on the path behind her, listening to Brooke's footsteps melding with his own. He watched the feminine sway of her hips beneath the black wool dress, the ties of her apron flapping seductively against her bottom. How he envied those ties.

His gaze moved higher to the thick, black curls bouncing down her straight spine. He remembered the softness of her hair against his fingertips, the taste of her mouth, the feel of her breast against his palm. Even now, his body burned from wanting her.

"Help! Help!"

Fitz glanced past the wall of boxwood that lined either side of the path and saw Lawford running toward him. His brows raised in surprise at seeing his son outside. Lawford's face looked paler than Fitz had ever seen it, his eyes filled with uncertainty and dread. Fitz and Brooke paused before him.

He grabbed his son's arms. "What is it?"

In between pants, Lawford said, "Miss Lackland is hurt. She fell."

"Where?" Brooke blurted, her eyes wide with panic.

"Come, I'll show you. Hurry!" Lawford waved at them to follow him.

They ran toward the house. Julia's moans grew louder.

"Oh, no! Julia!" Brooke ran faster.

Lawford paused at the steps that led to the wine cellar and looked afraid to go down them. The door stood ajar. He pointed and said, "She's down there."

"What the devil is she doing down there?" Fitz asked, following Brooke, who was already taking the steps two at a time.

"I don't know. I saw her go in and heard her scream."

"You saw her from your room?"

"No, I was outside taking a walk."

Fitz shot his son an incredulous look over his shoulder and followed Brooke through the door. Dank, moist odor hit him. The cellar ran the length of the old mansion and was half its width. Light from the open door cut a wide swatch over the cobwebs floating down from the ceiling.

"Julia, where are you?" Brooke called out, her voice shaky and frantic. She ran along the end aisle, past the many racks holding the wine.

Following Brooke, Fitz called out, "Julia! Dear God, say something."

Boom. Three inches of solid oak slammed closed behind them.

Fitz heard the bolt grind into place on the opposite side of the door. Darkness engulfed them.

"What the hell!" He turned, ran back to the door, and tried the latch. "Lawford, are you out there? Unlock this door!"

"I'm afraid Lawford isn't here."

Fitz recognized Julia's voice and said, "You'll open this door, young lady. Now!"

"Sorry, I can't do that, but we'll come back later and give you food."

"To the devil with food." Fitz tried to shake the door, but it wouldn't budge.

A shadow moved through the small shaft of light beneath the door. A giggle, then muffled footsteps died away. In the ensuing silence, he heard Brooke's rapid, uneven breath. He realized that she hadn't uttered a sound since they had become trapped.

"Are you all right?" he asked, striding toward her, feeling his way past the wine stands.

"I-I can't move," she said, her voice shaky with terror.

In three long steps he reached her side. He groped in the dark and touched her arm. "What is it?"

"I . . . have this fear of enclosed spaces," she murmured, her voice rigid.

"It'll be all right." Fitz wrapped his arms around her. "Hold me tightly." She gripped his neck. He found it impossible to swallow. "Not too tightly. That's it, now close your eyes and think about being in a garden." He rubbed the stiff muscles of her neck and felt the tautness of her body next to his, the heat of it seeping through his clothes.

"What kind of garden?"

"One with primroses, catkins, tall foxgloves, and roses."

"What color roses?"

"Red, pink, and white."

"I can smell them."

"Good." He felt her beginning to relax against him. The anger directed at Julia melted away. In fact, this couldn't have worked out better had he planned it himself.

"Are you with me in the garden?"

"Yes, escorting you. Our hands are locked."

Her hands, clasped behind his neck, loosened, and she laid her head against his chest. "What are we doing now?" she asked.

"We're walking. We stop. I pluck a rose and set it right

here behind your ear.'' He touched a spot behind her ear, feeling one of her curls twine intimately around his finger.

"What else are we doing?"

She raised her face toward his, her breath hot on his lips. He touched her face, running his fingers along the silken dip in her chin. "We are doing this . . ." He tipped her chin a little higher, bent, and kissed her.

CHAPTER SIX

Brooke felt his lips moving across hers, teasing, tantalizing her mouth with their urging pliancy. The image of them in the garden together had converged with reality, filling her as no mental image could. Her fear quickly melted beneath the sensations he awakened in her. She clung to him, kissing him back. It was dark here, a place not wholly real, a magical realm where he was making the fear go away. And if she imagined hard enough, she could be flawless in spite of her strange-colored eyes.

The cover of darkness made her bold. Her hands tangled in the crisp hair on his neck. He slipped his tongue between her lips and moved along the edge of her teeth. Brooke opened for him, and his tongue slid inside. The roughness of it glided against the roof of her mouth, below the tender spot of her own tongue, along the inside ridges of her teeth, exploring every inch.

She daringly glided her tongue between his lips, wanting to taste him, to somehow absorb him from the inside out.

"Brooke, don't push me away this time," he groaned against her mouth. His hand dropped to her bottom, and he pulled her hips closer.

"I can't," she assured him, feeling him splay his hand over her bottom and knead it.

He slid his thigh between her legs, tangling in the folds of her dress. Then his hips pressed tightly against her, moving with deft slowness. The urgent pressure of his erection roused the highly sensitive area between her legs, while he continued to make her dizzy with his kisses.

He nipped her bottom lip. Then his tongue traced the outline of her mouth and dipped lower to her chin. He trailed kisses along the edge and down her neck. She moved her head to the side, giving him free access to her throat.

With trembling hands, she explored his face, the hollows of his cheeks, the stubble on his chin. Her fingers slipped below his cravat, to feel the thick, corded muscle. She moved her hands over his chest, encountering the hard contours beneath his waistcoat and shirt. Brooke felt him trembling and knew he was holding back a fierce desire. She marveled at this power she had over him. With it came a budding confidence, a boldness that terrified her, yet one she never wanted to lose.

His hand moved up her back, along her side, the gentle, urging pressure of his fingertips sending tiny shudders through her. He slid his hand around and cupped her breast, stroking, kneading.

She arched her back and closed her eyes, drowning in the feel of his hands on her. He rubbed her nipple between his thumb and finger, making it harden instantly.

Unable to wait any longer, Fitz unbuttoned the back of her dress with an ease that surprised and fascinated her. His fingertips brushed the sides of her bare arms as he eased her gown and shift down over her shoulders. Tingles burned a line down her arms, her breasts, deep into the pit of her belly. He ran his lips along the hollow of her collarbone, slowly following the path of the material.

He paused, his lips pressed against the swell of one breast. "I can feel your heart pounding against my lips, my love."

"I'm sure you can," she said in a shuddering whisper, feeling his hot breath caress her.

Brooke felt him free her breasts. Then he took one of her nipples in his mouth. Fire erupted in her. Her knees weakened, and she felt the solid oak of a wine rack make contact with her spine. He had somehow moved her back without her knowing it. Her fingers tangled in the back of his hair as she held his face close to her breasts, each receiving equal treatment.

Brooke thought she would die any moment.

Then he was lifting her dress, pulling aside her undergarments to run his hand up her bare thigh, cupping her. He stroked her. Kissed her. Drove her to the edge of a precipice she had never before dreamed existed. She closed her eyes, letting him take her over the edge. He took her cry in his mouth.

"So sweet," he said against her lips. Then he pulled at the buttons on his breeches, lifted one of her legs, and slid slowly into her.

Brooke felt her flesh open to accommodate his hardness, an awfully huge hardness. She was glad it was dark and she couldn't see the size of him. A slight sting made her stiffen and hug him tighter.

Fitz paused and said, " 'Tis only your maidenhead. I promise it won't hurt long." He pressed deeper, sheathing himself fully inside her, easing her back and hips against the end of the wine rack.

She felt the cool wood stiff against her hot spine and his hardness pressing against her womb. The pain eased, giving way to the sensation of him filling her.

"Wrap your legs around me, my love."

She did his bidding. He lifted her hips and began to move inside her. From the stories Brooke had heard from eavesdropping on the women in the village, she had always believed copulation would be sordid and painful, but this was better than that first taste of chocolate, better than running barefoot on the beach on a spring day. This was like having wings and flying.

He moved faster and faster. Brooke held tight to his neck, searing heat burning inside her. The fireworks within her were coming again. She heard him groan. He kissed her, plunging his tongue in her mouth, matching the rhythm of his hips. They soared higher. Higher. As they burst together, their cries melding, she felt his hot seed enter her.

They clung to each other. He rested his head on her shoulder. His panting breaths burned the side of her neck.

"Thank you," she said, laying her hand along his face. "Feeling your arms around me, I've forgotten all about my fear."

"I'm glad I could be of service," he said, a rough, velvety quality in his voice as he pulled out of her and set her down on the floor. Slowly, kissing her bare shoulder, he pulled up the bodice of her dress and shook out her skirt.

"It is such a silly fear."

"Have you always been afraid of closed spaces?"

"No. When I was five, I fell in an abandoned well, and stayed there for two days before anyone found me. I've been afraid of closed-in spaces since. I've never tried to think of being somewhere else. That was very helpful, but I'm sure it wouldn't have worked if you hadn't been here with me." Brooke wanted him to never let her go.

"I'd have a bruised ego had you not thought so," he said with a smile in his voice. "But you needn't ever be afraid of the dark again. I'll always be here to hold you, Brooke." He bent and kissed her again until she was breathless. "You are mine now." He nipped at her bottom lip.

"What do you mean?"

"I mean we will marry when we are let out of here."

"You don't mean that."

"Of course I do. We must marry, I've taken your maidenhead."

"But—"

"No protests, my love. We'll announce our engagement at the Valentine's Ball—that is, if your sister sees her way clear to letting us out of here by then."

Brooke didn't know how she felt about marrying him—especially since honor and duty drove him. He was more than she could have hoped for in a husband, strong, agreeable, handsome—the man she had loved from afar for years. But could he ever love her? In a tight voice she said, "I'm going to strangle Julia for this."

"Do not be so hard on her."

"Hard on her? She'll be lucky to be alive when I'm done with her."

"I would not be so quick to admonish her. She is reckless and a little truant at times, but she brought us together. And is helping my son."

Brooke gazed up at him in the darkness and could see only the vague outline of his face. "I'm sure she has helped him, but you may not like the results if he continues in her society," she said, gazing up at the shadow of his eyes.

"If she helps Lawford deal with his grief and his fears, then I'm grateful to her and she has my blessing."

"I wouldn't give it so quickly. The very idea of Julia influencing anyone for the better is on the scale of miraculous, right up there with the parting of the Red Sea and Jonah living in the belly of a whale. You might regret Julia's influence on your son one day."

"Perhaps, but I'll always be grateful to her." He grinned and brushed his lips across hers. "Since we are to be down here for an indefinite period of time—thanks to Julia and Lawford's handiwork—I think we should make the best of it. Come," he said, buttoning his breeches. "Let us go and find a lantern and something to make a bed of, for I want to see every inch of your body.''

Brooke shuddered at the thought of the light. Darkness hid her imperfections. She could be gorgeous, desirable, anything she imagined, even as beautiful as Caroline. But light hid nothing and revealed only stark reality. ''Must we find a lantern?'' she asked, her voice laced with insecurity.

''Don't deny me the pleasure of seeing your body, Brooke. You have no need to hide it from me.'' He kissed her softly on the lips, then slipped his hand into hers and eased her deeper into the wine cellar.

She felt the strength of his fingers encompassing her hand, the heat of his palm, a balm against the cold, damp air swirling around them. If only she knew that he loved her, she might not fear the light. The moment he had saved Julia from Captain Ball and his crew, she had known she could truly love him, beyond her adolescent crush. But could he return her love? Her brows knitted together in the dark. She listened to his footsteps plod across the cold stone floor and realized her greatest fear wasn't the light, but the dread of losing her heart to him and having it crushed.

Above stairs, Julia and Lawford ran down the hall. Julia's laughter echoed against the wainscoting. Her companion merely looked pale and frowned. As they passed the ballroom door, Helms's voice rang out.

''Halt, this instant!''

Julia froze before the open double doors. She leaned against the stanchion. A circle of boxes filled with valentine decorations enclosed Helms's long legs. A pink heart protruded from one box, stark against his black breeches. Red table linens filled his arms. When she saw the scowl on Helms's face, her smile quickly straightened. ''Yes, sir?'' she asked, using her most diffident voice.

"Where have you been?"

"Master Lawford asked that I go for a walk with him. Isn't that right?" Julia elbowed Lawford's arm.

"Quite." Lawford moved his arm and shot Julia an indignant glance.

"You wanted to walk outside?" Helms shot Lawford an incredulous look.

"I–I . . ." At Lawford's hesitation, Julia eased her foot over and kicked his ankle. Abruptly, he blurted, "Yes, I did."

"And you have been outside?"

"Yes," Lawford said proudly.

"Good, Master Lawford. We shall have to tell your father." Helms looked pleased, until his gaze landed back on Julia. "Well, miss, why are you standing there? I need help emptying these boxes. And where has your sister got to?"

Lawford and Julia shared a glance. Lawford spoke first. "I saw Miss Lackland walking along the beach with my father."

Helms's gray brows made a disapproving line over his eyes. "I suppose there is nothing we can do about that now. But we can get busy on this room. We have only a week to ready it."

Julia strode into the massive ballroom and looked around at the bleak emptiness. "It'll take some doing," she said with a sigh.

Lawford followed, saying, "I'll help."

"Of course you shall. You didn't think you'd get out of it, did you?" Julia frowned at him.

Helms eyed Julia with a marked amount of respect and watched Lawford pause near her side. A smile broadened his cheeks.

Julia pulled out a large red streamer and handed it to Lawford. "Here. We might as well get started."

"Yes." Lawford grinned, but nervously.

Julia dug deeper into the box for another treasure and felt a prick from her conscience. Brooke would either be climbing the cellar walls by now, or in Lord Ridgefield's arms, bawling. Hopefully the latter. She hadn't meant to cause Brooke so much discomfort, but the situation called for drastic measures. Now all she had to do was connive a way to keep them in there for a while. She grinned deviously.

A long time later, Fitz hardly felt the dank, chilly air in the cellar with Brooke nestled in his arms. Her head rested on his chest, her leg slung over his thighs, her arm on his chest. She warmed him all over. They were wrapped in a tarpaulin he had found thrown in a corner of the cellar.

He could feel her warm breath against his neck, the heat of her body next to his own. Holding her, he realized he had never felt so possessive, even when he thought himself in love with Victoria.

He heard the door latch open. Fitz and Brooke had made their bed near the end of the third wine rack from the door, in plain view. They were fully dressed, so Fitz didn't have to worry about them being seen.

Hinges creaked. The door opened.

Julia appeared, carrying a huge basket. Lawford was behind her, his arms loaded with pillows and a quilt.

Fitz closed his eyes.

"Look, they're asleep and in each other's arms," Julia whispered, sounding pleased. "Come on, we'll leave this stuff."

"Are you going to lock them back in?" Lawford asked, trepidation in his voice.

"Nope. No need now."

"We should tell Helms. He said he was going to send out the servants to find Father."

"Let him, no one will look down here."

The door shut. Fitz grinned in the sudden darkness and eased out from beneath Brooke. Cold air seeped through his shirt. He missed the warmth of her body. The soles of his boots rang hollow on the brick floor as he strode over to the children's delivery. He picked up the quilt and pillows and searched the basket: A chunk of white cheese. Several boiled eggs on a plate of canapes. A bowl of rice pudding, with one spoon. Two glasses and a corkscrew. His fingers connected with a candle, holder, and tinderbox. He smiled. In spite of a long search of the cellar, he hadn't been able to locate a taper or lantern.

"Fitz," Brooke said in a sleepy voice.

"I'm here, my love, looking over our dinner."

"Is the door open?"

"No," Fitz lied, not ready to let the world intrude upon this intimacy with Brooke just yet. "I found it just a moment ago. The door is locked. Your sister must have left it while we were sleeping." He pulled out the candle and lit it. He glanced over and saw Brooke blinking away a seductive, heavy-eyed look.

"Oh, a candle." She gazed at the flame as if resenting it and swallowed hard.

"Wasn't that nice of the children to give us one? Now I can see you."

"I really wish we could stay in the dark. It was very romantic."

"True, but I want to see you."

"I'm starved," she said, quickly changing the subject.

"I have just the thing." Fitz smiled at her and picked up the basket and candle, aware of her unease. She had somehow reverted back to the shy, insecure young woman he had followed into this cellar. He wasn't about to let her leave here until she was aware of her own beauty and believed in it.

In three strides, he set down the candle on the floor near the tarpaulin and handed her the quilt and pillows. She laid them out, while he set out the fare and chose a bottle of wine.

At the end of their meal, Fitz fed her the last bite of rice pudding and watched her tongue flick out and lick a speck of it from the corner of her mouth.

He eyed her glistening lip, the long, raven curls that mantled her from head to waist. Her hair, blacker than her faded dress, shimmered blue in the candlelight.

"Why are you staring at me like that?" She raised her eyes and glanced at him from behind long, mink lashes. Looking uncomfortable because of his scrutiny, she grinned coyly. Two dimples beamed back at him.

"I can't get over your dimples. Where have you been hiding them? You look quite delectable when you smile."

"You have drunk too much wine." She reached over for the empty plate to put it into the basket.

Fitz captured her hand. "The only thing I'm drunk on is you. You are so lovely . . ." He ran the back of his hand along her soft, curved cheek.

"But I'm not. My eyes—"

"Are perfect. I like the two colors. The combination gives you a mystique that other women can never have."

She frowned and said, "You are only being kind."

"No, just very honest." He tangled his hands in the back of her hair, pulled her face toward his, then kissed her eyes. Her nose. Her lips.

She wrapped her arms around his neck and kissed him back.

Fitz worked open the first few buttons at the back of her dress.

Brooke broke the kiss. "Wait a minute." She leaned over toward the candle. . . .

"No you don't." He pulled her back into his arms.

"But we can't make love in the light." She leaned past his shoulder and blew hard.

The candle flickered.

He grabbed her chin, forced her face around to his, and kissed her.

She pulled back and hit his chest. "I don't want the light."

"You have nothing to be ashamed of, my love. I want to see your lovely body while I make love to you. Would you deny me this one pleasure?"

She gazed at him for a few moments, her eyes searching his

face, looking self-conscious and unsure. "I can't deny you anything," she whispered.

The softly spoken words touched something deep inside Fitz, for he knew what price she paid for them. "You honor me with your trust, my love," he said, tipping her face up and capturing her lips. He kissed her and continued to undress her.

The moment he pulled off her petticoat and she was naked, her arms clamped down next to her sides, and she tensed. She watched him closely for his reaction.

"God, but you are exquisite." He watched the dim candle-light flicker over her high, full breasts, with their dark peach tips, her flat waist, flaring hips, and the flawless triangle of black curls between her thighs.

"Do you really think so?" she asked, her voice wavering.

"I would not lie to you." He smiled encouragingly down at her and ran his hands over the soft, white skin of her breasts, feeling her nipples harden at his touch. He bent and placed a kiss on her flat belly, feeling her shudder. Lower still, he moved to kiss her woman's mound.

Brooke grabbed his shoulders and stiffened. "Oh, no, you mustn't."

"Do not be ashamed of your body, my love. I want to kiss all of it."

When he bent down again, she said, "But this is unfair. You cannot look at me like this while you are still dressed."

Fitz raised his head. "A very good point."

He made quick work of his own clothes, then eased over her. He was about to settle on top of her, but she put her hand on his chest and stopped him. "It is my turn to look at you," she said, none of the earlier shyness in her voice.

Her fingertips fluttered over his chest, along the corded muscle of his stomach, then lower. Her touch made his insides quake. When she touched his swollen manhood, running her finger over the tip, Fitz sucked in his breath and grabbed her hand. "Are you trying to kill me?" He smiled down at her.

"Just admiring you as you did me. It is only fair," she said in a newly found, impish tone.

"Enough admiring." He flipped half of the quilt over them and nestled down between her legs. As he nuzzled her neck, he grew aware of each one of her breaths, her nipples moving against his chest, the wild thumping of her heart next to his ribs.

He slid his body against hers, feeling a fine sheen of perspiration slick on their skin. Her woman's mound stroked his loins. The sensation made him groan and press his hardening erection between her thighs.

She whimpered and opened her legs, locking her ankles around the back of his thighs.

He pressed his lips along the side of her throat, feeling the pulse there throb against his mouth. "You have a lovely body and it belongs to me now."

"Not quite. We are not married yet." She grinned up at him and ran her hands over the muscles in his back.

"We shall be, my love. Never doubt it."

He eased his hand between them. The moment he stroked her, he felt a shudder go through her. A self-satisfied smile spread across his lips. He kissed her while he continued his intimate caress.

She arched her hips and moaned.

Unable to hold back any longer, he sheathed himself in her hot, moist center. He moved slowly at first, committing to memory the feel of her, the enticing, musky scent of her, the way her soft thighs felt against his own hard ones.

"Faster," she moaned.

"Like this?" He grinned at her boldness and did her bidding. His inhibited little virgin was quickly dying away.

She matched the rhythm of his hips. He felt her nails dig into his back. He gave and took of her sweet ardor. They both found their release together. Spent, he collapsed down on top of her.

At that moment the cellar door burst open.

CHAPTER SEVEN

Fitz turned, careful to shield Brooke's naked body with his chest and the quilt. Rollins stood in the doorway, a lantern raised in his hand, his eyes wider than his belt buckle.

Brooke gasped.

Rollins blurted, "Oh, me lord, Helms was worried. I've been searching the grounds."

"Yes, well, you've found me."

Rollins bowed, a wide, shrewd grin stretching over his ruddy face as he straightened. "I'll set Helms's mind at ease, me lord." He closed the door behind him. His heavy footsteps plodded away.

"I thought you said we were locked in here. I didn't hear the lock." Brooke tried to push him off her.

"Your sister unlocked it while you slept."

"What!"

"I didn't tell you because I wanted a little more time alone with you." He bent and nibbled her ear.

"What will everyone think of me?" She pushed his face

away. "All the servants will know. Gossip flies about Looe like wind."

"No need to worry, my sweet. We're to be married. What sort of gossip can harm us?"

"What did you say?" Lady Caroline's screech reverberated off the papered walls of her chamber. She snatched the brush away from her maid, Helen, and turned to glare at her.

Helen cringed. Her lady had a temper, and Helen didn't like to get on the wrong side of it. Lady Caroline's coiffure was not finished. Helen stared at the blond curls falling down over her nose and said, "I said, me lady, I heard that Lord Ridgefield and Miss Brooke were found in a wine cellar—"

"Yes, yes, I heard that part. What else did you say?"

" 'Tis only a rumor, mind, and ye can't believe a word of it, but they was found in a compromising position."

"What sort of position?" Lady Caroline snarled the question at Helen.

"One so's he'll have to be marrying her."

"Where did you hear this?" Lady Caroline's cheeks puffed out and turned the color of oxblood.

"From old Lady Bennings, she heard it from Jake Talbot, who heard it from Martha Rollins."

"Who the devil is she?" She slammed the brush down on the dressing table.

"The wife of Lord Ridgefield's driver."

"If you are lying to me . . ." Lady Caroline raised her hand to smack Helen.

She cringed and leaped back. "I swear it'd be the truth."

"We shall see about this." Lady Caroline jumped up from her seat and whirled around, the curls hanging over her forehead bouncing near her nose and mouth. She stormed out of the room, screaming, "Mother!"

* * *

Two days later, Brooke, Fitz, and Enid Lackland sat in the
parlor. A fire burned in the cottage's small fireplace, hissing
and cracking, at odds with Emily's off-key rendering of an
Irish love song as she fixed tea in the kitchen.

Enid sewed another stitch on the dress she was making for
Julia to wear to the Valentine's Ball, and said, "You must
forgive our housekeeper, my lord. Emily does get a little over-
zealous when she's happy."

"I can hear that, madam." Fitz shared a smile with Brooke.

"It is so very kind of you to give Brooke and Julia a position
at Glen Carion. I must admit I had reservations. I didn't like
the idea of my girls working; I had so hoped things would turn
out differently. But that was not to be." Enid's delicate brows
drew together; then she frowned pensively down at the stitch
she had just made.

"It was my pleasure, Mrs. Lackland." Fitz smiled politely,
but with a hint of impatience in his eyes.

Enid appeared to notice him and smiled. "I hope you will
not regret giving my younger daughter a position. She was
beside herself with excitement. Julia can be a handful, and she
has never worked before. She has not caused you any trouble,
has she?" The thimble on Enid's finger clicked softly as she
continued to sew.

"Not in the least. As a matter of fact, she has been quite
the opposite." Fitz glanced over at Brooke.

Their gazes locked. Fitz made sure her mother's attention
was on her sewing; then his hungry gaze roamed over Brooke,
lingering on her breasts. A familiar warmth spread through her.

"Has she?" Enid raised her eyes at him.

Fitz turned to gaze at Mrs. Lackland. "Indeed, madam, she
is partly to blame for the reason I've come."

"To blame?" Confusion slipped into Enid's delicate features.

"In a roundabout way she brought Brooke and me together. I've come to ask for your daughter's hand."

Enid's jaw dropped open. She looked too stunned to speak.

"It's true, Mama. We want to marry." Brooke glanced over at Fitz, who sat on a chair opposite her.

Enid's surprised face lit up with happiness, though there was still reservation in her expression. She found her voice. "My dear, this is so sudden."

"We just realized our love for each other," Fitz said.

"What of Lady Caroline? I thought that you and she were—"

"Only acquaintances, madam. They were the first people to call on me when I arrived at Glen Carion. They introduced me to the Society here, that is all. I've never given Lady Caroline any reason to believe we were anything other than friends."

"I see." Enid digested what had been said, taking in the glow on Brooke's face, the quiet determination in Fitz's gray eyes. The uncertainty left her expression, replaced by a genuine smile that beamed across her face. "I'm so happy for both of you. Of course I have no objections to this match. I hope you will be very happy."

"We'd like to marry within the week."

"A week? That's not enough time to post the banns." Enid worried her brows at Fitz.

"I don't want a large wedding, Mama. I only want you and Julia there."

"Well, if you feel that way." Enid gazed indulgently at Brooke.

"I'll go and get a special license. If you'll excuse me." Fitz rose and kissed Enid's hand.

"I'll walk you out." Brooke followed him to the door. She handed him his cape and set his hat on his head. She let her hands linger on the sides of his cheeks, feeling the rough stubble against her palms. "There, you look very handsome and distinguished."

"Don't tease me with compliments, my love." A wicked,

devouring light shimmered in his eyes. He grabbed her and kissed her.

Brooke felt his tongue ease into her mouth, and her insides melted. She wrapped her arms around his neck. He groaned softly and pulled back. "I had better go, before I drag you off and make love to you again. But I'll be back this evening." He winked at her and left.

Brooke watched him climb into his phaeton. He gathered up the reins and waved, his gaze locked on her as if he didn't want to leave her. Then he snapped the reins and drove off. She watched him until the carriage disappeared down the road.

Although she tried to shake the feeling, Brooke had the sense that something was bound to happen. She was too happy. Her smile faded, and she turned and strode back into the cottage, trying to ignore the growing feeling of foreboding inside her.

Brooke strode into the parlor and sat beside her mother on the sofa. She threaded a needle and began stitching Brussels lace along the edge of one of the cuffs.

Enid's delicate white hands paused, the needle poised between thimble and thumb. She glanced up at Brooke over the top of her spectacles. "Well, my dear, who would have guessed that you'd be announcing your engagement at the Valentine's Ball? I'm so very proud of you. What a handsome man he is, so gallant and amiable. Titled too, with a fortune. You will be very happy with him. I saw the way he looked at you. Just the way your father once looked at me." She lifted her hand and laid it on Brooke's cheek. A touch of sadness slipped into her eyes.

Brooke touched Enid's hand, feeling the frailness of it against her palm. "Thank you, Mama, I'm sure we shall." She didn't tell her mother what Julia had done, or that Fitz was marrying her because he had compromised her, or that the look had probably been lust. No, she could not rob the animated glow from her mother's eyes, for it had been too long since the poor lady had known any happiness.

The sound of a carriage made Enid put down her needle. "Visitors. I wonder who it is?"

"I shall see." Brooke jabbed her needle into the cuff, but pricked her finger instead. "Ouch!" She sucked the droplet of blood off her finger, rose, then strode over to the window.

Brooke gazed at the black lacquered side of the brougham, the yellow livery of the footmen and outrider, the yellow plumes on the trapping of the sleek black horses. The moment the footman let down the steps, Lady Josephine shoved him aside, her face pinched in anger. Caroline followed, looking more sour.

"Oh, dear, it's Aunt Josephine and Caroline," Brooke said past the growing lump in her throat.

"Ah," Enid said, sounding delighted. "Do you suppose they have come to congratulate us on the good news? My, how fast gossip does travel."

Bang. Bang. Bang.

The pounding rattled the door and reverberated through the small cottage like gunfire. Emily hurried past the doorway of the parlor.

"Afternoon, ma'am," Emily said, her voice drifting into the parlor.

"I'm here to pay a call on my sister-in-law."

"She be in the parlor, ma'am."

Lady Josephine filled the doorway. She wore a gray frock and matching woolen cloak. Caroline stood at her side, decked in a blue silk brocade dress, a short velvet, ermine-trimmed cape around her shoulders. A wide bow jutted out of the side of her fashionable new bonnet.

"My dear Enid, how are you?" Lady Josephine strode into the room.

"Very well. How nice of you to call." Her mother laid aside her sewing.

"It has been an age since we last visited." Lady Josephine's lips stretched with one of her nasty smiles. "And Caroline expressed a desire to see Brooke." Her gaze swung around and struck Brooke, narrowing.

Brooke flinched inwardly and swallowed hard. Lady Josephine knew; it was written on her face.

"Would you do me the honor of walking with me, Brooke?" Caroline asked, her words stiff.

Brooke wanted to refuse, but said, "Very well." She grabbed her cloak from a rack by the door and followed Caroline outside. Fluffy, gray clouds swirled overhead, blocking out the afternoon sun. A shadow hung over the landscape. Brooke felt the loss of the sun on her face, and a dismal feeling chilled all the warmth inside her.

In spite of her rigid posture, Caroline took long strides, and Brooke had to almost jog to keep up with her.

The moment they cleared the carriage and horses, Caroline asked, "I heard some alarming news today."

"Did you? What?" Brooke asked, bracing herself for what would come next.

"It makes me blush to speak of it . . ." Caroline's words trailed off.

Brooke could not see any evidence of her cousin's cheeks reddening. "Very well, let's forget it."

Caroline's lips pouted slightly. She eyed Brooke with a hint of awe in her eyes, then blurted, "It is of such an alarming nature, I cannot forget it. No one within a hundred-mile radius can forget it."

"Really?"

"Yes, really. And it involves you. I knew you would never do such a thing, and I told Mother those very words. So we came right away to hear you refute it and clear your name. That's why I asked you to walk with me. I couldn't broach the subject in front of your dear mother. I know how delicate she is. It would destroy her if she knew you'd robbed a carriage, and now to hear such a scandalous rumor—''

''What have I done that is so terrible?''

''Well, the rumor I heard said you allowed Lord Ridgefield to compromise you.''

Brooke smiled sweetly. ''Surely you don't believe rumors.''

''Say it isn't so, dear cousin, and set my mind at ease.''

''It isn't so.''

''I don't believe you.'' Caroline's patronizing facade dissolved behind a glower.

''Is there no pleasing you?'' Brooke said, losing her patience. ''It really is none of your concern, or anyone else's for that matter.''

''Then, it is the truth.'' Caroline stomped her foot.

Brooke stared hard at her. ''Think what you like, Caroline.''

''When I think how kind Mother and I have been to you and your family, and this is how you repay us.'' Caroline's nostrils flared, and she shook with rage.

''I've done nothing to you or your mother.''

''You have! He was courting me and was going to propose.''

''I don't think escorting you to one card party could be considered courting you. And if he entertained a notion of making you his wife, he would have proposed to you.''

''If you hadn't interfered, he was going to.'' Caroline stomped her foot yet again and shook her finger near Brooke's nose. ''And let me give you some advice. Stay away from him. You'll only get hurt. You really don't believe a small little insignificant mouse like you, with your odd eyes, could snag him, do you?''

''For your information, he wants to marry me.''

''Don't think for one moment I'll let you have him.'' She pounded a finger on Brooke's chest. ''I had him first, before you threw yourself at him and he took pity on you. If he is contemplating marrying you—Mama and I are prepared to go to the authorities and expose you for the thief you are. And he could possibly be arrested by the Crown for not doing his duty and arresting you. Highway robbery is a hanging offense. You wouldn't want that now, would you?''

Brooke couldn't get a word past the growing knot in her throat; she could only stare at Caroline.

At Brooke's silence, Caroline continued, ''Mama has found a governess position for you in Scotland. I suggest you take it. Here is the address. Be there at the end of the month . . .'' Caroline picked up Brooke's hand and slammed a piece of paper in it.

Tears stung Brooke's eyes, blurring Caroline's beautiful face, making it appear ugly and misshapen. Doomed from the start. All of it. Her happiness, her love for Fitz, the fact he was so handsome, she so flawed. It would never have worked. It didn't matter anyway, not with Caroline's threat hanging over her. Brooke couldn't let Fitz go to prison because of the kindness he had shown her that night. She wheeled around and strode back to the cottage.

''You'll never have him!''

Caroline's shriek rang in Brooke's ears as she slammed the door. She ran up the steps, trying to hold back her sobs so her mother wouldn't hear. But she couldn't.

In the parlor, Enid glanced toward the door, worry marring her pale brow. ''Oh, dear! Was that Brooke? I should go to her.'' She stood up.

A pleased expression passed over Lady Josephine's face, then quickly disappeared. She grabbed Enid's arm and said, ''I'm sure nothing is wrong. I believe I would give her a moment. You know how silly young girls can be. They've probably had a little spat. Come sit down and speak to me.''

Enid glanced once more toward the doorway, concern evident in her expression. Slowly, she eased back down on the sofa.

* * *

At that moment, two miles away, Fitz glared at Captain Ball. Ball's brown hair hung down to his shoulders in long, greasy ringlets. His shifty black eyes combed Fitz's study, stopping to gaze at the priceless pieces of porcelain on the shelves. His hands were thrust down into the pockets of a dirty coat. The odor of ale, perspiration, and cigar smoke permeated the air.

"Are you going to stand there staring at my study, or tell me why you've come?" Fitz asked, not bothering to offer him a seat.

The mantel clock struck two times, the bongs resounding in the silent room.

"I'm here to say I've heard the news of your marryin' Miss Brooke." His lips split in a black-toothed grin. "Now, seein' as how I know she tried to rob you—"

"Are you so sure of that?" Fitz's expression remained cryptic.

"Saw it with me own eyes."

"What exactly do you want?" Fitz leaned back in his chair and crossed his arms on his chest.

"What everyone else wants. A little extry blunt—just enough to keep me afloat."

"Are you blackmailing me?"

Ball shook his head, setting his greasy locks trembling on either side of his face.

"I don't like to be threatened, Captain. If you leave now, I might forget you were here." Fitz stood up. A head taller than Ball, he looked down on him.

"I'll go to the Justice. There'll be questions you'll have to answer. Your neck might be on the line. Seein' how you didn't arrest her."

"Go ahead, tell the Justice. Do you think he'll take a smuggler's word against mine?"

"I ain't the only one that saw it. The uppity Lady Caroline and Lady Josephine was there."

Fitz felt his gut tense, yet kept his expression impassive.

"Do you really think they want the scandal attached to their name? I think not. Now leave while you can still walk out." He shot Ball a look that made the miscreant take a step back.

He glared at Fitz. "I'll get me pay somehow." He turned and staggered toward the door, slamming it behind him.

Fitz frowned at the closed door. Captain Ball could be easily dealt with; he was nothing but a drunken sea captain out to make money any way he could. But Lady Caroline, and her overbearing, meddling mother? He wouldn't put it past them to try and cause trouble. Fitz quickly strode from the room and called to Helms to have his horse brought around.

Fifteen minutes later, Fitz stood in the parlor of the Lacklands' cottage, his back to the fire. He heard footsteps and looked at Enid Lackland. Her hands trembled as she clasped them in front of her. "She's on her way down," she said, her eyes glazed over with worry. "I'm afraid she's quite upset."

"What happened?"

"I don't know; she refuses to talk to me about it. She spoke to Lady Caroline, then came in crying—"

The sound of shuffling skirts made Enid pause. Brooke hovered in the doorway, in a black dress, looking very petite and slight and vulnerable. With shaking hands, she grasped a white cotton shawl around her shoulders. Her hair was pulled back in a tight bun. Wisps of raven curls framed her face. Her eyes were red and puffy. She wouldn't look at him, her gaze riveted to the floor, wearing the expression of a mourner at a funeral.

Enid's voice broke the awkward silence in the room. "I should go and see what Julia is about. If you'll excuse me."

Brooke stepped aside, allowing her mother to pass. As Enid did, she touched her daughter's arm in a reassuring gesture.

Fitz moved toward Brooke. "What is the matter?" he asked, his gut tensing at what he might hear.

"I don't want to see you again."

Fitz grabbed her arms. "Look at me, Brooke."

She pulled back from him and glanced up. There was a hard determination in her eyes that he had seen only one other time, when she had tried to rob him. The tightness in his gut moved up to his chest.

"Was I not clear? I do not want to see you again. I'll not marry you."

"You can't mean this?"

"I do. Do you think that because you declare it, I have no say in the matter? Do you think because I had a girlish crush on you that I'm still in love with you? Well, I'm over it. I don't love you. I never will love you. And I won't marry a man I don't love. Now kindly leave."

Fitz grabbed her shoulders. "Stop lying."

"It's the truth."

His eyes narrowed. "That is not what you said when you were in my arms. Have you forgotten that? They got to you, didn't they?"

"Who?"

"Your aunt and cousin."

"They have nothing to do with this."

"They threatened you, didn't they?"

"It's not what Caroline said to me."

"Something changed you."

She shook her head. "I just came to my senses. We shall never suit. Please leave it at that." She jerked her arms out of his grasp. "Now go." She pointed to the hallway.

He frowned down the hall at the door, then back at her. "Don't think I'll let you go that easily. You are still bound to work for me. I expect you there on the morrow, bright and early."

"I won't!"

"You bloody well will"—Fitz crossed his arms over his chest and pinned her with his gaze—"or I'll . . ." His words faded as he watched the hard facade she had tried to maintain crack.

Her lip trembled. Tears gleamed in her eyes. "That's blackmail," she said, her voice barely audible.

"I'm unscrupulous when it comes to what I want."

"How well I know it."

A rueful grin stretched across his lips. "I won't give up so easily on you. I intend to make you mine in every way, even if I must resort to blackmail. I can be ruthless when it comes to having you, my love, so don't cross me. We will marry."

Her lips hardened in a resolute line. Her eyes narrowed, at odds with the tears in them. "How dare you stand there and order me to marry you. Do you think for one minute, for one second, that I'll do as you command? I have bought my freedom from you with my maidenhead; that is enough."

Fitz stared long and hard at her, at the thin, determined expression on her beautiful face, at the unrelenting gleam in her eyes. "I assumed you'd be mine. Unfortunately, I made the same mistake with Victoria. Well, my love, I'll not force myself on you and face another loveless marriage. I learned my lesson the first time. You needn't worry that I'll bother you again." He slapped his riding crop against his boot, turned, and left without looking back.

The door slammed shut.

CHAPTER EIGHT

Julia crawled out from her favorite cubbyhole beneath the stairs. It was a perfect little closet for spying. If she put her ear to the floor, she could, with great clarity, hear everything being said in the parlor. She heard the creak of Brooke's rapid footsteps on the stairs. Her sobs, then. . . .

Bang. Brooke's chamber door shut.

Julia shook her head and stared up the stairwell. This called for drastic measures.

"Julia!" Her mother's soft voice drifted from the kitchen.

Julia turned and ran out the back way toward Glen Carion.

Half an hour later, she spotted Lawford in the ballroom, cutting out paper hearts for the Valentine's Ball. Several footmen struggled to set up tables. Helms stood on a ladder, stringing red garlands across the ceiling. Bright red cupids hung from the ceiling on strings, throwing sparkling red reflections from the chandelier.

As if Lawford felt her gaze on him, he glanced toward her. His face lit up. He grinned, then hurried over to her.

Helms paused from pushing a tack into a streamer and observed them. Grinning, he went back to securing the decoration.

Across the room, Julia grabbed Lawford's arm. "Listen, you've got to help me."

"What now?" His blond brows furrowed, and he pursed his lips.

"My plans have gone all awry. My silly sister has broken off with your father."

"I thought something was amiss. Papa stormed past here a few minutes ago and grumbled something about leaving Looe and going to London. He's locked himself in the study. He didn't look happy. I don't want to leave now that you're my friend." He glanced at Julia, a pout growing on his lips.

"I don't want you to go either. You're my only other friend besides Billy Swenson. We have to do something. Come on." Julia pulled him out of the room.

The next morning, Brooke sat at the dining room table, pushing the scrambled eggs around on her plate. In one mound she saw the image of Fitz's face, the hurt expression he wore after they had spoken. She would never be able to forget it. Feeling a knot growing in her throat, she jammed her fork at the pile, spreading it into little crumbles on her plate.

"Tonight is the Valentine's Ball. We are going, are we not?" Julia glanced over hopefully at her mother.

"I don't think so, my dear."

"Why not? We made dresses and have an invitation, and everything."

"Your sister does not feel up to it."

Julia gazed ruefully over at Brooke and stuffed a spoon of eggs in her mouth.

Brooke quickly changed the subject. "Mama, I've been meaning to tell you about the position Aunt Josephine was kind enough to find for me in Scotland. It's a governess position and pays twenty pounds per annum. I've written and told the couple I'd take it.''

Enid stared at her daughter, her jaw agape.

Julia dropped her spoon, and it clanked against the ironstone plate.

"My dear, that is so far away."

"Yes, but we need the money."

"Not that badly." Enid sighed and set down her fork.

Over the past few days, Brooke had noticed her mother's complexion had turned sallow, her eyes bleak. Now wasn't a good time to bring up finances. But the subject had to be broached sometime.

Julia leaped up from her chair and flashed her green eyes at Brooke. "Why don't you tell her the truth? You're a coward!''

"Julia!" Enid shot Julia a wan look of reproach.

"It's true, Mama. She is. She's letting Caroline run her away." Julia turned her gaze back on Brooke. "I thought I knew you. You had enough courage to go and rob a carriage—''

"Rob a what?" Enid grasped her heart and clung to the table, her gaze unsteady as if she might faint.

Brooke jumped up, snatched the smelling salts from the sideboard, and waved it beneath her mother's nose.

Enid shoved it aside. "I'm all right, my dear."

Brooke shot Julia an I-can't-believe-you-said-that look.

Unaffected by it, Julia continued, "Tell Mama the truth—''

"Be quiet! You're upsetting Mother."

"I'm not a china doll." Enid leveled an indignant glance at Brooke. "I want to know what is going on here."

Brooke remained silent and stared down at her eggs.

Always one to fill in a gap, Julia said, "Caroline and Aunt Josephine were at the hold-up and are blackmailing Brooke." She turned and scoured Brooke's face. "That's it, isn't it? 'Tis pretty obvious that they put this stupid notion in your head.

Can't you see she wants you to leave so Caroline can have Lord Ridgefield—''

Brooke glared at her sister, then saw her mother's lips trembling. "Say no more. My mind is made up. I'm going to Scotland."

"No! You're cowering to that sow and her daughter. It makes me sick. You have always been the strong one. You packed away Papa's belongings when you knew Mama and I couldn't help you, you arranged the funeral, you found this cottage for us to live in, you managed the household and on a very little bit of money. Out of all of us, you were the strong one. You had the courage to beg in the village for credit, to offer to work for our food. But now you are running away to Scotland and splitting up our family forever. I've looked up to you all my life. Now I wonder why." Julia shoved back her chair and ran from the room.

"Julia, wait!" Brooke stared at the empty doorway.

"I'll go to her." Enid rose.

"No, Mama, let me."

Brooke ran after her sister. Her heart ached as if Julia had driven a stake through it. But it wasn't Julia's words that hurt so much, rather the truth of them. Brooke was taking the coward's way out.

Brooke found Julia where she always went to sulk, in the attic, sitting on top of their father's trunk. She had her legs crossed, her lips set in a pout.

Julia glowered at her. "Go away."

"No. You have to understand."

"I'll never understand. You can't do this. We have to stay together. Papa would have wanted it. I heard you promise him you'd take care of us. How will you do that if you go away?"

"I'll send all my salary home to you and Mama."

"I don't want your money. I want you to stay here with us."

"I would like nothing better, but I can't. Caroline and Aunt

Josephine will make it impossible. If I stay, they'll report me and I'll probably hang, not to mention Lord Ridgefield will also get into trouble for not arresting me. Do you want that?''

"No, but—"

"You must accept it; I'm going to have to leave. We can't have everything we want, Julia. You'll learn that when you get older.''

"Then, I don't want to grow up.''

"You don't want to face anything—especially Papa's death. It's time you did. Mama will need you to be strong when I'm gone.'' Brooke heard the catch in her own voice. "Come on, I'll help you open the trunk.''

"No.'' Julia leaped up and backed away as if bitten.

Brooke slipped her hand in Julia's. "Come on, I'll be with you.''

With unaccustomed panic in her green eyes, Julia stared up at Brooke for the longest time, as if gaining courage from her sister. Julia swallowed hard, and whispered, "All right.''

Brooke guided her over to the chest. They knelt before it together, both wearing a reverent expression. Julia's hand trembled as she reached to open it.

Brooke helped her raise the lid. The spicy scent of her father drifted from the chest. On a small shelf, his Bible, with the tattered edges, lay next to his spectacles and watch.

Julia reached down and picked up his journal with all of his sermons in it. The pages breezed past her face as she looked at his bold handwriting. "Every time I went into Papa's office, he was always writing in this book.'' Julia's bottom lip quivered. She clutched the book to her chest and rocked back and forth. Her face screwed up as she tried valiantly to hold back her tears. "I miss him, Brooke.''

"I do, too.'' She reached out and hugged Julia, half expecting Julia to shove her away.

Surprisingly, the child clung to her and nuzzled her face against Brooke's neck. Julia had been her father's pet, and she had not shed one tear at the funeral. If she had, it had been at night, when no one was near. All the pent-up pain rushed out of her. Her little body quaked with violent, cleansing sobs. Brooke held her as she had held her mother so many nights, and together they wept.

After a long time, Julia drew back and wiped the tears away from her swollen eyes with the back of her hand. A blush broke out on her cheeks. "I'm done blubbering now," Julia said, sounding irritated with herself at her open display of weakness.

"You know, it's okay to blubber every now and then." Brooke wiped her own cheeks.

"If I had to blubber, I'm glad it was with you."

"Thanks for the compliment." Brooke grinned half-heartedly.

Julia frowned down at the chest, and her tone grew somber. "I want to go through the rest of it alone."

"All right, if you're sure you'll be okay."

"Of course." Julia smiled sadly.

There was something different in Julia's eyes. Perhaps an innocence lost, a maturity blooming. Whatever it was, Julia had just crossed one of life's many hurdles. Brooke was glad she had been there for Julia. She kissed her sister's cheek, smiled, then strode past boxes and crates and descended the stairs. Her smile faded as she thought of leaving.

The moment Brooke reached the hallway, she heard someone banging on the door. "I'll get it," she called to Emily in the kitchen.

Red-faced and panting, Lawford stood on the steps, his hot breath forming a cloud of white vapor in the frosty air, his windblown hair swept over to one side.

"Lawford! What an unexpected surprise. Please, come in and get warm. Julia's upstairs. I'll go inform her you've arrived."

"Please don't, Miss Lackland. I have to go. I just came to give you this." He pulled out a box and a rose he had been holding behind his back and thrust them at her. "It's from my father.'' Flustered and red-cheeked, Lawford turned and ran down the road, back toward Glen Carion.

Brooke smelled the rose and watched the hem of Lawford's coat flapping against the bottom of his boots. Then his form disappeared behind the wild nut trees growing along the road. After a moment, she closed the door.

"Who was it, my dear?" her mother called from the dining room.

"Lord Ridgefield's son."

"Julia will be disappointed he left without seeing her."

"He was in a hurry."

Brooke took the box into the parlor and sat on the couch. With great care, she laid the rose on an end table. Her hands shook with anticipation as she pulled off the brown wrapping on the box. Inside, she found a crimson silk dress, with a low décolletage. She laid the dress aside and found a transparent evening shawl, the same color as the dress, made of sheer gauze and trimmed in point de Venise lace. It was a beautiful gown.

An envelope in the bottom of the box with *Brooke* scrawled across it caught her eye.

She ran her finger over Fitz's seal, a flame with the letter *R* burning in the center. With trembling hands, she broke the seal and read the hurried, bold letters scrawled across the page:

Brooke,

My dearest, my love. How can I express the love and feelings I have for you? Words cannot convey it. All I know is that without you I'm like a ship adrift on the sea, a man without hope. Without you, I shall become an embittered man and die of loneliness. You don't know the pain and heartache you have caused me. I love you with every thread of my being, every thought is of you. Say you will end my suffering. I'm begging, pleading, you will reconsider my offer of marriage. I'll be waiting for you at the Valentine's Ball. Please make me the happiest man in the world. Say you will come. I hope you like the gown I've enclosed for you. When I saw it, I thought of you and how beautiful you will look in it. Wear it to the ball, my love.

> *Forever faithfully yours in heart and soul,*
> *Fitz*

Brooke crushed the letter in her hands and glanced over at the dress. Oh, Fitz! Even now she could feel his strong arms holding her, the heat of his lips against her own, the way the hair on his muscular chest brushed her bare nipples, the thickness of him inside her and the waves of pleasure that he caused to burn through her.

The thought of causing him such anguish tore at her. Julia's words came back to haunt her. *You're a coward.* Brooke straightened her spine and her resolve.

At the soft tread of footsteps, Brooke glanced up. Enid entered the parlor. She frowned at the dress, then observed Brooke's determined face. "My dear, what is it?"

"He's begging me to come to the ball. Caroline and Aunt Josephine threatened to have me arrested if I went near him again— I'm going, Mama."

Enid touched Brooke's shoulder. "Very courageous, my dear." A pensive, faraway expression drifted into her mother's eyes, as if she had reached some sort of resolve. She smiled serenely at Brooke. "Yes, very courageous, indeed. I'm very proud of you."

Brooke grinned back at her mother and noticed an animated, bright gleam in her eye, hinting at the spirited, lively woman Brooke had known before her father's death. Whatever had caused it was a puzzle, though Brooke welcomed it.

* * *

At Glen Carion, the voices of servants and caterers drifted from the ballroom. Lawford snuck past, ignored by the steady stream of people carrying trays of candies and potted ferns into the ballroom. Helms barked orders at them like a general.

The smell of lemon oil and beeswax on the recently polished wainscoting mixed with the enticing scent of food drifting from the kitchen. He paused near a small table that sat next to the door of his father's study. In the middle, a silver tray overflowed with the morning's post. His hands, still cold from running home, felt numb. He rubbed them and glanced right. Left. His gaze shifted back to the full tray. He pulled a letter out of his pocket. Before he could drop it . . .

The knob turned.

Lawford whipped the letter behind his back and stared into his father's face.

"Lawford? Would you like to come in and speak to me? I haven't seen much of you in the past few days. What have you and Miss Lackland been doing?"

"Nothing really. Playing," Lawford said absently, thinking he had never seen his father look so haggard and preoccupied.

"You have a good friend in Julia."

"I know."

"Has she spoken of her sister?" His father gazed hopefully at him.

"No, Papa." Lawford fingered the envelope and shuffled nervously on his feet. Somehow he had to get the letter in with the morning's post. He glanced past his father's broad shoulder and pointed into his study. "What's that?"

"What?"

The moment his father turned, Lawford tossed the letter on top of the overflowing pile of mail. "That . . . that paperweight there, with the lion head on it. It's new, isn't it?"

"It was your great-uncle's." His father turned and eyed him with a marked degree of suspicion. "Since when have you started to admire paperweights?"

"Since meeting Miss Lackland. She likes them. I'll have to show her this one. I'm supposed to meet her down by the cove in ten minutes. I'll bring her in directly to see it. Excuse me." Lawford bowed quickly, turned, and ran down the hall, leaving his father staring after him with a puzzled look on his face.

Grinning from ear to ear, he turned a corner and hurried toward the servants' entrance, aware Julia would be proud of him. Yes, she would. He had done all his tasks, even delivered the letters she had written. She had a flair with words Lawford envied. In fact, he was beginning to believe Julia had a flair with most anything.

Full of self-confidence, he stepped out the servants' entrance and into the cold again. The sun was beginning to set, painting the sky with swatches of pink and red. Soon it would be dark. In half an hour he was supposed to meet Julia down by the cove and give her a full report. He wanted to get it over with so he could get home before the Valentine's Ball.

For once in his life, he felt a sense of accomplishment. It had been a major achievement to deliver the package to Miss Lackland all alone. At first he had balked, not confident he could do it. With her usual saucy gall, Julia had threatened not to come to his room and keep away the ghosts. Right then and there, he had decided he could handle this particular fear—perhaps more to prove it to her than himself—but he wasn't ready to take on the ghosts alone. Not yet.

Let the specters come tonight. Julia would drive them away. She was better than a guard dog. This plan had to work. He didn't want to leave Looe and Julia. Frowning, he hurried past the garden and tall boxwoods.

Captain Hank Ball peeked out around one of the shrubs and watched the boy running toward the beach. He signaled to one of his crewmen, Henry Galding, a kinky-haired, burly man with no teeth, an ugly bugger and a mean drunk. But he would do for what Ball needed.

Crouched behind rock and bracken near the cliff that overlooked the cove, Henry watched the young lord's son run past him and down the path toward the beach. He nodded to Hank, then slithered out of his hiding place and followed the boy. A wide grin spread across Hank's face as he followed them.

Fitz shook his head at the empty hallway his son had just run down. There was still an air of reserve in Lawford whenever they were together. Fitz was at a loss to know how to reach him; the boy wouldn't even stop long enough to speak to him.

His brows furrowed as he remembered why he had come out of his office. He turned and grabbed the mail tray. A letter slipped from the tray and fell beneath the table. It escaped Fitz's notice; his mind was on Brooke and the way she had so coldly turned him away.

His frown deepened. With stiff strides, he walked back into his study, sat at his desk, and pulled the bellpull.

After a few moments, Helms's distinctive knock sounded at the door.

"Enter."

Helms bowed and said, "My lord."

"Yes, Helms. When Lady Josephine and her daughter arrive tonight, I want to know."

"Yes, my lord." Helms turned to leave.

"One more thing."

Helms paused, his hand on the knob. "What is it, my lord?"

"After the ball, I'm taking Lawford on an extended trip of Europe. A change of scenery will do us both good. Inform the staff."

"You've planned your honeymoon," Helms said, grinning from ear to ear. "How prudent of you, my—"

"It's not a honeymoon."

The grin gave way as Helms's brows furrowed over his nose. "I suppose this means you will not be announcing your engagement to Miss Lackland tonight."

Fitz rubbed his throbbing temples. "You assume correctly."

"I wish I had not, my lord."

"Yes, well, it appears marriage is not in my future." Fitz scowled at the mountain of mail on his desk.

In the tense silence that followed, Helms, vigilant as ever, sensed his master's need to be alone. He bowed, then left the room.

The click of the door's lock echoed in the silence.

Fitz squeezed his eyes closed and saw Brooke smiling at him, her dimples embedded in the pink bloom of her cheeks, her eyes glazed over with desire as he had made love to her. And her beautiful body, the taste of her nipples in his mouth, the womanly scent of her, her soft raven curls. If he imagined hard enough, he could feel the smoothness of her skin against his lips. She had been so adamant about not caring about him. In Brooke he had thought he had found something special, a woman who could love him fully, unlike Victoria. He couldn't help but wonder if Brooke wasn't of the same mold.

How could he have been so wrong about her? She had played him for a fool. Still, Fitz wanted to believe Lady Josephine and her daughter had brought about the sudden change in Brooke. They could have, though Brooke refused to admit it. He couldn't move to London until he was positive of it, nor could he leave Brooke to be blackmailed for the rest of her life by those two. Tonight he would face her relatives and force the issue. If Brooke truly thought nothing of him as she claimed, he would find out soon enough.

Julia's feet thumped on the wet sand. The wind lashed her short curls against her face. She shoved them out of her eyes and glanced out at the long stretch of bumpy beach, being quickly eaten by the rising tide. Several curlews waddled along the water's edge and took flight as she drew close. Their wings spread against the last hint of the setting sun. Pinks and purples bathed the horizon, reflecting in the sea, making it hard to tell where the sky stopped and the sea began.

Would Lawford still be waiting for her on the beach? She had spent several hours going through her father's things and had forgotten she was supposed to meet him. And she still could not accept the fact Brooke might leave them.

Running now, she hopped over a large piece of driftwood, skirted a jutting crag, and finally reached Carion Cove. She glanced up the sheer rocky cliff, at the small winding path snaking downward. She turned and spotted Lawford already on the beach, pacing near the waves.

"Julia!" Lawford waved to her and galloped toward her with his funny, awkward gait.

Julia took a step to meet him, and felt a hard tug on the collar of her coat. She wheeled around and looked into Captain Ball's glazed, hollow eyes. By the smell of ale on him, Julia was positive even the lice on his body must have been drunk. Another sailor was with him, one Julia had never seen before. He looked greasier and rougher than Hank.

"Well, well, if it isn't the little cheat. Did you think me so stupid I wouldn't know it were you trying to look like a boy?"

Julia tried to knock his hand away.

"You'll not be gettin' away this time." He lifted her off the ground and tossed her over his shoulder. His vicious laugh split the air.

"Leave her alone!" Lawford charged Hank.

The other man grabbed Lawford and wrenched his arm up behind his back. "Now ye'll be settling down, laddy, or ye'll be getting it good."

Julia felt her heart banging in her chest. They were in real trouble now.

CHAPTER NINE

Bats circled past a quarter moon, their forms dissolving into the surrounding darkness. Fitz stared up at them as he knocked on the Lackland cottage door. The anticipation of seeing Brooke again made his stomach clench. What reception would he get?

The door opened.

Brooke looked startled for a moment, as if expecting someone else. "Oh, Fitz." A mask of worry covered her face. "Do come in."

"What is the matter?" he asked, stepping through the doorway, his cape swirling around his legs.

"I thought you were Julia. We can't find her."

"Lawford is missing. I'd hoped he'd be here."

"I can't imagine where Julia could be. She did so want to go to the ball with us. She was upset with me. I hope she hasn't run away."

"You were coming to the ball?" Fitz raised a brow in a hopeful slant.

"Yes, you wrote and asked me to come. I had to." Her dimples beamed at him.

Distracted by her worry, he hadn't taken note of her appearance. He did so now. Her black hair, swept up, lay falling along one side of her shoulder in long curls. The transparent red shawl on her shoulder hid nothing of the crimson dress beneath it. . . .

His gaze fell on the low décolletage and the creamy white flesh of Brooke's high, proud bosom, hidden just enough by the sheer shawl to draw the eye. She looked good enough to eat.

"Where did you get this? It's lovely on you." He lifted a corner of the shawl with his riding crop.

"You sent it." She looked dumbfounded.

"I didn't."

"You did, along with a rose and a letter."

"That wasn't me."

"So all those things in the letter . . ." She squeezed her eyes closed. After a moment she stiffened her spine and gazed up at him, the pain on her face transforming into indignation. "When I get my hands on Julia and Lawford, I'm going to murder them."

Fitz stared at the provocative swell of her bosom. "You have to admire their creativity." He couldn't help but grin.

Footsteps sounded in the hall.

Fitz tore his gaze from the enticing sight of Brooke's cleavage. Mrs. Lackland stood in the doorway. A modest pink silk dress flowed down her slender curves. Her graying blond hair was braided and pulled back from her face. She looked younger somehow. Her gaze alighted on Fitz, and she smiled serenely at him. "Oh, my lord, how nice of you to come and escort us to the ball."

"We're not going to the ball, Mama," Brooke said, a severe stubborn look on her face. "Lord Ridgefield did not send this dress or the letter. It was Julia."

"Oh, Julia. What a clever child." Enid smiled proudly. In a determined voice, she said, "We must go, my dear. I've so looked forward to this evening."

Brooke opened her mouth to protest, but an abrupt knock on the door made her mouth clamp shut.

Mrs. Lackland stepped over and opened the door. Rollins stood in the doorway, clutching his hat, and bowed. "Ma'am. Is Lord Ridgefie—" His gaze landed on Brooke, halting his words. An appreciative grin tweaked the corners of his lips.

Unbidden jealousy stabbed Fitz as he stepped in front of Brooke and blocked Rollins's view of her. "Do you need something?"

"Me lord, I need to speak to you outside." He scratched his ruddy cheek and added, " 'Tis about Master Lawford and that certain person you had me to watch." Rollins cleared his throat and looked unwilling to say more in front of the ladies.

"I'll speak to you outside." He turned to Mrs. Lackland. "Allow me to have the carriage sent around for you, madam, and your daughter."

"Thank you." She smiled graciously.

He turned and followed Rollins outside.

"What is it?" Fitz asked.

Abruptly, the door opened.

Brooke stepped out behind him. "Now see here, if he knows something about Lawford, then Julia must be involved, too. I have a right to know what is going on."

"Very well." Fitz looked impatiently at Rollins. "Speak up, man. What do you know?"

"Captain Ball has the children. I followed him to a cave down by the cove. I left one of the footmen watchin' them and came straightaway to tell you."

"Bloody Hell!" Fitz banged his riding crop against his boot.

"Captain Ball will hurt them. I know it." Brooke gripped the shawl around her shoulders. The sheer material bunched in her white-knuckled grip.

"Don't worry," Fitz said. "I'll get them back safely."

"I'm going with you."

"No, I won't have you endangered. Stay with your mother and take her to the ball. I'll bring the children there."

Before Brooke could protest further, he mounted and galloped away. She watched him disappear into the night, then glanced up at the sky. "Please God, let him bring them back safely."

Mean drunks were capable of all sorts of cruelty. Julia realized now just how cruel they could be. She shivered in the cave and listened to waves hitting the rocks on the edge. In another fifteen minutes, the sea would cover the cave's floor. Through the thick wool layers of her coat, she could feel the jagged stone wall pressed against her spine.

Lawford sat next to her, working the bindings on his wrists. Was he almost free? Julia couldn't budge the ropes on her own hands.

A candle Captain Ball had stuffed in the top of an empty bottle threw eerie shadows along the craggy rock walls. He stood on the opposite side of the cave, his face distorted, ugly in the dim light. His greasy hair clung to his face. His cohort had passed out on the cave floor, hugging an empty bottle of rum against his chest. Julia wished Captain Ball would do the same, but he didn't show any signs of it. Yet.

She watched him take a swig of wine from a bottle and burp. As he tipped it up again, a mere drop hit his tongue. He squinted down the empty neck as if looking through a spyglass. Empty. With an angry thrust, he whacked it against the cave wall.

Glass shattered and pinged against the cave floor, raining down on his friend's legs.

Julia and Lawford flinched.

Captain Ball turned his wine-glazed eyes toward them. "Well, now, 'tis time to deal with the little cheater. Try to steal money from Captain Ball, will you? Better knaves than you have tried it.'' He waved a finger at Julia, then at Lawford. ''And you, with yer high-and-mighty pa. Well, he'll be givin' me money for you, too.'' He staggered over to Julia.

''You'll not get a farthing.'' Julia kept her voice full of bravado, though her insides quaked.

Captain Ball stepped closer. ''Is that what you think? I'll teach you to open yer mouth.'' He drew back to smack Julia. . . .

Lawford broke free of his bindings and yelled, ''No! Leave her alone!'' He charged Hank.

Julia screamed.

Hank and Lawford fell to the ground. It was as if a demon had been unleashed inside Lawford. He struck at Hank's face with relentless punches. Hank threw up his arms to protect his face.

Suddenly, Lord Ridgefield, Rollins, and another man she recognized as a footman ran into the cave. Lord Ridgefield charged Captain Ball. They fell against the side of the cave. Lord Ridgefield struck Captain Ball in the face. In the stomach.

Hank collapsed against the cave floor and didn't move.

Lord Ridgefield pulled Lawford into his arms. ''Are you all right?'' he said, crushing his son in a hug. He stepped back and checked Lawford over to make sure he wasn't wounded.

''Yes,'' Lawford said, grinning coyly up at his father.

Rollins cut the ropes from Julia's wrists. ''He saved my life. He's a Trojan,'' she exclaimed, grinning at Lawford, while frightened feelings still swirled inside her.

''I know. I couldn't be prouder of him.'' Lord Ridgefield gazed down at his son, looking overwhelmed and pleased.

''Are you really proud of me?'' Lawford asked, seeming to hang on the anticipation of his father's next words.

''Of course I am.''

''I'm sorry for the way I've acted, Papa,'' Lawford said, tears in his eyes.

''It's all right, son.'' Lord Ridgefield hugged him again.

Julia absorbed the look of complete contentment on Lawford's face. She felt the loss of her own father. An ache to feel his comforting arms around her again rose up inside her. She swallowed past the growing lump in her throat.

Lord Ridgefield must have sensed her distress, for he leaned over and drew her into his arms, holding her and Lawford in his embrace. Julia felt Lawford's arm go around her waist. Their heads touched as Lord Ridgefield hugged them tightly. Her sadness began to subside. It would come again, she knew, but as long as Lawford and Lord Ridgefield were nearby, it wouldn't be quite so unbearable.

"What do we do with this garbage, me lord?" Rollins kicked Hank Ball's limp foot.

"See that he and his friend find their way to a press-gang. A stint in the navy ought to set Captain Ball on the right path." Lord Ridgefield put his arm over Julia's shoulder and Lawford's. "Come, we have a ball to attend."

"But I can't go. Brooke and Mama are not coming." Julia's bottom lip stuck out in a pout.

"They are. I told your sister and mother I would bring you back to Glen Carion."

Julia smiled. Perhaps her efforts and Lawford's had not been in vain. She shared a glance with Lawford and by his expression knew he was thinking the same thing.

Helms opened the door for Brooke and Enid. The din of music and voices drifted from the ballroom. Looking pleasantly surprised, he bowed and waved them inside. "Please, come in."

Brooke removed her cape. Helms's gaze discreetly swept her. An approving grin spread across his lips. "You look lovely this evening, Miss Lackland."

"Thank you." Brooke nervously cleared her throat and handed him her wrap, her mind on the children. She hadn't told her mother what had happened, only that Julia and Lawford had run away and Lord Ridgefield had gone to fetch them.

Enid shot her daughter a concerned glance and took off her cloak, handing it to Helms. "Sir, could you tell me if Lady Josephine and Lady Caroline are present?"

"Yes, madam. I saw them only moments ago head for the powder room."

"Ah! Thank you." Enid patted the sides of her coiffure and said, "I should freshen up a little, my dear. I'll meet you in the crush."

Brooke strode to the entrance to the ballroom, the scent of cigar smoke, heavy perfume, and body odor wafted through the air. A country dance was in progress. People mingled in little groups along the sides. Against convention, couples and their children had always been invited to Lord Northdale's Valentine's Ball, and this year was no exception. Several boys and girls stood near the tables, cramming their mouths with candies and cakes.

Brooke was too worried about Fitz and the children to join the party, so she strode past the doors, down the hallway. When she neared Fitz's study, she sat on a bench and sighed deeply. A small mahogany table stood near the bench. Something below it caught her eye. She reached down and picked up an envelope that had fallen beneath it. It was addressed to Fitz. The parchment was redolent with lavender. Certainly a woman had written it. Curious about the return address, she turned it over. Lackland Cottage was written in Julia's small, perfect hand.

She opened the unsealed letter and read:

Dearest Love,

Such a fool I have been. I've thought and thought and now know that my refusal of your offer was foolhardy. Can you forgive me, my darling? I love you. Please say it is not too late for us. Please say you can forgive me.

*I'm coming to the ball just to see you. I await your answer
with bated breath.*

All my love,
Brooke

Brooke smiled down at the letter and shook her head at
Julia's creative deviousness. Abruptly her smile faded. She
wanted to tell Fitz she loved him. But how could she and not
incur the threats made by Caroline and Aunt Josephine? Even
if by some miracle those two shrews remained silent, she had
hurt Fitz so deeply he most likely wouldn't offer to marry her
again. She would never forget how devastated he had looked.
He was a proud man. He wouldn't repeat his offer. Brooke
hung her head. An unrelenting pressure squeezed her heart,
shot up to the back of her throat and into her eyes. She gazed
down at the letter. Her name blurred behind thick, stinging
tears.

Inside the powder room, Enid found Lady Josephine and
Caroline all alone, sitting at a dressing table, primping. Caroline
looked beautiful in a white dress with embroidered hearts on
it. Josephine wore basic black. A large turban and black plumes
towered on her head.

Josephine saw her and gaped in surprise. "Oh, Enid, I had
thought you would not be here with your weak constitution."

"Yes, well, one must have some pleasure in life." Enid
smiled placidly and looked in the mirror, patting a piece of
hair that was not out of place.

"Are you alone?" Caroline asked, cutting her blue eyes at
Enid.

"Oh, no. Brooke is here, and Julia will be along momen-
tarily."

"Brooke?" Caroline's face screwed up in a frown.

"Didn't you know? Brooke and Lord Ridgefield are getting married."

"But I thought—"

Enid pinched her cheeks and frowned at her reflection in the mirror. "I believe I put too much rouge on. What do you think, Caroline?"

"What do you mean they are getting married?" Lady Josephine blurted. She hoisted her wide body up from the chair and narrowed her eyes at Enid.

"Just what I said." Enid met Lady Josephine's gaze squarely.

"She can't do that!" It was Caroline's turn to leap up from her chair. "I want him."

"There are a lot of things we want in our lives, my dear, but we do not always get them." Enid smoothed out the folds of her dress. "Fortunately, for Brooke, she will get what she wants. And she does so love Lord Ridgefield."

"She can't have him!" Caroline stomped her foot, causing a rustle of silk and the string of beads around her neck to tremble.

"We'll see she doesn't, my pet," Lady Josephine said in a soothing tone. She glowered at Enid. "Do you know what your daughter has done?"

"You mean the attempted robbery of Lord Ridgefield?" Enid casually waved her hand through the air. "Yes, I know all about that."

"We shall go to the authorities and see she is punished properly," Josephine said.

Enid shot Josephine a warning look. "I advise against such action. I've kept quiet all these years, even hid the truth from my girls to protect your reputation and that of your family, but I'm not above divulging to the world that your husband impregnated the smithy's daughter and Walter had to see that the girl got on the next ship to America. Or the time Clive rode toward the village stark naked, and Walter had to fetch him;

or the time he stayed at a brothel for a week, and you appealed to Walter to bring him home.''

Lady Josephine's cheeks puffed out, and she shook from her barely contained fury.

Undaunted, Enid said, ''There are more stories I could tell—''

''You wouldn't dare.'' Josephine stiffened her back, rocking the quizzing glass on her chest.

''I have no compunction when seeing to my daughter's happiness. If Walter were alive, I'm sure he would be saying the same thing to you at this moment—even though you are his sister. By the by, where is my brother-in-law?''

''In London.''

''Yes, well on the verge of another scandal, no doubt. Who takes care of those these days, now that Walter is dead?''

''How dare you!''

A slow smile curved Enid's lips. ''I dare many things when you come after one of my girls. Remember that.'' She gathered up the hem of her skirt and breezed out of the door, leaving Josephine glaring at her.

''Oh, Mother!'' Caroline burst out.

Enid smiled to herself and closed the door, cutting off Caroline's dramatic sobs. As she turned she saw Brooke sitting alone on a bench in the hallway, her shoulders hunched, a letter twisted in her hands, streams of tears flowing down her cheeks.

Brooke glanced up. She wiped the tears away with the back of a gloved hand and tried not look as if she had been crying.

Enid pulled a handkerchief from her reticule and lifted Brooke's face, dabbing at the long, wet lashes. ''You shouldn't cry, my dear, you'll make your eyes puffy, and you want to look beautiful for Lord Ridgefield.''

''I want to go home.''

Enid clucked her tongue. ''You needn't fear your aunt and cousin any longer. You're free to have him.''

''But what did you say to them?''

"I merely pointed out some things that your aunt had forgotten. But everything is fine now. Trust me."

Brooke studied her mother for a long moment, appraising the new light in her eyes. "You seem . . . different tonight, Mama, like your old self again."

"It's about time for a change, don't you think, my darling?" Enid smiled down at Brooke and squeezed her hand.

"I do." Brooke beamed with pride, her eyes sparkling up at Enid.

"Now. Let us go into the ball and enjoy the rest of the evening."

"You go. I'm going to wait for Lord Ridgefield."

"I understand your desire to speak to him. I do so look forward to dancing tonight." Enid's eyes twinkled with a new-found intensity. She smiled, then tucked the handkerchief back in her reticule and floated down the hallway, the silk of her dress rustling.

Brooke heard a deep, familiar voice echo down the hallway. Fitz was home.

CHAPTER TEN

Brooke ran down the hall and saw Julia first. Smudges of dirt smeared the sides of her cheeks. Her blond curls stuck out in wild disarray around her face. Brooke hugged her. "Are you all right?"

"Of course," she said, grinning over at Lawford. "Nothing really happened. Right?" Julia shared a glance with Lawford and Fitz.

"Right," Lawford said, his handsome, boyish face lighting up with a sly grin.

"I know something must have happened." Brooke stared at the three of them. The moment she gazed at Fitz, her heart skipped a beat.

Julia ignored the question, raised her brows at Brooke's dress, and said, "I see you decided to come to the ball after all. I'm very proud of you. I take back what I said earlier." She hugged Brooke again, then pulled back. "Come on, Lawf. I'm starved." Julia grabbed Lawford's arm and tried to pull him into the ballroom.

He pulled back his hand. "You don't need to drag me everywhere. I can walk."

"All right. Though I don't like the way you're acting."

"I don't care if you do."

"Fine." Julia stomped off.

"Wait!" Lawford called after her and ran to catch up. Their forms disappeared into the crowded ballroom.

Brooke felt Fitz's intense gaze boring into her and looked at him.

An awkward moment stood between them. Brooke's pulse roared in her ears and drowned out the music and gaiety of voices in the background.

His expression was impenetrable, though a cynical light gleamed in his eyes. He looked devilishly handsome, with a thick afternoon stubble on his chin. He hadn't yet dressed for the ball and wore a fawn jacket, brown riding breeches, and knee-high black boots. Candlelight glistened in the spit shine on the leather.

Tap. Tap. Tap.

His riding crop hit the side of one Hessian. He stared at her, as if waiting for her to say something.

Unable to stand the awkward tenseness that seemed like a wall between them, she said, "I was very worried about Julia and Lawford. Captain Ball is a horrible person. Thank you for bringing them home safely. Something terrible must have gone on, since Julia would not worry me with the details. Would you tell me?"

"It's over and done with." He looked pointedly at her, the weight of his words heavy with meaning. "Captain Ball is finding his way to a press-gang. He'll never bother anyone again. Let's leave it at that."

Another long pause. The bittersweet harmony of Schubert drifted from the ballroom.

Leave it at that. Leave it at that. The words played over and over in Brooke's mind. In a calm voice that surprised even her,

she said, "If you'll excuse me, I should go and find my mother."
She wheeled around to leave, unknowingly dropping the letter.

When she was well inside the ballroom, a wide, powerful
hand clamped over hers. She gazed up at Fitz.

"You dropped something," he drawled, looking down at
the letter in his hand. Before handing it to her, he scanned it.
Then his gray eyes locked on her.

"I have to leave here."

"Just answer one question. Did you mean what you wrote
in here?" He waved the letter through the air.

"I didn't write it, Julia did."

The hope that had animated his face retreated behind heartache and regret. "I thought . . ." His words trailed off as he
turned to leave.

"Wait!" Brooke grabbed his arm, pulling him around to
face her. "I wish I had written that letter. I want to marry you
if you'll still have me." Her mouth went dry, and her heartbeat
seemed to halt as she waited for his answer.

His arms went around her, and he crushed her to him, then
kissed her. The moment his lips touched hers, Brooke felt her
knees weaken. She leaned against him and was forced to wrap
her arms around his neck. There was so much passion in his
kiss that it stole Brooke's breath. Her senses reeled. The sound
in the room faded, leaving everything still, as though only the
two of them existed.

He bent her back over his arm. His tongue slid into her
mouth. Brooke opened to him and was lost. She twined her
fingers in his hair, kissing him back, her passion matching his
own. Flames ignited within her. She ached from the feel of his
closeness.

The orchestra slowly ground to a halt, one instrument at a
time. People dancing paused and looked toward the couple
causing such a stir. The dowagers in the room gasped at such
scandalous behavior. Some of the more mindful mothers
grabbed their children and covered their eyes. Enid took a sip

of punch and smiled over her cup, while Caroline and Lady Josephine pouted, consumed with envy.

Julia looked down the length of the ballroom at her sister enfolded in Lord Ridgefield's arms. Her fists froze midair, and she paused from instructing Lawford on how he should have attacked Captain Ball. She had had little experience with fighting, only what Billy Swenson had told her, but that didn't stop her from giving her opinions. "Would you look at that, Lawf. We've done it. How long do you think they're going to kiss?"

"I don't know. Do you think they can breathe like that? They might suffocate. We should stop them." Lawford took a step toward the couple, but Julia pulled him back.

"Let them be. Kissing has never strangled anyone, silly."

"How would you know?" Lawford frowned over at her.

"Mature women know these things." Julia raised her jaw to a haughty angle and brushed back a curl that had fallen over her eyes.

Lawford grunted under his breath, making male noises just like an arrogant young boy should.

Julia scowled, not sure if she liked this new masterful, confident Lawford. He was acting more and more like Billy Swenson, and Billy wasn't someone she could manipulate very easily.

Fitz heard Helms clearing his throat and realized where he was and what he was doing. He ended the kiss and set Brooke on her feet. She stumbled, and he grabbed her elbow to steady her. Her eyes were still glazed with passion, her lips swollen from his kiss.

He gave her a tender smile and whispered, "You dazzle me with your beauty." He grinned at her, then in a voice that carried over the ballroom, said, "Ladies and gentlemen, it appears I have gotten somewhat carried away by this Valentine's Ball."

A round of laughter burst from the gentlemen in the room. Their wives shot them quelling glances. The laughter ended in a twitter of nervous coughing and clearing of throats.

"It is my great pleasure to announce my engagement to Miss Lackland."

Brooke smiled back at the crowd. For the first time in her life, she felt truly beautiful—the belle of the ball.

Everyone applauded, save two guests: Caroline ran out of the room sobbing, Lady Josephine trailing behind her like a mother duck.

Fitz turned to Brooke. "I'd forgotten about those two. They will be trouble."

"Mama has seen that they will not ever speak of my folly."

"A major accomplishment considering the waspish dispositions of those two. I would have thought they'd have eaten your mother alive. How did she manage it?"

"I don't know, but I have a feeling it had something to do with my uncle." Fitz glanced over at Enid Lackland. She raised her punch glass and saluted him. He smiled back at her.

The music started again. Fitz grabbed Brooke and swept her out onto the floor. He stared down at the hollow of her throat, the tiny pulse there throbbing in a delicate vein. He longed to run his tongue over it. After several spins around the room and the other couples had taken to the floor, Fitz whirled Brooke out onto the balcony.

Cold air hit him, but it did little to quench the heat Brooke ignited in his body. He swept her up into his arms and carried her down the steps.

"What are you doing? You're going to cause more scandal."

"You're my fiancée; that entitles me to a few scandals with you." He kissed her again.

Brooke forgot about everything, save his lips on hers and his strong arms holding her. When he broke the kiss, Brooke glanced around and saw they were in the wine cellar. In a small corner of it, a lone candle flickered on a crate. A pallet of quilts sat atop six inches of straw. Two glasses and a bottle of champagne glistened on the crate. Rose petals were scattered over the quilt top.

"When did you do this?" Brooke said, grinning.

"I sent someone trustworthy after I read your letter. I wanted some time alone with you, and since this seems to be the only place I can get it . . ." He kissed her again, all the while gently setting her down on top of the rose petals. Then he went to the door and bolted it from the inside.

"But we'll be missed."

"We shall put in an appearance later. Now, where was I?" His gaze roamed down her body and rested on her breasts. His eyes turned several shades darker with desire as he eased down on top of her. He ran his fingertips along the sensitive skin on the inside of her bare arms, slipping the shawl off her shoulders.

Brooke shivered at his touch. She glanced past his broad shoulder at the candelabra on the crate. "You didn't light all the candles."

"I thought the light would inhibit you."

"Not anymore. Light all of them."

He cocked a brow at her. "You have turned brazen on me."

"Are you complaining?" An impish grin spread across her lips.

"Absolutely not." He feathered a kiss over her lips. "You please me in every way."

"Show me, Fitz." She tangled her fingers in the wavy hair at his nape and pulled his head down for a kiss. The need to feel his hands on her, to feel his naked skin against her, grew overwhelming. With trembling hands, she tore at his clothes.

He sensed her need and with equal fervor undressed her. His hands caressed every part of her body, then his lips. He whispered, "Ravishing, gorgeous, the most divine creature in the world," against her lips, neck, breasts.

She believed him now. She would never doubt it again. Her thoughts quickly switched back to Fitz as he thrust inside her . . . again and again. They came together in a melding that left them both panting and weak and clinging to each other.

Brooke reveled in the feel of Fitz on top of her, their slick bodies touching. He nuzzled a sensitive spot below her ear, the coarseness of his chin brushing the side of her throat. "This is the best Valentine's Day of my life," she said, feeling a tingle shoot down her neck.

He raised his head and looked down at her, an adoring, proprietary gleam in his eyes. "For me, too, my love."

"And we have Julia and Lawford to thank for it. They will be happy their scheme reached fruition."

"Not as happy as I."

Fitz kissed her again, and Brooke forgot all about Julia and Lawford.

MEG'S SECRET ADMIRER

BY

CHERYL HOLT

CHAPTER ONE

"I hate Valentine's Day," Meg MacDonald muttered to herself as she stepped from the dressmaker's shop and onto the busy London street. The cold February air filled her lungs, and she heaved a sigh of relief at having made such an easy escape from her aunt, who was still inside in a fitting room.

The visit to the modiste had been as unpleasant as Meg imagined it would be. With the St. Valentine's Day Ball only eight days away, Meg was to have two new gowns, although how two would suffice for the myriad parties and teas they were scheduled to attend was a mystery. Meg hadn't minded receiving the new dresses—made by a London seamstress, no less—but her aunt had such abominable taste in clothing when it came to dressing Meg that the shopping excursion had been spoiled early on.

Even the modiste had found a brief bit of courage to point out that a red or green trim would have looked much better, but her aunt had stood firm on her choice of a shade which would help Meg blend in with the wallpaper. The dressmaker hadn't dared to contradict the stern, stuffy Lucinda Smythewaite, Countess Redding, so two dresses with pastel yellow trim it would be. No one would notice Meg during the next week. While other young ladies were being wooed and charmed by various swains, she would remain invisible.

"I hate Valentine's Day," she said with more emphasis this time, and the thought was a surprising one. For the most part, she considered herself the worst sort of dreamer, a romantic who truly believed with all her heart in grand passions, love at first sight, lifetime devotion and happily-ever-after. However, the silliness surrounding Valentine's Day never failed to irritate her. She hated the cards and the flowers and the candies, the poetry and words of endearment.

Most of all, she hated the dreaded St. Valentine's Day Ball hosted by her aunt, which had now become a yearly ordeal. Meg always spent weeks working like a slave to oversee the arrangements, then endured the entire evening in misery, standing alone and unnoticed with the widows and chaperones, a pathetic creature, yearning desperately to swirl by in the line of dancers.

Using her vivid imagination, it was easy to fantasize that she would be dressed in an exquisite gown, looking beautiful while acting witty and gay for some handsome gentleman who was completely smitten. The reality was that she would never have the chance because no one would ask her to dance in the first place.

Aunt Lucy had spent the past ten years drumming Meg's list of shortcomings into her—both the physical and the personal—until she believed every one of them. At age twenty, now three years past the time she should have found a beau and married, it was becoming quite clear that she would not. Standing at five foot ten without shoes, she was too tall, too big all over, her facial features too bold, her breasts too large, her legs too long, her eyes too green. And that list didn't even begin to include her exotic mane of red hair, one of the many distressing

Scottish attributes she had inherited from her dashing, wayward father, and which Aunt Lucy constantly assured her was too offensive to be shown in public. Meg spent hours of every week trying to think of new ways to hide or disguise it.

For all those reasons and more, the ball held on St. Valentine's Day was always a trial to be endured. This year would be no different, and, in most ways, would be much worse. The annual affair had been bad enough when it was held at the country estate with only the neighboring gentry available to attend as guests. Now they had come to London, and the party would be held in the main ballroom of the town house with all of Polite Society in attendance to watch Lucy's eighteen-year-old daughter, Patricia, make her debut.

Her cousin's coming out was the reason Meg was in the city for the first time. Patricia was a petite little thing, with shiny blond curls, bright blue eyes, and creamy smooth skin which made her look like a porcelain doll. With her dowry, looks, and being the daughter of an earl, she was considered the catch of the Season. Next to her, Meg felt big, clumsy, and mediocre.

Patty was hosting her first afternoon party that very day, as well as numerous small afternoon gatherings and soirées leading up to the ball. Meg was expected to attend the events, but she would watch from a distance and usually only after she had worked as hard as any of the servants at the preparations. After living with the family for the past decade, she felt tolerated though not particularly welcomed, but she never complained over her plight. Feeling lucky to have been taken in by her aunt and uncle after her parents' deaths, she always tried to be as pleasant and accommodating as possible.

Her mother, Eleanor, had been a Smythewaite, a daughter of the previous Earl of Redding, when she fell in love with Meg's father, Colin MacDonald. He was a singer, touring with a traveling show, whom she had met at a country fair. She had eloped with him three days later which caused her to be disowned and disinherited.

They died in a fire when Meg was ten, leaving her a penniless orphan, and the Smythewaites had taken her in. At the time, she had had no idea of the life her mother had given up in order to be with her father. All she remembered was that her parents had been in love. Deliriously so. She vividly recalled the affection and laughter that had permeated their life. She had spent the past decade listening to others talk about what a horrendous thing her mother had done, and while she always verbally agreed that her mother had acted egregiously, Meg had never quite taken the notion to heart.

Secretly, Meg viewed her mother's life as a magnificent adventure. Upon falling instantly in love with a flamboyant, handsome stranger, Eleanor had given up everything and run off with nothing but the clothes on her back. Together, they had taken every kind of chance in the name of love. The plot could not have been more fabulous if Meg had read it in one of the romantic novels she kept tucked under her mattress. If a chance for wicked happiness ever came her way, would she have the courage to grab for it as her mother had done?

Glancing down at her timepiece, she realized that she had daydreamed away nearly a half hour of her escapade. With two full hours of freedom to enjoy herself before making her appearance at afternoon tea, she planned to see as many sights as she could.

At a corner, she took stock of her location, knowing there had been a bookseller's near the dressmaker's. She planned to use a few of her meager coins to purchase another book or two. She especially loved the ones about foreign places, where the heroines met different kinds of people and experienced new ways of living, although she never passed up a chance to read a romantic tale. Accounts of pirates with daring, swashbuckling scoundrels as the heroes were also high on her list of favorites.

As she changed directions to head for the bookseller's, she passed a florist shop oddly tucked away in the middle of the busy avenue. A riot of colorful bouquets decorated the windows, looking inviting and decidedly out of place in the middle of London on a dreary February day. She couldn't resist stepping inside.

The place was delightful, crammed full of plants, blossoms, fragrances. She walked up and down the tight aisles, letting the leaves and stems tickle her nose, breathing deep of the fresh green-scented air, stepping around pots and watering cans.

At the back of the store next to the counter, there was a collection of bundled bouquets containing every kind of flower. She couldn't resist selecting the most colorful one, pressing the blossoms against her face and inhaling deeply. They were so lovely. Before she knew what she was about, she decided to purchase them.

"Do you make deliveries?" she asked, relieved when the clerk said yes.

She gave him the street number of the earl's town house while he handed her pen, ink, and a small square of parchment on which to write a note. As she leaned over the counter, some impish devil seemed to be sitting on her shoulder. She penned,

> *To My Dearest Meg*
> *From Your Secret Admirer*

No one had ever sent her flowers before. No one had ever sent her anything. She had no beau, no gentlemen callers, not even any male acquaintances other than her cousins, but oh, how she wished she had one. A daring, dangerous rogue who would sweep into the center of Patricia's boring musicale, meet Meg's eyes across the room, profess his undying love for her, sweep her off her feet, and carry her from the parlor as all the ladies in the room gasped and Aunt Lucy swooned. All the while, he would be showering Meg's face with kisses. . . .

Male voices and laughter coming up from behind brought her back to reality. Lest anyone see what she had written, she quickly sanded the card, then stuffed it into the envelope and was writing her name with a flourish on the front just as two men stepped next to her at the counter.

"So what will it be, Godfrey?" asked a deep male voice, the sound of which, for some odd reason, sent shivers down Meg's spine. "Roses? Daisies? Carnations? What will woo your fair maid's hand and make her beg you to marry?"

The second man let out a loud, embarrassing hiccup, and Meg could smell alcohol on his breath from several feet away. Foxed in the middle of the day! She couldn't help glancing out of the corner of her eye to see what sort of nefarious characters had joined her. What she saw was the second man searching through his pockets.

"What's cheapest, Sebastian?" he asked in a slurred tone. "I don't seem to have any money left. You don't suppose that little vixen we paid for last night pocketed it, do you?"

Meg's brows shot up. Foxed men who consorted with women of dubious reputation!

"I'd say that last hand of cards had a little more to do with it," the man next to her chuckled.

Foxed men who consorted with women of dubious reputation and who gambled away all their money! What an adventure this was turning out to be! She couldn't prevent herself from tipping her head slightly for a better look. Without being more blatant, all she could see was the hand resting on the counter which belonged to the man named Sebastian. Obviously, he was from a family of distinction, for the hand boasted a huge signet ring. There was a crest in the middle, but what it meant or whom it represented she had no idea.

The hand itself was fascinating—fingers long and slender, nails trimmed and elegant. The hair dusting the back was dark and disappeared under the cuff of his shirt. The shirt, surely meant to be immaculately white, was covered with all sorts of spots. Blood? Mud? A button was torn away as though he had been brawling.

He was standing very close, much closer than was proper.

She realized she couldn't actually smell alcohol on his breath, but it lingered about his person, along with numerous other odors, some pleasant, some not. Tobacco, whiskey, horses, and a hint of male distinctly his own were clearly present. Since she had never stood close enough to a strange man to notice such things before, the moment was a rush for her senses, but the titillation quickly vanished as she realized that overlying all was the distinct smell of cheap perfume.

She turned to step away just as she realized, to her horror, that he was speaking to her!

"What say you, Godfrey? Let's ask an expert." Somehow, he had moved closer without her noticing, and he leaned against the counter on an elbow. His breath, warm and sweet, brushed against her ear, sending goose bumps shooting down the backs of her arms. "Give us your opinion, please, *chèrie.*"

"About what?" She stared straight ahead, shocked to find she had answered him when she should have run away. Something about the way that French endearment had rolled off his tongue made her want to hear what else he might have to say.

"About flowers. If I wanted to convince you that you were the love of my life . . . that you had to marry me and no other . . . that you were the only woman in the world for me"—he was inhaling the scent of her hair, she was certain of it!—"what should I select which would convince you that I was the only man for you?"

Although she hadn't felt him move a muscle, she was certain he had shifted even closer. He wasn't touching her anywhere, but every single inch of her—flesh, bone, skin, hair—felt shockingly alive as though he were pressed against her from top to bottom.

She swallowed and found her voice, offering lamely, "Roses are always nice . . ."

"Ah, yes, roses. My favorite. But what color? Red for passion? White for innocence? Pink for . . . love?"

His lips were so near to her cheek, she could feel the heat

of them hovering as though he intended to kiss her. The very idea was ludicrous. He was probably slightly intoxicated, which would explain his forward behavior. Aunt Lucy had harangued enough times that a drunkard would act any despicable way, usually, when she was going on about Meg's father, who had been known to tip a few pints.

Lifting her head, she turned, finding his lips were right there. So very close. Warm and soft and inviting. His cheeks were stubbly with his morning beard; after his night of frolicking, he hadn't had time to see to his morning toilette. She couldn't help raising her eyes to meet his.

On looking at his handsome face, she gasped, frozen in place by the sight. Quickly recovering her senses, she stepped away, shaking her head and trying to clear her vision, for surely it was playing dastardly tricks on her.

He was the precise image of the hero in *Pirate's Pleasure*. All that dark hair, thick and wavy, was worn longer than proper and held back with a black cord. His eyes, blue as the deep ocean was said to be, had a cold, assessing gaze that took in every detail and missed nothing. Broad shoulders tapered down to a thin waist and long, long legs. He was even dressed in black breeches and boots, his long cloak slung casually over his shoulders, making him look every inch the pirate she had dreamed of as she had read and reread her favorite romantic novel. All he lacked was a large sword sheathed at his side and a gold earring looped through his ear.

That clinched it! Her fantasy life had led her so far astray that she could no longer distinguish dreams from reality. At that moment, she swore off the romances for the next six months. There would be no trip to the bookseller that day or any day for a long while.

"Have we met?" Sebastian Stuart stared into the most amazing pair of emerald eyes he had ever seen.

"Why do you ask?"

"Merely because of the way you're looking at me. As though you've always known me."

Meg instantly blushed bright crimson, remembering she was plain, dull, boring Meg MacDonald. Even her name was ordinary. "Beg pardon, sir. My apologies."

Sebastian had been aware of her from the moment he had entered the florist's shop. It was hard not to notice her. Even in that dreadful, worn cloak which covered her, it was easy to ascertain that she was incredibly shapely, with a tall physique and tiny waist. The fall of her skirts perfectly outlined her well-rounded buttocks and covered what he was sure had to be long, graceful legs.

Up close, she was lovely, a becoming blush brightening her smooth cheeks. Her face was heart-shaped with a dainty chin and upturned nose. Luscious, ruby red lips, the kind a gentleman dreamed about kissing, pouted at him. Full, round breasts, more than enough to fill a man's hands with some left to spare, pushed against the bodice of the dress, as though they longed to burst free. What he wouldn't give to see her in a fashionable low-cut gown, displaying an arresting amount of creamy bosom.

As it was, it appeared she was hiding her good looks. What little he could see of her hair was pulled back and braided so tightly it had to hurt, and it was hidden under a ridiculous hat. The locks looked red and were probably stunning when they hung down her back in loose disarray. And those eyes! Bright green, as verdant as a field of grass on a summer day. A man could lose himself in those eyes.

God, but he loved a pretty girl. After the past weeks of gambling, debauchery and loose women, she was like a breath of fresh air. He shifted closer, relishing how his presence unnerved her, which was the way it always went when he was around women—whether they knew who he was or not. Many flustered and swooned because of his family name, but others, like this unknown girl, reacted to his presence for very different reasons. While he didn't consider himself a vain man, it was simply a fact of his life that women found him exceptionally attractive. If he had been born a groom in his father's stables, he would still have had his pick of females. High-born and low.

"No apology necessary," he said. "When I first saw you standing there, I felt as though I might know you as well."

"You did?" she gulped.

"There's just something about you. Do I know your family, perhaps?"

"No." She shook her head. He was obviously a gentleman, and he probably did know some of her cousins, but she would never let on. She didn't want to share this moment with anyone. Plus, to say her family name, or mention her cousin, the young earl, might cause him to realize who she was. Knowing her station in life, he would end their brief encounter in a heartbeat. "I'm sure you don't."

Sebastian wondered if she was a governess or some noblewoman's abigail. She obviously knew how to carry herself. It had been quite some time since he had enjoyed a governess. The prim and proper young ladies were completely different once they let their hair down. He longed to see this woman's hair set free.

"What's your name, *chèrie?*"

"Meg MacDonald," she stated readily, as her heart did another flip-flop on hearing his French.

"May I call you Meg?" he asked. Without waiting for her response, he picked up her hand and studied it intently, running his thumb across the long, slender fingers, the callused palms. They were clean, strong hands and would feel so lovely roaming through his hair, across his chest and other more sensitive areas. Deliberately, he kissed the back, letting his breath skim across it, feeling her skin tighten and tingle in response. "But only if you agree to call me Sebastian."

What would be the harm? She would never see the rogue again after today. "I . . . I guess that would be all right."

"Meg, I must confess one of my deepest, darkest secrets."

His gaze penetrated hers, demanding all her attention. She couldn't have looked elsewhere if she had wanted to, which she didn't. There was something so absolutely delicious about having him stare at her like that. "What is it?"

"I love"—the word *love* rolled off his tongue as though he meant to caress her with it—"redheaded women."

If he had doused her with a bucket of cold water, the effect couldn't have been more immediate or more complete. The insolent cad was teasing her! If Aunt Lucy had told her once, she had told her a thousand times: men hated red hair on women, finding it unattractive in the extreme and believing it to be an indicator of bad moral character. Secretly, she had always loved the long, flowing chestnut locks, but she was continually terrified that some man would look at her and think her loose.

This man's false flattery gave her the strength she needed to end the encounter.

"Excuse me," she said, wrenching her eyes away from his and looking around for the florist's helper.

Sebastian's eyes darkened in consternation. The moment the words had left his mouth, he realized he had said the wrong thing, and was at a loss as to the reason. From his vast experience with the opposite sex, he was aware of all the ways to sway and charm. His sexual prowess was legendary. Complimenting a woman on her hair—either the style or the color—was an approach he had used often and well. It always worked.

"What is it, *chèrie*? What have I done?"

"Nothing, sir."

"Now it's 'sir.' I am Sebastian, remember?"

"I simply need to be going." Looking around for the clerk, she found him down the aisle, showing Sebastian's drunken friend a collection of potted plants. She waved and caught his eye, and he indicated he would help her in a minute. An extra minute spent standing next to Sebastian suddenly seemed like an eternity.

He leaned close again and slipped his hand in hers, smiling the smile that never failed to charm a female. She tried to jerk her hand away from the intimate and improper contact, but he held on tight, enjoying the feel of her soft flesh against his own. With his thumb, he made small circles in the center of her palm. "Tell me what I said to upset you so."

Meg wished the floor would open and swallow her whole. She jerked around with fire in her eyes, her furious gaze surprising him. "You're a cruel man, Sebastian. A wretched scoundrel!" There, she had told him!

"My dear Meg, I'm cut to the quick." He put his free hand over his heart, then chuckled at her fury, which only incensed her further.

"I'm sure you enjoy your fun, accosting one such as me in this public place. To tease me and toy with my affections. But to ridicule me! So blatantly. You're horrid!"

He had been called a cad and a villain by many women in his life, so the words were nothing new, but this woman continually surprised him. He thought they had been enjoying a bit of innocent flirtation, and he truly wasn't sure what he had done. "How did I ridicule you?"

"As if you didn't know!"

"Tell me!"

"My hair! I can't help it if it's red! I know I'm plain, but you don't have to be so mean about it." To Meg's great horror and shame, tears welled into her eyes, and she looked away, frantically trying to once again summon the clerk. Sebastian's hand, firm and insistent under her chin, forced her to look back at him.

"You think I was making fun of your hair?"

His consternation was so evident, she paused. "Weren't you?"

"No, you silly girl. Has it been so long since anyone's given you a compliment that you don't know one when you hear one?"

His remark was too close to the painful truth. No one ever complimented her—about anything. "You're teasing me, and it's very unbecoming."

"Really? Well, I'll have you know that red is my favorite color of hair on a woman. And I'm willing to bet yours is more auburn than red. Although it's hard to tell with the way you've hidden it under that absurd hat."

"Absurd hat!" she hissed quietly, as she surreptitiously glanced around, hoping no one was close enough to hear their appalling argument. Before she knew what he was about, he had reached for the pin in the back and removed it from her head. "What . . . what . . . ," she managed to sputter, "what on earth do you think you're doing?"

"Just checking to see if I'm right."

"You are the most rude, unconscionable boor I've ever had the displeasure to encounter . . ."

"Lovely," he whispered seductively, stopping her diatribe in midbreath. He toyed with a long strand which had come loose when he removed the blasted hat. It was soft and silky and smelled of roses. "Auburn, with gold highlights. Perfectly lovely."

Moving like a giant, predatory cat, until she was pinned against the counter, he leaned against her, pressed fully along her side. His chest was wedged against her arm, her thigh enfolded in both of his. She could feel him—there!—and blushed even brighter scarlet if that was possible.

She knew she should push him away, scream or run or slap him for his contemptuous words and audacious behavior, but something about the way he was touching her, the way he was looking at her, sent a wave of butterflies shooting through her stomach, out to all her limbs, until she felt so weak she could hardly stand. "Don't tease me."

"I never say things I don't mean."

He dipped his head so he was right next to her ear. She turned, and their lips hovered only inches apart, setting her heart to racing again. What would it feel like if he touched his to her own?

Raising her gaze, she could see far into those exquisite azure eyes. He looked so sincere, but then, Aunt Lucy had always warned her that a scoundrel could say any enticing thing and make it sound true. She shook herself back to reality once again. "You can't be serious. I don't care how much you insist the sentiment is genuine; it's heartless of you to say such a cruel thing to me."

"Meg," he growled in frustration, "I absolutely adore red-headed women. They have a fire in their blood which gives them an incredible passion not found in other females. Is that true with you, *chèrie?* Is there a raging fire inside, waiting to burst into flame for the right man?"

"Oh . . . you! Stop it! Just stop it!" She elbowed him hard, rewarding herself by pushing him away just as the clerk stepped behind the counter.

"Are you all right, miss?" the clerk asked, his eyes going from her, to Sebastian, to his friend who was weaving and swaying.

"I'm fine. My hat came loose and this . . . this *gentleman* retrieved it for me." While stuffing as much of her hair as she could under the brim, she gave Sebastian a furious stare, daring him to contradict her. For once, he kept his mouth shut. She turned back to the clerk with as pleasant a smile as she could manage, although her cheeks were so hot, she felt she might ignite. "I just need to pay for these flowers."

As she talked, she busied her hands reaching for her purse, refusing to look at Sebastian. Unfortunately, it was nowhere to be found. "Oh no, I've mislaid my reticule. It had all my money in it. This is most embarrassing."

"It's no problem, Meg. I'll pay for them," Sebastian offered.

"You most certainly will not." She tapped a finger against her lip, thinking back on her movements for the past hour. "I must have left it at Madame LaFarge's. I don't remember having it after I departed." She looked apologetically at the clerk. "Give me a minute, please. It's just down the street. I'll fetch it and be right back to pay."

She turned and hurried to the door which caused her to miss Sebastian laying his own coin on the counter to pay for the flowers. With a wink and a nod at the clerk, he followed her, chuckling over the way her hat barely contained her braids, how her hips swayed seductively under her cloak as she stomped away so angrily. He wasn't done tormenting the delectable Meg MacDonald. Not by a long shot.

CHAPTER TWO

Meg had not taken three steps past the door of the florist's shop before she realized she was not alone.

"What do you think you're doing?" she groaned in dismay as he took her hand and slipped it into the crook of his arm as though he had done it a thousand times before. Furtively, she glanced around, hoping to see no one she knew. What if word of this caper got back to Aunt Lucy? What if, heaven forbid, Aunt Lucy passed by right at this moment? The older woman would very likely suffer an apoplexy.

Luckily, only the faces of strangers stared back at her, and there was an added bit of good news. The drunkard, Godfrey, appeared to be nowhere in sight.

"I'm accompanying you to Madame LaFarge's dress shop."

"You most certainly are not."

"I most certainly am."

From his authoritative tone, she could tell he was a man used to giving orders and having them immediately obeyed.

Goodness, but he was in for a rude awakening. "I do not need an escort. Especially from you."

"Really? You appear to be cavorting about London by yourself. There's no telling what sort of scoundrel you might meet up with if left to your own devices."

"I hardly think any scoundrels I might chance upon could possibly be any worse than the ones I've already encountered today." He had the audacity to laugh heartily, which raised her ire and shortened her temper a few more notches.

"Darling Meg, what a refreshing girl you are."

"I am hardly a girl, and I am not, nor will I ever be, your darling." She tried to wrench her arm away, which was impossible with his tight grip, when she suddenly saw Lucy's carriage lumbering toward them. The shades would be pulled against the draft, so possibilities were slim that Lucy would look out and see. But what if she did? Or, more likely, what if the driver or one of the footmen noticed her?

Panicked, she looked around for a place to hide. Seeing none, she did the next best thing. She tripped, thinking to fall to her knees and be shielded from view by the passersby, but Sebastian acted the gentleman just when she least expected it. He immediately reached for her and caught her before she could land on the ground. Instinctively, her own hands grabbed for purchase to break her fall, and through no intent on her part, she found her arms wrapped around his waist.

Inadvertently, she had found the best and worst possible hiding place. Her ear was pressed over his heart, and she could hear its strong, steady beat. Her breasts pushed firmly against his chest, and she was disturbingly aware of them in a way she had never noticed before. They felt tight and hard and ached painfully.

Sebastian took full advantage of their precarious stance. Knowing their cloaks shielded them from curious eyes, he wrapped his arms around her tiny waist as well. She was taller than any girl he had held in the past, and the curious thought flashed that he had missed something in his female conquests by constantly seeking out petite women. She was luscious and full-figured, and all her soft places perfectly fit his hard ones.

"Are you all right?" he asked, his voice full of concern.

"Yes," she answered, raising her eyes to his, which was a grave mistake since he was looking at her with such fierce intensity. Still, she forced herself to hold his gaze as she listened to the jingle of the harness and the creak of the wheels as the carriage neared. "Just give me a moment."

"Are you hurt?"

"No."

Sebastian stared into those emerald eyes. He felt as though he could read her mind. She was hiding, from someone or something. He couldn't have received the message more clearly if she had spoken it aloud. "What's amiss, *chère?*"

Meg thought about lying, but she needed a few more moments for the carriage to rattle out of sight. Giving him part of the truth seemed opportune. "I thought I saw my aunt."

"She doesn't know you're out and about?"

"No. She thinks I went home an hour ago in a cab."

"Ah . . . I see." Sebastian looked around, wondering where the woman might be. "No one's watching."

"Another minute."

"Don't hurry on my account." Sebastian was enjoying every moment of the scandalous encounter. Although he was raised to be a gentleman, he rarely acted like one. He was used to behaving in any rude, brash way, with little or no regard for the feelings of others, and he couldn't see any reason to reform at this late date. Meg was effectively trapped, and she felt so bloody good in his embrace. Before she had time to realize what he was about, he lowered one hand from her waist to her buttock. It was soft and firm, and he rubbed his palm in a slow circle.

"What are you doing?" she managed to sputter.

"You are so delicious, *chèrie*. How can you expect me to resist when you tease me so unmercifully?"

"I am teasing you? I'm doing no such thing."

"You practically threw yourself into my arms."

"I did not. Unhand me this instant!"

"Or what?"

"I'll . . . I'll . . ." She paused, hearing the carriage passing directly behind her. For all intents and purposes, she was trapped for at least the next minute, and the rascal was taking every advantage. "I'll scream."

"Will you? I wonder. Let's see." His hand shifted lower and urged her groin into his. Although he had meant only to torment the sweet thing, he quickly found that the joke was on himself. There was something so delightful about the way her hips met his own.

With stunning clarity, he indulged in a flight of fancy, envisioning her naked and splayed beneath him on a soft bed covered with plump pillows and the finest silk sheets. Her auburn hair would be fanned out about her head, her creamy white breasts marked red from his hands and mouth, her nipples hard and begging further attention. She would be ready to receive him, her legs wrapped around his waist.

The idea was so enticing that his unruly body eagerly reacted. His maleness stirred and began to harden.

Meg's knowledge of the intimate acts that occurred between men and women was mostly gleaned from the whisperings of the maids who talked freely when they didn't know anyone was around to hear. However, some ancient, primal part of her received his sexual message loudly and clearly. She knew what she was feeling and what was happening to him.

Her body wanted to respond! There was suddenly a terrible, fluttering ache low in her stomach, and it took every bit of effort she could muster to keep from flexing her hips against his, somehow knowing that she could ease her agony by doing so.

Through the mix of intense physical pain and pleasure, she realized two scattered thoughts. The first caused her giddy excitement. To think that such a handsome, virile interloper found her desirable! The second flooded her with acute embarrassment. The blackguard was even more reprehensible than she had imagined.

With a jingle of harness bells, the carriage turned the corner behind Meg, and she gave Sebastian a hearty shove, hoping to be swept into the crowd. No luck. Before she could take a step, he was once again by her side, his arm holding hers.

The look of consternation she flashed him caused him to laugh aloud again. He couldn't remember the last time he had found such innocent delight in an afternoon escapade. "My, what a sinister look. Are you perhaps conjuring up ways I might meet my early demise?"

"No," Meg responded baldly, "I was thinking how much you remind me of some sort of vermin, like a leech or some other horrible creature who attaches itself to your person and won't let go."

"I have been called many things, but never a leech. My compliments on your ingenuity."

"I take it back. I think you remind me of something I stepped in once at my uncle's farm." His smile at her insult was infuriating.

"Your attempts to disparage my character will do you no good. I will not leave your side until you are safely home from this afternoon's daring adventure."

That was the last thing she needed! "You most certainly will not. And I would hardly call shopping an 'adventure,'" she insisted, although she was already considering it such. What luscious memories she would have of the knave. She hadn't felt so angry—or so alive—in years.

Just then, they arrived at the dress shop, and she turned to Sebastian, the move once again bringing the front of her body brushing dangerously against his. "Well, thank you for seeing me here. I'll just get my bag and be on my way."

"Let's go in, shall we?" he remarked, opening the door and setting off the small bell which announced their arrival and caused the modiste to come scurrying from the back.

In the three hours Meg had spent with the woman that morning, she had been polite, dignified and restrained, but when she saw Sebastian standing in her doorway, she suddenly became a different person, giving a shriek of delight that could have broken glass.

"You know her?" Meg asked out of the corner of her mouth.

"Of course."

"But how?"

"I have purchased many gowns from madame." Flashing Meg his most wicked smile, he couldn't help adding, "I am a generous man when the right female catches my attention."

Meg stared in wide-eyed amazement as Sebastian took the dressmaker's hand and kissed the back all the way to her elbow, all the while flirting and whispering playfully to the older woman in fluent French. Meg's cheeks were flushed just from watching. What would it feel like to have Sebastian's lips touch her like that, to hear those words spoken so softly and so deliciously?

The pair conversed for long minutes while Meg stood stoically invisible by his side, waiting for the warm welcome to be over so she could do her business and make some kind of gracious exit. The encounter lasted forever, allowing her ample time to ponder why he would be buying dresses for women. There could only be one reason. He kept them! Mistresses! He was the kind of man who kept mistresses!

She could just picture what type of women they were. Beauties. Voluptuous blondes with flowing locks, rosy cheeks, ruby lips and French accents. To her surprise, the images pained her. She didn't want to imagine *her* Sebastian in the arms of enticing wantons.

The pair was still talking rapidly in the foreign language when it gradually became apparent that they were talking about her! What were they saying? Oh, a pox on Aunt Lucy for not letting her have more schooling!

Sebastian and the modiste exchanged a significant look, and Meg could no longer stand it. She asked Sebastian, "What did she say?"

"Don't you speak French?"

"I never learned, and I find it quite rude for the two of you to be discussing me when I can't understand what you're saying."

"Well, I was simply remarking that you are a rare beauty—"

"Oh . . . stop it. I hate this incessant teasing which you find so entertaining."

"Are we back to that again? You will not tell me what I think of your looks."

"And you will not be so mean to me!"

The modiste, sensing they were about to have a full-blown argument in the front of her shop, intervened. "Mademoiselle, I am so glad you have returned. I did not know you were a friend of monsieur."

"Well . . . ," Meg said lamely, refusing to lie and say she would never befriend one such as he, but being too polite to tell the rude truth about the man.

Sebastian didn't hesitate, butting his nose right in and letting the woman think the very worst. "We are good, good friends, aren't we, *chèrie?*"

Meg elbowed him hard, appreciating the grunt of pain that followed. "We are acquaintances, madame, nothing more. Now if I could—"

"Monsieur will not wish to see you in the dress your aunt selected. It will never do. We will change it, no?"

"No," Meg said. "I just want to—"

Sebastian and madame engaged in another flurry of French, all the while looking at her as though she were some kind of abandoned street urchin. She wished the floor would open so she could fall through. Before she realized what was happening, madame had the offending cheap fabric and awful yellow trim in her hands and was showing them to Sebastian, whose distaste was obvious.

"Your aunt would dress you in this, Meg?" Sebastian asked.

"It's fine," she answered through tight lips.

"It's terrible. With your hair and height, you need something which demands attention."

"Mais oui, oui!" madame enjoined. "I tried to tell her aunt, but she would not listen."

Sebastian wondered again who Meg's family was. If they had the money to purchase a dress from Madame LaFarge, they were obviously well off. Perhaps her aunt was one of those commoners who was just making a fortune in the new day and age. She probably had plenty of money to spend but no taste.

"Look at this one," he said, picking up a bolt of dark green silk. He unraveled the end with a practiced hand and draped it across her shoulder and bosom. "Yes. This is you, my darling. It brings out the color of your eyes." He took a step back, admiring his work. "Umm . . . very nice."

Meg stood still as a statue, wondering why there was such an ache in her heart. The green he had selected was the exact one she had espied herself but didn't dare request of her aunt. It was exactly the bold sort of color that never failed to send Aunt Lucy into a tizzy.

The dressmaker came to his aid, offering him swatches of lace and various bolts of satin and silk which he draped and wrapped. Each one to catch his attention was one Meg would have selected herself if she had been given the choice. She was only rescued from the embarrassing scene when two other customers entered the shop. As Madame went to give them assistance, Meg was left alone under Sebastian's careful scrutiny.

Sebastian could imagine her in the flowing silk, how it would cling to her delectable curves, how it would hang and sway as she moved. He leaned closer, loving her smell and the wary look she gave him. "Let's tell madame to use the green silk."

His voice was soft and seductive, like one lover would use with another, and he talked as though they had purchased her dresses together forever. The pain around her heart grew fierce. "The dress my aunt selected will be fine."

"It will be awful."

Since he was so clearly correct, Meg could see no use arguing about it. "Still, it will have to be the yellow."

"You have such fire in you, girl," he asserted, wanting to shake her.

"Really, Sebastian . . ."

"You do," he insisted. "Are you always so pliant at the hands of others? You're a woman full-grown. Can you not refuse to wear what your aunt desires?"

Meg wished she could tell him how it was in her life. Long ago, she had learned that dissension was pointless. Her life passed smoothly, if not boringly, when she simply made things easier for everyone else by acceding to their wishes. She sighed, "No, I can't go against her."

Sebastian saw the look in her eye, the sadness and resignation, and for some reason, he wanted desperately to chase it away. He didn't know why the woman affected him as she did, but his afternoon of play had somehow turned into something more. "Let me buy it for you."

"You know how inappropriate such an act would be."

"Do I look like I care?"

"No, you don't." She smiled.

It was the first genuine smile he had received from her, and it was dazzling. "Then, let me buy it. You can wear it just for me."

The scandalous idea would have been shocking if it wasn't so ludicrous. She would never be alone with him. She would never see him again. A clock chiming the hour from the back of the shop brought her reeling back to the present. She glanced at her timepiece in horror. Tea would begin in exactly thirty minutes. Suddenly, she felt like Cinderella leaving the ball.

"I have to go." Frantically looking around, she caught madame's eye. Just as she was about to ask if anyone had found her reticule, one of the assistants came from the back room carrying it.

"I'll see you home," Sebastian reminded as she reached for it and secured the strap around her wrist.

"That won't be necessary." She hurried out the door, leaving so quickly that she did not see or hear Sebastian giving Madame LaFarge quick and explicit instructions.

Like an impossible shadow, he appeared by her side just as she opened her reticule to discover that her purse was empty. "Oh, no! My money."

"It's gone?"

"Yes." She would never be able to go back and pay for the flowers, but it was probably just as well. There wasn't time anyway. She sighed, the weight of the world pressing down on her.

"Let's go back and tell madame," Sebastian suggested, feeling horribly irritated that someone had taken advantage of his Meg. Odd, but he already thought of her as *his*. "She would want to know."

"No. I'm sure who ever took it must have needed it more than me." Up and down the busy street, cabs were bustling past, and one stopped right in front of them to let off a passenger. She raised her hand to motion the driver when her dilemma became apparent. With no money, how was she to get home? Why, oh why, had she ever wished for an adventure? They were not all they were cracked up to be.

Sebastian never passed up an opportunity. He would see her home now; she had no other choice. While she stood lost in thought, he hailed the driver. With the greatest anticipation, he wrapped his hands around her shapely waist and lifted her up. She was nearly all the way inside before she noticed what he was about.

"What do you think you're doing?" Hadn't she asked him the same question a dozen times already?

She was looking at him over her shoulder, giving him a delicious view of her backside and legs. If he could have been sure no one was looking, he would have run a hand along her flank, not just to feel her curvaceous leg muscles, but also for the reaction he knew his caress would elicit.

All innocence, he responded, "I'm seeing you home."

Meg bit back a retort. If he didn't pay her way, she would never make it on time, and her absence would be discovered. Her gaze was drawn to the dark interior. It was a small cab, built for two passengers, which meant they would have to share the seat. "Straight there, and no funny business, do you hear?"

"What kind of funny business could I possibly create?"

Meg snorted, then looked up at the driver, who was waiting for a direction "Mayfair, please. As quickly as you can. I'm very late." She glanced at Sebastian, wishing he wasn't there to hear, but it couldn't be helped. "The Earl of Redding's town house." Sebastian's interest piqued like a tangible thing, but she ignored him. "Pull up at the mews. I'll need to use the servants' entrance in the back." The driver tipped his hat as she ducked her head and sat.

"Does your aunt hold a position in the earl's household?" Sebastian asked, trying to sound casually interested.

"Yes, a very high position," she responded blithely. Only the earl's mother!

Sebastian smiled to himself. Probably the housekeeper or some other. "Do you work for the earl as well?"

She gave a funny little laugh which he couldn't begin to decipher.

"All the time."

Sebastian knew the young earl whose father had died when

he was a babe. He also knew the earl's mother, the pompous, insufferable Lucinda Smythewaite. If he hadn't had a clear plan before with regard to Meg, he had one now. He would spend his last few days in London seducing her, knowing how irritated Lucy would be if she ever found out that the renowned scoundrel, Sebastian Stuart, had worked his wiles on a Redding employee.

Meg scooted to the far corner which wasn't far enough. Sebastian entered and slid across as well, until he was touching her again the entire length from her shoulder to her feet. She didn't dare turn her head to give him the scathing look she knew he deserved. His lips would be too close to her own, and she couldn't help the overwhelming feeling that he would kiss her if he could. As it was, she was wedged against the squab, unable to move. "Must you sit so close?"

"Yes, I'm afraid I must. You see"—he shifted to the side and laid his arm across the back of the seat—"I simply can't behave when I have a beautiful woman so close and all to myself. I'm impossible, I know. It's my greatest fault."

"And I am so *beautiful,* you simply cannot resist me?" she remarked sarcastically.

"Ah, so now you finally believe me."

"I do not believe you—"

He cut off any further comment she might have made by moving his arm so it was resting across her shoulders. She was turned into him, and her breasts were forced up against his broad chest, where they once again swelled and began to ache. She meant to push him away and give him a verbal set down, but one look into those striking blue eyes instantly killed every dastardly remark she could have made.

In his arms, she felt wanted, desired, cherished. In her entire life, she had never experienced anything that prepared her for having Sebastian's full attention focused on her. She couldn't turn away; she didn't even consider it. Even if she had thought about it, all remaining resistance would have vanished when he raised his hand and ran a finger along her bottom lip.

"*Chèrie*, I was wondering . . ."

"Yes?" she asked breathlessly, staring into his eyes, but his gaze was on her mouth.

Gads, but she was pretty. So innocent and trusting, unaware she was looking up at him so lustfully. Her rosy red lips were slightly parted. She ran her tongue across the delicate skin where he had just touched her, wetting it and nearly wrenching a groan from him. His trousers were suddenly much too tight. "Have you ever been kissed?"

"No," she whispered.

"No? Then, perhaps, I should be the first."

"I don't think that would be wise."

"Close your eyes."

She did. Without thinking. Without considering the consequences. His warm breath was on her face, his finger on her chin, tipping her face up. Then his lips were against her own, feather light, the softest brush. A brief touch. It ended as quickly as it had begun.

Her heart was beating so hard she thought it might burst from her chest. Her eyelids fluttered open, and he was still there. So near. So intense. She could only think of one thing to say. "Again."

"My pleasure."

This time, there was no softness, no hesitation. His mouth covered hers, working with an experience and skill she could not resist. His lips were moist and soft; he invited and offered every delicious thing about which a romantic girl could ever dream. He nibbled and bit, sucked and tasted, until Meg was tingling from the top of her head to the tips of her toes and felt so overwhelmed she wondered if she might actually swoon for the first time in her life.

So, this is desire, she realized. No wonder the poets extolled its virtues so avidly.

Unable to resist, she started to kiss him in return. Her arms wrapped around his neck, drawing the kiss deeper. He instantly welcomed her reaction, responding in kind, encircling her in his embrace and running his hands up and down her back. Squeezing her buttocks. Massaging her thigh. Gliding over a breast on his way to her hair. Only when she realized that he was reaching for her hat and intended to pull the pins did sanity begin to return. If her hair came down, the heavy mass would be impossible to fix, and she would never be able to get into the house undetected.

"Wait . . . wait, please," she entreated, pulling his hand to her lap. She was the one to wrench her lips away. Breathless, aching and wanting, she searched his eyes, confused by the emotion she saw there. Was it anger? Annoyance? Impatience? While her world had just been turned upside down, he regarded her coolly, as though he kissed strange women every day.

Of course, he probably did. Waylaying one such as herself might very well be a daily occurrence. She had heard about gentlemen wooing and trifling with virtuous maids, and she could just imagine the jokes and laughter he would initiate later at his club as he regaled his friends with his latest conquest.

Her mortification was now complete, although not all of her humiliation could be laid at his feet. Hadn't she willingly thrown herself into his arms, reveled in his embrace, returned his kiss? She had acted the complete wanton with a man who was a virtual stranger, and she couldn't help wondering if perhaps Aunt Lucy was right. Perhaps the personality of a strumpet really did flow through her veins, just waiting to burst out at the first opportunity.

"What is it?" she asked accusingly. "Why are you staring at me like that?"

"Like what?"

"As if I were some kind of loose woman."

"I can tell you're not," he chided gently. "It's clear you're new to love games.

So that was it! He was offended by her innocence. "I told you I'd never been kissed before. I'm sorry if I didn't perform to your expectations."

He laughed.

"I'm sure this sort of thing takes practice."

He laughed again, louder this time.

"I'll not apologize for my inexperience simply because I've not had the chance to indulge myself with every dandy I pass!"

He was fairly giggling as he leaned his head back against the squab, rubbing his hand over his eyes to wipe away the tears of mirth. "Oh, Meg . . . ," he started, but couldn't seem to finish whatever horrid, insulting thing he wanted to say. Would he laugh this hard tonight when he was entertaining his drunken friends with his latest conquest? She shuddered to think.

Just then, the carriage rumbled to a halt. The driver, as if sensing she was sneaking in, had the good sense to sit quietly rather than announcing their destination. She peeked out and, seeing the familiar gate, grabbed for the door. "I hate you," she avowed fervently, not daring to look at him. "You're a rude, mean bully, and I hate you . . ."

"Meg, you don't understand . . ."

He reached out a hand to catch hers, but she leaped to the ground and took off running.

"Meg . . . wait . . . ," she heard Sebastian call, but if he said anything else, his words were silenced by the closing of the gate. She huddled with her back against the wood, taking in the stables, the gardens, the house, and all the other mundane landmarks that delineated her boring, structured life.

Composing herself, she steadied her breathing and prepared to return to the safety of her aunt's world where scoundrels like Sebastian dared not enter.

CHAPTER THREE

Sebastian Stuart entered the Earl of Redding's mansion with Godfrey by his side. They were just late enough to be quite rude, but Lucinda Smythewaite wouldn't think of turning them away. Sebastian would one day be a duke; Godfrey, an earl. Any woman with a marriageable daughter welcomed them with open arms, no matter how unacceptable their behavior.

Godfrey was more sober than he had been when they had parted a few hours earlier, and he was a hilarious sight, staggering up the steps under the weight of the huge bouquet he had purchased at the florist's. The clerk had offered to deliver the large arrangement, but Godfrey insisted on presenting them to Patricia Smythewaite himself. Desperately in need of a rich wife to fund his bad habits until he came into his title and the wealth which accompanied it, he was hoping Patricia would be the answer to his prayers.

Sebastian laughed aloud everytime Godfrey mentioned the possibility of marrying. He cared not a whit about his responsibility to his family's title, so he never intended to wed. Not a highborn aristocrat or anyone else, and especially not for money. His predicament was no less dire than Godfrey's, however, but no one would ever learn the depths to which he had fallen. A proud man, the situation would remain his secret, unless he refused to accede to his father's demands. Then all of London would find out.

His father was a difficult, cold man who had served the Crown in the military for most of his life. Born a third son with no hope of a title, when his two older brothers had died heirless, he suddenly found himself a duke, a designation for which he had not been reared and one he had never wanted. As a self-made man, who had always worked hard, he couldn't seem to change his ways. He still rose at dawn, insisting that a man's life was meaningless unless he was toiling at one task or another.

His father constantly tried to foist the same lifestyle onto Sebastian, but he refused to embrace it. Sebastian wanted to do nothing but what he already did so well. He gambled, he wagered, he drank, he loved women, he slept all day and played all night and could see no reason to change his ways at the ripe old age of one score and five.

The fights between father and son had been unending, growing progressively worse the past two years, until Sebastian had finally pushed the duke past his limit. Even Sebastian had to admit that frittering away his first quarter's allowance on the third day of January was bad form. Plus, there was the debacle over the married woman and the duel that followed, which only added fuel to the duke's fire.

Still, even Sebastian could not have guessed at the duke's finely tuned revenge.

Banishment.

To Jamaica. To work like a hired servant at the family's plantation for five years. If he didn't sail with the tide on the fifteenth of February, he would be disowned and disinherited. The duke also intended to notify Sebastian's creditors that he would no longer pay any of his son's bills. He was even going to place a legal notice to that effect in the *Times*. For all intents and purposes, Sebastian would be cast adrift with no money, no credit, and no means of getting either.

He was furious. More than that, he was terrified.

On occasion, he had toyed with the idea of telling the duke to take his threats and stuff them, that he didn't need his money or his name, that he could and would make it on his own. But the sad fact was that he had no idea how to go about making a living, and the very idea of having his comfortable life snatched away left him as fearful as a child trembling with night terrors.

In a desperate attempt to cover his growing sense of panic, he behaved wilder than ever. Spending recklessly, taking greater risks, drinking and gaming harder and longer. He spent every hour of every day acting as though he were a condemned man facing the executioner come the dawn.

Which was exactly how he felt. However much he longed to scorn the duke's threats, he knew he wouldn't. His pride would not let him remain in London, the pathetic poor child of Polite Society. He would be on the ship on the fifteenth, sailing off to a new life and a new world, his future as uncertain as any convict sent in chains from Newgate.

The butler opened the door just then, drawing him out of his reverie. The retainer tried to take Godfrey's bouquet, but the man refused to relinquish his hold until he could place the unwieldy burden in Patricia's hands. Sebastian chuckled as they walked to the drawing room, where the tension shifted and increased as the butler announced his exalted presence. None of the mothers wanted him there, unless, of course, his gaze shifted to their own little darling.

His eyes did a quick scan of the room, and he guessed there were sixty or seventy people present. He immediately moved to a far corner, refusing to kowtow to Lucy Smythewaite. Catching a waiter's eye, he waved away the offered champagne,

asking for a whiskey instead. Godfrey was on the other side
of the room, putting on a good show, offering the flowers and
fawning over Patricia. She and her mother were both obviously
delighted. His eyes casually roamed over those standing around
the settee when they landed on the tall redhead. Meg Mac-
Donald.

He was so surprised that he nearly dropped his drink. The
little vixen obviously belonged at the gathering, although she
was not much of a welcome addition if the attitude of the
Smythewaite women was any indication. She was standing
in a hideous hand-me-down dress, which was too small and
hopelessly unfashionable, with some kind of silly lace cap
covering her hair, holding a pretty bouquet of flowers which
looked suspiciously like the very one he had paid for earlier
at the florist's. Who was she?

He didn't have to wait long to find out. Portia Poundstone
slithered up to his side as smoothly as a snake, followed by an
entourage of female companions who were as tiresome as she
was.

He and Portia were the same age, but she had the distinction
of being a widow for the past four years. At one time, he had
made the dreadful mistake of taking her as his paramour. The
relationship had lasted several tempestuous months, until the
night Sebastian was late for a rendezvous and Portia demanded
to know where he had been. The row that followed had been
a public one, with Portia hurling a bracelet and several juicy
epithets no gently bred lady should know, and Sebastian taking
a slap in the face for his efforts. He had promptly ended their
liaison, but Portia seemed forever determined to start it up
again.

Why Lucy had invited them both to the same party was a
mystery, but then, she had been in the country and probably
hadn't been privy to the gossip surrounding their public spats.

"Hello, darling," she fairly purred.

"Portia," he greeted her, tipping his drink in her direction. "You look to be enjoying yourself."

"Oh, I am. I simply couldn't pass up the chance to see little Patty hosting her first soirée." Her words dripped sarcasm and malice. "Isn't she delightful?"

"Yes," Sebastian said noncommittally, nodding in agreement, although he found Patty quite plain in a conventional sort of way with her extremely British blond hair and blue eyes. His tastes had recently taken a turn for a more striking type of woman—tall and alluring with the temper and passionate nature to match her red hair.

As casually as possible, so as not to alert Portia to any special curiosity, he said, "I haven't seen the Smythewaites in Town in quite some time. Do you know any of the people with Patty and Lucy?"

Portia was in her element, tossing out bits of gossip and mean innuendo about several of the people, which he had to suffer through until she finally reached the only person about whom he truly wanted to know.

"And, of course, there's dear cousin, Meg."

"Whose cousin is she?"

"Patty's. She's Lucy's niece."

Keeping a straight face at learning that piece of information was incredibly difficult. He had wondered if he would see her in the house, but not like this, thinking instead that she would walk through with a serving tray during dinner. The possibility had given him several good laughs, and he had found himself greatly anticipating her reaction. He was willing to bet she thought she would never see him again, but he had designs on the woman. After the passionate kiss they had shared in the hansom, there was no way he was going to let much time pass without enjoying another—and much, much more.

He had to know more, but couldn't appear too interested. "I'm confused. How is she related?"

"Her mother was the young earl's auntie, Eleanor Smythewaite. Lucy's sister-in-law,'' Portia added, as though that piece of information was supposed to explain everything. Seeing that he still didn't know, she prompted, ''You remember, darling. She created a huge scandal years ago by running off with a commoner. A singer or some such. They had a daughter together, and Lucy had to take the girl into her home after she was orphaned. I shudder to think how awful it must be, constantly having her about.''

''Why is that?''

''Well, you've got eyes, haven't you? Just look! Isn't she the most pathetic creature?'' Her friends tittered along with her. ''Gads, that dress alone would be enough to keep me constantly abed. I'd never show my face.''

Sebastian made no response, but boldly stared across the room at Meg, daring her to look his way, but she was thoroughly engrossed in listening to whatever the older woman next to her was saying. He was irritated that she hadn't noticed him. For some reason, he desperately wanted her to.

In the meantime, Portia buzzed on, her voice like a bothersome insect. Something she said pierced through his inattention. ''What was that?''

''I said, I'd like to see the bloke who's idiotic enough to be attracted to her. Those flowers she's holding? They were delivered a short while ago. The card said they were from her 'secret admirer.' ''

''The flowers?'' Sebastian asked, completely baffled. ''But they were purchased by . . .'' Realization of what he was about to disclose suddenly hit him, and he didn't finish his sentence.

''You know who her secret admirer is? Do tell.'' Portia rested a hand on his arm as though they were together. ''I'm dying to be the first to learn his identity.''

''I don't have any idea who it is,'' he answered, although he clearly remembered Meg signing a card when he stepped next to her at the florist's shop. The little vixen! She had been sending herself flowers, pretending for everyone's benefit that she had a beau when it was clear she did not.

He surveyed more of the scene, taking in Meg, the family members, her clothing, remembering bits and pieces she had spoken about her aunt during their afternoon jaunt. Many things about Meg were abundantly clear. She was the dreaded poor relation; shunned, abused and mistreated by the very family who should be caring for her, while they never let her forget how put-upon they were by having to support her.

Was ever there a woman more in need of a little spice in her life?

Sebastian instantly determined to give her all she could handle.

Deliberately, he removed Portia's hand from his arm. "If you'll excuse me, ladies, I rudely neglected our hostesses upon arriving. I need to make my hellos to the countess and Lady Patricia."

He moved across the room, making a direct path to Lucy, but waiting only for the moment Meg looked his way.

Meg's nose was buried in the bouquet she had selected earlier in the day. The butler, Giles, had entered the room carrying them, and since Patty had been receiving flowers for days, Lucy had instantly thought the flowers were for her. Then when she had read the card—aloud, since Lucy had insisted on it—causing Lucy to snatch it out of her hand to read the words herself, every minute of the deception had been worth it.

Aunt Lucy was in a high dudgeon, imagining that Meg had caught someone's eye. Watching her as she pondered and vexed over the situation, Meg decided she was having more fun than she had had in a very, very long time. Too bad her "secret admirer" couldn't send her another gift, perhaps one every day to Valentine's Day. Wouldn't that put Lucy in a dither!

Two new guests were announced. Not caring who was joining them, she hardly paid attention to their names, although the older woman next to her instantly huffed at the arrival of the marquess, Sebastian Stuart. She and another woman started whispering about him, so, of course, Meg had to listen. How could she not?

Meg had heard all the delicious stories and loved every one, thinking how wonderful it must be to be a man and to have the power and courage to do any outrageous thing. He kept all of London constantly humming with gossip over his antics. The latest rumor was that he had gambled away twenty thousand pounds on the turn of a single card.

Patty had mentioned numerous times that he was desperately handsome, and, as a future duke, he was at the top of Lucy's list of husband candidates. Meg could only wince as she imagined the wiles her two female relatives would use to convince him to offer for Patty.

Craning her neck, she tried to catch a glimpse of him through the dinner crowd packed in the room, but there were too many people. Her view was further impeded by the arrival of another of Patty's besotted swains, who was fawning over her with a bouquet of flowers so big that Meg couldn't even see what he looked like. He was such a ridiculous sight that she had to bury her nose in her own bouquet to keep from laughing aloud, which gave her the perfect opportunity to turn her attention to her two elderly companions, who were regaling each other with more of the nefarious gossip about the marquess.

The women chattered on about this woman and that husband, this scandal and that duel. What an exciting life the marquess led!

As she listened, she gradually became aware that someone was watching her. The power of the person's gaze was so strong that it was almost a physical sensation. She couldn't keep herself from looking around, as though some sort of invisible force was drawing her eyes.

She located him across the room, staring down at her with all the arrogance, charm and daring he possessed. Her jaw dropped open, and she forced it closed. If the devil, himself, had been standing there, she couldn't have been more surprised.

Immaculately turned out, he was dressed in formal blacks as sleek and shiny as his ebony hair. The white of his shirt and cravat were blinding against the dark clothing. He was taller and broader than any man in the room. As he crossed in slow, measured steps, he looked to be the panther he resembled, and he was heading straight for her, ready to pounce.

People spoke to him as he came nearer, he nodded acknowledgments to a few, women whispered behind their fans after he passed, but he kept his gaze focused on Meg. Even as he stepped up to Patty and Lucy, his gaze didn't lower. He was waiting for something from her: Recognition? Embarrassment? Fear? Anger? Shock?

She was certainly feeling all those and more. The blackguard smiled at her as though they shared some special joke. The dimples creasing his cheeks made him look wickedly handsome. He winked! Right at her! What did it mean? Was he going to say something? Embarrass her in some fashion?

The flowers! What if he noticed? Instantly, she was heartsick over her little deception. What if he mentioned meeting her at the florist's? What if he commented on her bouquet? If anyone found out she had sent them to herself, she would die of shame.

As he tore his gaze from hers and shifted it to Lucy, Meg turned away, unable to watch. Panicked, she walked to the back of the room, to the door the servants were using to come and go with their trays. She stepped into the back hall, welcoming the cooler air and the chance to be alone for a few moments while she collected herself.

No, he wouldn't notice the flowers. He was too self-absorbed. Other than recognizing her face, he probably remembered very little about their rendezvous. There was no reason to fret or dread. Still, she handed the bouquet to a passing maid, asking her to put them in water and send them up to her room. Calm once again, she took a deep breath and stepped back into the parlor, leaning against the back wall where she hoped to remain hidden until the dinner bell rang.

"So lovely to see you again, *chèrie*," the deep, unmistakable voice poured over her like warm honey, and she groaned.

"What are you doing here?" she hissed through tight lips.

"Why, *chèrie*, I was invited, of course. I'm an honored guest. Your dear aunt, Lucinda, informs me that I will be leading the march into dinner, with your lovely cousin, Patricia, on my arm."

Sebastian chuckled, surreptitiously slipped something into her hand, then walked away.

Meg looked around, wondering if anyone had seen the short exchange, but she needn't have worried. As usual, she could have burst into flames, and no one would have noticed. Her fingers curled around whatever he had placed in her palm, and she realized it was a piece of paper. It seemed to radiate with his body heat until her hand felt afire.

Unable to bear the suspense, she stepped into the back hall once again and opened the folded square.

Meet me behind the mews at midnight.

SS

Through the partially open door, she heard dinner announced. Wishing she could head for her room, but knowing it was too late to escape, she rejoined the crowd and moved to the back of the forming, paired line. Despite the number of people between her and the dining room, she managed to see Sebastian as he took Patty's arm and escorted her through the door.

Perhaps she imagined it, but it seemed as though he paused for a moment to catch her eye, as though the two of them shared a secret jest.

She wanted to die.

CHAPTER FOUR

Dinner was the most tedious, lengthy, laborious event Meg had encountered in all of her twenty years. Even though Sebastian sat thirty people away, she was aware of his every action during the meal. Through the clatter of plates and the din of voices, she could hear him laugh, hear him talk, sense when he shifted or turned his head. She couldn't have been more cognizant of his presence if he had been sitting next to her.

Through it all, the scrap of paper which she had stuck in her cleavage seemed to be burning a hole between her breasts. There had been no way to dispose of it; she could not just drop it on the floor or hand it to one of the servants.

She understood the reason he wanted to meet with her alone in the dark of night. He would practice more of his physical wiles on her, humor himself over her inexperience, and add to the lurid stories he planned to tell others when he was boasting of his female conquests. Was there no limit to how low the man would stoop for his fun?

How dare he come into her home and continue to torment

her like this! By the time the last plates were whisked away, her nerves were frayed to the breaking point, and she wanted nothing more than a few minutes alone with Sebastian so she could give him the dressing-down of his life.

The ladies retired to the parlor while the men had their port. Although Lucy had several rooms open and arranged for entertaining, most of the women chatted quietly while waiting for the men to rejoin them. Meg managed to sit with them for a few minutes, until the sound of the pianoforte drew her away.

When Meg entered the music salon, Patty was playing the instrument, and one of her friends was singing. Meg sat unobtrusively in a corner, tapping her foot and listening. The piece sounded like something by that Mozart fellow whom everyone liked. Meg didn't. She had not had enough training to enjoy the classical compositions Patty insisted on performing. Meg would have chosen a ballad or even something bawdy every time. Not that she would ever have a chance to perform for a group like this.

Lucy had forbidden her from playing years earlier, once they both realized how people turned to stare whenever Meg opened her mouth to sing, so Meg confined her musical moments to those times when Lucy was gone from the house and wouldn't hear Meg secretly picking away in the conservatory. The restriction seemed so grossly unfair, for Meg loved singing more than anything.

She couldn't help it that she had been born with a voice that was too loud and too low. She had a gift for striking the right keys, finding the proper pitch, and her sense of rhythm was adequate. She didn't think she sounded any worse than some of the other girls she had heard wailing away. Still, people seemed to prefer this breathy, wavery soprano which never failed to set Meg's teeth on edge.

Patty accompanied several others while they sang, then stood to sing while her girlfriend played. Patty's singing was the worst by far, but Meg endured it patiently with a smile on her face so that anyone watching would have thought she was thoroughly enchanted.

During Patty's fourth, and Meg hoped her last, number, she realized Sebastian had entered the room. There was no need to turn around to see him; his presence overwhelmed her senses. Out of the corner of her eye, she could see his entourage. That Poundstone woman, to whom Meg had been introduced but couldn't stand, was on his arm. Godfrey was by his side, and several others fluttered about. Was it always like that? Were others drawn to him as she had instantly been? Was she the only person who knew what he was truly like? Or, more likely, was she the only one who cared about the genuine state of his character? Money and position could cause people to overlook many flaws.

He and his friends chatted openly while Patty was singing, and as their ruckus grew, Meg became incensed. While she didn't care overly much for Patty's feelings, she knew her cousin wanted to impress Sebastian with her musical talents. Didn't these people have any manners?

Finally, she could stand it no longer. As Patty's number came to an end, Meg stood and looked directly at Sebastian. Odd, but it seemed as though he had been waiting for her to rise.

Hoping to keep the argument between the two of them, she asked quietly, "Do you mind?"

"Mind what, *chèrie?*"

With his words directed her way, his friends turned to look at her as well, but Meg refused to back down. Someone should have taught the obnoxious boor some manners years earlier. "Some of us want to listen to the singing. Do you think you could step outside?"

"No. I wish to remain here."

"Then, please be quiet." To Meg's dismay, others were now watching the exchange. Sebastian was in his element.

"So far, I haven't heard anything worth being quiet about."

Meg hoped Patty hadn't heard what he had just said. Patty thought her singing was exemplary and would be so hurt. "Is there any ill-mannered, callous remark from which you will refrain?"

"No," he laughed, "there is not. Perhaps if you were to sing . . ." He let the challenge hang in the air.

"Me?"

"If you've any talent, I might be able to force myself to listen." He sipped his drink and eyed her carefully. "Are you any good?" Several people snickered, and a woman gasped, at his imprudent sexual innuendo. "At the pianoforte, I mean."

Meg didn't understand why people were chuckling as she assured him, "I don't sing."

"Don't or can't, I wonder." He shrugged. "It's probably just as well. I wouldn't want you to embarrass yourself in front of everyone."

The bastard! Her cheeks flamed bright red as her anger reached a new height. Everyone in the room had heard his remark. How could she refuse to perform after he had so nearly insulted her? Still, Lucy would have a fit if Meg so much as touched the pianoforte.

Just as she was about to back down and walk away from the argument, Portia Poundstone made her decision for her. With a smirk at Meg and a proprietary pat on Sebastian's hand, she said, "Really, Sebastian, you're tormenting the poor creature. Leave her be."

The last thing Meg needed or wanted was pity from the petite blonde. Her eyes blazing, she met Sebastian's gaze. "Do you have a favorite song, Lord Stuart?"

"Anything will do." He gestured graciously toward the keyboard.

Meg stormed to the piano with her fingers gripped together, wishing they were wrapped around Sebastian's neck instead. As she took the bench, Patty looked at her, her pretty brow creased in concern. "Meg, do you think you should be doing this?"

"Quiet, Patty," Meg said, behaving in a thoroughly disgraceful manner for the first time in her life.

Her fingers moved across the keys in a dashing arpeggio while she searched her mind for an appropriate number. Finding none that this crowd could possibly enjoy, she settled on one of her favorites, a song her father had written about a lusty barmaid. The lyrics were witty and the tune lively, and the melody matched her voice. She plunged ahead, completely immersed in her task and oblivious to the others in the room.

Sebastian wasn't sure what he had expected when he taunted Meg into playing a song, but it certainly wasn't anything close to what he was witnessing. He had simply wanted to tease her, to fuel her temper and watch those lovely green eyes burn with indignation. Instead, he listened in stunned amazement as Meg dominated the keyboard and belted out a bawdy, raucous song, the likes of which he had never heard. Her husky contralto filled the room, but before he had the chance to contemplate how gifted she was, her performance was interrupted as she was overcome by a huge coughing fit.

Her affliction looked and sounded real enough, but it certainly seemed timed to coincide with Lucy's entrance into the salon. She swooped down on Meg upon realizing what her niece was about.

"Meg," Lucy said, sounding pleasant enough, but Sebastian was unconvinced. "I thought I heard you singing."

"Yes, I just took a quick turn," she replied, staring at the keys.

"How nice," Lucy murmured without any enthusiasm. "Are you finished?"

"Yes," she choked.

"Good. I'd like a word with you." Lucy smiled at those around the pianoforte, focusing in on her daughter. "Why don't you take a turn now, darling. We'll only be a moment."

Sebastian watched Lucinda depart, with Meg following on her heels like a whipped dog. What was happening? Was she not allowed to sing? Had he unknowingly placed her in her aunt's disfavor?

He tried to resume his place in the conversation going on around him, but he couldn't help glancing up when Lucinda and Meg left the main parlor, looking to see which way they turned as they stepped into the hall. Patty was singing now, off-key and badly, and the classical piece seemed so boring after what Meg had just performed. Patty was trying to catch his eye, probably so he would be enchanted by her voice, but he was uninterested.

Casually, he wandered away from Portia, Godfrey and the rest. He walked through the crowd, passing a few card tables without talking or catching anyone's eye. Before he knew what he was about, he was alone in the exquisitely decorated hall. There were three closed doors, and he listened at each; but the rooms appeared empty. Thinking they could only have gone upstairs, he climbed to the next floor. At the first room on his right, he found what he wanted.

The door was cracked a few inches, and he could hear Lucy berating Meg, who was just visible in the opening.

"... I apologize again," Meg was saying as he stepped closer to blatantly eavesdrop.

"What were you doing, making a spectacle of yourself like that?"

"I didn't mean to. I didn't think—"

"That's the problem, Meg," Lucy cut her off. "You didn't think. You never do. I've told you time and again how poorly you sing. When I entered the room, everyone was staring at you."

"No, they weren't. I'm sure hardly anyone even noticed."

"For pity's sake, even the marquess was staring! You were making a fool of yourself," Lucy scolded. "Isn't it bad enough that I must still put up with the whispers about your mother after all these years? She always had to be the center of attention. If you continue to carry on this way, they'll be talking about you the same way they always talked about her. Is that what you want? For people to think you're just like her?''

With the mention of her mother, Meg's backbone suddenly stiffened. She said quietly, almost as though it were a threat, ''Heaven forbid that anyone think I'm like my mother.''

Sebastian received the distinct impression that Lucy had finally gone one step too far without even realizing it. To save the old bat from her own folly, he rapped on the door.

''Yes? What is it?'' Lucy asked as he pushed the door open.

''Countess,'' he said politely. On seeing who had entered, Lucy straightened. Meg turned her face toward the wall, so he could not read her expression.

''Lord Stuart,'' Lucy said sweetly, ''did you need something?''

''Actually, I was looking for you.'' Sebastian was a master at manipulating women. He could mold Lucy Smythewaite into any shape he wanted. If only Meg would understand and welcome his ploy to rescue her. ''I think I might have caused some trouble for Miss MacDonald, and I wanted to confess my sin.''

''What is it you think you've done?'' Lucy asked, all smiles.

''Several of the women had been singing, and I noticed Miss MacDonald sitting by the pianoforte. I'm afraid I encouraged her. She didn't want to; but I wouldn't take no for an answer, and I kept pressuring her until she felt she had no choice. I had no idea she had so little talent for the endeavor, and I wanted to apologize for pushing her into a situation for which she was so obviously unprepared.''

''Well . . .'' Lucy paused, obviously unsure how to respond. Finally, she admitted, ''She has a tendency to do things she oughtn't. It is a proclivity which we are constantly trying to curb.''

''I'm sure it's hard for her to endure her mediocrity when

Patricia's star is shining so brightly.'' Sebastian wanted to gag when he saw how Lucy's pride puffed up at his mention of her daughter.

''You're absolutely right.''

''If I may?'' He gestured toward Meg, and Lucy nodded her acquiescence. ''Miss MacDonald?''

Meg felt him step close, and she wished her heart would simply quit beating. He had hated her singing! Since her parents' deaths, her most fervent wish had been to inherit a small bit of her beloved father's talents. She had always felt it would be like carrying a piece of him inside her. Now, the very first time she had actually sung for a group of people, this man . . . this rude, boorish stranger . . . this marquess . . . dared to criticize her for it. Tears welled into her eyes.

Why, oh why, were these recent days so difficult? She had endured censure for the past decade. Through every bit of it, she had held her head high, but lately . . . the harsh words cut so deeply and made her so angry.

''Yes, Lord Stuart?'' she answered with a shaky voice. It took every ounce of fortitude she possessed to turn and face him without spitting in his eye. The rogue took her hand and held it in his own.

Sebastian couldn't believe the effect her tears had on him. She was too tough to let them fall, but they were there, making her eyes sparkle like diamonds. He wished they were alone so he could wipe them away. Or, better yet, kiss them away. What an odd sensation. Never before had a woman's tears moved him to any sort of emotion.

With a sincerity of which he didn't believe himself capable, he made his amends, hoping Meg would read between the lines to the truth of his words. ''Please accept my apology. When I pressured you to sing for me, I had no idea of your talent. I can't tell you how surprised I was.''

Meg stood as still as a statue, looking into that handsome face and those dashing dark blue eyes. His back was to Lucy, and she couldn't possibly see the look that he was giving Meg. He was smiling, like the blackguard he was, and he had the audacity to wink.

"I'm sorry I embarrassed you," Meg said, trying her best to sound contrite. "I should have remembered my place."

"No, no," he offered like a true gallant. "It is I who apologize to you. After hearing the other women sing . . . your cousin, Patricia, in particular"—he gave another wink at this—"I was expecting more of the same. I must say I was completely unprepared for your performance."

The sarcasm in his voice was so evident, she glanced quickly at Lucy to see if she had caught it, but her aunt was staring at Sebastian as if the man could bring the dead back to life. Through it all, he continued to grip her hand so tightly that she feared the bones might break. She looked into his eyes and experienced the strangest perception, feeling as though she could read his mind. It was almost as if he was telling her he really had liked her singing. Which was ludicrous, of course. No one knew better than herself how terrible she sounded.

Wanting only to be alone, so she could once again lick the wounds she had sustained at his machinations, she said, not meaning it, "I hope I've not ruined your evening."

"Hardly. It is my greatest hope that I have not ruined yours through my appalling lack of manners." He turned back to face Lady Smythewaite. "May I escort the two of you back to your guests?"

"I think Meg has had enough excitement for one night," Lucy responded tightly, glaring at Meg and daring her to disagree.

"My aunt is right. I believe I feel a frightful headache coming on." Meg pulled her fingers away from Sebastian's, hating how empty she felt when their physical connection was broken.

"As you wish, Miss MacDonald." He took her hand again and bowed over it, kissing the back. "Until we meet again."

Was it her imagination, or was there a blatant invitation in his words? Did the rascal seriously think she was going to join him at midnight? "Good night, Lord Stuart, Aunt Lucy." With a quick curtsey, she was out the door and scurrying toward the back stairs and the safety of her room.

As she went, she heard Lucy remark, "That girl! I don't know what's to become of her."

Sebastian chuckled in response, as though he knew something the rest of them did not.

CHAPTER FIVE

Meg took a deep breath as she walked outside into the cold, damp air. She had tried to be an obedient niece and stay in her room as she had been ordered; but the sounds from the party kept drifting up the stairs, and she couldn't overcome the feeling that she was being hidden away like some demented relative of whom everyone was ashamed.

The February night was a brisk but beautiful one as the fog swirled around the trees and bushes. Shivering, she pulled her cloak tighter. Her destination was the gazebo at the back of the garden. It was mostly hidden from the house by the rose bushes, and the thick fog was an added benefit, although no one would look for her. Not there, or anywhere for that matter. She could probably run off all night and no one would suspect or care.

Slinking along in the shadows, she passed under the back balcony and nearly groaned when she heard a familiar male voice up above. Sebastian was speaking to another man. His voice was tight and controlled.

"Are you worried I won't go, Father?"

Sebastian's father was here? She had not met him, and she was certain she would have heard the buzz if a duke had walked into the room. Perhaps he had arrived later after she had retired to her room.

"I never worry," the man responded to Sebastian in a deep voice much like his own. "I find it to be a horrendous waste of energy."

"Ah . . . that's right. The great Duke of Warren never worries about anything because he always gets his way."

"Always," the duke repeated with emphasis.

"Perhaps this time you've miscalculated. Perhaps I'll stay in London, where I can continue to be your ultimate embarrassment. Wouldn't that put a crimp in your plans for me?"

"I have no plans for you, other than to see to it that you amend your life."

"My life does not need amending," Sebastian replied, sounding bitter. "Especially not by you."

"That's where you're wrong." The duke's voice came from farther away. "What have you decided?"

"I've not made up my mind."

There was a heavy sigh. "I believe you think you are tormenting me by delaying your decision. Let me assure you that you're not. Your future is entirely up to you. Go or don't. It matters not to me what you choose to do."

Meg heard footsteps, then the sound of the door opening and closing as the duke went back inside. Above, she could picture Sebastian staring out into the dark. His disturbed emotions were so strong that it felt as though they were roiling over her: Anger. Betrayal. Disgust. Fear.

"Bastard," Sebastian muttered. Then he, too, returned to the party.

Meg slipped away to the gazebo, heartsick that she had stepped into the middle of such a private moment. It served her right for eavesdropping so brazenly.

She lit the lamp in the center of the gazebo, and in a few minutes had a small fire burning in the brazier. Sitting on a nearby bench, she found just enough light to read the book she had brought outside. She opened to the proper page, but quickly realized she couldn't follow the words.

With a sigh, she closed the cover.

What was the matter? For years, she had meekly existed in her aunt's household, hardly content, but fed and clothed. Was there something about reaching a full score of years that made a person wish for so much more? She felt so restless, so bored, her days maddeningly mundane. Always before, she had been able to endure the drudgery. Now ... what? She felt a shift coming, as though her world was about to spin off its axis.

Meg physically shook herself back to reality. What nonsense she conjured. Excitement and adventure never happened to a woman such as herself. There was something to be said for being warm in the winter, having your belly full, and knowing your bed was ready at night, even though it was a tiny cot in one of the attic rooms.

She stared into the fire, her mind in turmoil. It wasn't just her own state that worried her, but Sebastian's as well. Though she had only known him a few hours, she felt connected to him somehow, beyond anything she had ever experienced with another.

The words he had spoken with his father couldn't be silenced. She was sad for both of them, knowing she would give up all the remaining days of her life to spend a few moments with her own deceased father. Sebastian's was alive and well, and they despised each other. How tragic it was.

Just then, footsteps sounded on the stairs into the gazebo. For some reason, she wasn't startled or frightened. She knew exactly who it was. Their eyes met across the small fire. He looked older, tired, the rascally air which usually hovered about him no longer in evidence.

He leaned a shoulder against one of the beams which marked the entrance. "Are you very angry with me?"

"I should be."

"But are you?"

Meg would have loved to lay all the blame for the entire sordid singing episode at his feet, but she couldn't. She was perfectly capable of creating her own troubles without help from anyone else. All he had done was give her a little shove in the wrong direction. "No, I guess I'm not."

"Good. I'm glad to know it wasn't your anger keeping you away."

"From what?"

"Our rendezvous." A corner of his mouth lifted in a smile. "You're late."

"You didn't seriously expect me to join you."

"You might have." He shrugged. "A man never knows until he asks."

"Over the last few hours, I've had a great deal of time to consider your invitation, and I've come to the conclusion that you slipped me that note right before dinner simply as a means of tormenting me."

"You could be right," he chuckled softly.

"You really are quite wretched."

"I know."

"I haven't the faintest idea why anyone puts up with you."

"Because I'm irresistible?"

Meg had to admit that he was very close to being right. Being in his presence was stimulating and wonderful, even though she wanted to kill him at the same time. "Your vanity knows no bounds."

"It never has." He looked around, taking in the small fire, the lamp. "Why are you lurking about out here in the dark?"

"I might ask you the same question."

"I was waiting for you."

Meg's surprise was very great. She had been certain that his interest in his little joke would have waned hours earlier. "You're not serious."

"My carriage is parked behind the mews where I dropped you off this afternoon. I didn't know if you'd come to me, but if you did, it would have been incredibly rude not to be there, don't you agree?"

"Yes, I agree."

"I'd just about given up on you, but I decided to take a quick look about the garden. I saw the light." He took his first step inside the gazebo and noticed the book lying on her lap. "What have you there?"

"A book."

He took two more steps, bringing him next to her. "What's it about?"

"A woman . . . ." She was suddenly embarrassed and wasn't sure why. "A woman who went to India with her family."

"May I?" He reached down and picked it up, glancing over the title, then skimming through the pages. "It must be quite good. You've nearly worn it out."

"I just enjoy reading about different places. Different cultures and different lives," she murmured, wishing she could add how she longed for a life so different from her own.

"Would you go to India if you were given the opportunity?" he asked, handing the book back to her. She laid it on the bench, hiding it under her cloak.

"Me? No . . . I'd never . . . well, I'd never have the chance, so it's really a silly question to consider—"

He cut her off. "Pretend you could do anything you wished. You had the money, the time, and someone said, 'Go to India.' Would you go?"

"Well, yes. Yes, I would. I would love to see new places and new people. I think it would be heavenly."

He studied her for a long moment. "You're very brave."

"Not really," Meg denied, never able to take the smallest compliment. "It's easy to say I'd do something if it's all make-believe. If I truly had the chance? Who knows? I'm more bluster than anything.''

He studied her again. More intently this time. ''Do you mind if I join you?''

''Aren't you worried we might be seen here together and alone?''

''Should I be?''

''Well, people might be inclined to think the worst. My aunt might start demanding you marry me.''

''No offense, *chèrie,* for I am enamored of your many charms, but I would never do something I didn't want to do. Even if the likes of Lucy Smythewaite was screaming for it. I'm not afraid for us to be seen together.'' He paused. ''How about you? I would not want to do any grievous harm to your reputation, so I will do as you wish. Should I stay or leave?''

For the first time since they had met, there was hesitation in his voice. He was unsure of himself and how to proceed. Coming from the brash Lord Stuart she had grown to expect, this was definitely something new.

''Sit down,'' she said, sliding over to make room. ''There's no danger for you by remaining. If Aunt Lucy discovered us here, she would never insist on a marriage. She would spend the rest of her life apologizing to you for my lack of breeding.''

''Having seen the two of you together, I must say I'm inclined to believe you.''

He sat. Wearily, she thought. Much of his sparkle and flourish seemed to have evaporated. Staring straight ahead, he leaned forward and rested his arms on his thighs. She shifted to see him better, and the dim light cast his handsome face in profile. He looked anguished and sad.

''Are you all right?'' she asked gently. He hesitated for a long while, so long that she began to think he wasn't going to answer, which gave her plenty of time to wonder if she was mad for speaking the next, but she voiced it anyway. ''I heard you talking to your father.''

He stiffened. "When?"

"A short time ago. When I was coming outside, I was passing under the balcony."

"You heard it all, did you?" he asked, sounding resigned rather than angry. "It's so dreadfully impolite to eavesdrop, you little minx. I'm surprised you'd do such a thing."

"I didn't mean to listen. I was just . . . there."

He took a deep breath and heaved a sigh as though the weight of the world rested on his shoulders. Shaking his head, he said, "It doesn't matter."

"Yes, it does," she insisted. "And I'm sorry."

"You're sorry?" He turned to look at her. "For what?"

"That you and your father are at such odds. Has it always been like that between the two of you?"

"I can't say. Until I was twenty years old and my father returned to England to assume the title, I'd seen him a grand total of three times."

"Good heavens why?"

"He stayed long enough to plant a babe in my mother; then he went dashing off round the globe in service to the king. My uncles raised me. They always thought I was acceptable," he added bitterly. Sebastian couldn't believe he had just confessed such a thing to Meg, but he was upset and disconcerted. "I've never been able to please him, no matter what I do. I stopped trying long ago."

Meg saw many things clearly. "Where is it he wants you to go?"

"To Jamaica. To work like one of the slaves at our family's plantation."

"When?"

"February fifteenth."

Her heart ached at the thought. Jamaica was on the other side of the world. She would never see him again, and while she knew it was silly to be distressed, she couldn't help herself. She had known Sebastian one day; in nearly every way, she could consider him a stranger, except she didn't. "Will you go?"

"How can I not? If I remain in England, I am to be disinherited. My allowance stopped." He closed his eyes, seeing some horrible future she could only imagine. Quietly, he added, "I could not stand to have everyone laughing at me. There would be no end to it."

"You're right about that, I'm afraid." She reached for his hand and squeezed hers around it. "Is there anything I can do for you?"

"Just don't tell anyone. Please?"

Meg smiled, her heart warming to the idea of being in his confidence. "I won't. You have my word."

With that reassurance, he squeezed her hand in return. Another long, companionable silence passed; then he asked, "Have you ever wished you could become someone else? That you could just snap your fingers and change your entire life."

"I wish it all the time."

He turned his head to look her in the eye. "I loved your singing."

Couldn't he be serious for more than one minute at a time? "Please don't start doing that again."

"Doing what?"

"Teasing me." She looked away, staring out into the gray night. "I had myself convinced that I'd calmed my temper over your behavior inside. Don't dredge it up."

He placed a firm finger against her chin and turned her face to his. When she tried to pull away, he gripped her chin with his palm. "I loved your singing."

Could he really mean it? He sounded so earnest, and she yearned to believe him. For so long, she had wished to have some of her father's talent. If only one other person thought she was good. . . . "Why do you say that?"

"Because it's true. Your voice is so full and robust. You

have a natural flair and style of which other women only dream. I think you could succeed on the stage.''

"My father was a singer," she confessed.

"I can tell."

She wanted to hug him fiercely for saying such a kind thing. "I always wanted to be like him."

"You should sing more. All the time. Wherever you go."

"It's not that easy."

"Why? Because Lucy says you shouldn't? The woman has filled your head with nonsense."

"She has my best interests at heart."

"Does she?"

"Of course she does." The past ten years had been like a prison sentence under Lucy's watchful eye, so Meg had no idea why she was defending the woman's behavior. Habit, probably. Misplaced loyalty, certainly. "She's my aunt. My only family. My guardian. Why wouldn't she want the best for me?"

"Why, indeed?" Sebastian asked, daring her to consider the possibilities. "According to her, you're an untalented burden. I'm sure she's convinced you you're homely. Unmarriageable, as well. Am I close?"

"She didn't have to spend time convincing me of any of those things," she replied softly. "I'm well aware of my limitations."

"The only *limitations* you suffer," he growled, "are those your aunt placed in your head." He relaxed against the bench, stretching his arms across the back while he pretended to ponder the situation further. "What do you suppose her motive could possibly be?"

"She has no motive."

Sebastian continued as though she hadn't interrupted. "You don't suppose she might be worried, do you?"

"About what?"

"About Patty, you silly goose. Perhaps she's afraid that if she loosened your reins a bit, you would outshine Patty."

"The fact that you could give voice to such a preposterous idea tells me that you are completely deranged."

"Am I?"

Sebastian let the question hover in the air until it took on a disturbing quality. Through the years, Meg had often wondered why Lucy was so hostile. Meg had never been anything but a quiet, obedient ward who was easy to care for, yet, from the very first time Aunt Lucy set eyes on her, the woman's dislike seemed cast in stone. Her uncle might have tempered things between them, but he had died shortly after Meg's arrival, leaving her at Lucy's mercy.

"I'm sure you're wrong," Meg insisted once again, but this time she sounded much less certain.

He shifted, bringing an arm across her shoulder and down her back so her body was turned into his. Her breasts swelled as the tipped peaks felt the pressure of his broad chest.

"Is your hair down?"

"Yes."

The hood of her cloak covered it, and he pushed it back, pulling at the drawstring around her neck. The heavy fabric fell back off her shoulders, revealing her long, auburn tresses. Only the maids had seen her hair like this since the day she had moved to Lucy's house, and Meg suddenly felt free and scandalous. Grabbing a handful, Sebastian greatly pleased her when he wrapped it around his fist, rubbing the silken strands across his cheek and inhaling deeply of the scent.

"Lovely," he said, smiling into her eyes. He ran a thumb across her bottom lip, the simple gesture causing her heart to pound frantically. "How old are you, Meg?"

"Twenty."

"Do you know what men and women do together when they're alone?"

"I think so," she managed breathlessly.

"If we were in my apartments right now, I'd have you sing for me. I'd have you play the pianoforte for hours." His voice was deep and low; it tingled across her skin, sending signals of delight to every corner. One arm held her pinned against him while the other roamed down, moving from her lips to her throat. "First, I'd take off all your clothes . . ."

"Sebastian . . . ," she protested, glad the darkness hid her red cheeks. The very idea was too shocking to contemplate, but contemplate she did. Imagine being alone with him. And undressed! She felt hot and cold all over.

"Let me tell you my fantasy, *chèrie.* It's how I'll always think of you, when I'm looking at you across a crowded room. I'd dress you in one of my shirts, and I'd not let you button the buttons. I'd want to see you." As he talked, his hand drifted down the valley between her breasts, causing an exquisite pain to sear through her nipples. She wanted him to touch them, some primal part of her sensing that he could ease some of the ache, but he didn't stop there. His wandering hand continued across her stomach, hip, brushing the edge of a buttock.

"My shirt would be too long for you. It would hang to just about here, I think." He rubbed an imaginary hem in the middle of her thigh. "Your legs would be bare. Your feet as well. Your hair would be long and straight as it is right now. You'd tip your head back to sing, and your hair would sway about your hips."

"I think you should stop."

"Why? Am I upsetting you? I want to upset you." His hand began slowly working its way back up, resting on the lower part of her abdomen, loving the way her stomach muscles clenched at his touch. "The sight of your hair would thoroughly arouse me, and I'd walk up behind you and brush it aside so I could kiss your shoulder." His actions duplicated his words. He pulled the hair off her neck, sucking and tasting the warm saltiness of her skin.

The feel of his lips sent shivers coursing through her body, and she trembled.

"Are you cold?" he asked, knowing she wasn't.

"Yes," she lied.

"Let me warm you."

He lifted her onto his lap so her hip was balanced on his leg, and she was held between his strong thighs. With her cloak pulled over her back, she was surrounded by heat. Although she knew the answer, she asked, "Are you going to kiss me?"

"Yes. As thoroughly as possible this time."

"But you know I'm not very good at it."

"Then, perhaps it's best if you practiced a bit." The glint of mischief in his eye had been in hiding; now it was back.

"Promise you won't laugh at me again."

"Never. Never about this." He moved a hand down her back to her buttocks, pressing her forward into his groin. The hard bulge in his trousers was unmistakable. "Do you feel me there?"

"Yes." Without waiting for him to do it again, she pressed her hips forward against his. Perhaps she had turned into a complete wanton, but she couldn't seem to help herself. Her loins were hot and heavy. Her pulse pounded between her legs, making her moist there.

"This is desire, Meg," he groaned his pleasure as she found her mark. "Do you feel how I want you?" He took her hand and pressed the palm against his erection, guiding it up and down the length.

"Yes," she whispered, her eyes as wide as saucers as she eagerly touched his most private spot. "I had no idea . . ." She swallowed. "You . . . it . . . feels so big . . ."

"Not too big," he chuckled heartily. "Just the right size." He moved his hand up her stomach to her breasts, gauging the weight and size of one, then the other. Moving to the center, he squeezed a hard nipple between his thumb and finger. She sucked in an agonized breath. "Your body is telling me you want me, as well. Do you?"

"Very much."

"Put your arms round my neck." She complied, bringing her breasts and stomach into tighter contact. He hesitated a brief instant, his lips hovering next to hers, his eyes searching. As though in great turmoil, he asked, "What is it you do to me?"

His mouth covered hers, sampling the shape and texture. Her lips were soft and warm. She tasted like a honeyed wine, and he sipped his pleasure slowly, relishing the feel of her in his arms. His hands worked through her hair, freeing the long, heavy strands. They massaged her scalp and neck, her shoulders, down her back, to her buttocks, lifting her in a slow, steady rhythm against his raging phallus.

For some reason, the lass fueled a flame in him like none other he could remember, and his desire quickly reached a fevered peak. He could not hold her closely enough, kiss her deeply enough, press into her far enough. He wanted her physically—his body ached to be buried inside—but there was another, more disturbing need to join with her. An emotional one.

He needed Meg. For months, he had felt so isolated, so unsettled, so adrift. Somehow, he knew that she would hold him and chase away the demons who seemed to be hounding the corners of his long nights.

He moved his hand to her nape, teased her lips with his tongue. They parted as she welcomed him inside.

Kissing, Meg decided, was a dangerous, highly underrated endeavor. At first, she had been too stunned by the sensations he evoked to participate. But by the time his hands had drifted to her rear and started kneading the soft mounds of her buttocks, she had shaken off her stupor and begun to participate, following his lead the entire way.

As he played with her hair, she ran her fingers through his thick locks. When he kneaded her shoulders, she massaged his in return. His tongue begged invitation against her bottom lip, and she opened, her own tongue sparring with his, deepening the kiss beyond imagining. He traced her waist, her legs, and she did the same, stopping only when his hands moved to her breasts and began to fondle them. The searing pleasure was so mind-boggling that all she could do was force her lungs to move air in and out.

Sebastian was the one to finally end the passionate embrace, wrenching his lips from hers and moaning in frustration. When he had found himself inching her skirt up her legs, gradually exposing her long, graceful limbs, he had called a halt. If his hand had found its way between her thighs, there would have been no stopping. He would have stolen her maidenhead right there on the park bench.

"We have to stop." He rested his forehead against hers and said fiercely, "Now."

"I don't want to," Meg protested. Left to her own devices, she would have gladly spent the rest of her life sitting there, kissing him in mindless distraction.

"Trust me, *chèrie*. We must stop, for I no longer trust myself." His breathing was ragged, and he felt ready to spill himself in his trousers like a thirteen-year-old lad.

"It's all right, Sebastian. I like it." A flurry of doubt suddenly assailed her. "I was doing it correctly, wasn't I?"

"Oh, Meg . . ." He smiled, touched by her innocent desire to please him. "You are magnificent." What he wouldn't give to have her sprawled beneath him, on a fine bed, with her chestnut locks spread out in wild disarray, but he couldn't do it. He couldn't imagine pleasuring himself at her expense. "Hold me, would you? Just for a minute?"

She didn't hesitate, wrapping her arms around his shoulders, and burying her face in the crook of his neck. Loving the heat and smell of his skin, she could have lain there forever.

"I didn't know it could be like this," she whispered, and she was rewarded by being hugged more tightly, if that was possible.

"I don't want to spend tonight alone," he murmured, surprising himself at making such a personal confession.

"Then, don't," she responded, lifting back to look him in the eye. "Take me with you. To your apartments. No one will know."

"I cannot."

They both sat there, stunned beyond belief. Meg, because she had offered, Sebastian, because he had refused her.

She searched his eyes, hoping for an answer, but not finding it. Finally, she asked simply, "Why?"

"Because you deserve so much more than a man like me."

"But I don't want anyone but you."

Temptation was ghastly. He could snatch this bit of happiness from her, take what she was offering, but at what cost? For maybe the first time in his life, he acted like the gentleman he was supposed to be, grasping her shoulders and setting her off his lap and onto the bench. "It wouldn't be right, Meg."

Meg's usual self-doubt rushed to the fore. "It's because I'm so plain, isn't it?"

"No"—he winced—"it's not."

Feeling terribly hurt by his rejection, she turned away, straightening the bodice of her dress, adjusting her cloak, taking her time before she dared speak again. "I'm not stupid, you know. I realize it would just be for one night, and I'd never expect or ask for more. And I'd never tell anyone. I just want to know . . . once in my life what it's like to feel so . . . so . . . alive. Is that so terrible?"

"No," he was forced to admit. "But you deserve more and better." She looked lost and hurt; so he reached for her again, and she went willingly into his arms. Her body sprawled across his, and her face was pressed over his heart. He held her a long time, running his hand up and down her spine, until her breathing was so steady that he wondered if she had fallen asleep. Softly, he said, "Let's get you inside now."

"Yes, I suppose I'd better go." Meg looked at his chest, unable to look him in the eye.

He hooked a finger under her chin, lifted her gaze to his. "This was the most wonderful night I've spent in a very, very long time," he said, delighted to discover he meant every word.

Meg's initial reaction was to call him a liar and a tease, but

she held her tongue. For once, she was going to accept the
sentiment and hold his words close to her heart because she
so desperately wanted them to be true. She nodded. "Will I
see you again before you go?"

"I don't know. I have so many things to do in the next week."

"I understand." She nodded again as he helped her stand.
Then he stood with her.

"I'll miss you," she offered. When he didn't respond in
kind, she swallowed the hurt and held it close to her heart as
well. "Good night. And goodbye."

"Goodbye." He stared for a long while, memorizing her
face, then squeezed her hand reassuringly. "Go now. I'll watch
from here to make sure you're safely inside."

"I'll be fine."

"It will make me feel better to watch."

"All right." She kissed him on the cheek, then turned and
ran toward the house, pausing on the back step at the servants'
entrance. She couldn't see any of the gazebo from there, but
in her mind's eye, she could picture him clearly, waiting and
watching over her. It was a good feeling.

Clutching her book to her chest, she tiptoed up the back
stairs. The small window in her room looked down on the back
gardens. She rushed to it and peered out. For a brief moment,
the moon broke through the clouded sky, and she could just
make him out, leaning against the railing of the gazebo. He
was such a solitary figure, and her heart ached for him as she
wondered where he would go now, who he would see, what
he would do.

Would he ever think of her? Would he ever remember her
as she would remember him every minute of every day of her
life?

She waited breathlessly until he moved down the three steps
and toward the back gate. Like a phantom, he disappeared
through it, and her world felt empty and bleak once again.

Her first thought was that someone had found out about her ruse and was using the knowledge to tease her. Sebastian was the only one who might have had an inkling of how the first bouquet had originated, and she was initially terrified it was he. After she calmed herself, though, she realized that if he had been the sender, he would hardly have done it anonymously. He would have handled the entire affair in the most wretched way possible, trying to pique Meg's ire and stir a pot of turmoil. He would have been audacious, announcing his gift in the loudest possible terms, while sitting back to watch the disruption it caused.

Besides, at that very moment, he was across the room with Godfrey and Portia and a swarm of acquaintances who seemed to follow him wherever he went. Since he had entered a half hour earlier, he had never so much as looked in her direction. He appeared so far removed that they might have inhabited separate continents.

Someone else had sent them, but why?

Further reflection convinced her that the gift was genuine. The flowers were a holiday mixture of red, white and pink roses, with ribbons tied into little valentine hearts, and had probably cost ten times the paltry amount of the first bouquet. They were simply too dear for someone to have sent them as a joke.

Obviously, she had caught someone's eye, and her initial delivery had given him the courage and incentive to continue. But who could it be?

Lucy studied the card. Her lips tight, she sat rigid and tense on the settee, saying only, "Well, well . . . aren't they lovely." And even though she passed the card about and discussed the event with several guests, Meg knew her interest was feigned and her upset real.

Meg held the flowers for a time, inhaling deeply the scent of roses, her heart fluttering over the notion that she had captured someone's fancy. Suddenly, all the fuss over Valentine's Day

CHAPTER SIX

The first gift arrived the next afternoon.

Meg was in the downstairs parlor, helping Patty and Aunt Lucy entertain a steady stream of visitors, when the butler appeared with another bouquet. As he announced that they were for Meg, her first reaction was one of panic. Sebastian was the only man in the world she could think of who would send her flowers, and she couldn't imagine how she would explain a present from him without causing a disturbance.

Fortunately or not, depending on how one looked at it, they were not from Sebastian. As Meg stared at the card, her consternation was as great as her aunt's. Perhaps greater. It read much as the one had the day before when she had sent flowers to herself:

To Meg
From Your Secret Admirer

The script was bold and decorative, looking much like the signature she had used to sign her own card the day before.

didn't seem so silly after all. But, after a whispered word from
Lucy, she left to find a maid to put them up in her room. Before
Meg had met Sebastian, she would not have thought anything
of it, but now there was no mistaking the fact that Lucy was
angry because the mystery surrounding the flowers was generating too much attention, none of which was directed at Patty.

The next afternoon, to Meg's surprise and her aunt's dismay,
Meg received another gift, with the same type of card attached,
the same mysterious delivery. Lucy was prepared this time,
though. The butler whispered the news to Lucy, and Meg was
allowed to open the gift in another room, far away from the
keen assessment of Patty's guests.

The stratagem failed to stifle interest, however, for as soon
as Meg returned to the parlor, one of the women asked whether
she had received anything that day, forcing her to admit that
her clandestine devotee had sent the perfect Valentine's Day
gift, a book of love poetry. On learning of it, several women
sighed.

Lucy pretended to be intrigued, but Meg knew she wanted
to deny her niece permission to receive or keep the gifts. The
only reason she didn't was because she was afraid to take any
action without first knowing the identity of Meg's admirer. It
would never do to insult a family friend of rank.

The presents kept coming. A third gift was delivered on
Tuesday, a collection of colorful ribbons. A fourth on Wednesday, a silver pin shaped like an elephant. Each gift was more
valuable and more precious. The fifth, which arrived Thursday
afternoon, was an ivory cameo centered on a black ribbon, and
Meg gasped as she pulled the delicate carving from its small
box. She couldn't imagine owning anything so fine, let alone
wearing it for others to see, which she would never do. Showing
off any of the items might very well send Lucy over the edge.

That evening, she stood along the back wall of the ballroom,
wearing one of the new gowns Lucy had purchased for her.
Looking sallow and feeling distinctly out of place, she would

have given anything to join the line of gaily clad dancers, but as usual, no man had considered asking.

She knew how to dance, having watched dozens of dancing engagements in her life, but she had never had a lesson, nor had she danced with a partner. Her dancing had always been limited to times alone, unobserved and unnoticed. On a public dance floor, she would very likely make a fool of herself.

True to his character Sebastian stood across the room at the center of his adoring entourage. Five days earlier, they had met, fought, loved in the gazebo. Since then, her world had been turned upside down, and she wanted more than anything to talk to him about it, but he never noticed her presence. It was as though she didn't exist, which was hurtful to contemplate.

She thought they had formed a bond during the day they had met. Her body was still humming from the sensations he had evoked, her skin too tight, her breasts too full, but he seemed completely unfazed. Secretly, she wondered if he was embarrassed by the fact that he had confessed his greatest secrets and fears.

The ridiculous man! They were friends. Even though it was improper, she still wished they could spend some time together before he left. She would like to learn where he was going, find a way to correspond. The months and years stretching ahead would feel less lonely if she could expect an occasional letter penned in his hand.

She had toyed with the idea of dispatching a note to him, asking for another rendezvous, but she had no idea where to send it. And she certainly could not ask anyone how to contact him. Instead, Meg had taken to conveying mental messages from across the room, hoping he would understand what she was wishing. Just in case, she had gone to the gazebo each night at midnight, hoping he would come to see her once again. He hadn't, but she wouldn't quit hoping.

If they could talk privately, she would ask him what she should do about her newfound dissatisfaction with her circum-

stances. No doubt he was getting a goodly amount of enjoyment out of her predicament. As it stood, however, no one knew that they had befriended, so she could hardly walk up to him and begin speaking. Feeling more isolated by the day, she found herself staring in his direction like a lovestruck cow, mooning over what she could not have. The only eye she caught was that of Portia Poundstone, so she quickly looked away.

Sebastian was so keenly attuned to Meg that he knew exactly where she was in the room, how she was standing, to whom she was speaking. At times, he felt as though he even knew what she was thinking. She was longing for another clandestine meeting, but for once in his life, he had decided to hold his uncontrollable urges in check.

The simple fact was that she was much too fine to dally with. She was too trusting, too innocent, and her heart would be broken. Sebastian couldn't stand the thought of her being hurt. Particularly not by him. He would rather cut off his right arm than do something nefarious to her.

From the first, he had sensed their unusual connection. Where it came from, or why it existed, was a mystery, but he couldn't stop thinking about her, worrying about her. Gads, caring about her. He wanted her to be as happy and enthusiastic about life as she could possibly be. He wanted her delighted and surprised and angry and irritated. The pitiful fact was that he wanted her in all ways. Especially the physical.

She was such a pretty thing, standing there by herself, talking with the chaperones. Passion ran through her veins; he had felt her heart pounding as he had kissed her senseless. How he would like to do it again!

As a sort of parting gift, he wanted to build her self-confidence before he sailed away to Jamaica. He hoped to open her eyes, expand her options, show her some choices and new opportunities. Which was exactly why he had been sending her those silly trinkets.

The first day, he had done it simply to tease. He had wanted to torment her, to see her suspicions raised, her dander up, but the delight he had witnessed when she pressed the bouquet to her chest instantly made him change his mind. Her life had been one of lonely duty, with few joys or tender moments, and if he could brighten her world with a few foolish gifts, then he would do it gladly.

He wished he could shower her publicly, but because of the rule-bound, tightly controlled world in which they lived, he could give her nothing, could offer her nothing. He couldn't even chat or pass time with her. All he could do was stand at the opposite end of the room, pretending boredom and inattention while people around him spoke of her.

Portia and her friends had made numerous malicious comments about Meg and her admirer. Many of his male friends voiced observations as well, about her well-endowed physique, her prominent facial features. Distractedly, he listened, half hearing the rude remarks, knowing he could not respond without showing an emotional involvement, so he said nothing. Surreptitiously, he watched, eyeing her every move. She was dying to dance. Her foot was tapping to the rhythm, her fingers moving with the melody.

Without giving his next move much thought, he walked away from Portia and Godfrey and headed for the back of the room. As he approached the chaperones, everyone sat straighter, each wondering if he was going to ask her charge to dance.

He nodded a few times, said a few quick hellos, but was not deterred until he stood directly in front of Lucy and Meg. Patty was out on the dance floor, so he didn't have to bother with her. With only the briefest acknowledgment of Lucy, he turned the full force of his gaze on Meg.

"Miss MacDonald, may I have the pleasure of this dance?"

Stupefied, she stared at him, unable to credit his request.

"Miss MacDonald," he repeated, "I wonder if I might have this dance?"

She gave her automatic reply. "I don't dance."

"Don't or can't?" The question was the same one he had asked a week earlier about her singing, knowing it would get an instant rise out of her.

Lucy answered for her. "She cannot dance, Lord Stuart."

"Why?" He looked Meg over thoroughly, as though checking for flaws. "Is she physically incapable? Does she have no sense of rhythm? Does she move like a clod? Are her slippers too tight? What?"

He asked the personal questions lightly, as though they were meant to be one of his imprudent jests, but Lucy was no fool. She recognized the underlying tone, and two bright red rage spots appeared on her cheeks. Her lips were pinched together so tightly that he had to prevent himself from laughing aloud.

Quietly, Lucy responded, "She does not know how."

"Why is that?" Sebastian asked more loudly than he should have, wanting others standing nearby to hear. The woman deserved a dose of her own tonic.

"She has not learned, sir. I would ask that you not embarrass her."

"She hasn't learned?" The question sounded innocent enough, but both knew it was not.

"She leads a sheltered life," Lucy responded, wondering what was happening. If the despicable man wasn't careful, people were going to start listening. "I could see no reason to have her learn."

"You're her aunt. Why wouldn't you want her to acquire such an important social skill?"

"I see no need to explain my decisions regarding my niece's upbringing to you, Lord Stuart." Lucy straightened, looking away. "She cannot dance. She does not know how," she insisted once again, considering the matter closed.

"Then it's high time she learned, wouldn't you say?" Sebastian turned to Meg, who was looking more flushed and fair than he remembered from his previous encounters. "What say you, Miss MacDonald? Would you care to dance?"

Meg was mortified. Sebastian was back to his usual, ill-mannered form, and everyone nearby was watching to see how she would respond. Lucy was about to have a fit, and she knew her aunt would make her pay for this little episode.

She swallowed, trying to steady her breathing and calm her racing pulse. "Thank you, Lord Stuart. I appreciate your kind invitation, but I'm afraid my aunt is right. I'm not trained for dancing, and I would very greatly embarrass both of us."

"I don't care," he said, offering his hand.

Dear Lord, didn't he understand anything? She would cut off her right arm for the chance to whirl across the floor in his arms, but if she said yes, Lucy might be pushed to commit murder. The look in her eye said as much. "I'm sorry, I simply cannot."

"I realize I don't know you well, Miss MacDonald, but I never took you for such a timid little mouse." People either tittered or gasped at the open insult, but Sebastian ignored them, giving Meg his complete attention. Daring her. Challenging her. Torturing her.

Everyone was looking now, and Meg knew she had to defuse the situation. She was so angry with him, she could wring his neck for putting her in such a spot. As calmly as possible, she said, "I'm sorry you feel that way, but I still must refuse."

"What are you afraid of?" There it was! The reaction he wanted. Her green eyes flared, her lips pursed, and her fists clenched as though she would like to punch him right between the eyes.

"I'm not afraid of anything," she responded hotly.

"Really? You could have fooled me."

"I simply do not want to dance," she said, emphasizing each word clearly, throwing daggers at him with her eyes since she could not throw them with her hands.

"Because others might laugh at your awkwardness?"

"No, Lord Stuart. Because my aunt has asked me not to."

"Do you always do everything your aunt tells you?"

Why was he trying so hard to make her angry? Well, he would not succeed this time. As sweetly as possible, she said, "I try to be a dutiful ward."

"I'm sure you do," he responded, and no one could doubt his sarcasm. Just then, the orchestra finished its piece, and the room became increasingly quieter. The exchange would be more noticeable than ever. He decided for a parting shot. "My apologies, then, Miss MacDonald. I did not mean to point out such a social flaw in front of so many. I guess I'll go find someone with a talent for dancing."

Meg fumed. With a little practice, she could dance circles around any woman in the place. Sebastian had struck at her most vulnerable spot, and she couldn't seem to keep herself from responding. "I didn't say I had no talent for the sport."

"Then, show me that you know how." He reached out his hand again, just as the next piece was announced. A waltz. His eyes blazed the taunt. "What say you, Miss MacDonald? Shall we dance?"

Lucy interrupted. "She cannot possibly dance the waltz."

Sebastian looked at her as though he had completely forgotten she existed. "Why?"

"It will ruin any chance she has—"

"Any chance for what?" Sebastian cut her off. "A good marriage? I didn't realize you were trying to find her a husband. I'll be sure to tell all my friends." Sebastian grabbed Meg's hand and neatly maneuvered her into the swirl of dancers. Before she could protest or Lucy could stop her, they were sucked into the motion of the room.

For a brief second, she thought about stomping away and returning to her aunt's side, but she couldn't do it. They had already created enough of a scene. People were watching, staring and whispering.

Sebastian held her as closely as he dared. The first time around the floor was a little awkward; but as he had known she would, she quickly picked up the movement, and by the second time around, she glided with the ease of a practiced dancer. She wouldn't look at him though, and he desperately needed her undivided attention for the few short minutes she would be in his arms.

"I've missed you," he vowed truthfully.

"You have a funny way of showing it," she muttered to his chest, finally raising her gaze. His eyes were glowing with mischief and fun, and something else which she now recognized as desire. "Why do you do this to me?"

"Because I love to see the fire in your eyes," he responded without a bit of remorse.

"My aunt is going to kill me."

"Or me."

"No, it will definitely be me. I hope you're happy that you've precipitated my untimely demise."

"After dancing with you, I must say, it was worth the sacrifice."

Meg shook her head. What could a woman do with a rascal such as he? Nothing. As two unattached, single adults they could merely dance together. Once. No more would be proper or allowed. This was her one and only opportunity to savor his closeness. She smiled and relaxed, determined to enjoy their minutes together so she could always remember every single instant of the wonderful encounter.

Much, much too soon, the song ended, and they were only a short distance from Lucy, who was staring at them as though she were a thunder cloud ready to burst. In a moment, Sebastian would be lost to her, so there was no time for hesitation or regret. For once in her life, she was determined to be bold. She smiled pleasantly, looking up at him as though she were discussing something as benign as the supper buffet.

"May I visit you at your apartments before you leave?"

"No, *chèrie*. I could never let you."

Meg kept smiling past the hurt his rejection caused. "Then, may I write to you in Jamaica?"

"I would like that." He squeezed her hand.

"How will we accomplish it?"

"I will send the first letter to a servant I trust at my father's house, asking him to send it on. We'll work out details from there."

"Good. I like knowing I'll hear from you. I won't be so worried."

"I'll be fine."

"I know you will." She squeezed his hand in return. "Have you heard about the gifts I've been receiving?"

"Yes." He smiled. "You see? Someone else thinks you're as lovely as I do."

Meg's heart melted with the compliment. She felt she knew the answer to the next, but asked anyway, "Is it you? Are you my secret admirer?"

Lord, but he wanted to admit it, but not here. Not like this. "If I sent you a gift, *chèrie*," he lied, "everyone would know it was from me."

Just as she had deduced herself. She sighed, wondering which shy beau was watching her from afar. "Aunt Lucy is very angry about it."

"Let her be," he whispered as he deposited her once again by Lucy's side. Sebastian flashed Lucy his most charming smile, then bowed courteously, and Lucy had the good sense to let the matter drop. All on hand knew that it was fruitless to reprimand the marquess about his behavior. He would make her look like a fool, and others would simply eavesdrop so that they could viciously repeat whatever was said.

Meg remained silent, knowing Lucy's retaliation would come later and privately. Her goodbye to Sebastian was a tip of the head. He gave her a wink as he disappeared into the crowd. The minutes after his departure were the worst as she watched the dancers, pretending that nothing untoward had just occurred. He was gone again—for good, most likely—and each parting was more heart-wrenching. She stood, smiling blandly, as though her first and only dance with the man of her dreams had meant hardly anything at all.

It had meant something to others, though. Sebastian's attention stamped her with a mark of approval, and several young men decided to follow his lead and ask for a dance. While she wanted nothing more than to seethe alone and privately, courtesy demanded she accept the various requests. As for her aunt, after the ruckus Sebastian had caused, Lucy seemed hesitant to refuse any invitation, so Meg was whisked onto the floor by one gentleman after another.

The rest of the evening passed in a blur. She chatted occasionally, but mostly kept searching the crowd for a final glimpse of Sebastian. He was nowhere to be found.

As Meg scanned the assembly, Portia Poundstone focused on her. Portia's main goal in life was to win Sebastian back, and she had watched with a disturbing unease as Sebastian danced with the awkward Smythewaite cousin. Portia's dislike of Meg had nothing to do with Sebastian; she simply hated all the attention and gossip Meg was generating with her secret admirer, and she had wondered more than once if the ugly duckling might be sending gifts to herself. But she particularly did not care for the way Sebastian had smiled at Meg when they circled past where Portia was standing.

Listening carefully to those around her, she wondered if anyone else had noticed, but no one had seemed to. Most of the talk centered on what a brash, rude man Sebastian was, or why he would single out such a plain Jane for attention.

Portia knew Sebastian too well, and she was not imagining things. The country mouse held some sort of fascination for him, although she had no idea why. Obviously, they had met previously. How and where? And how could she use the information to rid herself of such an unlikely rival? As those thoughts spiraled through her head, she was so absorbed that she noticed little else.

So she did not see Lucy Smythewaite staring at Meg as well.

The very first time Meg had walked through the door, Lucy had known what trouble she would grow to be. Even at age ten, she had been much like her mother. Lucy was a realist, and she had known that as the girls aged, Meg would be prettier and brighter than Patty, and as a result, Lucy had done everything she could to hide the girl.

After all her years of hard work, in one brief instant, that wretched Sebastian Stuart had wrecked all her efforts. His unwanted attention had garnered more of the same from others, and in the limelight, Meg looked like what she was: an ill-dressed, crudely coifed, poor relation. If others looked too closely they would begin to notice and to wonder at Lucy's motives—motives Lucy did not want anyone examining too closely.

Meg was dancing perfectly and graciously, as though she had spent her life doing it. Her green eyes were glowing, her cheeks flushed from the exertion, her auburn hair glowing under the lights. Men were noticing her—just as men had noticed her mother years earlier.

By the morrow, they would have all sorts of callers at afternoon tea—callers for Meg as well as for Patty. Discreet whispers would start about whether Meg had a dowry and how much it was—as if Lucy would spend any of her own children's money on such a thing.

Gentlemen would start wondering if they should seriously consider her in spite of her parentage. After all, her grandfather had been the Earl of Redding; her first cousin was the current earl. Added to that lineage was the fact that rumors had always abounded that Meg's father had held a dispossessed title in his own right, his family having lost all in Scotland after the uprising back in the forties.

Lucy had always managed to quash the calumny, but chances

were good that it would surface again after the evening's debacle. One of Patty's suitors might shift his gaze and look—
really look—at Meg MacDonald. There was no telling where
the disaster might lead.

The girl had to be disposed of quickly, and Lucy had the
perfect solution.

CHAPTER SEVEN

Meg stood outside the library, waiting for Aunt Lucy's official summons. She had expected the ax to fall, but she hadn't expected it so quickly. After Sebastian's reckless invitation to dance the previous night, she had spent several hours with various partners. By the time the ball ended, Lucy had suffered through the requests of several gentlemen asking if it would be all right to call on Meg the next day.

Meg wished them all to perdition, wanting nothing more than to spend a few days easing her heartache over Sebastian's leaving. In three days' time, he'd board the ship to Jamaica. Meg was certain she would never lay eyes on him again, and she felt the distance between them growing hour by hour.

Lucy called to her, and she entered, going to stand in front of the desk. Lucy was seated on the other side, the massive oak between them. Meg felt ten years old again and unable to comprehend the reason for the scolding that was coming since she had done nothing to provoke it.

Lucy began without preamble. "I've decided you should return to the country."

"When?"

"On the fifteenth. A few servants are going home. You'll go with them."

"Good." Meg smiled, knowing she was perplexing Lucy by not wanting to stay in London. At least she was to stay for the next two days, so there was a chance she would see Sebastian one last time. And a chance to receive another gift or two from her secret admirer. "I've not enjoyed myself much. I'd rather be home."

"I've also made a decision about your future."

"What's that?" Meg asked, completely disinterested and, therefore, unprepared for the next.

"I've decided it's time for you to marry."

"I beg your pardon?" Meg was certain she had heard incorrectly.

"I know we've not discussed it, but the time has come to settle you for the future years."

"And you wish me to marry?" she asked, unable to process what Lucy had said.

"Yes." Her aunt nodded. "Some time ago, Squire Thomas asked if he could begin courting you."

"Squire Thomas?" she asked, completely aghast. A neighboring widower with eight children, he was twenty-five years older than she was, drank to excess, and was said to have beat his first two wives. Because he was several inches shorter than she, every time they spoke, she stared down at his bald head while he gazed lasciviously at her bosom. "You can't be serious."

"Oh, but I am. He wants to remarry. He needs help with his family."

"But why would he be interested in me?"

"He wants a local girl. Someone with whom people are

familiar. He's known you for many years, and he thinks you would be acceptable. I agree."

Meg had expected Lucy's retribution to take many forms, but never had anything like this occurred to her. "I don't want to marry him. I don't want to marry anyone."

"It doesn't matter what you wish. For many years, I've wondered what to do with you, considering your background. He's willing to overlook your personal failings and those of your parents."

"Isn't that grand of him?" Meg bristled.

"Yes, it is," Lucy agreed, completely missing Meg's sarcasm. "I've posted a letter to him this morning. The courting will begin immediately when you arrive home. I expect a wedding by Yuletide at the latest."

"Aren't you forgetting something?" Meg asked, fishing now for any aid she could find and greatly relieved when it came to her. "Perhaps we should wait to learn the identity of my secret admirer."

"Whatever for?"

"Perhaps he is someone who—"

"Someone who will what?" Lucy cut in. "Someone who might want to marry you?" She snorted as though Meg were the last woman on earth a man would ever desire.

"It could happen," Meg insisted.

"Even if his interest turns out to be earnest—which I seriously doubt, by the way—you have no dowry. Your appeal will wane quickly enough when he learns that fact." Lucy nodded toward the door, indicating the meeting was over. "You may go upstairs to begin packing."

"Am I to be allowed to go to the Miltons' ball tonight?"

Lucy thought for a moment, then shrugged. "I suppose it can't hurt. And I will expect you to help with Patty's ball tomorrow night."

"Yes, ma'am." Meg stood there completely dumbfounded, staring at her aunt and trying to read what could possibly be going on in the woman's head which would make her contemplate this final, horrid act. Lucy's attention was already drawn back to the papers on the desk, and several minutes passed before she noticed that Meg had not departed.

She looked up. "Was there something else?"

"One thing," Meg responded quietly. For once in her life, she was going to say what she was truly thinking and damn the consequences. "I have listened to your insults about my mother and father for the past decade. Should you ever again decide to speak so rudely of either of them, I will no longer be able to guarantee the consequences of my behavior."

She turned and stepped into the hall, shutting the door with an echoing click. At the foot of the stairs, she stopped, initially thinking that she would go to her room, but the thought of sitting in the small, stuffy enclosure was more than she could bear. Almost in a trance, she headed for the back of the house and walked outside. So distracted was she that she left without a cloak or hat.

The winter day was brisk and cold, but Meg didn't care. The world seemed to be closing in on her. She couldn't breathe and felt feverish. Desperately in need of fresh air, she walked through the gray, lifeless gardens, drawn to the bench in the gazebo.

Her first thought was to find Sebastian, but she quickly discarded the idea. He had made his feelings extremely clear; he didn't want to be alone with her, and he was leaving London, just as she was. Even if he wanted to help her, there would be no time.

There was a slight chance that her father's family might offer assistance. She remembered the name of the town where they lived in Scotland and would send them a letter in the post, although with the vagaries of the road, it was certainly possible that any message would never be received. Or if it was, they would very likely be unable to help her before the following

Christmas rolled around. So, she would hope to hear from them, but could not count on it.

Other than her unknown Scottish relatives, she could think of no one who would offer the least bit of aid, advice or comfort.

She shivered through the afternoon, alternating between rage and despair, as ideas spiraled through her mind. After several hours had passed, she was still confused about much of her future, but of one thing she was certain: no matter what, she would not marry Squire Thomas. Before that could happen, she would leave Lucy's house and find her own way. Perhaps she would join one of the missionary groups who were always off to America or some other savage place to aid the natives, or sign on with an East Indiaman and work her way to Bombay. Sing on the stage. Work as a governess. Play the pianoforte in taverns. She didn't know and didn't care, but she would succeed.

The cold eventually drove her back inside. By the time she returned to the house, the short winter day had faded; the sun had set. She was exhausted but resolved.

As she walked up the back steps, the butler opened the door as if he had been waiting for her. She hid her surprise. Although she couldn't be sure, she thought she saw pity lurking in his eyes.

"We're glad you've returned, Lady Meg. We were getting worried."

"Thank you, Giles," she said, amazed to hear the retainer use a title in conjunction with her name. Lucy had forbidden it years ago, saying Meg was no such thing.

"We've taken the liberty of ordering you a bath. It will be brought up shortly."

Meg was completely overwhelmed. None of the staff had ever done such a compassionate thing for her before. "That would be wonderful."

"We would hate for you to take a chill."

"You're very kind." At least she had a few friends, she

thought as she climbed to the top floor. The second of the two ball gowns Lucy had ordered from Madame LaFarge was lying across the bed, and she winced at the thought of how absurd she would look later that night while wearing it in the Miltons' elaborate ballroom.

Next to the dress lay an opened package with a bracelet inside—the latest offering from her unknown suitor. It must have come in the afternoon while she was out in the gazebo. In her haste to escape the house, she had completely overlooked the likelihood of receiving another gift. She had forgotten her admirer, but he had obviously remembered her. Had he been in the room when the package was delivered? Was he disappointed that she had been absent?

She scanned the note:

> *My dearest Meg,*
> *I hope you will wear this especially for me tonight at the Miltons' ball.*
>
> > *Your most devoted,*
> > *Secret Admirer*

She collapsed down on the lumpy mattress and held the bracelet in her hand. It was a beautiful, delicate piece of jewelry, a thin gold band decorated with three small rubies centered in settings that looked like roses. Mesmerized by its precious charm, she worked it back and forth between her fingers, and the gold glowed and felt warm against her skin. What a treasure, too dear to accept, but not knowing the identity of the sender, there was no way to return it.

In her whole life, she could not remember cherishing an object more. Its arrival on such a dreadful day made it all the more special. It was as though he had known in advance that she would need something to warm her heart.

Someone with exquisite taste had purchased the item. Who? Who would have anonymously gone to such extravagant expense? Obviously, he was a shy man with a great deal of money. The description did not match anyone she had met during her stay in London.

What she had started as a joke, he had continued, bringing a bright ray of sunshine into her dismal world. Meg didn't believe what Lucy had said about him. He was out there, and he thought she was a person of substance and value. Even if he couldn't bring himself to tell her, his presents spoke eloquently.

Up until now, she had hidden her new treasures in her room, not wanting to flaunt them and further inflame Aunt Lucy, but Meg had reached a point where she didn't care what Lucy thought. With only two nights remaining in London, she had to show him how much his attention had meant. Tonight and the next, she would wear as many of the trinkets as she could: ribbons in her hair, the pin on her bodice, the cameo around her neck, the bracelet on her wrist. None of them matched, and they would all look absurd with the dress—but the dress looked absurd in and of itself, so a few pieces of uncoordinated jewelry could hardly make it worse. Besides, no one would notice what she was wearing anyway.

Perhaps when the unknown gentleman saw her wearing his tokens of affection, he would find the courage to identify himself, and she would be able to thank him in person before retiring to the country.

Something was wrong with Meg.

Sebastian realized it the moment he entered the ballroom. In the past, as she had watched the people in the crowd passing her by, she had always looked interested and curious. Tonight, she looked lonely, forlorn, as though she had lost her last friend. Standing there in her ill-conceived gown, she looked as pallid as he had known she would. To make matters worse, she appeared to have decorated herself with items that didn't match her attire. It took him a few moments to grasp that she had decked herself out in every adornment he had sent her over the past week, as though sending some sort of desperate signal to her benefactor.

As he was announced and proceeded down the stairs, he took his time, walking slowly to give himself extra opportunity to thoroughly assess her condition.

That afternoon, he had gone to Lucy's for tea, accompanying Portia and Godfrey and a host of others, but Meg hadn't been there. He should have realized something was amiss, but propriety prevented him from inquiring to ensure she was all right. He was supposed to be hardly acquainted with her, let alone worrying about her welfare. But worry he did.

For some unknown, unfathomable reason, he fretted about her all the time. Whatever would become of her with her future in Lucy's hands?

He had quit trying to figure out why he was so obsessed with her. There was just something about her that had attracted and intrigued him from the very first. And, if he was honest with himself, he had come to treasure the afternoon teas and the various balls and soirees where he could keep an eye on her. When he sailed away to his new life, this silly, passionate, quiet girl, whom he had only known a matter of days, was the only person in all of England he would truly miss.

For the better part of an hour, he studied her. She didn't smile or laugh, she never looked around the room, and her eyes never followed the dancers or checked out any of the gowns or jewels. It was as though her rampant curiosity had fled. What the deuce had happened?

When she left the ballroom and headed for the buffet tables, he walked away from the group of people with whom he had been chatting. Matching his steps to hers, he tried to time his walk so he could enter the supper room at the same moment, thinking they could go through the line together, and she would have the chance to tell him about her situation. With a strange and sudden urgency, he realized he had to know what had occurred.

Meg moved to the end of one of the tables, and Sebastian quickly stepped behind her. Much to his dismay, he was accosted at that very moment by Portia. The timing was so perfect that he couldn't help wondering if she had been lurking nearby, waiting for the opportunity to join him.

"Sebastian, darling," she purred, stepping close and slipping her arm into his as though they were together.

"Hello, Portia," he responded, as he saw Meg stiffen at the sound of their voices. "Fancy meeting you here."

"I'm so glad you finally decided to eat. I'm utterly famished."

In a smooth move, she maneuvered him away from Meg and into the other line so they would be going down opposite sides of the long table. There would be no chance to whisper a question in Meg's ear or to have her whisper an answer in return.

Portia kept up her inane chitchat as they followed the people ahead of them, taking small steps toward the food. Sebastian ignored her, his attention completely focused on Meg, daring her to look his way. She only gazed morosely ahead, not acknowledging him or anyone else.

Finally, he reached the end of the table. Good fortune placed him there at the same moment Meg reached it as well. He continued staring at her, and because she had to reach for a plate and begin filling it, she was forced to turn in his direction.

"Well, hello there," Portia said to Meg before Sebastian could greet her. "Aren't you Patty's little cousin?"

"Yes, I am," Meg said, immediately looking back down at the table.

"We're all so excited about her come out tomorrow night," Portia gushed with false zeal. "You must be fairly bursting with anticipation."

"I can hardly wait," Meg responded with such a lack of enthusiasm that Sebastian wanted to laugh aloud.

"I'm sorry, but I believe I've forgotten your name."

"Meg MacDonald."

"Ah yes, Miss MacDonald. The woman with the secret admirer. It must be so exciting to have everyone talking about you."

"I hardly think everyone's talking about me."

"Of course they are! Have you identified your mysterious swain yet?"

Meg studied her for a long moment, trying to ascertain what hidden purpose lay behind the question. Unable to decipher the woman's true intent, she answered, "No," then went back to filling her plate.

Sebastian glanced down at Portia. She was playing at something. Meg sensed it, too. Whatever her game, it had to do with Meg, and Sebastian couldn't, for the life of him, think of why Portia would turn her ferocious attention in Meg's direction. He interrupted, hoping to deflect some of Portia's interest.

"Good evening, Miss MacDonald. It's nice to see you again."

"Lord Stuart." Meg nodded.

Portia asked, with what Sebastian felt was an unrestrained amount of glee, "Should we call you Miss MacDonald? Or Lady MacDonald?"

"Call me whatever you wish." Meg shrugged, disinterested. "I don't care."

Portia refused to let it go. "Well, your mother was the daughter of an earl, but then I realize there was ... well ... that *situation* with your parents." She let the insinuation hang in the air for a long, drawn-out moment, then looked up at Sebastian, trying to appear innocent when she asked, "What's the appropriate manner of address in such a circumstance?"

The insult to her parents finally brought a small flame to Meg's eye, and Sebastian couldn't help thinking that Portia

had probably met her match—if Meg ever decided to let loose
with her tongue and her temper. As usual, her manners won
out, and he could see her physically preventing herself from
rising to Portia's bait.

"Try some of this relish, Portia," he said, trying to steer
the conversation to a safer topic. "It looks good."

"Yes, it does," she responded absently, giving Meg a thor-
ough study that was near to insulting. "Don't you spend all
your time wondering who he is?"

"Who?" Meg asked.

"Why, your secret admirer, of course. It's so romantic. All
the flattery. All the attention. All the gifts. You must be dying
of curiosity."

"Actually, I really would like to know his identity," Meg
said, looking Sebastian full in the eye for the first time since
he had stepped to the table. "I'm returning to the country after
Patty's ball on St. Valentine's Day, and I'd like to thank him
before I go."

"In two days?" Sebastian asked. They would be leaving
London at the same time.

"Yes," she answered, sharing his thoughts exactly.

"Why, that's odd," Portia interjected. "You've hardly
arrived in the city. Has something happened?"

Meg wasn't sure why they were carrying on a discussion,
but if she didn't answer, Portia was the type who would suspect
the worst and spread stories even if they weren't true. "No,
nothing's happened. I just . . ." Trying for a smile, she hardly
found one as she started over. "My aunt has decided it's time
for me to marry. I'm going home to let a neighboring gentleman
begin courting me."

Sebastian felt as if he had been stabbed. His Meg? Married?
To another? The idea of such a thing happening had never
occurred to him. From the way Meg looked, he could just
imagine the sort of man Lucy had selected. To think that she

would do such a thing to his pretty, vibrant Meg! He didn't want her to marry. He wanted her to . . . What?

He broke out in a sweat. His hands were trembling as the truth finally struck like a bolt of lightning. He wanted her for himself! He truly did!

The idea was so shocking, his initial reaction was to push it away. He wasn't ready to settle down. Not with Meg or any woman. In fact, he would never marry. The thought of being shackled to a whining, complaining woman, who was always asking, taking, wanting more, was more than he could abide.

But then he looked at Meg, and couldn't help imagining a life with her. How lovely it would be to care for her every day, to listen to her talk of her outlandish dreams, watch her read her farfetched books of adventure, to hear her sing whenever he wished.

A crystal clear image appeared, and for several moments, he saw nothing else. It was as though he was seeing his future. It contained a small, healthy boy. His son! Their son! A child with his dark hair and Meg's green eyes, running along a sandy beach. The air was hot, the sun shining off an azure sea and Meg's chestnut hair. The lad ran into her arms, and she scooped him up and twirled him in circles as they laughed together . . .

His heart began to pound, and he had to force himself to breathe. Physically shaking himself back to the present, he once again heard Portia's annoying voice. Meg was watching him intently, as though she had just shared the same intense vision.

"Yes," Meg was responding to Portia while she eyed him carefully, "I'll be leaving on Sunday."

"Well, what a let-down for your dear secret admirer. After he's remembered you so faithfully."

"I'm hoping he'll approach me tonight or tomorrow. It will be my last chance to thank him for being so kind."

Portia couldn't seem to let it go. "Hasn't his attention made you feel special?"

"Well, yes. Yes, it has." Meg was hardly going to lie about it, even to the likes of Portia Poundstone.

The line had moved, and they were farther down the table. Meg juggled her plate and finally had to set it down because she needed two hands to spread butter on a piece of bread. As she did, Portia went stone-still, looking at the bracelet she was wearing on her wrist.

"What an interesting bauble. From your anonymous friend?"

"Yes, I received it this afternoon."

"May I?" Portia leaned across the table, rudely taking Meg's arm and lifting it to get a better look. She started to chuckle. Low at first, then longer and louder.

"I know it's not exquisite jewelry, but I like it anyway," Meg said, pulling her hand away. "It's the thought that counts."

"Really? Oh, this is rich. This is so rich."

Laughing harder now, she was causing people to turn and stare. Looking up at Sebastian, tears of mirth glistened in her eyes. "You horrible cad!" she chided, as though she and Sebastian shared a wonderful, crude secret. "What a cruel thing to do to the wretched little thing."

"What?" Meg asked, completely at a loss.

"The bracelet! Sebastian sent it to you," Portia declared loudly, wanting those standing nearby to hear. "I know because he gave it to me months ago, but I returned it in a fit of pique." She gestured around the table, saying, "Ask anyone here."

Meg could hear whispers beginning. *Stuart playing another joke . . . not a secret admirer after all . . . simply teasing the girl. . . .*

"Don't you see? It was all a joke!" Portia insisted. "He's been sending you gifts from his old girlfriends. Sebastian Stuart is your secret admirer." Laughing again, she turned to Sebastian. "Oh, you really are the worst. To pick on the poor girl this way."

Other people were listening. Turning. Meg could hear them

laughing as well. The talk was spreading through the supper room and out into the ballroom. Laughter was growing. She looked down at the bracelet and felt like the gold was burning a hole into her skin. Sebastian stood frozen in place, looking terrifically angry. She asked, "Is it true?"

"Miss MacDonald . . .," he began, trying to stand on polite form but failing. "Meg . . ."

"This was all just another one of your mean jokes?"

"Meg, listen to me. It wasn't like that . . ."

"Then, what was it like?"

"You don't understand . . ."

"I think I understand very well, Lord Stuart." She swallowed past the lump in her throat. "I'm just the plain niece of Lucy Smythewaite. Of course I'd embrace a little attention. And it was so easy to deceive me, because I'm so pathetic. Isn't that it?"

"You're wrong, Meg."

"Am I?" She glared at Portia, who was gossiping fiercely with the woman next to her, still giggling out of control. "I'm sure you and your friends had a huge laugh at my expense. I'm glad I could provide all of you such entertainment." As she spoke, she had been pulling the ribbons from her hair, the pin from her bodice, the cameo from her neck, and, finally, the bracelet from her wrist. She leaned across the table and dropped them in a condemning pile. "Here. I won't be needing these anymore, and I'd hate for them to go to waste. Perhaps you can use them for your next jest."

Tears overcame her then, but she refused to shed them in front of the horde of contemptuous strangers who were all staring. With her head held high, she turned from the supper table and headed for the doors. Through the ballroom, to the stairs, down the hall. Walking faster, faster. People parted as she passed, pointing, whispering and laughing. By the time she reached the front door, she was running, running away, free and alone into the dark night.

CHAPTER EIGHT

"Meg! Meg, wait!"

Sebastian's voice sounded through the darkness over the clopping of the horses' hooves, and she could sense the lantern light coming from his carriage. Paying him no heed, she kept running, until suddenly, like a bird of prey, he swooped down upon her. She struggled against him, trying to bite, kick and hit him, but he held her so closely wrapped inside his long cloak that she couldn't do any damage.

For a long while, she fought on until simple fatigue wore her down, and they stood in each others' arms on the quiet street. Their breath swirled above their heads, and a single street lamp cast eerie shadows over everything, making the moment seem unreal.

As she stilled, Sebastian's grip loosened until he was holding her tenderly, much like the lover she had fantasized he might become someday. She wanted to be shed of him, but every last bit of her strength had evaporated during the fight. If he let go of her, she might very well fall to the ground.

"I hate you," she whispered vehemently against the white of his shirt.

"I know you do, *chèrie,*" he whispered in return.

"I can't believe you would do such a despicable thing. I thought we were friends."

"We *are* friends." He placed a light kiss on the top of her head. "Let's get you out of the cold."

With no energy left to protest, she allowed him to lift her into the carriage. She huddled in the corner while he tucked a blanket over her lap and around her legs; then she stared out into the darkness while he settled himself on the opposite seat.

Silently, he watched her, wondering what to do. For once in his life, he had had only the purest of motives, so how could he have made such a mess of things? It was obvious she was not going to speak, being herself lost in some private misery he couldn't begin to fathom or share. He needed to break through her silence and the wall he had forced between them. An apology seemed the best way to begin.

Very quietly, he offered, "I'm sorry."

For the longest time, she said nothing, simply stared out into the night, wondering about things so far removed from Sebastian. Wondering where she would go now, where she would live, how she would put food on the table. Wondering how she would survive. Every bit of her life lay in ruins, as though it had been smashed into a thousand tiny pieces, and all he could do was offer meaningless platitudes.

"Do you have any idea what it's like to be me? What it's been like all these years?" She finally turned her gaze to meet his, sizing him up and finding him lacking.

"I have some idea."

"No, you couldn't possibly know," she said sharply. "I've tried so hard to make my way, to just endure, and now you've gone and made me the laughing stock of the entire city. How could you?"

"I didn't mean for any of this to happen."

"You never do. You go through life acting like an ill-behaved ten-year-old. You'll do and say any foul thing, and look what's happened to me because of it. I'll never forgive you."

He leaned forward, closing the distance between them, and took her hand in his. "Don't say that, *chèrie*. Please. I can't bear to have you so angry with me."

As though she hadn't heard him, she continued, "For once in my life, I thought someone had looked at me and found something worthwhile. I believed the gifts were real. I'd convinced myself that someone cared about me." In a whisper, she added, "I felt special."

"You are special."

"Stop it," she insisted. To her dismay, tears welled into her eyes once again and began splashing down her cheeks. She couldn't stop them, and they flowed freely.

"Oh, Meg . . . don't cry," he said, lifting his thumb and trying to dry them away, but he couldn't. There were too many. He had seen much female weeping in his day, but always it was calculated to gain some advantage. These were real, and the fact that they were Meg's and he had caused them made him feel like the lowest form of vermin. "Let me explain . . ."

"I don't want to hear any lame justification."

"But I need to tell you, so you'll understand . . ." He waited, and when she didn't respond, he took her silence as a good sign and rushed ahead. "It started as a joke."

"Why would you joke in such a fashion?"

"Because I knew," he sighed, not wishing to hurt her further, but knowing it was time for only the truth, "that you'd sent the first bouquet of flowers to yourself."

"Oh, dear Lord, I want to die." She pulled her hand from his and leaned her head back against the squab, closing her eyes against the crushing pain of humiliation. "How many people did you tell?"

"I told no one. I thought you were . . . I don't know . . . funny, sad . . . I wanted to do something to stir up your day, so I sent you a gift. I enjoyed watching how happy it made you. So I sent another and another. It wasn't a joke then. I came every day to see you receive them simply so I could see the joy in your eyes. I've wanted to tell you it was me for days now, but I couldn't figure out how without sounding as if I . . .''

"As if you cared for me?" she cut him off, adding sarcastically, "Heaven forbid that anyone think such a thing."

"I didn't care a fig what others thought about it. Only you. I was afraid I might hurt you somehow, and I didn't want to. That's all that mattered."

"But you hurt me anyway."

"Unintentionally! Look at me," he insisted, forcing her to open her eyes. "I was running late today. I've been so busy making arrangements, packing . . . but I wanted to be sure to send you something. There were trinkets on my dressing table, all sorts of things. I just grabbed one and had it wrapped. I didn't even look at the bracelet, really. I never meant to embarrass you."

"Was it truly a gift you'd given to Portia?"

"Yes, I realize now," he answered truthfully as his eyes begged for mercy. "I'm sorry."

"Is she your mistress?"

"No."

"But she was."

"A long time ago." Sebastian shrugged. He had no intention of discussing his lurid involvement with Portia. Meg would never understand some of the things he had done.

"Were you ever going to tell me about the gifts?"

"We were going to write one another, remember? I planned to tell you in a letter. I hoped I could find a way to make it sound wonderful."

She retreated again, turning her gaze to the window and staring out into the darkness, and he couldn't bear to witness the desolation in her gaze, knowing that he had put it there. In thirty-six hours, he would leave for Jamaica. There was no time to repair her reputation. No time to mend her broken heart or heal her damaged spirit. Worst of all was the thought that he would be leaving with the situation unresolved between them.

"What can I do to fix this, Meg? Whatever it is, just tell me. I'll do anything, whatever you ask." She didn't appear to hear him, and he was at a loss as to how to proceed; so they sat silently in the cold, dark coach as the minutes passed unnoticed.

On a long sigh, she finally turned to face him once again. There was enough light to make out his profile, the twinkle in his eye, the shock of hair falling over his forehead. His cheeks were darkened with what would become his morning stubble of beard, but he looked terribly young and vulnerable.

She believed him about the bracelet. Despite her humiliation at the ball, in her heart she knew he was a good person. He had done things she didn't particularly like, but with no malice. In his own way, he cared about her and what happened to her. She was certain of it. If he didn't, he never would have chased after her when she ran out into the night.

If only there was more time . . . But there wasn't. They would both leave London on Sunday and never see one another again. This was her one and only chance to find out what she had been longing to know. He had said he would do anything for her, and with searing clarity, she knew exactly for what she wished.

"I want you to take me somewhere."

"Where?"

"Somewhere private where it's just the two of us. I want us to be lovers."

Sebastian hesitated. There were many ways to play this, and he wanted to choose the best one which would hurt her the least. He leaned forward, his elbows on his knees. "Meg, I know I said I'd do whatever you want, but I can't do this."

"Why?"

"Because you don't know what you're asking. Or what you'd be giving up."

"I know enough."

"No, you don't. If you truly understood, you'd never offer such a thing."

"You'll lie down with the likes of Portia quickly enough," she responded bitterly.

"I took what Portia offered because I didn't care about her. I won't do it with you ... because I do." He took both her hands in his. They were cold, and she was trembling. "You're sad and you're hurting, and because of it, you want to give me your maidenhead. You think it will make you feel better, but it won't. Trust me."

"It's what I want more than anything."

"You only think so now. If we were to lie together, you could never marry. I can't take such a chance away from you."

"I don't care what my aunt is trying to do to me. I will never marry."

"You say that now because of her choice of husband, but you can't know what your heart may desire in the future."

"At the moment, the future seems a long time distant. It doesn't matter to me."

"But it does to me. You are offering me your most precious gift, and I don't deserve it. Nor could I ever hope to be worthy of it."

"Would you deny me this? After what you've done?" She closed the distance between them and brushed a soft kiss across his lips. "I want to know what it's like—what it's really like—and I want you to be the one to show me. If you ever had any kind feelings for me, you'll say yes."

Sebastian's conscience warred with his desire, and his conscience quickly lost the battle. He wished for the fortitude to say no, but he couldn't. The sad fact was that he was terribly frightened about his own future, and he didn't want to spend the night alone. Any number of women would have been happy to pass the time with him, but he knew that physical companionship alone would not assuage his restless spirit. He needed to be with someone who cared about him, someone who knew his secrets, understood him and liked him anyway.

In his entire, wretched life, Meg was the only one who fit the bill.

By taking her virginity, he would be using her in the worst possible way to satisfy his own needs; but the Fates that ruled the universe seemed to have determined the connection between them long ago, and he couldn't shake the feeling that whatever passed between them during the night would end up being a grand and wonderful thing.

Through the small window, he gave a quick one-word instruction to the driver, and the coach lurched away. Then his hands were on her waist; she was on his lap, his mouth covering hers, his tongue inviting, seeking. By the time the coach halted, her hair was down around her waist; her lips were wet and swollen from his kisses. Sebastian was straightening her clothing when one of the coachmen opened the door. A wave of air, smelling of salt water and rotted fish, filled the small space. Meg wrinkled her nose, looking at Sebastian.

"It's not the most romantic spot," he whispered, helping her to her feet and toward the door, "but it's very private, and no one will ever know."

As they stepped down, she looked around and realized they were at the docks. Directly in front was a large-masted sailing ship. Even in the darkness, the brass fittings of the magnificent vessel gleamed. It looked exactly like the one that her imagination conjured whenever she read one of her favorite adventure novels about pirates.

"Yours?" she asked.

"My father's."

"The one taking you away."

"Yes."

"I'm glad you brought me here. Now I'll be able to picture you on board during your crossing."

"What's your wish, Lady Meg?" he asked formally, offering his arm. "Shall we go aboard?"

"Yes," she responded without hesitation. No turning back, no worry about the morrow. There was just tonight and these blessed few hours with Sebastian.

A crewman, who had obviously been waiting for Sebastian's return, handed him a lantern. He used it to guide their way up the gangplank and across the deck. His cabin, down a short set of stairs, was small, with a narrow bed, one little window, a dresser, a desk and not much more. A tiny brazier lessened the chill, giving off a dim glow and making the room seem down-right cozy after sitting so long in the carriage.

Meg was shaking, from the cold but also from the thousand emotions cursing through her body. Staring down at the mattress, she realized that her brave attitude had vanished, and she suddenly felt shy and completely unprepared for what was about to happen. Sebastian busied himself in the cabin, setting down the lamp, removing his cloak; then he came up behind her and wrapped his arms around her. His nearness restored much of her bravado.

"I wish it was a grand bed with a deep feather mattress and silk sheets." He kissed her nape, sending shivers down her spine.

"It's perfect," she said, smiling at him over her shoulder. More determined, she added, "We'll make it perfect."

"That's my girl." He smiled.

He turned her so she was facing him, a hand resting on the small of her back bringing her body into full contact with his. He was already hard and wanting her. Unafraid, she rested her hands on his waist.

"I don't know what to do."

"I should hope not," he chuckled, "but don't worry. I'll show you the way."

"Promise me you won't laugh if I do something wrong."

"You can't do anything wrong here," he insisted, kissing her mouth, then her cheek. "No matter what happens, it will be all right."

She stepped fully into the circle of his arms, her breasts full and aching and pressed against his chest. "Promise me."

"I promise," he vowed, tipping her chin up so his lips could claim hers again.

"And I'd like to leave the lamp burning."

"An excellent decision," he agreed, kissing his way across her cheek, down her neck.

"I want to see everything."

The request wrenched a moan from Sebastian. Her head fell back, allowing him greater access to the spot where her pulse pounded so furiously at the base of her throat. "Something tells me, *chèrie,* that you are going to prove to have a natural talent for this sort of thing"—he dipped farther, nuzzling the tops of her breasts—"but I already knew that about you."

She wasn't sure how he had done it, but he had distracted her with kisses while his fingers were at work at the back of her dress. With hardly a flick of his wrist, the gown dropped to the floor. Another quick move shed her of her petticoats, and she stood before him clad only in her chemise. His hands slid over the fabric of her functional undercovering, and it felt rough and cheap.

"I wish I'd worn something prettier for you."

"It is not the garment which is fueling my desire," he insisted, pulling her closer and letting her feel his aroused state. "You're so beautiful, Meg. I can't wait to see you completely unclothed, to enjoy the touch of your skin against mine."

Blush colored her cheeks, making them rosy and warm. "I want to feel yours as well."

"So you shall, my beauty, so you shall." He sat her down on the edge of the bed while he removed his boots; then he knelt in front of her, kissing and touching her playfully as he removed her slippers and stockings. Meg discovered one new sensation after the next as he worked his hand up the inside of her thighs, stroking her in places no one had ever touched before, although his fingers never seemed to rise as far as her body wanted them to go.

When he started with his shirt, she quickly took over the task until she had him bare-chested. The sight of his shoulders, chest and stomach was amazing. Dark hair was matted across the top. It descended until it became a thin line, drawing her eyes to the waist of his trousers and what lay below.

Sebastian understood her need to explore. Before she made a move, he took her hands and placed them, palms open, on the furry pile. She worked her fingers through the springy growth, then up across his shoulders and down his arms. Each trip caused her to grow more bold, until she found herself not only touching, but pinching, biting and tasting as well.

When her confident hands reached for the front of his pants and moved across his swollen phallus, he could no longer bear her examination. His painful groan stopped her busy fingers. "Am I hurting you?"

"I'm dying," he admitted, "but to such sweet torture, I gladly succumb." He covered her hand with his, helping her learn the rhythms and the locations that could drive him to a fevered pitch.

"Like this?" she asked.

"Exactly like that," he managed, before pushing her onto her back and joining her, his long body stretched along the length of hers. He went to work, with a skill and finesse that never failed to captivate the most experienced of women. Meg gave herself up to his capable hands, following his lead wherever possible, but mostly, letting him indulge himself until her body felt as though it was being swept away on some new and dangerous tide.

Before she realized what had happened, her chemise was crumpled about her waist from top to bottom. Her breasts were bared, and he held them in his hands, in his mouth, until she was writhing and fighting in sweet agony. Her hips and thighs were bare as well, and he had centered himself between, her legs splayed wide in a most shocking display; but she didn't care.

He had ignited a fire deep in the pit of her stomach, and it was quickly surging out of control. So consumed was she by the flames that she hardly noticed that he had begun touching her there, in her woman's spot. With his fingers, he teased and stretched until she was open, moist and rotating her hips in a steady rhythm with his hand.

When he finally halted his incessant touching and coaxing, he was poised over her, his weight balanced on one arm, his jaw set, his eyes filled with desire, every muscle in his body taut with strain. His male part had replaced his hand. Hard and relentless, it rested against her opening, demanding entry.

"I can't wait another moment, *chèrie,*" he said, nudging against her so that the tip was inserted inside her body. "Are you sure?"

"I want this more than I've ever wanted anything."

"It will hurt for a moment, when I enter you."

"I know," she said impatiently, wishing for him to just get on with it. An explosion inside her body seemed imminent, and she sensed that Sebastian would know how to ease the torment she was experiencing.

"God, you're lovely," he told her, letting his eyes rove across her face, her breasts, her stomach, to the spot where he perched so tremulously. The sight of his solid and pulsing member eagerly waiting to join with her was his undoing. He dragged his gaze to hers. "Come with me. Now."

He dipped his head to her breast, sucking the aching nub deep into his mouth. At the same time, his thumb began making slow circles across a painful spot in her woman's hair. "Sebastian . . . ," she groaned out.

"Let go, Meg. Let go, just for me." He shifted to her other breast.

The feeling that had been growing spiraled out of control, and Meg arched up off the bed, crying out his name as her universe shattered into a million pieces. The riveting sensations went on and on until she dazedly wondered if they would ever end. As reality gradually returned, she found herself safely sheltered in his arms. His eyes were bright with tension, but they were smiling down at her.

"It's done," he said softly.

It took her a moment to realize what he meant. He had entered her. She was completely filled with him, in more ways than just physically. In awe, she whispered, "It didn't hurt."

"I'm glad."

"We're not finished, are we?"

"No. We've hardly begun." He grinned. "We just got the difficult part out of the way." He moved inside her, pulled back, entered fully, and her eyes widened with joyous surprise. "Follow me again?"

"Anywhere," she answered, quickly picking up his tempo.

In a matter of minutes, Meg reached another glorious peak, and Sebastian joined her, emptying himself into her body with several dramatic pushes. As he spilled his life seed, something monumental flooded through her heart, and she couldn't hold back the tears of wonder which sprang to her eyes.

"I'm sorry," she sobbed as he held her tight and kissed them away. After what had just occurred, she knew she could never lie down with another, and she wondered how she would go through the rest of her life without experiencing this blessed glory ever again. "I feel so silly. I don't even know why I'm crying."

"I do," he soothed, some deeply ingrained male part of him reveling in the fact that he had managed to thoroughly undo her with his loving.

"Is it always like this?"

"No, *chèrie*," he responded, knowing he spoke the truth when he said, "it's never like this."

He loved her twice more before they finished. Lying together, exhausted and sated, they began to notice the chill in the cabin. They were both naked, and Sebastian covered them with a blanket. Touching, kissing, and cuddling, they faced each other on the narrow bed, breasts, bellies, and thighs connected, legs and feet entwined. Through the tiny window, they could see it was still dark night. Sebastian brushed his lips over hers as his eyes drifted closed. "Let's rest for a few minutes; then I'll see you home."

"I'd like that," Meg whispered in return, cherishing the excuse to hold him one last time. Her arms were wrapped about his shoulders, and she pulled him closer as his breathing steadied and slowed. His face was pressed against her chest, and each warm exhale felt like a special caress. She closed her eyes and held him tight, imprinting every sight, every sound, every smell into her memory.

Just when she thought he was sleeping, he spoke.

"I don't want to go to Jamaica."

"I know you don't," she agreed, kissing his forehead.

"I'm afraid . . . ," his voice drifted off, sounding young and so very insecure.

"Don't be. Everything is going to be all right," she soothed, wishing it to be true.

She laid with him as long as she dared, not trusting herself to fall asleep. When the first morning bird cooed in the distance, she knew her time with him had ended. Quietly, she slipped out of the bed and dressed. A last look around told her she had not forgotten anything.

"I love you," she pledged, leaning forward and stealing one last gentle kiss. "I'll love you forever."

He smiled, seeming to have heard and understood even in his sleep.

Taking the lamp, she made her way to the deck, relieved to find his carriage and its attendants faithfully waiting on the dock. One of the liverymen helped her climb inside, and she was whisked away into the approaching dawn.

CHAPTER NINE

"I hate Valentine's Day," Meg muttered to herself as she huddled alone in her tiny room, staring down into the gardens. The gazebo was barely visible at the back. Despite the cool late afternoon air, there were windows open downstairs, and she heard the occasional voices of servants or the rattle of china and glassware as last-minute preparations were made for Patty's come out ball which would begin in a few hours.

No one had noticed when she slipped in the back door and up the servants' stairs at dawn, just as no one had noticed that she had been absent all day from the preparations. She should have been there, guiding the servants and overseeing the final details, but somehow, she couldn't work up the least bit of interest. For the entire day, she had sat on her bed, staring out the window, reliving every moment of the previous day, from Lucy's announcement that she had found Meg a husband, to the disastrous ball where she had learned the identity of her secret admirer, to the bliss-filled hours she had spent with Sebastian.

In awe over what he had done to her and how he had made her feel, she could only sit and brood. With her fingers splayed wide over her abdomen, she dreamily wondered if she might be, at that very moment, carrying his babe. She didn't know if it was possible from the first time, but she hoped so. In most peoples' opinions, such an eventuality would be considered a catastrophe which would ruin her life. In her own, having Sebastian's child would be a miraculous circumstance.

Sometime during the unending day, Lucy had sent a note upstairs, telling her that she was not to attend the ball. Any other time of her life, the message that she was not welcome at this most important of family gatherings would have shattered her tender heart beyond repair. Not today.

Lucy thought she was meting out punishment for Meg's indecorous behavior at the Miltons' ball, but Meg secretly embraced the opportunity to hide from the rude stares, snickers and awful gossip which awaited her at Patty's fête. She needed the quiet hours to love and mourn Sebastian, for his father's ship was ready to work its way down the Thames, and before she knew it, he would be on the high seas.

How lucky he was! To be leaving this dreadful place, building a new life full of new friends and new experiences. He didn't think so, and he was frightened about the changes his father was forcing on him. But he was so lucky to have the chance for such an adventure.

Would he ever think of her? She hoped so, for she would love and think of him every moment.

A knock sounded at her door, and she was irritated that someone dared interrupt her solitary reverie.

"Who is it?" she asked, more rudely than she meant to.

"Giles, Lady Meg," came the response.

Since she cared for the old retainer, she rose off the bed, wondering what had brought him up so many stairs. She opened the door, surprised to see several women standing behind him. "Whatever is happening?"

"You've received several packages, milady. From your secret admirer."

"I'm sorry, Giles, but you must be mistaken."

"I'm not," he said with a twinkle in his eye as he handed her a card.

"I'm surprised you didn't hear. It was all a joke."

"I don't think so, Lady Meg," he offered kindly. "Read the card."

She stepped closer, looking out at the women standing behind him, her eyes widening when she saw the dressmaker, Madame LaFarge. With shaking hands, she turned the card over and ran her thumb under the seal.

Wear these tonight. Just for me.

SS

Standing frozen in the doorway, she was unable to grasp the meaning of the note or the arrival of the well-known modiste and several members of her staff. Her consternation was so great that she might have stood there forever if madame had not taken charge.

She shooed Meg back inside, taking a quick, disapproving look about. "The room is too small, but it will have to do." She looked over at Giles. "We will need better light. Many lamps. And a good wine, to calm the lady's nerves. Only the best." She sniffed at this, as though Giles would not be able to select a fine one. "And food. A full tray."

"I'll see to all of it immediately." He bowed in agreement. "Let me know if there is anything else."

"We have much work to do," she said, turning her focus back to Meg, "and only a few hours to do it."

"A few hours to accomplish what?" Meg asked.

"To prepare you for the ball."

"I'm not going to the ball."

"But of course you are." She signaled with her hands for the other women to enter. *"Vite, vite.* There is not much time."

Meg watched in amazement as they began to unpack parcels containing all manner of women's things: brushes, combs, ribbons, curling irons, facial paints, jewelry, undergarments of the finest silk and lace. But she didn't truly understand the significance of what was happening until madame, herself, opened the largest box and removed a ball gown. It was the most exquisite thing Meg had ever seen, and, she realized, made from the fabric and trim Sebastian had admired during their disastrous visit to the shop on the day they had met.

How had he done it? Why had he done it?

"It is very beautiful, *n'est-ce pas?"* asked the formidable dressmaker.

" 'Beautiful' doesn't begin to describe it," Meg responded, cautiously running her hand along the shiny dark green of the silk, the green velvet of the trim, as though she was in the middle of a fairy tale and the gown might magically disappear.

"Monsieur was right," Madame LaFarge said, holding the gown against Meg's chest so the dress unfurled and the flounces of the skirt swirled to the floor. "The color matches your eyes perfectly." With a disdainful sniff as she assessed the plain gray day dress Meg was wearing, she added, "Let us begin. Off with your clothes."

"I don't know . . ." Meg sighed, gazing longingly at the panoply of gifts Sebastian had sent. What she wouldn't give to appear downstairs dressed to the nines, looking like a beauty, but she doubted her humiliation from the prior evening had been forgotten by the party-goers. There was a slim chance that a fresh look would help her to be admired and treated with respect. More likely, despite the exquisite apparel, they would still think of her as plain Meg MacDonald, the charity case of the Smythewaites, for whom they had all been waiting so they could, once again, make merry at her expense.

"What is there to know?" Madame LaFarge snapped. "If

you are to dance the night away in the arms of the most handsome man in the kingdom, you must be dressed accordingly.''

With her words, a small spark ignited in Meg's heart. Sebastian would be downstairs. His last night in England, and he wanted to spend it with her! He had sent all the finery so he could go to Jamaica with this memory of her. They would dance all night, laugh and talk as the lovers they were, and Meg didn't care a fig what anyone thought or said. Only Sebastian.

''You're right, madame,'' Meg agreed. ''I'm ready.''

''We will do it all. The hair, the face . . .'' The older woman began giving rapid directions to the others in French, and they went to work immediately. Meg was pushed onto a stool and surrounded by a whirlwind of hands and utensils, and she determinedly gave herself over to their care.

Sebastian walked up the steps of the Smythewaite mansion. The place was teeming with activity, all the windows lighted and glowing, the front doors open wide as fashionable London descended on the place. Tired of the jam of carriages, and too impatient to sit idly and wait for his future to descend, he had exited his own several blocks back and walked the remaining distance. The wet night air had been the ticket, helping to calm his pounding heart and his jangled emotions.

He had always been a gambler, loving the game, the stakes, the excitement. His only problem had been that he never cared about the outcome. He had so much, that to lose some of it on something as frivolous as the turn of a card or the speed of a horse had never concerned him overly much. Tonight was different.

For the first time, outcome was everything. He was prepared to take the biggest gamble of his life, to risk all, knowing full well that if he lost, the results would reverberate throughout whatever sorry events shaped the rest of his years. He would never be the same. But if he won—oh, if he won—then the greatest treasure of all would be his for what he hoped would be a very long and fruitful life.

Heads turned as he leaped up the steps, but he hardly noticed. People always turned to look when he passed, so the assessment was nothing new. Their gazes were different tonight, though. Everyone was obviously wondering what he was doing in attendance and if he had more shenanigans planned. His garb alone was enough to set the tongues wagging. Dressed for traveling, in black boots and trousers, shirt and cape, he felt like a pirate, ready to seize the riches waiting inside.

Before taking three steps across the foyer, he was accosted by Portia.

"Darling, I'm so glad you've come." She slipped her arm through his, trying to make it look as though they had entered together.

"Leave off, Portia. I'm not your 'darling,' and I never have been."

"My, aren't we testy this evening." She patted his arm. "Your attire is certainly interesting. Did we dress in a hurry?"

"I'm leaving for Jamaica in a few hours." He took distinct pleasure in seeing her mouth fall open with surprise. Rarely was a secret kept from the woman.

"You're leaving?" She tried to sound unconcerned, but her shock registered before she had time to straighten her face and summon her usual air of bored disdain. "Why didn't you tell me?"

"It's none of your business, really." He was being intentionally cruel. For years, he had silently put up with her vicious tongue, as did everyone else, not caring most of the time and actually enjoying it on occasion, but after she had hurt Meg in front of so many, the gloves were off.

"How can you say that? After all we've meant to each other . . ."

"You've never meant anything to me."

"Well . . ." Her cheeks reddened. Several of her friends

were standing nearby and heard what he said. How could he embarrass her like this? After she had exposed the Smythewaite cousin at the Miltons', she had thought they would get together, have a good laugh over the entire affair; but he had vanished, and she hadn't been able to find him all day.

It took her several moments to realize that he wasn't paying any attention to her at all. Instead, he was scanning the crowd ahead. A sinking feeling stole over her, the one she had had when she saw him dancing with Meg MacDonald. "She's not here."

"Who would that be?" Sebastian asked, trying to sound uninterested.

"The gigantic frump you're so fond of." In a full-blown snit, she asked bitterly, "Did you send her any trinkets today?"

"As a matter of fact, I did," he responded coolly. He leaned over and whispered wickedly, "Emeralds. A necklace and earrings," not mentioning that he had the matching ring in his pocket.

Portia understood the significance of the gift without his saying more. "You'll be the laughingstock of London, tying up with that silly thing."

He shrugged and yanked his arm free of hers in a determined gesture he wanted everyone to see. "And let me give you a word of advice before I depart. You really should be more careful about who you insult. You never know who they might become in the future." He let the crowd swallow him up so he didn't have to hear any of her retort.

At the rate the receiving line was going, it would take another hour to get to the front. He didn't have the time. Everything else about his appearance was rude, so he started pushing past those who were waiting politely. As he reached the door to the ballroom, he could see Lucy, Patty and several other family members at the bottom of the stairs. Meg was not with them.

No matter. He would search the bloody house room by room if he had to.

Pushing past people, he created a stir with his clothing and presence as he made his way down the stairs. Couples parted to let him through, and the crowd hushed as he passed. It took several moments for Lucy to look up and see him coming, and he loved the determined look in her eye. She had just met her match, but she didn't know it yet.

"Where is she?" he demanded, stepping around those who were at the front of the line.

Lucy smiled tightly, wanting to strangle the dastardly marquess for having the audacity to show himself. She didn't want people talking about him or Meg; she wanted them focused on Patty. "I'm sure I don't know who you mean."

"Where is she, you old bat?"

The people standing closest gasped. Lucy pulled herself up to her full height, ready for the fight that she would not hold in front of the assembled company. "If you'll excuse me," she said, nodding graciously to those nearby, "Lord Stuart and I need to speak alone."

"No, we don't. Tell me now, or I'll start searching for her. I'll take this place apart brick by brick."

"If you are referring to my niece," Lucy said tightly, trying to retain control of the situation, "she is indisposed and will not be joining us. Now, I must get back to my guests . . ."

"Why is she 'indisposed'? Did you lock her in her room?"

"I most certainly did not! I simply refuse to let her appear in public where you could make another spectacle of her. She was so emotionally overcome by your outrageous behavior that she's resting before she returns home to the peace and quiet of the country." Doing her best to look offended, she added, "If I were a man, I'd call you out for what you did to that poor girl."

"Oh, spare me the theatrics, Lucy. Your acting is atrocious."

"I will not be mocked in my own home, Lord Stuart. In case you haven't noticed, we are hosting a party. You were invited, but are no longer welcome. Leave at once or I will have you thrown out.''

"I would love to see you try." He flashed a malevolent look to those standing closest, daring anyone to step forward. No one did. "Besides, force will not be necessary. I'll leave as soon as Meg and I have spoken." He turned toward the stairs. "I'm sure I can find her room. It must be on the top floor with the rest of the servants."

Before he could make a move, his father stepped through the crowd into the small circle of space around the receiving line. He was a tall, striking man, who looked much like Sebastian would in another two decades, with the same blue eyes and dark hair, although his was silvered with streaks of gray.

"Sebastian," he growled, "I thought you'd be . . ." He paused, not wanting to say the rest in front of the throng of onlookers.

"Bound for Jamaica?" Sebastian finished for him, no longer caring who heard the news. "I have a few hours yet, but don't worry. I'll be out of your hair shortly. First, I must take care of a most pressing appointment."

"What are you doing here?"

"As you can see, Father, I'm insulting the countess in front of her guests."

"Then, I insist you apologize at once."

"Or what? You'll banish me? Disown me? We're a little past that, wouldn't you say?" He leveled a stare at Lucy. "Besides, she doesn't deserve an apology. If anything, she should be horsewhipped for how she's treated Meg all these years."

"Meg? Who is Meg?"

"You'll find out soon enough."

"Meg is my niece, Your Grace," Lucy butted in, "and the marquess has inflicted himself into her life in the most horrid way. I shall demand reparations on her behalf."

"Do stop, Lucy. I'm prepared to take her off your hands.

You won't have to spend any more of your precious coin feeding her.''

Just then, a flurry occurred at the top of the stairs. Guests started whispering and turning. The crowd began to part. Meg appeared, looking radiant and regal. With her head held high, she paused, letting everyone look their fill. As she had suspected, she could tell from the murmurs spreading out in front of her that everyone had been hoping she would make an appearance so they would have something to gossip about. Well, she was certainly ready to give them all the talk they desired.

Taking in the scene below, she carefully assessed the situation before stepping into the middle of it. Lucy commanded attention at the front of the receiving line containing her family. She was vexed and angry. Sebastian, dressed for traveling, stood in front of her, defiant and ready to do battle. A man, who could only be his father, brooded next to him, looking thunderous.

Like a royal princess, she began her descent, taking her time with each step. Tipping her head to acknowledge this person and that as she passed, she moved closer to Sebastian with each step.

''God, isn't she magnificent?'' Sebastian vowed softly as he watched her come to him. She was as breathtaking and radiant as he had known she would be, and he felt a huge wave of pride welling inside as he heard many others standing nearby whispering much the same sentiment.

''Aunt Lucy, Patty,'' she acknowledged as she reached the group, giving them both a polite curtsey. Patty looked stunned, and Lucy furious. For once, Meg didn't care. Sebastian was the only one who mattered, and from the way he was staring at her, she could tell he greatly approved.

She rose and faced him. He held out his hand, which she grasped instantly. It was her lifeline in a sea of hostile faces. ''Hello, Lord Stuart.''

"Hello, *chèrie.* You look lovely this evening."

"Thank you." She blushed prettily. He took her arm and turned toward his father. "Father, may I present my very, very good friend, Lady Meg MacDonald." Each word he used was calculated to raise brows, and he succeeded. People were standing on tiptoes, peering over shoulders, trying to see what he was about.

"Good evening, Your Grace," Meg added, deciding to join Sebastian in his charade. If he wanted to act like they were longtime companions, she had no problem with the image. She was proud to let everyone know they were close.

She started to curtsey once again, but Sebastian stopped her. "There is no need," he whispered, his warm breath tickling her cheek, and she gave him a puzzled look. "Father," he said, returning his attention to the duke, "Meg is the earl's first cousin. Her mother was Eleanor Smythewaite . . ."

"Well, now that you say it," the duke interrupted, "of course I see the resemblance. I knew your mother. An exceptionally gracious woman. She was a great beauty."

"I always thought so," Meg agreed.

"You look just like her."

"What a generous thing to say." She smiled, squeezing Sebastian's hand tightly.

"I might have married her, myself, if your father hadn't come along and swept her off her feet."

Meg braced herself for a scathing remark. Weakly, she asked, "You knew my father?"

"Yes, I met him years ago in Portsmouth. A grand fellow. I liked him very much. It was easy to see why your mother was so taken with him."

Meg fell in love with him on the spot. "You're very kind."

"How are your parents? I've not seen them in ages."

"They're gone, Your Grace. Over a decade now."

"I'm so sorry to hear that."

"Actually," Sebastian offered, "she's been living with Lucy ever since. But I'm hoping that's about to change."

He winked at his father, and Meg had no idea what it meant. She was even more confounded when he turned to her and took both her hands in his. The look in his eye was completely unreadable. "What?" she asked softly. "What is it?"

Sebastian thought his heart might burst. Since he had awakened in the early morning to find her gone from his side, he had known that he must have her back. He could not sail away from England without her, and he could not leave her behind to face scorn and ridicule from others because of his actions. And, no matter what, he couldn't leave her in Lucy's clutches one more day. There seemed only one way to fix the situation.

So he had spent the day preparing for this moment, although he couldn't shake the feeling that perhaps he had been preparing for it all his life. Wagering all, his pride, his freedom, his future, hoping against hope that words would not fail him, he started.

"My dearest Meg," he said, his eyes searching hers. "I am bound for Jamaica with the dawn tide. I'm to start a new life in a new world, and I can't imagine going without you.

"Oh, Sebastian . . . ," she gasped.

"Will you come with me, *chèrie?*"

"You want me to go with you?" she asked, thoroughly confused.

"I want much more than that," he chuckled. "Meg, I never imagined that I could find a woman such as yourself, and now that I've found you, I can't let you go. Will you take a chance on me? Will you let me show you how much I love you? Will you let me spend the rest of my life making you happy?"

"What are you saying?" she asked in a shaky voice. She thought she knew, but she dared not hope that he meant what she thought he did.

He dropped to one knee. "Meg, I know you deserve better, but I swear to you in front of our families and this assembled company that I will love you and cherish you all the days of my life. Would you do me the great honor of becoming my wife?''

The room seemed to hold its collective breath as Meg waited the longest time before answering, not because she didn't know what to say or how to say it, but because she needed time to savor every delicious moment and to thoroughly imprint all of it into her memory. Finally with a trembling smile, she said, ''The honor would be mine to have you as my husband, so my answer is yes. A thousand times yes!''

''Then, I have just become the luckiest man in the kingdom.'' He stood and took her in his arms, hugging her tightly as many people standing close by applauded the exchange.

''Well done, well done.'' His father patted Sebastian on the back.

''I don't want to leave you behind,'' Sebastian whispered to her, pulling back slightly to look in her eyes. The next was as important as the first. ''The captain tells me he can marry us as soon as we set sail. Will you come with me tonight so we can go to Jamaica together?''

Meg thought she had died and gone to heaven. The chance to marry Sebastian was a dream come true, but to marry immediately, then run off to start a new life together in an exotic, untamed land! It was like something out of a storybook. ''I can't think of anything more wonderful.''

The duke leaned close to the two of them. ''You better ask Lucy first. She looks ready to blow.''

Meg's heart sank. Technically, she was still many months away from twenty-one years. If Lucy wanted to refuse her permission to marry Sebastian, she could.

Sebastian turned to face Meg's aunt. She had always used wicked intent when dealing with Meg in the past. It was entirely possible that she would rather continue her harsh treatment than to see Meg happily married and facing the future as a duchess. Would the woman dare to refuse his suit? ''What say you, Countess? May I have your ward's hand in marriage this night?''

"This is highly irregular," she huffed, trying to retain some of her dignity. To think that if she said yes, Meg would someday be a duchess! The idea was ludicrous, and she frantically tried to think of a reason to delay. Finally, it came to her. "If you truly desire to marry her, there is no need for haste. You should be betrothed at least a year; then we would normally need another six months to plan the wedding. I'm willing to shorten the time, and agree to a ceremony twelve months from now."

"But, Aunt Lucy," Meg said, her heart sinking by the moment, "I've no desire for a lavish wedding or a lengthy engagement."

"Still, I am your guardian. I know what's best, and marriage to the marquess needs some serious contemplation before you charge ahead." Lucy could not have cared less if Meg was shackled with Sebastian; she just didn't want the blasted girl to make a marriage higher than Patty.

"Why, Lucy," the duke intervened, "if I didn't know better, I'd swear you had just cast public aspersions on my son's character." Although he rarely approved of Sebastian's antics, he would never let Lucy publicly belittle his only son.

"Why no, Your Grace." She flushed bright red. "I simply meant that this is happening so quickly, and Meg needs more time to think it through carefully. I'd give the same advice to any young girl about to make such a major life decision."

Sebastian rolled his eyes in disbelief. "You have only her *best* interests at heart, am I right?"

"Of course," Lucy insisted.

"Then, think on this: In six months, Meg will be twenty-one. If you won't let her come with me tonight, she'll sail alone at that time. Wouldn't it be safer to let her come now?"

The duke didn't understand all the nuances of what was truly happening, but he had never seen Sebastian so adamant about anything. Marriage and impending parenthood were the best

ways the duke could think of to settle him down. Plus, the fact
that Meg was Eleanor's and Colin's daughter made Sebastian's
choice an excellent one.

He stared meaningfully at Lucy. "They are in love, Countess.
Surely it's better to let them go together than to make them
wait. Sebastian will take good care of her." A month ago, a
week ago, a day ago, he could not have made such an assertion.
But now, seeing how Sebastian looked at Meg, the duke knew
it to be true. He played the card he knew Lucy couldn't ignore.
"And look to the benefits for your children with Meg as a
member of my family. Surely, this is the finest match you could
possibly have made for her and for them. And we're both lucky
that it's a love match as well."

"So," Sebastian interrupted, unable to stand the suspense
any longer, "what is your answer?"

Lucy caught her bottom lip between her teeth. Knowing she
was outmaneuvered, she couldn't refuse. It would simply look
too suspicious if she refused to let Meg marry a marquess.

"Go, go," she said, shooing her hands toward the stairs.

Sebastian smiled, then swooshed Meg away as though he
wanted to get her out of there before Lucy changed her mind.
Hand in hand, they raced toward the stairs. At the bottom one,
Meg paused to look over her shoulder. She felt as though she
should have made her goodbyes to the Smythewaite family,
perhaps hugged Patty or thanked Lucy, but from the glares she
was getting, it was obvious no goodbyes were welcome.

They started up, people stepping aside as they passed, clapping Sebastian on the back and shouting words of encourage-
ment to the two of them. As they reached the top, Sebastian
pulled her to a stop.

"I had Madame LaFarge pack two trunks for you. They're
in my cabin on the ship. I think I have everything you need."

"You were awfully sure I'd go."

"I refused to fail." He pulled her palm to his lips and kissed it. "If I forgot anything, we can get it for you once we reach Jamaica, but is there anything you want to take from here?"

Meg paused in the doorway to the grand ballroom. Below, the room looked magical, decorated with thousands of pink, red and white roses in celebration of Valentine's Day. Candles flickered in sparkling chandeliers over the hundreds of guests who were turned out in their finest clothing, their most dazzling jewels. At the front of the crowd, her family stood stiff and unbending, and the receiving line had begun moving once again as though nothing of consequence had just occurred. None of them looked up for a final wave.

"No," she said, without a hint of regret, "there's nothing here I want."

They walked out together and found Sebastian's carriage had finally made its way to the front door. A coachman settled them in, and they raced for the docks. Sebastian had just helped her down and was saying goodbye to the liverymen when another carriage rattled up behind. On the door was the ducal crest. Sebastian stiffened, and Meg squeezed his hand. "It will be all right." She smiled. "Just wait and see."

The duke stepped out, looking older than he had at the ball, as though the events of the past hour had aged him considerably.

"Hello, Your Grace," Meg called and waved. "I'm glad you came to see us off."

"Hello, Meg," he said gently as he walked next to them, "and please, I would be honored if you would call me Father." He blushed slightly. "If that's not too forward."

"I would like to," she said. "Thank you." A bit awkwardly, she added, "Father."

"What are you doing here?" Sebastian asked.

"I came to tell you goodbye, and to . . . well actually . . ." The duke, never at a loss for words, was suddenly choked by emotion. Now that his son was truly leaving, with his new wife by his side, he didn't want them to go. "I was thinking that I may have been too hasty. I hate to see you dragging Meg to

Jamaica, and I was wondering if you'd like to . . . that is . . . I'd like you to remain in England.''

Sebastian stood silently for a long, dumbfounded minute, wondering what he had done to bring about such a dramatic change in his father's attitude. He looked over at Meg and found his answer. There was just something about her that made a man want to keep her close by.

Visually asking her for advice, his eyes widened as she gave a quick shake of her head. He read her message clearly and knew she was right. ''No, thank you, sir. I am looking forward to the journey. I know you have expectations for me, and I plan to meet each and every one.'' Sebastian swallowed hard, unable to believe he felt a prickle of tears lurking behind his eyes. ''I want to make you proud of me.''

''I am proud of you,'' the duke insisted, ''and I'm so very happy for both of you.''

Meg stood on tiptoe and kissed his cheek. ''We'll miss you.''

''I'll miss you, too,'' he admitted. ''When will you come back?''

Meg and Sebastian looked at each other. At the moment, neither had any desire to set foot in England again. Too many adventures lay ahead.

''I don't know,'' Sebastian finally said. ''I don't know if we'll be back.''

''We'll write, though,'' Meg said. ''All the time. And perhaps you could come visit some day.''

''I'd like that very much.'' The duke smiled wistfully.

Just then, a pipe sounded on board the ship, and the man guarding the gangplank politely mentioned that the marquess needed to board. Meg and the duke stared at each other for a moment; then Meg leaned forward and hugged him tightly. ''I wish we'd had more time.''

''We will find the time. In Jamaica,'' the duke insisted. ''I promise it.''

"Goodbye, Father," Sebastian said, finding the moment a thousand times harder than he had ever imagined it would be.

"Goodbye, my son." Surprising them both, the duke clutched Sebastian in a strong embrace, and Sebastian couldn't prevent himself from hugging his father in return. "Take good care of her, or you'll have to answer to me."

"I intend to take very, very good care of her, sir, every day of what I hope is our long life together." He stepped away from his father and turned to Meg, who would become his wife within the hour. She looked spectacularly out of place standing on the old, stinking dock in her ballroom finery, but no woman had ever been a more beautiful bride.

He offered his arm. "What say you, Lady Meg? Shall we go aboard?"

"Yes," she said, smiling in return. "Let's do."

They walked on together, holding hands all the way.

ONE SPECIAL NIGHT

BY

JACKIE STEPHENS

CHAPTER ONE

January, 1849

"Sounds like a dang fool thing to do, if you ask me, Doc."

Grant Radnor's temper flared at the flagrant shock in his friend's strained voice. He pulled the next stitch, drawing together the wound on the blacksmith's muscled arm, then paused and glanced up. "I *didn't* ask you," he said. "And what's so foolish about it?"

"Well, for starters," Tollie Culver began, "I thought ya swore off women after that Boston gal decided not to get hitched."

Grant frowned. His betrothed had decided not to get hitched all right. She had been more interested in the wealth and status she thought to obtain through their union, and quite disappointed to learn Grant would never inherit a dime from the prominent Boston physician who refused to acknowledge his bastard son.

But the seamstress, Cara Martin, didn't strike him as a woman on the search for an open door into society. She was quiet, and aloof . . . and her alluring beauty had captivated his senses the moment he set eyes on her after arriving in Texas.

Grant turned back to his work. "I've had time to get over being mad, and rethink some things."

"Time to get plenty horny, too, I reckon," the blacksmith retorted.

Grant jabbed the needle harder than necessary through the three-inch slice the blacksmith's young apprentice had accidentally inflicted with a poker. Tollie flinched.

"If that was the problem," Grant replied, poking the needle into the pale flesh again, and not bothering to hide his sardonic grin, "I'd take care of it at the saloon with one of Tyler's girls."

He tugged the needle through, pulling the last stitch, then tied a knot and snipped the end of the suturing thread.

Tollie eyed the wound with a relieved smirk. "Why don't ya?" he challenged. "Might improve this foul mood you've been in lately."

"There's nothing wrong with my mood," Grant huffed, stepping back from the wooden examining table where Tollie sat. He flung the needle and scissors into a white porcelain bowl of soapy water, heedless of the suds that sloshed over the side.

"Sure there isn't," the blacksmith grumbled, slipping his arms into the sleeves of his red flannel shirt and shrugging it onto his shoulders. "So buy yourself a woman, and see if it improves your thinkin' any."

Grant planted his fists low on his hips and narrowed his stare. "What's so all-fired wrong with wanting to invite Miss Martin to supper?"

Tollie stopped buttoning his shirt. "I've told ya about Miss Cara." He lifted one hand and rubbed at the dark stubble on his chin. "Course, I heard tell she ain't had a bad spell in quite a while now. Still . . ." Tollie's voice trailed off, the unspoken words clearly etched on his ruddy face.

A tinge of guilt edged its way into Grant's annoyance. Not long after moving to Blue Plains, he had heard about Cara's "spells" from Tollie and several of the other townsfolk. He couldn't ignore his medical interest in her ailment, but that didn't have a blasted thing to do with wanting to buy her dinner.

Turning away, Grant crossed the planked flooring of his office with stiff strides and stopped at the square-paned window overlooking the main road through town. Bright sunlight filtered through the scattered gray clouds, coating the community in its soft winter glow. Several large oaks reigned majestic beside the distant church and schoolhouse, and over the three-story hotel directly across the dirt street. A light breeze rustled the reddish brown and orange leaves, sending them over the short, winter-dead grass in a fanciful dance. Glancing down, Grant was surprised to see the very person under discussion emerge from her father's newspaper office.

Dressed in a simple, high-buttoned indigo dress, with a matching ruffled bonnet atop her upswept chignon of cinnamon brown hair, she was the prettiest sight he had ever seen. She bent to speak with the towheaded Johnson boy who delivered papers once a week around town, then hiked her skirt, revealing ankle-high black boots, and stepped from the wooden walkway. Dodging wagons, riders, and horse droppings, she hurried across the road. Grant followed her progress, his breath catching as his sight fell to her full, round breasts.

She climbed the steps to the walkway out front and passed his window without a glance in his direction. Not the least discouraged, and still entranced by her beauty, he swept an appreciative stare from her smooth oval face, over her slender waist, the gentle flare of her hips, and watched her enticing sway until she stopped outside her dress shop next door.

What was this power she held over him? Grant wondered. A man of science, he knew her enchanting presence had nothing to do with witchcraft, or demonic possession, as some folks in town hinted as being the cause of her seizures.

"I happen to think Miss Martin is nice," he said, "and I wouldn't mind the opportunity to spend time with her."

"Why, she's sweet and mild as barnyard milk, and pretty as a basket of flowers, but she just ain't right, Doc." Tollie's ominously lowered tone drew Grant's attention. "You've only been here a few months. I've known Miss Cara a long time, and I've seen those spells of hers. Why, it can scare a man bad enough to make the skin get up and crawl all over him."

Grant curled his fingers into a tight ball. He liked Tollie—they had become fast friends after Grant moved to Texas four months ago—but right now, he was damn close to punching the blacksmith in the face. "You're being mighty harsh, aren't you?"

Tollie shook his head. "Don't get me wrong, Doc, I like Miss Cara right fine. But—"

"You know, Tollie, it might be better if we don't discuss Miss Martin."

Shrugging, Tollie jumped down from the table. "Have it your way, Doc. He grabbed his hat off the wall peg. With one hand gripped around the door handle, he stopped. "Seems to me, though, if you're lookin' to have supper with a woman, you'd pick from the swarm of butterflies chasin' after your hide, instead of the one gal who won't give ya the time of day."

"I don't see you rushing out to take that advice," Grant taunted. "Or have you finally gotten up the nerve to speak to Brigitte since the last time I saw you?"

With a fierce growl, Tollie slammed his hat on his head, then yanked the door open and stormed outside.

"You owe me for the stitches!" Grant hollered as the blacksmith passed by the window in long, clipped strides.

Tollie had been mooning over Brigitte Raineau since she came to town three months ago, and he still hadn't stammered a word beyond hello to the hotel barmaid. At least Grant had spoken with Miss Martin—several times in fact, when he could corner her for a minute or two after church or at Yancy's Mercantile. So far, he knew some about her family, a lot about her father's paper, more about Texas weather than he cared, and not one thing about her . . . except the townsfolk's ignorance of her medical problem.

Somewhat familiar with the condition he suspected plagued the young seamstress, several weeks ago Grant set aside his personal dislike of Dr. Grantham Hayward, a renowned scientist in the study of brain disorders, and wrote a letter asking for the man's advice. Unsure if the Boston physician would respond, Grant also posted a second letter to a friend working at the Medical Institute in France where studies were also being conducted. He still anxiously awaited a reply from either man.

Grant stared at the connecting wall separating his office and small living quarters in back from Cara's shop next door. He heard her moving about, and not for the first time pictured her busy at her sewing—laying out her fabric, cutting, stitching. As always, his imaginings quickly turned to other, more exciting thoughts of Miss Martin—thoughts that would earn him a well-deserved slap if the little seamstress ever found out.

He shook his head in exasperation. After his broken engagement, Grant swore his interest in women would never progress beyond the pleasure he could buy. But Cara Martin had bewitched him the moment the reverend introduced them, and his attraction had only increased over the months.

Tollie was right. She was sweet and mild. She wasn't shy though, and on a few occasions Grant thought he had seen a spark of desire in her amber gaze. If the gossip and fears of her neighbors had reached her ears—as Grant figured they must have over the years—he suspected she also hid a strong spirit beneath the calm, passive facade she displayed, a strong enough spirit to keep herself at arm's length from people, him included. But he wasn't one to give up easily.

Right now, though, he had patients to check on. After cleaning his needle and scissors, Grant returned them and his suturing thread to the proper drawers in the glass and wood supply cabinet, then pulled a silver watch from his vest pocket. Eleven forty-five. Just enough time to grab some dinner at the hotel, then head out to the Houghton farm and check on young Samuel's broken leg.

Plucking his heavy black jacket from the wall peg beside the door, he slipped it on. As he reached for the handle, the wooden barrier flew open.

"Oh, yoo-hoo, Dr. Radnor."

Grant cringed as the high-pitched voice sailed through the doorway as fast as the determined woman. Jumping back before she could plow into his chest, he placed his hands on her wool-wrapped shoulders to prevent her from advancing, then stared down at the cloth-covered plate in her hands. He stifled his groan as the spicy smell of nutmeg assailed his nose. Just what he needed—more baked goods. With the exception of Miss Martin, the single ladies of Blue Plains had brought a constant parade of food through his office since he arrived. More than once, he had shared his overabundant bounty of sweets and breads with Tollie and several families he had met on the surrounding plantations, but always with the utmost secrecy to avoid any hurt feelings.

"Good morning, Miss Peterson." He lowered his hands to his sides, forcing a smile for the young blonde whose calculating blue eyes reminded him way too much of his former fiancée's.

"Hello, Dr. Radnor. I brought you some cookies Annie baked this morning."

"Please give your cook my thanks, Miss Peterson." He took the china plate from her, set it on his desk, then turned back to the woman invading his office. She flapped the folds of her sable wrap aside, exposing the low neckline of her pink gown.

Grant looked away from her revealing décolletage and met her widened stare. "Is there something I can help you with?"

"Nothing medical, but I do have another problem." She pursed her thin lips into a pout.

Grant bit back his urge to say that he didn't have time, or any interest, if her dilemma wasn't medical. "And how can I be of assistance?" he politely offered.

Her lips parted in a smile as she slipped her hand through the unoffered crook of his right arm. "Well, Doctor, I'm glad you asked."

Cara Martin froze at the simpering satisfaction in Henrietta Peterson's tone. *Don't look,* she silently admonished. *Don't!*

Cara cut her stare toward the doctor's opened door. Her heart lurched at the sight of the woman's possessive hold on Dr. Radnor's arm, at the smug grin on her upturned mouth. Chiding herself for her unwanted reaction, Cara hurried down the steps, not stopping until she reached the saddled sorrel mare tied out front. Covertly, she watched the pair continue their discussion as she lifted the saddlebags from her shoulder onto the horse, then untied the reins from the hitching post.

Stop it. She forced herself to look away. *It's none of your business what might be transpiring between Henrietta and the doctor.* She wasn't interested.

Liar! She *was* interested . . . in seeing that the handsome doctor didn't become an unwilling victim in Henrietta's selfish clutches!

And? her conscience demanded. Cara bit the inside of her lip, as she reluctantly admitted she couldn't completely ignore the doctor's engaging kindness, and warm jade eyes.

Tall and sinewy, with wavy strands of sandy brown hair brushing his neckline, and a rakishly confident smile, the doctor had caught her eye the moment he sauntered off the river steamer that brought him to town. Though she had fought her attraction over the months, his presence still played constant havoc with her senses. That in itself surprised Cara. At twenty-three, she had thought herself long past foolish wishes and dreams. Betrayed by her former beau, Bernard Hampton, as he had sailed away nearly four years ago in disgust and embarrassment at her illness, she had accepted the truth of what she couldn't change. Since then, she had peacefully resigned herself to spending the rest of her days alone. She would never risk her heart again—ever.

Turning away, Cara lifted her foot to the stirrup.

"Miss Martin, there you are. I've been waiting for you."

Dr. Radnor's deep voice sent a slow radiance through Cara's veins. His rushed words roused her curiosity. Why did he sound so desperate?

Lowering her foot to the ground, Cara looked back, startled to see the doctor fast approaching, with Henrietta disengaged from his arm and hurrying behind.

"You're ready to leave? I thought you were coming by the office first." His widening smile stole her breath.

Cara swallowed the lump in her throat. Frowning, she shook her head. "I'm sorry, I don't know—"

His gaze narrowed to a flinty stare. His smile faded as he silently mouthed two words: *Help me!*

Henrietta stopped beside the doctor and quickly took hold of his arm again. She took several breaths that heightened the decadent display of her bosom, which Cara noted with surprise Dr. Radnor didn't bother to view. "Hello, Cara."

"Henrietta," she responded warily, wondering what the woman had done to cause the doctor such distress.

"Grant asked me to dine with him." A pink flush rose in Henrietta's cheeks. She looked up at the doctor and batted thick, pale lashes. "We're on our way to the hotel."

"I'm very sorry, but I'm afraid we'll have to partake of lunch together some other time." The doctor removed Henrietta's hand from his arm.

Cara coughed lightly, covering her chuckle at the other woman's angrily stricken face. "Um . . . yes, the . . . um . . . I mean, Dr. Radnor offered to escort me this afternoon."

"Escort you where?" Henrietta demanded, daggers blazing from her narrowed stare.

Should she tell Henrietta the truth? Cara pondered, biting at her bottom lip. She knew how the woman would react. Cara glanced at the doctor, then back. *Oh, why not.* A smile lifted one corner of her mouth. "I'm riding out to visit Lucinda Weaver."

"What on earth fo—" Henrietta cut her stare up to the doctor's arched brows. "I mean, how nice of you."

Cara cocked her head. "Someone in this town should be nice to her, don't you think?"

Henrietta jerked her head high and glared down her nose. "I think if she needs a friend, you're the perfect person," she responded haughtily, then turned toward the doctor, her voice much sweeter as she continued. "But why are you going, Dr. Radnor?"

"I'm headed out of town anyway," the doctor responded, his curiously amused gaze softening when he turned and pinned Cara with his stare. "I promised to see her safely there. As I mentioned earlier, I was only waiting for Miss Martin to let me know she was ready.

Cara's pulse fluttered at the suggestion in his deep voice of more than just an excuse to escape Henrietta. She refused to dwell on his sincerity, or any hidden meaning.

Henrietta's pale features pulled taut as she looked at Cara. "When are you returning? I planned to stop by your shop. I'll be needing a new dress for the St. Valentine's dance."

Cara choked back her groan. She hated sewing for Henrietta. The woman was far too demanding, and annoyingly indecisive. "It'll have to wait. I promised Lucinda I'd visit today."

"And we really should be going," the doctor smoothly interjected before Henrietta could voice another protest.

"What about my problem, Doctor?" the blonde whined.

"Come by my office tomorrow. We'll discuss it then." Dr. Radnor turned and took the reins from Cara's hand. Retying the leather straps around the hitching post, he gripped her gently by the elbow. "Come with me. I need to get my bag; then we'll stop at the livery for my horse."

His firm hold penetrated the layers of Cara's clothing and sent a strange, warmth tingling along her arm. Every instinct told her to break free and run the other way. She glanced at Henrietta instead. "We'll discuss your dress tomorrow, as well."

As Cara allowed the doctor to lead her back up the steps, Henrietta's shocked face was the only comfort to her jangling nerves. He opened the door to his office, released his hold, then stepped aside and motioned for her to proceed.

"I think you're safe now," she whispered, crossing the threshold.

"I thank you for your assistance." His warm breath brushed the back of her neck, raising goose bumps along her skin. "But just to be sure, do you mind if I ride out with you?"

Did she mind! Cara wheeled around, ready to refuse. The words died on her lips. How could she say no to that gorgeous smile? Or that serious pleading in his eyes? No man had ever looked at her with such intensity.

"I suppose there'd be no harm." She heard the words, surprised they were her own. A sudden hollow pit formed in her stomach. What was she doing? She didn't want to be alone with this man. What if . . . Cara swallowed the rise of panic. "Well, maybe it really wouldn't be such a good idea."

"It's a fine idea," he assured her, glancing briefly over his shoulder. "Besides, you can't desert me now. Henrietta's still watching."

CHAPTER TWO

Creaking leather and the steady clip-clop of the horses' footsteps blended peacefully with the birds chirping in the sparse trees, the rabbit scurrying through the sun-coated grass, and the lone eagle soaring high overhead. Grant shifted in his saddle, peering behind at the distant town spread along the banks of the Brazos River. The wide, slow current trailed a path alongside the well-traveled road. Thick, bushy cedars and tall pines dotted the vast countryside of sloping hills and valleys. After living twenty-nine years back east, Grant couldn't imagine ever growing tired of this openness, or sense of freedom. He harbored no regrets about leaving his past. In fact, he realized answering that ad had turned out to be the best medicine for his angry soul.

Still awed by his impetuous genius and good fortune this afternoon, Grant adjusted his hat brim lower and turned his gaze to the woman riding silently astride her sorrel mare.

He peeked at her trim, stocking-clad ankle displayed above the bunched hemline of her skirt, then slid his gaze over the long black cape which blocked his view of her shapely figure. She held the reins in both gloved hands, her back stiff, shoulders squared. Several wayward strands of her silky brown hair danced playfully about her shoulders.

"Thanks again for your help with Miss Peterson."

"It was no trouble." Her soft, sultry voice sent his pulse racing. She tucked her head down slightly and glanced sideways at him. "And it's not necessary for you to escort me to Lucinda's."

"You really shouldn't travel alone, Miss Martin," Grant cautioned. "Besides, it's my pleasure."

"I should hate to take you out of your way."

Grant smiled, not caring in the least that the Weaver farm was in the opposite direction of the Houghton plantation. For the next mile and a half, he aimed to put good use to every second of Cara's company. "I'll take this opportunity to enjoy the nice day." He followed the line of her small, straight nose, the lush curve of her cupid's bow mouth. "And the lovely view."

A soft blush sprang into her cheeks and made his heart beat faster. She turned away. "I'm sure you have more important things to do with your time, Doctor."

"I could say the same of you, Miss Martin." She shot him a look of puzzlement. "You're very kind to take time from your own responsibilities to visit Miss Weaver," he explained.

Cara tilted her chin higher. "I don't share Henrietta's opinion of Lucinda."

Grant knew it wasn't just Miss Peterson's opinion, but nearly the entire town's. Tollie had told him about Lucinda Weaver's unexplained disappearance five years ago, calling it as mysterious as her sudden return a while back with a four-year-old illegitimate son in tow. She had returned when her parents took ill, and stayed on at the farm after they died.

"I assure you, neither do I."

"That's very generous of you, Doctor." Doubt hung heavy in her tone.

Being born on the wrong side of the sheets, Grant knew what it was to be shunned, talked about, rejected. He had witnessed firsthand how a woman suffered shame and degradation when she made a mistake that resulted in a lifelong reminder.

"Life's full of choices, Miss Martin. No one makes the right decision all the time. Truth be told, we're all bound to make a mistake or two before we depart from this world. Personally, I think Miss Weaver and her son are lucky to have you as a friend."

"You do?"

He nodded. She adjusted the reins to one hand, ran a gloved palm along the mare's neck, and stared at the road ahead. But he could tell by the taut lines on her brow she wasn't quite sure whether to believe him. "We're not put here to judge, Miss Martin, that's God's job. But it takes a big heart and a strong will not to fall in with everybody's line of thinking. You've made up your own mind to be her friend. I admire that."

She stopped rubbing the horse's neck, sat up straight, and rested her hand on the saddle horn. Tension slowly tightened her jaw and stiffened her back. "I'm hardly anyone to admire, Dr. Radnor. But I do thank you for the compliment, and for not having a bad opinion of Lucinda."

"More often than not, women like Miss Weaver are guilty of nothing more than trusting in the wrong man."

Silence reigned for several seconds as she worked her lip between her teeth and stared thoughtfully ahead. Finally, she relaxed her seat in the saddle, then sighed and looked over at him. Grant sat back, surprised and pleased at the softening in her warm stare.

"You're very kind, and I suspect accurate, though Lucinda never talks about Jacob's father." One corner of her mouth lifted in a sly grin. "Do you by any chance have a potion in your black bag that could make Henrietta, and a few others around here, as kind and understanding?"

Grant chuckled. "No, ma'am. I'm afraid there's no simple cure for the Miss Petersons of this world."

Her deep, gentle laughter sent a wave of hot pleasure crashing over him. He looked away lest she see the desire he couldn't hide in his eyes. Grant stared at the pines lining the bank of the distant river and considered taking a dip in the cool stream when he parted company with Miss Martin. But time was wasting, and Cara's destination drew near. Grant turned back and found her watching him with a quizzical brown stare.

"Since we're talking about Miss Peterson, I want to thank you again for your help."

She shook her head. "I didn't mind."

"Well, I'm glad for that, but still, I'd like to return the favor."

"That's not necessary," she responded sincerely.

"I disagree."

She furrowed her thin, mink brows. "I neither expect, nor want anything in return, Doctor."

He leaned forward slightly, resting his palm against his thigh. "Perhaps you should reserve your decision until you know how I'd like to repay you."

Grant smiled at the skeptical glimmer in her eyes. Her light, flowery scent carried across the narrow distance between them. He breathed in deeply. "Have dinner with me at the hotel tomorrow night."

Her pulse kicked up its already rapid pace. She raked her gaze from the light dancing in his eyes, along the bridge of his straight nose and smooth jaw, stopping at the smile on his firm, full mouth. Cara's throat went dry. Goodness, but his handsomeness was a distraction to her senses.

It didn't help that the slight breeze kept blowing his manly scent of spice and bay rum her way, that his black pants snugly defined his muscled legs, or that God's glorious greenery constantly reminded her of his eyes. Nor did it help that he had turned out to be so charitable of character, that he sounded so determined to have his way in this matter . . . or that she wanted to say yes.

That wouldn't do at all! Having dinner with the doctor was much too risky. The ride to Lucinda's farm had taken hardly any time, yet already she couldn't control her traitorous thoughts, or her body's strange, warm response to his presence. How on earth could she expect to spend an entire evening in his company and still keep her sanity?

"That's very kind of you, but it doesn't change my mind. You don't owe me anything."

"Then, take pity on me." His velvet-edged insistence sent a ripple of heat coursing through her veins. "I get tired of eating alone."

Her heart stopped. What was he doing? "Alone, Dr. Radnor?" she accused, arching her brows. "According to Brigitte, you and Mr. Culver take your meals together at the hotel almost every night."

His slow smile revealed his pleasure at her admission. "You and Miss Raineau discuss me and Tollie?"

Heat flooded Cara's cheeks. Swarming flutters churned through her stomach. She lowered her gaze to his opened jacket and swallowed hard at the expanse of his broad chest. She stared at the road and nervously ran one hand along the mare's neck. Goodness, how had she gotten herself into this mess? What was it about this man that made her forget everything when he was near? Most recently, her good sense.

"We don't *discuss* you and Mr. Culver," she defended. "Brigitte only mentioned it. Once. That's all." Once a day. Truth was Brigitte talked to her about Tollie all the time, and occasionally the doctor's name came up. But there was very little discussion, because the shy serving girl was too busy pining away for the blacksmith, and Cara didn't dare admit her

feelings for the handsome doctor to anyone . . . not even herself.
"So, why did you lie, Doctor?"

From the corner of her eye, she watched his smile thin. He
leaned back in his saddle. "I didn't, not really. I'm afraid my
boredom with Tollie's company has grown to the point where
I hardly even remember he's sitting across the table. A woman's
presence would definitely be a welcome change."

"I'm sure there's any number of women who would happily
take Mr. Culver's place." *Any* woman in town, if the barrage
of food she had seen delivered over the last four months was
any indication.

"Including you, Miss Martin?"

Her breath lodged at his tenderly whispered inquiry. She met
his probing green gaze. She was definitely tempted.

"Miss Martin?" Grant asked, taking in her frozen, blank
stare. Her eyes rolled slightly back.

He came instantly alert, recognizing the symptoms even
before the muscle in her cheek grew taut, then twitched. Reaching over, he grabbed the leather strap alongside her mare's
neck and brought both horses to a halt.

She blinked, and her eyes were once again alert. "No, Doctor,
that doesn't include me."

Grant wasn't surprised she continued the conversation as if
nothing happened. He knew these types of absence seizures
struck without warning, lasted less than a minute, and left the
afflicted with no memory of the lost consciousness. He was
highly disappointed in her answer, though.

She frowned. "Why are we stopped?"

"I thought you might like to get down and rest a minute?"

"Why would you think that?" The same hint of cautious
fear in her tone crept into the honeyed depths of her eyes.

Grant sat up straight, and braced his hand on his thigh. "You
had a mild seiz—"

"I did not!" She turned away. A bright flush crawled up
her neck, then flooded her face.

Grant hesitated, not wanting to embarrass her further. He could only imagine what she had suffered mentally and physically because of her attacks. The controversy between evil forces and physical disorders being the cause of seizures dated back to the medieval ages, but Grant knew there were studies being done, new remedies being tried, that strongly supported a treatable medical problem. That was why he had written the letters. That, and this unexplainable, desperate urgency to make things better for her. "You did," he softly insisted. "And I'd like to help."

"I don't need help," she snapped, her brown gaze turning cold. "Thank you for the escort, Doctor. I can find my way from here."

Before he could respond, she kicked the sorrel to a gallop, then into a flat-out run. He knew the Weaver farm was just around the bend in the road ahead and watched until she disappeared. The resigned sadness in her clipped tone haunted him. A cold fist tightened his gut at her dismissal . . . and at the anticipation of her response when she learned he had sought advice she obviously didn't want.

"Miss Cara! Miss Cara!" The childish voice squealed from the porch as Cara reined the horse to a halt in front of the weathered frame house.

She nodded at the tall, auburn-haired woman dressed in a faded brown calico, then smiled at the boy jumping up and down beside her. "Hello, Jacob. I take it you're glad to see me."

He nodded, his blue eyes widening beneath the unruly strawberry blond locks feathered across his brow. "Did you bring me something?"

"Jacob Adam Weaver! You mind your manners."

Jacob's mouth drooped. His shoulders slumped under the

threadbare shirt covering his thin frame. He looked up, sighing. "Sorry, Ma."

"Of course I brought you something. Don't I always?" Cara stated, pleased to see the boy's joy return.

Lucinda stood, hands planted on her rail-thin hips. "You shouldn't spoil him." She shook her head in disapproval, but the sparkle in her light green eyes at her child's excitement spoke the truth of her gratitude.

Cara shrugged, thinking about the new pants and flannel shirt she had sewn for the child—necessities Lucinda could ill afford, not frills. Now, the stick candy she had securely wrapped in brown paper and tucked inside the folded clothing was another matter, but hardly enough to be considered spoiling. "I brought you something, too."

Lucinda frowned and crossed her arms, but she couldn't hide the pleased curiosity in her stare. "You do too much for us, Cara. And why were you riding in like the devil was chasing your heels?"

Cara's thoughts jumped instantly to Doctor Radnor: the disturbing memory of his handsome company, his kindness, his charming words . . . his offer of help. A surge of bile rose in her throat. She had feared something like this might happen when she agreed to ride out of town with him. How many times had her father sought advice for her ailment? How many times had the answer been the same? Well, Cara had no intentions of being sent to an institution, and no interest in what the doctor thought about her ailment.

Cara shook aside her thoughts and forced an easy smile. "I was just anxious to get here." She dismounted, removed the saddlebags from the horse's rump, and climbed the three narrow steps to the small porch. Stopping in front of Lucinda, Cara frowned as she peered closely into her friend's pale face. "You look tired. Are you feeling all right?"

CHAPTER THREE

Cara stepped outside her shop into the early morning sunlight streaming over the walkway. A brisk chill seeped through the high-collared bodice of her emerald calico.

She stared at the sun hanging low on the horizon, listened to the birds chirp, singing their revelry from the trees scattered about town. Cara liked mornings best, watching the start of a new day and the slow stirrings as people ventured about, finding comfort in the familiar sights and sounds of her home. The rhythmic pounding of iron drifted from Tollie's shop at the west end of town. Loud male shouts floated from the warehouse down by the river where a steamboat bringing supplies and mail from Houston stood docked. The sound of Yancy's bell jingling above his door as two farmers emerged from the mercantile drew her attention, and she waved at their called-out greeting.

She glanced toward Dr. Radnor's office. Firelight glowed through his window. Biting at the inside of her bottom lip, she nervously adjusted the bonnet ribbons tied beneath her chin, then ran her shaking hands down the sides of her skirt. She prayed he wouldn't want to talk about her, or her ailment. She was only doing this for Lucinda.

Cara squared her shoulders and, with far more determination than she felt, covered the short distance next door. Taking a deep breath, she closed her eyes and raised a tightly clenched fist.

Hurriedly shoving his hat on his head, Grant opened the front door. Small, curled fingers flew inside, clipping him on the chin as Cara stumbled forward. He sucked in his breath as her soft breasts pressed against his chest.

Wide amber eyes revealed her shock. Her cheeks paled as white as the bonnet covering her head. She stepped back. "Oh, my goodness! I'm so sorry . . . I didn't mean . . . are you all right?"

Grant gripped her arms in a steadying hold and hid his smile as she leaned in, intently searching for damage.

"Just fine. I've got a pretty tough chin, Miss Martin," he assured with a slight chuckle, breathing in her sweet, delicate scent. "But this is a nice coincidence." The quivering feel of her arms beneath his fingers set his blood pounding. "I was on my way over to speak with you."

Caution flamed in her brown eyes. She drew her brows together. "You were?"

He nodded, unperturbed by her less than enthusiastic response. Actually, he had wanted to go over and see her ever since he heard her arrive at her shop earlier, and had only been waiting for a more decent hour. Then he had heard someone call out to her and, fearing her departure, quickly shoved his boots on and grabbed his coat. He never dreamed he would find her standing outside.

"Please, come in." He released her arms, and stepped aside, his interest more than a little piqued. She had obviously been coming to see him, yet she now looked as though she had had a change of heart and was ready to run.

She hesitated, then tilted her chin defiantly higher and crossed the threshold. Grant slid his gaze over her slim waist, and held fast to the gentle sway of her hips. A wave of excitement settled hard and low in him. *How did she learn to walk like that?* he wondered.

Shaking his head, Grant turned and rehung his hat. "Would you like some coffee?" He crossed to the hearth on the far side of the room.

"No, thank you." She stared at him through narrowed eyes, her hands clasped together in a white-knuckled clench. "Why were you coming to speak with me?"

Grant cocked his head at her suspicious tone. It bothered him that she sounded almost afraid. "Why were you coming to see me?"

Her face grew pensive. She chewed on her bottom lip. Grant wanted to reach out and save the tender flesh from more abuse. Instead, he lifted the blue enamel pot from the low flames and poured coffee into a tin cup. He replaced the pot close to the fire, then took a slow sip of the hot brew, meeting her impatient stare over the rim of the cup. "Well?"

She planted her hands on her hips. "I'd like an answer to my question first."

Grant held her stubborn gaze and took a lingering sip of coffee, then set the cup on the corner of his desk. "All right." He crossed his arms and stepped closer, glad she stood her ground and didn't retreat from him. He balled his hands into fists to keep from reaching out and tracing his finger over her trembling mouth. "I was hoping you'd reconsider my dinner invitation."

She sucked in a sharp breath, then eyed him warily. "That's all?"

Grant nodded, guessing she thought he wanted to discuss her seizure yesterday. He had definitely thought about it, but since she adamantly denied anything even happened, he didn't figure she would be receptive to his plea for her company if he started out trying to talk about her illness.

"Now," he whispered, daring to step closer when she relaxed her shoulders and lowered her hands to her sides, "why are you here to see me?"

Cara swallowed, still unsure why she trusted his response, or why he insisted on standing so close. She stepped back. "I came to talk to you about Lucinda." She turned and walked toward the hearth. "And I think I will have a cup of that coffee."

She bent over, grabbed a handful of her skirt with unsteady fingers and wrapped the material around the warm metal handle. As she lifted the pot from the fire, a strange sensation of being watched made her stop and turn. The doctor's back faced her as he leaned forward to retrieve his cup from his desk. The movement hiked the bottom edge of his coat and pulled his pants taut across his lean hips.

Quickly, Cara averted her gaze and blamed the sudden heat flowing through her on the yellow flames in the hearth, and not Dr. Radnor's firm backside. She poured her coffee, then straightened. Turning, she found the doctor now propped against the edge of his desk, his arms crossed over his broad chest. There was a gleam in his darkened jade stare that gave her pause.

"You wanted to talk about Miss Weaver?"

Cara nodded. "I thought she looked tired, and maybe feverish, though she said she was fine."

He arched one sandy brow. "But you're worried?" he inquired in a soft tone.

"Well, I know if she is ill, she won't say anything, and she won't send for you."

"Why not?"

"Because she can't pay you." Cara watched him nod, saw the understanding of pride flicker in his eyes. "However, I can, and I would like for you to go see her."

He slowly shook his head.

Cara's heart pounded with confusion. "Why?"

"I'd see Miss Weaver whether she could pay me or not, and I don't want your money, Miss Martin."

"Bu—"

"Now," his deep voice cut her off. He rose to his full six-foot height and sauntered over to where she stood. She had to look up to meet his stare. A smile lifted the corners of his mouth; his nearness heightened the pounding in her breast. "If you want to thank me for riding out to see your friend, then agree to have dinner with me tonight."

Every nerve in her body tightened. "Oh ... well, I ... I don't think that's such a good idea. Perhaps I could bake you something?" She stepped back.

He reached out before she could take another, and lightly gripped her arm. The warmth of his touch penetrating through her sleeve reminded her why she had said no to his invitation the day before. The smile that stole across his lips and sparkled darkly in his eyes sent her breath into retreat.

"It's a great idea, Miss Martin, and the only payment I'll accept." He leaned closer, his breath brushing smoothly across her cheek. "So what do you say?"

Gray clouds coated the afternoon sky, but did nothing to dispel Grant's mood. Whistling a tune as he sauntered along the grassy incline away from the blacksmith's shop, he headed toward the saloon on the opposite side of the road. Hearty gratification pumped through his blood as he remembered the shock on Tollie's face when he had learned Grant was having dinner with Miss Martin. Feeling rather confident, he had even gone so far as to offer his friend advice about talking to Miss Raineau.

Grant hadn't bothered to mention that he had practically shoved Cara out the door earlier, then ridden fast out of town before she had a chance to follow through with that sudden fear on her face and change her mind. He had stayed away, riding out to check on a few families in the area, his first stop being Lucinda Weaver. He still had three hours, though—three hours in which the little seamstress could learn her friend was going to be fine and then politely decide not to dine with him . . . but she would have to find him first.

Grant strode into the road and quickly regretted his curiosity when he glanced at the far end of town toward his office. The whistle died on his lips. His steps slowed. His shoulders sagged. He groaned at the sight of Henrietta Peterson standing outside his door. Remembering his promise to hear her problem, Grant reluctantly picked up his stride, dodging the sparse wagons and riders as he crossed the road. He climbed onto the walkway in front of the barbershop, then made his way past the mercantile.

She stood with arms crossed and tapped the toe of her boot against the wood. Her blue hem peeked out from beneath the long sable coat, fluttering in time with the rapid motion of her foot. Grant frowned, recalling how his ex-fiancée used to do the same thing, which was only one of the reasons he found little to like about Miss Peterson. She was beautiful, there was no denying that, but she reminded him way too much of the woman he had almost married. Not only were they both blonde and blue-eyed; he suspected they both pumped blood through a selfish heart.

She spotted his approach, and her face lit with relief.

Grant plastered on a phony smile. "Good afternoon, Miss Peterson."

"Dr. Radnor." She smiled. Bowing, he took the hand she presented and lightly pressed his lips to her lace-gloved fingers. "I was beginning to think you'd forgotten your invitation."

Grant released her hand and straightened. "Of course not. I hope I haven't kept you waiting long."

"Not too long. I stopped by Cara's shop after Father and I

ate lunch at the hotel. We only just finished with the details for my dress a short while ago.''

Grant wondered how Cara had fared being cooped up with this woman for the last few hours. Opening the door to his office, he ushered the blonde inside. His thoughts again jumped to the evening ahead with the seamstress, rekindling the pleasure that Henrietta Peterson's presence had dimmed. But the feeling faded when he turned from hanging his hat just as Miss Peterson loosened the string tie securing the wrap at her neck and revealed the low-scooped neckline of her dress. Grant wondered that she didn't take ill exposing so much flesh in the winter, even in the milder climate of Texas, and considered telling her of the dangers of pneumonia. Judging by the predatory look in her stare, he decided his advice would only fall on deaf ears. Besides, the last thing he wanted was to get into a discussion about her exposed breasts.

He took her coat and hung it on an empty peg. Motioning for her to take the chair in front of his desk, Grant slipped behind and sat down, grateful for the barrier of the smooth oak top between them.

''Now, if I remember correctly, you wanted to discuss some sort of problem.''

She nodded, her eyes widening with excitement. ''The annual St. Valentine's Day dance.''

Grant tensed, arching one brow. ''And how is the dance a problem?''

''Well, the dance is always held at our plantation,'' she boasted, her lips lifting in a pretentious smile. ''And hosted by the ladies' quilting bee. The last couple of years we've had a masquerade ball. This year we wanted to do something different, and we were hoping you might have some ideas.''

''Me?'' Grant didn't bother to hide his shock, but hoped his irritation didn't show. This was hardly a ''problem'' that warranted his time and attention.

She nodded eagerly, blond ringlets bobbing at her neck.

"Since you're so recently from back east, we thought you could tell us what they do in Boston."

Grant frowned. Growing up poor, he had attended very few dances. It wasn't until he had made a name for himself as a physician that any doors had opened. But Grant searched his mind for a helpful response, figuring the sooner he came up with an answer for Miss Peterson, the sooner he would be rid of her.

"Well, I attended a dance once where they adopted an old Roman custom called 'name drawing' for choosing partners." It was also how he had met his former fiancée.

Henrietta clapped her hands together. "Oh, how intriguing," she squealed, the high-pitched noise grating on Grant's nerves. "Tell me more."

"It's really quite simple. The ladies who wish to participate write their name on a piece of paper and place it in a jar. Each man draws out a name, thus choosing his partner for the night."

"It sounds delightful. Perfect, in fact. I told the ladies in the quilting bee you'd know what to do. They're just going to love this idea." The woman stood, placed her hands flat on his desk, and leaned over, giving him a generous view of her cleavage. "Of course, you will participate, won't you, Doctor?" she cooed.

Grant wondered how long into dinner he should wait before asking Cara to attend the dance with him. "I'm afraid not. But you tell the ladies in the quilting bee I'm glad I could help."

CHAPTER FOUR

Grant frowned at his reflection and with a damp cloth dabbed at the nick on his chin. He hadn't cut himself shaving in years, but tonight his hand shook as he had scraped away the light growth of beard. Fumbling with his tie for the fourth time, he swore under his breath. Neither could he recall having this much trouble since he was a boy and his mother had so patiently taught him how to knot the required male adornment.

Growing irritated with the resurrected surge of schoolboy nerves, Grant gave the ends one final tug beneath his starched white collar and turned away from the mirror. He shrugged into his black wool jacket, reached for his hat, then sauntered out the back room. Passing his desk, he grabbed the late winter flowers he had ridden out and foraged for along the riverbank.

After dealing with Miss Peterson, then the unexpected arrival of the reverend's daughter with a cloth-wrapped loaf of fresh bread, followed by the schoolteacher's offering of apple pie and an invitation to take supper with her and her folks after church the following day—which he politely declined—he had needed some peace. At the time, picking purple verbena and pink asters for the woman he looked forward to dining with this evening had seemed a much better option than slamming back a few drinks. But now, he almost wished he had stopped into Tyler's saloon for at least one shot of the nerve-steadying whiskey.

Promptly at six o'clock, he stood in the graying darkness outside Cara's door and swallowed the lump in his throat. There was no answer to his first knock, nor his second, then third. Frowning, Grant sidestepped to the window. Cupping his hand to his face, he peered through the glass. Banked ashes glowed in the hearth's fire, their red embers giving just enough light in the shadowed interior for Grant to verify the room was empty.

A stark sadness pummeled at his chest. She had changed her mind.

His hand fell limply to his side. He had thought for sure she would want to know about her friend. Thought for sure she would stay committed to this evening, if for no other reason than to avoid feeling indebted to him. His heart pounded fast and hard. Obviously, he had thought wrong.

Grant marched past his office, intent on reaching the saloon and drowning this deep sense of loss as quick as possible. He drew his hand holding the flowers close to his chest, then flung his arm in a hard thrust toward the road.

"Dr. Radnor, wait!"

Grant's step faltered at the sound of Cara's frantic plea. His eyes shifted to the flowers arcing high into the air. He dove for the bouquet, catching the ribbon-tied bundle at the same moment his feet left the walkway in front of the mercantile. Grant hit the dirt on his side, groaning as a sharp pain sliced up his arm into his shoulder. He quickly rolled out of reach of the hooves belonging to the spooked horse tied out front.

"Ya all right, Doc? Didn't hurt my horse, didya?"

Heat flooded his cheeks at Yancy's chuckled inquiry. Grant

sat up and saw the mercantile owner leaning against his long broom handle and staring down from the walk. Climbing to his feet, Grant dusted the dirt from his coat and pants, straightening when Cara came to a stop at his side. Concern etched her soft oval face, glowed in her warm amber stare.

Swallowing the sudden dryness in his throat, he held out the rescued flowers. "These are for you." The smile which curved her mouth as she reached for them made him forget all about looking like a fool.

At the last second, she pulled her hand back, and frowned. "You were throwing them away?"

"I'd thought you changed your mind about dinner."

"You two are having dinner?"

The shop owner's incredulous tone ignited a spark of temper in Grant. Slowly, he turned and narrowed his stare at the short, middle-aged man. "Is there something wrong with that?" He held his voice low and even, but there was no denying the intent to do bodily harm if the man said one degrading thing about Miss Martin.

Yancy raised his hands, palms out, and stepped back. No . . . not at all, Doc." The drawn look on his thin, angular face said just the opposite.

Grant turned to find Cara working at her bottom lip again, and looking ready to bolt.

"Maybe this wasn't such a good idea," she whispered, her eyes darting to the store owner.

"The only bad idea, Miss Martin, was me not trusting you to hold to your word. I hope you'll accept these flowers, along with my apology." He pressed the slightly rumpled bouquet into her raised hand and offered a smile he was pleased to see she returned.

"Is there something going on 'tween you two?" Yancy interrupted.

Reluctantly, Grant pulled his gaze away from Cara's beautiful smile and met the store owner's puzzled look. "Nothing that needs discussing,'' Grant stated, knowing it was useless. Anything worth talking about in town was done so at Yancy's store. Grant didn't doubt his plans with Cara this evening would definitely warrant discussion, especially after the flower incident. A slow smile spread across his mouth.

Let 'em talk. And let them get used to seeing him and the seamstress together, because Grant didn't intend for this to be his only night with Cara.

''Now, if you'll excuse us.'' He turned, giving his full attention to the woman at his side. Grant deepened his smile in hopes of easing her continued look of uncertainty and gently took hold of her arm before she could decide to run off. ''Shall we?''

She darted her gaze toward the store owner and back, then to his immense relief slowly nodded. ''How is Lucinda?'' she whispered as they made their way across the road.

He wasn't surprised at the urgency in her voice, and now that he had her where he wanted her, there was no longer any reason to avoid what she wanted to know. ''You were right to be concerned about Miss Weaver. She did look tired. Of course, it took a while to convince her I was just making a courtesy visit, no charge, before she'd let me close enough to find out she had a slight fever as well.''

''What's wrong with her?'' Cara's distressed gaze tore at his conscience.

A surge of guilt lodged in his chest. He had been so desperate to have this date with her, he hadn't thought about the depth of her anxiety, and knew the bout of nerves wasn't good for her ailment. He gave her arm a reassuring squeeze. ''Nothing to be alarmed about. Just a touch of the ague. She's probably not getting enough rest.''

Cara nodded. ''She's been worried a lot lately, but she won't say why. And Jacob can be a handful sometimes.''

''I left some Peruvian bark for the fever, and some laudanum to help her sleep. I'll ride out tomorrow and see how she's doing." He glanced down and let a mischievous grin lift one corner of his mouth. "Free of charge, of course."

She cocked her head. "You're too kind, Doctor. Are you sure I couldn't bake you something?"

Grant arched a brow at her knowing tone. Her sudden teasing smile was all the reward he needed. The sparkle in her golden stare convinced him she had seen the female visitors parading through his office this afternoon, and he wondered if she might be jealous of the attention. He certainly hoped so.

Grant waited for Brigitte to finish pouring another glass of the dark red wine he had ordered for this special night. Raising the tall, delicate crystal, he drank slowly and stared over the rim at Cara seated across the white linen-covered table.

Her modest green calico complemented the amber flecks in her almond-shaped eyes. The ivory lace around her wrists and the matching collar at the base of her slender neck looked as soft and smooth as her creamy skin. She was beautiful. He hadn't been able to take his eyes off her all evening. During dinner, he kept the conversation between them light and impersonal, hoping she would relax. She finally did, close to the end of her second glass of wine. He enjoyed her company, found her engagingly witty and knowledgeable about a variety of topics, politics included. A couple of times, he considered bringing up her ailment and easing his conscience about the letters he had sent, but afraid to risk spoiling the evening, he didn't.

She tucked her head down, away from his appreciative gaze. Grant smiled as he stared at the top of her small black hat, and released a sigh. What he wouldn't give to see her without the bonnet, to remove the pins securing the thick knot of brown hair at her nape, and run his fingers through its shiny length. He shook his wayward thought aside and turned his attention to Brigitte. "I trust Tollie managed to find his way over without me this evening?"

Glancing upward through her lowered lashes, Cara frowned at the smile the handsome doctor gave Brigitte, more bothered by the innocent gesture than she wanted to admit.

Brigitte grinned, her delight reaching into her violet eyes. "Oh, yes, he came same time as always, five o'clock. Even commented on the food tonight. I passed his compliment on to Miss Sally."

Before Cara could wonder about the doctor's perplexed expression, he looked at her, and warm pleasure washed over his face, stealing her breath. "Would you care for more wine, Miss Martin?"

Goodness no! She had already indulged in two glasses. She could count the times she had partaken of wine in her whole life on three fingers, including tonight, which no doubt explained the easing effect it was creating on her senses. The last thing she needed was more spirits clouding her mind. "Yes, please."

Brigitte arched dark brows beneath her fringe of black curls. Cara rolled her eyes away from her friend's curious stare and nudged the glass closer to the edge of the table. *Just one more,* Cara told herself. To steady her nerves. The doctor had no idea how close she had come to going home and forgetting this whole evening.

Cara still wasn't sure what had possessed her to call out when she saw him storming away from her shop. Or why his thoughtfulness in bringing her flowers had brought a tear of joy to her eyes. But it was the hurt in his dark stare when he had claimed he thought she changed her mind that had startled and confused her even more . . . and still did.

Brigitte carried their empty plates away. Cara fidgeted with the wineglass, took a sip, then twirled the thin stem between her fingers. Hushed conversations from the few remaining diners filled the room. She didn't doubt their talk at some point had included her and the doctor. Strangely though, tonight she didn't care what they said, or thought, but she hoped Dr. Radnor wasn't embarrassed. He certainly didn't act as though he minded being seen with her—quite the opposite, in fact—and she couldn't help but wonder why, or what he wanted. To her relief, he hadn't once mentioned her illness.

He leaned back in his chair and sipped his wine, his burning gaze never once straying. Cara shifted her stare to his slightly askew necktie and oddly wanted to reach over and adjust it for him. Gripping the glass tighter, she brought it to her lips. As she drank, her gaze lifted to his sandy brown hair. He had bound it back with a strip of leather in the same fashion he wore to church every Sunday, and she liked it best this way because it revealed the corded column of his tanned neck.

The warm liquid clogged her throat. Goodness gracious, what was she doing? She set the glass down and lifted a hand to cover her choking cough.

"Are you all right, Miss Martin?" Grant sat forward, setting his wineglass down. Several people glanced over at their table.

She nodded, coughed again, then took a hurried swallow of the strong Bordeaux. Grant would give anything to know what she had been thinking a second ago. He wanted to make sure, whatever had brought that desirous gleam to her eyes, it happened again.

"Thank you for dinner, Doctor." She placed the glass on the table, then slowly slid one finger up and down the narrow stem.

"It was my pleasure." He tore his gaze away from the sensuous movement of her finger before his body grew any harder, only to have his blood fired by the pretty flush in her cheeks. He swallowed, finding no relief from the heated dryness in his mouth, and reached for his wineglass.

"You're most kind." She paused, then pulled her hand away from her glass and began fingering the ribbon on the bouquet of flowers lying off to one side. "And I truly appreciate that you went out to check on Lucinda."

Grant frowned slightly at the reminder that he had had to blackmail her into this dinner. Just as quickly, he recognized a possible new avenue for seeing her again. "Would you like to ride out there with me tomorrow?"

Yes. No! Cara's nerves tingled. "I . . . suppose that would be all right. I was planning to ride out there anyway." What on earth was she doing? That wasn't at all what she had meant to say. Why couldn't she keep her wits around this man?

"Good. We can leave after church." Grant took another sip of his wine, then set his glass on the table and leaned forward. "Now, there's something I've been wanting to discuss with you this evening."

She immediately sat up straighter, her face drawing taut. "What?"

Grant recognized her cautious tone and realized he should have phrased his words a little better. He would have to remember that in the future. "I wanted to ask you a question. I heard there's going to be a St. Valentine's dance."

One brow shot upward, but she said nothing.

Undaunted by her widened, wary stare, he proceeded. "I was wondering if you'd like to attend . . . with me?"

Cara's heart pounded so hard she thought for sure it was going to catapult right from her chest. She had never been asked to the dance before, had only attended the annual event once, when she turned eighteen and her father insisted she go with her older sister and brother-in-law. She had always dreamed of attending, dancing to the sweet love ballads and slow waltzes while being held in the arms of a handsome escort. But her brother-in-law was the only man who had approached her for a dance the entire night. Then she had met Bernard Hampton . . . and now she knew better than to indulge in her fantasies. "You're quite kind to ask, Dr. Radnor, but—"

"Don't say no." He leaned over and placed his large hand on top of hers. His touch sent a hot jolt shooting up her arm. "At least think about it while I see you home."

Cara swallowed, and glanced nervously about the room, catching the eye of several patrons observing them. She pulled her hand from his gentle grip and tucked it in her lap. If he was going to be as persistent about this as he was about dinner, perhaps it would be best to save her denial until they were alone. She hesitated only a moment longer, then nodded her agreement.

Heart pounding with the force of a hammer to an anvil, Grant settled the bill. After retrieving her wrap, he escorted her from the hotel. The clear sky allowed the bright quarter-moon and sparkling stars to light the night. The cool temperature, unlike the frigid cold back east this time of year, was comfortably bearable. It was a perfect night for a leisurely stroll to the edge of town where she lived with her father. Now, if he could only figure out a way to change Cara's mind about the dance.

She had seemed to enjoy dinner, and hadn't acted as though she minded his company—once she started to relax, anyway. She had even talked a little more about her family, and her love for them was quite evident. So was the sadness when she told him her mother died ten years ago giving birth to her stillborn brother. He was positive he had made progress with the seamstress, but the second he had mentioned the dance, the smooth lines in her forehead had deepened with returning tension, and he had seen the amber glow leave her eyes.

Cara hurried down the steps in front of the hotel and continued on as though she had been shot from a cannon. Obviously, she was of a different mind than a leisurely stroll, he realized.

Grant followed for several quick steps, then gently gripped her arm and forced her to stop. "I don't run well on a full stomach, Miss Martin."

She looked up at him with widened eyes. The moon's glow softened the blush coloring her cheeks. "Sorry," she whispered.

It took every ounce of strength not to lean down and kiss her full, trembling lips. "Quite all right. Shall we try this again?" Grant took hold of her hand and slipped it through the crook of his left arm, resting her cool fingers on his coat sleeve.

Cara tried to ignore the warmth of his hand closed securely over her fingers, tried to forget the pleasing smell of bay rum and manliness that assailed her nose. She looked away from the moonlight glistening in the dusting of hairs on his large hand and fought the whirlwind of heat the strength in his soft touch kicked up. How on earth was she supposed to remember to say no to this man? She fell into step with his slow, sauntering stride.

"Much better." He turned, and gave her that gorgeous smile that always stole her breath.

She sighed, wondering if he had any idea how he affected her. A shiver that had nothing to do with the cold night air raced through her limbs. Heated flooded her face. Cara didn't know she could grow so hot without being feverish.

They walked along for several minutes, and to her relief he made no attempt to engage her in conversation. She assumed he was giving her time to think about his invitation—not that she needed any. The answer was no. No to the dance . . . no to the longing in her heart.

They rounded a slight bend in the road, bringing into view her white, two-story clapboard home. Yellow candlelight glowed brightly through the front windows. Grant knew Cara's sister and family were staying with her while their father was in Georgia on his honeymoon, and his time alone with her was coming to a fast close.

He stopped, forcing her to do the same, and stared down into her pretty face. "I had a fine time tonight. Your company was a definite pleasure. And I would very much like to escort you to the St. Valentine's dance, Miss Martin."

A flicker of hesitation flashed across her eyes, giving him hope, but it died an instant death when she blinked and looked at him with her clear, defiant gaze. He raised a finger to her lips, stopping the words he didn't want to hear, but knew were coming. "Before you tell me how kind and nice I am, let me assure you this has nothing to do with either of those virtues, and I really don't want you to say no."

She bit at her bottom lip and stepped back. Grant let his arm fall to his side, feeling defeat close at hand.

"Let me think about it," she whispered.

CHAPTER FIVE

"You talked about the blasted food!" Grant grabbed the glass of whiskey and downed the contents in one gulp.

"What's wrong with that? You said to compliment her, and I did!" Tollie shouted back from across the table.

Grant shook his head in exasperation. After seeing Cara home, he had headed for Tollie's place, intending to set the man straight about compliments. "Sally cooked the food, you fool. By the way, Miss Raineau passed your compliment along to *Harold's wife*."

Tollie sat back in his chair and crossed his arms over his burly chest. "So whadya want me to say?"

Grant frowned his disbelief. "You might have started by telling her how pretty she looked tonight."

"I ain't no good with fancy words like that," he snarled.

"You better start practicing, because women like to hear that kind of stuff."

"Oh, and I guess you're the expert on women. All right,

Mr. Fancy Educated man, just how did you fare with Miss Cara? She goin' to the dance with ya?"

Grant looked away from his friend's knowing stare, circled his hand around the neck of the whiskey bottle, and poured another measure. "Not yet," he said, downing the alcohol, and setting the glass on the scarred wood with a hard clunk as the liquid scorched a path to his gut.

Tollie slapped one palm against the square oak top, jostling the glassware. "Told ya she'd say no."

"She didn't say no," Grant defended. "She said she'd think about it."

"Same thing."

Grant was afraid his friend might be right.

Tollie shook his head, letting his satisfied smile slip away. "Since that fella skipped town on her, she hasn't looked twice at a man. Course, even 'fore that, them spells of hers kept us boys from gettin' too close."

Grant paused, his fingers still inches from the bottle. "What fella?"

"Bernard Hampton. I told ya 'bout him."

Grant knew better, but didn't waste time arguing. "Tell me again." He leaned forward and snagged the bottle. The muscle in his cheek tightened as he poured another shot, then scooted the whiskey within Tollie's reach.

The blacksmith frowned and poured himself another drink. "He's from Austin. Ran for governor when Texas got statehood. He was here campaigning then, and stayed with the Petersons for a while. Started courtin' Miss Cara. But one day, she had a real bad spell in church, and before ya know it, Hampton was hightailin' it outta here like his pants were on fire." Tollie shook his head. "She hasn't so much as looked at another man since."

A dull, empty ache for Cara's suffering gnawed at Grant's heart and mingled with his bitter anger at the faceless bastard. At least Grant now understood why he had had to blackmail his way into spending time with her. And no doubt why she wouldn't agree to go to the dance.

Well, Grant decided, he would just have to change his strategy and prove he was no Bernard Hampton. He wasn't the least bit afraid of her ailment. He intended to help her, and he had no plans of running anywhere.

"You're wrong about that last part," he told Tollie. "She was looking at *me* plenty during dinner. She'll go to the dance," he stated with confidence.

Tollie picked up his full glass and leaned back in his chair. "I've only known Miss Cara to attend a dance one time. No one danced with her 'cept her brother-in-law. My money says you don't stand a chance of changin' her mind, Doc."

"Don't be so sure, my friend," he cautioned, lifting his glass and staring at the dark liquid. "I agree with you. She's probably going to say no. But if she does, I have a plan. And if you agree to help me, I'll make it worth your while."

Tollie leaned forward over the table. "What are ya offerin'?"

Grant went in for the kill. "I'll guarantee you a date to the dance with Miss Raineau."

A clear blue sky reigned over the crowded churchyard. The sun's bright rays chased away the chill which had greeted the day at dawn. Grant adjusted his hat brim lower, then cut his glance sideways, grateful to see Miss Peterson still occupied with her lady friends a good escaping distance away. He had seen the women eyeing him a few moments ago, then giggling and whispering, and had a gut feeling he was about to be pounced upon with a request for another favor. He hoped Cara would hurry up before that happened.

Looking up the front steps of the church where she lingered in the doorway talking with Reverend Watkins, he raked his gaze over her shapely figure, admiring the generous swells beneath her dark blue calico. Her simple black bonnet came to just above her ears and was secured with shiny black ribbons tied in a bow under her chin. She had draped her wrap over one arm. Grant thought about the day ahead he had planned, and hoped she wouldn't try to back out of her agreement.

Finally, Cara started down the steps. Her sister, holding her sleeping eight-month-old son in her arms, and her brother-in-law followed her. Grant took off, reaching the bottom step of the church at the same time as Cara. He swept his hat from his head.

"Good morning, Miss Martin, Mrs. Delaney." Grant glanced up at the tall, redheaded man. "Ian." He brought his gaze back to rest on Cara's wary stare. "I was hoping you might be ready to head out to Miss Weaver's place."

"You're riding out to Lucinda's together?" Beatrice Delaney's widened gaze matched the surprise in her voice. Ian Delaney was quietly just as curious.

"Yes," Grant responded.

"No." Cara's heartbeat kicked up double time when the doctor turned to her and deepened his smile.

"We agreed, last night, remember?"

Of course she remembered, but she had quickly come to her senses once she got home. And now there was that matter about the dance to clear up. What on earth had she been thinking when she agreed to consider his invitation? Well, that was the problem. She hadn't been thinking, not with her head anyway. His handsome presence, his charming wit, his seemingly intent interest all through dinner had swept her away on a cloud of dreams, and temporarily given her heart free rein over rational thought. But she was clear-headed this morning.

"I've decided not—"

"I took the liberty of packing a lunch." She gaped at his interruption. He smiled. "I thought after our visit, we could have a picnic."

A picnic? Butterflies fluttered in her stomach. Cara clasped her hands together behind her back and glanced about at the curious stares of the townsfolk milling around the church. Horses and wagons littered the yard, and a few lined the roadway as people left, headed for home, or an afternoon of visiting with friends and family.

Cara opened her mouth, a firm, definite no poised on her tongue.

"Well, that sounds like a splendid idea," Bea stated.

Cara glared at her sister.

Bea stared back undaunted. "It's a beautiful day. Plenty warm enough for a picnic." She shifted the sleeping infant in her arms, resting the child's head against her shoulder. "Have fun, dear, we'll see you later."

Cara stared dumbfounded at her sister and brother-in-law's retreating backs, still not believing how easily they had abandoned her, especially Bea. At least Ian had shown some resistance, until Bea grabbed his arm and jerked him into motion.

What had gotten into her sister? Any other time, she would have agreed Cara shouldn't go. Bea had always been her protector, always been there to defend when others made fun or said hurtful things. It was Bea who had warned her about Bernard Hampton from the beginning, then wiped away her tears when she hadn't listened.

"I rented a buggy for the day." Grant's deep voice pulled her attention. "I thought that would be more comfortable."

Cara gasped. How could she share the same seat with this man? She could barely think when there *was* some distance between them. She would be doomed in a buggy.

She stared at his handsomely chiseled face, the hopeful boyish glint in his jade eyes, and swallowed, realizing just how hard it was going to be to decline. But that was exactly what she intended to do. "I really don't think—"

"We'll invite your friend and her son to join us, if you'd like. I packed plenty."

His thoughtfulness melted her restraint. "All right," Cara

whispered on a sigh, even as her thoughts pounded with growing force.

Doomed. Doomed! DOOMED!

Cara sat so close to the side edge of the seat, Grant feared she would fall off every time they hit a bump. The delicate fringe lining the ends of her black shawl draped over her shoulders and brushed against her breasts as the buggy rolled along the dirt road. She held her hands clenched together in her lap. Grant hid his exasperation; she hadn't relaxed in the slightest, or spoken more than three words since they had ridden out of town.

He turned his attention to the pair of bays pulling the small open carriage and adjusted his hold on the reins. "I know a nice little spot not far from Miss Weaver's place where we can have our picnic."

"Why are you doing this?"

Grant pulled back on the reins, bringing the horses to a stop in the middle of the road. Shifting his seat, he faced her, glanced quickly to make sure no one was riding up behind, then placed his arm along the backrest of the bench seat and looked into her eyes. "I'm doing this because I want to, Miss Martin. I enjoy your company."

"You do?" Her voice was barely above a whisper and held more than a hint of disbelief.

He nodded. "Very much."

Not for the first time since he learned about Bernard Hampton, Grant wondered just how badly she had been hurt. His own heartache over his broken engagement was painful, but at least he had had his anger of betrayal to ease the burden. From what Tollie told him, all Cara had to fall back on was embarrassment.

"If you're uncomfortable with that, I'll take you back to town."

She bit at her bottom lip. Grant couldn't resist. He reached up and touched one leather-clad finger to her mouth. Slowly, he traced the full line of her lip, paused, then swallowed his desire to kiss her and lifted his sight to her widened amber gaze.

"Do you want me to turn around?" he softly asked. She didn't say anything. Reluctantly, he lowered his hand from her mouth, but held her unsure gaze.

She slowly shook her head.

He smiled. "Then, will you please stop looking as though you're going to jump out at any moment?" His calm tone and reassuring smile warmed her inside and made her feel strangely safe.

The affirming smile she offered in return faltered beneath her trembling lips.

"And will you please talk to me?"

She nodded, then swallowed. Just as soon as he stopped devouring her with his gaze and she could find her breath.

"Good." He looked away and, with a click of his tongue and a slap of the reins, set the horses into motion.

When the buggy jerked forward, Cara grabbed for the empty space of seat between them. He wanted her to talk to him! For the life of her, she couldn't think of a thing to say. She was still trying to recover from the heated wave his gentle touch on her mouth had created. His declaration that he enjoyed her company wasn't helping her remember her vow to keep her distance and guard her heart, either.

He pulled back on the reins, slowing their pace. Cara turned her attention to the road ahead, surprised to see they were already approaching Lucinda's house, and realized she hadn't been paying attention to anything but the doctor's presence since they left town.

"Oh, no!"

"What's wrong?" Grant jerked his head around, instant concern etching the lines on his wide forehead.

Cara glanced toward the small figure standing on the porch. "I forgot Jacob's surprise. It was only another piece of stick candy, but he'll still be disappointed."

"Perhaps some of Miss Sally's cinnamon cake will make up for it."

Cara swung her gaze to meet his amused green stare. "Sally fixed our lunch?"

He nodded, grinning slyly. "This morning, but only after I bribed her with a free loaf of bread and an apple pie."

Cara couldn't stop the chuckle that bubbled from her throat. She wondered what the reverend's daughter and the school-teacher would think if they knew their efforts were being tasted by the hotel patrons instead of the town's handsome doctor.

"Well, what a surprise." Lucinda called out from the front porch as they came to a stop. Cara noted with pleasure that her friend was dressed in the new yellow calico she had brought the last time she came out, and Jacob was wearing his new pants and shirt. She also saw the curiosity in her friend's expression and knew Lucinda wondered about her keeping company with the doctor. Not that she was, Cara quickly reminded herself, and when they were alone, she would make sure to inform her friend of that fact.

"We came to see how you're feeling." The doctor responded as he secured the reins, then jumped to the ground.

Cara rose from the seat and started to climb down on her side of the buggy. Grant was instantly standing in front of her, giving her no choice but to accept his offer of assistance as he slipped his gloved fingers around her waist and lifted her easily. She tried to ignore the feel of his hands on her waist, the strength in his hold as he lowered her to the ground, but it was no use. Even after he let go, she could feel the heat of his touch burning through her wool-lined dress.

Cara climbed the steps to the narrow porch and stood in front of her friend. "How are you?" she asked, grateful to see the woman's cheeks held more color today, and her eyes looked rested.

"Still a little tired. But better." Lucinda stared over Cara's shoulder. "Thank you for the medicine, Doc."

"I'm glad it helped."

Cara hadn't realized how close Grant stood at her back until his warm breath brushed across her neck and sent goose bumps tingling down her arms. She stepped away from his distracting presence, and her friend's delving gaze, and knelt in front of the little boy shifting anxiously from one foot to the other, waiting for someone to notice him.

"Hello, Jacob. How are you?"

He smiled. "I'm fine, Miss Cara. But Mama says I can't ask if you brought me something."

Cara peeked up through her lashes at Lucinda's poor attempt at a stern expression, then turned her attention to the boy and frowned slightly. "Well, I'm afraid I left your surprise at my shop this time." His little face fell, and would have broken Cara's heart if she hadn't had something even better to offer the lad. "But Dr. Radnor brought you a big surprise. He's invited us all on a picnic."

"Oh, that's quite nice of you, Doctor," Lucinda hedged, darting her stare from Grant to Cara, then back, "but I'm afraid I'm not feeling up to an outing today."

The excited light in Jacob's eyes burned dim at his mother's announcement. Cara frowned, uncertain whether her friend spoke the truth.

Dr. Radnor arched one brow. "Anything I should know about?"

Lucinda shook her head and smiled. "You two go ahead."

Cara stood, and glared at the pleased gleam in Lucinda's eyes. She strongly suspected her friend was intentionally forcing her to spend the afternoon alone with the doctor—which Cara *did not* want to do.

"I'm not feeling bad," Jacob piped up with youthful innocence. "Can I go?"

CHAPTER SIX

"Look, Miss Cara," Jacob whispered excitedly. "A bunny rabbit."

Grant watched as Cara's gaze followed where the boy pointed to a brown and gray hare sitting contentedly on his back legs in the short, faded grass near the creek.

"You know, Jacob," she spoke low, turning back to look at the boy, "if you're very quiet, maybe you could sneak up and take a closer look."

"I can do that," the boy assured, nodding eagerly. Hunched over slightly, he took small, slow steps away from the blanket where they had enjoyed their meal.

Grant smiled as he watched the lad intently inch his way closer toward the animal, then settled his gaze on Cara's beaming face. Twin spots of color rose in her cheeks as though she sensed him staring. She looked toward Jacob still making his way down the sloping hill to the creek, then pulled her knees up close to her breasts and wrapped her arms around her legs.

Grant sat up from his reclining position and propped himself with one hand. "You're good with him." All through the ride out here, and while they ate, she had been so patient and loving with the boy. Grant found himself envious of her attention to the kid a time or two . . . and more than once wondered what it would be like to have a family of his own. "Your mother must have been a wonderful teacher."

She turned amber eyes his way, and nodded. "I still miss her sometimes."

"I know what you mean. I lost my mother several years ago."

"Were you close?" Cara asked.

Grant nodded. "It was always just the two of us when I was growing up."

She arched her brows in surprise. "What about your father?"

He frowned and looked away, wondering how he had blundered his way into this subject. Grant didn't want to talk about his father. "He's been . . . gone for a long while."

"I'm sorry," she whispered.

Grant knew by her sympathetic tone she thought the man was dead. Saying nothing, he tucked away the stab of guilt at the lie and watched as Jacob slowly gained on the jack rabbit. The animal twitched its long, pointed ears. Another few feet and Grant knew the hare would pick up the boy's scent and scurry along.

"I'm afraid I owe you an apology, Dr. Radnor."

Surprised, he shifted his stare around to meet hers. "For what?"

"I realized after I got home that I never explained why I wasn't at my shop last night when you came."

Grant realized it had never even occurred to him to ask.

"I went to talk with Brigitte."

He smiled, his blood pumping a little faster. "Dare I hope about the topic of discussion?"

The color in her cheeks deepened. "Not you," she quickly responded, much to his chagrin. "But Brigitte was full of talk about Tollie.'' She cocked her head. ''I wonder, since you and Tollie are friends, could I ask if he's even the least bit interested. Because if he isn't, I think Brigitte should know, and quit pining over him.''

Her sultry voice was as soft as a lullaby. ''Oh, I'd say Tollie's more than a little interested.''

''Well,'' she huffed slightly. ''He certainly doesn't show it.'' She pursed her lips in thought.

He couldn't tear his gaze away from her mouth. Perhaps that was his problem as well, Grant pondered. Before he could stop himself, he leaned forward and lightly took hold of her chin with his hand. ''You know, Miss Martin, I owe you an apology as well.''

''You do?'' She blinked her surprise, but didn't try to pull away.

He nodded, following the line of her small, straight nose to her full, slightly parted lips. ''I never thanked you for granting me the pleasure of your company last night.'' Closing his eyes, he gently touched his mouth to hers. Feeling no resistance, he pressed his lips harder against her warm, yielding flesh.

''What are you doing?''

Jacob's interruption made Grant sit back with a start. Releasing Cara's chin, he slammed his hand over his pounding heart. ''Jeez, Jacob!'' he snapped. ''You shouldn't sneak up on a man like that.''

The boy's bottom lip trembled. Grant felt as small as the lone red ant he spotted crawling across the blanket, and even smaller when he saw Cara's tight frown of disapproval. He prayed she was only upset about his harshness, and not their kiss.

''I'm . . . sorry, Mr. Doc,'' Jacob mumbled, ducking his head down.

Grant placed his hand gently on the boy's shoulder. ''No, I'm sorry. You just startled me, and I shouldn't have snapped like that.''

The boy smiled, and to Grant's relief, so did Cara.

"The bunny ran away." Jacob jabbed his finger toward the creek, then looked back at Grant and planted his tiny fists on slim hips. "Why were you kissing Miss Cara? Mama kisses me when it's time to go to bed, and sometimes when I get hurt. Is Miss Cara hurt?"

"No, Miss Cara's not hurt." Grant glanced at Cara's flushed face and smiling mouth. God, what he wouldn't give to kiss her again right now. He forced his attention back to the lad. "Has your mama ever given you a kiss when you did something that made her happy?"

Jacob drew his brows together in thought, then nodded. "She was happy that I gave her a hug after that bad man came and made her cry. She kissed me then."

Grant turned his puzzled frown to Cara, only to see the same expression mirrored on her face.

They questioned the boy in unison. "What bad man?"

The bell jangled above her shop door. Cara looked up from her sewing, stark disappointment settling in her breast at the sight of Henrietta crossing the threshold. Much as she hated to admit it, she had been hoping to see Grant.

"Good morning, Henrietta." Cara secured her needle into the hemline of Eliza Smith's ivory-laced wedding gown, stood, and laid the dress aside on the long wooden counter occupying one wall of her shop. "I wasn't expecting you today." She wasn't in the mood to deal with her, either. Or perhaps, she was.

Cara narrowed her stare. She wanted some answers, and maybe Henrietta could give them to her.

The woman tugged her gloves off, then holding them in one hand, tapped the black kid leather against her free palm. She tilted her chin up and peered haughtily down her long, narrow nose. "I've changed my mind about the blue wool for my dress. I want you to use the yellow gingham instead, and I've decided I want a different style."

Cara stifled her groan. Just this morning, she had cut the wool to Henrietta's measurements.

Henrietta stepped over to the table on the opposite wall laden with various colors of calico and silk, then turned her attention to the latest *Godey's Lady's Book* on top. Idly, the blonde began flipping through the pages.

"While you're deciding, there's something I'd like to ask you."

The woman continued studying the pictures. "What?" she asked, disinterested.

"Why did your father visit Lucinda Weaver?" Cara bluntly asked.

The woman's hand froze in the process of turning the next page. Slowly, she shifted a hard glare on Cara. "I have no idea what you're talking about." Henrietta snorted unladylike, waved a dismissive hand, then returned her attention to the book. "My father wouldn't step foot anywhere close to that woman. Why, everyone knows she's not respectable. Just look at that boy she's got, and never been married a day in her life."

"Lucinda says he was there," Cara challenged. She and Grant had pried that much information from Lucinda when they had confronted her about the "bad man" Jacob spoke of, but nothing else. Cara also recalled that her friend had been nervous when she admitted it. And after the doctor was called away to deliver a baby, Lucinda had strangely made Cara promise to take care of Jacob should she have to leave, but had offered no further explanations.

Henrietta released a heavy sigh and dropped her hands on her hips. "Oh, pish posh, who's going to believe Lucinda Weaver. The woman disappears without a word to anyone, including her own folks, then returns without a single explanation of where she's been. Why she's as strange as y—"

"Get out!"

Henrietta's eyes widened. "What?"

"I said, get out," Cara seethed, pointing toward the door.

The blonde arched her pale brows in utter disbelief. "But, what about my dress?"

Cara shrugged, concealing the bottled rage building inside. "Sew it yourself."

Henrietta jerked her head up indignantly, then squared her shoulders "You might be interested to know who stopped by Riverwind last evening."

"No, I'm not." Cara crossed her arms. Her gut tightened at the sly grin forming on the woman's lips.

"Dr. Radnor."

Cara tensed. He had gone to Riverwind?

"He came to see me."

He had gone to see Henrietta? She hadn't seen Grant since they returned to the Weaver farm with Jacob. Not that Cara really expected him to come by, but after the kiss they shared. . . .

Her cheeks heated as she recalled the gentle warmth of his mouth on hers, how his touch had sent her stomach into a wild swirl. His continued absence since their picnic two days ago bothered her more than she liked. Not for the first time, she wondered why he had kissed her. Obviously, it hadn't meant much to him, if Henrietta was telling the truth.

Cara chided the sadness that engulfed her heart. It certainly wouldn't be the first time a man had second thoughts about her. Hadn't she learned her lesson with Bernard? She needed to stop wishing for things that were better left alone.

"The doctor stayed for dinner," Henrietta stated with a simpering confidence that grated nastily at Cara's nerves. "We had a lovely time."

Cara's right hand tingled. She froze as the sensation trailed up her arm to her shoulder. *No. Dear God, not now,* she prayed. *Please not now! Not in front of this mean-spirited woman.* The tingling stopped. She released a long, grateful sigh and steeled herself to meet Henrietta's satisfied stare.

Her fury at this pretentious woman was as sharp as the unexpected knot of pain in her throat. "And so did we, the other night at the hotel."

"Oh, yes, I heard about that." The blonde waved the news away as unimportant, but the frown tugging at her lips belied her indifference "Did Dr. Radnor tell you his wonderful suggestion for the St. Valentine's dance this year?"

Cara lowered balled fists to her hips and squared her shoulders. She shook her head, eyeing the woman with cautious curiosity.

Henrietta smiled. "He suggested we participate in a delightful old Roman custom where the men draw names to choose their partners for the night. Doesn't the whole thing sound like a great deal of fun?"

Not to Cara it didn't. If he planned to participate in this name drawing, then why had he invited her to attend with him? Her plaguing uncertainty about the doctor's interest returned doublefold, pounding in her head. She had been right to question his sincerity, right to guard her heart. And she needed to tell Grant Radnor she definitely *wasn't* going to the dance.

Henrietta's face took on a hard, fearful look that Cara immediately recognized. "Oh, dear, perhaps the doctor didn't mention it out of politeness. He must have known you wouldn't want to join in."

Cara's anger boiled to the surface. "And what if I do?" She tightened her fists to keep from reaching out and smacking the smugly distressed look from Henrietta's face.

"You can't." The blonde's high-pitched worry sent a strong, familiar ache arching its way through Cara's breast. "Why, the menfolk may decide not to risk the chance of getting your name. Then there wouldn't be a name drawing at all.''

Heart hammering, Cara stormed past the woman and yanked open the front door of her shop. "Get out of here, Henrietta. And from now on, find someone else to make your dresses.''

CHAPTER SEVEN

Grant strode outside the hotel, his boot heels tapping against the planked walkway. He lifted his hat to his head, and froze as he stared across the road.

"Blast it," he mumbled, spinning sharply around. He returned toward the safety of the hotel just as Tollie emerged. Shoving the startled blacksmith aside, he hurried through the open door.

"What in blue blazes ya doin'?" Tollie questioned, following.

"Shut the door!" Grant ordered in a harsh whisper, then did it himself when the blacksmith just stood there shaking his head in confusion. Turning, Grant smiled and tipped his hat at the couple who stared their surprise from the dining room doorway.

Stepping to one side, Grant looked out the window. "Miss Peterson's out there." He glanced over at Tollie.

The blacksmith arched one black brow. "And you're hidin' from her?"

"Darn right I am." Grant frowned. "I want to talk to Cara, and I don't need that blonde sidetracking me with her prattle. There's no telling what kind of damage she's already done."

"Damage? What are ya talkin' 'bout?" Tollie chuckled.

Grant had seen Henrietta's angry expression as she stormed from the dress shop, then stared at Cara's tempered sneer before she roughly shoved the door closed. "I'm sure she's told Cara I had dinner at Riverwind last night."

"You did what? Why?" Tollie's incredulous tone rose with each word.

Grant cringed. "Keep your voice down," he grated, looking around and meeting the curious stare of the clerk at the front desk. "I had a reason."

Tollie nodded, a smirk gracing his ruddy face. "Part of that plan of yours, I reckon?"

Grant let out an exasperated sigh. "Yeah, part of my plan," he snarled. A bad part.

Tollie leaned forward. "Well, I don't know how having dinner with Miss Peterson figures into gettin' a date with Miss Cara, but I gotta say, Doc, that was some pretty smooth talkin' ya did back there with Brigitte." He spoke low, the smile on his face deepening. "She swallowed the hook to participate in this little name drawin' like a starving fish."

Thanks to Cara asking on the barmaid's behalf about Tollie's interest, Grant knew he wasn't going to have any trouble. But the seamstress was another matter. Cara Martin was definitely going to be a much harder sell ... especially after Miss Peterson's visit.

"You just let me know when ya want me to help out with Miss Cara. Right now, I'm leavin'." He grinned, and shoved his hat farther on his head. "I ain't got a reason to hide from pesky Miss Peterson." He nodded once. "Most likely cuz I'm not as educated as you when it comes to women." Tollie chuckled, and headed out the door.

Grant glared briefly at his friend's retreating back, then turned his attention to the wealth of sunlight shrouding the town in its bright rays. Scanning the faces of the folks on the walkway, and the riders on the main road, he thanked his lucky stars Miss Peterson was nowhere in sight.

Hurrying from the hotel, he crossed the road, climbed the steps, and strode purposefully to Cara's shop. Being the middle of the day, and not at all sure she would answer, he decided not to knock. The bell tingled. Grant crossed inside and closed the door, then leaned back against it.

"What are you doing here?" She slammed a large pile of ivory silk and lace down onto the counter.

Grant swept his stare over her tense figure. Small clenched fists rested on her generously curved hips. Her breasts heaved beneath the high-buttoned brown spencer that reached to the waist of her brown calico skirt. Her tightly drawn face was flushed a pretty pink, and her eyes blazed golden fire. Damn! She was beautiful, and madder than a wet cat. He wanted to smile at the display of what he hoped was jealous anger, but figured he already had a big enough hole to climb out of.

He raised his hands. "I want to explain why I went to Riverwind."

"Explain?" She straightened, and raised her chin. "I don't need an explanation," she responded blandly. "It's of no matter to me whose company you choose to keep."

"Sure it is." He pushed away from the door. "Because I choose to keep company with you, not Miss Peterson." Grant stepped closer, drawn by the pain in her dark eyes she tried so hard to conceal. He stopped when she took a step back.

She cocked her head and stared at him through narrowed eyes. "*I* don't reside at Riverwind, Dr. Radnor, nor did I request your company."

Grant arched one brow. "Then, why are you so mad?"

"I'm not mad," she shouted.

A smile hovered at the corners of his mouth. "And this little outrage isn't a case of jealousy, either?"

Her cheeks paled. "Absolutely not," she hissed, turning around and storming toward the hearth.

Grant let his smile roll full blown over his mouth, thrilled to realize she wasn't as immune to him as she pretended. He removed his hat. "Mind if I have a cup?" he asked, pointing toward the blue pot hanging over the flames.

She glared at him. "You won't be staying long enough to finish it."

Grant hung his hat on a wall peg, then sauntered over to the fire.

"What are you doing?" She sidestepped across the planked flooring into his path and crossed her arms.

"I'm getting a cup of coffee."

"You're leaving."

Grant shook his head and crossed his arms over his chest. "Not until you let me explain."

"I don't care why you went to see Henrietta, or—"

"I did *not* go to see Miss Peterson." He frowned. "Although she did hoodwink me into staying for dinner. I went there to talk to her father." Her eyes darkened with surprise. "I wanted to hear what he had to say about visiting Miss Weaver." As she lowered her crossed arms and leaned slightly closer, Grant breathed in her light, flowery scent. "It was most interesting."

Her eyes widened. "What did he say?" Her voice dropped several octaves, the sultry softness turning his blood to liquid fire.

Grant arched his brows high and nodded downward. "Can I have that coffee now?"

She sighed her exasperation. "Oh, all right. Half a cup." She turned and bent over, using a handful of her skirt to lift the enamel pot free of its hook. Grant rocked back on his boot heels, trailing his gaze over the revealing sight of her small, low-heeled kid boots and shapely stocking-clad calves, then up to her rounded backside. A pang of guilt at his blatant perusal stabbed at his conscience. The reminder that he had almost been caught staring at her in his office the other day made him look away and focus his attention on the table filled with several neatly stacked bolts of cloth and a ladies' fashion book open on top.

"Here."

Grant turned back and smiled. It was no accident that his fingers brushed hers when he took the tin cup she offered, and no surprise that the feel of her soft skin stirred a pool of heat low in his gut.

She started at his touch, then quickly drew her hands behind her back. "Now, tell me what he said."

Grant took a slow sip, drawing out the pleasure he found in her eagerly awaiting stare, and thinking about the kiss they had shared. He would have liked it better if she was standing there waiting for him to do that again. He sure as heck wanted to do it again.

"Interestingly enough, Miss Martin, he denied the visit. Called Miss Weaver a liar."

She started to pace along the narrow aisle in the center of the shop. Grant lowered his gaze to the sway of her hips.

"Henrietta did the same." She paused. He jerked his gaze up in time to meet her challenging stare. "You don't believe him, do you?"

Grant shook his head. She paced again. He wasn't quite sure what he believed yet, but Wes Peterson *had* gotten pretty nervous when Miss Weaver's name came up.

"I just don't understand why Lucinda wouldn't say anything," Cara murmured.

"Have you given any thought to the possibility they don't want folks knowing?"

She stopped, confused. "Knowing what?"

"Well, Miss Martin"—Grant set his cup down on the counter, and came to stand in front of her—"perhaps they don't want folks knowing they're keeping company."

"Keep . . . comp . . . are you crazy?"

Grant shrugged. "I've been called worse. But you have to admit it's possible. She's got no one . . . and Peterson's wife has been dead a long time. She may have been crying because of a lover's spat."

"No," Cara challenged heatedly, shaking her head. "There's been bad feelings between Lucinda's family and the Petersons for years. The only one she ever spoke to was the son, Wade."

"People get lonely." Grant stepped closer. "You ever get lonely, Miss Martin?" he whispered.

Cara's heart pounded faster. She stared into his handsomely chiseled face and felt her breath lodge in her throat when he smiled. She wondered if he would kiss her again.

Stop it! She didn't have any business wondering such things, or reacting at all to Grant Radnor. He was wrong about Lucinda. And he was wrong about *her* being lonely.

And why did he insist on standing so close?

Cara turned away. "Not lonely enough that I wish to participate in your name drawing for the St. Valentine's dance," she spat.

Grant placed one hand on her shoulder. Cara chided herself for not putting up more of a struggle when he turned her to face him.

"Good. Because I'd rather you go to the dance with me instead."

She swallowed, mesmerized by the fire dancing deep in his green eyes. "Why?"

"Same reason I've been wanting to do *this* ever since I walked in the door." He lowered his head and settled his mouth gently over hers.

The feel of his smooth, warm lips sent her pulse racing, fire licking at every fiber of her being.

His tongue traced her parted lips, then slipped inside to find her own. A spark of wondrous delight flared in her heart. Warning bells clanged in her head.

"Oh, dear, have we come at a bad time?"

Cara jumped back, realizing the bell she heard was the one above her door. She swallowed the knot of embarrassment clogging her throat. Telling heat crept into her cheeks as she stepped around the doctor and hurried toward Yancy's wife and daughter.

"Not at all, Mrs. Smith. Eliza." She forced a calmness to her voice that was foreign to the rest of the tide racing through her. "I've been expecting you. I'm almost finished with Eliza's wedding dress." She glanced nervously behind her, meeting Grant's hooded gaze. "And Dr. Radnor was just leaving."

To her relief, Grant bid the ladies farewell and left. Cara couldn't bring herself to look at him as he sauntered past, but she had no trouble feeling his probing gaze, and didn't doubt he would be back. She wouldn't be here, though. The last thing she wanted to discuss with him was that kiss. It shouldn't have happened. It certainly couldn't keep happening!

"Dang, Doc, you've gone and done it now." Tollie shook his head in disbelief as he walked through the doorway of Grant's office several hours later. "It's all over town that you were caught kissing Miss Cara this afternoon."

Leaning back in his chair, Grant groaned, rubbing at the tension that throbbed in his temples. "So what if we were caught," he commented dryly, a heavy sigh escaping his lips.

"So what!" Tollie echoed incredulously. "Why, folks are already fearing you'll up and leave just like that Hampton fella did, and we'll be without a doctor." He shook one finger and grinned. "And you're darn lucky Jack Martin's out of town, or I guarantee you'd be sportin' a black eye right 'bout now." He stopped pointing and shoved his hand on his hip. "As it is, I'm here to warn ya that Mrs. Delaney is headin' this way."

Grant noted the ominous note in Tollie's voice and sat up straighter in his chair. "What for?"

Cara's older sister hadn't struck him as a short-tempered

type of woman. Frowning, he shifted his gaze, keeping the blacksmith under close scrutiny as he sauntered over and sat down on the opposite side of the desk.

"My guess is she's gonna want to know why ya were kissin' her sister." Tollie removed his hat and scratched his head. "What made ya do it anyway, Doc?"

Grant leaned over, resting his arms on the oak surface, and narrowed his stare. "If you need an answer to *that*, Tollie, then you're the one who's been too long without a woman, and I'm wasting my time helping you with Brigitte."

The blacksmith stilled, then released a hearty chuckle. "You better lose that temper before Miss Beatrice gets here. And I know *why* ya did it, I just don't know why ya were fool enough to do it in broad daylight, where Yancy's wife and daughter could walk in."

Grant sat back and ran his fingers through his hair. He had asked himself that exact same thing at least a hundred times. After the curious peeks through his window, and more than a few snide remarks offered while he hid out at Tyler's saloon, he would be surprised if Cara ever spoke to him again after causing her this embarrassment. But even so, Grant couldn't dredge up any regrets.

He sighed. He liked kissing Cara. She was soft and warm, and tasted better than anything that had ever touched his lips before. The memory stirred a pleasing flow in his veins that came to a fast halt at the dam of his guilt. Her horrified expression at seeing the two women standing in her shop flashed through his mind.

"I didn't plan it that way." Hell, he hadn't planned it at all. It had just . . . happened. He had gone over later to talk with her, wanting to apologize for the results his impulsive action had caused. But she hadn't been there, and he hadn't seen her all afternoon.

A knock sounded at his door.

Tollie shoved his hat on his head and leaned forward over

the desk. "It might not be a good idea to suggest ya *planned* anything, when you're talkin' with Miss Beatrice," he whispered, then smiled wide and stood.

The blacksmith strode over and opened the door, letting in the sparse graying shadows of early dusk, and Beatrice Delaney with her infant son wrapped in a blue quilt and propped on one hip. "Evenin', Miss Beatrice." Tollie tipped his hat. "I was just leavin'."

Grant rose, and swallowed the dryness from his throat. "Good evening, ma'am." He offered a polite smile to match his tone.

She closed the door behind Tollie and turned. A sly grin lifted one corner of her mouth. "Evening, Doctor." Without waiting for an invitation, she marched over and sat down in the chair, placing the smiling baby on her lap.

Grant puzzled at the humor in her light brown eyes. After Tollie's warning, he had expected . . . well, he wasn't sure what he expected, but it certainly wasn't laughter. He sat back down and folded his arms on top of the desk. "What can I help you with?"

"I wanted to invite you to supper tonight."

Grant's mouth gaped open. He stared wide-eyed.

She tilted her chin stubbornly in the same fashion he had seen Cara use. "Why did you think I was here?"

He forced his lips together and leaned slowly back in his chair. Confusion swirled in his head like a fog. "I . . . well . . ." He sat forward again and gripped the edge of the desk. "To be honest, Mrs. Delaney, I thought you wanted to talk about your sister, and . . . well, what happened."

"You mean kissing Cara?" Little Jackson grabbed a fistful of her white ruffled bonnet and giggled. She patiently pried his fingers loose, never veering her steady stare.

Grant nodded, not trusting his voice.

She chuckled, a smile pulling at her lips even as the baby tugged a handful of her dark brown hair loose. "Contrary to what you might have heard, I'm not angry. My husband, however, is another matter. He feels a little overprotective with Father out of town. But I'm not here to discuss whether or not you've ruined my sister's reputation.''

Grant tensed. "I never meant to bring harm to her reputation, I assure you,'' he spoke low.

"Oh, I believe that, Doctor.''

Grant arched a brow at her confident tone.

Beatrice smiled, looked down at her son, and started to bounce him on one knee. The baby cooed his delight. "I've seen you watching Cara. I've noticed the way you look at her. I was afraid to get my hopes up when she told me about agreeing to have dinner with you, then the picnic, but in light of what happened today''—peeking up through thick, dark lashes, she met his stare—"I thought we should have a talk.''

Grant steepled his fingers and narrowed his eyes. He had an idea where all this was finally leading, but that part about her getting her hopes up still didn't make sense. "Is this your polite way of inquiring after my intentions toward your sister?''

"Do you have intentions toward Cara?'' she questioned in a soft, quiet voice, catching Grant slightly off guard.

He paused, unsure exactly what he wanted at the moment, then answered honestly. "I intend to get to know her better.''

"And I intend to help you, Doctor.'' The baby squealed when Beatrice tickled his side.

Grant was grateful for Jackson's distraction which covered his shocked intake of breath. He leaned farther over the desk. "Did I hear you right, Mrs. Delaney? You want to help me?''

"Yes,'' she stated without a moment's pause. "Regardless of what Tollie might have led you to believe, that's why I came over to invite you to supper.''

Grant sat back and shook his head in bewilderment. "I don't understand.''

She shifted her slender frame in the chair and began bouncing the fidgeting infant on her knee again. "About Tollie, or my visit?"

"Well, both."

She chuckled. "I boxed Tollie's ears once for stealing a kiss, and Father chased after him with harmful intent."

Grant was flabbergasted. "You . . . and Tollie?"

She shrugged. "We were young, still in school, and it was before Mr. Delaney came to town. As for my visit, it's really quite simple. My sister made a mistake trusting once, but I don't believe she should give up the rest of her life because of it."

Grant clenched one set of fingers into a tight fist. "You're talking about Bernard Hampton?"

She nodded.

"I'm not going to hurt your sister, Mrs. Delaney. I can promise you that."

For the first time since she stepped into his office, Grant saw her hesitate, her action reminding him of Cara. But in the blink of an eye, confidence returned in her darkened stare. "I've heard good things about you, Doctor. Folks are real pleased to have you here. The fact that Cara let you get close enough to kiss her says a lot. I'll trust you to keep your word." She lifted the baby in her arms and stood. Grant did as well.

Beatrice looked up at him. "I think you might be just what Cara needs . . . to solve a good number of her problems."

Grant pondered her words. "Does that include her . . . medical problem?"

She nodded. "Among other things. But you mustn't tell Cara. She won't be happy to think I asked for your help."

Grant didn't doubt Cara would be displeased, and he didn't want to think about her anger when she learned he had sent inquiries concerning her ailment. But he had her sister's support, Grant realized. Maybe between the two of them, they could make Cara see reason about getting treatment—provided Grant ever received an answer. He shoved aside his anxiety. "As I recall"—he grinned—"you didn't ask."

"That's right, I didn't." Beatrice Delaney smiled, her brown eyes glinting with mischief. "So Cara can't get mad. Dinner is at seven, Doctor. I hope I'll see you there."

CHAPTER EIGHT

"You did what!" Cara's heart kicked up its already rapid force as a hard knock resounded at the front door. She spun around and pinned Ian with her glare, whispering harshly, "Don't answer that!"

Bea skirted around the dining table, untying the white apron from around her waist. "Cara, calm down. Ian, answer the door."

"Calm? You invite the doctor to dinner and don't bother to tell me until he shows up. Ian, get away from that—"

"Evening, Doc." The redheaded Irishman offered the greeting with little enthusiasm.

Cara wondered if her brother-in-law had had a say in this evening's dinner guest, or if this was something her sister had cooked up all on her own. Ever since Grant invited her on that picnic, Bea had been hinting that Cara should show more interest in the doctor. After today, Cara was sure she had shown plenty—too much, in fact.

"Ian."

At the sound of Grant's voice, Cara's face heated to a fiery flame. She wanted to flee. Her feet refused to move. Ian stepped back, opening the door wider. Grant sauntered in, black boots tapping against the planked flooring, black pants hugging his long legs, defining the tight muscles in his thighs. He stopped. Cara's unblinking gaze lifted to the dark jacket buttoned over his tapered waist, the slightly askew black tie around the collar of his white shirt . . . the wide smile that shaped his full mouth. Her breath lodged.

"Good evening, Miss Martin, Mrs. Delaney. I want to thank you again for inviting me."

Cara opened her mouth. Her voice failed.

"We've been remiss in waiting so long." Bea stepped forward and took Grant's arm. "Please come in and have a seat." She led him to a chair near the fire in the front room. "Dinner's almost ready. Ian, would you get the baby? I hear him fussing."

Ian cocked one red brow. "I don't hear him."

Bea widened her eyes. "I do," she insisted.

"I'll get him," Cara offered, grateful for the escape.

"No," Bea rushed to command, holding up one hand to block Cara's departure. "Ian can do it," she insisted.

The man shook his head in puzzlement and headed for the stairs.

"Cara, dear, would you mind keeping the doctor company while I finish supper?" Bea hurried past, then disappeared through the narrow doorway into the kitchen.

"I was hoping to have a chance to talk to you," Grant stated.

Cara watched him cross the distance between them in quick strides, purposeful intent darkening his stare. "We don't have anything to talk about," she whispered, sidestepping around him. She half walked, half ran the length of the spacious room and stopped in front of the large hearth. When she spun around, he was standing right beside her.

"I disagree." He placed one hand on the wooden mantel,

his sleeve brushing the side of her face. "I think we need to talk about that kiss. Everyone else is."

Blood rushed to her cheeks. "It shouldn't have happened."

Grant leaned closer, his distracting mouth inches from her own. "You didn't like it?"

"I . . ." She started to walk away. He brought his other hand up to the mantel, capturing her between his arms. Cara swallowed.

"You're not sure?" his low tone rocked her senses. "Perhaps we should try it again."

"No!" she hissed, ducking under his arm and quickly scooting to the other side of the room.

Placing cool palms to her warm cheeks, she stared at his broad back and watched with growing trepidation as he slowly turned around. She wrapped her arms protectively around her middle and forced herself not to think about how warm and manly he smelled when he had trapped her in his arms.

"What are you afraid of, Miss Martin?" He swept her with a slow, appraising gaze that heated her blood and twisted her stomach into knots. "I think you liked that kiss, and the first one, more than you want to admit." His challenging tone gave her pause. The braided rug covering the planked flooring cushioned the sound of his steps as he approached. "Am I right?"

Cara straightened, planting her hands on her hips. "I'm not afraid of anything, Dr. Radnor, and what I *think* is that you need to leave."

"Dinner's ready." Bea emerged from the kitchen and placed a steaming platter of potatoes and beef on the table.

He leaned down, his lips brushing gently against her ear. "You're not getting rid of me that easy, Cara."

Her name rolled softly from his lips, caressing her as his warm breath on her skin melted her insides. His spicy scent of bay rum assailed her nose. How was she going to get through this evening?

"The baby's fast asleep, honey." Ian descended the stairs.

"I told you I didn't hear anything. Supper smells good." The Irishman crossed the room, staring through hooded eyes as he passed by where Cara stood with the doctor.

"Shall we?"

Cara bit her bottom lip and stared at the arm Grant offered.

"Come on, you two," Bea coaxed from where she stood behind the chair on the far side of the table.

Cara looked back to find Grant watching her and wondered what he would do if she just walked through the front door and hid out until dinner was over. The boyish gleam in his jade eyes suggested he had guessed her thoughts and was more than willing to give chase. Cara's heart pounded against her breast. Would he kiss her again?

No, she sternly rejected the wistful idea. Because she wouldn't let him. Reluctantly, Cara discarded the idea of fleeing. At least here, she realized, she wouldn't be completely alone with him . . . or her foolish desire to think with her heart where he was concerned, instead of her rational good sense.

Ignoring his offer of escort, she turned and walked toward the table. Grant lowered his arm and watched the sway of her hips beneath the brown calico. No bonnet covered her head tonight, and Grant stood mesmerized as the candlelight glistened off her brown hair. The thick, long strands reached nearly to her waist, and she had bound the mass together at the base of her neck with a single ribbon—the same ribbon, he noted with growing pleasure, that had been tied around the flowers he had given her Saturday night.

Grant followed, reaching the table in time to hold her chair out while she seated herself. He wasn't discouraged by Ian's disapproving scowl, or the sideways glare Cara shot him, not after seeing the blue silk tied around her hair. He understood Ian's protectiveness, mirrored it in fact as he learned more about this woman who was slowly haunting his every waking thought and consuming his dreams at night. And he was beginning to understand how cautiously Cara guarded her heart. A sudden rush of anger welled in his gut. What he wouldn't give to get his hands on Bernard Hampton and beat some sense into the man. How could anyone walk away from this sweet, lovely woman? Hurt her so badly she never wanted anything to do with men again? In the blink of an eye, Grant's anger dissipated. He smiled inwardly. Hampton's loss was definitely his gain. He would show Cara she could trust him and prove to her that Hampton was never the man for her anyway.

Grant wasn't surprised Cara sat silently through most of the meal, letting Bea, and eventually a more relaxed Ian, carry the conversation. She hardly looked up from the tin cup she gripped in a white-knuckled clench as they lingered over coffee and bowls of Indian pudding Bea solicitously admitted Cara had made earlier in the day.

While Bea and Cara cleared away the supper dishes, Grant joined Ian by the fire and indulged in a cheroot and another cup of coffee. It was after nine when he finally forced himself to rise from the chair and proclaim his intent to depart. Bea bid him good night, then taking her husband firmly by the arm, pulled him along up the stairs, leaving Grant alone in the flickering firelight with Cara.

Without a word, she walked to the front door and opened it. "Good night, Doctor."

The cool night air swirled through, brushing her skirt and seeping through his wool pant legs. Grant smiled, braced one hand on the wood barrier, and softly closed it, shutting out the breeze.

"I had a great time tonight."

"I'm glad." She looked down and reached again for the door handle.

He took her hand in his and refused to let go when she tugged at his grip. He rubbed his thumb along the inside of her soft, smooth wrist. "Are you?"

She looked up through thick lashes, her amber eyes wary, and nodded.

"I'd like to kiss you good night, Cara."

"I don't think that's a good idea."

"Then, don't think," he whispered. Tilting her chin with one finger, he closed his eyes and brought his mouth down on hers in a slow caress. She tensed; then her lips moved ever so slightly beneath his. Encouraged by the heated sensations she stirred with her light action, he circled his free hand around her waist, pulling her closer. Her fingers pressed resistively flat against his shirtfront, then ever so slowly slid upward to his shoulder and around his neck. Grant trailed his tongue along the rim of her mouth and felt the shudders ripple through her body with the same force that sent his blood pounding, his heart racing. Her lips parted invitingly, and he took what she offered. She tasted of warm molasses, and all he could think about was having more.

"I knew I should have punched him the second I opened the door," Ian whispered.

Bea straightened from her crouched position on the stairway and scowled up at her husband. "You sound like Father," she scolded in a low voice.

"Yeah, well, maybe Jack's right to be so protective."

Bea shook her head. "He's part of Cara's problem. She needs Dr. Radnor."

Ian lifted one brow. "How can you be so sure?"

Bea smiled up into her husband's dark blue eyes. "He's persistent. Just like you were."

Ian arched both brows playfully and grinned. "A man's gotta be with you Martin lasses." He bent and scooped her into his arms.

Cara's eyes flew open at the sound of Bea's muffled squeal and met the doctor's surprised stare. She tore her mouth away, then struggled to free herself, but Grant's hold on her hand and waist remained firm.

He glanced upward at the sound of muffled laughter, then the closing of a door. Cara's cheeks heated. When he smiled

down at her, the warm gleam in his eyes renewed the fire he
had stoked with his kiss.

"Next time, I'm aim to finish kissing you without any inter-
ruptions, and without an audience."

Before she could fully register his intent for this to happen
again, he released her, tipped his hat, and sauntered out into
the darkness.

Cara climbed the steps, pulling her wool wrap tighter around
her body to ward off the chill which seemed to blow colder
along the narrow walkway. The town stood bleak and deserted
under the billowing gray clouds blanketing the early morning
sky. A shrill whistle down by the river broke the gloomy silence,
sounding the arrival of the steamboat from Houston.

She noted the lack of firelight glowing through the window
as she paused outside Grant's office door. Her courage disappeared, sailing away on the breeze that seeped through her
clothes straight to her bones. She couldn't see him, not yet,
not after the way she had responded to his parting kiss last
night. Her body tingled at the memory. She still couldn't believe
the way she had wantonly clung to him as he so skillfully
probed her mouth. Probed at her willing invitation, she chided,
recalling how she had wrapped her hand around his neck to
pull him closer. What on earth had gotten into her?

Cara sighed. She knew the answer. Her heart was growing
way too fond of Grant, and if she wasn't careful, she was going
to get hurt again.

But that kiss . . . She smiled, then frowned.

Stop it. Stop it. Stop it! She had come to clear up the little
matter about the dance. Nothing more. And as soon as she
told Grant Radnor she had no intentions of attending, she was
hightailing it out to Lucinda's for the day—to hide out, pure
and simple. Cara admitted it. She wasn't in the mood to deal
with any of the townsfolk who might stop by to chat about

that kiss the Smith ladies had witnessed, and she needed some time to sort out her heart. Time away from the doctor's distracting presence. Time to remind herself why she couldn't, wouldn't let her feelings get any more involved. But first, she needed to get hold of her courage. She swallowed, tucked her head down, and hurried on, unlocking the door to her shop, then slipped inside.

Coffee. What she needed was some coffee; then she would be ready to face Grant. She walked over to the hearth and stirred the bed of glowing ashes.

Cara jumped at the firm knock on her door. Butterflies winged their way through her stomach as her thoughts instantly leaped to Grant. She shook her head at her lack of emotional control and squared her shoulders. If it was him, then she had best get this over with and put some distance between them quickly.

Crossing to the door, Cara gripped the handle. "Lucinda?" She blinked her surprise, then gazed down at the smiling boy holding his mother's hand.

"Mornin', Miss Cara. Mama says I get to stay with you for a while, if that's all right."

Stunned at Jacob's excited announcement, Cara swung her widened stare to the boy's mother, for the first time noticing the pinched set of Lucinda's mouth and the stark worry in her eyes.

"Can I talk to you?"

Cara nodded, and opened the door wider, allowing the woman and child entrance. "What's wrong?" she inquired, closing off the winter cold that rushed in behind her visitors.

Lucinda spun around. "I need to leave town, and I was wondering if you would watch Jacob for me. I don't know how long I'll be gone."

"Of course I will, but where are you going?"

Lucinda shook her head. "It's best if you don't know."

Cara frowned, recalling what she and Grant had learned the

day of their picnic. "Does this have anything to do with Wes Peterson?"

"Please." Lucinda placed a gloved hand on her arm. Cara saw the shimmer of tears glistening in her pleading stare. "Don't ask anything. Just promise me you'll take care of Jacob. You won't let anything happen to him?"

Cara nodded her promise. A disturbing fear clutched at her gut. "Do you need any money?"

Lucinda quickly shook her head, then squeezed Cara's hand. "Thanks." She kissed Jacob goodbye with a promise to bring him back a surprise, then hurried out the door. Cara glanced down at the innocent boy's beaming blue eyes.

Well, so much for hiding out at Lucinda's.

"You Doc Radnor?" the stranger inquired.

Grant braced his hand against the edge of his office door and nodded at the aging, gray-bearded captain.

"Brung you a letter."

Grant's heart missed a beat. Finally, a response to his request for medical advice. Was it from his friend . . . or Dr. Hayward?

The man stuck out an envelope, then hooked a thumb over his shoulder when Grant relieved him of the missive. "Got a crate for you, too. My men are unloading it down at the warehouse."

Grant thanked the man and closed the door. He stared at the letter, frowning as he slowly crossed to his desk and sat down. He didn't know an attorney in Boston named Bryan Thompson. So, why was the man writing him? Grant's stomach tightened with trepidation. His hand shook as he broke the seal and pulled out the folded sheets. Unfolding the letter, he read:

Dear Dr. Radnor,
    It is with deepest regret I must inform you that your father, Dr. Grantham Hayward, and his wife both per-

*ished in a carriage accident shortly after your departure
from Boston.*

*Their two surviving sons, of course, will inherit the
bulk of your father's estate. But before his demise, Dr.
Hayward added a codicil to his will, to include you. The
conditions are as follows. . . .*

CHAPTER NINE

"Go to your shop." Bea looked up from the mound of dough she was kneading, and swatted Cara's hand away from the plate of fresh-baked cookies.

"But—"

"No." Bea raised a flour-coated finger in front of Cara's nose. "You've been cooped up in this house for nearly a week using the rain, and Jacob, as an excuse to stay away from town."

"That's not true," Cara argued.

Bea planted her hands on her aproned hips. "Then, why are you doing your sewing at home when I've offered more than once to watch Jacob? And why didn't you go to church yesterday, or out to the Potters' for supper with Ian and me?"

Cara glared back at her sister. "Jacob's not your responsibility. And yesterday, he wasn't feeling well. I couldn't take him out. Besides, I wanted to finish sewing that stuffed rabbit for him." And as long as she stayed home, giving Jacob far more attention than she knew he needed, she didn't have to listen to the same gossip about her and the doctor that Ian shared each evening when he came home from the newspaper.

A few times, she was even able to forget about Grant as well, and the dance . . . and the fact she still hadn't spoken to him. Not once all week had he tried to seek her out. She chided herself for being bothered by that. Hadn't she known all along his interest wouldn't last? She should be glad he hadn't come around.

Cara sighed. So why wasn't she?

"The boy is plenty well enough this morning."

Cara followed Bea's nod to where Jacob sat at the table eating, his new stuffed bunny perched beside his plate of eggs and biscuits. The boy's short, thin legs swung back and forth under the chair, and he giggled between bites as he watched the baby rolling from side to side on a blanket spread on the floor.

"The rain stopped two days ago," Bea added, plowing her fists back into the dough. "And frankly, I'm tired of having you underfoot."

It was on the tip of Cara's tongue to remind Bea who exactly still lived here, and who had gotten married and moved out until recently, but she knew her sister was right. It was time to stop hiding. "Fine," she huffed. "I'll leave."

Cara placed another log on the fire, then brushed the bits of dirt and wood from her hands into the flames. Standing, she smoothed out the folds of her indigo skirt. The shop bell jangled loudly, drawing her attention. Wes Peterson shoved the front door back against the wall with a heavy thud.

"Where the hell is she?" Peterson demanded, his large, burly form filling her doorway.

Cara's eyes widened as the plantation owner whipped his hat from his blond head and stormed into her shop. The mottled rage on his angular face made her back up as he approached. She snatched her skirt from the reaching flames in the hearth, then stepped down the narrow aisle to her right, placing the long table laden with bolts of fabric between them.

"Where's . . . who?" she croaked, certain she already knew the answer. She had never seen Henrietta's father behave this way before, but if he had acted like this around Lucinda and Jacob, she understood why the boy had called Wes Peterson a "bad man."

Narrowed blue eyes blazed with anger as he stopped and faced her across the waist-high piles of cloth. "You know damn well I'm talking about Lucinda Weaver. Where'd she go?" he sneered.

"I don't know," she responded, grateful for the honest reply that would keep her friend safe from this man.

"You're lying," he seethed, leaning over the table. "You're her only friend in this town, and I hear you're keeping her bastard brat. You must know where she went."

Cara's temper flared at his bullying. "I wouldn't tell you if I did. Now, get out."

With lightning speed, he grabbed a handful of her bodice at the neck and jerked her across the table to within inches of his face. Cara screamed, then groaned when her legs scraped across the wooden edge, and bolts of fabric bit into her stomach. She pulled her head back from the hateful daggers blazing in his eyes.

"You can't get rid of me as easily as you did my daughter, Miss Martin," he ground out, his hot breath blasting her face. The stale smell of whiskey and cigar smoke made her slightly nauseous. "I'm not leaving until you tell me where Lucinda went."

Cara's quickened breath rubbed raw in her throat. She clawed at his hand.

Grant stormed through the doorway, grabbed the man's thick

neck, and squeezed hard. Peterson's blue eyes bulged with surprise.

"Let her go," Grant ordered in a low, deadly voice. "Before I rip your fingers from your hand and cram them down your throat!"

Peterson dropped her, then shoved his elbow into Grant's gut.

Grant doubled over at the impact, losing his hold on the man's neck. Cara's loud gasp echoed in his ears.

"I don't have any quarrel with you, Doc."

Grant looked upward. "You do now," he grated. Straightening, he shoved his right fist up under the man's chin.

Peterson's head snapped, and he stumbled backward. Grant started after him. The sound of metal clicking made him freeze. He lowered his sight from the indignant anger blazing in the plantation owner's narrowed stare, to the gun Wes leveled at his gut.

"With all due respect, Doc, this really isn't any of your business."

Grant's blood pounded in his veins. He met the man's glare with one of his own. "You made it my business when you started this commotion. You ever lay a hand on this woman again, I'll kill you."

Peterson leaned his head back and peered down his long nose. "Well, I guess those rumors about you being sweet on Miss Martin are true." He shook his head, sneering. "I took you for a better educated man, Doc."

Cara's sharp intake of breath made Grant grit his teeth even tighter. "Get out' " he commanded harshly.

"Oh, I'm going." Peterson uncocked his gun, and shoved the barrel into the waistband of his pants. He looked over Grant's shoulder. "And I'll find Lucinda Weaver. You can count on that, Miss Martin."

Frowning, Grant grabbed Peterson's arm as the man headed past. "What do you want with Miss Weaver?"

One corner of Wes's mouth lifted in a grin. "That *is* none of your business, Doc. I think you best stick to what you know, and check on the lady." He jerked free of Grant's hold and sauntered out, closing the door as he left.

Grant spun around. Cara was nowhere in sight. He glanced down, and his heart stopped at the sight of her crumpled form lying on the floor. A cold chill crawled up his back as he rushed around to the other side of the table. Kneeling, he stared into her taut face. Her eyes were closed. One side of her mouth twitched rapidly, as did her right arm. He ran his hand along her slender limb, frowning at the stiffened muscles. Her breath came in sharp gasps, then sometimes not at all.

He pressed his hand to her face. Her skin felt sharply cool against his touch. Heart aching with anger at his inability to do more than observe, Grant rubbed his palm over her narrow forehead, brushing away the loose strands of her silky hair. Several minutes later, her mouth relaxed. Grant touched her still arm, smiling his relief at the softened flesh under her cotton sleeve. Slowly, she opened her eyes.

"How do you feel?"

"Fine." She squinted. "Except for a small headache." She darted her eyes from side to side. "What happened?"

"You fainted."

She drew her brows together in concern. "Any . . . thing else?" Her voice was barely above a whisper, but Grant heard the fearful caution in her tone.

He placed his hand against her smooth, flushed cheek. He pondered whether to tell her the truth, but knew he had no choice. "Yes," he answered.

She groaned, and raised one hand, warding him off from saying more. "Did Mr. Peterson see?"

Grant had a gut feeling that the truth—he didn't know what the man had seen—would upset her the same as a yes, and he didn't want to do anything to distress her more. "No," he assured, offering a smile as he stroked her soft skin.

Cara sighed her relief and closed her eyes. The talk of her illness had finally started to die down since her spell two years ago. She wasn't eager for it to resurface. Because he was a doctor, or perhaps because he was so kind and patient—she didn't know which—she trusted Grant not to say anything. His gentle, comforting touch made her feel safe. She wanted to stay like this forever, drawing strength from his nearness.

What on earth was she doing?

Her eyes flew open. Cara braced herself up on her elbows. Before she could venture a guess as to his intent, Grant lifted her in his arms, then rose to his feet.

"You're not getting up, and you're not working today. You're coming to my office."

"But I'm fine," she protested, linking her arms around his neck for balance as he carried her toward the back of the shop. "Where are you going? Please, put me down."

"Not until I make sure you're all right." He shoved the rear door open and stepped into the alleyway, then headed next door.

"I'm fine," she insisted, grateful he hadn't gone out the front where folks could see.

Ignoring her protest, he entered the confining space he used as his living quarters, crossed into his office and carefully laid her on a long, narrow table covered with a clean sheet. Cara immediately propped herself up on her elbows. He braced his hands against her shoulders and gently pushed her back down.

"Stay put," he ordered in a soft whisper, then turned and shrugged out of his jacket.

Cara stared at the broad expanse of his back. A visible darkening of tanned flesh shadowed the thin white cotton of his shirt. The material pulled taut across his muscles as he rolled back first one sleeve, then the other. A tingling started low in her stomach. He turned around, revealing the corded lines of his forearms as he planted his hands on lean hips. His concerned smile stole her breath and clouded her thoughts. She suddenly longed to be held in his arms again, wanted to feel his lips touching hers.

Cara sat up and brought her legs over the side. The pounding in her temples increased. She would have hopped down if the doctor hadn't stepped over, preventing her escape. He placed his hands on the table, his arms brushing the sides of her hips.

"Where do you think you're going?"

She looked down at her hands clasped in her lap, needing to break contact with the close proximity of his intense jade stare, and swallowed hard. "I've already told you, I'm fine."

He touched her chin lightly and forced her to look up. "Since *I'm* the doctor"—his deep voice stirred her blood to flow faster—"why don't you let me be the judge." His teasing grin started a strange, desirous fire building low in her belly that both intrigued and frightened her.

Grant decided she did look just fine, and quickly became much more interested in kissing that beautiful cupid's bow mouth of hers than discussing her ailment. If she didn't stop staring at him with those soft, shimmering brown eyes, he was going to do just that.

" Is it true?"

Grant frowned, wondering just how long he had been daydreaming to have missed this jump in the conversation. "Is what true?"

She blushed. "What . . . Mr. Peterson said," she rushed on breathlessly.

Grant smiled. "You mean about me being sweet on you?"

She nodded, her cheeks turning a darker shade of red.

"Would that bother you?"

To his chagrin, she nodded again, and chewed at her bottom lip. He moved his finger over her chin and gently tugged the delicate flesh free.

"It shouldn't. I'd never do anything to intentionally hurt you," he whispered.

A small spark of trust sprang into her eyes, replacing some of her uncertainty, and making his heart soar.

He leaned slightly closer. "I've missed seeing you these last few days. I've been wanting to talk to you about the dance." He ran his finger along the line of her smooth cheek, down the column of her slender neck. "I heard Miss Weaver left town, and you've been taking care of Jacob."

She nodded.

Grant paused, letting his finger rest on the soft cotton collar at the base of her throat. "I'd have to say you were right. After the way Peterson behaved today, whatever's going on between him and Miss Weaver is more than a simple lovers' spat. Did she leave because of him?"

"Lucinda wouldn't say, but I suspect so." She stared at him with her innocent gaze. "You could have come by the house."

Grant straightened, drawing his hand back to his side. Guilt put a swift end to the delightful flight in his heart. "You're right, and I'm sorry I didn't." He stepped back, raking his fingers through his hair.

"Is something wrong?"

The painful catch in her voice tore at his conscience. He had avoided seeing her this week because he needed time to think, time to digest all the lawyer had written, and time to figure out a way to explain what he had done. His stomach knotted into a tight ball.

"Cara, there's something I need to tell you."

Her eyes dimmed cautiously. Grant wanted to reach out and smooth the lines in her furrowed brow, but didn't.

He took a deep breath, knowing he could put it off no longer. "When I first learned about your ailment, I wrote a letter to a doctor in Boston."

Her face drained of color. "How dare you," she gasped, and jumped off the table. Grant stepped closer, determined not to let her escape.

"He was a well-respected man, and world-known for his

study and treatments of brain disorders. I thought he could help."

"I don't care. You had no right."

Grant reached for her, but she sidestepped from his grasp, slapping his hand away. He followed, grabbing her arm and holding her in spite of her efforts to pull away. "I know I should have talked to you first. But I wasn't at all sure I'd hear from the man . . . even though he was my father."

She stilled her struggles and turned her puzzled stare up at him. "Your father? I thought he was dead."

He nodded, sighing. "I let you think that because I was never close to him. He was from a prominent family, and a dedicated physician. I was the illegitimate son he never acknowledged. But I received word last week that he died a few months ago."

Cara's eyes softened. She reached out and touched his arm. "He was wrong not to acknowledge you. You're a fine man, Dr. Radnor. Even if I don't agree with you going behind my back to send that letter."

Her kind words and soft tone were like a bucket of cold water hitting him in the face. How fine would she think him when he told her the rest? He swallowed the knot of tension in his throat. "It's that letter I want to talk about. And in light of what just happened in your shop, I think we need to discuss your ailment."

Her muscles tensed beneath his hold. "There's nothing to talk about." She looked away, lowering her hand from his arm.

"There's a great deal to talk about."

She pinned him with her blazing amber stare. "We have nothing to discuss," she adamantly stated. "Please let go of me."

Grant shook his head. "Not until you listen to me. My father was experimenting with a new theory. A new treatment. Something I thought might help."

She jerked her arm from his hold. "I appreciate your concern, but I don't need help. And besides, your father's gone now, so it doesn't matter.''

Grant blanched at the pain in her eyes, at the hurt in her forceful voice. ''It matters, Cara, and there's still a way.''

She raised one brow in a questioning slant. ''What are you talking about?''

He sighed. He had known this wasn't going to be easy, but he had to tell her. ''In the event of his death, my father requested I carry on his studies.''

Her face tightened with indignation. Angry tears shimmered in her stare, and tore at Grant's heart. ''And you thought to test his theory out on me?''

CHAPTER TEN

"Are you sure you know what to say?" Grant paused at the front door inside his office and gripped Tollie's shoulder. "She won't go willingly."

"I know what to do," Tollie growled his frustration, knocking Grant's hand away. "You've been over it a hundred times."

Grant didn't care. He couldn't allow for mistakes. He hadn't seen Cara since she had stormed from his office, impossibly resistant to his desperate pleading that he didn't think of her as an experiment, and that he only wanted to help because he cared. His added explanation that he hadn't decided whether to honor his father's request, since it could mean moving back to Boston, had only fueled her anger more. Before leaving, she had vowed never to trust him again.

All week she had thwarted his efforts to speak with her, rushing over to talk with Brigitte, staying away from her shop, refusing to receive his visits at her home. The written apology he had slipped under her shop door one night had been returned unopened the following morning, same as the package of stick candy he had left for Jacob the day before. And along with his weekly copy of the *Blue Plains Gazette,* the towheaded Johnson boy had delivered a brief note. In one curt sentence, Cara politely explained that she wouldn't be attending the dance.

"It's important, so let's make it a hundred and one." The name drawing was taking place tonight. Grant feared this might be his last chance with the stubborn little seamstress.

Tollie shook his head. "Don't bother, I got it." The blacksmith jabbed one finger into Grant's chest. "You just make sure Brigitte's name *isn't* in that damn drawin' jar."

Grant shot his friend a warning glare. "Do *your* part right, and I will."

Cara frowned her stunned confusion at the man standing in the dusky shadows on her front porch. "You can't be serious, Tollie. It's your best Sunday shirt, and you didn't know before now?"

The blacksmith nodded, and turned the brim of his hat through his fingers. "I went to put it on, and there it was. A big rip clean down the side. But it's mostly on the seam, so it shouldn't take ya too long. I've really got to have it for the name drawin' tonight, Miss Cara."

She stiffened at the mention of the event that had been the talk of the town all week, as had the doctor's agreement not only to participate, but to assist Henrietta in presiding over the whole blasted thing. A sense of betrayal as cold as the sudden gust of wind that swept across the porch seeped into her bones. How could she have let her heart get involved? Hadn't she learned from Bernard that no man could ever be serious about her? She wasn't normal, wasn't that what he had said? What most of the townsfolk thought? But Grant had seemed interested. Hadn't seemed to care what folks thought. Grant had a reason, though . . . her ailment. Cara shivered. She never should have trusted him.

Cara tightened the wool shawl across her shoulders to ward off the cold and shook aside the sadness that threatened to engulf her again. Instead, she concentrated on Tollie's request and the memory of Brigitte's hopeful excitement that the blacksmith would draw her name tonight. Sighing, she held out one hand. "All right, let me have it, and I'll see what I can do."

Tollie's eyes widened. "I didn't bring it with me."

Cara arched one brow. "You need me to fix your shirt so you can wear it in half an hour, and you didn't bring it?"

"I thought we could go into town and you'd fix it at your shop."

"Can I go?"

Cara spun around at the sound of Jacob's eager voice and saw the lad standing in the doorway, a hopeful glint in his blue gaze. The same type of boyish gleam she had seen before in Grant's eyes.

Stop it! She had no business thinking about the doctor. Whatever fantasies she had foolishly let herself harbor were gone, locked back behind the protective wall she had built around her heart.

"Not this time, son," Tollie responded in a harsh, hurried tone.

Jacob's smile fell at the same time his shoulders slumped. Puzzled, Cara shifted her stare to the blacksmith. "Why not?"

Tollie twisted his hat a little faster. His mouth screwed up in seeming concentration. Cara had an overwhelming sense there was more to this visit than a request for her sewing services.

"Well, um ... you see ..." The blacksmith shifted his stance, glanced down at the boy with sad, guilty eyes, then back at Cara. "Oh, heck, Doc didn't tell me what to do if the kid wanted to come along."

Cara straightened with surprise. Her heart pounded. "What does Dr. Radnor have to do with this?"

Tollie ran one hand through the black curls on his head.

"Oh, hel—heck, I'm makin' a huge mess of this. Doc's gonna have my hide."

"Jacob, go inside where it's warmer," Cara calmly instructed, placing her hand on the boy's shoulder to make sure he obeyed; then she closed the front door. Anger rose in her with the speed of a flooded river as she reeled around to face Tollie. She planted her hands firmly on her hips. "You tell me right this minute what's going on," she demanded.

Tollie ran one finger along the inside of his collar. "I can't. Doc swore me to secrecy."

Cara narrowed her stare. "Do you want your shirt fixed, or not?"

"Next week will be soon enough, ma'am." Tollie dropped his shoulders slightly and stared at her with pleading eyes. "But I really need ya to come with me, or Brigitte's gonna end up goin' to the dance with someone else. And I'm gonna be sweepin' the floor with Doc's head."

Grant scanned the faces inside the crowded town meeting hall and tried not to give in to the anxious pain knocking at his heart. *Where the hell is Tollie?*

"Everyone's here," Miss Peterson commented, touching his arm. Grant forced himself not to cringe and peered down at the woman he wished was standing anywhere else. "Shall we begin?" She smiled wide.

Grant shook her fingers from his arm and reached inside his vest pocket for his watch. He took his time popping open the silver engraved lid. "It's not quite seven. Let's wait."

"Oh, pooh, what's a minute or two," the blonde scoffed, and flicked her hand as though shooing away a pesky fly. "Everyone's eager to start, and we've already put the ladies' names into the jar."

Grant shoved his free hand into his pants pocket and continued to stare at his watch. He fingered the slip of paper with

Brigitte's name on it that he had withheld from the cloth-covered jar. Tollie had a similar slip tucked safely in his coat. Grant glanced at the barmaid and saw her nervously watching the front door of the building. He knew exactly how she felt.

"I know Tollie's planning to come, and we'll still need another female to make the drawing come out even."

Miss Peterson pulled her lips into a slight frown and shook her head. "We've got an even number already, and surely by now it's seven, which means your friend is late."

Grant stifled his groan at her accuracy and snapped the watch lid closed, then replaced it inside his pocket. Obviously, Tollie hadn't been able to convince Cara. Grant's stomach clenched in a hard knot. Defeat slowly edged its way into his thoughts, his body. He released a deep, heavy sigh. "All right, Miss Peterson, let's—"

The door opened, emitting a large gust of chilling wind that brought squeals from the ladies, then a descending hush as Tollie and Cara rushed inside.

Her cheeks were flushed, her amber eyes wide as she took notice of everyone's stares. Grant's heart pounded furious relief at the sight of her. He smiled when she met his gaze.

"Hope we're not late," Tollie offered with a cheery smile as he took hold of Cara's arm and guided her over to where Brigitte, all smiles now that the blacksmith had arrived, stood with the other ladies along one side of the room.

"Just a little," Miss Peterson piped up in a none too friendly tone. "But you're here now, so let's get started."

Grant swallowed his urge to respond just as rudely, saying instead, "At least allow Miss Martin a chance to drop her name into the jar."

"No!" Henrietta squealed. She turned away from the doctor and glared at Cara. "You told me you weren't participating."

The fact that the blonde dared to protest riled Cara's temper. "If I remember correctly, Henrietta, that was your suggestion, but I never agreed with it. In fact, it's part of the reason I threw you out of my shop." Cara ignored the surprised murmurs springing up from the crowd, and Henrietta's heated stare. "Let's not hold up the event any longer. If you don't mind, Dr. Radnor''—she pinned him with a hard, knowing look— "would you place my name in the jar for me?"

Grant hesitated long enough for Cara to see understanding of her knowledge dawn in his eyes before he nodded, then bent over the square table and wrote her name. His hand disappeared inside the wide opening of the cloth-covered container. When he removed his fist, Cara had no doubt the white slip was still clutched in his grasp. And she was quite hopeful that the deathly pale look on Henrietta's face meant she was going to faint quite soon.

Cara refused to look at Grant as the drawing proceeded. Each man filed past the jar, drew a name, and announced his partner for the upcoming dance. There were few disappointments and many flirtatious giggles as the men then came to stand beside their designated partner. Brigitte gripped her arm with shaky fingers when Tollie walked up to the jar, then squealed her delight and hugged Cara when the blacksmith drew the bar-maid's name. Cara wasn't the least surprised at Tollie's luck, and quite happy for her friend. Another man took his turn, then announced his partner, leaving Henrietta and Cara the only two left.

Cara glanced at the freckle-faced, sixteen-year-old Whorton boy, his toothy smile wide as he stepped up to the drawing jar, then at Henrietta. She almost felt sorry upon seeing the hopeful, praying look on the blonde's face, until she saw a strange, confident gleam in her narrowed blue stare. Cara knew there was only one slip in the jar, but Henrietta didn't. What was the woman up to?

Joshua Whorton stuck his hand into the jar.

"Hurry up," Henrietta snipped.

"I'm trying, but the paper's stuck."

Henrietta stepped over and smacked the boy on the arm. "Not that one, take the other one," she hissed.

Curious whispers rose among the crowd.

"Got it," Joshua declared.

Cara lifted a hand to hide her smile as Henrietta snatched the slip from between his fingers. Her howling screech was all the response everyone in the room needed to know whose name the boy had drawn. Undaunted, Joshua stepped up to Henrietta's side and swept his hat from his wild shock of red hair.

"It's my pleasure to be your escort, ma'am."

Henrietta scowled.

Grant snatched the jar before Henrietta could and tucked it under his arm. "And, I guess that means you're my partner, Miss Martin." He smiled, his voice low and even, but Cara saw the concern in his jade eyes.

"I suppose it does, Dr. Radnor," Cara responded calmly, crossing her arms and ignoring the curious stares and looks around her. She remained rooted to the same spot as folks filed past and left. The reverend's daughter and the schoolteacher led a still fuming Henrietta out. When everyone was finally gone, Cara looked up where the doctor stood at the front of the room.

"Tollie told you, didn't he?" Heavy remorse laced his tone, his look.

She nodded.

He winced, then took a deep breath. "I'm surprised you came."

"You went to a lot of trouble." Cara's insides shook with longing. She wanted to believe what Tollie said about Grant's interest being personal not medical, wanted to trust his reasons for rigging the drawing to ensure her as his date. But a part of her couldn't be sure. After all, Grant hadn't told her about seeking advice for her ailment, or the truth about his father. How could she know what his real motive was for suddenly being so persistent? "And Tollie was pretty worried you'd mess things up for him and Brigitte. He threatened to do you bodily harm."

Grant arched one brow. "So, you came to save me?"

Cara lowered her gaze from the hopeful gleam in his eye and his breath-stopping smile. "No," she whispered. She had come because she realized how badly she wanted to attend the dance . . . with Grant. "I came for Brigitte and Tollie."

"Just so you know, Tollie had nothing to worry about. It was an empty threat. And it looks like I'm indebted to you again. I should have known Miss Peterson would try something sneaky. Thank you for saving me from her clutches."

She looked up through her lashes and saw the grim set of his jaw. "You're welcome."

He ran one hand through his hair, pulling the long, loose strands away from his face. "I don't suppose you'd consider going to the dance with me anyway, would you?"

"Yes, I would." Cara raised her chin and saw the pleased glint in his widened stare. "But I'm not agreeing to be your experiment . . . or anything else."

"Before we disperse," Reverend Watkins's voice boomed from behind the oak lectern at the front of the church, "I understand Mr. Peterson has something he wishes to discuss."

Wes Peterson stood from his seat in the front pew, glanced directly at Cara with his heated stare, then moved to stand beside the reverend. The small hairs on the back of Cara's neck rose. Instinctively, she gave Jacob's thigh a reassuring pat, then shot Bea a worried look over the top of the boy's head. She hadn't seen or spoken to the plantation owner since that day he had grabbed her in her shop and Grant saved her, but every fiber of her being suggested whatever the man was about to say, it concerned her and Lucinda.

"As I'm sure most of you are aware by now," his voice

echoed with irritation, "Miss Lucinda Weaver has abandoned her son, leaving the lad in the care of one Miss Cara Martin."

Startled murmurs and some nods of agreement rippled through the packed church room. Jacob fidgeted at Cara's side, his bottom lip sticking out and trembling.

Rankled by the accusation, Cara jumped to her feet. "Miss Weaver most certainly has not abandoned Jacob, and I resent your implying so, Mr. Peterson."

"Then, why don't you tell us where she went," Wes challenged sarcastically. "And when she's planning to return."

"I don't see that's any of your concern." Grant's deep-voiced defense drew Cara's attention, as well as the curiosity of the rest of the congregation. He stood in the center aisle near the back of the church, hands planted on his hips, his hair secured back with a length of rawhide strip revealing the vein throbbing at the corner of one temple.

"I'm only looking out for the boy." The plantation owner responded. "His ma's been gone awhile. And frankly, I'm concerned Miss Martin isn't the proper person to care for a small child. For one thing, she's not married, and for another, well . . ." He scanned the others in the room, his insinuation of Cara's illness clear in his light blue stare.

Jacob started to cry. Cara fumed.

Bea handed her son to Ian and rose to her feet. "My sister is fully capable of taking care of Jacob. And Lucinda *is* coming back. She loves her son."

"With all due respect, Mrs. Delaney, everyone in this town knows you've always come to your sister's defense. But the truth of the matter is, she's sick. We all saw what happened right here in this room a couple years ago. And I saw her fall to the floor and start twitching just the other day in her shop."

Her heart stopped. Warm blood drained from her veins, replaced by a cold, sweeping flow. Grant had lied . . . again. Cara refused to look away from Peterson's accusation. "I fainted, after you attacked me."

Startled gasps and murmurs rose among the crowd.

"I did not attack you, young lady," Peterson hotly defended.

"Looked like it to me." Grant's heated affirmation created a new stir of conversation.

"I'd say your opinion is biased, Doctor. We all know how you feel about Miss Martin."

"Good. I never intended for it to be a secret."

The plantation owner narrowed his stare. "That doesn't change the fact Miss Weaver left—"

"Lucinda left because of you," Cara accused.

Henrietta quickly jumped to her feet and glared at Cara. "My father would never have anything to do with *that* woman," she spat.

"Why she left isn't the point, Miss Martin," Peterson snarled. "The point is you. How can you care for a child when you can't even control yourself? And furthermore, you don't know Miss Weaver's intentions any better than anyone else in this room. It's my belief that under the circumstances, the child should be sent to an orphanage."

Cara's breath caught in her throat.

"No! I want to stay with Miss Cara," Jacob wailed.

A pandemonium of conversations, looks, and pointed fingers stirred throughout the room. Jacob's tears fell faster. Cara grew tense, desperate to spare Lucinda's son this awful display. The tingling started in her hand, then shot up her arm. She closed her eyes and prayed for the sensation to stop, then breathed a sigh of relief when it did.

The reverend pounded the lectern with his gavel, silencing the room. He looked at Cara, then over the rest of the congregation. "There's only one person here qualified to say whether Miss Martin is able to care for the boy. Tell us, Doc, and keep your personal feelings out of it. Is it your medical opinion that given her ... problem, Miss Martin can or cannot take care of this child?"

CHAPTER ELEVEN

"That was a great meal, Mrs. Delaney. Thank you."

"It's the least we could do, Doctor, after the way you stood up for Cara today." Beatrice rose, and began gathering dishes from the table, then disappeared through the narrow doorway into the kitchen.

Ian stood, his sleeping son cradled in the crook of one arm. "Gotta hand it to you, Doc, that was a real pretty speech you gave in Cara's defense. Sure shut up that loudmouth Peterson in a hurry."

"I only said what I believed." Grant leaned back in the chair and took a sip of hot coffee as Ian left to lay the infant down for the rest of his nap.

Outside the large, square window, Jacob stood on the porch in the sun's golden rays. In one hand, he protectively grasped the stuffed rabbit Cara had made for him, and he used the other to throw sticks one by one off the front porch with youthful determination. Grant knew the boy didn't understand all that had happened at the church and hoped he would never have to.

Grant shifted his stare to Cara sitting across from him and staring down at the table. She hadn't spoken much beyond her thanks for his support, and barely responded to his sincere apology for not telling her earlier he didn't know whether Peterson had seen her spell. He realized now what a mistake it had been. She couldn't have possibly been more hurt and embarrassed than she was today.

Grant placed his arms on the table. "It's warm enough for a ride this afternoon." He leaned down to better see her face and met her eyes peeking at him from beneath her long, thick lashes. "If you're interested?"

She sat up straight. "I really shouldn't leave Jacob."

"We'll take him with us," Grant offered, surprised she had given him even an ounce of hope.

Half an hour later, Cara paced the length of the porch waiting for Grant and Jacob to return from the livery, desperately searching for a way out of her rash decision. She frowned at the sorrel mare Ian had saddled and tied out front. Jacob would be disappointed she had changed her mind, but she would find a way to make it up to him. There was no way she could spend the afternoon with Grant. After this morning, her defenses were weakened. There had been such intense pleading in his stare as he watched her, but addressed the plantation owner. Did he really think she had the kindest heart of any woman he had ever met? That he would trust her with his own life, and saw no reason to doubt her capability as a parent, substitute or otherwise?

She had never loved him more than at that moment. Cara straightened with a start, then sighed. There was no use denying it. She was in love with Dr. Radnor, had been practically from the moment the handsome man stepped foot in town. It was her wayward heart that made her agree to spend time in his company and to finally participate in the name drawing. Truthfully, she was flattered by Grant's persistence. She was even able to forgive his lie about what Mr. Peterson had seen, believing his entreaty he just hadn't wanted to see her upset by the cruel man anymore. But it didn't erase the doubts. How could she trust him? How would she ever know if he saw her as a woman . . . or a means to follow in his father's footsteps?

She paused, and lifted a gloved hand, shielding her gaze from the sun as she watched Grant ride up after retrieving his horse from the livery. The excited boy seated on his very own mount beside the doctor made Cara waver in her decision to declare her change of mind about this outing. Jacob's widened blue eyes shimmered his delight. The cloth rabbit she had made him sat perched between his legs.

"Look, Miss Cara," he shouted, his grin amazingly large. "Mr. Doc let me have my own horse. I've never ridden my own horse before. Wait'll ma gets back. Is she gonna be surprised."

Now how could she possibly tell that little boy they weren't going riding?

"She sure is," Cara responded, tugging on her gloves as she climbed down the steps and walked over to her mount. She glanced at Grant's pleased expression and for a second thought she saw a gleam of awareness in his gaze. Had he guessed she would change her mind? Was that why Jacob sat on the gentle-looking, gray gelding?

She climbed into the saddle and guided her mare over to where the pair stood waiting in the road, positioning herself so that Jacob rode between her and the doctor. "So where are we going?"

"I thought we'd ride out to where we had our picnic. I want to show you something."

"Mr. Doc says he's got a surprise," Jacob offered.

Cara looked from Jacob to Grant. The older man's smile was as infectious as the boy's, and she had no resistance to either one. Thankfully, Jacob's constant chatter made conversation of a personal nature between her and Grant impossible, and Cara found herself relaxing as they rode in the afternoon warmth. She admired the doctor's patience in answering the young boy's curious questions about the workings of nature. She listened with close interest when Jacob asked the man if he planned to kiss Miss Cara again when they got to the picnic spot. Her mind relived the velvet touch of his mouth on hers that first time, recalled the passion that had warmed her body, her heart. His response that he would if she let him pulled at her conscious effort to remain immune to him, to guard herself from being hurt any more. She realized Grant Radnor could damage her beyond repair if she let him get close, only to walk away . . . as Bernard had. She also knew her despair would be much worse. She had never really been in love with Bernard Hampton; she knew that now. She had never felt this intense longing, this tingling heat, except in Grant's presence. Bernard had never stirred her senses to distraction, but Grant could set her aflame with just a look, could make her melt with desire from his touch, his kisses. Still, though he might care for her, he saw her as a means to continue his father's experiments. She wasn't his love.

Pain gripped her heart.

"Think we'll see that bunny rabbit again, Mr. Doc?"

Grant reluctantly tore his gaze away, wondering what had brought that sadness to Cara's amber gaze even as he formed an answer to another of Jacob's curiosities. "We might. He looked pretty smart to me, and I think he'll take advantage of this nice weather. Winter's bound to arrive eventually, even here in Texas." He glanced up and smiled at the blush on Cara's cheeks. So, she did recall telling him months back there wasn't much winter here. The thought that she remembered his first attempts at trying to talk with her pleased him immensely. "He'll have time enough to stay burrowed away when the cold does hit."

Jacob nodded his agreement, then pursed his lips. "We're here, Mr. Doc," he announced. Grant beamed his approval when the boy sawed back on the reins just the way he had shown him at the livery and brought the horse to a stop.

He thought of what it would be like to have his own son someday, and let his stare fall on Cara. "So we are," he answered.

"What's the surprise?" Jacob inquired, squirming anxiously in his seat, and latching on to his stuffed rabbit as it started to fall.

"Well . . ." Grant braced one gloved hand on his thigh and leaned closer to the boy. "You see the cabin up on that hill?" Grant pointed to the small, slightly dilapidated frame house in the distance. "I bought that, and this land."

"You did?"

Grant looked up at Cara's startled inquiry. "Yes, ma'am."

"What about Boston?"

Grant sighed. The idea of delving into the more scientific side of medicine still intrigued him. He wanted to help others, to help Cara, and he couldn't completely ignore the fact that it made him somewhat proud that his father had finally acknowledged him, thinking enough of Grant's ability as a doctor to trust him to carry on this study. But his heart wasn't ready to leave Texas . . . or Cara. He lowered his eyes from her probing gaze. "I haven't decided."

"Does that mean you own the rabbit, too?" Jacob piped up.

Grant chuckled at the same time Cara did. Their eyes met over the top of the little boy's black felt hat. He saw curiosity and doubt burn in her brown stare. It ate him up inside knowing he was to blame for both. "Naw, just the hole he's burrowed in is all. He's free to come and go."

"Can I go look for him?"

"Don't you want to ride up and see my house?"

Jacob frowned. "It really don't look like much, Mr. Doc."

"Jacob," Cara admonished.

Grant smiled, and waved a dismissive hand. "Boy's right. In fact, I thought maybe I'd tear it down and build a new one." He swung his leg over and dismounted, then reached up and lifted Jacob from the gray gelding. He set the child on the ground, but held him by the shoulders. "Don't get too close to the creek. It's deep."

"I won't," Jacob promised, wide-eyed. Clutching his stuffed rabbit in one arm, he turned and trotted through the knee-high grass.

Grant shifted his attention to Cara still astride her horse. She bit at her bottom lip, and he wondered if her nervous action had anything to do with them suddenly being alone.

"Why did you buy this place?"

Grant shrugged. "I'd been thinking about it for a while." Long before he received that letter, in fact. Buying this place two days ago had still seemed right, though. And, Grant told himself, it wasn't just to prove to Cara she meant more to him than any damn experiment. No matter the pride he felt, he didn't owe his father any loyalty.

But what about the medical profession? Grant shoved the troubling thought aside. "Would you like to get down?"

She nodded, then didn't bother to wait until he could get there to assist her from the horse. Grant took hold of her gloved hand before she could walk away and forced her chin up with one leather-clad finger. "Answer something for me."

She lowered her lashes and stepped back from his touch. "I should really watch after Jacob."

Grant held fast to her hand, halting her retreat. He glanced over the top of her head at the boy happily searching for the rabbit's hole. "Jacob's fine." Grant's heart pounded as erratic as a spring storm. "Tell me why you agreed to go to the dance with me."

She arched one brow. "Have you changed your mind about being my escort?"

The challenge in her tone, the daring fire that sprang back into her amber eyes, and his own burning need all converged together and pierced his composure. He grabbed her arms, pulling her flat against his chest, then circled her in his embrace. His devouring lips seared hers and left him breathless.

"I think that should answer your question, sweetheart," he whispered, releasing her. "Now, please answer mine."

Cara's breath lodged. She missed the comfort of his hold, missed the feel of his hard, broad chest pressing her breasts flat between them. Held in his arms, kissed, she forgot everything but her need, her desire to be with him. She swallowed the sudden dryness from her throat. "I . . . wanted to go with you."

One corner of his mouth lifted in a smile. "Because I rigged the drawing?"

Her pulse fluttered. "Does it matter why?"

Grant leaned down, his lips moving tantalizingly closer. "It matters a great deal."

His warm breath fanned across her chin. He closed his eyes and pressed his mouth ever so lightly against hers. Cara let her eyes drift shut, giving in to the sensations swirling in her veins. She wound her arms around his neck, melting in his strong embrace as he parted her lips with his tongue . . . praying he would kiss her again like he had a moment ago.

"I found it! I found it!" Jacob shouted. "Hurry Mr.—are you kissing Miss Cara again?"

Grant pulled away, and smiled, his smoldering gaze as soft as a caress.

"I'll be there in a second," he called out, then gently placed his forehead on hers, the brim of his hat bumping her bonnet. "One of these days, I'm going to kiss you and never stop, no matter who's around."

Cara set the steaming cup of tea on the table next to the burning candle. Climbing between the cool sheets, she sat back against the pillows propped at the headboard and pulled the covers up to the waist of her white flannel nightgown. A sharp wind rattled the two windows in her bedroom. The banked fire in the small hearth warded off the sudden northern chill which had blown in shortly after the sun disappeared. Now, close to midnight, the cold threatened to permeate through the solid wood walls.

Cara looked up as the door to her room slowly opened. Jacob peeked around the edge, agony contorting his small face. The soft, yellow candlelight glistened in the drops of moisture on his cheeks.

"Jacob, what's wrong?" Throwing the covers back, Cara left the bed.

Jacob rushed inside, burying his face into her stomach. Racking sobs shook his tiny shoulders. "I left my . . . bunny rabbit at Mr. Doc's new place," he cried.

CHAPTER TWELVE

A deep chill coated the air, and heavy gray clouds hovered low in the morning sky. The first slow drops of cold rain started as Cara reined her horse to a halt beside the sparsely timber-lined creek where Jacob insisted he had left his rabbit. She pulled the hood of her black cape farther over her face, warding off the moisture and the wind that kicked up, then dismounted. Walking along the stream's edge, she prayed this wouldn't take long and she could return home before the threatening weather worsened. As though reading her thoughts, and laughing, the rain came harder, sharp pellets of freezing water slapping her cheeks. Within minutes, a thin layer of ice began to form on the ground. Cara turned around, intending to climb back on her horse. Jacob's tears crashed into her memory. He had been so upset when he came into her room last night, and for the first time since Lucinda left, the boy had cried for his mother. It wasn't until Cara suggested he stay in her room, then promised to ride out first thing this morning and find his rabbit, that he finally settled down and went to sleep.

She turned around and searched again, heading back to the water's edge. Ice pelted the ground, sounding like a thousand crystal glasses breaking at once. Where was that blasted rabbit?

"Ouch!" Cara jerked her foot up, away from the sharp rock digging into the bottom of her boot.

"Are you hurt?"

Startled by Grant's shouted concern, she reeled around on one foot and lost her balance. Flinging her arms out, Cara tried to regain her footing, but slipped again and screamed as she fell backward. She hit the icy water hard, knocking the air from her lungs. Something struck the back of her head, and blackness engulfed her as thoroughly as the deep stream.

Grant cursed the howling wind seeping through the weathered walls of the near empty cabin and tossed another log onto the blazing fire. Sparks flew in wild disarray; shadows danced in the darkened corners of the room. He glanced out the only window in the single-room house. Barely mid-morning, yet daylight gave way to the graying darkness of the storm. Snow fell thickly, covering the ground in a soft, shimmering white.

He turned his sight to Cara's still form lying on the pallet he had used for his bed last night—not that he had slept much. Thoughts of his father's will, his request, troubled him long into the late hours. If he honored Grantham Hayward's request, he would have to move. He couldn't do research in Texas. He needed equipment, a hospital, patients. And was that even what he wanted? He liked Blue Plains. He liked Cara Martin. He didn't know just how much until today. When he saw her fall in the creek, then float facedown to the surface, he had never been so scared in his life. At that moment, he realized she had laid a claim to his heart like no one ever had before. Love and fear mingled as one, telling him with all certainty he would be lost without her.

Firelight glistened on the long strands of brown hair he had fanned out behind her to dry. After fishing her unconscious body from the creek, he had carried her up the long trek to his cabin, then piled blankets on her, trying to warm her. But still he could see her lips quivering.

Dammit! He needed to make it warmer in here. He didn't want her taking a fever. Grant poked at the fire and threw another log into the flames. She had been unconscious for almost an hour, and he was starting to worry. The knot he had found on the back of her head wasn't that big, but it didn't lessen his concern the longer she stayed out.

She groaned softly. Heart pounding with tension, Grant stood and crossed the distance between them in two lengthy strides. He knelt down, staring into her pale face.

Her eyes fluttered open, then closed. She pushed her arm from under the covers and pressed her palm against her forehead, moaning again.

Grant touched his hand to her cheek, thankful to feel only cool flesh. "Cara?"

She blinked several times.

"That's right. Wake up for me," he coaxed.

"Grant?" she croaked, closing her eyes.

"Yeah, it's me. Now, I want you to open your eyes again. C'mon, sweetheart, open them for me." He ran his hand along her cheek, her forehead, smiling when she did as he requested, then leaned closer to examine her dilated pupils.

"What are you doing?" she whispered.

Grant paused. He was concerned for her on a medical level, but right now his profession had nothing to do with this overwhelming need to take care of her and keep her safe. Or this powerful desire to kiss those sweet, tempting lips of hers. He smiled. "Well, I'm looking into the most beautiful eyes I've ever seen, and staring at the prettiest face on God's earth . . . and praying you won't slap me when you realize you're not wearing your dress."

"What?" Her eyes widened. She peeked under the blankets,

then grabbed them up tight around her neck and glared at him, twin spots of pink filling her cheeks. "Whose shirt am I wearing?"

"Mine."

She glanced down at his bare chest. Grant's blood pumped faster.

"You undressed me?" she whispered incredulously.

His own embarrassment surfaced on his cheeks. Even though his sole interest had been to get her warm, Grant hadn't been able to completely ignore her soft, luscious curves. "I had to get your clothes off to get you dry."

He pointed to her feminine attire draped over two spindly chairs set close to the fire. His own wet clothing hung on pegs on the far side of the wall and dripped puddles of moisture onto the planking.

She sat up slowly. His wool shirt hung loosely off her narrow shoulders. The front opening dipped low, revealing the shadowed cleavage of her breasts. Closing her eyes, she lifted one hand, the blue sleeve sliding down to reveal her pale arm, and rubbed at her temple with two fingers. "I remember. I fell into the creek."

Grant sat back on his heels, more than a little relieved she recalled what had happened.

Her long, dark lashes lifted. Her amber gaze captured his. "You startled me. I didn't expect you to be out here."

"Good thing I was." His voice caught. A sickening wave of fear welled in his gut at the thought of what might have happened to her if he hadn't been looking out the window when she rode up, and gone to find out why. "What made you come out in this weather?"

"Jacob," she answered softly.

"The rabbit." Grant nodded, realizing he should have guessed. He knew the boy was attached to it, and if Jacob hadn't been asleep when they headed back yesterday, the stuffed animal would never have been left behind. "I found it last night and was intending to bring it by on my way to town, if the weather cleared.''

"I was hoping to get back home before the storm hit.''

"Afraid you didn't make it, sweetheart.'' His velvet-edged voice washed over her like warm silk. Cara stared into the heartrending tenderness of his gaze. She wanted him to touch her, wanted to feel the soothing comfort of his soft, warm hand on her face again.

"Bea's going to worry if I don't come back.''

"The storm's gotten worse,'' he responded. "We can't go anywhere right now.''

Cara glanced toward the dim light coming through the window and saw the large flakes of snow falling. A loud wind buffeted the walls of the small room. Pecking noises she knew were ice sounded sporadically against the outside frame of the house. He was right. They were stuck. She turned back to look at Grant.

He stared at her with darkened eyes that devoured her in a single sweep and made her long to know the feel of his arms around her again, the taste of his firm, warm lips on hers. Cara shivered at her wayward thoughts.

Grant stood. She sucked in her breath at the sight of his broad chest. Flames shimmered in the thick matting of brown hair that swirled across his tightly bunched muscles and tapered to a thin line down the center of his flat stomach. The firelight gave his tanned skin a deep, healthy glow. Black wool pants hugged his hips. She had never seen a man half-dressed before, certainly never been alone with one. She drank in the sight of his tall, powerful frame. A dizzying current raced through her veins and pooled hotly at her very core, stirring a powerful longing in her heart for him to join her on the pallet.

He looked up at the ceiling, then raked one hand through his hair. She puzzled over his look of unease.

"Uh . . . I'll get some coffee. That'll help warm you.''

He turned and crossed to the fire, giving her an unobstructed view of his sleek back. A sudden chill made her look down. She saw where his shirt had slipped off, exposing her right shoulder, with the front opening hanging dangerously low on her breast. Her cheeks burned with understanding at his action a moment ago. Quickly, she tugged the soft wool back in place, drawing the collar up close to her neck and breathing in the scent of his distracting manliness.

"I brought a few supplies with me last night. Are you hungry?" He stared at her over one shoulder.

Cara swallowed the thick knot in her throat at the unexpected gleam of desire in his gaze. Could he tell she wanted to touch him? Wanted to know if his skin was as hard as his muscles indicated, or as soft as the feel of his hands on hers, on her face . . . ?

"Cara?"

She blinked. "What?"

His lips curled down. Slowly, he turned around. "I asked if you were hungry." A glint of alarm sprang into his narrowed, searching gaze.

The look reminded her of the seizure he had witnessed the first time they had ridden out of town together. But Cara knew this time her distraction had nothing to do with her ailment, and everything to do with Grant.

She shook her head, then moaned when the movement caused a sharp pain to slice across her skull and stab at the backs of her pupils. She closed her eyes and seconds later felt Grant's hand rest gently on her shoulder.

"You need to take it easy. You hit your head when you fell."

What she needed was to get away, before she did something foolish. The handsome doctor had occupied a good portion of her thoughts last night, and all her dreams when she had finally slept. She had awakened at dawn no more certain of his motives than before—but achingly positive of her love for him.

Peering through her lashes, Cara stared at his stocking-clad feet poised in a squat beside her, then raked her gaze over his powerfully muscled legs, his broad, masculine chest. His musky scent sent her heart beating faster, and wild swirls of heat stirred low in her stomach. She swallowed, looked into his intense green gaze, and smiled weakly, trying to ignore the delicious shudders coursing through her limbs and the rapid thud of her heart.

"I really should go home. If you'll just sadd—"

He chuckled low. "Sweetheart, your horse ran off when you screamed. And there's a veritable blizzard coming down at the moment. He stuck one hand inside her shirt collar and slid his smooth palm up her neck, across her cheek, and behind, stopping at the base of her skull. "What you need to do is relax. You're perfectly safe here." He rubbed lightly with two fingers, creating a slow circle that eased the dull throbbing in her head.

"That feels good," Cara sighed, enjoying the tingling warmth of his soothing touch.

God, if she only knew how good. Grant stifled his groan. If he didn't stop touching her, he was going to do something he would regret. He stilled his hand.

Slowly, she lifted her long lashes. Grant stared into her smoldering amber gaze. "Thank you for coming to my rescue . . . again." Her soft, sultry whisper sent a shiver coursing through his heated blood.

"Anytime, sweetheart." He leaned closer. She closed her eyes and raised her lips to meet his. Grant froze at the rush of desire swelling in him, hardening his body. He feared if he kissed her he wouldn't be able to stop. There was no one to interrupt them, no one watching.

Cara could stop him, though. One word from her, and he would be across the room in a flash.

Grant lowered his mouth on her full, soft lips, drinking in her sweetness. She pressed herself closer, her tongue boldly tracing the shape of his mouth, coaxing what he was more than willing to offer.

He tasted his fill, delighting in her eager response. Falling to his knees, he cupped her face in his hands, pulling her to him, sampling deeper. He ran his hands through her soft hair, then lowered his touch to her shoulders, running his fingers over the soft wool, down her arms. One palm brushed the side of her breast, and she tensed slightly.

With a harsh groan, Grant tore his lips away from hers and stood. What the hell was he doing? He drew in a ragged breath. "I better get you that coffee."

"I don't want coffee," she whispered.

Several long seconds passed. Grant studied her flushed, innocent face, watched the firelight dance in the depths of her honey eyes. "What do you want?" he finally inquired in a deep, strained voice.

Cara swallowed at the sudden dryness in her throat. Her pulse pounded. She wanted Grant. Wanted him to hold her, kiss her, love her. She had fought her attraction for this handsome man for months, but still he had coaxed and charmed her into loving him. He owned her heart.

He had told her he cared. She truly wanted to believe his declaration was more than just caring for a patient. Why else would he have come to her defense before the entire congregation, and persistently finagled his way into her company? Did it matter why he had sought out her company in the beginning? Or did it only matter that she loved him? Loved the way he made her burn with such unstoppable passion every time he stared at her with his warm eyes, held her in his arms . . . kissed her.

She was driving him crazy! Desire raged through Grant, threatening to overpower his good sense. Crossing the short distance between them, he knelt and placed his hands on her cheeks, staring into her eyes. "I'm trying real hard to be a gentleman here."

"Don't try," she whispered.

He tensed, feeling the tight rein on his fervent ardor slipping fast. He drew his brows together. "Do you know what you're saying?"

She nodded.

Grant took a deep breath. God, how he wanted her. But what if she changed her mind? What if he couldn't stop? "I don't think—"

She silenced him with a slender finger pressed to his mouth. "Don't think. Just kiss me." Her shy smile made his heart stop as effectively as her whispered reply. Her gaze sparkled with tremulous courage, then flared with innocent desire.

"With pleasure." Hot waves raged through his blood, pounded in his loin. Grant lowered his mouth, capturing her lips and tasting of her sweetness, her warm desire. He circled her in his embrace, pulling her up to kneel in front of him. Her hands slid slowly up his bare chest, burning him with her silky touch. Grant stroked her back through the wool fabric, traced the soft, curving shape of her waist, her hips. His fingers touched her warm flesh below the shirt's hem, and he felt her thighs quiver as he ran his hands over her smooth skin. Finding the bottom shirt button, he unfastened it, then slowly worked his way up until the garment hung open. He pulled back from their kiss and saw the apprehension in her gaze. "I'll stop if you want."

Tension laced his voice. He lowered his hands to his sides, and Cara watched his chest heave with every deep breath he took. She knew he meant it, though his taut face suggested it wouldn't be easy. The fact he cared enough to ask made her love him more . . . want him more. She shook her head.

He smiled reassuringly and gently drew the shirt away from her shoulders, letting the fabric slip down her arms. He sucked in his breath at the sight of her full, round breasts, the rosy nipples pebbled with desire. His eyes drifted lower to her small waist, flat stomach, and the mound of dark curls that marked her womanhood. He swept his stare back to her flushed face.

"You're beautiful," he whispered, capturing her lips again.

He pulled her close in his embrace. Her soft curves melted with scorching enticement against his harder form. He pressed her down toward the pallet, never breaking contact with the sensuous feel of her tongue delving and dancing with his in one accord.

Her nipples tingled in the soft hair on his chest, then hardened when he pressed his heated skin to her breasts. Wild jolts of pleasure shot through her blood.

She sucked in her breath when his large, warm hand caressed her breasts, closing her eyes at the feel of his gentle fingers, kneading, stroking. Exquisite heat flared in her stomach and rushed to pool lower as his hands roamed over her body, drawing pleasure she had never known before.

Grant left the delicious softness of her mouth and dropped light kisses along her cheek, down the column of her smooth, creamy neck. He touched his lips to the hollow of her throat. Her soft moans assailed his ears, igniting the building fire in his hardened body to a throbbing crescendo. He ran his palms over her narrow shoulders, then down, brushing the sides of her breasts, outlining her shapely fullness with his hands, then circling her taut, rosy nipples with one finger. He took the pebbled nub into his mouth, thrilling at her throaty moan of pleasure, then sucking, lavishing his attention on first one, then the other.

Cara ran her hands through his long, soft hair, over his broad, smooth shoulders. She wanted, needed to feel more of him, know more of this craving, this fire he stirred in her body.

Grant captured her trembling mouth in a slow, lengthy kiss. Her tiny cries of pleasure fueled him on. He trailed his hand over her thigh, then up, touching the mound of soft curls, finding her hot and ready for him. She arched into his palm. He slipped one finger inside, swallowing her cry of surprise and meeting the darkened, amber fires of desire blazing in her narrowed stare. Her pleasure made him harder, driving him with an urgency he fought to control. The first wave of her heated release was as vibrant as the moans that escaped her slightly parted lips. Grant reveled in her abandonment, her warm moisture, her surprised but satisfied smile. Wasting little time, he shed his pants and lowered himself back to her side. He stoked the fire in her again, touching, kissing, tasting the sweetness of her luscious curves as he marked a path from her face, to her breasts, then lower still. He parted her legs with one knee, then shifted himself between her thighs.

The sudden worry in her eyes gave him pause. "The pain won't last," he whispered. "I promise."

She nodded trustingly, then wound her arms around his neck, drawing him closer. Grant probed the core of her velvety heat, easing slowly into her silky moisture, and broke through the barrier of her femininity. She stilled, then slowly relaxed as he devoted his attention to her body, kissing, stroking, bringing her to the edge of glorious passion once again.

White-hot pleasure swept over Cara, blinding her with its brilliance, sending her flying into a vortex of ecstasy as wave after wave of liquid heat made her tremble with crashing force.

Nothing in his life had prepared Grant for the sweet rapture he found with her. Nothing had ever felt so right before. He cried out her name, unable to hold back any longer as the satiny feel of her sweet release made him spill himself inside her with such power he wasn't sure he would ever find his way back to earth . . . and wasn't the least interested in doing so.

CHAPTER
THIRTEEN

"Can you ever forgive me?"

Cara opened her eyes at Grant's softly spoken request. He stretched out beside her, his head propped up in one hand, his finger tracing her face around her hairline. His saddened stare ripped through her heart. A dull, empty ache filled her stomach. Please God, don't let him regret what they had shared. She had given herself to him freely, twice as the morning waned into early afternoon, and she didn't want to hear him say he was sorry. Not when it was the most beautiful experience of her life, and one she would cherish for as long she lived.

Cara blinked back the threatening tears. "For?" her voice shook.

Grant's breath stilled at her shimmering amber gaze. "For not being up front with you about the letter," he whispered. "For giving you even the slightest hint that I would ever want to *use* you for anything." For taking advantage of her sweet innocence when there were still things to settle between them. For not telling her how he really felt, fearing she would perceive his declaration of love as only another means to garner her agreement to help with his father's studies. "Cara, I want to explain to you about my father."

"You don't have to ex—"

"Yes, I do," he insisted, leaning over and kissing her briefly on her sweet mouth. The fire burned low, the flames glistening in her hair and setting her smooth, flushed cheeks aglow. God, how he loved her.

"I grew up thinking my father was dead, until eight years ago. When my mother was dying, she wanted to ease her guilt about the lie before she passed on."

Cara's eyes widened. "She lied to you about your father?"

Grant nodded, lowering his hand to trace the curve of her neck, along her shoulder. "She told me about a doctor she met. He was only in Philadelphia for a few days, and only sought comfort in a scullery maid's arms because he thought his beloved new bride had perished at sea. But Dr. Hayward's wife was found about the same time my mother learned she was pregnant."

"Didn't she tell him about you?" Her voice barely rose above an incredulous whisper.

"She wrote him a letter the day I was born. He paid for her silence and never contacted her again. Mama said she kept the money and used it to arrange an apprenticeship for me and to pay for my studies." Grant recalled the numerous times he had asked his ma where she found the funds, but always she just told him not to worry.

Cara rolled to her side, facing him, and pulled the blanket up over her partially exposed breasts. "Did you try to contact him when you found out?"

Grant nodded. He focused his attention on trailing his hand along the blanket's edge, finding comfort from the painful memories in the quivering feel of her skin as he nudged the cover down and skimmed his finger along the tops of her breasts. "I was upset, and angry he had never wanted anything to do with me. And, I wanted revenge. So I moved to Boston. Got a job at the hospital where Hayward often did his research. It took a while, but I managed to meet the right people and finally finagled my way to a dinner party he was attending. When we met that evening, I brought up my mother's name. I saw the guilt in his eyes, the shame, and he saw the hatred in mine." Grant shrugged. "That was enough. I realized I didn't want to know him. I just wanted him to know I knew the truth." He paused, arching one brow. "And possibly, I took a little more satisfaction than allowed in knowing he would always wonder when and if I'd publicly reveal it."

"You never did?" Cara's breath fanned across his cheek like a warm wave.

He sighed, frowning. The man was a brilliant doctor, a dedicated scientist . . . a devoted husband, and out of respect for his mother's silence all those years, Grant couldn't bring himself to cause Hayward trouble.

"No, only to a close few." Grant recalled his ex-fiancée. "He had a wife, and two other sons. I decided to spare us both a lot of gossip."

"I'd say you did more than that." She smiled, reaching up one hand.

His heart kicked up its pace as she stroked his face with her delicate touch. The corners of his mouth lifted. "You're right, I did. I answered that ad your father sent to the Boston paper . . . and I met you." Grant lowered his head and kissed the tip of her nose. "From the first moment I met you, I was drawn to your sweet charm and the stubborn fire I could see burning in your beautiful brown eyes. When I heard about your illness, all I wanted to do was try to help, and maybe have an excuse for getting to know you. I kept hoping you'd come by my office seeking advice, but you never did. You didn't even bother to bring me so much as a slice of bread, either."

She chuckled softly. "You hardly needed more baked goods."

He smiled, enjoying her velvety caress. "I assure you, I wouldn't have given any of yours away. That day I begged your assistance in aiding my escape from Miss Peterson, I was already giving strong consideration to asking you to dinner. I realized by then you weren't coming to see me about anything, and it was time I made a more aggressive move." His smile lowered, as did his tone. "Please believe me, Cara, I never had any medical motive for wanting to be with you. But I am a doctor, and it is my job to help. I sent those letters—"

"Letters?" Her hand stilled on his face. Her brows arched high, even as her smile faded. "You sent more than one?"

Damn! How was he ever going to win her trust? Grant sighed. *By stopping the lies right now, that's how.* He swallowed the knot of tension from his throat.

"Yes," he whispered.

Betrayal flashed across her stare and ripped the breath from his lungs. She started to roll away from him, but Grant stopped her, pressing his hand to her shoulder.

"Since I wasn't sure about getting a response from my father, I sent a letter to a friend in France. He's doing research at the Medical Institute there. I was hoping he might be familiar with Hayward's new studies." She stiffened, and Grant rushed on with his explanation, desperate to make her understand. "I wrote asking for advice *as* a doctor, and like I told you, because I care about you, and I want to help." He could see belief wavering in her stare.

"Why didn't you tell me sooner?"

"I started to, the day we rode out and you suffered that brief seizure, but you weren't real receptive to talking about your ailment. And I didn't want to spoil any further chances to get to know you."

Cara remembered her withdrawal, then riding away. She also recalled waving him off from explanations in her shop that day, and the concerned pain that had hovered in his eyes. She couldn't deny any longer what her heart had been saying all along—she had misjudged his motives in the beginning. But what about now? "What are you going to do about your father's request?"

Grant raked one hand through his disheveled hair and sat up, pulling the blanket with him. "I've read through his notes, and I think his theory of a connection between the nervous system and seizures is valid, and worth exploring."

Cara sat up beside him, drawing her knees to her chest under the blanket. Nerves? Was it possible? Cara thought back to that day in church two years ago when she had had her last major seizure. Just that morning, she had overheard Henrietta telling her friends in the quilting bee that Bernard was only using Cara because he wanted her father to support his political campaign for governor in his paper, and that he never intended to marry her. She was terribly hurt and angrily nervous about confronting him after church. Her seizure kept her from having that chance. After Bernard left, she hadn't suffered any more spells . . . until Grant came to town. Her feelings for him certainly made her nervous.

"Now it's a matter of deciding where and who I want to turn the information over to for study."

"You won't do the work yourself?" Cara didn't hide the surprise in her voice.

Grant sighed heavily and shook his head. "I gave it some thought. But that kind of research has to be done in a hospital, with a laboratory . . . and patients. I'm not so sure I want to leave."

"You're not?"

"Not if there's a reason to stay."

What was he saying? That he would choose her over his father's request? Before she could ask, the noise of several hoofbeats crunching through the snow and ice sounded outside the house. She met his widened stare with her own.

Grant muttered an oath and jumped up from the pallet, grabbing for his pants. Cara gasped, scrambling to adjust the blanket

over her. Footsteps pounded across his porch. Grant fastened
the remaining buttons on his pants and was just shrugging into
his shirt when Tollie burst into the room, followed by Ian,
Yancy Smith, and Wes Peterson.

"Doc, something's happened to Miss Cara—Whoa!" Tollie
spun quickly around and tried to herd the other men back out.
"C'mon boys. Don't think we need that search party after all."

Peterson sidled his burly frame around the blacksmith. "Well
now, what do we have here?"

"Not a damn thing, Peterson." Still buttoning his shirt, Grant
stepped in front of where Cara sat on the pallet, her face bright
red, her hair loose and wild from their lovemaking, the blanket
clutched over her nakedness in a white-knuckled clench. "Why
don't we take this outside?" he hotly suggested.

"What's going on?" Ian demanded, pushing his way between Tollie and Wes, and pinning Grant with a hard glare.
"Why'd Cara's horse come back without her?"

"The mare spooked when Cara fell into the creek." Grant
offered no further explanations. He crossed his arms and narrowed his stare. "Now, why don't we all get out and give Miss
Martin some privacy," Grant suggested in a tone that brooked
no argument.

Ian shook his head, muttering his irritation as he spun around
and grabbed Yancy and Peterson each by one shoulder and
forced them to precede him outside. Tollie followed behind.

Grant looked down at Cara and started to tell her how sorry
he was about this, but she shook her head and told him with
her weary gaze she didn't want to hear it.

"Please, just go," she whispered, wrenching his heart.

Damn! How much more could he hurt her?

Grant nodded, grabbed his boots, and stepped outside, closing
the door. A cool wind sifted through his wool shirt, but did
nothing to freeze the guilt in his chest for causing Cara yet
another embarrassment. Wrapped in the warmth of the cabin,
cradled in her arms for the last few hours, he hadn't realized

the clouds were clearing and the sun was struggling to shine through. Melting snow dampened the bottoms of his feet. Grant shoved his boots on. Turning his back on the curious stares of Ian, Yancy, and Wes, he crossed over to where Tollie stood alone on the opposite side of the porch.

"Dang, Doc, you've gone and done it now," Tollie stated ominously, shaking his head.

"What the hell did you bring Peterson for?" Grant snarled.

Tollie shrugged. "He was at Yancy's when Ian came looking for men." His doomed hazel stare did nothing to comfort Grant's anger. "Peterson's gonna have a heyday with this."

"Tell me something I don't know," Grant grumbled.

Grant opened the door to Cara's shop without knocking. The bell jangled, causing her to spin around where she stood in front of the hearth. He hadn't seen her since Ian took her home the day before. Judging by the dark circles under her eyes, and her pale cheeks, she hadn't slept much. But then, neither had he.

Worry lines wore a path on her brow, but she held her head high. The simple yellow calico modestly covered her shapely curves and highlighted the amber flecks in her eyes. Her clenched hands rested against the front folds of her skirt. He knew she was concerned about the town meeting Wes Peterson had called for noon today. The plantation owner was going to make another run at having Jacob sent away, Grant was sure of it. And this time, more than Cara's illness would be on display.

"You shouldn't be here." She crossed her arms in a stubborn defiance that matched the tone of her voice.

Grant frowned. In another half hour her reputation was going to be bandied about by the folks of Blue Plains, with details of how she was found naked in his cabin.

"This is exactly where I need to be." He closed the door

and crossed the room to stand in front of her. "I'm not going to let Peterson do anything to hurt you, or Jacob." Grant hated the fact he had caused Cara this scandalous embarrassment and had pondered all night how to fix it. There was only one way.

"What are you going to do? Deny what happened?" Cara sighed.

She started to turn away. Grant grabbed her by the arms and pulled her against his chest, surprised as much as she was by his action, but driven by a need stronger than he could control. "No, I'm not going to deny it. I'm going to marry you. Today if I have to."

CHAPTER FOURTEEN

Cara's pulse pounded with apprehension as she watched Grant rise from his seat beside her in the front pew and step forward. He stopped, standing with feet wide apart, his hands planted firmly on his hips, his hair hanging loose and brushing over the collar of his black coat.

"We're getting married, Peterson."

A renewed burst of curious conversation filled the crowded church at Grant's strongly determined announcement. Cara heard her sister's surprised gasp and Ian's low mutters that it was about damn time the doctor did what was right, but refused to look at her family.

"So, you can call off this meeting," Grant continued.

From his spot beside Reverend Watkins at the lectern, Wes Peterson arched one blond brow. "Well now, did you decide on this because we found the two of you practically naked together?" he taunted, grinning. "Or because you're worried about keeping Lucinda's brat here?"

This isn't right. The thought hammered furiously in Cara's mind. They shouldn't be having this meeting. She glanced at Jacob fidgeting nervously beside her. Lucinda would return;

Cara had no doubt in her heart. But Grant was doing more than trying to save the child from Peterson's heartless intentions. He was trying to save her, and she couldn't let him go through with it. She would keep her promise to Lucinda some other way. She wouldn't let anything happen to Jacob.

Cara rose, and stepped to Grant's side, gripping his arm. "We can't do this," she whispered in a shaky voice, ignoring the murmurs rising among the congregation, and meeting the confused, tempered stare he turned on her.

"We've already decided." He kept his tone low.

She bit at her bottom lip. He had decided. She never agreed, though her heart had screamed yes so loudly it rang in her ears. But now, she was thinking with her head. She couldn't marry Grant. He was a kind, honorable man, and he was only suggesting marriage to save her reputation . . . and because of Jacob. He had waved aside her arguments that she had survived gossip in this town before, and would again, and offered up his own persuasions that she might already be carrying his child. But not once had he mentioned love. No matter how much her heart yearned for him, or how strong her gratitude that he was gentlemanly enough to do the right thing, she couldn't marry him, not when he was doing this because he felt he had no choice.

"Something wrong?" Peterson sneeringly inquired.

"No," Grant assured in a strained voice, his hurt gaze piercing her before he turned his attention to the front of the church. "We're getting married . . . right now."

"Wait," Cara insisted, willing the tears in her eyes not to fall.

"If you don't want to get hitched, Miss Martin, that's fine." Peterson smiled slyly. "We'll just go ahead and make the arrangements for Lucinda's brat to be sent to the orphan—"

"You're not sending that boy anywhere!" a harsh male voice boomed from the back of the church, drawing everyone's attention.

Cara gaped at the man standing at the opened door of the

church, then at the auburn-haired woman beside him. A rush of relief swept through her at the sight of Lucinda, even as ripples of shocked whispers at the couple's unexpected presence together moved among the gathered crowd. Before Cara could stop the boy, Jacob jumped up from the first pew.

"Mama!" He ran down the center aisle where Lucinda Weaver stood with the tall, blonde man at her side. Lucinda gathered the boy in her arms and hugged him against her shoulder. Cara could see tears slipping down her friend's face.

"You know that man with Miss Weaver?" Grant whispered in her ear.

Cara nodded, then glanced up to see the pale shock on the plantation owner's face before turning to Grant. "It's Wade. Wes Peterson's son."

"Just what do you think you're doing, Father?" Wade Peterson sauntered up the aisle, guiding Lucinda by the elbow and ignoring the curious stares of everyone he passed.

"I don't know what lies that woman has told you," Peterson blustered. "Bu—"

"Be careful, Father," Wade seethed. "Lucinda is my wife now."

"What?" Wes Peterson's face turned red.

Henrietta shrieked loudly from her seat near the front of the church, and startled bursts of conversation rose among the onlookers. Cara's eyes widened at Lucinda's slight nod of agreement and the soft smile that lifted the corners of her mouth.

Grant's hand settled gently on her arm. Cara looked up and met his perplexed stare. She shook her head, as confused by this turn of events as everyone else.

"That's impossible," Wes blustered. "You're marrying Senator Randall's daughter next month."

"Not anymore," Wade stated in no uncertain terms. "Lucy and I were married in Austin last week. Now, unless you want the whole town to hear the details of how you kept us apart five years ago with your lies—"

"I never—"

"And your blackmail against Lucy to keep my son a secret so her parents could keep their farm," Wade continued in a forceful voice. "Not to mention your threats against her since she returned. I suggest we take this conversation home."

"Did you have any idea?" Grant whispered to Cara as they stood at the front of the now empty church and discreetly watched Wade Peterson meet his son properly for the first time.

Cara shook her head. "I didn't even know they'd liked each other back then." She wiped the tears of happiness from her face. "I should have guessed, though. Jacob resembles Wade a great deal. No wonder Wes Peterson wanted to send him away, before anyone guessed the truth."

"Miss Cara. Mr. Doc," Jacob's gleeful voice resounded off the walls of the church as he ran up the narrow aisle. "I got me a pa."

Cara smiled, and knelt down, pulling the boy into her embrace when he stopped in front of her "You sure do, and I'm so happy for you, Jacob."

"Thanks for taking care of him, Cara, and for everything else you did. You too, Doc," Lucinda said.

"We really appreciate it," Wade added with all sincerity.

Cara looked up into Lucinda's smiling face. There was no denying the happiness in her friend's brilliant gaze, or the love shining in Wade Peterson's eyes when he glanced from his wife to his son. A hurtful pang stabbed at her heart, and just as quickly guilt knocked at her conscience. She had no right to wish for the same fulfillment Lucinda had found, and no reason to envy her friend. It was enough that Grant had been willing to marry her, even if it was for all the wrong reasons.

"Glad we could help," Grant responded, then looked down at her with his suddenly heated stare. "But if you'll excuse us, Cara and I have some things we need to discuss."

Cara stood, blood pounding riotously in her ears. She swallowed, suspiciously certain his renewed anger had to do with her earlier protest about getting married, and no doubt what he wanted to talk about.

Wade nodded. "We need to head out for Riverwind, anyway, and get our own things settled." He turned and smiled at Lucinda. "Once and for all."

They parted company with the Petersons at the bottom of the church steps. Cara inwardly cringed at Grant's tensely clenched jaw and firm grip on her arm as she allowed him to lead her across the road, then into his office.

He shoved the door closed and whirled around. "Why the hell did you tell Peterson you didn't want to get married?" he ground out through clenched teeth.

His bullying accusation grated at her temper. "I didn't say I didn't want to get married," she argued.

He straightened, and cooled his tone. "Then, what were you saying?"

Cara sighed, wishing he would just leave her alone, but knowing he deserved an explanation. Butterflies fluttered in her stomach, making her nauseous. "I couldn't let you go through with it. It wasn't fair."

"Let me?" he stammered incredulously. "Fair?" He stepped closer. "If I remember correctly, I'm the one who suggested we get married."

"Because you had to, or thought you did, anyway." Cara clutched her hand over her racing heart, unbelieving of how easily she had blurted out the truth. Why was it she could never think straight around this man? She jerked back with a start at the devilish gleam that sprang into his jade stare, at the heart-stopping smile that slowly curled his mouth.

"Of course I had to marry you." Grant closed the distance between them and ran his finger along her furrowed brow as he had longed to do so many times before. "Because I love you," he whispered, lowering his hand to her chin and swallowing her gasp of surprise as he tasted of her sweet lips. He tried to resist pulling her into his arms, but when her hands found their way around his neck, he couldn't. He pressed her against her chest, reveling in the feel of her softness, then left her mouth and trailed a path of kisses across her cheek, to the corner of her eye. The salty moisture on his tongue made him draw back. Her eyes shimmered with wetness.

"Do you? Really?" she whispered.

Grant tightened his hold around her, hating that he had given her any reason to doubt him in the first place. "With all my heart, Cara, and I'm truly sorry you ever had any reason to think my feelings, or motives, had anything to do with your illness. Will you forgive me?"

She nodded. Her soft smile further warmed him inside. "I love you, too." Her sultry voice set his soul aflame as much as her words.

He wiped her tears with his thumb and smiled. "I'm glad to hear it. And it would be my honor, and definite pleasure, if you'd change your mind again and agree to be my wife."

"Yes," she whispered.

Grant's heart soared. He pulled her into his embrace. A wave of unfettered love washed over him, settling comfortably in his soul. "I want to get married tomorrow night, at the dance. We'll surprise the whole town. Really give them something to talk about."

She drew back slightly, her eyes widening. "You're not serious . . . are you?"

He nodded, grinning wider.

She frowned. "I don't think—"

"Don't think." He kissed her with a searing passion that swept him away from reality, to a place he wanted never to leave.

* * *

Cara hiked her skirt, racing down the stairs as the fervent knocking sounded again, this time on the front glass. She smiled as she drew closer and saw Grant peeking through the window of her home. His boyish smile stole her heart all over again. God, how she loved this man. She hurried to the door, opened it, and unabashedly swept her gaze over his muscled frame, admiring the hugging fit of his tailored black suit. Her smile deepened when she saw his black tie perched askew at the neck of his white shirt. Reaching out, she adjusted the necktie, then lifted her stare to his handsome face. Beneath his hat, his darkened gaze blazed desire, heating her blood and firing her thoughts with memories of their hours in his cabin . . . and the night ahead that awaited.

"You look lovely." Grant boldly raked his gaze over her curves, remembering how soft and perfect she was beneath the egg-shell blue silk covering her from neck to toe . . . and wondering how quickly he could get her out of it and into the bed Tollie had helped him set up at the cabin earlier.

"Thank you," she whispered, tucking her head down, but not before he saw the blush fill her cheeks.

Tilting her chin up, he kissed her briefly. "Are you ready?"

She bit at her bottom lip.

Grant frowned. "What's wrong?"

"Are you sure we should go through with this?"

It took him a moment to catch his breath. "You don't want to get married?"

Her eyes softened. "Of course I want to marry you," she whispered, smiling. "I just meant surprising the town. Bea's going to be furious I didn't tell her, and—"

"And she'll get over it." He pulled her into his arms. "I don't want to wait another day, another minute. Besides, I went to a lot of trouble getting the dance moved to the Meeting Hall, and making sure Tollie and the reverend held to their promise not to tell."

"Well"—she cocked her head and grinned teasingly—"if

you went to all that trouble I guess we better go and get married."

"With pleasure, sweetheart."

He helped her with her wrap, then followed her out into the night and aided her up into the buggy he had rented from the livery. His heart pounded with anticipation as he gathered the reins and set the horses to a slow walk. He had a little more on his mind than just their wedding, and he needed to talk to Cara before they got to the Meeting Hall. Moonlight glistened in her upswept brown hair; twinkling stars glittered in her eyes. He swallowed hard, catching his breath, and his courage.

"Care, I've been giving some consideration to my father's studies." Grant sighed. He had given it a lot of thought, in fact.

"So have I," she stated with a strong confidence that took him by surprise. "You should do as your father wanted. I don't mind moving to Boston, or wherever you need to go to do your research." Her eyes softened, turning dark gold under the moon's bright glow. "And I won't mind your ... help with my ailment."

Grant hadn't known he could love her more ... until this moment. Offering the very thing that had nearly kept him from having her, from knowing of her love, told him of her trust better than any words. "I love you, Cara."

"And I love you."

Grant smiled. "How would you feel about moving to Paris?"

She blinked her surprise. "France? Did you hear from your friend?"

He nodded. "Pierre had no advice to offer about you, but was interested to know if I heard anything from Dr. Hayward. He asked me again to come there and study with him at the institute for a while."

"And do you want to?"

Grant reined the horses to a stop in front of the Meeting Hall. Candlelight spilled from the windows, and loud voices and laughter echoed from behind the walls. He turned his attention back to Cara and grinned. "More importantly, do you?"

She frowned, and bit at her bottom lip. Grant felt a moment of panic slam into his chest. He really wanted to make this move. But no matter how much he might want it, Cara meant more to him. If she didn't want to leave Texas, her home, he would understand.

"Would we have to leave right away? It's bad enough I'm getting married without Father being here. I couldn't leave the country without saying goodbye."

Relief washed over Grant that she wasn't saying no; then guilt at his selfishness settled heavy in its place. "We can wait as long as you want, Cara. To move . . . and to get married."

She arched a playful brow. "Are you trying to back out tonight, Dr. Radnor?"

He grinned. "Not on your life, Miss Martin." He sealed his lips over hers.

"Look, Mama, Mr. Doc's kissing Miss Cara again."

Grant tore his mouth away at Jacob's joyous pronouncement and met Cara's soft, warm gaze. Startled murmurs, then booted steps pounding across the walkway in front of the Meeting Hall pulled their attention. Wade and Lucinda stood beside their son, their grins as wide as the boy's. Curiosity drove several to gather outside and others to peer out the door and the windows on either side. Tollie stood at the end of the walkway, his arms stubbornly crossed over his chest.

"Dang it, Doc," the blacksmith grumbled. "Would you two stop that kissin' stuff long enough to hightail it in here and get hitched? You're ten minutes late, and I'm runnin' out of excuses why we can't start the dance."

"Well, by all means. Let's get this wedding started." Grant turned, and winked at Cara. "I want to get back to that 'kissing stuff' as soon as possible."

Derek glanced aroun[...] moment before still s[...]ddle of the control room, paying no attention at all to what was happening. Two Phillida stood behind him, blocking any thought of escape.

"So tell me this, Billie," Derek said, turning to squarely face the gun. "Why will the Phillida let you get away with killing me?"

Billie laughed. "Oh, they'll let me just fine."

With his free hand, Billie reached up and took the flesh under his chin and pulle[...] revealing an alien face that mad[...] throw up. Never in all his worst n[...] ever seen or imagined something [...]

He choked and turned away.

"You see, my stupid human b[...] said in Billie's voice, "the Phillida [...]

THE GRAZER CONSPIRACY

Dean Wesley Smith

BANTAM BOOKS
New York   Toronto   London   Sydney   Auckland

MEN IN BLACK: THE GRAZER CONSPIRACY

A Bantam Spectra Book / January 2000

ISBN 0-553-57769-7

Published simultaneously in the United States and Canada

Bantam Books are published by Bantam Books, a division
of Random House, Inc. Its trademark, consisting of the
words "Bantam Books" and the portrayal of a rooster, is
Registered in U.S. Patent and Trademark Office and in other
countries. Marca Registrada. Bantam Books, 1540 Broadway,
New York, New York 10036.

PRINTED IN THE UNITED STATES OF AMERICA

OPM   10 9 8 7 6 5 4 3 2 1

Human history becomes more and more a race between education and catastrophe.

—H. G. Wells
—An Outline of History

For

Jim Kiser, Pat Morgan, Bobby Young,

Shannon Meyer, Susan Bolland,

and the interesting years of 1967–1972.

Memories often return in the most

fascinating ways.

The lights of the city of Hood River spread out along the Columbia Gorge below nineteen-year-old Anthony Davis like a strand of jewels sparkling in the cold night air. Behind him the chair lift clanked as another empty chair swept past the off-load ramp, spun around the big wheel, and headed back down the mountain. The lights that lit the snow swept off to the left of the chair lift, carving a path of shadow-light, shadow-light on the slope down through the trees to the lodge below. In twenty-eight minutes those lights would be turned off, after the patrol swept the hill for any stragglers. There wouldn't be any, since Anthony was the last one up here. In fact, in the last hour he'd been the only one skiing on the entire hill.

P
R
O
L
O
G
U
E

He treasured nights like tonight. They didn't happen often, especially during the height of the ski season. But since most people had turned their attention to baseball or golf by the end of March, he was often the only one on the hill at ten at night, and always the last off the slopes, often helping the ski patrol with their closing duties.

He stood, leaning on his ski poles, studying the small town two thousand feet below and the mass of lights from Portland in the distance. There were very few places on this mountain from which you could look down on the lights of Hood River. He'd found this spot two years before. He skied five nights a week after work and never grew tired of the view on clear nights. He loved the feeling of standing over the entire world and just watching it. And he loved the intense silence of the nights, as if the laughs and shouts of the skiers during the day had never existed.

He took a long, deep breath, trying to clear the last grease from his nose and lungs with the crisp cold air. His job during the winter was cooking in the lodge. He had grilled thousands of hamburgers over the winter season. Earlier tonight, in preparation for closing part of the kitchen the second week of April, he had helped clean out one of the exhaust fans over the grills. It had been coated with grease so thick they ended up filling buckets with it. He needed this time in the cold, clean night air to clear his lungs.

And to think.

At the moment his girlfriend was mad at him.

That seemed to be a regular occurrence. For some reason they argued just about every other day about something. It was always stupid, and often pointless. But the making up was always fun. The argument yesterday, however, had been about getting married, something he had no desire to do.

The worst thing in his life at the moment was that the draft board was after him. They wanted to send him to Vietnam and he had no idea what he would do. Or could do. He couldn't imagine being a soldier and killing people.

Skiing had been his entire life. On the mountain, on snow, was the only time he really felt alive. Vietnam was a hot jungle on the nightly news where people died. It had never occurred to him that he would do anything but work around ski resorts. And ski. The war in Vietnam seemed so distant, the social and racial revolution in the cities around the country so alien.

And so confusing.

He took another deep breath of the clear mountain air and let the cold push the thoughts back. He would figure all that out tomorrow. Girlfriend, Vietnam, everything.

Right now he still had time for at least two more runs before having to store his skis for the night and head down the curving miles into town in his Volkswagen. And since there weren't many days left in the season, he shouldn't be wasting time worrying about things he couldn't do anything about.

With one last look out over the lights below, he

turned and started toward the ski run, pushing off with his poles and skating over the packed surface.

Suddenly a rainbow of colored lights shimmered in the darkness to the right of the chair lift.

"What?" Anthony said, stopping and staring, half leaning on his ski poles.

The lights swirled faster and faster, expanding, seeming to come down from the sky. Other than the clicking of the lift delivering empty chair after empty chair, there was no sound.

Or heat.

Just sparkling lights that spun in the crisp night air.

Suddenly the lights snapped into a shape, forming what looked like a door in the side of a weird-looking dark oval.

"*Candid Camera* or *Twilight Zone,* I hope," Anthony said. His voice didn't carry far down the mountain.

Slowly the door opened just above the smooth-packed snow.

Anthony half expected it to creak, or air to go whooshing past him, but nothing happened.

The swirling lights filled the door, so he couldn't see anything through it. But there had to be an inside to that oval.

Anthony knew he should turn and head down the mountain as fast as he could go, but fear wasn't something that usually moved him. At least not while he was standing on a pair of skis. No jump was too big, no run too steep for him. He attacked them all head-on.

So now, at the top of this chair lift, he wasn't about to suddenly ski away in fright, even if he didn't know what had just come out of the night sky to hover near him.

He swallowed the shadow of fear, just as he did when faced with a large jump and stood and watched the swirling lights and weird door, coldly, as if studying how to attack a steep slope.

After what seemed like an eternity, but was actually only a few seconds, a man stepped through the door and onto the snow, sinking slightly. He wore coveralls and tennis shoes. He had dark hair covered with a golf cap. Even in the faint light, Anthony could make out the words BANDAN DUNES across the front.

The sudden appearance of the man made Anthony back up, shoving himself away from the door with his poles. He didn't know exactly what he had expected to emerge from that strange ship, but it wasn't a regular-looking man in coveralls and a golf cap.

"Glad I caught ya, Anthony," the man said in a southern accent. Then he looked around. "Man, it is *cold* up here on this here mountain."

Now Anthony really wanted to bolt for the lodge and escape from this impossibly normal man, but again he didn't move. Instead he said, "Who are you? How'd you get here? How do you know me?"

The guy shrugged. "None of that matters much at this point," he said. He reached into his pocket, then held something up so Anthony could see it.

It looked like a gas credit card, only larger.

As Anthony was trying to figure out just what it was the guy was showing him, the man put something over his eyes with his other hand.

"Nice havin' ya with us, Anthony."

"What?" Anthony asked. "With you? I'm not—"

There was a bright flash.

From that moment on Anthony had no memory of that last run of night skiing. He remembered having gone skiing that night, but not the last run.

In the lodge he put his skis in his locker and headed into town without even saying good night to anyone in the kitchen.

On the way down the mountain he didn't notice that the only car he passed was a black sedan, speeding up toward the lodge.

The next morning he didn't go back up the hill to work. Instead he called his boss and quit.

Then he walked into an army recruiting office in downtown Portland and signed up to go to Vietnam.

He did two tours in Vietnam and thirty years later was a two-star general.

He never skied again.

Or had any desire to.

There's nothing like a warm, sunny day in early May in New York City. It brings out the people like bees to sweet-smelling flowers. Hordes of people. The sidewalks fill elbow to elbow, everyone walks instead of taking the subway or cabs. Every terrace, deck, and fire-escape landing is covered with a partially clad body enjoying the warmth. But it is the city's parks that take the brunt of the spring attack, as anyone with a little extra time wants to stroll among the budding trees and inhale the smell of freshly mowed grass to forget the winter just past.

MiB Special Forces Agent Jay, formerly New York Detective James Edwards, didn't even know the day had turned beautiful. With his partner, Elle, formally Dr. Laurel Weaver, city mortician, Jay sat at a long

1

metal table, deep inside the gray walls of MiB head-quarters in downtown New York. In front of him was the manual on the ritual habits of the Abosins, only one of a thousand alien races that visited or lived on Earth.

Abosins were a new race to Earth, with the first due to arrive in two days for a projected stay of three years. Jay and Elle had been given the assignment of showing them the "ropes" of living among humans. It wasn't a job either of them looked forward to. In fact, Jay had complained to Zed, saying, "What about ridding the earth of the scum of the universe and all that? When did we become tour guides?"

Zed had only snorted and didn't answer, which meant Jay and Elle were stuck. So now they were studying. Actually, they weren't going over the manual in a traditional sense. Instead they were doing what Jay called "absorbing the manual."

The MiB Special Educational Unit called it "Pattern Learning by Cellular Rearrangement."

No matter what the name, Jay hated doing it. He didn't like the idea of someone scrambling anything inside his head, either for pain, pleasure, or learning. As he told Elle, he had "moral objections" to anyone but him killing his brain cells. So he only used "absorbing" when they were pressed for time, which they were with the Abosin situation.

Elle didn't really trust the device either, even though she claimed to understand the principle of its operation. She had tried to explain it to Jay one afternoon, and only succeeded in losing him after two sentences. After that he and Elle just agreed they would use both ways of learning when they needed to. They would submit to "absorption" then test each other with the written manuals, just to make sure they knew what they needed to know.

Jay was just about to quiz Elle on the Abosin eating ritual, a disgusting cross between the way a pig rolls in mud and a female spider eats her mate. Thanks to "absorption," Jay could see in his mind exactly what activities the Abosin engaged in during this ritual, and this was, as far as he was concerned, already way too much information.

Thankfully Zed's voice broke in over the intercom, filling the room without being loud. To Jay, Zed's voice commanded authority. In all his years as a New York City cop, Jay had never had a boss with a voice like Zed's.

"We have a Grazer," Zed said. "Central Park. Containment teams on the way."

"On the road, boss," Elle said into the air as both agents sprang to their feet and headed for the door at a sprint.

Jay and Elle didn't even have to ask for specifics about the problem. They had dealt with one Grazer about two months after both of them had joined the MiB Special Services. A Grazer was an alien that stood about the size of a cow and looked like a mad scientist's idea of a cross between a grasshopper and a pig. They were also the dumbest aliens ever to take a ship through interstellar space.

The problem, though, was that Grazers simply loved Earth. There was something in the chlorophyll in the grass and plants that acted like an intoxicant to them. One sniff of Earth grass or any green-leafed Earth plant, and they would start eating and eating and eating. Nothing besides getting knocked out or killed could stop them.

The Grazers had another trait that compounded their love of chlorophyll. There was no limit to the amount of food that they could eat. Or at least none anyone had heard of.

That constituted a large containment problem to the MiB Special Forces. Grazer bodies simply grew bigger and bigger and bigger while the Grazer ate, expanding like a child's balloon in the hands of a mad clown. The biggest Grazer on the MiB records had been found by a man named Kay, who had trained Jay. That Grazer had been eating for days and had grown to the size of an elephant by the time Kay shot him. The resulting explosion of half-digested leaves, flaps of Grazer skin, and green alien blood covered a half-block area of the old World's Fair grounds in Spokane, Washington. Jay had thought the slime that had resulted from the exploding bug on his first mission had been bad. Compared with the pictures Kay had taken in Spokane after the big Grazer explosion, however, the bug guts looked almost appetizing.

Out in the Galaxy, Grazers had the reputation of dumb guests who always come to the party, eat too much, and never seem to want to leave. They were mostly ignored. And because of the effect of Earth vegetation on them, they were not allowed anywhere near the planet for any reason. Nevertheless, a chlorophyll-junkie Grazer usually managed to slip in at least once every six months, causing a containment nightmare for MiB.

Elle monitored the police radio bands as Jay weaved their special black LTD in and out of afternoon traffic, headed for the west side of Central Park. Jay swerved into a parking lane, then yanked the LTD hard right through a red light, turning with traffic to the sounds of a dozen cab horns.

"Police problems at the park," Elle said as the police scanner filled her in on the police plans.

"Better tell the boss," Jay said as he shoved a cab to one side and scraped past a bus before running a red light, all this to the accompaniment of more honking and fist waving.

Elle ignored his driving as she punched a button on the dash and Zed's face appeared on the screen.

"Police have ten cars ahead of us," Elle said, relaying the information she had received from the scanner. "Plus they're bringing in a chopper."

Zed frowned. "Understood. We'll stop the chopper from here. And all the news choppers, too. But you'll have to handle the newspeople on the ground. One containment team is on-site, six more are en route."

Elle nodded and cut the connection.

"Goin' ta be a mess," Jay said, cutting the LTD up onto the sidewalk just inside the park entrance and blowing his horn to warn off the pedestrians. Most of them scurried out of his way, but he had to swerve to miss an elderly couple, plowing the LTD through a garbage can in the process.

"You want me to drive?" Elle asked calmly as she worked on the monitor in the dashboard in front of her.

"I'll be gettin' us there," Jay said, accelerating across the grass toward the reported location of the alien. He would, too. Elle was a good driver, but he was better. And he had told her that often. She had disagreed. They had settled on taking turns driving. It was just easier that way.

Ahead, on the far side of a stand of trees, Jay could see a kind of shimmering area of air, as if he were looking through a layer of clear water around the space. The shimmering always indicated a shielded alien ship.

Jay sighed in relief. A shielded ship meant almost no one saw it land and normal radar couldn't follow it. Shielding didn't prevent alien ships from being detected by MiB orbital scans, but it did keep the level of containment down to only the park and those who had seen the alien.

Jay pointed at it. "We got lucky."

Elle glanced up from her computer and nodded. "That we did." She glanced back at the computer terminal, reading off the information. "There's a carnival out in Brooklyn right now. We'll use the idea that an escaped animal was caught in the park for reprogramming. Make it a trained water buffalo. It says they have one of those out there, if you can believe that. Weird."

Jay just shook his head as he swung the car around a tree and headed toward the mass of people. "Not very original."

"Original is not the point," Elle said.

"At least make it a whale," Jay said.

Elle glanced over at him like he had lost it. "A whale, like in 'thar she blows'?"

"Don'tcha see?" Jay asked. "We got the perfect chance to start one of those urban myths. The whale was washed up through the sewers and learned to eat grass to survive while staying wet in the sprinklers. They breathe air. It could happen." He gave her his best innocent smile.

She just shook her head. "Escaped carnival animal. Harmless escaped carnival animal. Understand?"

"I like the whale better," Jay said as he slid the car to a stop short of the crowd and just beside the shimmering air that was the Grazer ship. Even though he liked his idea better, he knew Elle's cover story was going to be the one they used. The last time he'd come up with a containment cover story Zed had yelled at him for thirty straight minutes. It had been a funny idea to give the entire neighborhood a friendly ghost, but not thirty-minutes-of-Zed-yelling-at-him funny. Who knew how long Zed would yell about a whale in the New York sewers?

Elle relayed her cover story to the containment teams, then they both climbed out of the car and slipped on their sunglasses. They were dressed in the MiB standard black suit, white shirt, black tie, and black shoes. And today, with the bright sun, the sunglasses felt right to Jay.

Jay did a quick check to make sure his Series-4

Atomizer was charged and tucked inside his jacket. Grazers weren't known to be dangerous, but there was no point in taking any chances. One of them might go rogue and it was a good idea to be armed.

It was clear where the alien was. A large mass of people stood around it in a large circle, watching it eat the lawn like a vacuum cleaner sucking up dirt. The grass was going to have to be replaced in an area three-foot-wide-by-sixty-foot-long. If you didn't know better, you'd think the Grazer was preparing an area for a new sidewalk.

A dozen policemen were already on the scene and Jay could see the first containment team slowly working its way around the perimeter, making sure no one got away without a new memory to replace their experience of an alien. And making sure no photographs survived to document the alien's presence. Two other containment trucks were just pulling up in the trees. Another few minutes and they'd be ready. It would take him and Elle that long to get into position.

Jay and Elle shouldered their way through the crowd and stepped toward the Grazer. The alien was already the size of a small milk cow. A very fat, grasshopper-legged milk cow that had pink skin like a pig and smelled like stagnant water. No wonder the people were staying back a pretty good distance. Jay had forgotten how vile Grazers smelled.

"Hey, you two!" a cop shouted as Jay and Elle stepped toward the Grazer. "Just where do you think you're goin'?"

The cop was solid, stood about six feet tall, and

had thinning red hair under his cap. His hand was resting on his gun, but he hadn't pulled it. Jay didn't recognize him as anyone he used to work with.

"Getting our dog back, Officer," Jay said, stopping to face the cop. "Hope he hasn't been too much trouble."

"That don't look like no dog to me."

"Are you insulting our poor dog?" Jay asked. "Fido there has had a really hard life, if ya know what I mean. He hates it when people insult him, don't you, Fido?" He glanced over at the Grazer.

The cop glanced at the Grazer.

The alien kept eating, ignoring them.

Around them people laughed.

The cop sneered, his face red.

"Sir," Elle said, stepping past Jay toward the police officer while she flashed a badge. "I'm CIA Special Agent Barbara Hanna." She flipped the badge closed before he could see too much of it. It was a real-looking CIA badge, but there wasn't any reason to take extra chances.

Jay gave her an odd look. In all of their first year together, it was the first time she had given a different cover name. He always gave different names, relying on their Carte Noir badges to change with him into what he needed. But she had always stayed consistent until today.

"That poor creature is our responsibility," Elle said, smiling sweetly at the cop. "Just call it a genetic experiment gone horribly wrong."

A dozen or so of the bystanders who heard these

words instantly took a step back from the Grazer. From the scared looks on their faces, they clearly had memories of those fifties sci-fi movies where the hideous results of botched genetic experiments broke out of labs and ate screaming people. Before he joined MiB, Jay used to watch those movies all the time. He loved them, especially the ones with the big spiders eating entire cities.

The cop swallowed and nodded. "Is it dangerous?"

"We're trying to determine that now," Elle said. "If you and your men could just keep everyone where they are, we'll let you know as soon as we know."

"Go right ahead," the cop said.

"Thank you," Elle said, again smiling sweetly.

"You're really good at that sugarcoatin'," Jay said only loud enough for her to hear as they both turned toward the Grazer.

"I'm a woman," she said, smiling at him. "We get a lot of practice."

"Cute," he said.

The closer they got to the alien, the worse the smell, as if all the toilets in the city had backed up. If there was one thing Jay had learned in his rookie year as an MiB agent, it was that aliens usually smelled. And always badly. So far he had yet to run into an alien that smelled like a rose. Or chocolate-chip cookies.

The Grazer's stomach rumbled as it munched, swallowed, burped. And then started over.

Munch.

Swallow.

Burp.

The Grazer stripped the grass from the lawn like newlyweds ripped off clothes on their honeymoon night.

Jay moved over and stood in front of the Grazer. "You want to cool your assault on the salad bar and tell us why you're here?"

Between the swallow and the burp, the Grazer grunted the Grazer word for *no*. Then went back to eating.

"Man, that's some breath you got there," Jay said, fanning the air in front of him.

The Grazer said nothing.

"If you don't stop eating," Jay said, kneeling so he could look into the four brown eyes of the alien, "you know what we have to do, don't you?"

"Don't care," Grazer said.

Jay stood and stepped back to ease the smell before he choked.

"Five full containment teams in place," Elle said, glancing around. "Let's do this."

"Enjoy your last meal," Jay said to the Grazer.

"Buzz off," the Grazer said in so many words. And considering that the Grazer vocabulary consisted only of two hundred and six words, that was pretty good communications as far as Jay was concerned. He got the meaning exactly.

With Elle at his side, they moved back toward the cop.

"Ready?" Elle asked into her communications link with the containment crews. "Count off."

By the time the containment teams were finished checking in as ready, Jay and Elle had reached the cop.

"Fido out there has a really bad case of it," Jay said.

"Of what?" the cop asked.

"Stupidity," Jay said. "Terminal, I'm afraid."

"Do it," Elle said into her communications link.

Three small rockets launched simultaneously into the air over the crowd from three sides, whistling loudly as they went.

The whistle made everyone in the crowd look up.

A moment later a bright flash blanketed the crowd and everyone seemed to just freeze in place.

Flash grenades.

They worked on the same principle as the flashy-thing in Jay's pocket, only they were used for crowd situations where it just didn't make sense to use the handheld devices.

A containment-team member moved through the people and handed Jay a megaphone.

"Okay, everyone," Jay said, loud enough for all in the crowd to hear. "The creature you have been watching eat is an escaped water buffalo from the circus."

Elle smiled at him, but he ignored her and went on.

"It was nothing more than that. A simple rene-gade water buffalo. Now I need you all to turn slowly and move toward a park exit, checking in with a person in a black suit before you go."

As one, the entire crowd, including the cop who had tried to stop them, turned and moved like walking zombies.

The Grazer just kept munching, eating his way toward his own death.

"So now what do we do with Dumbo out there?" Jay asked. He didn't much mind killing aliens who were threatening him or Elle, or trying to take over the planet. But the Grazer was basically benign, seeming to want nothing more than a good meal. In the past MiB had killed a few and had shipped a few others back into space. And there was no standard method for their removal. At least he hadn't read about one when he glanced at the manual. Now he wished he had looked at it a little closer.

Elle shrugged. "Let's ask Zed." With that they moved back over to the LTD as around them the containment crews slowly gave each member of the crowd a new and different memory of the last few minutes and blocked anyone else from coming in the area, including a news crew that had started to get angry before being flashy-thinged.

"Yes?" Zed said, his face appearing on the screen the moment Elle called for him.

"Containment in place," Elle said. "Ship was shielded. What do you want us to do with the Grazer?"

"Try to find out why it came here," Zed said. "Then toast it and get back here fast."

"Kill it?" Elle asked. "Why?"

Zed frowned and Jay was glad that Elle was the

one questioning Zed's orders this time. Usually it was him. Nice to have the shoe on the other foot for a change.

"At this moment we have tracked twenty-one Grazer ships on the ground in the last thirty minutes," Zed said. "There may be others already on the ground."

"Shit," Jay said. "The invasion of the grass-eaters."

Zed nodded. "We don't know how many more are on the way. They're invading us for some reason and we have to get it stopped at once. See if you can find out why they're doing it, then kill the cow and get back here. I need you both. Let containment take care of the mess and the ship. Understood?"

"Understood," Elle said, cutting the connection.

"Invading us?" Jay asked. "Grazers?" It was the strangest thing he had ever heard of.

"That's what the boss said." She pulled out her Atomizer and checked it. Then she stared out the front window at the Grazer now alone in the middle of the Central Park meadow. "Got any idea how we're going to get it to talk?"

Jay nodded. "I sure do. Ever heard of cow-tipping?"

Elle laughed. "It just might work," she said.

"We need two of the containment team and some rope."

Elle nodded. "I'll get them."

They climbed out of the car and Elle moved off

toward a containment truck while Jay headed back across the grass toward the Grazer.

At this point the Grazer had a three-foot-wide swath across the Central Park lawn for sixty paces and its stomach was clearly expanding. And the smell was getting worse, if that was possible.

Jay stopped about ten feet away from the creature and waited for Elle and the containment crew to join him. He didn't much like the idea of killing this Grazer. He didn't have any special love for it either. But it just seemed too helpless to gun down in cold, alien blood. Maybe if he gave it a weapon and let it make a move to shoot him, then he could kill it. But he doubted that the poor, dumb space traveler could even hold a weapon, much less shoot it.

Grazers were just the Galaxy's losers.

Elle moved up beside Jay. "Ready."

Two containment agents stood nearby with rope.

"Each of you wrap up a hind leg and pull when I tell you," Jay said to the containment agents.

Both nodded.

"Kick it on the count of three," Jay said to Elle as they moved together toward the Grazer.

"One."

They were three steps away.

"Two."

Two steps away. The smell was overwhelming. Jay felt as if he had stuck his head in a public toilet that hadn't been flushed in three days.

"Three."

One more step and both agents used their speed

and momentum to plant kicks squarely in the side of the eating alien. Jay's foot caught the beast just behind its front legs. Elle's kick just in front of its hind legs.

To Jay, the alien's side seemed extremely soft, as if he had kicked a large pillow.

The alien let out a combination of a loud burp and a high-pitched scream and went on its back like a fish out of water. Its two large, grasshopperlike hind legs flailed at the air while its shorter front legs tried to get a hold on the grass to pull itself back on its feet.

Both containment agents instantly moved in and roped a hind leg, one pulling in one direction while the other pulled in the opposite direction as if they were trying to split the Grazer like a turkey wishbone. With its legs up in the air and its fat stomach protruding, the Grazer looked like a grotesque, outsized version of a pregnant woman about to give birth.

"Let me go!" the alien grunted, then let out a loud and extremely smelly burp.

Jay moved around so he could look into the Grazer's four brown, watery eyes.

"I'll think about maybe not killin' you," he said, "if you tell me what you are doin' here."

"Eating," the alien said. "Now let me go!"

Jay pulled out his Atomizer and held it so the Grazer could see it with every eye. "Now, you wanta try that answer again?"

"I tell reason," Grazer said, trying to shake the

containment agents loose without luck. "Here to eat."

"But you know this planet is restricted to your people," Elle said.

"You invite," the alien said. "We come to eat."

"Invite?" Jay asked, glancing at Elle.

"Invite," the Grazer repeated, then burped again before going on. "All invited to come. Eat all we want. Let go so can eat."

"And just who sent you this invite?" Jay asked, moving the Atomizer to his other hand right in front of the Grazer's eyes to stress the importance of the question.

"Human wearing black," Grazer said. "Say can eat. Now say can't eat. Not understand."

"Shit," Jay said, stepping back and looking at his partner.

Elle just shrugged, also clearly stunned.

In his first year as an MiB agent he'd been shocked about a lot of things, but that answer rocked him.

"He's telling the truth," Elle said.

"I know," Jay said. Even though he had only glanced at the manuals, he knew that Grazers had no real ability to lie. That meant that all the Grazer ships that were landing on Earth were not part of an invasion. They were coming by invitation.

But who would invite them?

And why? No one that Jay knew needed their lawn mowed that badly.

Derek Comstock stood on the deck of the Phillida trading ship, staring out at the view of Saturn far below. Unseen winds in the huge planet's atmosphere seemed to swirl and blend the yellows and faint reds of the clouds like a slow-speed blender mixing different flavors of yogurt. Derek had no idea what that atmosphere was made of, nor how the rings of rock and dust and ice that circled the planet were formed. But he had to admit, the view from here, in an orbit just inside the famous rings of Saturn, was fantastic.

Plus, here a ship was impossible to detect by any Earth monitoring system.

He stared at the view again, trying to take it all in at once. In all his years of working for the Earth Expansion League,

2

he had never expected to get off the planet, let alone be orbiting Saturn. This was a real treat that all Earth men should experience, and if he had his way, they'd get the opportunity.

Behind him the Phillida crew rustled as they went about their duties. The Phillida were a race of what he and others around the League called "plant men." Actually, they weren't a plant, yet they were covered with what appeared to be a green, mosslike substance. They bore no resemblance to humans at all, with their six arms, six legs, and a head with twelve eyes mounted on stalks. They rustled when they moved, making the sound of a large person's jean-clad legs rubbing together on a hot summer's day. But around the League, everyone for some reason just called them the "plant men."

Maybe it was because they smelled like potatoes. Derek doubted he would ever eat another potato after this mission was over, since the odor was slowly becoming nauseating. A spudless existence would be a small price to pay to free all humanity from the surface of Earth and get them out into space in their rightful positions among the stars and the races of the Galaxy.

He loosened his tie and unbuttoned the top button on his black suit, letting the ship's thick air get to his skin. He'd worn the black suit of an MiB agent as a disguise while he sent out the invitation to all the Grazers. But the Phillida kept the temperature of their ship just under sauna level and a black suit was far, far too hot to wear for long.

He'd have to change soon. But first he wanted to wait to see how his invitation was received. There was an outside chance he might have to send it again.

None of the so-called plant men were headed his way, so he went back to staring out at Saturn. If all those idiots back in the offices of Schofield & Rose could see him now, wouldn't they be surprised? For fifteen years he'd been an attorney in Portland, during the week going about his dull, routine business. But on weekends he went on his "fishing" trips east into the mountains. Of course, he never fished. He had also never married. For all those years since he'd first met the alien he called "Frank" out on the desert outside of Reno, he'd worked every weekend and every vacation for the Earth Expansion League. The League was an underground secret organization whose mission was to tell one way or another, all of Earth the truth about aliens. Now all those years of hard work were starting to pay off.

"Incredible, ain't it?" Billie Floyd asked as he moved up and stood in front of the port beside Derek. "Seen it twice. I swear it's prettier the second time around."

Billie was the only other human on the Phillida ship. A southern hick from Alabama, with a third-grade education and the ability to fix just about anything that had an engine in it, he wore dirty tennis shoes, coveralls over a stained T-shirt, and a golf hat with the name Bandan Dunes on it. Derek had somehow managed to put up with Billie the few times they had been together, but not much more. And now, being trapped here on this Phillida ship with him was quickly growing old. As old as the smell of potatoes.

"When were you out here before?" Derek asked.

"Two months ago," Billie said, seeming to smile fondly at the memory. "Can't tell ya why. Secret, ya know?"

Derek knew all too well. One of the ways that the League had managed to survive was by never letting one member know too much about anything other members were doing. That way if one member turned traitor, or got caught, no one else, and the organization as a whole, was jeopardized. It was a smart policy as far as Derek was concerned, but at times like this when his curiosity was aroused, it galled him a little.

"I sure had myself a good nap," Billie said, yawning. "Any news yet?"

"Nothing," Derek said. He almost told Billie he should go back to sleep, then didn't.

"Want me to ask one of them plant men?"

Derek shook his head. "I'll do it."

With one last long look at the beautiful view of Saturn and the rings spread out before him, he turned and moved to the center of the room, heading toward a Phillida. Phillida were one of the top trading races in the Galaxy, a kind of interplanetary alien Wal-Mart. They liked to go into backwater planets, set up exclusive trade agreements, and reap all the profits. The League had convinced them a few years back that if Earth was free, if humans knew about the aliens living among them and were able to join the races in space, the Phillida would harvest the profits of all the trade that would follow.

Since coming aboard, Derek wondered if the Phillida didn't have another objective also. He didn't know why he wondered that. It was just a feeling. But after years of battling in courtrooms, he had learned to trust his feelings. And this time his feelings told him there was much more going on here than he understood. And if he just kept his eyes and ears open, he'd learn about it.

"Is the mission going as planned?" he asked the Phillida standing in the middle of the control room.

The Phillida clicked and clucked back at him in its own language. Derek had learned the language before starting this mission. He couldn't speak it, but he could understand it, just as the Phillida in charge could understand English.

"Twenty-six Grazer ships have landed on Earth," the Phillida clicked at him.

"Only twenty-six?" Derek asked. He was disappointed. The MiB might be able to handle twenty-six. It had been almost six hours since he had broadcast his invitation to the Grazers. Should he do it again?

"Only twenty-six close," Phillida said. "Hundreds, maybe thousands more en route. Three Earth cycles they arrive."

Derek could feel himself smiling. "Thank you," he said to the Phillida, then turned away. Hundreds and hundreds of Grazer ships all landing on Earth at once would be impossible for the MiB to contain. They would be forced to admit the presence of aliens among them. And then Earth could take the first step in forming a trading alliance with the Phillida.

The grand plan was off and running. All the years of work were about to pay off, thanks to the chlorophyll addiction of the stupid Grazers.

He moved back over to where Billie had sat down, his tennis-shoed feet up, his hands on his protruding stomach, his golf hat shoved back.

"It's working," Derek said. "Twenty-six Grazers have already landed, hundreds more are coming in the next few days."

"Perfect," Billie said, smiling. "I thought it would." Out of the side of his coveralls he pulled a nasty-looking alien pistol and pointed it at Derek.

"What?" Derek said, stepping back.

At that moment two plant men rustled up behind him and stopped so he could go back no farther, as if there was anyplace to run to on this alien ship anyway.

"Nasty-lookin' little gun, ain't it?" Billie said, indicating the weapon in his hand. "Shoots real good, let me tell ya. Kinda melts skin, burns everything so there's no real mess."

"Why are you pointing it at me?"

"Your mission is plum over," Billie said, smiling so that Derek could see his rotting teeth. "You made your phone call to da Grazers, now the League can't let you just hang around and get caught and give away the entire plan. You claim to be a smart attorney. I'm sure you understand."

"But I don't know the entire plan," Derek said. "And who put you in charge of this mission anyway?"

"The League," Billie said, smiling. "And the plant men here. And this little gun in my hands. I'd say that's pretty darned good authority, wouldn't you?"

Derek glanced around. The Phillida he'd talked to a moment before still stood in the middle of the control room, paying no attention at all to what was happening. Two Phillida stood behind him, blocking any thought of escape.

"So tell me this, Billie," Derek said, turning to squarely face the gun. "Why will the Phillida let you get away with killing me?"

Again Billie laughed. "Oh, they'll let me just fine."

With his free hand, Billie reached up and took the flesh under his chin and pulled it up and aside, revealing an alien face that made Derek want to throw up. Never in all his worst nightmares had he ever seen or imagined something so hideous.

He choked and turned away, fighting to keep his stomach from spewing its contents all over the ship.

"You see, my stupid human buddy," the alien said in Billie's voice, "the Phillida work for me."

The shot caught Derek squarely in the chest and the last thing he ever heard was the sickening laugh of Billie the alien.

The news that the Grazer had been invited by some human in black had rocked Elle. She knew it couldn't be anyone in the MiB Special Forces, but if not MiB, then who? Who, outside of MiB, could contact an alien in space, or even know they were there?

Let alone know *how*?

That last question really had her worried.

Around them the spring day was turning almost hot and she was sweating in her black suit. The two members of the containment team had the Grazer's hind legs roped and pulled apart so it couldn't climb back to its feet. The rest of the team had finished clearing the last of the crowd and were moving the perimeter back with police

3

help, keeping people and news crews away from the entire area.

She took three steps toward where her partner Jay was standing and knelt down in front of the face of the Grazer, ignoring the rotting smell of sewer. Speaking slowly, she said to the alien, "I've got to be sure what you are telling us. It is important."

"Want to eat," Grazer said in its own language. A language that was simple and one that Elle knew completely.

"You can eat in a short time," she said. "But first please tell me how you came to be invited to Earth."

"Already spoke of it," Grazer said.

"Speak again," Elle said. "Was it a human who invited you to this planet?"

"Human. Yes," Grazer said. "Black-clothing human."

"Like we are wearing now?" Elle asked.

"Yes. Look same."

She glanced up at Jay, who, for the first time in a while, seemed almost speechless. Finally he said, "I bet we all look alike to them."

"Yeah, but it was still a human," Elle said.

"Good point."

Elle turned back so that she was again looking into the eyes of the upside-down Grazer. "How many of your people did this human invite?"

"All."

"All?" Elle asked.

"All," the Grazer answered. "Many come soon. Eat."

"We're dead," Jay said. "Shit! Shit! Shit!" He turned and paced away, then stopped after about ten steps.

"Want to eat," Grazer said.

Elle stood and moved back away from the stifling smell of the alien. Sweat dripped down her face and her shirt was sticking to her back. And at that moment she wasn't sure if the sweat was a result of the warm day or of the information they'd received from the Grazer. Jay was right. They were dead if they couldn't stop this.

"We've got to tell Zed and fast," Elle said to Jay.

"You ain't kiddin'," Jay said. "This is one party we gotta cancel before the guests start arrivin'."

"Cut him lose," Elle ordered the containment agents, pointing at the Grazer. "Let him eat for a few minutes while we find out what to do. Keep him in the trees out of sight of nearby buildings and roads."

"Zed told us to toast him," Jay said as they both took off at a run for the LTD.

"Yeah," Elle said, "and lose our one source of information. How smart is that?"

"Another good point," Jay said.

Thirty seconds later, with the air-conditioning running full blast in the LTD, Jay told Zed what they had learned.

"Invited?" Zed asked, sounding as shocked as Elle had felt. Elle wasn't sure if having the boss shocked made her feel any better.

"You're not pulling one of your stunts here, are you, Junior?" Zed asked.

"Not on something this serious," Jay said.

Zed nodded. "Damn. Invited by humans in black, huh? Who the hell could do that?"

Both Elle and Jay said nothing. Elle figured Zed wasn't asking them for an opinion. Which was okay by her since she didn't have one at the moment anyway.

"Well then," Zed said, "we're just going to have to *uninvite* the grass-eaters."

"Boss," Elle said. "How about we go over the Grazers' ship here. Might find something that would give us an idea who'd try to throw this party."

Zed nodded. "Do it. Keep the containment in place. You killed the Grazer yet?"

"No," Jay said.

"Good," Zed said. "Keep it contained there and out of sight. Most of the other Grazers landed in remote areas and we're taking them out easily. We just might need that one."

"Understood," Elle said as Zed cut the connection.

"You want us to go *inside* a Grazer ship?" Jay asked. "Woman, are you nuts? You know what it's going to smell like in there?"

"Like the men's rest room at a strip bar," Elle said. "You'll be right at home, I'm sure."

What she didn't say to Jay as they climbed out of the car was that she agreed with him. Entering the

Grazer ship wasn't going to be a pleasant experience and more than likely it would be worthless. But there was always a chance that they'd find something that would help. And at this point she really wanted some answers. She imagined Zed did also.

The containment crew had the Grazer chewing on grass under the trees near its ship. The police and other containment crews had set up a barrier far enough off so that if anyone did catch a glimpse of the Grazer, calling it a renegade water buffalo wouldn't appear too farfetched. A very deformed water buffalo, but close enough for the moment. The police were telling people they had to stay out until Animal Control and the carnival people got here. So far the cover story she'd come up with was holding.

Elle and Jay moved over to a nearby containment truck where Pro stood. He was the head of what she considered the best containment crew working for MiB. Pro's agency name was JayEe, but since he'd been a golf pro before joining up, everyone just called him Pro. He was a solid, powerfully built man who wore his suit as if he belonged in it and came naturally to the authority it implied. People just sort of automatically followed Pro. Elle liked working with him and his team. Jay did, too. And since Zed knew this, he tended to put Pro with them.

The other two members of Pro's team were KayBe and R'Elle. KayBe was called Captain because he loved to read *Star Trek* books during his breaks and R'Elle was called Partner as a result of a bet he'd made years earlier with another MiB agent. Captain also looked as if he belonged in his suit, while Partner, an expert in computers and alien weapons, seemed like he would be more comfortable wearing a golf shirt.

"We're going to need your team's help," Elle said to Pro.

"Run now," Jay said, "while you still can."

Pro laughed. "What can we do, Elle?"

Elle pointed at the watery area in the trees where the Grazer ship was. "We're going in."

"Inside a Grazer ship?" Pro asked, his eyes growing bigger. He turned to Jay. "She's kidding. Right?"

Jay just shook his head sadly.

"Inside," Elle said. "We've got to try to find out who invited it here and how."

Pro shook his head, then glanced up at Jay. "You were right. I should have run."

"Told ya," Jay said.

"Oh, quit complaining and let's get going," Elle said.

"Not without equipment," Pro said. With a wave he motioned for Partner and Captain to join him. Then he quickly explained to them what they were doing.

Elle watched as the containment team set to work in their van, emerging quickly with masks and other equipment. Pro tossed one mask to Elle, then another to Jay. "Trust me, you're going to need these. We won't last two minutes in a Grazer atmosphere. More sulfur than just about anything else."

"So how do they breathe out here?" Jay asked.

Pro shrugged. "Beats me. Someone at headquarters could tell you that, I'm sure." Then he turned to Elle as the five MiB agents formed a circle on the grass beside the ship. "What exactly are we going to be looking for in there?"

"Not sure," Elle said. "We need to find any record of the invitation the Grazer got to come to Earth."

"Invitation?" Pro asked. "The grass-eaters were invited? By whom?"

"A human wearing black," Elle said.

Pro's face went white.

Behind him Captain said, "You're kidding?"

Partner just shook his head in clear amazement.

"Zed is trying to stop the party now," Jay said.

Pro nodded. "Let's all hope he can do it. Partner, you got what you're going to need to download everything off that Grazer computer?"

Partner patted a case hanging from a strap over his shoulder. "I can do it in my sleep," he said.

"Captain," Pro said, "you stay with the Grazer. I don't think the insides of that ship will hold more than four of us."

Elle laughed at the relieved look on Captain's face as he handed Pro a bag of tools.

"Ready when you are," Pro said to Jay and Elle.

"Let's do it," Elle said, heading toward the shimmering air that was the shielded ship.

She reached the edge of the shield and just went through. She knew the theory of shielding, but had never been through one before. It felt like the air was electrified slightly around her. The hair on her arms stood up and her throat went suddenly dry.

In front of her the Grazer ship suddenly seemed to appear, its dented gray sides making it look more like an abandoned trailer than a spaceship. A ramp extended from the side of the ship to the grass. At least the Grazer hadn't started eating until he got outside the shield.

"Weird," Jay said beside her. "You just sort of vanished."

She turned around. She could see Captain and the other two agents near the Grazer, but it looked as if she were looking through a thin film of water. But they couldn't see her.

"Masks," Pro said.

"I'll lead," Elle said, slipping the mask over her head and making sure it was tight over her nose and mouth. Then she slipped the earpiece from the mask into her ear. Each mask had a communications link with the other masks. Easier than shouting through the masks to each other.

"Hope this cuts smells, too," Jay said as he put on his mask and adjusted it.

"Some," Pro said. "But we'll all need new suits when we come out."

"Oh, just great," Jay said. "I just got this one broken in."

"Took three months, right?" Pro asked.

"Six," Elle said. Then, to the sound of chuckling, she headed up the ramp into the blackness of the Grazer ship.

It was not a place she wanted to go.

Beach-Grass-In-Limbo eased back the resting unit that kept him above the floor and turned to face the communication screen that linked the Moon Observation Base with the humans on the surface of the planet. He was a Sashanian, one of a dozen on the base at the moment. And for the next two cycles of the planet he was the acting commander of the entire base. He took his duties under the treaty seriously. And right now his three eye stalks and many tentacles were moving in an agitated manner, not at all in their normal smooth fashion.

He was angry with the humans.

Very angry.

He could not understand why they had done what they had done. It made no sense to his logical mind why any race would

4

want to destroy itself. But the humans were a strange race by any standards. He had known that already when he accepted the assignment here. But this action seemed even beyond anything the humans had taken it into their perverse heads to do before.

They had destroyed themselves.

Just thinking of it tangled his tentacles.

He forced himself to calm. The Human-Who-Called-Himself-Zed wanted to talk with him. He needed to be calm for such a conference with a member of a Race-That-Would-Soon-Be-Dead.

After a moment he massaged the communication screen on, letting the human's face fill the image before his eye stalks. But before the human could growl-speak, Beach-Grass-In-Limbo put his thoughts forward.

"Why do you break the treaty? Why do you invite Those-Who-Eat-And-Are-Worthless to your planet?"

"We did not invite them," the human said, his growl-voice firm. "We do not want to break the treaty. This is a trick of someone who would gain from the treaty breaking."

Beach-Grass-In-Limbo considered these words, then asked, "Who would be in such a position?"

The human growled, "I do not know. But I must beg for your help in stopping the ones you call Those-Who-Eat-And-Are-Worthless from coming to Earth."

This was not at all how the Sashanian had expected the conversation with the human to proceed.

Was it possible such an event as a trick of this nature had actually taken place?

"What would you ask?"

The human showed his teeth for a moment, then growled, "Broadcast to Those-Who-Eat-And-Are-Worthless a message from Earth that they are not wanted and must turn back."

The Sashanian's eye stalks swiveled toward the screen. "Do you have such a message prepared?"

"It is prepared," the human said.

"Send it."

The human made a motion with one of its ugly, thick tentacles and then growled, "Message sent."

"If the message is as you say, it will be sent."

"Thank you," the human growled, bowing slightly as it should to a superior race. "We will eliminate Those-Who-Eat-And-Are-Worthless who have already arrived here."

"Understood. But I must warn you and your tiny-minded race that it must surely be, as you would say, too late to stop what must happen."

"Are you saying that Those-Who-Eat-And-Are-Worthless might not be turned back by the message?"

"Some will continue forward, but our ships will easily turn them away or destroy them. But you clearly do not understand what has happened. You tiny-minded humans are clearly in need of our protection, as it was ordered by the treaty. But now it must be too late. A sad event in the time of the stars."

"I am afraid I am not understanding," the human growled.

"The great Sashanian fleet is progressing in this direction, along with other fleets of those who feel you must be protected. We will do our best to hold the others away by our very presence. We will not fight for you."

"What others are you referring to, O great friend?" the human growled.

All Beach-Grass-In-Limbo's tentacles waved in agitation for a moment then abruptly calmed. "Your invitation was to the lowest of the low—Those-Who-Eat-And-Are-Worthless."

"It was not our invitation," the human growled, breaking into the commander's time to speak.

The commander continued, ignoring the rudeness of the human. "You have insulted many, many powerful races by inviting such creatures. They must now visit Earth also to feel superior to Those-Who-Eat-And-Are-Worthless. Your planet will be destroyed in the process of many thousands of such visits. I have seen it happen many times before, to many planets and races."

"The message I have sent to you will not stop such an event?" the human asked.

"It will stop many. Those of us who are your protection will also warn away others who do not dare anger us. I fear it will be far too little and the great Sashanian fleet will not fight for your planet. Many others know this as fact. Sending such an invitation was a mistake from which your people will not recover."

The connection with the human broke with a flick of a tentacle. It did not feel comfortable to Beach-Grass-In-Limbo to be talking to a member of a Soon-To-Be-Dead race. Conversations with the humans would have to be limited until the extinction process had run its course.

The human's message was reviewed and sent out at once, spreading through the inhabited universe.

As the commander of the moon base, Beach-Grass-In-Limbo, knew it would be, the message from the human was too little.

Too little and far too late.

Throughout the inhabited universe ships had already started the voyage toward the backward planet Earth, to take their races' rightful place in the way of things above Those-Who-Eat-And-Are-Worthless.

Every space-traveling race in the Galaxy was above Those-Who-Eat-And-Are-Worthless in the way of things in the Galaxy.

And there were hundreds of thousands of space-traveling races.

All now had ships—if not fleets—headed toward Earth.

Jay was glad he had put the breathing mask on because the smell inside the Grazer ship was choking even with the protection. It was as if someone had broken about a million rotten eggs inside a hot tin building and then closed the doors and let the sun thicken the air inside. Elle glanced at him and he made swimming motions as if he were moving upstream in a river of sewage.

Plus the place was darker than a tomb, the only illumination coming from the lights attached to the side of their masks.

"Nice place," Jay said. "Pro, you know how to find a light switch in here?"

"Sure," Pro said, moving past Jay and tapping a panel twice. Dim yellow light filled the small main cabin of the ship, causing the odd-shaped instruments to cast eerie

5

shadows. Every piece of equipment or furniture was designed to fit a Grazer's body shape. Thus the main control panels were placed only a few feet off the ground, while extra equipment seemed to hang at odd angles and seemingly random positions from the walls and ceiling.

"Not sure if that helped," Elle said.

Jay completely agreed. Not only did the place smell, but it was a cluttered mess. Some kind of grime that felt like oil to the touch coated every surface. Trash and half-eaten plants littered the floor and was piled up in the corners. There were pools of fluid on one side of the room that Jay didn't even want to ask Pro to identify.

"The trash ghetto of spaceships," Jay said. He knew from his short glance at the manual that a Grazer lived and died in his ship, leaving it only to eat or find supplies. But how any creature could exist in this was beyond him. In his days as a New York cop he had seen a lot of poverty and filth, but no depth a human being could sink to came close to this. No wonder the Grazers were treated with contempt Galaxy-wide. They were stupid *and* messy.

"Are all Grazer ships this bad?" Elle asked.

"From what I've heard of the Grazer ships we've captured over the years," Pro said, "they all are. Sometimes worse."

"Much worse," Partner said. "I trained in one that made this one look clean."

"Killing a Grazer is like a mercy killing," Elle said.

"If I had to live here," Jay said, picking up a

scrap of something and dropping it quickly, "I'd want someone to shoot me, too."

Pro and Partner knelt and went to work on one area of what looked to be the main control board. Pro held the case while Partner attached connecting cables.

While they did this, Jay and Elle explored. Jay had no idea what they was looking for, but they looked anyway. The Grazers had been invited to Earth for a reason and there just might be a clue to that reason somewhere in this mess.

A short hall, walls dripping oil and slick with moistened dirt, led to another room with a closed door. After a quick look around the items stored on the walls and ceilings of the main cabin, they headed toward the door.

"You won't want to go in there," they heard Pro call out to them, his voice carrying clearly to Jay's ear microphone just as he reached down for the release that would open the door. It was a latch about a foot off the ground, right where the front feet of the Grazer could reach it easily.

"Why's that?" Jay said, standing and looking back into the main room at Pro. The containment-team leader was staring at him while Partner worked.

"Don't remember your manual on Grazers, do you?" Pro said, laughing.

Jay glanced at Elle and she shrugged. Obviously she hadn't read all of it either.

"It's where the Grazer sleeps," Pro said. "Makes

this room look like it was scrubbed with ammonia and steel wool."

"How much worse can it get?" Jay asked.

"You don't want to know the answer to that question," Pro said.

Jay looked at Elle and pointed at the door.

She nodded. "Doesn't hurt to see it once."

Jay leaned forward and went to push the hatch open. Down the hall in the main cabin Pro was shaking his head, laughing softly. "Don't say I didn't warn you."

Jay flicked the latch to open and the metal door slid sideways into the wall. Instantly his nostrils filled with a stench even more disgusting than what he had just smelled.

Inside, a yellow light came on, showing Jay a room filled with the rotting corpses of other Grazers.

"Oh, shit," Jay whispered.

Two or three Grazer bodies were still pretty much in one piece. It was clear—from the positioning of the stinking corpses, and from the fact that this room was clearly used as sleeping quarters— that the Grazer eating outside had been using both of the bodies as organic mattresses, curling up inside their rotting intestines.

Another five or six Grazers in various stages of decomposition appeared to have been used then discarded as beds long ago. Grazer flesh either decomposed much more slowly than human flesh or the rotting here had been slowed by the controlled atmosphere of the room. But not slowed to anywhere near a stop.

The floor of the room was littered with hundreds of bones from more Grazers than Jay wanted to think about. Some of the skulls had been hung on the walls, their huge mouths hanging open as if waiting to eat anything that came within snapping distance.

Elle made a choking sound and both of them turned and shoved back into the hallway.

The door to the cabin slid closed, blocking off direct sight to the horror, but not clearing it from Jay's mind.

They both turned as one and returned to the main cabin. Jay was sweating and was suddenly very afraid of closing his eyes. Very afraid he would see that room again.

"Understand now why we kill the Grazers and destroy their ships?" Pro asked.

Elle coughed and nodded.

Jay completely understood. Right now all he wanted to do was run, get the hell out of this nightmare ship and then blow it up, along with its grass-eating pilot. But they weren't done yet, so he couldn't act on the impulse.

"Sorry you saw that," Pro said. "MiB uses it to train containment crews when a Grazer's ship is available. I suppose they figure if we last through seeing that, we can clean up anything."

"I think they just may be right," Elle said, her voice still shaking.

Jay completely agreed. If Kay had shown him

that room his first day, there'd be no way in hell he'd have taken this job. No way at all.

"Each ship is passed down from one Grazer to another," Elle said. "So those Grazer bodies are relatives? Right?"

Pro laughed without looking up from his work. "Like the manual says, a Grazer very seldom leaves its ship, even after death. They only live about five Earth years and breed like rats. Chances are the ship's current occupant is sleeping inside the remains of his mother or father. Maybe both."

Again Elle coughed, then said softly, "I thought I'd seen it all at the city morgue."

Jay could think of absolutely nothing to say, funny or otherwise, so he just stood there and tried to breathe evenly and not close his eyes or even blink.

"Got it," Partner said, after what seemed like an eternity to Jay.

"Watch the screen." Partner pointed to a smudged flat surface about waist-high.

It flickered, then came to life. On the screen they saw a human wearing a black suit, white shirt, and black tie. He smiled, then said, *"This message is to all Golgothas."*

Partner froze the image and glanced at Jay with a puzzled frown.

"Golgothas are what the Grazers call themselves," Jay said. "I remember that much from the manual. That room just taught me that I'm going to read all the way to the end, though."

"You recognize him?" Pro asked, pointing to the man on the screen.

"Nope," Jay said.

"No," Elle said.

Partner backed up the playback and started over. The man on the screen smiled again, then said, *"This message is to all Golgothas. Earth welcomes you. Come, eat all you want."*

The man smiled again and then the message repeated.

"You got that recorded?" Elle asked Partner.

"Got it," he said.

"Including when and where it was recorded and where the message was broadcast from?"

"Got it all," Partner said, standing. "Including the type of carrier band it was sent on. Not one of ours, that's for sure. I can tell that right off."

"Then let's get the hell out of this stink," Jay said, turning and heading for the ramp and the fresh, clean day that lay outside. All he really wanted to do was get as far away from that room as he could. He was going to have nightmares for years simply because he had opened that door.

At the bottom of the ramp he tossed aside his gas mask and walked right through the shield and into the warm sun of the afternoon. Central Park stretched out around him. A few buildings could be seen through the trees. The sun was warm, the air fresh.

Without even pausing, he pulled out his Atomizer and with one shot dropped the Grazer in its tracks, surprising the other agents standing nearby.

Behind him another Atomizer fired, frying the body of the Grazer into so much ash.

Jay glanced around to stare into the sweating face of Elle as she finally stopped firing. Her eyes looked almost haunted.

He understood exactly how she felt.

"Toss that ship into the sun," Jay said to the two containment agents that had been standing guard over the Grazer. Then Jay turned to face Pro and Partner as they gathered up his and Elle's gas masks. "Give that information to Captain."

Jay turned to Captain as Partner handed him the case. "Get it to Zed as fast as you can go. We'll tell him it's on the way and we'll be not far behind you."

Captain nodded and turned and headed for the truck at a run.

Through the trees Jay saw a fire truck parked along the perimeter. "Captain, on the way out send that fire truck in here."

Captain waved his acknowledgment as he jumped into the cab of the containment truck and took off for MiB headquarters.

A minute later, as the fire truck rumbled to a stop in the sun, Jay was digging through the trunk of the LTD for new suits for him and Elle.

Two minutes later he, Elle, Pro, and Partner were all standing in their underwear on the grass, basking in the sun in Central Park as they were hosed down by wonderfully cold, wonderfully clean cold water.

Jay knew without a doubt it would be only the

first of many showers he was going to take over the next few days to get the feeling of dirt and sewage and rot out of his mind and off his skin.

He had no idea how long it would take to clean it out of his memory.

Billie Floyd stood in the central control area of the Phillida ship and watched the viewscreen as Zed's message was broadcast over and over from the Sashanian moon base.

"We did not invite the Golgotha to our planet. No Golgotha is welcome on our planet. The invitation was a trick to hurt humans. Please accept our apologies for any misunderstanding this may have caused. No Golgotha is welcome on Earth, now or ever."

Zed's stern face started to repeat the message yet again and Billie leaned forward and clicked it off with a pass of his hand. Then he turned to the Phillida and in their clicking language said, "Humans are too stupid to be allowed to live."

The Phillida in charge of the ship started

6

to shake slightly, a sign he was laughing at Billie's comment.

Billie laughed with him for a moment.

Then the Phillida captain said, "For humans, being alive at all is only a temporary condition now."

Billie again laughed in his human voice, then said, "Too true. But I must continue this charade for a short time longer. Put me in touch with my base on Earth."

The Phillida bowed and did as he was ordered.

Billie stepped in front of the camera and the Phillida moved back out of the way so only Billie would be seen. As the link to Earth was connected, Billie's posture changed. Instead of standing straight, he slumped, became a little more agitated.

A woman's face filled the screen in front of him. Her name was Sarah Wallace. She was middle-aged by human standards and had been working with Billie for almost twenty Earth years now. Her hair had slight streaks of gray and wrinkles were starting to fill the corners of her face.

For Billie's race, twenty years was only a brief span, but for the woman it was half of her lifetime so far. He had recruited her from a small town in Utah when she was only nineteen, barely a human adult. He liked getting them young. They were even dumber and believed almost anything he told them.

"Sarah," he said. "It was just awful, let me tell ya."

"What?" Sarah asked, clearly afraid.

"Derek had gone and sent the message just fine

when suddenly he went wild, tried to kill a Phillida."

"What?" Sarah asked, clearly shocked.

Billie nodded real hard. "Then he tried to run hisself right out an airlock. He's dead, Sarah."

Sarah covered her mouth, but said nothing.

"The message was sent, though," Billie went on.

Sarah nodded, hand still over her mouth.

"Derek died a hero and that there is how I'm a-gonna tell it," Billie declared. "That all right with you?"

She took a deep breath. "Fine. Good idea."

"Okay," Billie said. "I'm gonna be comin' back."

"Did MiB send out a retraction of our invitation to the Grazers?" Sarah asked.

"Just like we thought they would, so we have lots of work to do."

"I understand," Sarah said. "We'll be ready here when you arrive."

"Good," Billie said.

He cut the connection, then leaned back and laughed, long and hard. Like a human would laugh. He had impersonated one for so long, it almost felt natural to laugh like one.

But in a very short time humans would be wiped off the face of their planet. The entire ball of rock and water would be all his. And with what he had found thirty Earth years ago buried deep underground, he would be the most powerful and richest entity in all the Galaxy.

He had found what he called the Power.

Pure and simple Power.

But first he had to get rid of the humans, their MiB organization, and all the aliens that watched over them.

He couldn't use the Power for that. They had to be gone. It had taken thirty years to bring his plan to this point. And everything so far was working perfectly.

A few more Earth days, maybe a week or two, and they would all be wiped from the surface.

And the great Power would be his for the taking.

Jay and Elle headed through the Immigration Cen-ter toward Zed's office. Hundreds and hundreds of aliens and humans filled the vast space, standing in lines, talking, or just sitting and waiting. Much, much busier than normal.

The Immigration Center was the hub of the MiB headquarters. Every alien who visited Earth or lived on the planet had to pass through the cavernlike space. And it was the job of the MiB to keep track of them all during their stay on the planet. No ship entered Earth's atmosphere without the MiB orbital tracking satellites following it.

On the surface, it was another matter entirely. A massive screen filled one wall of the room, towering at least three stories high. At a huge control board in front of

7

the screen sat two octopuslike aliens. They were called the twins since their real names were nothing a human could say. Jay knew that for certain because one day last month he'd tried, without success. Zed had stopped him just before he insulted them both by mispronouncing their names. The last thing anyone on the planet Earth wanted to do was insult the twins.

The twins each had eight arms, which were in constant motion over the controls, tracking every alien on the surface of the planet, all the time, thirty-six hours a day. Their long eye stalks jerked, watching the screen in front of them, apparently assimilating all the activity it rendered at once. Jay knew for certain that those eyes didn't miss much. The twins were very good at what they did.

As Jay and Elle walked by, the twins looked busy, as always. And the lines of departing aliens looked a lot longer than usual. Jay wondered if that had anything to do with the Grazer invitation. He suspected it did.

They took the stairs up to Zed's office two at a time and didn't bother to knock at the open door. Jay knew Zed was expecting them.

Zed's office was above the Immigration Center, a wood-and-glass throwback to the 1970s. He had a huge desk and a notepad, but nothing else in evidence. Jay knew the room was stocked with the most high-tech equipment available to humans. Surveillance equipment the government could only dream about having.

Zed's office might look like a standard office in

any New York building, but from it Zed ran the vast, secret MiB organization assigned the task of safeguarding the planet Earth from the alien scum of the universe. And he ran it with an iron hand.

As Jay and Elle entered, Zed was standing at the window looking down into the heart of the center. He was a stout, middle-aged man who filled out his black suit like a linebacker filled out a football uniform. At the moment his large hands were clasped behind his back, his head down.

Usually Zed had some alien secretary-in-training bumbling or zipping around the office when they arrived, but today it was only Zed.

"Yo, boss," Jay said.

Without looking around at them Zed said, "They're starting to leave in droves. Only going to get worse. Can't say as I blame them. I wouldn't mind going with them."

Jay glanced at Elle, who only shrugged.

In the year Jay had been with MiB, he had never heard Zed sound so downbeat. Zed had seemed worried, although only slightly, only once before, when the bug had taken the Galaxy and the Achturians were going to blow Earth from the sky to keep the bug from escaping. Today Zed seemed truly worried.

"Hey, boss," Jay said, making sure his voice was light and upbeat, "want to fill us in on the bad news so we can be depressed, too?"

Zed snorted and turned from the window. "Good job getting that tape out of the Grazer ship. Hope you showered."

"Twice," Elle said.

"Good," Zed said. "Hate that smell."

"New suits, too," Jay said, turning from side to side like a model on a runway. "I really look good in these things, don't ya think?"

Again Zed just snorted and dropped into his chair, staring at the paper in front of him.

"All right, then," Jay said. "I admit it. Elle looks better in them than I do, but don't quote me on that."

"Well, thank you," Elle said, smiling at him.

"Junior, would you stop cracking jokes and sit down?" Zed said. "We got a serious problem here."

"Yes, sir," Jay said, holding the chair for Elle, then dropping into one beside her.

Jay sat and watched as Zed seemed to be lost in thought for a long half minute, then he leaned forward and looked them both right in the eye, Jay first, then Elle. "Look, I'm going to be straight with you two, so listen up."

Jay only nodded. Zed's intent stare did that to people: made it almost impossible to talk.

"The human race has about one chance in a million of surviving the next week and that chance is you two."

Jay glanced at Elle, who looked shocked, then back at Zed. "Boss, you're not starting this out real well here. You lost us in the second sentence. The part where the human race has one chance in a million of surviving."

"Yeah," Elle said, her voice cracking a little. "You want to explain. Please?"

Zed shoved himself away from his desk and stood, moving over to the window overlooking the Immigration Center. There, hands behind his back, he gazed into the distance for a moment before starting to speak. "The Grazers are the lowest form of all interstellar-traveling life."

The image of that Grazer sleeping room flashed back into Jay's mind and he could feel himself breaking out into a sweat. Beside him Elle coughed, also clearly remembering. Zed would get no argument from either of them on that statement.

Zed kept staring out over the Immigration Center below. "Out in the vastness of space there are hundreds of thousands of space-faring races," Zed said, "all more technologically advanced than humans. All of them are above the Grazers on the pecking order of things."

"Okay," Elle said. "We got that. Go on."

"The treaty that keeps the human race going forward blissfully in the dark was signed by a few hundred or so of those races. MiB came into being as the human enforcement arm here on the planet, to keep scum like the Grazers off the surface, keep humans in the dark until we all advanced enough as a species to join the big party out there."

Zed was going over basic history, stuff that Kay had explained to Jay his first day on the job, but clearly the boss was headed somewhere with this, so Jay didn't interrupt. He just looked at Elle and she shrugged.

Neither of them said a word.

"Some human, posing as an MiB agent, sent an invitation to all Grazers to come to Earth."

"And you canceled that invitation," Jay said. "Right? Closed the door on the party."

Zed nodded and turned around. Slowly he moved back over to his desk and sat down hard in his chair, as if the weight of the world was crushing him. Jay had no doubt it was.

"I talked to the Sashanians on the moon," Zed said, "and they broadcast a retraction of the invitation. But that will make no difference."

"Okay," Jay said, "I was followin' ya right up to that last sentence."

"The first invitation pissed off every race in the Galaxy," Zed said, leaning across the desk and staring at Jay intently. "We invited the scum of all races to our planet without inviting the rest of them. So, basically, they're all headed here to either crash the party or teach us a lesson in manners."

"Even though the bogus invitation has been canceled?" Elle asked.

"Yup," Zed said. "They're all coming to eat, drink, and take what they want. Hundreds of thousands of races. We won't survive it. I doubt there will be anything left on the surface of this planet in ten days."

Jay was having trouble wrapping his mind around the idea of hundreds of thousands of alien races all headed here. Let alone one hundred thousand pissed-off alien races.

"Can't the Sashanians and other treaty signers turn them around?" Elle asked.

"They'll do what they can," Zed said. "They'll wave their arms and ask others nicely to go away, but it will be like throwing a handful of sand in a river and expecting it to stop the water. It's not going to happen. And unless we can come up with something on our end, they won't even bother fighting for us."

"And that 'something' is our job," Elle said.

"She's fast," Zed said to Jay. But there was no smile behind his kidding.

"I heard that from guys down at the morgue," Jay replied, just to stay in the spirit of it.

Elle made no move even to punch him, but instead stayed focused on Zed. "What can we do?"

Zed leaned back in his chair. "I honestly don't know. I've got every other agent out working to stick a finger in the dike to hold off the flood of Grazers and other aliens starting to drop in."

He took a deep breath. "I've also apologized to half the Galaxy in the last half hour and called in every favor from every race we've ever met to help turn the tide out there. I figure, at best, we have four or five days. More than likely one or two."

"But we don't know why all this even happened, do we?" Jay said, finally catching on to what Zed wanted them to do.

"Exactly," Zed said. "A human sent that invitation. A human who knew about MiB enough to look like us."

"Why and who?" Jay said. "Those are the really big, important questions.

"And don't forget: how?" Elle added.

Zed nodded. "I can spare you two, plus one containment team to try to find the answers to those questions on the outside chance it might help."

"Pro's team," Jay said.

"Already assigned to you and waiting for your orders," Zed said.

"Any idea where to start?" Elle asked.

"Agent Elle," Zed said, looking sternly at her, "if I knew the answer to that question, wouldn't you think someone would already be on the road."

"Understood," Elle said.

"We'll figure it out," Jay said, and stood.

"Junior," Zed said, "I hope you're right this time. And I hope it makes a difference."

"Well, how's that for pressure?" Jay asked Elle as they headed down the stairs and made their way through the noise and activity of the Immigration Center. "Up to us to save the entire world. All in two days."

"If Zed thought there really was a hope," Elle said, ducking around an alien carrying a large bag of something that smelled like wet dog hair, "he wouldn't have assigned it to two rookies."

"Too true," Jay said. "And he'd have put a dozen teams on it instead of just us."

"Agreed," she said.

And she really believed that, too. Zed was the smartest man she had ever met. Her and Jay's chances of finding anything that might help were worth one team and not one person more.

8

"Good point," Jay said, giving a multihorned Imatey with two suitcases a wide berth and catching up to her. "So what do you say we prove him wrong and find something."

"Fine by me," Elle said, stopping to face Jay. "Where do we start."

"Elementary, my dear Ms. Elle," Jay said, smiling at her with that impish grin he got. "We start with our only lead."

"The invitation?" Elle said, knowing exactly where he was going. It was the same thing she had already thought of.

"The invitation," Jay said, smiling at her. He led the way toward a private screening room just off the main concourse of the center.

The room was long and thin, with a table down the middle and windows along one side overlooking the Immigration Center. It smelled of cleaning solution and new electronics. Elle had been in here dozens of times over the past year, studying, getting assignments, watching films about some infraction or other an alien was committing against the rules.

Inside Jay punched a communications link and set up the showing while she pulled the curtains to block out light from the center. Zed was right. There were a lot more aliens suddenly leaving, all looking very much in a hurry.

And no one was in the check-in line. Made sense. Why check into a hotel that was days away from being whacked by the wrecking ball?

Rats deserting a sinking ship, aliens leaving a dying planet, it was all one and the same. Well, she and Jay and the entire human race were going down with the ship, unless they could plug the hole somehow.

She finished closing the blinds and sat down in the chair at the end of the table while Jay dropped into the chair to her right.

Ten seconds later the image of a middle-aged man dressed in a black suit was on the screen that filled the end wall of the long room. Quickly the man ran through the invitation to the Grazers, then it started over.

It was hard for Elle to imagine how such a short little invitation could mean the death of all humanity. But that's exactly what those few sentences were going to mean.

"Okay, first things first," Jay said, freezing the film with the guy's mouth open. "Is this guy human?"

Elle stared at the open mouth on the screen, the man's eyes, his nose, then shrugged. He was a decent-looking guy. The type that could almost be trusted. The type that would fit as a nine-to-five husband, or maybe doctor, or a lawyer.

"No way to tell quickly," she said, then punched a communications button on an inlaid panel on the table that hooked her directly to Research. "Let's see if that has already been determined."

"Yes, Agent Elle." A man's voice filled the room almost instantly.

Elle had been down to Research a number of times. The department took up three full floors the size of the Immigration Center below them. As far as she could tell, the seemingly hundreds of people who worked there had unrelentingly thankless jobs. But for some reason, they all seemed to really love it. Or at least the ones she'd talked to had seemed to love it.

"Can we have two printouts of the analysis of the invitation footage retrieved from the Grazer's computer?" Elle asked. "Including any summary findings."

"Coming up now," the voice said.

"Thank you," Elle said.

There was a click and a faint rustle of paper. She reached into a slot in the base of the table and pulled out a small stack of paper. She gave one printout to Jay and kept the second for herself.

"He's human all right," Jay said after a moment of quick reading.

Elle had already seen the same piece of information. According to the page-long conclusion of the study, there was no chance at all that this invitation was made by an alien in a human body. The guy who did the inviting was one of them.

A human out to destroy his own race. She wondered if he realized what he was doing.

She stared at the frozen image of the guy filling the far wall. He looked so damn normal.

So MiB.

Black suit, white shirt, black tie.

The same as she was wearing now.

Almost.

His suit collar was thinner than hers. And if you looked closely, his tie seemed to have a faint pattern in the blackness. There *were* differences. The guy was clearly trying to look MiB, but had missed in slight ways. Ways that just maybe gave him away.

The report said that MiB was running a scan of all photo databases to try to find a match, but it would take some time. They had no name at this time.

Elle punched the communications button again.

"Yes, Agent Elle?" the same male voice said.

"How long until the photo database scans are complete on the human on the invitation retrieved from the Grazer ship?"

"Six hours, ten minutes," the voice said without hesitation. "Unless a match is found sooner."

"Too long," Jay said, and Elle nodded.

"Has an analysis of the man's suit been completed?"

There was a pause. "No."

"Please do so quickly," Elle said. "And his tie. I want probabilities of type and brand and likely purchase locations as soon as possible."

"Understood," the voice said.

"Good thinking," Jay said, staring at the man's image on the screen. "Never would have thought of that."

"Neither would I." Elle said, "If you hadn't left his image up there. See the difference in the lapels?"

Jay nodded. "Sure do. Nice spot."

Elle leaned forward over the table slightly, staring at the man's tie. She kept seeing a pattern in it, even though it didn't seem as if there was one. "Enlarge the image of his tie, right above where it tucks into his coat?"

"Got it," Jay said, working the image controls in front of his chair.

With a flick the guy's black tie almost filled the entire wall.

"Focusing," Jay said, working the controls in front of him, pulling the image in clearer and brighter as he went.

"It's a horse," Elle said. "Would you look at that." An image of a horse rearing back was embossed in black on the black tie. Up close, it would be noticeable, but on the invitation to the Grazers it looked solid black.

"You're right," Jay said.

Elle again punched the communications link to Research and this time didn't wait to hear the man's voice. "Focus your photo database scans on western states if not already done. Washington, Oregon, Idaho, Montana, Wyoming first. Then go Nevada, Arizona, Utah, Colorado, and New Mexico."

"Understood, Agent Elle," the man's voice answered.

"And add into your data that the man is wearing a tie with the image of a horse on it."

There was a pause, then the man said, "Understood. Thank you."

Jay laughed. "I think you just beat Research at their own game."

"Now if they can just repay the favor quickly."

"In the meantime," Jay said, "I'm going to run this thing again."

Elle nodded as the man's face again started to extend his invitation to the Grazers.

"He's dead," Jay said after the entire thing ran a few more times.

She knew exactly what he meant. She had been getting that same feeling watching the film. Anyone who would attempt such a thing would be killed. Whoever was behind this scheme couldn't allow the messenger to survive. A face was too easily tracked, even if the process was slow.

"I think you may be right," Elle said. "That would be perfectly logical."

This time it was Jay who punched his communications link with Research. Before anyone could answer, he said, "Also match the man on the invitation with missing persons' files. Start in the western states."

"Understood, Agent Jay," the voice from research said.

"Well," Jay said, leaning back and smiling. "We got them going in about three different directions. Something should pop pretty soon."

"Let's hope," Elle said. "It's going to be next to impossible to wait very long."

"That is the truth," Jay said. "In fact, maybe we should get some lunch so we're ready to—"

"Agents Jay and Elle," the man's voice from Research said, "we have found a match. Information coming up to you now."

The rustle of paper filled the room as the silent, high-speed printer in the table spit out a page. Elle pulled it out and looked at the face on the paper, then again at the one frozen on the wall in front of them. It was the same face.

"Derek Comstock," Jay read. "Attorney in Portland, Oregon. Last seen four days ago headed into the coastal mountain range to go fishing."

"Bingo," Jay said, jumping to his feet.

Elle beat him to the door. With the fastest suborbital plane MiB had, they'd be in Portland in less than two hours. Two long hours to figure out what they had to do next.

Two hours closer to the end of the world.

Spring in downtown Portland seemed to be in full bloom. Bright green trees covered many of the roads in what was called the northwest section, forming tunnels of leaves that shaded the street. Flowers were planted everywhere, along every house, in planters in front of the buildings, at the base of carefully groomed shrubs.

Nothing seemed out of the ordinary and Jay couldn't believe how clean the place was. It was almost creepy, as if littering might be considered a capital offense in this town.

"Never seen a city without trash on the streets," he said to Elle as she wound their LTD past the old train depot and down into the main part of town. Behind them Pro and his team followed in a containment truck.

9

"Neither have I," Elle said. "Not even a gum wrapper. Didn't know they made such a place. Maybe we're just in a good section of town."

Jay shrugged.

The boulevard they were driving along dead-ended into a street in front of a statue of some strange guy who was standing with his hand tucked into the front of his vest.

"Wonder what he did?" Elle said, pointing at the bronze figure as she drove past.

"Says on the plaque he shot a litterbug," Jay said, pretending to read the sign.

Elle laughed.

"I'm not kidding," Jay said, trying to give her his best serious look.

She wasn't buying it. She very seldom did.

They worked their way up the hill. Portland was built in a river valley, at the point where two rivers converged. The larger buildings had been built closer to the water, while the homes seemed to spread up the side of the mountain. They had decided to try Derek Comstock's workplace first, then his home second.

Finally Elle pulled the LTD up in front of an old thirties-style two-story house that had been converted into legal offices. A wooden sign stuck out of a flower bed: SCHOFIELD & ROSE. ATTORNEYS.

"Nice place to work," Jay said. "Wonder what made good old Derek run off to Saturn and destroy the world?"

"I'd like an answer to that question myself," Elle

said as they climbed out of the car into the warm afternoon air.

In the distance Jay could see a big, arching bridge and the river. This was his first visit to Portland. It was a pretty city, that much was for sure. But he'd still take New York any day, litter or not.

Inside, the reception area was exactly what Jay would have expected from the outside, a former residential vestibule, framed in highly polished wood. A large wooden staircase swept away from the desk where a young woman sat staring at a computer. A half-dozen chairs were arranged around the space with magazines neatly sorted on end tables between them. The place smelled of fresh air and furniture polish.

The receptionist looked up and smiled as they entered. "Can I help you?"

"We're from the FBI," Elle said, flashing a badge and then quickly closing it. "I'm Agent Place, this is Agent Kincaid. We're here looking for an attorney who works with your firm. A man named Derek Comstock."

Jay was shocked again. Elle had changed their cover names for the second time in two days. Amazing.

Jay watched as the receptionist's face went pale. "Is he all right?"

"We don't know the answer to that question," Elle said. "May we talk to one of your senior partners?"

"Certainly," a woman's voice said from near the top of the stairs. "Come on up."

The receptionist smiled weakly as Jay and Elle marched past her desk and began to climb the stairs.

At the top Jay was surprised when he saw the person that matched the voice. The woman was young, maybe Jay's age at most, and stunningly beautiful, with long brown hair and brown eyes that could melt his heart any day. He couldn't remember when he'd had so strong a reaction to a woman.

Elle reached the top of the stairs first and the woman smiled and shook her hand.

"I'm Kathy Rose," she said.

"Agent Place, FBI," Elle said, then indicated Jay. "Agent Kincaid."

Jay shook attorney Rose's hand and returned her smile. The woman's handshake was firm, yet soft. And there was a lot of intelligence in her eyes.

Cold intelligence.

"You don't mind if I see your ID?" she asked.

"Not a bit," Jay said as he flipped his wallet open, glancing at it to make sure it said FBI and Agent Jay Kincaid. The badges always did. They were another gift from an alien race, like the flashy-thing. No matter what name he gave, or what organization, the badge somehow responded to his verbal command and transformed into the appropriate agency. The MiB Agency called them Carte Noir badges, but Jay just called it his badge-thing.

He handed his ID to the woman and she studied it for a moment, then handed it back with a nod and a smile. As always, the badge-thing had passed the test.

She then motioned that they should follow her into a large, comfortably furnished office. She didn't ask to see Elle's ID.

She indicated that they should have a seat in inviting-looking chairs facing her desk, then she went around and sat down in her high-backed office chair. Law books filled a floor-to-ceiling oak bookcase behind her desk and her framed law degree was hung on the wall near the window. Jay noted that there were no family pictures on her desk and no ring on her finger.

She was the perfect picture of an attorney. Jay figured she was almost too perfect.

"We're looking for Derek Comstock," Elle said, sounding very official. "Any information you might be able to give us would be helpful."

Jay watched Attorney Rose's face; it didn't even flinch. The woman was either very, very good, or had nothing to hide. He couldn't figure out which at the moment.

"I've been looking for him, too," Attorney Rose said, frowning. "He went on a fishing trip four days ago, promising to be back for a meeting in two days. He missed the meeting and we haven't seen him since."

"Can you fill us in a little on his background?" Jay asked, giving her his best I-really-am-attracted-to-you smile.

She shrugged. "Not much to fill in. Born here in Portland, went to law school at the University of

Oregon in Eugene. Decent grades, not outstanding. He worked as a clerk for a district judge, then with another firm downtown for about ten years. We hired him three years ago when we wanted to expand. He's always done us a good job until now."

"Wife? Children? Friends?" Elle asked.

Attorney Rose shrugged. "Not married. Never was, to my knowledge. Except for his fishing, he didn't seem to have many passions at all. And few friends, now that you mention it."

"So"—Elle glanced at Jay—"you have any idea where Derek went on his fishing trips?"

Attorney Rose laughed, which made Jay immediately smile along with her. It was that kind of laugh. He couldn't help liking her at the same time as he didn't trust her at all. Weird how he was reacting to this woman. Total attraction, total distrust.

"Not a clue," Attorney Rose said. "But every so often he'd mention Tillamook, a little town over on the coast. So it must have been up in that direction somewhere. Guess the fishing is pretty good in the mountains above there."

Elle nodded.

"I think that's all we're going to need for now," Jay said, standing. "We want to thank you for your time."

She stood and took his extended hand. "My pleasure, Agent Kincaid. Please keep me informed if you discover anything about Derek. Everyone in the firm is deeply concerned."

Jay didn't really want to let go of the attorney's

very soft hand, but somehow he managed to do so before he made a total fool of himself.

"We most certainly will," Elle said, standing and shaking Rose's hand. Then with a friendly pat on Jay's back, she turned him and sort of eased him toward the office door and the stairs beyond.

Something was bothering him.

And bothering him a lot.

He just couldn't get past Kathy Rose's looks and put his finger on it.

At the door Elle stopped, did an about-face, and went back to the attorney, handing her a card. "Would you call us at that number if Derek does return? It would be for his own safety."

The attorney nodded, glanced at the card, and then frowned. "You never did say why you were looking for Derek."

Elle glanced at Jay, then smiled at Attorney Rose. "Just trust me when I say it's for all of our own good that we find him. And find him fast."

Elle moved out the door and toward the stairs, going past Jay as he watched the attorney's expression. The woman didn't flinch at Elle's comment.

"Sounds to me like this is very serious," Attorney Rose said calmly, following the two agents to the top of the stairs.

"More than you could ever imagine," Jay said. "Don't be afraid to use that number if you need to."

With that, he turned and left Attorney Rose, following Elle down the stairs and out the front door. He knew exactly what was bothering him now.

That woman was a walking shell, nothing more. And something had clearly made her that way.

Outside, Elle shook her head at him as she climbed in behind the wheel. "Can't get past the good-looking brunette, can you?"

He grabbed the phone and picked it up. "Pro?"

"Go ahead, Jay," Pro said.

"Quickly put a trace on all calls coming in or out of that office in the next twenty-four hours. In fact, I bet she makes a call the moment we leave."

"Understood," Pro said.

Jay turned to see a puzzled frown on Elle's face. "You're the one who gave her my phone number."

"I gave her *our* phone number," Elle corrected, pulling the LTD away from the curb.

Jay glanced back at the building. Sure enough, Attorney Rose was watching them from the second-story window, a phone resting against the side of her head. This might not even take as long as he thought. She would call her boss immediately and tell him or her that the MiB had come.

"Now, you want to tell me what I missed?" Elle asked.

"You just got to have an eye for beautiful women." Jay laughed.

"Cold women," Elle said.

"Exactly," Jay said. "Empty and cold. Just like Derek Comstock."

Elle looked at him for an instant, then smiled. "Exactly like Derek Comstock."

"Besides," Jay said, "if the world's going to end,

Attorney Rose could represent me at the pearly gates anytime she wanted."

"Yeah, as if you or her are going in that direction," Elle said, laughing.

"It's possible," Jay said.

"But not likely," Elle said.

Jay had to admit, she had a point on that one.

Twenty minutes later they had wound their way across Portland and exited the freeway and were climbing up a hill heading south to Derek Comstock's small house in a nice suburb. It was just like the northwest section: shaded street, meticulously mowed lawns, and everything looking very clean. Tucked off to one side of a major street and hidden under two large oak trees, Derek Comstock's house looked to Jay like a perfect dwelling for the Brady Bunch.

As Jay walked up the front sidewalk, he had the feeling he was walking onto a movie set. The place was generic to the point of becoming almost surreal. Everything he was seeing was for show and nothing more. There really wasn't any personality in this house, no details that made it uniquely one person's home.

He doubted they would find anything of importance inside.

As things turned out, he was right.

But they also found no fishing equipment.

No lures, no rods, no reels, no flies.

No frozen fish in the freezer.

And not one fishing magazine in the entire place.

The shadows of the moss-covered pine trees were long and the mountaintops blocked most of the sun from entering the steep valley. Along the coastal range mountains, the snow had all melted, except in the highest areas. Spring had come late for this area this year.

An old log cabin sat among the trees, hidden by overgrown berry bushes and thick underbrush. Billie Floyd swung open the door to the cabin and walked inside, glancing around to see if anything had been disturbed in his absence. Nothing had.

The room felt almost deserted, even though there were dishes on the counter and blankets on the bed. Props and nothing more, to keep unwanted snoops away. No one had lived in this place for over thirty years.

10

Billie owned the old log cabin and the six hundred acres of prime timberland around it, stretching down to the river on one side and up into the mountains on the other. He had bought it thirty years earlier, right after he had stumbled onto the presence of the Power while passing this backward little planet.

He opened an empty old medicine cabinet in the small bathroom and then clicked the back of the cabinet forward, exposing a sophisticated control panel. Quickly he keyed in a few well-practiced numbers, then swung the panel closed and stepped back. The wall opened between the sink and the rusted old toilet silently, just enough for him to step through.

A modern-looking staircase led downward into the side of the mountain behind the cabin. Lights were spaced evenly along the walls. He was actually whistling a human tune as he descended the stairs, the door closing behind him, returning the old cabin to its usual innocuous appearance, the perfect shield from intruders.

Two hundred and six steps down, the stairs ended in a long corridor extending back into the mountain. The sides of the corridor were concrete and reinforced by a special mixture of steel and plastic that could support almost any amount of weight. It had taken Billie ten long years, with the labor of humans now long dead, to build this staircase and corridor. And another ten long years to build living areas down here for his new human companions, and even more years to expand the room at the other end, to surround and contain the Power that was there.

But now it was finished.

And his plan to clear the humans from the surface of the planet almost complete. They had been so easy to manipulate. They had been nothing more than wooden puppets, jerking this way and that when he pulled their strings.

In a few short years, with the humans gone and the other races no longer interested in this ball of dirt orbiting this weak yellow star, he would be able to dig the Power out of its resting place and return it to the stars, where it belonged. Only this time the Power would be his to command.

He moved into the large room and stared at the shining alloy of the Power, curving away from him in two directions. Every time he saw it, shivers ran through his body, causing the human shell that encased his form to loosen.

This time was no exception and he quickly adjusted his "Billie" disguise, then running his hand along the smoothness of the Power's hull, he felt along to his right, enjoying the feel even through the human skin.

Ahead he could see the hatch, the entrance to the Power. Once, far in the distant past of the Galaxy, a race called the Numen had stepped through that hatch and ruled the stars for eons. They were never challenged and their strength never questioned. Their name was now legend in almost every civilization, and they were considered by some to be a race of godlike beings.

But, as the legend went, they became so powerful as to merge and become one with the stars. Soon after this mystical event, they vanished, leaving nothing behind except a few relics.

But every race who traveled the stars knew of them, knew of the material they used in their ships, knew that meeting a member of the Numen would be like meeting one of the Galaxy's gods.

He had never thought of meeting a god, or finding an intact Numen ship. Yet he had done exactly that, discovering a vehicle buried here for eons under tons of rock on this backward little world. And the find had been purely accidental. Even with thousands of alien ships coming and going from this little planet on a regular basis, no one had even noticed the Numen material here until he stumbled across it.

He called it the Power, for power was what the Numen ship, flying among the stars, meant. Power for him and for those who followed him. So, for over thirty cycles of this planet, he had slowly dug out the Power, getting it ready to again fly as it had millions and millions of cycles before the humans ever walked the Earth.

Soon the time would be at hand.

"Billie!"

A human voice echoed through the cavern surrounding the Power and he paused. Sarah and three others were moving toward him, smiling.

He let his hand drop from the side of the Power, then moved toward them. It was time to report in, to act human again, to keep his plan moving until the time when he could kill these stupid creatures and fly the Power into space.

He put on a human smile, then said, "Sure is real good to be back."

They all smiled and greeted him and he acted his part, as he had done for thirty years. For the moment he needed them.

But it was only for the moment.

The image of Zed's face clicked off the screen built into the dashboard of the black LTD. Jay shook his head at what they had just heard from their boss. He was having a hard time grasping all the details of what was happening.

Grazers, it seemed, were landing everywhere, even though Sashanian warships were blowing many of them out of space before they even got near Earth's orbit. They were completely ignoring Zed's retraction of the invitation.

Two dozen other races had tried to land on Earth, but the Sashanians had turned them around, too. But, as Zed had explained, those races were "minor" ones coming from the local area. Thousands of "major" races from the Galaxy's core area

11

were headed this way as well, either one ship at a time or in fleets. And the Sashanians and the rest of the treaty signers would not be able to help stop them.

They wouldn't even try.

Zed figured they had tomorrow at most. Not much longer.

Jay glanced around. They were parked in front of an old office building near the Portland airport. The building had a fresh coat of paint, fresh flowers along the sidewalk, and air conditioners sticking out of the windows, but it was still clearly a very old government office building.

"Not much time left," Elle said, commenting on what Zed had just told them. "We'd better get moving."

Jay nodded. "It's time to take the gloves off, I'd say."

"Agreed," Elle said.

They both climbed out of the LTD into the warm, dry air of the Portland spring evening. Jay put on his sunglasses, took out his flashy-thing, and headed for the door. Inside that building was General Anthony Davis. The general was the very first person Attorney Kathy Rose had called after her meeting with Jay and Elle. In fact, he was the only one she had called.

They needed answers from the general if he was involved in all this, and they needed them fast. Military types were not known for willingly giving information, and Jay and Elle didn't have time to deal with any of their tricks.

Their MO was simple: flashy-thing the general, get the answers they needed, then move on. Jay liked that idea the best.

The inside of the old office building was in sharp contrast to the outside. Instead of wood floors, as Jay would have expected, they stepped onto clean carpet, surrounded by pictures of mountains on the walls, and cool, clean-smelling air. A receptionist sat behind a desk, smiling past a pitcher full of fresh flowers. A fairly new computer filled a corner of the desk beside her.

"May I help you?" she asked sweetly.

"Everyone in this city is so *nice*," Jay said to Elle, gritting his teeth. Then he turned to the receptionist. "We're here to see General Davis."

"Is he expecting you?" she asked, making a motion to flip through an appointment book near her phone.

"No," Elle said.

"Then I'm afraid he won't be able to see you at the moment." The receptionist's smile hadn't shifted a fraction throughout.

"Sure he will," Jay said. He glanced at Elle to make sure she had her sunglasses on, then flashy-thinged the woman.

What Jay called a flashy-thing was actually a Neuralyzer, given to MiB by a friendly alien race. When flashed at a person, it caused them to forget what they had just seen and allowed an MiB agent to plant fresh memories. It could erase years' worth of memories or just minutes', depending on how it was set. This woman was going to have a fine half hour or so this afternoon. Fine but forgettable.

Elle opened her phone and without dialing a number said, "Pro, we got one for you. Receptionist just inside door. Soon to be two or more."

Elle flipped the phone closed and nodded to Jay. He knew Pro and his team would be right behind them to help cover their tracks and give people new, consistent cover memories.

"Let's have a talk with a general," Jay said. "I think we just got an appointment."

"I'd say that," Elle agreed.

Jay led the way down the short hallway beyond the receptionist's desk to a door labeled GENERAL ANTHONY DAVIS. He didn't bother to knock, but went straight on in, moving to the left out of Elle's way.

"Greetings, General," Jay said, not surprised at all to be facing the barrel of a service-issue revolver. The general was still sitting at his desk, the gun resting easily on the blotter in front of him, pointing directly at Jay's stomach. Jay had no doubt that the man knew how to use it.

He was a thin man, with broad shoulders and dried-looking skin. He wore the standard army dress shirt and his jacket and hat hung on the coatrack beside the door.

"Looks like we had an appointment after all," Elle said, moving in and standing beside Jay. "We were clearly expected, that's for sure."

"Now that you've broken into my office," the general said, "I can shoot you at will."

"Maybe," Jay said, smiling at the general. "Maybe not. But why would you want to?"

"To stop you MiB types from giving our world away to the aliens, that's why."

That sentence chilled Jay right down to his toes. It was not at all what he expected the general to say.

"*What?*" Elle asked, also clearly shocked.

"You heard me," the general said.

Clearly this guy was involved in the invitation to the Grazers. He knew too much to leave this conclusion in doubt. And that meant Attorney Rose was also involved. And who knew how many others? But Jay hadn't expected the general to just come right out and admit it like that.

"Mind if I close the door so we can talk?" Jay asked.

The general shrugged. "Go right ahead. Whatever makes you the most comfortable in your final few minutes of life."

"I'm sure getting tired of people telling me I'm about to die," Jay said.

"Yeah, me, too," Elle agreed. "Wears on a person."

Jay reached around and flipped the door closed while at the same time he turned the flashy-thing in his hand so that it was aimed at the general. He flashed it, not caring what length of time it was set for.

For an instant the general froze. Then he shook himself and laughed. "Bet you thought that

Neuralyzer would work, didn't you? Nice move, too."

Jay wasn't sure if his mouth dropped open or what. This general was full of all sorts of surprises.

"Alien, huh?" Elle said to the general. "How'd you get the human construct? What race are you?"

The general laughed. "Oh, I assure you, I'm perfectly human. And I care a great deal more about humanity than you two do, I can tell you that."

Jay eased his finger to the left on the flashy-thing, increasing the intensity of the flash. The guy had shuddered for an instant on the low intensity. Let's see how he did on high.

"Oh, so you destroy us with your love," Elle said, stringing him on. "Sort of sick, don't you think?"

"The Grazers aren't going to destroy Earth. They will simply wake humanity up to the fact that there are aliens out there."

"True," Elle said, "about one day ahead of the thousand other races who are angry at your invitation coming in here and destroying everything."

The general started to laugh again.

Jay flicked up his wrist and flashy-thinged the general again, turning the office into bright, white intense light. This time the guy actually froze.

Jay jumped forward and knocked the gun from the general's hand, then moved to the left as Elle kept him covered with her weapon from the right.

Three seconds later Anthony Davis shook himself and glanced around, getting his bearings. "Again, nicely done."

"Coming from you," Elle said, "it's a compliment I'll treasure forever and ever."

"Uh-oh, General," Jay said, "when she starts a talking like that, you're gettin' her angry, and trust me, ya don't want her angry."

Elle glared at Davis for a moment, then flipped open her phone. "Pro, we have a Neuralyzer resistant one in here. We need full equipment."

"You won't get anything out of me," the general said, glaring at Elle like a second-rate actor in a bad movie.

"Oh, I think we will, General," Jay said, smiling. "I don't know what you've heard about our little group, but we usually get exactly what we need from scum like you, alien or human. Makes no difference to us."

Jay kept the smile on his face and kept staring at the general until the guy finally looked away.

A moment later the door opened and Pro and Partner entered, carrying two briefcases. Jay moved off to one side to give them room, making sure he kept a clear eye on the general at all times.

Within thirty seconds they had Davis hooked up to a headset. The guy wasn't happy about it, but Pro made sure that wasn't an issue by tying the general's hands behind his back and securing him to the chair.

"Okay," Elle said to Partner, "let's find out what makes this guy tick."

Partner flipped a switch and the general's eyes went wide, then after a moment his face softened. It was the weirdest thing Jay had seen in some time. It was as if someone else had moved in and taken over the man's face. A nicer person.

"Amazing," Partner said, staring at the screen in his case. "The guy has been completely brainwashed for thirty years."

"Thirty years?" Jay said. "Are you sure?"

Partner nodded. "Completely. Over thirty, actually. His core personality is only twenty, stunted and boxed up out of the way of the one controlling the general."

Jay shook his head in disbelief. This conspiracy had been going on for thirty years. Why would someone plan all this for so long? And to gain what? None of this was making any sense at all. The more information they uncovered, the more questions they had.

"Will he still remember recent events if you break the control?" Elle asked.

"Mostly," Partner said. "It will all seem like a distant memory. To him it will suddenly be as if he woke up from a long nap and can remember a vivid dream. The memory should get better as time goes on."

"Then get what we can before we break it," Jay said.

"Can't," Partner said. "We prod any more than I already have and the entire thirty-year control snaps like a dried stick."

Jay glanced at Elle and shrugged. "Havin' dreamlike memories is better than nothin'."

Elle nodded, then glanced at Partner. "Do it."

Partner nodded.

The general's face softened even more, years of age seeming to drop away as his expression grew calmer. Finally Partner nodded and flipped a switch. "The brainwashing is completely cleared."

Pro untied the general and stepped back.

Davis blinked, then opened his eyes and looked around.

"You all right?" Jay asked.

The general nodded. "How'd I get here? How'd I get off the mountain?"

Jay looked at Partner.

"He's taking up right where he left off," Partner said. "That's normal."

"Man, that was some weird dream," the general said, his eyes losing focus for a minute. Then he seemed to notice his hands, then his uniform. "Oh, shit," he said softly. "Oh-shit, oh-shit, oh-shit."

Elle knelt beside the general. "When was your last clear memory?"

Davis kept staring at his wrinkled hands as he spoke. "Skiing," he said. "Night skiing. And this weird light came out of the sky and landed near me."

"What year?" Elle asked.

"Nineteen seventy," the general said. He looked at his uniform, then up into Elle's eyes. "Am I really a general?"

Jay was very glad he was standing back at that moment. It wasn't a question he wanted to answer.

"I'm afraid you are," Elle said, both softly and firmly. "Something from that ship brainwashed you and has controlled your every action for the past thirty years."

"Thirty *years*?" Davis repeated. It sounded as if he was about to cry. "All I ever wanted to do was ski. Why would someone do that to me?"

"Clearly they wanted something from you," Elle said, patting the general's shoulder. "But we've freed you now."

"Well," Jay said, moving over so he stood directly across the desk from the seated general, "if we all survive this, you can retire from the army and ski every day for the rest of your life without a money worry in the world. But first things first. We have to survive this. Who brainwashed you? Do you have any idea at all?"

"Billie," the general said softly. "Billie stepped out of those lights and flashed something at me. I remember that clearly. I didn't know his name at the time, but I do now."

"Anyplace in particular we might be able to find this Billie?" Jay asked.

The general nodded. "In a cabin above Otis, out near the coast. It covers an underground facility. We meet there. Billie lives there, I think."

Jay nodded. "Good. Now let's start over and see just how much you can remember about what exactly is going on. Okay by you?"

Davis nodded again. "I'll try."

"Best we can ask for," Jay said. He glanced at Elle. He didn't know exactly what question to start with. Or even how to start, for that matter.

She shrugged. Clearly she didn't know either.

MiB training manuals didn't provide how-to lessons for debriefing someone who had been brainwashed for thirty years. Jay figured it wasn't something MiB ran across an a regular basis. It certainly wasn't something a New York cop encountered.

So he started from the beginning. He asked the general what happened after he met this Billie on the mountain.

"I joined up," the general said. "Never skied again. Went through two tours of Vietnam, worked my way up to a general."

"And when was the second time you saw Billie?" Elle asked.

"Two years ago," the general said. "I took over the office here, sort of an out-of-the-way assignment, off the base, and he showed up three days later. He flashed me with something and told me the time was getting close."

Jay couldn't believe what he had just heard. This Billie person had brainwashed a young kid and then not returned to see what the kid had turned into for over twenty-eight years. Why would anyone do that? For what possible reason?

And how many other people had he done it to?

The last question made Jay shudder.

He had no doubt that there were maybe hundreds of humans out there who were walking time bombs, moles buried in the population by this Billie.

"Close?" Elle asked. "The time for *what* was getting close?"

Davis shook his head slowly. "Makes no sense," he said. "Billie said we were close to humans taking their rightful place among the stars. He brought me into what he called the Earth Expansion League."

"Which is headquartered below this cabin in the mountains?" Elle asked.

"Yes," the general said. "There is an alien ship there, too." He shook his head and looked up at Jay. "Did I dream that ship?"

"Probably not," Jay said. "There really are aliens. What did the ship look like? Can you remember?"

"Oval. Strange glowing gold metal that was warm to the touch. Billie called it the Power."

"And it's underground, too?" Elle asked.

"It was buried there for millions of years," the general said. "Or at least that's what Billie told us. He said it would bring freedom for all mankind." Davis shook his head. "I believed him. How could I believe him?"

"You were brainwashed to believe him," Elle said. "It was out of your control."

"Hang on a second," Pro said. "General, you said something about a ship buried for millions of years?"

"Billie told us that, yes," the general said.

"Did he ever say who made the ship?" Pro asked.

Jay had no idea where Pro was heading with this questioning, but clearly it was important. And when an agent has been with MiB as long as Pro had, he just knew things rookies like Jay and Elle didn't, couldn't, know.

The general shook his head slowly, then said, "Only name I heard attached to the ship was Power. Oh, and Numen."

At the mention of the word "Numen," Pro's face drained of color and he almost staggered back, catching himself on the edge of the general's desk. Now Jay felt like he had seen everything.

"You want to fill the rest of us in on what he's talkin' about?" he asked Pro.

"Please?" Elle said.

The veteran MiB agent shook his head. "I think I better let Zed do that."

Jay glanced at Elle, then at Partner, who just shrugged. Clearly only Pro knew what the general was talking about.

"General," Jay said, "I just have one more question for you."

"Anthony," the general said. "Call me Anthony."

Jay nodded and sat on the edge of the desk. "Are you willing to help us catch this Billie person?"

Davis replied without a moment's hesitation. "Absolutely."

"Even though when we came in here you were going to shoot us because we were MiB agents?"

For a brief moment the general looked puzzled, then shook his head. "I don't even know what an MiB agent is, except that they wear black suits and ties. Billie just told us we had to hate them all." He shrugged. "Sorry."

Jay nodded. "More brainwashing. Come on, sir. We've got a Billie to catch. You've just resigned your commission and are about to take up skiing full-time."

The light that filled the general's eyes was like a kid seeing mounds of presents under the tree on Christmas morning. All Jay could do was smile.

As they walked General Davis out to the car, Pro pulled Elle aside. "You really need to tell Zed about the buried ship at once."

"Planning on it," Elle said, staring at Pro's face. She had been shocked and mystified by his reaction to the general's mentioning the word "Numen." "I was guessing it was important by how you reacted."

"Not sure what will kill us first," Pro said. "The Grazer invitation or the Numen ship—if it *is* a Numen ship. Either way we're doomed."

He shook his head and turned away before she could even ask him what the hell he was talking about.

Elle watched him head toward the containment truck, walking slowly, head

12

down. He looked like a broken man. Not at all like Pro.

Jay helped the general into the backseat and slipped in behind the wheel as Elle slid into the passenger side.

"We may be in bigger trouble than we thought," she said.

Jay laughed. "Bigger than all humanity getting wiped off the face of the planet tomorrow or the next day? This I got to see."

"Wiped out?" the general asked from the backseat, leaning forward so his head was between Jay and Elle. "What's going on? You didn't tell me anything about this."

"Anthony . . ." Jay turned to face the general. "Your ex-friend Billie and the organization you were involved with invited the scum aliens of the universe to a party on our little planet. You remember that?"

The general nodded. "We called them Golgothas, right?"

"Right," Jay said. "We call them Grazers. By inviting them, you pissed off about six billion other aliens, who are going to destroy this planet in a few days if we don't stop them. You help us find Billie and the rest and save the planet and I can guarantee you all-expenses-paid skiing vacations for the rest of your life."

The general swallowed and nodded. "I'll do what I can."

"Good," Elle said. "For the moment we need to

contact our boss. So sit back and relax for a minute."

General Davis did as he was told and Elle punched up the communications link with Zed. It took a little longer than normal, but finally his image appeared. He looked harried and grouchy. He was standing behind his desk and Jay could see the Immigration Center behind him. It was in a state of total chaos.

Jay quickly filled him in on the general's brainwashing and explained about the underground facility in the mountains—at least what he knew about it.

"Go get 'em," Zed said, then glanced down at his desk at something. "We had a report of a shielded Phillida ship landing and taking off in that area a few hours ago. My guess is your Billie is back from his trip to Saturn. Chances are he's an alien. Get me proof of the existence of this conspiracy and I'll present it to the treaty signers. Never know what might happen."

"Zed," Elle said before the boss broke the connection. "There's one thing we haven't told you yet, but Pro says is very important."

"Go on," Zed told her, clearly slightly annoyed.

"There's an alien ship in the mountain hideaway. The general says that Billie and the others call it the Power."

Elle watched to see if Zed had a reaction. He didn't.

"They also said it might be a Numen ship."

Now Zed had a reaction.

And an instant one.

He snapped his finger down on a button on his desk and the connection was cut.

Elle glanced at Jay.

"What was that?" Jay asked.

"Not a clue," Elle said. And although she really didn't have a clue, she had a sneaking hunch she and Jay had just stumbled onto something big.

Suddenly Zed's face again filled the communication panel between her and Jay in the dashboard. "We're on a secure link now," he said. "And my office is secure."

"Understood," Jay said.

Sweat was running down the sides of Zed's face and was beaded on his forehead and he looked as if he was on the verge of a heart attack. Given his size and shape, that could easily be the case. Elle had no idea what would cause their boss to have such a reaction.

"Pro had that same reaction," she said. "You want to fill us in on this?"

"Or at least send us the manual?" Jay said.

"You two never heard of the Numens or their ships?" Zed shook his head in amazement. "We got to train our new agents better, I can see that now."

"Numens?" Jay asked.

Zed snorted. "There hasn't been a Numen alive in millions of years—at least that anyone knows about."

"Wiped out like we're about to be, huh?" Jay asked.

Zed frowned. "Not hardly. Numen civilization

controlled the entire Galaxy for millions of years. They were the most powerful civilization to ever exist. They were called gods. Then one day they just vanished."

"Oh, shit," Elle said. "And one of their ships is sitting under a mountain here."

"If that *is* a Numen ship," Zed answered. "We're more than screwed if anyone else knows it's there. Every race will fight to get it."

Suddenly Jay understood. Forget the minor problem of a giant alien party. Try a giant alien *war*.

Zed seemed to be staring off into space. In the year Jay and Elle had been a team, working for MiB, he had never seen Zed hesitate about making a decision. Now he was taking long seconds.

Very long seconds.

Finally the boss looked back at them. The firm, in-control Zed was back in his eyes. "From this moment on, the word 'Numen' is not to be mentioned until I give the all clear. Understand?"

"Gotcha, boss," Jay answered for both himself and Elle.

"Make sure Pro and the team know this, too. Only the six of us will know of this inside MiB. Understand?"

"Yes," Elle said.

"I'm sending in every bit of help I can find," Zed continued. "I want that ship under our control as soon as possible. I don't care what it takes. Understood?"

"Got it," Jay said.

"Clearly we're dealing with some alien here who knows exactly what he's got in his possession," Zed said. "And wants us out of the way so he can use it. So be careful. He might be ready for you. He only has to hold out another day or so and we're no longer factors."

"We'll get the ship, boss," Jay said.

"Call me when you do," Zed said, and snapped off the connection.

Jay glanced at General Davis, who was sitting in the backseat, looking extremely pale, then at Elle. "Sometimes not knowing shit is just flat better, ain't it?"

She nodded. "I'm starting to believe ignorance is truly bliss."

"Well, Anthony, my friend." Jay turned to face the general. "Think you can take us to this ship?"

Davis nodded. "Not a problem."

Elle opened her door. "I'll fill the guys in about Zed's orders, and make sure they leave a good cover story for the general being gone. We don't want anyone tipped off too early that we're coming."

"I have a sneaking hunch," Jay said, "this alien has been expecting us . . . for thirty years."

It had taken them just over an hour, with Jay driv-ing the black LTD as fast as he could on the crowded two-lane roads, across Portland and up into the coastal mountains toward the ocean. They had sped through at least a half-dozen small towns, many with Indian names, and now they were on a fairly well-traveled road that worked its way down a large, winding stream. Jay was managing to keep a speed of between eighty and a hundred miles an hour. Next stop, the signs said, was the ocean. But General Davis had said Otis, Oregon, and the location of the buried spaceship was less far away than that, just at the point where they emerged from these mountains.

On the screen Elle had the locations of three MiB helicopters and six more contain-

13

ment teams besides Pro's coming in from different directions. But Jay could tell they were clearly going to be the first on the scene by a good fifteen minutes.

On the way they had quizzed Anthony about what he remembered of the security surrounding the ship. He had managed to recall the code for the security system, which was, he said, hidden in the bathroom. And he said that as far as he knew, there were no cameras surveiling that area. At least he had never seen any below in the living area. He told them there just wasn't much else down there beside the small living area and the ship.

Jay listened but had a hard time believing there wouldn't be surveillance cameras and other high-tech apparatuses to get past.

Just to be sure, he and Elle had decided that they would approach the site in a different car from the LTD. Better and safer to take what precautions they could easily take.

"Rest area coming up," Jay announced. "Pro still behind us."

"Less than a minute," Elle said.

"He did some good driving, then," Jay said, laughing as he swung the LTD off the road and into the parking lot of the rest area. It was a beautiful spot, alongside the stream. Towering old pine trees blocked what little light was left of the day, giving the picnic tables and rest room an almost creepy look.

Jay noticed two other cars in the rest area. One was a pickup that belonged to a guy taking apart a fishing rod, the other a Cadillac containing two elderly passengers.

"Any of your people own a pickup?" Jay asked Anthony.

"Two of them drive pickups."

"Perfect," Elle said as Jay stopped beside the guy with the fishing rod.

Elle got out and flashed her badge. "FBI. We need your truck."

The guy looked to be around sixty, with a soft white hat full of hooks and flies. "You can't just go taking a man's truck!"

Elle flipped on her sunglasses and Neuralyzed the guy. "Sorry," she said to the fisherman as Jay climbed out and flipped open the trunk of the LTD. "No time to talk."

As Jay loaded guns and equipment into the back of the truck, Elle walked over to the Cadillac and did the same number to the two scared-looking elderly people as she had done to the fisherman.

Anthony climbed out, shaking his head at the sight of the zombie fisherman standing there. "You people really know how to get what you want."

"With other humans," Jay said. "But with aliens, we aren't worth shit."

"Good point," Elle said, moving the fisherman out of the way and making sure his keys were in the ignition. Then she went to help Jay load weapons into the back of the truck.

At that moment Pro and the containment truck skidded to a stop beside them.

"Borrowing his truck." Elle pointed to the guy.

"Two witnesses need new memories in the Cadillac."

"Got it," Pro said, motioning for Partner to take care of the fisherman and Captain to take care of the old folks. "What's the plan?"

"Anthony here is driving the truck up to the ship site," Jay said. "Then we're going in. You hang back and we'll be in touch. If we haven't contacted you in thirty minutes from the moment we get inside, come in with everything blazing. Until then stay back and out of sight."

"Got it," Pro said.

"And bring the LTD up closer," Elle said. "We might need it quickly."

Pro nodded. "See you inside."

"Ready, Anthony?" Elle asked, patting the general on the back. She gave him a little shove toward the cab.

He nodded like a scared kid. "I think so."

"Good," she said, smiling at him. "Drive carefully."

Elle climbed over into the back of the pickup while General Davis jumped in from the other side. Besides their weapons and supplies, the bed was covered in a thin layer of dirt and had three fishing poles strapped to one side.

"No seat belts back here," Jay said, dropping down so his back was against the cab.

Elle joined him.

The bed of the truck felt hard under his thin pants. Even with only a few miles remaining, this wasn't going to be a comfortable ride by any means. In all his life he had never ridden in the back of a truck. He wasn't especially excited about having the experience now.

Anthony managed not to get hit by another car as he pulled out onto the highway and then accelerated, running the loud pickup engine through the gears. The wind whipped around them, cold and very intense, like a winter's day on Broadway. The wind could really blow in those canyons between the buildings and right now Jay wished he were back there instead of in this truck. He glanced over at Elle. She seemed to be trying to hold herself off the bed of the truck with her hands.

"Ain't this fun," Jay shouted over the noise, smiling as the trees flashed past.

"Sure is," she said. Jay could barely hear her answer over the wind and engine.

After what seemed like an eternity, but was actually only a few minutes, Anthony slowed down and turned off the highway.

Instantly both Jay and Elle lay flat, facedown on the bed of the truck, ready to move at a moment's notice. Elle kept her hands under her to ease some of the shocks and bumps as the truck bounced up the gravel road. Jay just let it ride, ignoring the bumps.

Dust swirled around behind them, some of it settling into the bed. Elle coughed once, then stayed silent.

All Jay could see above the edge of the truck bed were pine trees whizzing past, sometimes turning into a dark green blur as Anthony gained speed, other times becoming individual trees as he jarred down through a creek bottom or around a sharp corner.

He kept watching the trees, trying to spot any cameras looking down on them, but he didn't see anything. And he was sure if Elle had noticed any, she would have pointed it out to him.

Finally Anthony stopped the truck and shut off the engine. Grabbing the Phaser rifle he called Beauty and making sure his Atomizer was in his belt, Jay rolled over one side of the truck and out onto the ground, rifle up and ready to fire.

Elle went out the other side, in much the same manner.

Anthony slowly climbed out of the cab, also looking around.

Nothing that Jay could see moved. The place was quiet. In the distance there was the faint sound of a running stream or river, but nothing else. And the shack looked almost abandoned.

Anthony moved toward the front door of the shack and both Jay and Elle followed, keeping him covered.

Inside, the place had a lived-in appearance, but it was all phony to a trained eye, like the props of a play. No one lived here, that was for sure.

"Staged," Jay said, pointing at the plates.

Elle nodded and pointed to the bathroom, gesturing for Anthony to lead the way. She went with him while Jay stayed in a cover position so he could watch the one dirt-covered window and the front door. He alternated between doing cover duty and

watching what was happening in the small bathroom.

Anthony opened the old medicine cabinet, then
opened the back to it, exposing an electronic panel.
He glanced at Elle and she nodded.

Slowly, carefully, he keyed in the code.

Then closed the panel.

The instant he finished, a section of the wall slid
open beside the old toilet.

"We're in," Elle whispered to Jay. Jay knew Pro
was also listening to every word they said.

She pulled Anthony back out of the way.
"Thanks," she whispered, pushing him toward the
front door.

"Good luck," he said.

Then Jay watched as Anthony headed back out
to take the truck the rest of the way down the highway to the coast to a prearranged meeting spot
with Pro.

Jay went past Elle and into the wall first, rifle at
ready.

Elle was right behind him.

Then the wall slid closed silently, locking them
in.

A modern-looking flight of stairs led downward
as far as he could see. Lights were spaced evenly
down the walls, but there didn't seem to be anything else. Jay knew without a doubt that if they
were attacked in here, they wouldn't stand a chance
in hell of winning. He didn't like this.

Not one bit.

Elle quickly put on a mask that allowed her to

see any laser trip beams or hidden light sources. After a moment she took it off and shook her head. "Looks clear."

Jay moved down quickly, as silently as he could go. His police training took over in situations like this. MiB did some building-entry training, but nowhere near as much as he had had with New York City police.

Elle followed, checking their backs.

Nothing moved.

Nothing came at them.

He couldn't believe there wasn't a security system in here. But so far there didn't seem to be anything. Maybe, just maybe, this Billie person didn't think he needed much more than the phony shack and the lock in the bathroom.

Maybe he didn't think anyone could ever break one of his people.

Maybe.

Maybe.

Maybe.

Too many chances, too many questions.

And absolutely no choices.

Down they went into the mountain.

Quickly.

One silent step at a time.

Billie sat on the couch, his human feet up on the coffee table, in the living area of the underground living quarters he'd had built next to the ship. The human Sarah and three others sat with him, making what they called "small talk" about nothing important. Always boring.

Actually Billie didn't much care. In just a short time they would all be gone, he'd be rid of this human construct he'd been wearing for years, and at last he could be alone with the Power.

"I can't believe the plan is working," Sarah said after a moment of silence. She was, at the moment, sitting in a large, overstuffed armchair, a cup of tea in her hand.

The human beside her, a woman named Bright, laughed. "Isn't it great!"

14

Bright was the youngest of his current human helpers. Billie had seen her walking on a beach down in California ten years before and recruited her, as he had many, many humans over the years. He just never knew when one of his recruits might come in handy in one fashion or another. He had directed and kept track of them all.

Many had ended up serving him in one fashion or another. Many had worn out their usefulness. But since he had recruited hundreds over the years, there was always another to take their place.

Two years ago Bright had become very important among the humans working on computers. Although an expert as far as human technological resources went, she had barely enough knowledge to help him. He'd brought her here to see if she could understand the computers of the Power. So far they had made great headway. For a human, she was very smart.

Across from Bright was the oldest of his current recruits, an electrical mechanic named Charles who had spent the last six years helping him study the many circuits and controls of the Power. Both Charles and Bright thought they were going to take all the knowledge and great devices they had discovered and share them with the rest of their species. Little did they know their species would shortly cease to exist.

The thought made Billie so happy, he almost started laughing again, which wouldn't have been good if his human-construct skin came loose.

"Soon," Billie said, "this here place will be the most famous place in the *en*-tire world."

Sarah laughed. "It is hard to believe."

Sarah helped Billie in just about all phases of his operations, and pretended to be in charge of the so-called Earth Expansion League along with General Davis, a pawn Billie had used to make the humans believe that high-level officials in the government were behind the organization.

In reality, there *was* no Earth Expansion League; all there was, was a bunch of puppets recruited to play parts and make the alleged meetings look bigger and better attended.

Now all Billie needed the three humans around him for was to get the Power started after the rest of humanity was gone. Once the ship was going, Billie wasn't even going to need Sarah and Bright and Charles to fly it.

He would then have everything he needed.

A faint chime filled the room. Sarah picked up what the humans called a phone from the table. Only a handful of his human people knew this number.

She listened for a moment, then said, "Better warn General Davis." There was a pause, then Sarah said, "Good. Thanks for telling us."

She hung up the phone and looked around. "MiB agents were in Portland this afternoon asking questions at Derek's law firm."

"They didn't learn nothing?" Billie asked.

"Nothing," Sarah confirmed. "And Kathy warned General Davis. He's making himself unavailable."

Billie smiled and sat back. He had known the MiB agents would track Derek to Portland fairly quickly. But even with that they were too late. Far too late. They had been too late the moment Derek transmitted his message. Suddenly Sarah let out a gasp.

"Sorry to interrupt the party," a voice said from behind where Billie sat.

He jumped up and spun around. Two MiB agents stood, Phaser rifles leveled at them.

"Not possible!" he snarled in his native language.

One of the MiB agents laughed. "Seems we know for sure which one is the alien here."

The MiB agent swung his rifle slightly and the next thing Billie knew the human had fired, not even giving him an instant to move.

The blast sent him smashing back against the wall, almost knocking him out, but not quite.

The pain filled his entire body.

Over him his human construct began to melt away like so much putty, dripping down onto the floor.

Sarah screamed.

"Stupid humans," Billie snarled, the human words splattering off his liquefying human lips.

"Not as stupid as you look right now," one MiB agent said. Then he fired again and the world around Billie went black.

They had made it down the long flight of stairs without a problem and past the gold ship without so much as giving it a second look, except to check to see if anyone was inside.

It seemed empty.

At that point, as far as Jay was concerned, their first priority was to get to whoever was down here, get them under control, and find the Billie person Anthony had told them about. Later they would have time to deal more directly with this possible ship of the gods.

Voices had led them directly to what looked like a small living room, with a television, a couch, five or six chairs, and a small kitchen off to one side. Four doors led off the other side of the living area, all closed. The faint smell of steak still filled

15

the air from their dinner, but no dishes were in sight.

Everything seemed exactly as Anthony had said it would be.

Two women and two men were in the room as Jay and Elle stepped into the doorway, Phaser rifles ready.

"Surprise!" Jay said.

All four seemed to move at once, three diving for cover. Only Billie reached for a gun.

Jay didn't want to hurt the brainwashed humans if he could help it, but he would if he had to. What he and Elle were after was Billie. And he was easy to spot, golf cap and all.

Billie drew what looked to be a normal Earth pistol and Jay hit him solidly in the chest with a blast of his Phaser rifle, smashing him back against the wall.

"Don't move!" Elle shouted.

The other three froze like statues, staring at Jay and Elle as if they were the most hated criminals in the world.

"On the couch!" Elle said, motioning them to move as Jay quickly searched each of them. Nothing. Only Billie had been armed.

After thirty seconds, all three were sitting together on the couch, looking stunned. They kept staring at the remains of what had once been Billie.

Jay quickly checked the four doors that led into nothing but small, cold bedrooms, then came back into the living area. The place was clearly not meant to hold too many people. Their three prisoners were the only ones down here.

"Remember this race?" Jay asked Elle, pointing at the smoking remains of the alien called Billie. His human construct had mostly melted under the Phaser rifle blast. His golf cap had been knocked off and was currently filled with false human flesh. Jay had never seen anything like it.

"He's—was a Florian, I think," Elle said, covering their human prisoners while glancing at the alien. "Real scum."

"Pro," Jay called into the air, "can you hear me?"

"Every word," Pro's voice came back in his ear.

"Get the area sealed and get your team down here fast. We're going to need some help. Three possible humans, more than likely Neuralyzer resistant. One dead alien. Bring only your team and the general."

"All others stay on the perimeter as per Zed's orders," Elle added. "Anyone other than one of us comes out, they have orders to shoot first and ask questions later. We want this site completely contained. Only secured transmissions allowed from this moment forward."

"Understood," Pro said. "On the way."

Jay nodded to Elle, then sat down on the chair beside the youngest woman. She was good-looking in a nerdy sort of way. She looked like the type that sat for hours at a computer without moving. "What's your name?"

She shook her head, clamping her teeth on her lip.

"We're the bad guys to them," Elle said. "Remember? They're not going to talk."

Jay shrugged. "True. But I bet they didn't know old Billie there was an alien."

All of the prisoners' gazes immediately went back to the now somewhat smelly remains of the alien. It was becoming clear as the human skin finished melting off that his normal skin color was a faint green, and that he had four eyes on stalks. All four were looking blank at the moment. Actually they would be permanently blank.

"Sorry I had to kill him," Jay said after a moment of watching the prisoners stare at the alien. "But he was trying to destroy all of the human race and that sort of pisses me off."

Elle laughed. "You were lucky you got off the first shot. I wanted to kill him."

"Just faster on the trigger," Jay said. Then laughed.

The older woman started to say something angry, then obviously changed her mind.

"Like aliens with four eyes, huh?" Jay asked her.

He watched the hatred in the older woman's eyes turn on him as her face became red. But she remained silent.

At that moment Pro and Partner entered the room, carrying equipment. Anthony, who was accompanying them, stopped cold at the sight of Billie. Then he dropped silently into a chair, his face white with shock.

Captain stopped and took up a guard position in the door.

Pro did a quick scan of the three prisoners with a handheld device, then nodded to Jay.

"Good news," Jay said to the three on the couch. "You're all human."

They all shifted from side to side at hearing that news, glancing at the remains of the alien as they did, then staring with hatred at Anthony.

Pro pointed to the melted form of Billie. "A Florian. Not allowed here. Mostly known for petty thievery and murder. Not a well-liked culture by any of the races."

"Think that's going to help Zed convince the Galaxy to stay away?" Jay asked. At this point he was grasping at straws.

Pro shrugged. "Couldn't hurt."

Elle nodded. "I'll report to him." She picked up their secure link computer from her pack and told Captain to take up watching the prisoners. Then she went out to the area that contained the ship to talk to Zed in private.

Partner set up the equipment quickly on the kitchen table, then put the older woman in the brain-scan device first. Jay thought for a moment they were going to have to stun her to get her to move, but finally she allowed Pro to put the headset on her.

"She's been under the alien's control for over twenty years," Partner said after a moment, shaking his head.

"Under the alien's control?" the young woman on the couch asked. "What are you talking about?"

Partner shook his head no to Jay. Clearly Jay wasn't supposed to answer this question for some reason, so he just shrugged and smiled at the woman.

"You'll understand in a minute," Anthony told her.

The young woman only glared at him.

"Break the brainwash," Jay said. They were going to have to break the alien's mind locks on all three of these poor people. But Jay hoped they remembered enough afterward to provide some help.

The gray-haired woman strained for a moment, then sagged in her chair, her face seeming to grow younger, just as the general's had. Partner nodded and took off the helmet. The woman looked around for a moment. "Where am I? This is a dream, right?"

"We'll explain everything to everyone in a minute," Partner said.

"This way," Jay said, helping her stand and move over to a chair.

"What did you do to her?" the young woman demanded.

The older woman stopped and looked at the younger one. "Trust them, Bright," the older woman said. Then she let Jay help her sit down in the chair. She sat there for a moment, then broke into tears, crying softly. Anthony reached over and put his hand on her arm, comforting her.

Jay put his hand on her shoulder gently. What

could he say to people who had just realized that over twenty years of their lives had been stolen from them. There was really nothing to say. He just let his hand rest on her shoulder, let her know someone was there for her, at least for the moment.

Captain forced the young woman into Partner's headset next. Her mind control seemed to break more easily.

"She was only controlled for about ten years," Partner said.

"I was on the beach," Bright said. "This light came out of the sky over the waves."

Jay couldn't believe how young and alive Bright now looked. The anger was gone. The years of trained hatred melted away. Too bad more of the hatred in the world couldn't be deprogrammed like that.

Jay moved across the room and helped Partner stand Bright up and get her to a chair beside the older woman.

"My turn?" the man asked.

"It is," Captain said, keeping the gun leveled on him.

"I gather that alien was controlling all of us," he said, "and you're clearing out the control. Right?"

"Quickly," Partner said, shoving the man down into the chair and putting the helmet on him. Then without even taking time to set the machine, he flipped the switch.

As with the women, the guy's face became younger.

Partner looked relieved. "Why the hurry?" Jay asked.

"MiB was programmed in very firmly in all of them to be the enemy," Partner said. "Having him think of us in any other way might have caused brain damage."

"Got it," Jay said. Now he understood why Partner didn't want him talking to the young woman about what was going on. "Is he all right?"

"He's fine," Partner said.

At that moment Elle came back into the room. "Zed thinks the information about the Florian might help a little," she said. "He's going to try."

"Good," Jay said. Then he turned back to Partner. "And what do we need to do now?"

"For them?" he asked, pointing at the prisoners. "Nothing but help them regain their memories."

"Orders from Zed?" Jay asked Elle.

"Keep this bottled up tight and wait for his orders."

"Perfect," Jay said. They were stuck down here doing nothing while above them the entire human race was going to be destroyed. There had to be something they could do. He just didn't know what. But maybe the three they had just saved might suggest an idea.

He turned to Partner. "No problem talking to them now? No possible damage?"

"All yours," Partner said.

"Let me," Elle said.

Jay nodded and sat on the edge of the couch, the Phaser rifle resting across his leg.

"First off," Elle said, "some names. I'm Agent Elle of the Men in Black Special Forces. That's Agent Jay."

Jay bowed slightly and smiled.

"Containment Agents Pro, Captain, and Partner," she said, going around the room. Then she turned to the younger woman. "What are your names?"

"Bright Wilson," the younger woman said.

"Charles Benson," the man said.

"Sarah Wallace," the older woman said.

"Anthony Davis," the general said, joining in.

"Good," Elle said. "We'll get more information later, but first a little history. That all right with all of you?"

"Please," Sarah said. "Anything to explain what happened to me."

"From what we have put together so far," Elle said, "that dead alien there, a member of the Florian race, somehow discovered that ship out there and decided he wanted it all for his own. It might be a very, very special ship."

"The problem was," Jay said, "humans, MiB Special Forces, and hundreds of other alien races were already here on this planet."

"Exactly," Elle said. "He had to get rid of humanity and the other alien races before he dared try to take that ship away from here. And he needed help to do that."

Elle went on to give them a quick overview of Billie's plan as they had figured it out so far.

Jay watched the growing shock on the faces of the three prisoners as they listened to her words.

"So basically," Elle finished, "the alien races headed this way will destroy Earth in a matter of days."

Sarah looked as if she might be sick.

"All to steal a buried old spaceship?" Charles asked. "He'd kill every human for *that*?"

"He would," Elle said.

"I'm afraid if those aliens that are headed here because of the Grazer invitation, if they learn about that ship out there," Pro said, "humanity will also perish very, very shortly. That ship, if it is what we think it might be, is that special."

Jay laughed. "Yeah, we came here to see if we could find a way to help stop the destruction of Earth and discovered a second reason why we should all be dead."

"I don't find that very funny, Mr. Jay," Sarah said.

"It's not," Elle said. "He just tends to laugh when the going gets really bad."

"Ya ought ta hear my jokes when I'm 'bout ready ta die."

Elle just shook her head. "You're not helping, Agent Jay."

"Sorry," Jay said. He glanced around at the four they had just rescued. He couldn't imagine what they were feeling right now. The last clear memory they had was of events that had occurred decades ago, yet it must seem to them as if only moments had passed. The last several years seemed, as they said, like a long, vivid dream.

"We need to ask you all some questions," Elle told them softly.

All three nodded.

"First off, do any other humans outside of this place, besides the attorney Rose, know about this ship?"

Sarah slowly shook her head. "She's the only one. There were a lot more members of the Earth Expansion League, but none of them knew about this place."

"Good," Elle said. "What were you doing on the ship?"

"Trying to get it ready to fly," Charles said.

"I was working on the computer guidance systems," Bright said.

"What?" Jay asked, actually standing.

Pro also jumped to his feet. "Billie planned to fly that thing out of here?"

Charles nodded.

Jay couldn't believe such a thing was possible. But if it was, it just might change a few things.

"I think so," Bright agreed.

Jay looked at Elle, who was looking at him with a light in her eyes.

"You two aren't thinking what I think you're thinking?" Pro said.

"If the Florian could fly the thing, why couldn't we?" Jay asked.

Pro just shook his head. "I know you never got to read the special manual about the race that owned that ship. You might want to check it out before you do anything hasty."

"He's right, Jay," Elle said. "We don't have enough information."

Jay pointed at the helmet they had just used to clear the brainwashing of their three prisoners. "That work for a quick absorption session?"

Partner nodded. "I could download the basic information about the Numen race for you."

"I'm game," Jay said, sitting down. He still hated this way of learning, but right now he had no choice. There was no time and no library of manuals nearby. It was either "absorption" or not very blissful ignorance.

Partner glanced at Pro, who nodded.

Partner quickly adjusted the helmet and fit it on his head. "Ready?"

"Fire away," Jay said, smiling at Bright. "A little more knowledge won't hurt anyone."

Pro laughed. "You may come to regret those words."

Very quickly Jay did.

Beach-Grass-In-Limbo, commander of the moon base and the great Sashanian fleet in this area of space, used two of his many tentacles to pull himself closer to the viewscreen.

He did a quick summary scan of the dealings in nearby space, his three eye stalks moving as a unit at times, at other times working apart.

The data he gathered was not good for anyone concerned with the salvation of the humans.

So far his ships had kept many of the weaker and more worthless races from breaking the treaty with the race of the Soon-To-Be-Dead. And his ship's captains were taking great sensory pleasure destroying the ships of Those-Who-Eat-And-Are-Worthless. No great fleet had yet threat-

16

ened, but the coming would be soon, from all he could see with his eye stalks.

And now the Human-Who-Called-Himself-Zed wanted to communicate with him again. He said it was urgent, but to a member of the race of the Soon-To-Be-Dead, everything was urgent.

And understandably so.

At that moment another ship of Those-Who-Eat-And-Are-Worthless was destroyed outside the orbit of the ringed planet. Beach-Grass-In-Limbo watched the ship's captain's obvious relish as he came in for the kill.

It gave the commander pleasure to have his captains experience pleasure. In honor of that pleasure, the commander owed the Human-Who-Called-Himself-Zed another audience.

He flicked on the viewscreen. "Proceed."

The human bared his eating teeth in a gesture known as a greeting by humans. Strange race, humans. He was going to miss commanding this post when they were gone.

"We have discovered," the human said, "that it was a Florian who deceived the great races of the Galaxy and invited Those-Who-Eat-And-Are-Worthless to our planet."

Beach-Grass-In-Limbo prided himself on his ability to remain calm under pressure. But the human's words sent his tentacles into fits of jerking and twisting. He had had dealings with the Florian world. They were called by his people Those-Who-Rob-And-Cheat.

"The Florian is now dead," the human reported

in his growling manner. "His motive was to trick the great races of the Galaxy into destroying humans, then take our planet for profit. The great races of the Galaxy should not be controlled by a Florian only interested in profit."

"There is no other motive for Those-Who-Rob-And-Cheat," the commander replied. But silently he marveled at how resourceful this human was. He had learned much of the ways of the Galaxy very quickly.

"Does this information help, O great friend of humans?" the human growled.

The commander forced his tentacles to calm, then focused his eye stalks on the human. "I will form a message and send it with this information. It will cause a few, maybe many of the races who do not like being tricked by Those-Who-Rob-And-Cheat, to turn back and return to their home planets. But not all."

"We will still be destroyed?" the human questioned with a higher-pitched growl.

The commander pulsed his three eye stalks in a motion of sympathy to the human. "Of course. But my race will do what it can. We are not fond of Those-Who-Rob-And-Cheat. We do not enjoy the treaty being broken by one of their kind. We will do what we can."

"Thank you, great friend of the treaty," the human growled.

The connection was cut and the Sashanian commander pushed himself away from the communication panel. Quickly he composed a message. Then put his personal Note-Of-Purpose on it to put extra pressure on those who knew of his position and his great power.

More races would turn back when they got the message. Many would turn and attack the Florians for pleasure. The destruction of the planet under his care would be slowed slightly. But not postponed.

Even with this knowledge, and despite their enjoyment of destroying Those-Who-Eat-And-Are-Worthless, the mighty Sashanian fleet and the fleets of other treaty signers would still not fight for the Earth.

The humans were just not worth losing a ship over.

Beach-Grass-In-Limbo put his three eye stalks together in a gesture of deep compassion for the humans. Besides sending the message, it was all he could do.

Jay hated having facts jammed into his head like ground meat being stuffed into a sausage sleeve. He'd much rather take the knowledge in slowly, one hard-learned fact at a time. But at the moment comfortable reading was a luxury he couldn't afford.

He glanced around the living area at the others. Bright, Anthony, Charles, and Sarah all sat quietly, watching with puzzled and sometimes confused expressions on their faces. After what the four of them had been through the last few hours, after all the years of brainwashing they had endured, Jay understood their puzzlement. He wasn't far behind them on that score.

"Scramble away," Jay said to Partner as the agent flipped the switch that started the absorption process.

17

Instantly the images of a beautiful and powerful people filled his mind, seemingly all at once.

Numen.

Tall and thin, with two arms and long, flowing robes, they seem to float as they move through beautiful, tall-spired cities made of glass, their faces hidden by the hoods of their long and flowing robes. Their faces are no longer remembered.

Only their myth.

Facts: They ruled all of space in the Galaxy with a soft hand and powerful, golden ships. Those ships could destroy an entire planet if the Numen were pushed. No race ever pushed them.

They ruled for millions of years, almost as gods. They were seldom seen and no one ever questioned their authority when they spoke.

Then, almost overnight in the Galaxy scheme of things, they vanished from their home, leaving the races they ruled in a dark age of war and confusion. Fighting filled the Galaxy. Fighting that continues to this day. No one knows for certain what happened to those early gods of the Galaxy. Many believe they still exist on another plane.

Many believe they are still among the stars.

Rumors of their appearance are reported all the time.

Very little of their world survived their disappearance. No ship was left intact. Races are willing to go to war to acquire even the smallest bit of Numen technology.

Jay took off the helmet and glanced at Elle. "We're screwed."

Pro only nodded. "We are for sure, if anyone ever finds out that that ship is here—if it *is* one of their ships."

"How will we know?" Elle asked. "Wait, I need to get that same information."

Jay stood and handed her the helmet.

She put it on and nodded to Partner, her eyes closed. Thirty seconds later she took it off and looked at Jay. "Amazing."

Jay nodded. "Hard to imagine beautiful aliens, isn't it? I'll bet they even smelled good."

Elle didn't even smile. Her eyes looked distant, still lost in the information she had just been fed.

Jay glanced around at the four people they had rescued. "What did Billie the alien call that ship?"

"The Power," Bright said. "Everyone just called it the Power."

The others nodded. "The race that built it were called Numen," Charles said.

"At least that was what the general told us," Sarah added.

"The general?" Elle asked, glancing at Partner, then at Anthony.

"Just a false command structure," Anthony said, shrugging as if it didn't much matter. "Billie was the one who recruited me. He fed me the information I was supposed to know. Of course, I didn't realize it was coming from him at the time." The general shook his head. "Weird what the mind can believe, isn't it?"

The three other prisoners nodded, lost in memories.

Jay completely agreed. He still had a very clear memory of his first visit to the Immigration Center in MiB and his meeting with the three Vermars who loved their cigarettes and coffee.

"So Pro," Elle asked, "you have any idea how to tell if that really is one of *their* ships sitting out there?"

"Let's go take a look at it," Pro said.

"How about we all go?" Jay suggested, glancing around at the others. "You folks have been workin' on the ship for years. Help us out with whatever you can remember."

"It's all fuzzy," Charles said. "But I'll try."

"Like a bad dream," Bright said.

Elle waited with Jay until everyone had filed out toward the ship, then she asked him, "What exactly are you thinking here?"

"Honestly," he said, "I don't know. We're stuck inside a mountain with an alien ship while all of humanity gets its ass destroyed because of a small-time crook tryin' ta cop a ship. I'm just tryin' ta do something. Anything."

She smiled. "Then let's go do it."

"What?" he asked. "The *something* part? Or the *anything* part?"

"Both," she said, "sound good to me."

The inside of the main cabin of the ship was round and actually bigger than the living-room area of the sleeping quarters. Captain stayed outside on guard duty near the ship while the rest of them went inside.

Jay was struck by the sleek "clean" lines of the

ship's design. Its structure and details were all smooth, curving, simple yet elegant. The walls and floor seemed to be made of the same, golden-tinted substance. Eight different panels with built-in chairs in front of them were spaced evenly around the circular space. It was almost exactly the opposite of the Grazer ship they had entered in Central Park. This one was light, smelled good, and everything seemed perfectly in order, even after being buried underground for a million years.

Bright stood behind one chair, her hands on the back of its soft leatherlike upholstery. "Billie always sat here when we worked," she said.

She pointed to the next chair over. "I sat there, where I could work on the computers."

"This ship has power?" Pro asked, glancing around, seeming to notice for the first time that the light was emanating from inside the ceiling; the fixtures were built in instead of being strung in from outside.

"Sure does," Charles said. He moved over to another chair and touched a spot on the panel. Every panel around the room lit up with soft lights and odd symbols.

Jay damn near jumped out of his skin. In all his life he had never been so thoroughly creeped out before. And why turning on the power to a long-dead ship would do that to him, he had no idea. But it sure did.

"Impressive, isn't it?" Anthony asked, his voice breaking the hushed air. "First time I came in here with the power up, I remember feeling like I was walking into a sacred church."

"Many races of the Galaxy would agree with that assessment," Pro said softly, looking around.

"Let's just make sure they don't all come here to worship," Jay said. The last thing he wanted to happen was that Zed and the MiB forces would succeed in saving the planet from the Grazer invasion only to have him and Elle destroy everything by their discovery of this ship.

Partner moved over beside Bright and just stared at the panel where she had worked on the computers, his mouth open.

The silence in the ship gave Jay goose bumps. He rubbed his arm through his suit jacket to get rid of the feeling. It didn't go away easily.

Jay glanced at Elle. She was looking as creeped out as he was feeling. There was clearly something uncanny about this ship.

"So Billie-the-alien thought he could fly this thing, huh?" Jay asked, moving over and forcing himself to sit down in the chair Billie sat in.

Amazingly, it felt comfortable to his body, as if it quickly molded to fit him perfectly.

"He said it would fly itself once we had the engines on-line," Charles said. "I remember that much clearly."

"Means you four were dead the moment he got those engines started," Elle commented, standing to one side of Jay.

Sarah snapped around and looked at Elle.

"Sorry," Elle said, shrugging slightly. "Truth and

you know it now. Same thing that happened to Derek Comstock after he sent the message Billie needed him to send."

Sarah slowly nodded, the memories clearly coming back to her.

"Okay, people," Jay said, standing and facing everyone. "Here's the plan for the moment."

Jay glanced at Elle. "Go ahead," she said, "if you have an idea."

"Our assignment from the big boss is to keep this ship under wraps until the world is destroyed or we get other orders," Jay said. "We might as well make the best of the time. Partner, you and Bright see if you can get a handle on the ship's computers."

Partner nodded and Bright turned and dropped into the chair she said she had sat in before.

"Pro, you and Charles see what you can do about the engines. I want to know what it would take to start them."

Both nodded.

"Anthony, I want you and Sarah to help me and Elle here with anything you can tell us about this ship, the history of it, and how to fly this thing."

"How about weapons?" Elle asked.

Jay turned around and looked at her. Until she said that, he hadn't even thought of weapons. And that wasn't like him at all.

"Remember the absorption session?" she asked. "The manual said these ships had powerful weapons."

"She's right," Anthony said, and pointed to a

chair in front of a panel on the other side of the round room. "That's why we all called the ship the Power. Because of the weapons."

"You remember anything at all about them?" Jay asked Anthony.

The general's eyes looked a little distant for a moment, then he half nodded. "A little."

"Better than nothing," Jay said. "Elle, you want to work with him on that?"

"Sure," she said. "You thinking we might use this ship to try to defend Earth?"

Pro laughed. "Right, one ship against all the ships in the Galaxy. And, of course, the minute the other races saw this ship they would all want it and do anything to get it. So I don't think that idea would work."

"I don't have any idea what I want to do with it," Jay said, smiling at Elle. "As Pro said, I don't think, even if it could fly, there would be any way we could actually fly it. But this beats sitting around and waiting for the world to end, doesn't it?"

"True," Elle said.

"Besides"—Jay smiled at her—"what better time to play around in a ship of the gods than right before you're about to die?"

"Not funny," Pro said.

"He seldom is," Elle said.

Elle sat in the soft, plush-feeling alien chair, letting its support wrap around her like no other chair she'd ever sat in before. She couldn't believe that something designed for an alien could be this comfortable.

In front of her the alien weapons-control board was a curved moon, with almost everything set at a comfortable distance from the chair. She had thought the controls would be farther away from her memory of the picture of the Numens. They appeared to have such long arms, but the more she thought about it, the more she realized that it was only the sleeves of their robes that were long. Their hands, just like their faces, were not visible in those learning images she had been fed earlier.

Anthony leaned forward and pointed to

18

a control area on the smooth surface. "I think," he said, "if my memory serves me, that this brings up a diagnostic of the weapons systems."

"I'm not sure I should be touching anything here," Elle said, suddenly very afraid of setting off a weapon by accident and destroying them all.

"Good point," Anthony said. "That spot is the only button anyone was allowed to touch on this board. I remember that much now, also."

She nodded. "Go ahead."

He gently touched the smooth surface of the control board near its upper corner. Nothing happened.

"I'm not sitting in the chair," he said, laughing. "Doesn't respond unless the person sitting in the chair touches it."

"What?" Elle asked, looking up into the smiling face of the general. "The ship has that sort of sensors?"

Anthony shrugged. "I don't know. I'm just getting bits and pieces of memory. But I tend to remember it worked that way. I wasn't in here that much, to be honest with you."

She nodded. If this truly was a Numen ship, anything was possible. She reached out and touched the same spot Anthony had touched on the smooth surface of the control board.

Instantly a holographic image of the entire ship appeared in front of her, floating over the control panel. It was a diagram in three dimensions of every space in the ship, composed of blue lines that showed the shapes and outlines and doors. Red spots were shown in a dozen places around the holographic ship, clearly indicating weapons status of some sort.

A green spot indicated which chairs around the main room were currently occupied. But it wasn't so much the weapons that startled her, or the image of them, but the outline of the ship itself floating in the air over the board. It showed the big room they were in, plus six more smaller rooms below it.

This was only one of two decks!

She had thought it was the entire ship. Of course the Numen would need places to sleep and eat. What was she thinking? How stupid could she be?

"Jay! Pro!" she shouted. "You better take a look at this. Fast!"

"Amazingly cool," Jay said, moving up beside her. Then he said, "Wait—"

Without really getting anywhere near the holo image, she carefully pointed at the other areas of the ship he had clearly seen, too. Then she glanced up at Anthony. "You know what's down in those rooms?"

"Never been down there," he said. "At least that I remember."

"Has anyone," Jay asked, turning to the others. "been down to the lower deck?"

"Just the engine area in the back," Charles said. "But I went in through a panel under the ship."

"Billie was in here a lot by himself," Sarah said. "I remember a few times I called for him in here and he didn't hear me, but then came out later. So he must have been down there."

"Damn," Elle said softly. There was no telling who or what was on that lower deck.

"Anyone know how to get down there?" Jay asked, drawing his Atomizer.

"Through that panel, I think," Sarah said, pointing to a plain-looking panel between two control stations. "Touch it on the right, about waist-high. Billie said it was never to be opened by any of us."

"Billie's orders?" Jay asked.

"Sort of," Sarah said, a puzzled expression on her face. "I really don't remember who gave that order. It just was sort of a standing order for us to never go down there. Odd."

"Me either," Anthony said. "But I remember it, too."

Elle stood quickly and pulled her gun. The holographic image vanished.

Pro and Partner both took up positions near the door, guns ready.

Their movements clearly spooked the others. But Elle knew they had no choice. Suddenly there was an area down here that had not been secured.

An area on an alien spaceship.

A secret area that Billie hadn't even allowed the humans to enter.

"All of you get out and wait near the base of the stairs," Elle said. "Move it."

"Pro, you stay inside here by the door," Jay ordered. "Partner and Captain stay with the rest. Something goes wrong I want you all out of here and this ship sealed under a few tons of rock."

"Com links on secure channel," Elle added. "We don't want anyone on top listening in down here."

As they were leaving, Elle sat down in the chair again and tapped the same spot on the control board. Again the holographic image appeared floating over the board.

She studied the layout of the lower level of the ship. The stairs were clearly shown behind that panel. And the six rooms, two on each side of a short hallway at the bottom of the stairs, one under the stairs, and one at the end of the hallway. No green marks showed in any of the rooms, as the green mark indicated where she was sitting on the main deck. But that didn't mean anything. Jay and the others weren't shown on this display either. Only when a person was sitting down did a green mark light up.

Jay leaned in beside her and studied the layout for a moment, then asked, "Ready?"

"Let's go," Elle said, standing and heading with Jay toward Pro and the door. She wasn't really ready, but they had no choice at this point.

Without hesitation, Jay nodded to Pro and touched the spot on the panel.

It whisked back almost instantly, showing a lit staircase beyond. The stairs were steep, but otherwise normal-looking human stairs, with a soft railing on both sides. Elle could see nothing but a clean hallway at the bottom.

"Back in a minute," Jay said.

"Make sure I don't have to wait up for you two," Pro said, smiling.

Jay led the way, staying to the right of the stairs, his gun up and ready.

Elle followed closely, staying left, keeping her back against the railing on the way down.

Pro kept his body inside the door at the top, making sure it stayed open.

The hallway was empty and clean at the bottom. For a ship that clearly had been buried in rock for millions of years, there was no decay, not even any dust. Even the air was fresh down here, with a faint smell of ocean breeze. When the Numen built something, they had clearly built it to last and keep working. And they had succeeded.

There were no sign of any doors. It seemed the Numen didn't like obtrusive openings marring the smooth "high-tech" surface of their interiors.

It was clear under the stairs, Elle could tell just by the shape of the short hallway, where the door to that room was, so she pointed in that direction and Jay nodded.

Silently, they moved to either side, then Jay palmed the area about waist-high on the left hand side.

The door whisked back quicker than Elle could even get her gun lowered into position.

"A bunk room," Jay whispered.

"Eight bunks," Elle filled in. Same number as chairs upstairs in the big control cabin. Jay stayed in the door, blocking it open while she moved carefully inside.

The beds were covered by some sort of cloth blankets. They all looked carefully made and about queen-size. Elle was just glad there were no signs of any long-decayed bodies. She wasn't sure exactly why she was expecting that. She supposed it came with the territory when you found a long-buried spaceship. And then again, she had only recently experienced the horror of the Grazer ship.

There were blank-looking areas between each bed and Elle bet they were closets. She moved over and palmed the wall between one bed, keeping her gun at the ready. A section slid back, showing robes.

Numen robes, if the absorption she had undergone earlier was to be believed.

"Shit!" Jay said, seeing what she was staring at.

"Something wrong?" Pro asked in Elle's ear.

"All fine so far," Jay said. "Everyone stay in position."

She moved away from the closet and it slid closed. Until that moment she didn't want to think they might actually be on a Numen ship. But it was clear they were.

Very clear now.

They moved down the hallway and Jay touched the wall opening the next room.

In it looked to be a shower and bathroom setup, only they were like nothing Elle had ever seen before. It might take her a month to figure out how to use everything in there. Or even find out how to turn on the water.

If the Numen used water.

The next room was also another bathroomlike room. Eight people, two bathrooms. Maybe the

Numen were a two-sexed race, like humans. There were three- and four-sexed races living on Earth, but with two bathrooms, Elle would bet on two sexes for the long-dead gods of the Galaxy.

The larger room at the end of the hall was filled with comfortable-looking chairs set in groups. A few tables were scattered around the large space.

"Game-and-relaxation room," Jay guessed.

"Looks that way," Elle said. "And eating." She pointed to one table with eight chairs placed around it. The room had a very comfortable feel to it, that was for sure. But there was no kitchen in sight. She bet it was in the wall and perfectly clean.

Four rooms down and two to go. Elle was starting to relax just a little. But she had no idea what they would find in the last two. Bedroom, bathrooms, food-and-relaxation room. What was left?

They opened the next door and the reason for that room was instantly clear: medical. It was sterile white, unlike any room on the ship. Two beds filled the center of the room. Both, thankfully, were empty. No doubt an Earth doctor could spend a lifetime in this one little room, making medical discovery after medical discovery.

Elle felt a massive wave of relief when they opened the last room. It contained four tables, one on each of the four blank walls, plus a chair in front of each table. Nothing else.

No one was inside.

She didn't know what she was expecting, but finding this extra deck had caused her more worries than she had imagined.

"Ship secure," Jay said, also clearly relieved.

"Captain, Partner," Pro said in Elle's ear. "Bring them all back in here."

Elle moved into the last room and looked around. The purpose of all the other rooms had been clear and obvious, but this one baffled her. Four chairs, four desks, one facing each wall. A blank-looking desktop was in front of each chair. There was nothing else in the space except a golf cap sitting on one counter.

One of Billie's golf caps. Clearly the Florian had been in here for some reason.

"Strange room, huh?" Jay said, moving over and putting his hand on the back of one of the chairs. "Movies, maybe?" he asked, pointing at the blank walls in front of each chair.

Suddenly Elle knew what she was looking at.

"You're right," she said. "Movies. And education. This is a training room, I'll bet."

Jay laughed. "You just might be right. Wonder how you turn it on?"

Elle remembered what Anthony had said about the panels upstairs not responding to anyone but the person in the chair. "You sit down," she said.

"A butt switch," Jay said, dropping down into the nearest chair.

The desk in front of him became a control panel and on the wall an image appeared.

The image of a Numen.

Talking in the Numen language.

All Elle could do was gasp.

Jay wanted to jump out of the chair in the last room they had explored, but he ignored his racing heart and forced himself to sit there, the Numen talking on in front of him. So far nothing in this ship seemed designed to hurt anyone. More than likely this movie he was seeing wasn't going to hurt him either.

A light was shining on him from the wall. And the Numen, a very human-looking alien, was talking to him in a strange language, his robe sleeves pushed back, his hood off his head. A completely different picture of a Numen than Jay had gotten from the absorption of the manual summary. If they all survived the next few days, MiB would have to update their library a little.

Even though there were similarities be-

19

tween the Numen and humans, Jay could still see large differences. First off, the guy had no hair and a very large head. He did have two eyes, but they were also large, almost bug-eyed, and slanted upward. The Numen had no chin and didn't seem to move his lips much when he spoke. He did have two arms, but only four long, multijointed fingers with no thumb. He looked more like the aliens made up in the tabloids than a real one.

Or maybe, the tabloids had known something Jay hadn't known.

The Numen was going on in some language that sounded like a cross between Arabic and Chinese, with a lot of soft clicks added into the mix. It sounded hard to pronounce, but the alien in the picture clearly wasn't straining.

"Can't understand a word he says," Jay said, looking up at Elle. "But that's the closest to human I've ever seen an alien look. Bet that guy is taller than I am, though. And those hands look strong."

She nodded, clearly stunned by what she was seeing, just like he was.

Just then the guy in front of Jay stopped talking.

The light over his head got brighter.

"Jay!" Elle shouted, reaching for him.

But it was too late.

The light seemed to blind him for a moment, then flashed off. And the guy started talking again. Only this time Jay could understand him.

Completely.

The alien was listing possible choices Jay could pick on the desktop in front of him.

"What just happened!" Elle demanded, her hand still on Jay's arm, where she was about to yank him from the chair.

"I'm not sure," Jay said. "I think I was just taught the Numen language."

"You're kidding?" Elle asked, letting go slowly.

Jay watched the Numen image in front of him keep explaining the options the library they were sitting in offered. "Can you understand him?" Jay pointed at the alien.

Elle shook her head. "Are you kidding? Not a word."

At that moment the door whisked open and Pro poked his head inside the room. "You all right in here?"

"Have Partner come down here with his brain-equipment," Elle said. "I think Jay here just got a quick absorption lesson from our long-dead hosts."

Pro glanced at Jay, then left quickly.

"Want to see if I've been brainwashed?" Jay asked, laughing. He didn't feel brainwashed, but he didn't like the idea of an unknown, ancient, and alien technology scrambling around inside his head any more than he liked MiB technology doing it. Of course, MiB had acquired its absorption technology from some alien race somewhere, so he supposed there was little difference.

Still, he decided it was better to be safe than sorry.

Jay got up from the chair and the guy disappeared. Jay followed Elle outside into the hallway, where Partner was setting up his equipment on the stairs. Jay sat down on the second step and slipped the helmet on.

"How come it is," Jay said, "that when MiB sticks stuff in my head, no one worries, but when an alien does it, you're all concerned?"

"Because, my dear Jay," Elle said, "we know how small your brain is and that makes you, shall we say, a 'quick study.'"

Pro and Partner laughed.

Jay just pointed at Elle and said nothing as Partner scrutinized his screen for a moment, then shrugged. "Same brain patterns as your last absorption, same everything. Looks normal to me."

"Nicest thing anyone's ever told me," Jay said.

"Notice he said normal not perfect," Elle said, smiling at him. "But now you can understand the Numen language. Strange, don't you think?"

"You calling me strange?" Jay asked, trying to get himself to calm down a little. He had to admit, suddenly knowing how to understand an alien language had bothered him more than he wanted to admit.

"Of course I am," Elle said, smiling.

"This isn't really that odd," Partner said. "Our absorption techniques are primitive by Galaxy standards. These Numens were considered the most advanced race ever. Seems logical their educational stuff would be top-of-the-line, too."

"But is it logical that it would work on us?" Elle asked. She was clearly worried about Jay and fearful of the consequences of brain tampering by an unknown technology. Jay could see the concern on her face, but at the same time he felt okay, undamaged. Or at least, from the inside out, he felt all right. He supposed the four prisoners with Captain upstairs had thought the same thing all those years they were under Billie's control. This line of reasoning made him shudder.

Partner shrugged. "From what I've gathered about this race, they dealt with thousands of other races. Chances are that device was set up to work on just about any walking, talking creature. But that's just an educated guess."

"Better than nothing," Elle said.

Jay knew right then that if he didn't immediately climb back into that chair, he was never going to do it. He turned and marched into the library, followed shortly by Elle, Pro, and Partner.

Jay dropped down into the chair again and the man appeared.

"Wow!" Pro said. "No one is supposed to know exactly what they looked like."

"Select a broad category," the Numen said in his native language. "Entertainment."

A green light on the board blinked.

"Medical," the Numen guide said.

Another green light blinked next to the first. Jay glanced at the markings. He could understand the Numen language, but he still couldn't read it.

"Maintenance."

Another green light.

"Education."

Then the guy started over.

"I'm going to try education," Jay said aloud. He

reached out and touched the place where the education light had blinked.

"Fine," the Numen guide said. "Select the area of interest."

The board in front of Jay changed, the writing changed, the lights all changed inside the smooth surface of the desktop. The Numen said nothing.

Jay waited, but nothing happened. The Numen guide didn't go on.

Jay studied the board, but couldn't make heads or tails of any of what he saw.

"Problem?" Elle asked.

"Can't read the language," Jay said, "and he's—"

The Numen said, "Language. Reading. Fine."

Again the board changed.

"Please select the language desired," the Numen said. On the board there looked to be over a hundred choices. "More selections are available."

"It understood me," Jay said to the three watching. "But do any of you know what their language was called?"

All three shook their heads.

"Great help you are?" Jay said.

"Help?" the Numen said. "Certainly. An image of each race will be displayed here. A light will illuminate beside the choice."

"Numen."

A green light flashed on inside the desktop beside a term he couldn't decipher and the Numen on the screen bowed slightly.

Jay, without hesitation, reached up and touched the green-lit area.

Again, almost instantly, a bright light flashed down from an unknown source in the ceiling and covered him, blinding him just for an instant.

Then it was gone.

"You all right?" Elle asked. Both she and Pro looked as if they were ready to yank him from the chair.

"Would you like to learn how to read another language?" the Numen asked.

Jay glanced at the board. Now he was able to understand everything he saw written there. It all made sense to him now. How it made sense, he didn't know, but somehow his brain had suddenly learned how to understand and read the long-dead language.

"No, thank you," Jay said to the Numen, and stood.

The image flashed off.

"Well," Elle asked.

"I can read their language," Jay said, smiling. "Who's next?"

"Not until I check you again," Partner said.

"You're not going to find anything wrong," Jay told him, laughing. He was actually starting to think this Numen method of learning was a good thing. Certainly quick and painless.

"Humor him," Elle said.

"Humor it is," Jay said.

He was right. There was nothing wrong. Nothing had changed inside his head except that he could understand and read Numen.

And more than likely, it was right here in this room that Billie had learned enough about Numen technology to think he could fly this ship.

Thirty minutes later every human on the ship knew how to read and understand the long-dead language of the Numens.

And for the first time in over a million years, this Numen ship had a crew.

The Supreme Controller of the great Zulla fleet sat in his chair, his four, thick, stumpy legs raised on a foot lift in front of him. His body covered a massive area of the main room of his ship, contained by four walls that kept his bulk from flowing everywhere. Gentle massage machines in his bed worked his thick, pink skin, wiped him down, kept his underside from rotting under his glorious weight.

His giant digestive system rumbled as it always did, comforting him and those around him.

The giant viewscreen in front of him showed nothing but the blackness of space as they sped forward. He found such blackness soothing, a good background for the fattening of his large body.

20

Two feeders, one stationed on either side of him on extended platforms that were raised over his bulk, dropped the nut fruit from the planet Hansee into his gaping mouth, letting the juices drip exactly a T-unit down his thick chin before wiping them from his fat neck with the softest of fabric. He was so large, only his head extended above his bulk.

He chewed slightly, savoring the taste while allowing most of the fruit to simply slide down his wide throat.

He was the Largest-of-the-Large. The Supreme Controller of a thousand ships, all following him now to a backward little planet called Earthling, or something close to that. It made no difference to him what its name was. The pitiful little race there had insulted His Largeness. They would pay.

"Message, O Largest-of-the-Large."

The feeders dropped two more nut fruits in his mouth before he allowed himself to glance over his massive bulk at his second-in-command.

The creature still weighed so little that he could move around on his four thick legs, even possibly leave the ship. The Supreme Controller had not left this ship for half his lifetime, which was as it should be. He had not seen his legs in many units of time. But he could remember being so small. He hated to dwell on such unpleasant memories too often.

"Who sends a message?"

"Sashanian commander, O Largest-of-the-Large. Stamped with his importance."

The Supreme Controller knew of the power of

the Sashanian fleet. They were his ship's match, although he would never admit such a thought even to a feeder. The Sashanian had taken on the task of protecting the creatures before they suffered the full consequences of their stupidity in inviting Golgothas to their planet. The Sashanian had forwarded the false message from the pitiful creatures declaring the Golgothas uninvited.

"What does the message say?"

His second dropped instantly to the floor, his head down, his giant bulk covering a large area. "I would not dare read such a message intended for only the Supreme Controller of all the gathered Zulla fleet."

"Of course you would not," the Supreme Controller replied. But he knew his second had read the message. As a second, he had read all the messages for the previous Supreme Controller. His second would not be performing his job if he weren't devious enough to do at least that much. And the Supreme Controller had picked his second because he was the most devious of all the Largest. And his size made it easier to keep an eye on him.

"Give me the message," the Supreme Controller ordered.

His second slowly shoved his large bulk to his feet, grunting and straining. It would not be long until his second would be of good size, also. The Supreme Controller must watch his second's girth. Size was everything.

With an extension stick, his second sent the message over the Supreme Controller's massive body to his upper thick hand. The movement sent ripples of skin against his bed's walls.

The message was still sealed. Smart of his second. A good ploy, well played.

He let the feeders drop more nut fruit into his mouth, then he opened the message and read about the trick of the Florian.

He read it twice, as protocol dictated, then placed the message back on the extension rod so his second could also read it just once, at least officially.

The feeders dropped more nut fruit into his mouth as the Supreme Controller thought. The puzzling action of inviting the Golgothas now seemed to make sense. And the Florian was dead, as he deserved to be. But turning back now would not show his, the Supreme Controller's, great skills of leadership.

They had traveled too far for his ships, his troops, not to have the enjoyment of destroying a planet.

The Sashanian message did not say that they would defend the earth. There was no reason not to continue. It was such a short distance away now.

"Time of arrival?" the Supreme Controller asked his second.

"Two short feedings," his second replied.

"Good," the Supreme Controller replied, chewing the last of the nut fruit. His stomach rumbled, the sound echoing through the ship. "Our great fleet will be glorious in the feeding."

"As is your wish," his second said.

The Supreme Controller said nothing as the feeders began on the first of the two short feedings. In front of him on the large screen the blackness of space would soon be replaced by the image of the destruction of the Earthlings.

The thought was enough to make any creature hungry.

Elle glanced over at Jay where he stood in the little kitchen area of the underground living quarters, staring into the refrigerator. One of the containment team had bagged up the remains of old Billie and hauled him to the other side of the ship so he didn't smell up the place. This left the living area almost comfortable, like a good-sized apartment furnished in Early Student decor.

They had spent the last hour exploring the ship's functions, checking out its status, now that they could all read the Numen language. Surprisingly, the ship was almost in operational condition. Except for starting up the engines, Jay was convinced the thing could fly. So was Pro.

Elle wasn't so sure, but she always

21

required more proof on most things than Jay did.

Jay came out of the kitchen area chewing on a carrot as she opened up the secure link between them and MiB headquarters. "Zed's not going to talk to you," he said between bites. "My bet is right now he's buried up to his eyebrows just trying to buy the planet one more night of blissful peace."

"We need to check in," Elle said. She firmly believed they did. Learning how to understand and read Numen was an important discovery that Zed needed to know about.

It took a moment before Zed's tired face appeared on the screen.

"Problem?"

"No," she said, "but—"

"Keep a lid on your location and that ship," Zed said. "I've pulled all of the surface agents out of there, so guard it from below. We got a mess up here."

With that the link went dead.

"Don't say it," Elle said, snapping the lid closed on the secure communications unit.

Jay just shrugged and kept chewing.

She leaned back on the couch and sighed. She hadn't felt this helpless, this out of control, in a long time. "It's wrong that we should be down here when we could be out there helping."

"Got that right," Jay said. "I'd love to do a little more Grazer tipping."

"I'd be up for just shooting a few of them," she

said, remembering that Grazer sleeping room. She would never, ever hesitate to kill a Grazer again.

"No argument there," Jay said.

"Safe to come in now?" Pro asked, knocking on the door that lead out to the ship.

"Safe for the night," Jay said.

"We're stuck here, huh?" Pro said.

"Keep a guard on the stairwell and stay put," Elle said, surprised at how disgusted she sounded repeating Zed's orders. "Everyone's pulled out up top."

"Captain's already got a dozen alarms set throughout the cabin above and another dozen more on the staircase," Pro said. "Nothing can come down those stairs that we won't know about."

"Great," Jay said, finishing off the carrot.

"MiB meeting or can anyone attend?" Bright asked from the doorway.

"Come on in," Elle said, moving the communications unit off the couch and putting it on the end table.

Bright, Anthony, Sarah, and Charles all filed in and took chairs. They looked tired and very washed out. All of them slumped. And considering that Anthony still had his general's clothes on, he looked even odder slumping like a teenager in a chair.

After the day they had all had, Elle could understand their exhaustion. Plus they were on the normal twenty-four-hour clock and it was getting late for them. For the MiB agents it was still the middle of their day.

The silence filled the room. None of them seemed to have enough energy left to talk.

"Looks like you four could use some sleep," Pro said. "We're locked down for the night, so you might as well turn in."

"You remember which bedroom belongs to whom?" Elle asked.

They all nodded except for Anthony, who said he had never spent the night here.

"You can use Derek's bed," Sarah said to him.

"Thanks," Anthony said, "if someone could show me which one it was."

"I'll show you," Sarah said, standing slowly, as if she were an old woman. "Any of you need beds?"

"We aren't allowed to sleep," Jay said, smiling at her.

Sarah frowned.

"Thanks," Elle said, overriding Jay. "We're fine. We're just on a different schedule."

Sarah nodded and Anthony followed her into one of the side bedrooms. A moment later she returned, waved a tired hand at them, and moved into the next room over. Both Bright and Charles stood to head to their rooms.

At the bedroom door Charles stopped and looked back at Elle and Jay and Pro. "Don't really know how to thank you for rescuing us."

Elle smiled at him. "We don't need thanks. It's our job. Now get some sleep."

"Thanks anyway," Bright said. Then both she and Charles were gone, doors closed.

"We need to watch them at all?" Elle asked, turning to Pro, then glancing at Jay.

"Already set up," Pro said. "Cameras and sensors in all four bedrooms. Captain set it up while we were in the ship. They can't send out any messages from in there, and we'll hear and can watch any attempts to do so. But I doubt we need to worry. They're clear."

"Glad we're making sure anyway," Jay said, putting his feet up on the coffee table and stretching out. "Comfortable little place they got down here."

"Glad you think so," Elle said. "I just hope we're not riding out the end of the world in this bomb shelter."

"Yeah," Jay said. "Hope Zed can get this one stopped in time."

"There's got to be something we can be doing." For the first time she realized just how angry she was they were stuck down here. It was her planet out there in danger, other MiB agents needed their help, yet here they were stuck guarding a million-year-old ship that wasn't heading anywhere fast.

"I wouldn't know what it might be," Jay said, glancing at Pro. "But if anyone thinks of somethin', I'm game."

"Don't look at me," Pro said, laughing. "I just clean up the mess. You two are the hotshots with all the ideas."

"Yeah, right," Elle said.

They sat there in silence for a short time, all lost in their own thoughts.

Elle kept coming back to the fact that both Jay and Pro thought the old ship might still fly. Yet they didn't know anything really about the race that owned it. Or even why it had ended up here in Oregon. What happened to the original Numen crew? How did the ship survive the tons of rock that had buried it without a scratch on the hull? Or had it been put here purposely?

Too damn many questions for her taste.

She liked answers.

Suddenly it dawned on her that she was not without recourse. The answers to her questions were in the ship's library. And they had the time to try to find some information that might help.

She suddenly stood and headed for the kitchen. In the refrigerator was a bag of carrots. She grabbed two and shut the door. Then taking a small bite of one, she tossed the other one to Jay.

"Come on, there just might be something we can do."

"What?" Jay asked, catching the carrot and sitting up.

"I don't know yet," Elle said. "That's what we need to find out. And when you need information, what's a good place to go to get it?"

Jay looked puzzled.

Pro laughed. "Didn't spend much time in the library as a kid, I see."

Jay nodded. "Oh, I understand."

He didn't sound happy, but he wasn't objecting, so Elle ignored him.

"Where are the rest of the team?" Elle asked, moving toward the door.

"Partner's outside the ship," Pro said, "Captain's got the stairs and monitor duty. I'll stay in here and keep an eye out on our friends."

"You know where we'll be," Jay said. His voice clearly showed no excitement.

"Looking forward to getting more brain cells scrambled, huh?" Pro said, then laughed.

Jay pointed to his head. "It's not much, but it's all I got."

"Come on, big fella," Elle said, also laughing. "Let's go fill it a little fuller."

"Yeah," Pro said, "half a tank is better than a quarter tank."

Jay frowned. "Why's everyone pickin' on me?"

"Because we can," Elle said, laughing and shoving him toward the door and the alien ship beyond.

"Good reason," Jay said.

Jay had learned far more than he had ever wanted to know about an alien race after spending over two hours of sifting through the alien ship's library, picking a topic he wanted to learn, then having the library shove it into his head.

The Numen were a gentle race, who hated fighting. Got it.

The Numen developed massive weapons that could wipe out an entire fleet so no one would ever fight with them. Got it.

The ship they were on was equipped with such a weapon. Got it. Didn't like it, but got it.

In fact, he didn't much like any of this, mostly because he had slowly become convinced, no matter what Elle or Pro told him, that he was hurting himself by shoving the

information into his brain this way. He knew what the Numen ate, how long they lived, even how they mated, a fact that no matter how hard he tried to forget, just wouldn't go away. And nowhere on the panel in front of him could he find an erase or delete button.

Elle had told him he was just afraid of learning, period.

That comment had hurt. He'd done his share of learning new stuff over the years. But sometimes the old ways of doing things were the best. And thinking such a thought made him sound like an old man already. And he hated that, too.

Elle, on the other hand, was going at this as if they had the chance of a lifetime tonight. The old kid-in-the-candy-store description fit her just right. He hadn't seen her so excited in the entire year they'd been working together. Even though they didn't have a clue what they were looking for.

Or even why.

"Jay," she said from the chair next to his. "I think I found something here." Her voice was hushed and clearly she was shaken by something.

He stood and moved over beside her, glancing down at the topic she had been studying. *Numen History. Exodus.*

"What ya got?"

"Go back to your chair and take this in." She pointed at the title. "You won't believe it."

"Can't you just summarize it for me?" he asked, hoping to avoid another head-cramming experience.

She laughed. "Trust me on this one. You want to know this."

He moved over and sat in his chair. The Numen library guide appeared. Over the last hour Jay had come to call the guy Bud, and it seemed as if the guy was almost answering to the name.

"Well, Bud," Jay said, his hands tapping on the control panel, running through the menus he'd become familiar with. "Numen History, Exodus section it is."

"Numen History: Exodus," the holograph said.

The white light blinded him, as it always did, then let him go.

Suddenly he knew exactly what Elle had been talking about.

The Numen had chosen to leave their posts as gods of the Galaxy on purpose. And for a reason Jay understood completely. They had become tired of hanging around the old neighborhood Galaxy and wanted to get out and explore. They had built massive ships, planet-sized ships that they could live inside for millions of years in the long trip between galaxies. Their first stop: Andromeda Galaxy.

They had taken along many of their ships, but in the end this became impractical; there were just too many to take. So they began to bury the ships in groups of a hundred on remote, distant planets, leaving them shielded so they would never be found by other races.

Then they had simply piled into their planet-sized ships, all of them, and left this Galaxy on the greatest exploration into the unknown ever under-taken.

"Hundreds of ships?" Jay said aloud, turning to look at Elle. "All armed and ready to fly."

She was looking at him, nodding. "All here on Earth."

Jay suddenly thought back to Zed's reaction to their discovery of the Numen ship. He had known exactly what to do. And had been almost annoyed and afraid that an alien had found it first.

"You think MiB knows where more of these ships are hidden?" Jay asked, standing and leaning against the desktop.

"Of course," Elle said. "And I'll bet in here somewhere is the record of where they all are."

"And MiB would know that, too."

"Of course," Elle said. "If it's in one ship, it's in them all. More than likely MiB just hadn't gotten to this one yet. No hurry when something has been buried for millions of years."

"So old Billie snuck in under our noses. No won-der Zed was so annoyed when we told him what was happening."

"Makes sense, doesn't it?" Elle asked.

"All except one thing," Jay said. "Why hasn't Zed ever played this card? We almost lost the planet last month with those flowering meat-eaters, remember?"

"But we didn't," Elle said. "We saved the planet without using these ships."

"And what about that bug and those Achturians

that Kay and I stopped? Why didn't he use it then? We were seconds from getting toasted."

"You—actually we stopped them," Elle said. "Remember? He didn't have to play the ultimate hole card."

Jay just shook his head in amazement. This idea actually had him excited. "Well, he might have to use them today. What do you say we get this ship ready to fly completely? That just might help to have one more in the fleet."

"Sounds like the best idea you've had all night," Elle said. "So what do we need to do that?"

"Three things," Jay said, walking back and forth and ticking off the items on his fingers. "We need to know how to get this ship out of this mountain. There has to be a way."

"That's one," Elle said.

"Two, we need to know how to start the engines."

"That's two," she said.

"And we need a trained crew and someone to fly the thing into space."

"That's a good one," Elle said. "I'll bet we can find all the training we need in here."

"True," Jay said. "Looks like it's time for our crew to wake up from their naps."

"You thinking we should use everyone?" Elle asked.

Jay smiled at her. "At this point I think we're going to need everyone we can get to help us. There are eight chairs up there. We might as well fill them all."

"And we're not telling Zed, right?" Elle asked, smiling.

"Not until we're ready to join the rest of the ships in the air," Jay said. "Or morning check-in, whichever comes first."

"I love it," she said.

"So do I," he said.

And for the first time since they captured the ship, he felt as if they were again finally doing something important. Something that just might help save Earth from the scum of the universe. After all, wasn't that their job?

"Zed's calling," Pro said, sticking his head into the spaceship's main door.

Elle glanced around at Jay, who nodded.

They were ready. She knew it. It had taken them all night, but they were trained and raring to go.

Around the spaceship's cabin five heads turned as Jay pushed himself out of the pilot's chair. All were at active stations and all knew what they were doing with those stations.

Sarah was at the internal-systems monitoring station.

Anthony was at weapons.

Charles was at the engineering station, and Bright was at computers.

Partner had taken over navigation and Elle was in the overall control seat.

23

If the time came, Pro would sit in the remaining chair as the ship's second-in-command.

It had been a long night of learning and practice, but Elle was pleased with their progress. If they had to, they just might be able to get this ship out from under this mountain and into orbit.

With a great deal of luck, they wouldn't have to. Not playing on this strength was better. Much better. But at least now they had it ready to play.

But the next step was to convince Zed of their idea, of their readiness to fly and join the other ships she was sure MiB had ready. And that was going to be some trick.

Elle moved down the ramp and into the living-quarters area. The secure link had been set up there on the kitchen table, facing out toward the ship. They had planned a little charade for Zed to help convince him and now she was getting nervous about it. Very nervous, actually.

She sat down in the chair and then glanced around at Pro.

He nodded that she should go ahead, so she turned back to the secure link and punched the on button on the laptop-size communications device.

"Sorry for the delay," she said as Zed's face appeared on the screen. "We were in the ship. How's the status?"

"Not good," Zed said, looking up at her. His eyes had deep circles under them and he seemed just about as overall tired as she had ever seen him. And Zed never really looked tired. Harried, maybe, but both she and Jay had come to believe that Zed never slept. At least they had never caught him at it.

"We managed to keep things contained last night across this country," Zed said, "but China and Europe are having problems right now. They should hold on and keep it wrapped up, we hope."

"Hold on for what?" Elle asked. "Are the major fleets turning back?"

"No," he said blankly, glancing down at something on his desk, then looking up at her. "The first of the big ones will go right past the Sashanian fleet in about three hours. Who knows how long we have after that. I'd say almost no time at all."

"So," she said, "you're telling me the human race is finished?"

"Short of a miracle," Zed said.

"Worse than last month with the man-eating plant invasion?"

"Much worse," he said, his voice tired. "What are you driving at?"

"How about the Achturians and the bug? This worse than that?"

"It's worse," he said. "Much worse."

"So what about pulling out your secret weapon?"

Now Zed was really looking puzzled and starting to get angry. Jay usually managed to get Zed angry at him. Elle very seldom did, and she wasn't at all pleased about it.

"Please explain," he growled. "And make it quick."

"What about the Numen ships?" she asked.

"The other races find out about that ship and we're even deader," Zed said. Then he laughed. "If being deader than dead is even possible."

Elle glanced back at Pro, who only shrugged. He had been as convinced as she and Jay that MiB knew about the other ninety-nine Numen ships buried around the world. Suddenly it seemed as if they had been wrong in their assumption.

She turned back to the link with Zed. "Are you telling me MiB doesn't have a fleet of these ships sitting somewhere?"

Zed blinked twice, then started laughing. "Fleet? Are you kidding? Why would we have a fleet of million-year-old spaceships?"

"Damn, you're not kidding, are you?" Elle asked. She could feel her stomach twisting and her heart racing. This wasn't good. Not good at all.

"Why would I kid about a thing like that?" Zed asked, his voice low and very, very controlled. Which meant he was very, very angry.

Elle took a deep breath. Their only real hope now was to push ahead. There wasn't a fleet of ships, but there was still the one sitting in the other room.

"We have an idea about how to stop the ships that are coming to destroy Earth," Elle said. "Take a deep breath and just listen to it. All right?"

Zed frowned, but before he could say anything, Elle turned and nodded to Pro, who shouted, "You can come in now."

Elle moved slightly to one side as the hooded figure moved into the room and stood where Zed on the secure communications link could see him. To the uninitiated, the figure looked mysterious and a little menacing, a cross between grim reaper and some kind of monk. Actually, though, it was Jay, but she wasn't going to tell Zed that just yet.

The face was hidden in the shadows of the hood and the figure's hands were nowhere to be seen. It looked exactly the way the Numen looked in the MiB records.

Then Jay did something he had practiced a number of times during the night. He started speaking in Numen.

"The treaty involving this planet must be enforced," Jay said. *"We, the Numen, will not be pleased if it is not. We will enforce it if we must."*

Elle glanced back at the screen.

Zed's face was almost white, as if he had seen a ghost, or was having a heart attack. Clearly this image of a Numen looked real enough for him.

"Here's our idea," Elle said after Jay stopped his short speech. "We take this ship out of here shielded. There's so much going on, no one is going to notice."

Zed's mouth opened but no words came out, so Elle rushed on. "Then we circle back and come in unshielded from what looks like deep space. We put the Numen ship between the coming fleets and the planet, and Jay there goes into his speech, which says, basically, that the Numen support the treaty and no one should break it. He's fluent in Numen, you know."

At just that moment Jay pulled the hood back and smiled at Zed.

Zed's mouth opened again, then closed, then opened again. Again, nothing came out.

"To answer your questions," Jay said, stepping forward to stand beside Elle so Zed could see them both, "yes, we can fly the ship. Yes, it is armed and has a weapon on board that can destroy an entire fleet of ships. Yes, we know how to fire that weapon. And yes, we can get the ship out from under this mountain. The Numens left us a way to do it without leaving a crater the size of a football field."

Zed just sort of stared at them, saying nothing.

Jay glanced at Elle. "I'm gathering here that MiB doesn't know about the other Numen ships."

"It doesn't," Elle said. "We were wrong." She smiled at Zed. At the moment she didn't know what else to do.

"Well, that's going to be a headache when this is all over," Jay said, his voice light.

Elle nodded, deciding to play along to break the tension. "Especially the one buried a mile under the Bronx."

"Yeah, or the one under the Astrodome," Jay said. "Yow, not a good scene there."

"If you two are joking, I'll personally fly out there and strangle you both before the aliens blow everything up!"

"No joke," Elle said.

"Would we kid you on something like this?" Jay asked, his face very serious. "We actually thought when we discovered that there were a hundred of these babies buried around the planet that MiB had a fleet of these things. We just worked all night to get ready to join the troops."

Zed leaned back in his chair and took a deep breath. Elle was happy to see some color return to his cheeks. After a moment he said, "Give me two minutes to clear off a few things here, then I want you to start over and tell me everything you've been doing. Understood?"

"Perfectly," Elle said, but the connection had already been cut.

"You think he liked our idea?" Jay asked Elle.

"I think you knocked his socks off and he has to go looking for them," Pro said, laughing. "I've never seen Zed so shocked."

"He's going to regret the day he hired us," Elle said, shaking her head. It was one thing to consider taking a ship into space when she thought MiB had a fleet of the things parked somewhere. But knowing they would be the first to try to fly one of these ancient vessels suddenly had her very, very worried.

"Oh, you save Earth's butt and he won't regret anything," Pro said, still laughing.

"Yeah," Elle said. "If. There's a lot of those little if-words between this idea and saving Earth."

"Won't matter," Jay said. "We either make it work or we'll all be dead."

"He has a good point," Pro said.

Elle knew he did. She just didn't like the odds suddenly. A million-year-old ship that might not fly going up against fleets of advanced aliens. Suddenly nothing at all sounded good about their idea.

Nothing.

It took Zed exactly six minutes to get back to them. And when his face reappeared on the secure communications link, Jay was glad to see the old man looking better. He had color back in his skin and he seemed once again very much in control.

"Now," he said, his voice sounding as it would on a normal day during a normal briefing. "Tell me what you two have been up to?"

Jay and Elle spent the next fifteen minutes explaining carefully everything they had done and learned, with Pro in the background adding details they missed that he thought might be important.

Through all of it, Zed just nodded, letting them talk. But Jay knew their boss wasn't missing a detail. He seldom did.

24

"So, now what, boss?" Jay asked when they finished their explanation. "We gonna go give them all a little scare?"

"Not yet," Zed said. "We're not taking the chance with your harebrained idea until there are no other options."

"Remember," Jay said, "it's goin' ta take us at least a half hour to get the ship out of this hole, then fly it away from the planet so we can look as if we're coming in from deep space."

"And that's if everything goes as planned," Elle said.

Zed nodded. "I understand all that. But you need to understand a few things, too. Humans aren't allowed to have interstellar spaceships. Or fly them. It was part of the treaty we and a bunch of friends signed."

Jay laughed, not believing what he had just heard. They and the whole human race were all about to be blown to bits and Zed was still worried about a stupid piece of paper. "I don't think the fleets of alien scum comin' here to destroy all us humans worry much about that treaty."

"Don't you think I know that?" Zed growled. "But I'm going to wait until the last possible minute *before* I violate the treaty from our side. There's still an outside chance the Sashanians and other treaty signers might defend us."

"So we sit and wait?" Elle asked.

"No," Zed said. "You make doubly sure that ship is ready to fly and you make triply sure you know how to fly it. If we need it, you two and your charade are going to be humanity's last damned choice."

"Got ya," Jay said. His stomach suddenly felt as if he'd been slugged.

Elle only nodded.

"So go double-check everything," Zed ordered. "I'll be in touch."

The connection broke, leaving the three of them in silence.

"Well," Jay said after a moment, "we wanted to be able to help . . ."

"Let's hope we don't have to," Elle said softly. She stood slowly, as if she were tired, and moved toward the door.

"I'm with Elle," Pro added, also standing.

Jay agreed with both of them. It was one thing to think they were going to fly the ancient Numen ship to help a whole fleet of ships defend Earth, but being only one ship between Earth and fleets of alien ships wasn't what he had in mind.

He followed Elle and Pro back into the ship, then dropped into the pilot's chair. The comfortable feel wrapped around him, giving him a false sense of security. He had never flown a plane, or even sailed a ship. But after absorbing the pilot's information on this ship, he was convinced Billie had been right. The ship could almost fly itself.

It was going to have to, Jay had a sneaking hunch.

"Okay, everyone," Elle announced, "we might be humanity's only chance. So we're going to practice what we can practice, double-check what we can double-check."

"And hope we don't get tapped to go into the game," Jay said.

"Is she kidding?" Bright asked Jay, her eyes full of worry and fear.

"Afraid not," Jay said. "Listen up, everyone. We were wrong. The MiB haven't found any of the other buried ships. This is the first one. If we have to go up against the aliens out there, we do it alone. And the only way MiB is going to send us is if there's no other choice. Period."

Everyone around the alien control room was silent. Then Sarah said, "We helped Billie start all this, we can help you end it if this is the only way."

The other three humans Jay and Elle had rescued all nodded.

"Thanks," Elle said.

Jay smiled at Bright. If she felt she could do this, then he could do it. It was that simple.

For the next two hours they reviewed every bit of data they had learned and rehearsed every action in the event of every possible contingency Elle, Jay, Pro, or anyone else could think of. Three times Jay had run down to the library to absorb another chunk of knowledge about flying a Numen ship. And he hadn't been the only one running back and forth between the main cabin and the library.

By the time the two hours were finished, Anthony was convinced that all the weapons were armed and that he could fire them if he needed to. And actually hit something.

Charles was sure the engines would start on command, without problems. And the Numen-built ground cover would open them a hole big enough to permit the spaceship to launch.

Bright and Partner were sure they could program the computer course needed to get them off the surface of Earth without being seen, to carry them away from the planet, then to bring them back.

Only thing was, Jay felt he wasn't so sure he could fly the thing. In his mind he knew he could. It was no harder than moving a small joystick on a video game. And if stupid aliens like Grazers could fly interstellar ships, he could do it, too.

He had repeated that a dozen times over the past two hours.

But in his gut he still wasn't so sure. He didn't tell that to anyone. Better to let them think he knew exactly what he was doing, because he was the one steering. They needed to believe him to be competent and confident. After all, they all had enough to worry about already.

"Okay, everyone," Elle ordered, rising from her command chair. "Quick break and then get into the Numen robes. We want to be ready to move at a moment's notice."

Jay watched as they all stood and headed for the living quarters. They all looked very solemn and very focused, even Pro and Partner. And those two were trained for dangerous stuff, just like he and Elle were. But this was different.

This wasn't just their own lives or deaths. The whole planet was at stake.

"We have a great crew," Elle said, when only the two of them were left.

"Never thought I'd need a crew," Jay said. "This idea is a long ways from the streets of New York."

"And the city morgue," she said. "Whoever would have thought I'd go from cutting up dead bodies to being the commander of a starship of the gods."

Jay glanced around at the control room he was getting very, very used to. "Ya think humans will ever get advanced enough to develop somethin' like this?"

"I hope so," Elle said.

"But one step at a time, right?" Jay said.

"Right," Elle said.

"First we fly it, then we build it."

"Feels backward," Elle said, then laughed.

"Sure does," Jay said. He didn't want to tell her just how backward it felt to him.

Just then Captain shouted from the living quarters. "Zed's calling!"

"Shit!" Jay said, heading out at a run, beating Elle to the door by just inches. He just hoped he didn't come running back through that door in a few minutes as a pilot.

Beach-Grass-In-Limbo watched the monitor in front of him, all three of his eye stalks at full attention.

On the screen he could see the Zulla, the Fattest-of-the-Fat in all the Galaxy, approaching, slowing as they neared the outer planets of the system. Although they had received his message, they were clearly not turning back. Their round, thick, ugly ships seemed to fill all of space, blocking out the stars in many places.

Many other major fleets followed.

The Bonka fleet, with an even larger number of ships, was only two hours behind.

Behind them were the Horsanakii, the most powerful of races on this side of the central Galaxy core. There had not been a

25

race as powerful since the disappearance of the Numen.

None of them were turning back.

Beach-Grass-In-Limbo knew that very soon the planet below him would soon be cleared of anything of value. No human would survive. It would be a sad day in the history of the Galaxy, to be added to many other sad days of other races who had met the same fate.

He keyed in his command code with one tentacle. His orders went out to his ships, and to the many other treaty ships standing by, helping with the cleanup of Those-Who-Eat-And-Are-Worthless.

The orders were very simple.

"Do not engage. Pull back and re-form. We will soon be going home."

He cut off the command code and again focused his eye stalks on his monitors. His ships were doing as he had ordered. Soon his job here would be finished.

He regretted it had to end in such a fashion.

Just then a light blinked on his communications board.

He used one tentacle to check it. It was from the human He-Who-Called-Himself-Zed. There seemed no reason to take such a call, but honor deemed it appropriate to grant the Soon-to-be-Dead one final communication.

He keyed the switch with the tentacle, then focused his eye stalks on the image of the human.

"Are the large fleets stopping?" the human inquired abruptly, without bothering to employ formal speech patterns. Normally the human had maintained some degree of formal speech, but not this time. His lapse was understandable under the present circumstances.

"No," Beach-Grass-In-Limbo said. "Your gods will soon be greeting you."

"The treaty means nothing to you?" the human asked.

"The treaty is only as strong as those who defend it," Beach-Grass-In-Limbo said, his tentacles making soothing motions in the air around his head. "We cannot and will not stand against the coming fleets."

"Why?" the human demanded. "I know the great Sashanian fleet is strong. The cause is just."

"True," the commander said. "But the fight is not ours."

"In other words," the human said, "we are not worth losing ships over."

Beach-Grass-In-Limbo had often been shocked at the blunt perceptiveness of the humans. This was one of those times. "You are correct."

"I understand," the human replied.

He paused, then asked, "Have you considered, O great friend of the treaty, that such a negative assessment might be wrong?"

"I have," Beach-Grass-In-Limbo replied tensely. "It is not."

"Is there nothing humans can do to stop this?" the human asked, his face full in the screen.

"You are a proud race," Beach-Grass-In-Limbo said. "Die proudly, also."

"Understood," the human said. "But dying is not something humans do easily."

"Then fight well," the Sashanian said.

"We will," the human answered.

This time the human cut the connection.

With all three eye stalks, the commander stared at the blank screen. It was a pity the humans would become an extinct race. There was so much he and others did not understand about them, so much in them to arouse curiosity and reward study.

His ships had all pulled back into position.

The fat ugly ships of the Zulla were about to arrive.

It would soon be over.

Jay approached the secure communications de-vice and opened the connection between himself and Zed. Gathered around him were Anthony, Charles, Sarah, Bright, Pro, Partner, and Elle. Only Captain wasn't present, since he had drawn guard duty for the stairs and hadn't trained for a position on the ship. One MiB agent was going to be needed to stay behind on the ground and keep people away from the hole they were going to leave when they lifted off.

If they lifted off.

Zed's face appeared. He was angry.

Angrier than Jay had ever seen him.

Behind him the Immigration Center looked deserted. Jay had never seen it so empty. All the rats had left the ship, it seemed.

26

"They aren't lifting a damn finger to help us," Zed said, his voice low and mean sounding.

Jay felt his stomach clamp down into a tight knot. The human race was dead if the treaty signers didn't help them.

"Nothing?" Elle asked.

"Not one damn ship is willing to stop the coming fleets," Zed said.

Sarah choked back a sob. "What have we done?"

"Damn," Anthony muttered.

"How long do we have?" Jay asked.

"The Zulla fleet of about a thousand ships will be in Earth orbit in less than a hour."

"Then we don't have much time," Jay said grimly. "Let's go try to stop them."

"I'm afraid"—Zed looked directly at them as he spoke—"we don't have much choice. Maintain communication silence and stay shielded until you're coming in from space. If anyone in all the Galaxy besides us ever discovers it's humans flying that ship, they'll kill us. A second time."

"Understood," Elle said.

"And good luck," Zed added.

The connection broke, leaving them all standing there in shocked silence. Finally Jay said, "You heard the man. We got a planet to save. Everyone to the ship! Pro, get Captain out of here and up to his position on top."

"Got it," Pro said, sprinting for the door.

Jay was right behind him, only he was headed for the ship.

Behind him Partner gathered up the communications equipment.

Within fifteen seconds everyone except Pro was swathed in Numen robes, hoods back, sleeves rolled up, and seated in their chairs.

"Secure the hatch," Elle ordered as Pro came in.

"Got it!" Pro said. "Captain will be on top and in the clear in thirty seconds."

"Everyone ready?" Jay asked.

Heads nodded hesitantly around the ship. They all looked odd in the Numen robes, as if they belonged in those chairs, yet, at the same time, didn't.

"People," Jay said, "look at it this way. We can die when a thousand Zulla ships smash up our homes, or we can die taking some of them with us."

"How about we not die at all?" Elle said firmly.

"I like that idea even better." Jay laughed. "Take it away, She-Who-Sits-In-The-Big-Chair."

"All systems on and ready?" Elle asked, starting the drill they had practiced earlier.

"Computer systems on. Check," Bright called, her voice a little louder than it needed to be.

"Navigation systems on and ready. Check," Partner said, seemingly calm.

"Weapons armed and ready. Check," Anthony said, sounding like a general.

"Ship's general systems all go," Sarah said.

"Engines and electrical on-line," Charles said. "Engines ready to start up."

"Shields on-line and ready," Pro said. "No one is going to see us leave."

"Ready as I'm ever going to be." Jay sighed, easing his hands forward to lightly hold the pilot's controls. The central control was a round ball-like device that was set into the recessed panel. His right hand went around it and he could feel its granular surface, which had somehow been constructed to prevent his fingers from slipping. The ball moved in all directions. The ship moved in all directions, depending on how he moved the ball.

Simple. Like a mouse on a computer, only the cursor was a spaceship.

He hoped it was that simple.

His left hand was on a slide control for speed. Forward for faster, full back for stop.

Also simple.

In front of him, at least in theory, would be a three-dimensional display when they got flying. It would include the information Bright and Partner would be feeding him from the computers. His course, unless he decided to stray off it, would be marked in the three-dimensional display by a green line. All he had to do was keep the ship on the green line and he was fine.

He had no idea how hard that was going to be. In the simulations given him by the library downloads, it had been easy. But he knew that nothing in real life was ever as easy as simulations.

"Let's get into space," Elle said. Then laughed a nervous laugh. "Never thought I'd hear myself say that."

"I wish I wasn't hearing you say it," Jay said.

Pro laughed.

No one else did.

"Open the gateway," Elle ordered. "Start the engines."

To Jay's right, Pro's fingers did a quick tap dance on the flat panel, then stopped. If all went well, Pro should have started the earth splitting above them.

A slight rumble shook the ship, but otherwise Jay couldn't tell if anything had happened or not. The tunnel through which they would exit was supposed to be formed by a force field, pushing the earth back out of the way long enough to allow the ship to slide through.

Beyond him in the next chair, Charles moved his fingers on the panel, starting the engines.

Suddenly the ship seemed really alive.

There was no extra noise.

No shaking.

Nothing except the feeling of power flowing through everything.

"Engines on-line," Charles announced, his voice high and sounding extremely nervous. "It worked. I'll be go-to-hell."

"Haven't heard that one before," Jay said, laughing.

"Tunnel open and stable," Pro announced.

Suddenly in front of Jay a holographic image appeared on his screen.

It took him a moment to understand what he was seeing and relate the small scale of the image to the enormity of the reality. What he saw was an image of the tunnel and the shape of the ship. A green line moved from the ship up through the tunnel. A green dot was imposed on the image of the ship.

How the hell was he supposed to get that ship up through that hole?

"Shielding up and working," Pro announced.

"Okay, Jay," Elle said. "Get us out of here, slow and careful."

"Easy for you to say," Jay muttered, staring at the screen in front of him. He wondered if the sweat forming on his right palm would make the ball slippery.

"Don't think," Elle said. "Just do it."

"Got ya," Jay said.

She knew him too well.

He was thinking too much, which was getting in the way of the training he had gotten last night. It was like it was on the streets. If he stopped and really thought, he often screwed up. But if he trusted his instincts and postponed thought until later, he was usually right.

He took a deep breath and let the knowledge from the library well upward to the front of his mind.

As Elle had told him sometime during the night: "Don't question. Just know you know how to do something and do it."

It had worked when he spoke Numen for Zed. He hoped it was going to work now.

He eased the thrust forward while at the same time moving the ball backward to tip up the front of the ship.

There was no sense of movement at all inside the

ship. No sense that the ship was now tipped up-ward. Weird.

"We're moving," Partner announced.

The ship on the holographic image in front of Jay was moving, the green dot following the green line up through the tunnel that had opened in the earth.

It seemed to take forever, but actually less than three seconds passed.

He didn't bang the ship into a wall, or crash it in the narrow space.

Three long seconds of torture.

Three seconds to get a ship out of its million-year-old tomb and into the air.

The instant they cleared the tunnel the holographic image in front of Jay changed. It was now an image of the planet Earth, with a small green dot showing the spaceship's location on the surface.

But there was no green line on the image.

Jay pulled the speed control back and tipped the ship's nose down so that they were a hovering golden saucer, just off the ground above the tunnel. With luck they were shielded. But just in case they weren't, or if the shielding malfunctioned, they had left Captain to take care of any sightings.

"Great job," Elle said, letting out a sigh of relief. "You can drive all the time from here on out."

"Got yourself a deal," Jay said. "But I need directions."

"A man saying he needs directions." Pro said. "You've shamed all men."

"Funny," Elle said.

"Feeding course now," Partner said.

"Got it!" Bright shouted, clearly excited.

On the holographic display a green line appeared leading from the green dot on the surface of the planet, off into space directly over the North Pole.

"Here we go," Jay said. He took a deep breath and let his instincts again take over. Slowly he eased the nose of the ship up while shoving the speed control gently forward.

Again there was absolutely no sense of motion at all.

The green dot moved along the green line on the holographic image. Quickly they were above the pole and headed out into space. Jay focused on keeping his hands steady and the speed moderate. He wanted to go a ways out, but not too far out.

"Any chance of finding a viewscreen around here?" Partner asked.

"Got it," Pro said.

Suddenly the rounded walls between and above each control station seemed to just vanish as if they weren't even there. Stars peppered the black sky ahead of them.

The vast and spectacular view made Jay jerk his attention away from the holographic image and stare into the blackness ahead.

The walls were so invisible, or the screen images so good, it was as if they were all suddenly just sitting on a platform shoving its way through space, with nothing between them and all of the universe.

Jay quickly forced himself to focus on the holographic image in front of him, not on the stars shown ahead. He knew if he looked back, past Elle and Pro, he would see the disk that was Earth receding into the distance below them.

"Holy shit!" Charles exclaimed.

"Wow!" Partner whispered.

No one else said a word. Jay wasn't even sure he could hear the others breathing back there behind him. Beside him Anthony sat with his mouth open.

Partner's mouth was also open and he stared around them.

Bright was looking just plain scared.

If they were like Jay, going into space was not something they had ever expected to do. Even after he discovered there were aliens out there, Jay had never even considered the possibility. And it wasn't something he really wanted to do, either. His world, his universe, was the streets of New York. And right now he very much wanted to be back on them, chasing a simple mugger. Or arresting a car thief.

Instead he was flying an ancient spaceship away from Earth.

Life was strange sometimes.

Just plain strange.

The Supreme Controller of the Zulla fleet listened to his stomach rumble, his mouth open as two feeders squeezed the drippings from the Umaxian beetle into his mouth, one luscious droplet after the other. He knew the rumbling had a calming influence upon his staff. They calmed him.

Underneath his massive pink flesh, the massage rollers increased their tempo. They always did this after each of his fifty meals per cycle and he always enjoyed the sensation.

On the huge screen in front of him the images of the pitiful planet called Earth grew larger. They were the first to arrive, beyond a few unimportant stragglers. Even sooner than the mighty Horsanakii, who would not be pleased when they learned of it.

27

His stomach rumbled and he smiled at the taste and joy of it all.

"Supreme Controller," his second said, grunting to move into his direct line of vision so his master would not have to move his head. It was a good sign that his second was thinking of such simple pleasures.

"I have good news."

The feeders ended their course of Umaxian-beetle drippings and began to pour the thick paste of the Sulyts love gatherings into his mouth. He often craved the taste of this delicacy, savoring the saltiness combined with the intense sweetness of the nectar. It was the most expensive food in all the Galaxy and he only indulged his passion for it for a few moments every cycle.

His second bowed and waited until the feeders were done and moved to drop several chunks of Bacoon meat into the Supreme Controller's mouth before he spoke. "The Sashanian fleet stands aside, as do all the others in this region."

The Supreme Controller waved away the news with one thick hand. "Of course. I expected nothing else. Sashanians are not a stupid people. Just ugly. No flesh and all those tentacles. Terrible creatures to gaze upon."

"I agree completely," his second said.

"Of course you do," the Supreme Controller said.

On the screen the white and blue of the small planet started to be clearly seen. He hoped they would find lots of new animals, new plants to eat here. It would be a glorious day for his fleet.

Suddenly the image of the small planet ahead was washed clear, the giant screen went blank.

"What has happened?" he demanded. His stomach grumbled and he belched in impatience.

Then, just as suddenly, the screen cleared and he was greeted by an image that in all the time he'd spent gaining weight, in all his years of gorging and scheming to achieve his position of Largest-of-the-Large, he had not expected to see.

There, on the screen, stood a Numen, face covered in shadow, hands hidden in the long Numen robe. A god from the Galaxy's past, millions of meals ago.

Then the Numen began to speak in its long-dead language, a language the Supreme Controller did not understand. He had seen no reason to learn it. But he did recognize the sound of it.

Then the image vanished and the small blue planet was again visible on his screen.

For the first time in many cycles, the Largest-of-the-Large brushed aside his feeders. "Where did that image come from?" he demanded of those within earshot of his giant voice. "And what did it say?"

"It comes from a ship moving in from deep space to a location between us and the planet ahead," his second replied.

"A Numen ship?" the Supreme Controller demanded.

No one said anything as his second worked to

obtain the information from the board in front of him. Then the second moved to a place beside the Supreme Controller and dropped to the floor in complete submission.

"Well?" the Supreme Controller asked.

"It appears to be a Numen ship," his second said. "The message states that the Numen agree with the treaty protecting this planet and will defend it."

"*What?*" the Supreme Controller shouted, actually shifting his bulk from the position he had sat in for more years than he could remember. Under him the moving rollers worked to adjust to his massive movement. Waves rolled over and through the flesh of His Largeness, banging on the walls of his bed.

Again his second hurled his bulk to the floor and kept his eyes averted.

"Put this intruding ship on my screen," the Supreme Controller ordered.

Instantly the single ship moving into a position between the mighty Zulla fleet and the planet beyond filled the screen. The smooth lines and the unmistakable gold color of the vessel told him at once that it was a Numen ship.

The first Numen ship to be seen in the Galaxy in over a million years. Had they returned?

Had they never left?

And why would they wish to protect this puny little planet?

He had no answers to these questions, and when the Largest-of-the-Large had no answers, it made him hungry.

"Halt the fleet. Hold position!"

His orders echoed over the vast spaces of his ship.

Then he motioned for the feeders to come back in on their extension platforms, reposition themselves over his body, and feed him. He needed food to think. Such decisions as he now faced could not be rushed.

"Fleet is holding position," his second said from his place on the floor, the information relayed to him through his implants.

"Get up!" the Supreme Controller yelled between large hunks of Dovian snake slithering down his throat. "This is not your fault, you fool."

His second grunted and somehow managed the herculean task of getting himself back onto his four feet.

The Supreme Controller thought while eating, staring at the golden Numen ship. One single ship stopping his fleet. If he returned to the planet of the Zulla, he would be starved out of his position for allowing one ship, Numen or not, to stop him.

Yet he dared not attack it alone. He knew of the weapons power the Numen ships were rumored to have had. How much more power would a single ship have now, after a million years? He didn't want to make his people the laughing stock of all the Galaxy by going up against a single Numen ship, and losing.

He chewed on this for a moment, then understood what he must do. "The Bonka and Horsanakii fleets are close behind us. Correct?"

"Yes," his second replied.

"Send them a message that we will wait and let them join in the honor of taking this planet with us."

"Yes, Supreme Controller."

After two bites, his second announced, "Message sent."

"Good."

His feeders moved to large hunks of fat-dripping Vortonian spider intestines, stuffing them into his mouth every six beats.

"Sir," his second said. "The great Horsanakii have thanked you for your offer and say they will join us soon. However, the Bonka have refused and have offered their help to the Sashanian defenders of the treaty."

"They change sides in fear of a single ship," the Supreme Controller said, laughing, sending waves rolling through the pink wonderfulness of his giant body. "How soon until the Horsanakii arrive?"

"One feeding cycle."

"Good," the Supreme Controller said.

"Sir, will the Sashanians now defend this puny world?"

"Of course not," he said, the rumbling of his stomach growing louder in protest against the interruption of a feeding cycle. "We only worry about one ship and how much new food we can carry back to our space with us."

"Good," his second said.

Just then the feeders jammed a large, whole Sanda bird into the Supreme Controller's mouth and he allowed them to force it down without attempting to chew. He needed the strength it would supply him for the enjoyment that would soon be his.

On the screen in front of him, the single golden ship hung in space, waiting with the patience of the gods.

"We have about fifty incoming calls," Pro said, scanning his board.

Elle looked at the massive fleet stopped in space in front of them. Because of the Numen ship's weird viewscreen system, it still felt as if they were just sitting exposed on a platform in space. Very exposed and very weak.

She couldn't shake the feeling.

For the first few minutes after Jay had spoken his message, the feeling of victory had sent the spirits of the humans soaring. The oncoming fleet had stopped cold in space. Jay had kidded about how his voice could stop anyone. But the other fleets behind it were still coming.

The euphoria had quickly yielded to sober reality.

28

They were one ship against fleets.

They stood no chance.

"Who is calling?" Jay asked.

Pro shrugged. "I have no idea," he said. "I only recognize the Sashanian name from the moon base."

"The alien guy Zed is always talkin' to?" Jay asked.

"One and the same," Pro said.

Jay glanced around at her, but she shook her head no.

"Look," she said. "At this point we've played our bluff. We stand by it and fight if we have to."

Jay nodded. "Agreed."

Elle glanced around at the others. Everyone seemed to be doing very well at their post. The only one she had been worried about at all was Bright, but even the young computer expert had remained fairly calm. And Elle had to admit, she was getting used to the feeling of just sitting out in space. It was beautiful in a strange way.

Actually beautiful didn't even come close to covering it. Spectacular was closer. It was no wonder the astronauts coming back from space when she was a kid always had so much trouble describing this beauty. There was nothing on the surface of Earth to compare to it.

She looked at the shapes of the attacking fleet. It made no sense that such a beautiful place as the Galaxy could have so many really ugly races in it, including the one sitting facing them now.

"Uh-oh," Pro said.

"What?" Elle asked.

"The Zulla fleet in front of us has invited the two fleets behind them to join in destroying our phony ship and looting the Earth. In so many words."

"Shit!" Jay said.

Elle didn't like the sound of that. Their main hope was that the fleets would see their ship, hear their message, freak out, then turn tail and run. Seems that wasn't going to happen. All they had accomplished was forcing the fleets to join up before attacking.

"Good news, bad news," Pro said. "The next fleet in line, a race called the Bonka, have turned down the invitation and offered their help to the Numen and the Sashanian in defending the treaty."

"Good news," Jay said.

"The next fleet a few hours back agreed to join the jerks in front of us."

"And that's the bad news," Jay said.

"How many ships do they have?" Elle asked. "Can we find that out?"

"Looks like a couple thousand," Pro said. "One hour until arrival."

"Plus the thousand ships in the fleet in front of us," Jay said. "Just great. One against three thousand. I'd say we have about one hour left to enjoy the view."

Elle stared out at the stars and caught faint images of the ships waiting to destroy Earth. She didn't like Jay's attitude, but she agreed with it.

Their bluff hadn't worked. They needed a plan B, and they needed it fast.

She turned to Anthony. "What kind of weapons does this ship really have?"

Anthony snorted, then looked at her, a haunted look in his eyes. "This really was a ship of the gods," he said. "There are weapons here that could destroy all of those ships out there with one touch on this panel."

Jay glanced around. "You're kidding us, right?"

Elle watched as General Anthony Davis shook his head no. She could see it in his eyes: he wasn't kidding. But the real Anthony, the one they had rescued, was just a kid who wanted to ski. He had said at one point yesterday that he couldn't believe he had become a general in the army. He hated the thought of killing anything.

"Jay. Pro," Elle said. "Go with Anthony down to the library and absorb the information he shows you about the weapons systems."

"Good idea," Jay said. He tapped a button on his board and stood.

Anthony and Pro followed him down the stairs.

If there was going to be shooting, she didn't want a civilian to be doing the killing. It was the MiB's job to rid the Earth of alien scum and they would do it if they had to. Asking a kid in a general's body to assume the task wasn't right and just wouldn't work.

But firing a single weapon at an alien who was trying to kill humans was one thing. Firing and destroying entire ships full of aliens was another. And while she and Jay had downed their share of alien ships over the past year, Elle was now faced with the possibility of destroying an entire alien fleet.

And she knew that if it came down to doing that and saving Earth, she would do it.

Jay felt shaken after his session in the library with Anthony and Pro. There was no doubt, none at all, that the ship they were taking their little joyride in could blow the fleet of alien spaceships right out of space. In fact, the ship had about four or five different ways of doing it.

And it could blow up the second fleet that would soon be joining the first one just as easily.

As long as they had this ship sitting up here, there was no chance at all that Earth would be invaded by a fleet of ships.

None.

Zero.

Zip.

If any of them here could pull the trigger.

Jay moved back up the stairs and out

29

onto what appeared at first glance to be a deck sitting in space with counters and chairs in a circle around the outside. The Numen viewscreen system was so good at making the eye believe the walls and ceiling weren't there that Jay felt as if he was hanging out on a rooftop in the city. The sensation was both disconcerting and really cool at the same time. The highest possible rooftop, with no other taller buildings around it. He'd never actually been up on one like that, but he was sure this was what it would feel like.

Only difference here was that there was no wind and no smell like there would be on the rooftop in the city. Just the fantastic view of space around them and the Earth behind and below them.

Anthony took his old position at the weapons board, but didn't touch anything. Jay had assured him in the library that if any weapon had to be fired, he would fire it. For a moment there Jay thought the general was going to break into tears, he was so relieved.

Now, after seeing what the weapons of this ship could do, Jay understood Anthony's feelings completely. He flat out didn't want to fire them either.

"Okay," Jay said to Elle, stopping beside her chair to talk. "I see it this way. We have two options."

"One?" she asked.

"We blow that fleet of alien ships out of space, then warn any other fleets that we will do the same thing if they challenge the treaty on this planet."

Elle nodded. "Option two?" Elle asked.

"We wait until they attack, then blow all of them away."

"Weapons are that strong, huh?" Elle asked looking him in the eye.

Jay nodded. "Those poor suckers out there don't stand a chance against us."

"Amazing," Elle said, "and I thought only one ship against fleets didn't stand a chance."

"No, fleets don't stand a chance against ships once built and owned by the gods," Jay said.

"Oh," Elle said.

"Believe him," Pro said. "They don't stand a chance."

Elle nodded.

"I don't like either option," Jay said. "But I honestly can't think of a third."

"I don't like them either," Elle said.

Jay didn't like the two options because both involved the destruction of entire fleets of alien ships. Granted, those ships out there were about to destroy all of humanity, but that still didn't shake Jay's feeling of being a child playing with a loaded pistol. They fire the shot and they'd have no idea what the final outcome of their act would be.

"Isn't there something we could blow up instead of the ships?" Sarah asked from her chair. "Show them how powerful we are without taking so many lives?"

"Option three," Jay said, clapping his hands.

"Perfect," Elle said.

"But we got to be doing it quickly," Jay said.

"Before that second fleet gets into position and we lose option one."

"And what do we blow up?" Elle asked.

Jay turned to Anthony. "I didn't get to the range lessons on these weapons. How far are we good for?"

Anthony shrugged, clearly happier with the idea of blowing up something other than ships. "Mars orbit safely, with any kind of accuracy."

"Wow!" Jay said.

"But there's nothing to blow up, I'm afraid," Elle said, "unless you want to destroy the moon and our friends on the far-side base there."

"Mars has two small moons," Jay said. "Would one of them do?"

"No," Pro said, staring at his screen. "Both on the far side of Mars at this point, plus Mars is on the other side of the sun. Too far away."

"Any asteroids—big ones—nearby?"

Pro studied his board, then shook his head. "Nothing."

"Back to option one and two," Elle said, sighing.

"Damn," Jay said, slamming his hand on the back of one chair. For an instant there he had felt better, but now the weight of this decision was bearing down on him again. He just wished they could contact Zed, get *him* to make the decision. But they didn't dare take that chance. There were too many alien eyes on them at this very moment.

"How about a game of chicken?" Bright asked, looking back at Jay.

"New option three," he said, smiling at her. "Just might work."

"You two want to explain it to the rest of us?" Elle asked.

"We give the fleet out there another Numen threat," Jay said, flipping the hood of his Numen robe up to make the point. "This time we add a ticking clock whose time runs out just before the second fleet gets there."

"Exactly," Bright said.

"And what happens when they call our bluff?" Elle asked.

"We threaten to blow one of their ships out of space every Numen second until they leave."

Elle nodded. "It just might work. Better than blowing up their entire fleet. But what happens if they start firing first? Can this ship take it?"

Jay glanced at Pro and both of them laughed. "That entire fleet out there could fire at us at once and they wouldn't hurt this ship," he said.

"You're kidding, right?" Partner asked.

"Nope," Pro said. "He's actually underestimating the shielding on this thing. All the ships coming in here wouldn't even put a scratch on this thing."

"I'm starting to like this ship more and more," Elle said, laughing.

"Sort of like our LTD," Jay said. "Looks simple, but has all sorts of really cool stuff."

"Okay, everyone," Elle said, "let's play some chicken with the big bad aliens."

"Pro, I need to know in Numen time how long

until the other fleet arrives. I'll set the clock just ahead of that."

"Seventeen Dons," Pro said. "About twenty minutes."

"So I say fifteen Dons and we're in," Jay said, moving over and standing by one station of the wall near Pro's station. The ship's communication system would send his image from that point, with nothing but a plain background behind and around him. Another cool feature.

But just to make sure, Elle said, "Hoods up, hands out of sight, everyone."

Jay did the same, making sure his hood was tilted far down in front of his face and his hands were far up inside his sleeves. Over and over in his head he repeated the words in Numen, making his voice low, calm, and clear.

"Ready when you are," Pro said.

"*Okay*," Jay said in Numen.

Keeping his head down, he counted to three as they had done with the first message, then spoke in Numen slowly and clearly.

"*The fleet standing off this planet is in violation of the treaty governing this world. You have fifteen Dons to leave or we will take action. One of your ships will be destroyed every MaDon after that point until you leave or no ships remain. It is your choice.*"

Jay counted to three, standing very still.

Then Pro said, "Clear."

"Great job," Elle said.

"*Start the clock ticking*," Jay said in Numen,

then realized what he had done and laughed, pushing the hood back.

They were all looking at him with questioning looks.

"You all right?" Elle asked.

"You sounded great," Bright said. "Kinda spooky, though."

"Sorry," Jay said, shrugging. "Method acting. Got carried away."

"Well, don't do it again," Elle said. "I don't want you turning into a god on us."

Pro laughed.

Jay just glared at him.

Beach-Grass-In-Limbo could not believe what his three eye stalks had just seen on the monitor. He had been prepared to watch the destruction of a planet he had sworn to guard; instead he had witnessed the return of the gods.

The Numens were back.

Or at least one ship was. But from his understanding of the Numen race, one ship was all that was needed to stop any fleet of ships.

More than enough, actually.

And then They-Who-Hated-All-Violence had stood where he had not dared stand: between the powerful fleets and the planet Earth.

Beach-Grass-In-Limbo's tentacles had become so agitated and twisted when this hap-

30

pened, it had taken him a short calming session to untangle. But his profound embarrassment would not allow him to raise an eye stalk to his heaven for some time.

The Numen had come back to teach the way of peace again, using this backward planet as an example.

He, Beach-Grass-In-Limbo, commander of the Sashanian fleet and keeper of the treaty, vowed he would learn the lesson well, and not fail again.

But the Zulla fleet still challenged the gods' ship, and the prideful Horsanakii were going to do the same.

Such stupidity. It twisted his tentacles, it angered him so much.

Beach-Grass-In-Limbo let two of his tentacles wave in agitation, but managed to keep the others in control. Didn't the Zulla and Horsanakii know of the power of They-Who-Hated-All-Violence? Not even a race as undeveloped as the humans would be so foolish as to stand up to a Numen ship.

But it seemed that a million years of time had dulled the memories of the Zulla and the Horsanakii. But those years had not dulled his race's memory. Beach-Grass-In-Limbo and his people would stand with the Numen, never against them.

Now the Numen ship had informed the Zulla that they had only a short time to effect their retreat.

This was so like what he had understood of the

ways of the gods. They never killed unless they had to. And never more than they had to.

Ever.

It was what made them gods.

Beach-Grass-In-Limbo moved up close to his monitor screen, his eye stalks focused on the task, and sent his order.

"Move all Sashanian and treaty ships into position flanking the Numen ship, facing the Zulla.

"We will stand and fight with the gods."

His order was quickly obeyed.

The great Sashanian fleet moved into position.

Many other ships that were nearby joined the treaty fleet. All stayed back and to the side, out of the way of the gods' ship. It was as it should be.

The gods must lead.

Then, while the Numen countdown continued for the Zulla, the Bonka fleet joined the Sashanian fleet, standing with the treaty and the gods.

Beach-Grass-In-Limbo smiled and made soothing motions as he acknowledged the intelligence of the Bonka commander.

Again he let two tentacles wave. No fleet dared stand against the gods and the combined ships that now supported the treaty that protected the humans.

Yet the Zulla fleet did not leave.

The Numen countdown continued.

His tentacles moved in greater and greater agitation at the stupidity of the Zulla fleet commander.

No amount of pride was worth challenging the

gods, They-Who-Hated-All-Violence. They could destroy entire fleets, all worlds, if needed.

And he knew they would do so.

He remembered the history.

They had done so in the past.

They would do so today. He knew it.

Beach-Grass-In-Limbo focused all three eye stalks on the monitor and watched and waited, as everyone in all the thousands of ships watched and waited.

It was a time of great tension, of great tanglings of tentacles.

"Six Dons left," Pro said.

Elle glanced at him, then out at the fleet facing them. Why weren't they moving?

Why were these aliens being so stupid?

Behind them and on both sides, great metallic Sashanian ships moved into position, facing the Zulla fleet. After a few minutes she knew there must be at least a thousand ships behind and around them. But all the ships clearly deferred to them as the leader and Elle didn't much like that at all.

"Sure feels better not to be alone out here," Jay said, studying the ships around them from his chair.

"Yeah," Elle said, "it does. Except they are all waiting for us to do something."

"We're playing chicken, remember," Jay

31

said, laughing. "Chicken is a game of waiting until the last moment before blinking."

"Well," Elle said, "my stomach doesn't much like the game." Her stomach actually hadn't much liked anything about this flight except the spectacular view.

"I'll agree with that," Sarah said. "And the problem is, we can't blink."

"I know," Elle said. She had been thinking about that very problem. If the Zulla were stupid enough to call their bluff, they would have to start taking out ships, one at a time, every 1.7 seconds. And when that happened, who knew what the ships around them would do?

Chances were it would be a major bloodbath.

If she and Jay made the wrong move here, a lot of beings were going to die on both sides of this fight.

That thought cramped up her stomach even more.

"Five Dons," Pro said.

Around the control room that felt like a sundeck in space, the silence was thick. Not even Jay was his usual wisecracking self at the moment.

The silence dragged on.

More ships joined the fleet behind them.

The Zulla fleet still did not move.

Elle sat and stared at the ships, as if by her very will she could cause them to retreat and she and Jay could go back to being regular old MiB agents on good, solid ground.

"Four Dons," Pro said.

"Time flies when you're having fun," Jay said.

None of the civilians around the room looked as if they could speak. Anthony, who was still at the weapons board, looked like he was going to sweat himself right into a giant puddle.

"Jay, you'd better relieve Anthony," Elle said. "Just in case things fire up faster than we want."

Jay nodded, tapped a place on his board, and stood. Then he moved over and patted the general on the back.

"Thanks," Anthony said, the relief clear in his voice as he stood and let Jay drop down into the chair.

Elle was glad she wasn't sitting there. Both she and Jay were responsible here. But she didn't want to be pulling the trigger on an entire fleet of ships unless she had to.

She was sure Jay didn't want to any more than she did.

"Three Dons," Pro said.

"They're not blinking yet," Elle said.

Jay shrugged. "Still time."

The thick, heavy silence again filled the room.

Suddenly the openness of space and the unique viewscreens of the ship seemed to have the opposite affect on Elle. The blackness, the stars seemed to be shoving down on her, pushing her into the seat.

She forced herself to take a deep breath and the feeling receded a little.

But not much.

She sat, breathing steadily as the silence and the blackness of space pushed at her.

Around them the massive fleet was standing poised, waiting for their first action.

In front of them a massive fleet waited to attack them and then destroy Earth.

Standoff.

Draw.

A lot of beings were going to die very shortly. And if they didn't win, then humanity was going to be added to that list.

"Two Dons," Pro said.

"Blink," Jay said to the Zulla fleet. "Blink, damn you."

"They're not going to," Elle said softly. And she knew deep down inside that she was right.

The Supreme Controller let the feeders slip two gi-ant Beenor slugs down his throat before he looked down at his second, who was at the moment cowering in front of him.

"Only three C-units left," his second said.

The smaller creature had been reminding him of the countdown every unit since the Numen had started it. It was boring him, making his digestion slow, and that he didn't like. It was time to take action, to seize the day, fling wide the gaping Zulla maw, and swallow what came with gusto.

"Be prepared to attack on my command," the Supreme Controller ordered.

"What?" his second cried. "You want us to attack a Numen ship, plus the combined power of the Sashanian and treaty signers' fleets?"

32

"Surprise is a very powerful weapon, my dear second," the Supreme Controller said, ignoring the outrage of having his orders questioned by a junior officer. "We will scatter them before they are aware of being hit."

The feeders dropped two more snails down his throat, one after another. Then he looked directly at his second. "Now give the order."

"I will do as you—" He paused, looked pained, then stared at the Supreme Controller. "Another fleet approaches at high speed."

Then his second did something that in all the years of history the Supreme Controller had never heard of being done. His second simply screamed, a high-pitched gurgling noise, and dropped to the floor, his mass spread out like a mate in heat, waiting to be mounted by a Larger-than-Large.

The Supreme Controller could see others in the ship's control room doing the same, dropping to the floor, whimpering as if lost.

"Put the other fleet on the screen!" he shouted, smashing the feeders out of his way.

The image appeared on his monitor.

It was another small fleet of ships coming in very, very fast. Faster than anything he knew of in all the Galaxy. Three hundred, maybe four hundred ships at most.

Why would a mere four hundred ships cause such problems with his second and the others.

Then he understood what had caused his second to scream. And the knowledge caused him to release his bowels far ahead of schedule, emptying fluids in a flood through the units below. Fluids and mass that would take him many units of time to replenish.

"Send the order to retreat at once!"

He actually hadn't needed to send such an order. All of his ships were already turning and fleeing.

The massive Horsanakii fleet was also turning and racing away as the four hundred new ships took up positions near the first Numen ship.

At first the Supreme Controller hadn't believed that the gods had actually returned. He would never run away from one ship.

But now he knew for sure the gods were here.

And they had brought an entire fleet with them.

He knew the legends. Not even the combined forces of all the races in all of the Galaxy could stand up to the four hundred ships of the Numen fleet.

And he wasn't about to be the one to prove that point again.

"Food," he demanded, glancing out of the corner of his eye for his feeders. "I need food for the long trip home."

On the floor near his massive bulk, his second continued to sob.

He would need a new second, it seemed, as well.

"We are so screwed," Jay said, standing beside Elle and staring out at the fleet of Numen ships that had come in and taken up positions around them.

Elle said nothing.

All the ships looked identical to the ship they were in. Only he couldn't believe there were four hundred of them. And then there was the biggest question of all: where had they come from?

"The Zulla and Horsanakii fleets are running like scared rabbits," Pro said. "Earth is saved."

"Maybe," Jay said, turning slowly to stare at the Numen fleet.

"Maybe not," Elle said.

"So what happens next?" Jay asked,

33

more to the ships out there than to anyone in the room.

"I'd say we're in big trouble for borrowing their ship, that's what," Elle said.

Jay laughed. "Well, it was a good idea at the time."

"Famous last words," Elle said.

"Let's hope not," Jay said. "Now who's being discouraging?"

She just shrugged.

"Got a message coming in from one of the Numen ships," Pro said. "You want to take the call, or should I say you're out?"

"Is it secured so none of the other races can listen in?"

Pro stared at his board for a moment, then nodded. "It is."

Jay slipped off his Numen robe, adjusted his black suit and tie, and then quickly moved over to the correct place to stand. Then he nodded to Pro.

In front of him the holographic image of a Numen, hood covering his face, appeared.

In Numen, Jay said, "We are honored to meet you. Your quick actions saved our planet and our race. Thank you."

Jay hoped that thanking them for their help was a good way to start a conversation with a god.

The Numen pushed its hood back. Its large, black eyes seemed to radiate warmth and comfort, even though it was only a hologram. Instantly Jay felt far less fear than he had a moment before.

"We did nothing but return for our ships. The activation of this ship signaled us that it was time."

"We will gladly help retrieve all the others on the surface," Jay said.

"Thank you," the Numen said. *"We will need your help, to stay within the treaty that covers the dealings with your culture. You did promise our support of the treaty, did you not?"*

"I did, posing as one of you," Jay said. "And for such actions, I beg your forgiveness. I did it only to save our planet."

"You and your race have done well for such a remote part of the Galaxy. Your actions are understood. We will honor the promise made on our behalf. One of our number is asking if you understood the power of the weapons of the ship you now stand on?"

"We did," Jay said. "We hoped never to use them. We worked not to use them."

The Numen nodded. *"Your race shows promise. We will be watching. Now, please follow us into deep space, away from these other ships so that we may maintain the secrecy of your actions. We will return you to your home base shortly under shield."*

"You are more than kind," Jay said, bowing slightly.

The image of the Numen vanished.

Jay allowed himself to lean against the back of the nearest chair and breathe. In all his years he had never, ever been so nervous.

Around him the others broke into applause.

"Ten seconds until departure," Pro shouted.

"Jay, you need to fly this thing," Elle said. "Remember?"

"Oh, yeah."

Jay jumped into the pilot's chair and let the feel of the controls snap his mind back to attention.

In front of him their flight plan was marked by a green line on the holographic display. The other Numen ships in the fleet were marked on the display by blue dots. He just hoped they went slow enough for him to keep up.

"Three," Pro said. "Two . . . one . . . *now!*"

Jay moved the ball upward and around, pushing the throttle up so that the ship turned with the rest of the fleet and sped into deep space, away from the planet Earth.

"Amazing!" Elle said as the Earth shrank to a point behind them almost instantly.

Around them the stars moved faster and faster as they gained speed, Jay keeping their ship in perfect position with the rest of the Numen fleet.

Then, as his hand eased on the controls, letting the ship move almost on its own, he realized he was smiling.

In all his life he had never imagined doing such a thing as this. But from now on, when fighting a smelly alien, or getting basketball-game tickets for an important visiting dignitary from another planet, he would remember this moment.

The moment that he, Jay, a street-smart cop from New York City, had flown among the stars with the gods.

The familiar smell, the roughness of the seats, ev-erything about the LTD felt just great to Jay as they sat and talked with Zed on the secure link. The air-conditioning was running and the sun was beating down through the Oregon trees around them. Pro's containment crew were in their van parked behind them. Anthony, Sarah, Charles, and Bright had all been flown by helicopter to Portland, where they would be given new memories and cover stories for the time they had spent with Billie.

Both Jay and Elle had wanted to accompany their civilian crew to help them adapt to a real life, but Pro had convinced them that they would just get in the way. As he had put it, "The best thing we can do for

34

them is return them to at least a part of their old lives in the quickest fashion possible."

Finally both Jay and Elle had agreed, after Jay had remembered how well it had worked for Kay.

Jay and Elle had given a summary report to Zed of what had happened, even though he'd been following much of it from his office, almost totally alone in the MiB Immigration Center. Only he and the twins had hung around, it seemed.

"I just about peed my pants when that Numen fleet showed up," Zed said, laughing.

"You?" Elle said. "You ought to see four hundred of those ships up close in space. Scared the hell out of me."

Jay had to admit it had scared him, too. And talking to them hadn't helped that much. He had been convinced that he and Elle had committed a deadly sin by taking their ship and that all humanity was going to have to pay for it.

But, as things turned out, they had made exactly the right moves all the way down the line.

Luck. Just plain simple good luck.

"And," Zed said, "I thought I'd lost you all when you and the entire fleet vanished into deep space. That was some sight on the big board, let me tell you."

"What?" Jay asked, laughing. "You thought we'd joined up with them? Or that we were kidnapped? Or maybe were going to be punished?"

"All three," Zed said.

Elle laughed. "We had the same thoughts before they told us what they were going to do."

Jay had to admit that the flight into deep space had been something he would always remember. He never wanted to do it again, but he was glad he got the chance once.

"So what all happened out there?" Zed asked.

"Nothing, actually," Elle said.

"True," Jay said. "A few hundred light-years out, another Numen craft linked up with our ship."

"In mid-flight?" Zed asked. "Impressive."

"Everything about them is impressive," Elle said.

"Also true," Jay said. "One of the new crew asked us to move downstairs into the kitchen-and-lounge area."

"Got no argument from you, I'll bet," Zed said, again laughing.

"Not a word," Elle said. "And twenty minutes later there we were, standing outside the car here in the trees in Oregon."

"Captain was sure glad to see us back," Jay said.

Zed laughed. "I'll bet. And Junior, that was one great talk you had with them. I got the meat of it from Pro's report. I want a word-for-word from you later. But for now, nice job."

Jay smiled. It was rare when Zed gave a compliment. He wasn't even going to make a joke in return. "Just told them the truth, boss. Figured that was the safer way to go."

"And you were right," Zed said, the smile still filling his face. "Good policy never to lie to a god."

Smoke from a cigar slowly curled up along the edges of the picture, but Zed didn't puff it in front of them. Clearly a cigar was a private moment thing for him.

"You talk to the Numen yet about their other ships?" Jay asked.

"Yup," Zed said. "They're going to come back and start getting them in a couple of years. They figure things will have cooled down in this area by then. They want us to guard the ships for them until then. No touching, of course."

"Of course," Elle said, laughing.

"Actually," Zed said, chuckling to himself, "there's only going to be about ten of us total in all of MiB who know where the ships even are. Or that they even exist."

"Another classified file, huh?" Jay asked.

"You got it in one, Junior."

"And I assume the treaty is in good condition now?"

"Perfect," Zed said. "The Sashanians are bending over backward to help us now. We're still cleaning up the mess all over the world, though. Which reminds me, there's work for you two to do near there."

"No rest for the weary space travelers, huh?" Elle asked.

"Nope," Zed said, the smile still filling his face. "I'll download the information on your new assignment to you. Clean it up and get your asses back here."

"Gladly," Jay said, thinking about walking the streets of New York again. It would be wonderful.

Zed signed off and Elle picked up the com link

that put them in touch with the containment truck behind them. "Heads up, boys," she said. "We're back to work."

"Got it," Pro said. "We're right behind you."

Twenty minutes later, with Jay driving, they had wound their way up an old logging road to a clearing high in the coastal mountain range. There, a Grazer had landed and had been eating for almost two full days. He'd been so far away from civilization that MiB hadn't cared about him until the cleanup phase was under way. There was no sign of the alien's ship, though.

"He's as big as a small trailer," Jay said, totally disgusted, climbing out of the LTD and staring at the giant alien eating the brush.

"Got any ideas?" Elle asked.

"None," Jay said. And he didn't.

"There's no chance we can stuff him back in his ship," Elle said.

"Are you willing to try?" Jay asked, shocked.

"Not in the slightest," Elle said. "I'm never getting near one of those Grazer ships again."

"Found the ship," Pro said, coming back through the trees toward them. "About a hundred yards in that direction. Got a tow ship coming in to toss it into the sun."

"Perfect," Jay said. "Better take cover."

Moving back and standing in the door of the LTD, he took out his Atomizer.

Elle opened the other door of the car and stood in the same fashion.

Pro quickly climbed into the backseat and closed the door.

"Ready to uninvite a guest?" Jay asked.

"Ready," Elle said.

"On three," he said.

"Three," she said.

At the same moment they both fired, the image of the rotting carcasses in that Grazer spaceship clear in Jay's mind. His job was to rid the planet Earth of alien scum and that was exactly what they were doing.

The beast exploded like a kid's balloon being popped by a pin.

The sound was a sickening *kerrr-thump!*

"Duck!" Jay shouted, and dove behind the steering wheel of the LTD, slamming the door closed behind him just in time.

Elle did the same on the passenger side.

Grazer guts, half-digested food, and green slime rained down on the car, pounding it hard for a second before stopping.

"It be rainin' gopher guts," Jay said.

"Yuck," Elle said.

"Good fertilizer for the forest, though," Pro said.

"That reminds me." Jay glanced over at Elle as the slime and Grazer fat ran down the windows around them.

"What?" she asked.

He smiled. "We haven't had lunch yet."

Anthony Davis stood on the top of the hill, his skis adjusted comfortably under him on the new snow. Behind him the night-skiing lights bathed the slope in a warm glow. In front of him, a thousand or more feet down through the trees, the lights of Hood River were brighter than he remembered them being thirty-one years earlier. The town was bigger; more people lived along the Columbia River near there, too.

Things had changed. Actually, a great deal had changed, but he was discovering that he didn't mind so much.

It felt good to be back.

Skiing this run, at this time of night, was the last thing he remembered clearly. His doctor had said it was a good idea to return to the scene of the "accident."

E
P
I
L
O
G
U
E

Even to the very time.

Thirty-one years before, as a young man, he'd fallen on a night-skiing run and hit his head, changing his personality. After that he had quit skiing, become a general in the army, or so they told him. He had to believe them, even though he didn't much remember. They had pictures.

His doctor had said it was normal in cases like his for his original personality, his original memories, to suddenly return, erasing the years of being a general as if they had never happened. But the accident had taken thirty-one years of his life from him, made him into a different person during those years. It had also given him a very generous retirement from the army, enough to permit him to ski all the time if he wanted.

At least that much was good.

He had decided that skiing all the time was exactly what he wanted to do with the rest of his life. He had spent the summer skiing in Australia, and now he was back here, in his old hometown, on his old hill, night-skiing on the now much-expanded and modernized hill.

But changed or not, it was still his home. And he cherished the memories of skiing here. They felt almost as if they were just yesterday.

Above him the stars shone clear. The night was cold, without much wind.

He stared at the sky for a minute, thinking about what might be out there. Since his original personality had returned, he had had an odd yearning to look at the stars. He didn't know why. He just accepted it, just as he was learning to accept so much else.

With one more long look at the stars, then a quick glance at the valley below, he turned and started down the mountain, to finish the run he hadn't finished all those years ago.

He was skiing.

Life was good.

Everything was as it should be.